Caring for Your Teenager

This invaluable volume was prepared under the editorial direction of distinguished pediatrician Donald Greydanus, M.D., and draws on the contributions and practical wisdom of 57,000 pediatric specialists and a five-member editorial review board. Written in a warm, accessible style and filled with helpful hints, this book gives you the information you need to safeguard your child's most precious assets: his or her emotional and physical well-being.

Anyone who has ever raised a teenager knows the challenges—and joys—that lie ahead. But while helping your teenager become a healthy, happy, well-adjusted adult can be difficult—it doesn't have to be impossible.

Here is the information you need from the people you trust, based on the very latest medical and psychological findings in the field of family and childcare, to help you make your teenager's transition into young adulthood safe and successful.

INSIDE YOU'LL FIND ANSWERS TO ALL YOUR TEEN PARENTING QUESTIONS:

- Hormones—easing teenagers' anxieties about their changing bodies

- Improving motivation and providing consistent discipline

- Talking to your child and learning how to keep the communication flowing

- Adapting to different family types—from single-parent to adoptive to blended

- Your teen's everyday health—nutrition, exercise and sports, and instilling the healthy habits that will stay with them for life

- The latest information on learning disabilities, attention deficit hyperactivity disorder, depression

- Helping your teenager cope with serious illness or death in the family, sibling rivalry, separation, or divorce

- Helping your teenager find the right college—or make an alternative choice

- Your teen's physical growth and development—the expected and the unexpected

- A comprehensive medical guide to common ailments—how to deal with everything from acne to sports injuries

Child Care Books from
the American Academy of Pediatrics

CARING FOR YOUR TEENAGER

The Complete and Authoritative Guide

Editor-in-Chief

Donald E. Greydanus, M.D., FAAP, FSAM
Pediatrics Program Director
Michigan State University/
 Kalamazoo Center for
 Medical Studies
Professor, Pediatrics &
 Human Development
Michigan State University College
 of Human Medicine
Kalamazoo, Michigan

Writer

Philip Bashe

Editorial Board

Roberta K. Beach, M.D., MPH, FAAP
Professor Emeritus
Department of Pediatrics and
 Adolescent Medicine
School of Medicine
University of Colorado Health
 Sciences Center
Denver, Colorado

Suzanne Boulter, M.D., FAAP
Assistant Professor of Community
 and Family Medicine
New Hampshire Dartmouth Family
 Practice Residency Program
Concord, New Hampshire

George D. Comerci, M.D., FAAP
Professor Emeritus
University of Arizona College
 of Medicine
Tucson, Arizona

Robert B. Shearin, M.D., FAAP
Private Practice, Capitol
 Medical Group
Chevy Chase, Maryland

Victor C. Strasburger, M.D., FAAP
Professor of Pediatrics
University of New Mexico
 School of Medicine
Albuquerque, New Mexico

BANTAM BOOKS
New York   Toronto   London   Sydney   Auckland

CARING FOR YOUR TEENAGER
A Bantam Book / May 2003

Published by
Bantam Dell
A Division of Random House, Inc.
New York, New York

Library of Congress Cataloging-in-Publication Data

Caring for your teenager : the complete and
authoritative guide / the American Academy of
Pediatrics and Philip Bashe ; editor-in-chief,
Donald E. Greydanus.
p. cm.
"A rewrite of the American Academy of Pediatrics'
book Caring for your adolescent, ages 12 to 21 . . .
published in 1991"—Frwd. Includes
bibliographical references and index.
ISBN 0-553-37996-8
1. Parent and teenager—United States.
2. Adolescence. 3. Adolescent psychology.
4. Teenagers—United States. I. Bashe, Philip.
II. Greydanus, Donald E. III. American Academy
of Pediatrics. IV. Caring for your adolescent.
HQ799.15.C373 2003
305.235—dc21   2003040349

Manufactured in the United States of America
Published simultaneously in Canada

RRH   10 9 8 7 6 5 4 3 2 1

Reviewers and Contributors

Patricia A. Treadwell, M.D.
Susan E. B. Tully, M.D.
David E. Tunkel, M.D.
Surendra Kumar Varma, M.D.
Richard P. Walls, M.D., Ph.D.
Sally L. Davidson Ward, M.D.

Reginald L. Washington, M.D.
Morris A. Wessel, M.D.
Lani Wheeler, M.D.
Timothy E. Wilens, M.D.
Mark Wolraich, M.D.
W. Samuel Yancy, M.D.

This book is dedicated to
every parent who recognizes that children are our greatest inspiration
in the present and our greatest hope for the future

ACKNOWLEDGMENTS

Dr. Donald E. Greydanus would like to thank his beloved wife, Katherine, for over a quarter century of happiness. Thank you, Kathy, for sharing your life with me.

Philip Bashe would like to thank Robert and Rochelle Bashe, the late Evelyn Bashe, my son and teenager-to-be, Justin, and, as always, Patty Romanowski Bashe, for everything.

Thank you to the staff at Bantam Books: our wonderful editors Toni Burbank, Robin Michaelson, and Beth Rashbaum; copyeditor Faren Bachelis; art director Jim Plumeri; and designer Glen Edelstein.

PLEASE NOTE

The information contained in this book is intended to complement, not substitute for, the advice of your child's pediatrician. Before starting any medical treatment or medical program, you should consult with your own pediatrician, who can discuss your individual needs and counsel you about symptoms and treatment. If you have any questions regarding how the information in this book applies to your child, speak with your child's pediatrician.

The information and advice in this book applies equally to children of both sexes (except where noted). To indicate this, we have chosen to alternate between masculine and feminine pronouns throughout the book.

This book has been developed by the American Academy of Pediatrics. The authors, editors, and contributors are expert authorities in the field of pediatrics. No commercial involvement of any kind has been solicited or accepted in the development of this publication.

Contents

FOREWORD

Caring for Your Teenager is a rewrite of the American Academy of Pediatrics' book *Caring for Your Adolescent, Ages 12 to 21,* which was first published in 1991. *Caring for Your Teenager* is part of a series of child-care books developed by the Academy that includes *Caring for Your Baby and Young Child: Birth to Age 5, Your Baby's First Year* and *Caring for Your School-Age Child: Ages 5 to 12.*

What distinguishes this book from other reference books that address issues surrounding the teenage years is that pediatricians who specialize in these matters have extensively reviewed it. Under the direction of our editor-in-chief, the material in this book was developed with the assistance of numerous reviewers and contributors from the American Academy of Pediatrics (AAP) and its committees and sections. Every effort has been made to ensure that this book contains the most up-to-date findings, but since medical information is constantly changing, readers may want to visit the AAP Web site at www.aap.org for the latest information. Readers may also access consumer health information from the AAP at www.medem.com, an e-health network created by the AAP and other leading medical societies.

It is the Academy's hope that this book will become an invaluable resource and reference guide to parents. We are confident that parents and caregivers will find the book extremely valuable. We encourage its use in concert with the advice and counsel of our readers' pediatricians, who will provide individual guidance and assistance related to the health of children.

The AAP is an organization of fifty-seven thousand primary-care pediatricians, pediatric medical subspecialists and pediatric surgical specialists dedicated to the health, safety and well-being of infants, children, adolescents and young adults. *Caring for Your Teenager* is part of the Academy's ongoing educational efforts to provide parents and caregivers with high-quality information on a broad spectrum of children's health issues.

Joe M. Sanders Jr., M.D., F.A.A.P.
Executive Director
American Academy of Pediatrics

PART I

ADOLESCENCE:
A TIME OF CHANGE

1

PARENTING TEENAGERS IN TODAY'S WORLD

"Adolescence is when children start bringing up their parents."

—Anonymous

What if parenting a teenager were a job like any other, advertised in the want ads? Imagine picking up the classifieds and finding this:

We have an exciting, demanding position open in our department of growth and development. You will be in charge of grooming a small but dynamic team of up-and-coming young adults. Be prepared to put in endless hours and expect your authority to be challenged frequently. Fluency in two languages required: yours and theirs. Other prerequisites include infinite patience and a working knowledge of psychology, sociology, popular culture and all secondary-school and college curriculum. *Must have car!* Zero room for advancement; compulsory demotion in several years. Don't bother sending salary requirements; there are none.

If you didn't already *have* this job, you'd probably keep moving right on down the page.

Adolescence can be a challenge for parents. Your youngster may at times be a source of frustration and exasperation, not to mention financial stress. But these years also bring many, many moments of joy, pride, laughter and closeness. Too often, though, our culture seems to overemphasize the pervasive stereotypes of adolescence, many of them negative. Countless books, movies and news accounts create sensationalized portraits of disaffected youth flouting authority at every turn and often getting into serious trouble. As a result, the accomplishments of the good youngsters who make up the majority of America's approximately sixty million adolescents tend to be overshadowed.

Denver pediatrician Marianne Neifert objects to the barrage of disparaging messages parents receive about adolescence. As the mother of five children now grown to adulthood, she observes a parallel between the so-called "turbulent teens" and what is known as the "terrible twos." Just as not all toddlers go through the terrible twos in the same way, not every kid transforms into a defiant, capricious creature upon turning twelve. To assume that the teen years will be fraught with conflict can distort our perception of our children's behavior and result in a self-fulfilling prophecy, says Dr. Neifert, "because kids tend to rise or fall to our expectations of them."

Recent studies dispute the long-held belief that adolescence is inherently a time of turmoil. Four in five youngsters negotiate adolescence without any major problems, while in a 1998 nationwide poll of more than one thousand thirteen-to-seventeen-year-olds, 97 percent claimed to get along with their parents "very well" or "fairly well."

PARENTS MAKE A DIFFERENCE!

Granted, adolescence is a time when kids come under the pull of their peers and fall susceptible to the attitudes and values promoted by TV, movies, morning-radio personalities, advertisements, sneaker-peddling sports stars and the latest brooding rock singer. But as a large nationwide study demonstrated, mothers and fathers still exert a great deal of influence in shaping their children's moral and ethical beliefs and character.

The National Longitudinal Study on Adolescent Health, published in 1997, surveyed nearly twelve thousand students in grades seven through twelve. Across the board, youngsters who said they felt secure in their parents' love and caring were far less likely to experiment with tobacco, alcohol and drugs, engage in sex or violent behavior, or contemplate suicide than those who claimed not to feel emotionally connected to their families.

What does the study tell us? "It says that parents have a tremendous influence on their kids," says Dr. Robert W. Blum, one of the researchers. "And that influence remained constant across the age group." Adds Dr. Lia Gaggino, a pediatrician in Kalamazoo, Michigan, "Parents don't appreciate how important they are."

HOW THIS BOOK CAN HELP YOU

Not only do parents need to prepare their youngster for the journey from childhood to adulthood, but they need to prepare themselves as well. *Caring for Your Teenager* contains the collective wisdom and experience of the approximately fifty-seven thousand primary-care pediatricians, pediatric medical subspecialists and pediatric surgical specialists who belong to the American Academy of Pediatrics. In it you'll find practical advice for helping teenagers adjust to the changes of adolescence and make good decisions about drugs, alcohol, tobacco, premature sexual activity and other threats to their physical and emotional well-being. You'll also learn strategies for helping teens who have struggled with these or other problems to reclaim a happier, more fulfilling future. Consider this book a guide to what these years may hold in store.

Naturally every youngster is unique, but the biological changes that occur in adolescence are accompanied by certain predictable psychological changes. This is a time when behaviors that are considered inappropriate in both young children and adults have to be accepted as normal, healthy manifestations of growing up—even if they age *you* in the process. Once you understand the de-

The American Academy of Pediatrics: Who We Are

Perhaps you associate pediatricians with infant or child care. Most people do. But did you know that pediatricians are trained to care for children from birth, through adolescence and into young adulthood?

The American Academy of Pediatrics, founded in 1930, is an organization of pediatricians and other health-care professionals dedicated to upholding and improving standards of medical care for youngsters under age twenty-one. This mission takes myriad forms, including public education, continuing medical education for pediatricians, conducting research and advocating for legislation that benefits children.

velopmental mechanisms at work, you may find that you're better able to identify which situations warrant your concern and which you can take in stride.

The following examples of adolescents in action may have you nodding in recognition at least once. The good news? Barring extremes, these behaviors are perfectly normal. The bad news? *These behaviors are perfectly normal.*

It's a Friday night, and your seventeen-year-old daughter is going to a friend's party. She trots downstairs wearing the vampiric makeup and all-black uniform of the self-proclaimed "gothic"-rock movement.

"I'm *goth*," she intones solemnly, while you struggle to suppress a grin. Or, if you're not sufficiently up on teen subcultures, perhaps you mistakenly think she said, "I'm *Garth*," leaving you scratching your head as she kisses you good-bye and heads out the door.

Cause for alarm? Not beyond the normal concerns you would have about any teenage party; namely the availability of alcohol and drugs—and parental supervision. In sculpting her own identity, a teenager routinely experiments with different personas. Each incarnation, expressed through fashion, hairstyles, interests, beliefs, a particular group of friends and so on, is typically short-lived. By next year she may have adopted an altogether different look and attitude.

As a boy, your son seemed to hang on to your every word and saw you as infallible. Remember how proud that made you feel? Now this fourteen-year-old points out your every shortcoming, and "Boy, Dad, you know everything!" has been replaced by an exasperated, "How would *you* know?"

It is common for adolescents to suddenly cast a critical eye on Mom and Dad, as they seek to separate from their parents and form their own system of values. Try not to take it too personally, but do make it clear that expressing himself disrespectfully is unacceptable.

Lately your thirteen-year-old daughter has been fixated on her ever-changing body and bodily functions. She's constantly asking her mother: "Do you think I'm too fat?" "When am I going to get breasts?" "Am I pretty?"

The body is a source of endless fascination—and anxiety—for self-conscious teens. This is also a time when kids tend to behold themselves as the center of the universe; consequently, the discovery of a pimple can seem like a catastrophe.

Since the start of the school year, your seventh-grader has grown moody and irritable. He spends increasing amounts of time barricaded in his room, and your attempts at finding out if something is bothering him are met with a testy, "I'm *fine*. Just leave me alone."

Should you be alarmed? That depends. Some boys and girls are introverted by nature, and perfectly content to be by themselves. Does this describe your youngster? Or is this behavior out of character?

Rising tides of hormones and the struggle for self-identity may account for his moodiness, which is normal. Sadness and emotional withdrawal, too, are not uncommon during adolescence. But as with adults, depression that persists for more than two weeks should be brought to the attention of your pediatrician, who may in turn refer you to an adolescent mental-health specialist.

THE STAGES AND GOALS OF ADOLESCENCE

Adolescence, these years from puberty to adulthood, may be roughly divided into three stages: *early* adolescence, generally ages twelve and thirteen; *middle* adolescence, ages fourteen to sixteen; and *late* adolescence, ages seventeen to twenty-one. In addition to physiological growth, seven key intellectual, psychological and social *developmental tasks* are squeezed into these years. The fundamental purpose of these tasks is to form one's own identity and to prepare for adulthood. Table 1.1 shows a condensed preview of how these events typically unfold during adolescence.

Physical Development

Puberty is defined as the biological changes of adolescence. By midadolescence, if not sooner, most youngsters' physiological growth is complete; they are at or close to their adult height and weight, and are now physically capable of having babies.

Table 1.1
Tasks of the Teenage Years
1. Learning to feel comfortable with their bodies.
2. Becoming emotionally independent from their parents.
3. Learning to think and express themselves conceptually.
4. Developing a personal set of values: ideals, priorities, concepts of right and wrong.
5. Forming meaningful relationships with members of both sexes.
6. Defining their sexual orientation, and deciding whether or not to become sexually active.
7. Working toward economic stability.

Intellectual Development

Most boys and girls enter adolescence still perceiving the world around them in concrete terms: Things are either right or wrong, awesome or awful. They rarely set their sights beyond the present, which explains younger teens' inability to consider the long-term consequences of their actions.

By late adolescence, many youngsters have come to appreciate subtleties of situations and ideas, and to project into the future. Their capacity to solve complex problems and to sense what others are thinking has sharpened considerably. But because they are still relatively inexperienced in life, even older teens apply these newfound skills erratically and therefore may act without thinking.

Emotional Development

If teenagers can be said to have a reason for being (besides sleeping in on weekends and cleaning out the refrigerator), it would have to be asserting their independence. This demands that they distance themselves from Mom and Dad. The march toward autonomy can take myriad forms: less overt affection, more time spent with friends, contentious behavior, pushing the limits—the list goes on and on. Yet adolescents frequently feel conflicted about leaving the safety and security of home. They may yo-yo back and forth between craving your attention, only to spin away again.

Social Development

Until now, a child's life has revolved mainly around the family. Adolescence has the effect of a stone dropped in water, as her social circle ripples outward to include friendships with members of the same sex, the opposite sex, different social and ethnic groups, and other adults, like a favorite teacher or coach. Eventually teenagers develop the capacity for falling in love and forming romantic relationships.

Not all teenagers enter and exit adolescence at the same age or display these same behaviors. What's more, throughout much of adolescence, a youngster can be farther along in some areas of development than in others. For example, a fifteen-year-old girl may physically resemble a young adult but she may still act very much like a child since it isn't until late adolescence that intellectual, emotional and social development begin to catch up with physical development.

Is it any wonder that teenagers sometimes feel confused and conflicted, especially given the limbo that society imposes on them for six to ten years, or longer? Prior to World War II, only about one in four youngsters finished high school. It was commonplace for young people still in their teens to be working full-time and married with children. Today close to three in four youngsters receive high-school diplomas, with two in five graduates going on to college. "As more and more teens have extended their education," says Dr. Joseph Rauh, a specialist in adolescent medicine since the 1950s, "the age range of adolescence has been stretched into the twenties."

Reflect back on your own teenage years, and perhaps you'll recall the frustration of longing to strike out on your own—but still being financially dependent on Mom and Dad. Or striving to be your own person—yet at the same time wanting desperately to fit in among your peers.

Adolescence can be a confusing time for parents, too. For one thing, they must contend with their children's often paradoxical behavior. How is it that the same son given to arias about saving the rain forest has to be nagged repeatedly to sort the recycling? Or that in the course of an hour your daughter can accuse you of treating her "like a baby," then act wounded that you would expect her to clear the table after dinner?

But beyond learning to anticipate the shifting currents of adolescent emotion, mothers and fathers may be struggling with some conflicting emotions of their own. The pride you feel as you watch your youngster become independent can be countered by a sense of displacement. As much as you may accept intellectually that withdrawing from one's parents is an integral part of growing up, it *hurts* when the child who used to beg to join you on errands now rarely consents to being seen in public with you, and then only if the destination is a minimum of one area code away.

It's comforting to know that feeling a sense of loss is a normal response—one that is probably shared by half the moms and dads standing next to you at soccer practice. For pediatricians, offering guidance and advice to parents makes up a considerable and rewarding part of each day. In the course of shedding light on your child, *Caring for Your Teenager* will help you be more attuned to *your* evolving feelings as you guide your youngster through the adolescent years.

TODAY'S UNIQUE GENERATION OF PARENTS AND TEENS

Perhaps it's human nature for each generation to inevitably find fault with the next. But take a look at a group of teenagers milling about outside school, and chances are that aside from clothing baggy enough to accommodate a family of four and the ubiquitous beepers and cellular phones, the scene looks oddly familiar. Who'd ever have thought that chunky-heeled shoes and bell-bottom pants would come back in style?

You belong to a unique generation in that unlike your parents or your grandparents you probably had an adolescence very similar to your teenager's, because the teen years of today bear a strong resemblance to what they have been since the 1960s. Now, as then, the times are relatively affluent, our current recession notwithstanding. Culturally and socially, teens are still consumed by many of the same interests you probably had: TV, sports, music, dating, movies. Unfortunately, they still face many of the same social problems, including widespread substance and alcohol abuse, unplanned pregnancies and sexually transmitted diseases.

Compared to parents of a generation ago, you probably have a greater understanding of the obstacles confronting your child. And while today's moms and dads aren't going to agree with everything that teens do in the name of expressing their individuality (if we did, our kids would never forgive us), perhaps we're more inclined to be accepting of their need to do it.

The common ground you share is a great place to begin establishing and nurturing communication, closeness and trust. In a stereotype-shattering 1998 survey of thirteen-to-seventeen-year-olds, two-thirds felt that their parents were "in touch with what life is like" for today's teens. So you may be more in tune with your teen than you realize. For all the similarities, though, this *is* a different world. Strains of marijuana are far more potent, unprotected sexual intercourse can infect a youngster with the human immunodeficiency virus (HIV) and the proliferation of violence throughout our society has fomented a climate of fear and anxiety in many communities. Not only are the stakes higher for teenagers today, but the age of innocence has become shorter and shorter. Kids face having to make critical decisions at increasingly younger ages—often before they are mature enough to fully assess the risks involved.

Probably the most significant difference between being a teenager today versus when you came of age is the diminished presence of the family in many adolescents' lives. Approximately half of all marriages end in divorce, almost twice the rate of the early 1960s. While nearly nine in ten children lived with both their mother and father in 1970, today at least half can expect to live in a household headed by a single parent at some point before they turn 18. And because three in four mothers of school-age children now work outside the home, many adolescents spend the afternoon hours unsupervised, with no adult at home to greet them and ask, "Hi, how was school today?"

The cumulative effect of these changes is familiar to all of us: a more stressful, less stable environment. And yet recent statistics paint a healthier portrait of our young people than you might expect—especially if compared to the beginning of the 1980s, when the final procession of baby boomers was entering adulthood.

- From 1981 to 1996 illicit drug use among high-school seniors dropped by 15 percent. Over the same period, alcohol use fell 14 percent and tobacco use, 7 percent.

- Teenagers are demonstrating more reproductive responsibility. From 1991 to 1996, the adolescent birth rate declined steadily, from 62 births for every 1,000 girls ages 15 to 19, to 55 per 1,000. Experts attribute the lower figures to a combination of more teens abstaining from sexual intercourse, and more sexually active teens using birth control (including more who are using condoms correctly).

- Contrary to figures purporting to show a disturbingly sharp rise in teen suicides, the numbers have actually gone *down* since the 1970s. In reality, the seemingly higher rates reflect improved identification of adolescents who died by their own hand. Years ago, suicides by drug and alcohol overdose, self-inflicted bullet wounds and so forth were virtually always ruled as accidents. Still, homicide and suicide remain the second and third causes of death respectively in Americans ages fifteen through twenty-four. Homicide is usually the second cause of death in African American teens, while suicide is usually the second cause of death in Caucasian teens.

The heartening message behind these statistics is that if we communicate to kids the adverse consequences of drugs, alcohol, tobacco, premature sex and so on *in a way that reaches them,* the message can have an effect. Nonetheless, a youngster's adolescence presents a frightening paradox for mothers and fathers, in that the time when you must learn to let your teenager go is the very time their need for guidance is the greatest because the consequences they potentially face are the most dire.

Though adolescence is a trying time for parents, take heart from one who has been there. Dr. Marianne Neifert offers a view of the road ahead that is both inspiring and realistic because it is based on her own experience of shepherding five children through the teen years. "How was it? It was great. Looking back, though, I would say that whatever struggles we did have were due to my lack of parenting skills. And here I was, a pediatrician! Had I been a little better prepared, I could have done a much better job. But even so," she says, "we had a ball! And, of course, the gift that you get at the end is adult children who are also your friends."

2

ESSENTIAL PARENTING SKILLS

Adolescents need their parents more than ever, only in a different way. Accordingly, mothers and fathers may discover that hard-won parenting techniques that succeeded so well in the past have suddenly been rendered obsolete. "We don't instruct parents on how to deal with teens," says Dr. Adele Hofmann, a pediatrician since 1955. "They continue to treat them like they're still children, which often doesn't work. Then the parents wonder, 'What's happened?' "

It's true that the basic aspects of raising and nurturing teenagers are the same as when they were little. Your kids still need you to shower them with love, establish discipline and provide emotional support and direction. But just as teenagers are works in progress, you must be open to revisions in your parenting program. Now is the time to expand your repertoire of parenting skills to fit this new person your son or daughter is becoming.

Get ready: You're in for quite a learning experience. "You will probably grow more as a parent during the teenage years," says pediatrician Dr. Marianne Neifert, "than at any other time."

LEARNING TO LISTEN SO THAT TEENS WILL TALK

Getting teenagers to express themselves—at least to their parents—can sometimes seem like an exercise in futility. "Yeah." "Nope." *"Whatever."*

The first rule for fostering communication between you and your child is simple: Never stop trying. "Parents shouldn't misinterpret a lack of response to mean that their kids aren't listening," says Dr. Robert Blum, director of the adolescent health program at University Hospitals in Minneapolis, and a father of three. On the contrary, says Dr. Lia Gaggino, a pediatrician from Kalamazoo, Michigan. "Kids want to talk and want your feedback"—even if their facial expressions and body language appear to say otherwise.

"I try to talk to my son, but I barely get more than one-word answers out of him. 'Hi, how was the game?' 'Fine.' Then he disappears into his room, and that's the extent of our 'conversation.'"

The tips below will help you both listen and talk in ways that will keep the doors of communication open between you and your child.

Listen.* Really *listen. "The parent who listens is the parent who gets heard," says Dr. Roberta Beach, director of Denver's Westside pediatric and teen clinics. She, like many other experts, recommends practicing *active listening,* also known as *reflective listening.* Pay close attention to your youngster's body language, the tone and inflection of her voice and her facial expressions, all of which convey important information.

After your teenager finishes speaking, clarify the problem or question by repeating back to her your interpretation of the central idea or emotion she is trying to express, without being judgmental or critical: *"I want to make sure I'm hearing you correctly, so let me repeat what you just said. Your geometry teacher made fun of you in class for giving the wrong answer, and all the kids laughed."*

You can go farther and gently suggest how you think she might be feeling. This requires the ability to empathize—to put ourselves in our youngster's unlaced high-top sneakers and reflect on how we might have felt at that age under the same circumstances. A parent's broader vocabulary and insight can help a teenager to sort through conflicting feelings and express herself more accurately.

"It sounds like you were really hurt, and angry at your teacher. I know if that had been me, I'd certainly have felt that way."

Tread carefully, though. If you're on target, your teen might reply (in astonishment, no doubt), "Wow, Mom, you really understand!" But mislabel a child's feelings, and she's likely to become even more upset, perhaps accusing you of not listening or not caring. Should she say in exasperation, "You just don't get it," Dr. Adele Hofmann suggests replying, "Well, I would love to understand. Why don't you explain it to me?"

Refrain from offering advice until you're sure you've digested all the details. Then ask, *"Would you like to know what I think might be the best way for you to handle this?"*

"Okay . . ."

Only then do you give your opinion on how you think she could resolve matters.

TEEN TIP:

To help calm an excited or upset youngster who is talking loudly and rapidly, counter by using a soft voice and speaking slowly.

Look at your teen when the two of you are talking. You'd be surprised how many times we don't bother to glance up from the newspaper, the TV or washing the dishes when talking to our kids. Maintaining eye contact is just one way that we silently communicate, "I am genuinely interested in what you have to say."

Don't interrupt. The same admonition we give our kids applies to us as well. Respect their right to express an opinion, even if you disagree with it. And if their viewpoint is based on a misconception, hear them out before correcting them—tactfully, without being condescending.

Watch your tone of voice. Asking questions is one thing; interrogating, using an accusatory tone, is another. And let's do our best not to bark at our teenager, as we sometimes do when we're pressed for time or worn out at the end of the day.

Ask questions that elicit conversation. Be resourceful! Create opportunities for discussion by asking questions that compel youngsters to describe, explain, share opinions—and the more specific these questions, the more based they are on what you already know is on your child's mind, the more effective they will be. "How did your English class like your speech this morning?" will go over much better than "How was school today?"

Grab opportunities for conversation whenever you can. Sometimes we put off talking to our kids, waiting instead for that perfect time to chat. Given today's fast-paced lifestyles, those ideal moments arrive far too infrequently.

Car rides are terrific times to talk, if for no other reason than both of you are a captive audience, in an environment free from many distractions. Another benefit is that when you are in a car you're usually sitting parallel to each other, not face to face, which makes for a less confrontational setting.

Feel free to share your own life experiences, even those that may not cast you in the most glowing light. We say this with some reservation. Sometimes parents reveal details from their past inappropriately. Before you regale your youngster with lurid tales of your past, ask yourself, "Is knowing this about me in my child's best interest?"

That said, your teenager may appreciate hearing how Grandma and Grandpa once grounded you after you skipped out on school to go joyriding with your buddy in his new car. Just prepare yourself for the possibility of an unreceptive audience, and responses ranging from, "Oh no, here we go again . . ." to, "But that was when you were a kid!" That's *okay:* At some point your teen will reflect on what you've said.

Repeatedly reassure your youngster that she can come to you with any problem, then make good on your promise of unconditional acceptance. Convey shock or disgust, even non-verbally, and you've just torpedoed the bridge of communication between you. "I may not approve of everything that you do," you say, "but no matter what, I'll always love you."

Pediatrician's Perspective

DR. TASNEEN ISMAILJI: "When teenagers come home, they often say hi and go straight to their room. They might not even say hi! And parents really shouldn't violate that space. But at some point they're going to come out—if nothing else, for food. And when they do, that is the time to talk.

"Right now, the only time I can really connect with my sixteen-year-old son is late at night. I hang out reading the paper, because I know that he's going to come out to watch TV. And when he does, we start talking. It's the only time out of the entire day. If I said, 'I'm tired; it's time for me to go to bed,' weeks might go by without any substantial conversation. So if I want to know what's happening in his life, that's the time I stick around."

Keep your antenna raised for signals that your teenager wants to talk. Your child might secretly be aching to confide in you but is too self-conscious, or scared, or simply doesn't know how to begin. Clues that he might have something on his mind include:

• Questions concerning "a friend" (often anonymous) with a problem: *"Mom, this kid I know at school shoplifted a Chicago Bulls jersey. If he'd gotten caught, would he be in really big trouble?"*

• Questions about your own adolescent experiences: *"Dad, how old were you when you first had sex?"*

• A magazine left open on your youngster's bed, turned conspicuously to an article. For instance, "Teenagers Get Depressed Too" might be a cry for help.

If you're too uncomfortable to discuss certain subjects face to face, write your son or daughter a letter. "Letters are a great way to get your thoughts out in an uninterrupted fashion," says Dr. Ray Coleman, a pediatrician in Rockville, Maryland. "It also gives you a hard-copy record of your feelings and advice."

A letter shouldn't be regarded as a substitute for verbal communication, but when addressing potentially volatile issues they can enable you to express yourself more thoughtfully than you might in person. What's more, stating your concerns in writing is less likely to provoke a defensive response or spark a conflict, simply because you're not physically there. This is also the perfect forum for saying "I love you" or paying a compliment.

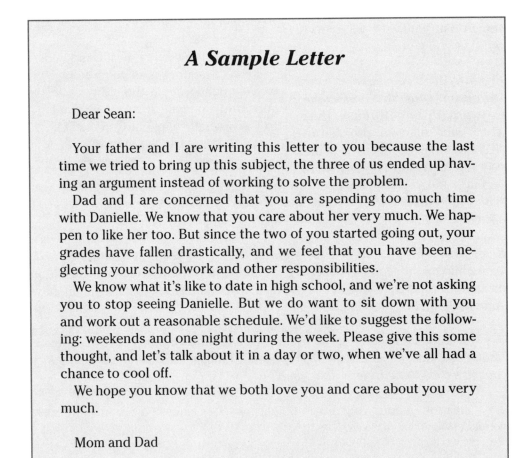

A Sample Letter

Dear Sean:

Your father and I are writing this letter to you because the last time we tried to bring up this subject, the three of us ended up having an argument instead of working to solve the problem.

Dad and I are concerned that you are spending too much time with Danielle. We know that you care about her very much. We happen to like her too. But since the two of you started going out, your grades have fallen drastically, and we feel that you have been neglecting your schoolwork and other responsibilities.

We know what it's like to date in high school, and we're not asking you to stop seeing Danielle. But we do want to sit down with you and work out a reasonable schedule. We'd like to suggest the following: weekends and one night during the week. Please give this some thought, and let's talk about it in a day or two, when we've all had a chance to cool off.

We hope you know that we both love you and care about you very much.

Mom and Dad

Find other adults with whom your child can speak freely. Even if you have an exceptional rapport with your youngster, there may be times when she needs another supportive adult's perspective. What if you're a single mother whose twelve-year-old son has questions about his changing body? He might prefer talking to his uncle, an older cousin or his best friend's dad than to Mom.

MAKING DISCIPLINE WORK

The word *discipline* is so often used interchangeably with *punishment* that we tend to lose sight of its true purpose and meaning. "Discipline is not intended to be punitive," explains Dr. George Comerci, an Arizona pediatrician and former president of the American Academy of Pediatrics. "The object is to teach self-control and to prepare teenagers for entering adulthood and society."

You and your youngster will both benefit if you approach discipline as a system of setting and

"Our fourteen-year-old son used to be an obedient kid. But now it seems like the only way to get him to listen to us is for my wife and me to issue threats and take away privileges. It's made life at home pretty unpleasant. There's got to be a better way."

enforcing effective *limits* through incentives and deterrents rather than issuing *ultimatums*. An ultimatum is a do-it-or-else statement: *"Joe, put away your bike, or you can't ride it for the rest of the day."* It is condescending to teens and may be interpreted as a challenge.

Establishing boundaries, on the other hand, communicates respect.

- You spell out the desirable:

  "Joe, I want you to put away your bike . . .

- Then specify a positive consequence for compliance:

  "If you put it away now, you can ride it later . . .

- And a negative consequence for noncompliance:

  "But if you don't, you cannot ride it for the rest of the day."

First parents must establish and clearly identify what constitutes permissible and unacceptable behavior in everything from conduct, to school performance, to curfew. Instead of calling these rules and regulations, let's refer to them as a teenager's *rights and responsibilities*. It may seem a small difference in semantics, but these terms more accurately reflect the goal of imposing discipline at home: to teach children the self-discipline they must master to achieve happiness and success in later years.

Youngsters who have little or no structure at home may be the envy of their peers, but as Dr. Renée Jenkins observes, "They often feel ignored by their parents." Teens will never admit to it, but secretly they *want* and need us to set limits—even if they don't always abide by them. In time, most come to realize that we do so out of love, not merely to flex our adult muscles. Just don't expect to receive any expressions of gratitude until they become parents themselves.

Rules for Making Rules

Adolescents, so intent on asserting their independence, tend to see themselves as tyrannized by rules, rules and more rules. Although consistency in the enforcement of your rules is key to discipline, not all rules are equally important. Now and then parents can bend the regulations pertaining to such matters as TV viewing, curfews, bedtime, dating, homework habits, car privileges and similar matters. Learning to prioritize household rules gives both you and your teenager room to practice the arts of negotiation and compromise. As Dr. Adele Hofmann explains, in a discussion of establishing a curfew: "It's like buying a rug at a Turkish bazaar; you bargain your way down." A curfew negotiation might proceed along these lines:

"I've given a lot of thought to what your weeknight curfew should be during the summer. Nine o'clock seems fair."

"Nine o'clock? But Mom, all my friends get to stay out till eleven!"

Suppressing your skepticism, you reply, *"Well, I think eleven o'clock is much too late for a fifteen-year-old. What if we compromised and said ten o'clock? That gives you an extra hour. . . ."*

As with a commercial transaction, it helps if you enter the negotiation with an idea of where you're willing to end up.

However, there should be no negotiation when it comes to restrictions imposed to safeguard youngsters from risky behaviors such as substance abuse, premature sexual activity and reckless driving.

Your policy on matters that affect health, safety or well-being should be stated clearly. For example, make sure that your child understands that tobacco, alcohol or other drug use will not be tolerated, and that any breach of your trust will result in serious consequences. It's wise to spell out your expectations early on in adolescence, if not sooner, to help avert problems down the road. And your chances of having these expectations met are higher if you are prepared to explain your decision. "I can't ride my bike to the mall across town? But *why not?*" your teen is likely to demand.

An appropriate response would be: "Because your father and I think that it's too far away and there's too much traffic. You can take the bus, but biking it is too dangerous. We love you, and we're concerned about your safety."

Teenagers are more inclined to comply with a rule when they understand the logic behind it, as opposed to receiving a flat "Because I said so, that's why."

Curfews and Bedtimes

Curfew and bedtime are two of the more negotiable household rules. During adolescence, when boys and girls are getting their first taste of independence, they probably spend the equivalent of a law-school education making their case to Mom and Dad for just a *little* extra time to stay out or to stay up.

What is not negotiable are the consequences for disobeying curfew, except in the event of unforeseen circumstances. So that the punishment conforms to the crime, deduct time from future curfews, depending on the severity of the infraction. If your youngster straggles in an hour late, perhaps the next time he goes out with his friends, he has to come home an hour earlier than usual. Two hours past curfew buys a teenager a Friday or Saturday night confined to home. Long-term punishments, such as grounding the offender for one month, amount to overkill and will very likely do more harm than good.

Q: When setting a curfew, how do I know what's reasonable and what's not? All of my son's friends have to be home at different times, so it's hard to base my decision on what other parents do.

TEEN TIP:

"Sorry, Mom, I lost track of the time. I'll be home in half an hour. You're not too mad at me, I hope. Are you?" A phone call from your teen explaining why she'll be late for curfew demonstrates enough responsibility to get her off the hook, so long as this doesn't become a recurring pattern.

Let's help our kids do the right thing: If you can afford it, buy your teen a beeper or keep a cell phone in the car, but with the provision that it be used *only* in an emergency or if he expects to be delayed getting home. And should you ever page him, he'd better call back within ten to twenty minutes.

A: You can start by consulting the following table, which gives parents *general* guidelines appropriate for each stage of adolescent development.

Let's use as an example a fourteen-year-old boy. If he has school or other early morning commitments the next day, he really should be home no later than nine o'clock at night; if it's a vacation day coming up, between 10 P.M. and 11 P.M. is reasonable.

That's your *starting point.* Now factor in the following:

1. *How mature and responsible is he overall?*
    If you feel confident that he knows how to watch out for his own safety and you trust he is where he tells you he will be, perhaps you extend the curfew. Some kids may not need a curfew beyond a community or state law regulating when adolescents must be off the road.

TABLE 2.1

Basic Guidelines for Setting Curfews

	DURING EARLY ADOLESCENCE AGES 12 TO 13	DURING MIDDLE ADOLESCENCE AGES 14 TO 16	DURING LATE ADOLESCENCE AGES 17 TO 21
On most nights *prior to school* or other morning activities or responsibilities:	7 P.M. to 8 P.M.	8 P.M. to 9 P.M.	10 P.M. to 11 P.M.
On most nights *not followed by school,* or other morning activities or responsibilities:	9 P.M. to 10 P.M.	10 P.M. to 11 P.M.	12 A.M. to 1 A.M.
Following a special event, such as a basketball game, a rock concert and so on, he must be home by _____, depending on distance and travel time:	Negotiable — No later than 12 A.M.	Negotiable — No later than 12 A.M.	Negotiable — No later than 2 A.M.

2. *Does he usually comply with curfew?*

Again, his past behavior will influence how lenient or strict you are.

3. *What activity is he engaged in?*

If he is shooting hoops in the park, he should be home by sundown, but if he's studying with a friend, he can stay out later.

4. *If he's attending a baseball game, concert, school function or other event, what time does it let out and how long will it take him to get home?*

This will help determine whether or not you allow him some extra time to perhaps get a bite to eat before heading home.

5. *How much sleep does he usually need?*

The average adolescent requires about nine hours of shut-eye a night, some more, some less. If your youngster is drowsy in the morning, you'll want to move up his bedtime, and with it, his curfew. See page 532 for advice on sleeping problems in adolescents.

What Are Fair and Reasonable Limits?

How do you know if the boundaries you've set are reasonable? Your pediatrician may be a valuable source of advice on general age-appropriate ground rules. You might also try networking informally among other parents. Ask, "What time does Meredith go to bed on school nights?" Don't be surprised if it's not as late as your youngster led you to believe. But even if it is, the limits you set for your son or daughter must ultimately reflect your own values and priorities, no one else's.

However, we do suggest consulting one other expert on what comprises sensible restrictions—namely, your teenager. Whenever possible, youngsters should have a say in developing the rules that they're going to be expected to follow. You may be surprised how reasonable your son or daughter can be.

Always listen respectfully to your child's point of view; kids have a right to vent frustration ("You're always treating me like a baby!"), even anger ("You're the meanest mom and dad in the world!"). But in the end, if you feel you must say no, don't back down.

Other Suggestions for Setting Limits

Be specific. Again using curfew as an example: "You are to be home no later than eight o'clock on school nights." Not: "I don't want you out late during the week."

Be concise. Setting a limit shouldn't take more than a few sentences.

Put all important rules in writing, to counter selective memories. "But you never told me I'm not allowed to have friends in the car when I'm driving!"

"Oh yes we did. Remember this?"

An adolescent's rights and responsibilities are subject to change. Standards of discipline must suit not only a youngster's age, but her behavior, emotional maturity, capabilities and developmental understanding.

As she demonstrates increased responsibility, we grant her more freedom. If she shows bad judgment, however, or breaks the existing rules, we impose more restrictions until she regains our confidence and trust.

Pediatrician's Perspective

DR. LANI WHEELER: "I have an older teenage son. When he was younger, I used to wait up until he got home. Now when he goes out at night, I set an alarm clock for ten minutes past his curfew, leave it near the front door and go to bed. If my son comes home on time, he turns it off, and I continue sleeping. If he didn't come home on time, I would be alerted by the alarm.

"I say 'didn't' because since I started this system, he's never been late!"

A parent's expectations must be reasonable and achievable. Realistically, a chronically disorganized youngster who has always kept a messy room is not going to be instantly transformed. His improvement is likely to come in increments, which should then be the yardstick for praise. Perhaps the stack of comic books beneath his bed is still accumulating dust, but he *did* straighten out the bedcovers before leaving for school today, making this a milestone worthy of a compliment. And a snapshot?

What Are Fair and Reasonable Consequences?

Effective punishment is neither too lenient nor too harsh, but commensurate with the severity of the "crime." To merely scold a teenager after he returns the car with empty beer cans stashed under the seat sends the message that you don't truly take the infraction seriously, and neither should he. Conversely, to forbid a youngster from attending the big fall homecoming dance because she missed the due date for an important social-studies report will undoubtedly stir up resentment toward Mom and Dad—and school—more than it will impart a lesson about the importance of handing in work on time.

Methods of Punishment

MILD MEASURES

• **Actively ignoring:** This is for addressing minor behavioral problems on the order of whining, yelling and sulking. To "actively ignore" is not the same thing as giving the silent treatment, a passive-aggressive tactic that we strongly discourage. In a firm voice, you tell your teen, "I will not talk to you until you stop _____." Then you proceed to do just that.

• **Time out!:** Time-outs, so effective for defusing impulsive, aggressive or hostile conduct in younger children, can still be applied to adolescents, including older teens. Implementing a time-out prevents youngsters from commanding any more attention for their behavior.

Q: How long should time-outs be?
A: For younger teens, experts recommend one minute for each year of life. That's twelve minutes for a twelve-year-old. Older teens can decide for themselves when they have calmed down sufficiently to return to where you are and continue the discussion rationally and courteously.

Q: Where should youngsters take a time-out?
A: Time-outs are ostensibly for reflection—even if in reality your youngster sits there muttering under his breath. Preferably, the designated time-out area should be someplace away from the hub of household activity, quiet and free of distractions (in short, *boring*), but within your sight.

• **Scolding and disapproval:** Reprimands should be administered sparingly, and never when our emotions are out of control. The point is to focus on the transgression, not the transgressor, and to do so without resorting to "charged" language or a tone of voice that is sarcastic, disrespectful or demeaning. For a youngster to feel ashamed of something he said or did can discourage similar behavior in the future. But nothing productive ever comes from humiliating a child.

Say: "I am saddened by your actions."

MORE SEVERE MEASURES

• **Imposing additional responsibilities:** When time-outs and reprimands fail to change behavior, more drastic consequences become necessary. One approach is to assign adolescents additional household tasks. If for example your teenager didn't deliver on a promise to rake the leaves last weekend, then this weekend he must not only rake the leaves but weed the flower beds, regardless of whatever plans he may have made.

• **Imposing additional restrictions:** Another highly effective one is to rescind privileges or possessions that are meaningful to them, be it watching TV, using the car or attending an upcoming hockey game.

One way of deciding upon an appropriate punishment is by consulting with that previously mentioned expert—your teenager. Just as adolescents can participate in setting the limits they will be expected to follow, they can also be allowed to help determine the penalty for overstepping those boundaries. Dr. Tomas Silber, a pediatrician at Children's Hospital in Washington, D.C., suggests that if breaking curfew was the offense, you might ask, "What do *you* think is a fair punishment for a kid who came home late and didn't call?" Sometimes, he says, the sentences teens hand themselves are stiffer than what Mom and Dad had in mind. "The parents actually find themselves saying, 'Well, you have to suffer a consequence, but that's overdoing it! How about this . . .' " According to Dr. Adele Hofmann, a youngster may accept his punishment less grudgingly if he's played a part in deciding it, "because then it becomes his own rather than something that is imposed upon him."

The American Academy of Pediatrics

Where We Stand on Physical Punishment

The American Academy of Pediatrics strongly opposes any form of physical punishment, including spanking. The risk of injury—to the child or to the parent—is one concern. But just as damaging, if not more so, are the psychological wounds corporal punishment often inflicts on the victim.

Mothers or fathers who become physically aggressive with a teenager should seek the help of a mental-health specialist. The right therapist can show them more effective, nonviolent methods of discipline, as well as teach them techniques for anger management.

Positive Attention

Some parents resist the concept of positive attention, likening it to bribery. "Why should I reward my son for good behavior?" they ask. "Isn't that what he's *supposed* to do?" Certainly children learn from having their mistakes pointed out to them in a constructive manner, but reprimands not offset by praise—and the occasional treat—inevitably prove demoralizing.

It's easy to shine too unforgiving a light on our kids' misdeeds and to overlook the many, many things they do right every day. Here's a healthy and not-unrealistic ratio to strive for: For every reprimand, try to find two things your youngster did that merit compliments. *You've taken out the trash for two weeks without my having to remind you. Good job. I appreciate it."* Just watch his face light up.

"Grandma's Rule": Stealth Discipline

It's true that one way to prompt kids to behave is to remind them of the consequences they will face if they do not toe the line, as in: "Mister, you're not leaving this house to meet your friends until the lawn is mowed, like we'd agreed yesterday." However you can impart the same message using the kinder, gentler approach aptly referred to as "Grandma's Rule." Rephrase the previous statement this way: "As soon as you've finished mowing the lawn, you may go out with your friends." *Voilà!* You've transformed a perceived threat into a reward.

When a Teenager Breaks the Rules
General Rules of Administering Discipline

Never punish when you're angry. In the heat of the moment, you may say something you'll regret later or you may set too harsh a restriction. This leads us to rule number two . . .

Never impose a penalty you're not prepared to carry out. It is important to imagine your teen's possible reactions to the discipline you have in mind, particularly if it's on the extreme side. Example: grounding for one month because you caught him and a friend smoking out back. Might he challenge you verbally? Run away? Become depressed, or perhaps suicidal? Then ask yourself if you could live with any of those outcomes. If the answer is no, you should moderate the penalty. Not following through damages your credibility and serves to reinforce the very behavior you intended to punish.

Another point to consider: Could the punishment conceivably damage your relationship with your youngster?

Short-term consequences work best. By "short-term," we mean punishments lasting several hours, or several days for major violations. To ground a youngster for a month can set the stage for him to act out in some other way, such as sneaking out of the house. He may figure, *What have I got to lose? I'm already grounded for a month.* Most punishments lose their effectiveness if they last longer than twenty-four hours.

Punish the guilty party only, not other family members. Example: If the whole clan has been looking forward to spending a day out on the boat, don't let the fact that your teen is grounded scuttle those plans. Arrange for him to stay home with a friend or family member.

Don't use guilt as a means of discipline.
"Why do you do this to me? I think you secretly enjoy torturing me."
"How can you go out in public looking like that, with all those holes in your jeans? Everyone will think I'm a bad mother!"
If you can hear yourself in these lines, you're probably cringing right now. In general, guilt should not be used as punishment. It often fails to produce the desired outcome, and even when it works, teenagers (like adults) resent it and find it unjust.

Help youngsters learn from their mistakes. Confronting a teenager about a breach of conduct doesn't have to become an inquisition. "It should be a dialogue," advises Dr. Hofmann. In order for an adolescent to learn from her mistake, first she has to reflect on what she did and her reasons for doing it:
"Honey, you know full well that we don't allow you to ride in a car being driven by anyone we don't know. And yet you and your friend Jennifer went ahead and accepted a ride from two boys who don't even go to your school. I'd like to hear your side of things and why you did that."
The next step is to restate and clarify the problem, then help her to come up with one or more solutions:
"So the two of you were up at the shopping center, and it was hot out, and you didn't feel like walking home. But you know that you are forbidden from riding with strangers. How do you think you could have handled the situation differently?"
"Well . . . I suppose we could have taken the bus. Or we could have called you or Jen's mom."
"Right. And if the bus was late, or no one could drive you, what should you have done?"
"I should have walked."

There are two essential messages to convey: First, every problem has a solution. Second, your child is responsible for her own conduct.

Impose discipline consistently. To set limits but not enforce them is akin to installing an elaborate security system in your home but failing to turn it on at night. We're not implying that discipline be applied dogmatically. One reason it's essential to replay events with your youngster is because sometimes you learn that extenuating circumstances contributed to the misconduct. But as a general rule, when parents dispense punishment erratically, they are reinforcing the negative behavior.

Sending mixed signals does one of two things. "It may confuse the child," explains Dr. Tomas Silber. "Worse, it can breed disrespect for the parent." Once you've settled on a limit, stick to it.

This presumes that both parents regularly agree on where to draw the line, which isn't always the case. In fact, a couple may hold radically different views, either concerning an isolated situation or across the board.

The good-cop/bad-cop routine may be useful for prying confessions from criminals on TV, but it's a formula for trouble when practiced by mothers and fathers. Kids quickly learn to get their way by manipulating the more lenient parent against the stricter parent. There is no simple solution to this, other than sitting down together and negotiating a list of boundaries and consequences you can both live with. Putting rules into writing, as suggested earlier, is perhaps less for the child's sake than it is for helping Mom and Dad maintain a united front. If you can't seem to reach a compromise, consider soliciting the advice of a marriage and family counselor.

> ### *When Your Teenager Says . . .*
>
> "Cory's parents let *him* watch TV before he does his homework!" (Be prepared to hear countless variations on this theme throughout the teenage years.)
>
> **YOU MIGHT REPLY . . .**
> *"What goes on in Cory's family is their business. We don't live at Cory's house. We've set certain rules for you because we love you and believe they are in your best interest—like doing your homework as soon as you come home from school. We expect you to abide by those rules."*

To the extent that you can, enlist the cooperation of other mothers and fathers. Trying to steer your child in the right direction can sometimes feel like swimming against the current, especially when rules that prevail in your home aren't shared by other families.

Surely you know many, if not all, of the parents in your teenager's circle of friends. Perhaps a group of you can agree upon some relatively uniform guidelines regulating such issues as curfew, X-rated movies and videos, etc.

But whatever you do, don't cave in on the core standards of behavior that you've set for your son or daughter. We ask you to heed the same admonition that parents have been handing their children for generations: the immortal, "If Johnny jumped off a bridge, does that mean you would too?"

Parenting: It's Never Too Late to Make Adjustments

If you would describe yourself as overly strict (or perhaps it's been pointed out to you by your spouse—or by your teen), begin your shift toward the middle by learning to *choose your battles.*

"Parents must prioritize what they're going to try to control," advises Dr. Margaret Blythe, director of adolescent medical services at Indiana University Medical Center in Indianapolis. "Everything can't be a power struggle." For parents and children to butt heads constantly is not healthy.

Perhaps you have the opposite problem, however, and are overly permissive. The role of disciplinarian doesn't come naturally to everyone. No parent enjoys being on the receiving end of a teenager's hurt and angry glare. But for mothers and fathers who have tended to overindulge their youngsters and are now seeing warning signs that a change is in order, remember this: *Kids need us to be their parents first, their pals second.*

Consistently maintaining boundaries and following through on consequences takes on added importance when permissive parents attempt to become more authoritative. Until now, their children have been used to manipulating Mom and Dad. They can be expected to rebel against these new limits. In fact, their misbehavior may grow worse for a time. Once they come to see that their parents are serious about enforcing discipline, they will usually learn to respect the rules of the household.

RESTORING THE PEACE:
HOW TO RESOLVE CONFLICTS AND MANAGE ANGER

Sometimes it seems as if adolescence sets parents and children on a perpetual collision course. As much as we love our kids, their seesawing moods, penchant for challenging authority and lapses in judgment can be maddening at times. Of course, to hear them talk about us (and if you've never listened in on teenagers' discussions about their parents before, you're in for a humbling experience), we can be equally exasperating: basically lovable, but overly demanding and oftentimes clueless about what really matters—to them, that is.

Place adults and children under the same roof, and some conflict is not only inevitable but normal. Disagreements and verbal skirmishes aren't necessarily symptomatic of an unhealthy or unhappy household, unless arguing becomes the standard mode of communication. It's certainly preferable that family members

"I don't like arguing with my daughter; I really don't! But it's as if the two of us are locked into a pattern of continuous conflict. I'll innocently remind her about something: 'Please be home by four o'clock to help me with the cooking; all the relatives are going to be here around six.' She'll say something snippy in response or accuse me of nagging her, and before you know it, I've lost my temper and we're having another shouting match."

feel free to express their feelings honestly—including airing grievances—than to repress them. That's how problems get resolved before small misunderstandings snowball into more serious conflicts. But in order for confrontations to ultimately be constructive, everyone needs to observe certain ground rules. As parents, it falls to us to model the behaviors and attitudes conducive to healthy disagreements and, we hope, resolution.

Rules of the Ring: How to Fight Fair

Before George Munson has even hung up the phone, he can feel his face reddening.

"David!"

His sixteen-year-old son appears in the doorway, absentmindedly working the buttons of a handheld video game.

"Yeah, Dad?"

"David, did someone from the camera store call here yesterday?"

The computerized beeping stops, and the teenager studies the tops of his desert boots.

"Oh. Uh, yeah. I guess I forgot to tell you."

"My camera was ready to be picked up today; I could have stopped by there on my way home. You know I need that camera for the wedding I'm shooting tomorrow. Now I'll have to make a separate trip over there at nine o'clock, which barely gives me enough time to get to the church. How many times have your mother and I asked you to write down all phone messages?" It's a rhetorical question, but for those keeping score: twice this week and countless times before that.

Time-out for parents. If you feel your temper start to flare out of control when you confront your teenager about some lapse, excuse yourself until you regain your composure.

TEEN TIP:

All actions are reciprocal. If you stay calm during a conflict, your youngster is more likely to stay calm.

Take five to ten minutes. Walk around the block if you need to, march outside and dig a new flower bed in record time or barricade yourself in the bathroom, the private sanctuary of parents everywhere. After that you should be ready to address the issue at hand more calmly and rationally.

Dr. Helen Pratt, director of behavioral and developmental pediatrics at Michigan State University's Kalamazoo Center for Medical Studies, has an expression to describe those moments "when you're not ready to be 'on'; to be reasonable, loving and nurturing. My husband or I will say, 'I'm not ready for prime time.' " (The Pratts probably have more experience in prime time than most of us: In addition to raising five children, they've opened their home to thirty-five foster children over the years.)

"When you feel that way," she continues, "you need to be able to separate from the rest of the family and actively do something to bring yourself around. And children should have the same opportunity," she points out.

Use "I" statements that reflect your feelings. Sentences that begin with the word *you* sound accusatory and threatening, and will elicit a defensive response. Just look at the difference between the following statements:

"I'm upset about not receiving my phone messages, because they're very important to me and my business."

"David, you took four phone messages for me last week and forgot to tell me about them."

If you do make an accusation, be specific: *"David, you forgot to give me four phone messages last week."* Not: *"You never take phone messages when you're supposed to."*

Explain why the behavior makes you upset or angry: *"When I don't get a message like this one, it creates a lot of problems for me that could have been avoided. I work very hard, and the prospect of having to get up early tomorrow makes me angry."*

Don't dredge up events from the past. Complaints are like yogurt: They have an expiration date. It's unfair to confront someone about something he can no longer change. If it bothered you then, *then* was the time to say so.

Never belittle the other person's feelings. You may not agree with how your youngster sees the situation. You may not believe he is even entitled to feel the way he does. But there can be no disagreements about *how* he feels.

Ask your youngster to offer his solution to the problem.

No Hitting Below the Belt

- ***Don't*** overgeneralize, using words such as *always, never* and *every time.*
- ***Don't*** give the other person the silent treatment.
- ***Don't*** resort to name-calling and put-downs.
- ***Don't*** presume to know what the other person is thinking or feeling.
- ***Don't*** assume the other person should know what you're thinking or feeling.
- ***Don't*** play a game of tit for tat, responding to a complaint with one of your own.

Our ultimate goal isn't to win the argument, it's to resolve the conflict. David's family worked out the following compromise: David promised to make sure that there were paper and pencils next to each telephone. He also agreed to get up early enough the following morning to drive down to the camera store for his father and still be able to get to school on time.

You're wrong? Admit it. The scene: *six-thirty on a Tuesday.*

"Denise, where on earth have you been? Dinner's been waiting for half an hour."

"Mom, we had a meeting of the yearbook staff after school. I told you all about it yesterday."

"Today? Oh. I thought you said that was next week."

"See? You and Dad are always accusing me of stuff I didn't do! Around here I'm guilty until proven innocent. It's really, really unfair."

"Well, maybe I'm too quick to assume the worst because until recently you never used to tell me where you were going after school."

Mothers and fathers sometimes resist apologizing to their teenagers when they are wrong, in the mistaken belief that to do so would somehow compromise their authority. If anything, the opposite is true: Being big enough to say you're sorry only deepens your youngster's respect for you. Teenagers detest hypocrisy, and they figure out right away when a parent was wrong.

In the example above, an appropriate and fair response would have been a simple, "You're right. I jumped to a conclusion, and that was wrong of me. I apologize."

To be able to say to our teenagers, "Can you forgive me?" is a humbling experience for us, but esteem-building for them. It models for teenagers how to apologize and also sends a comforting message: Mom and Dad aren't perfect. Whether we realize it or not, our children are continually measuring themselves against us. When kids know that you're not perfect, they realize that you don't expect them to be perfect either, which takes some of the pressure off them.

The preceding pages have presented strategies for resolving conflict. Knowing when it's best to *sidestep* conflict is another essential parenting skill. Often our natural inclination is to pick up the scent of confrontation like a bloodhound and go chasing after it. We wag a finger and sternly admonish our youngster not to act so disrespectfully, or else. And we're absolutely correct in doing so. Sometimes, though, keeping the peace is preferable to diving into a power struggle—for everyone's sake. "Parents can choose to disengage from the power struggle," suggests Dr. Pratt, "and decide not to argue."

SHARE YOUR VALUES

Today, teenagers are bombarded with conflicting, ever-shifting standards of ethics and morality, at the very time they're in the process of formulating a system of beliefs. This is not only confusing for them but troubling for their parents because they can no longer rely on society to reinforce the values they teach at home.

Previous generations depended upon a complex matrix of people and institutions to uphold the community's moral codes. Extended family members, neighbors, religious and civic organizations, and schools expanded a parent's sphere of influence beyond the home. What's more, most mothers and fathers felt they could depend on other parents and adults in the community to back them up, to adhere to the same basic values and rules of conduct for their children. In many cases, that safety net has been stretched thin, a consequence of the high divorce rate, longer work weeks and other societal changes that have taken place over the last several decades.

"How can I tell my daughter not to become sexually involved with her boyfriend, when she knows that her father and I lived together before we were married? I can just hear her saying, 'Oh, sure, Mom, you're one to talk!' "

Exacerbating matters, we often find ourselves competing with the ever-more-invasive influence of media, which tries to unify the increasingly fragmented audience by an appeal to its insatiable appetite for sensationalism, sex and celebrity worship. If we're to counterbalance these outside influences, it's up to parents to build their youngsters a sturdy moral and ethical foundation. Though it may not always seem like it, you are *the* guiding influence in your teenager's life. Don't hesitate to express your views on drug use, sex, racial intolerance, hate crimes and other matters that affect your children, especially when setting a limit or administering discipline. First, however, you must thoughtfully reflect on your positions. Discuss with your youngster what you believe and why, as in the example below. He may not like the rule or punishment, but at least he may come away satisfied that it's not being imposed arbitrarily.

Children need to know where Mom and Dad stand, if only to have a belief system from which to craft their own. They may disagree with you—defy you, even—but eventually they will probably respect you for your convictions. According to a number of studies, most kids return to and adopt their parents' values by their midtwenties.

The Most Effective Way to Instill Values? By Example

Your words will carry more weight if you model the values and habits you want your teenager to emulate. Walk the talk, so to speak. Adolescents whose parents smoke, for example, are three times more likely to take up cigarettes than children from homes where tobacco is not used.

Nevertheless, the fact that parents may fail to practice what they preach—either now or in the past—does not preclude them from imparting ethics and morals to their children. Being perfect is not a prerequisite of parenthood. The inevitable protest, an indignant "But *you* do it!" (surely you saw that one coming), has a surprisingly simple comeback. In the box at right, "it" happens to be smoking. But you can tailor your response for any behavior or attitude that is inappropriate, unsafe or illegal for a minor.

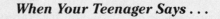

> ### *When Your Teenager Says . . .*
>
> "How come I can't smoke? *You* smoke!"
>
> **YOU MIGHT REPLY . . .**
> *"You're right, I do smoke. I wish I didn't, and I'm trying to quit. But besides the fact that it is* illegal *for you to smoke cigarettes, I love you and don't want to see you become addicted to tobacco like I am. And the best way not to become hooked is to never start. I am doing what I believe is best for you. You are not to use tobacco."*

Parents who perhaps experimented with drugs, alcohol or sex years ago face a similar dilemma. Is it hypocritical to prohibit your teenager from doing things that you did when you were his or her age? In a word, no. You are acting as a concerned parent who has learned from experience and wants to protect her child.

Earlier in this chapter we cautioned parents against volunteering stories from their youth too freely. But what if your child asks you point blank, "Did you ever _____ when you were a kid?" When it comes to run-of-the-mill teenage dilemmas involving sex, drugs, smoking, school and so forth, speak up. A parent's admitting to previous lapses in judgment or ethics can make for powerful testimony about the advantages of traveling the proper path. Don't overdramatize or resort to scare tactics. Just be honest:

"When I was sixteen, I let a boy I was dating pressure me into having sex. Looking back, I realize I wasn't mature enough to handle it. I got hurt pretty badly. I wish I'd waited until I was older."

"During my sophomore year in college, I was getting high every weekend. One night I drove home from a bar drunk and crashed into a parked car. The police and the paramedics were amazed I wasn't killed. It took me a couple of years to straighten myself out. That's what drugs and alcohol did for me. I hope you'll be a lot smarter than I was and not get into that stuff."

However, there may well be aspects of your personal life that you would rather not divulge, particularly if your youngster is emotionally immature, a gossip or prone to throwing things back in your face when tempers flare. Consider relating your experience as if it happened to someone you "knew," provided it's not anyone your child could identify. The point of this type of discussion is to raise your teenager's awareness of what's at stake and how her decisions can have consequences, not to gain her trust by baring your soul or airing your dirty laundry. Parents who do that too often or indiscriminately risk losing their children's respect and undermining their authority. Use common sense.

LET TEENAGERS KNOW HOW MUCH THEY MATTER

When a teenager seems to be pushing his parents away, they may think that he doesn't want their affirmation—or perhaps that he doesn't *deserve* affirmation from them. But what children need more than anything else, at any age, is for their parents to convey to them over and over again, both in words and in actions, *I delight in you, and I am thrilled that you're my child.*

As you're probably all too aware, mothers and fathers today have less time to devote to raising children than their parents did. One unfortunate consequence of longer work weeks and the increase in dual-income families is that parents and children spend ten to twelve fewer hours together per week than they did in 1960. When parents and children become disconnected from one another, cracks can form in the family foundation. According to Dr. Robert Blum, making the most of what time they do share can compensate for the lack of it, for "quality overrides quantity in importance."

Let's define "quality time." To some parents it's weekend family outings to an amusement park or the movies, when in fact it describes any moment of closeness, affection and connection between you and your youngster. The setting could be raking leaves together, jogging, playing chess, fishing, setting the table or shopping. Major family expeditions, as fun as they are, aren't necessarily conducive to communication. Every exchange doesn't need to be serious or deep, incidentally; the "quality" we refer to lies in the quality of your attention.

"I'd been putting in long hours at work for weeks on end, then spent five days out of town at a business convention. My wife told me that our twelve-year-old son was feeling neglected and, frankly, was a little angry with me.

"When I got back home, I said to him, 'Marc, how about you and me hitting the Brewers game this Sunday? I can get us box seats right behind the dugout. We'll gorge ourselves on hot dogs and soda and peanuts. Sound good?' He said, 'Sure, Dad,' with a surprising lack of enthusiasm.

"The next day he asked me if I would mind skipping the ball game. 'You know what I'd rather do? Remember when you and I used to go bike-riding down by the lake? Could we do that instead?' More than anything, he just wanted my undivided attention."

Family members sometimes seem to pass each other like the proverbial ships in the night. Make the effort to squeeze in quality time whenever you can. Perhaps you're driving your daughter to ballet practice. Instead of sitting in silence, half-listening to the news, turn off the radio and use the time to chat. What could be more interesting than what's going on in your teenager's life?

Simple Ways That Say "You're Special to Me"

Pay attention! What teenagers want most of all from their parents, says Dr. Blum, "is their psychological availability." As part of the National Longitudinal Study on Adolescent Health, which he coauthored, the young participants were asked, "How do your parents show you they care?"

"The kids said they do it by *remembering what goes on in their lives.* Remembering that they had a history test last Tuesday and asking how they did. Remembering that they went out with Jimmy—not Sammy—last night, and asking how the date went. Remembering the names of their friends when they call or come over, and not asking, 'Who's that?' even though they've seen that friend half a dozen times."

Show up! Their grumbled protests to the contrary, most kids secretly want their parents to attend special events in their lives such as school plays, parent-teacher conferences, sporting events and recitals. And when that's not possible, it's a good idea to line up other adults who can stand in for you in a pinch: aunts, uncles, grandparents, close friends—anyone who has a meaningful relationship with your youngster.

"When my daughter was in elementary school," Dr. Renée Jenkins recalls, "I had a group of people I could depend on. If there were seven important events to attend, I could usually make two of them, and her dad could go two times. The other three were spread among her godmother, her godmother's son and her aunt."

Be available even when you're not home. With more mothers working outside the home, so-called "latchkey kids" are no longer an anomaly of American life, they are the norm. With a little creativity on our part, youngsters who come home from school to an empty house can still feel that we're accessible to them.

Want to warm the heart of even the most outwardly jaded teenager? Leave a note on the refrigerator that says, HOPE YOU HAD A GREAT DAY AT SCHOOL. I'LL BE HOME AROUND 5:30. LOVE YOU, MOM. Thanks to technology, we can be available by phone, fax, e-mail and pager. If possible, set aside ten minutes each afternoon to check in with your child and inquire about her day.

3

YOUR TEENAGER'S PHYSICAL DEVELOPMENT

Looking at any seventh-grade class picture, it can be hard to believe that the (mostly) smiling faces all belong to children the same age. The boy on the far left looks as if he's still in grade school, while the girl standing next to him could pass for a high-school senior. Several girls tower above the rest of the students. Most of the boys are still smooth-cheeked, but a few already have the faint beginnings of sideburns and mustaches. Pimples and other evidence of the dreaded acne can be seen in many.

These differences do not go unnoticed by the teenagers themselves. The *growth spurt* of puberty shifts into high gear during the early to middle teens, a time when youngsters are striving for approval from their peers. They are constantly comparing themselves to other kids to gauge where they stand on the scales of physical development and attractiveness.

Small wonder, then, that adolescents can seem obsessed with their changing bodies and faces, which inspire a combination of fascination and anxiety. They critique themselves in the bathroom mirror with the ruthlessness of an art critic studying a painting, acutely sensitive to imperfections both real and imagined. As a parent, you may find yourself fielding some disarmingly frank questions:

"Doesn't my nose look funny to you? I think there's something wrong with it."

"Mom, am I gonna be tall like Dad, or a shrimp like you?"

"I am, like, so ugly! No boy is ever gonna want to go out with me . . ."

"Some kids want their parents to look at *everything*," observes Dr. Renée Jenkins of Howard University Hospital in Washington, D.C. "Mom and Dad may see this as an attention-getting ploy, but teenagers need a lot of reassurance that they are normal. It's important to treat their concerns seriously, look when they ask you to look and patiently answer their questions."

Youngsters' fears about puberty usually stem from not knowing what to expect. It's up to parents to educate them—or, if you're not comfortable having this conversation, to find someone who is, like your pediatrician, an aunt or uncle, a mature older cousin and so on. This may require brushing up on the fundamentals of adolescent physical development, which is the focus of this chapter. However not all adolescents prance around the house, calling attention to each and every new physical development. Some are deeply embarrassed by these changes. They go to great lengths to conceal their maturing bodies by wearing baggy clothes and adopting a stooped posture.

As for how to initiate a discussion with a self-conscious or reticent teenager, Dr. Marianne Felice suggests casually asking questions, the same technique she uses to draw out shy youngsters during office visits.

"I might ask a girl, 'Have you noticed that one of your breasts is slightly larger than the other?' " says Dr. Felice, who is a pediatrician at the University of Massachusetts Medical Center in Worcester. The young patient will usually nod. "Next I'll ask, 'Have you ever compared yourself to other girls and wondered if that's normal?' Then I reassure them that it is very common. And from there I go on to talk about normal progression and what they can expect. 'In about six months to two years, you're probably going to start menstruating. Do you know what it means to have your period?' "

PHYSICAL DEVELOPMENT: WHAT'S NORMAL? WHAT'S NOT?

Two boys exactly the same age can begin or complete puberty years apart, yet still fall within the broad parameters of "normal" growth. The timing and pace of a child's physical development varies greatly, because it is determined largely by the genetic programming that he inherited from his parents.

For a boy or girl to be slightly less developed or more developed than other kids the same age rarely warrants cause for alarm. But if a youngster seems significantly outside the norm, parents should raise their concerns with their pediatrician, so that he can evaluate for—and most likely rule out—any medical disorders. Chances are, it's the doctor who will bring this to the parents' attention.

Whatever timetable a teen's growth pattern follows, it is dur-

---

Puberty/Pubescence

The physical transition from childhood to adulthood. This includes sexual maturity, at which point a boy or girl is capable of reproduction.

Prepuberty/prepubescence simply refers to the period prior to puberty.

ing adolescence that your son or daughter grows more rapidly than at any time of life except infancy. On average, a girl's growth spurt occurs around age eleven and a half, but it can begin as early as eight or as late as fourteen. Boys usually trail behind by about two years—hence the comical sight of thirteen-year-old boys slow-dancing with thirteen-year-old girls a head taller.

Here's what typically happens:

The hands and feet grow first, resulting in a frequently awkward appearance. Until the arms and legs catch up, teenagers may literally trip over their own feet. Next the thighs widen and boys' shoulders and girls' hips broaden. Then the trunk of the body lengthens. The bones in the face grow too—particularly the lower jaw—bringing about a noticeable transformation.

To help you appreciate the dramatic changes that take place, consider that every year since the age of two or three, your youngster has grown an average of two inches and gained about five pounds. During adolescence, however, you can expect that rate to double. A boy may sprout four inches in twelve months, and by the time this surge is complete he's likely to have added thirteen to fourteen inches and forty pounds. Girls' growth is significant too, cresting at three-plus inches in the six to twelve months before they begin having menstrual periods. Growth slows considerably soon afterward. In all, they gain nearly ten inches and twenty-five pounds.

Once the peak period of development is over, you can trim the

> - Over the course of two to four adolescent years, teenagers gain up to 25 percent of their adult height and up to 40 percent of their adult weight.
> - Major organs such as the heart, lungs, kidneys, liver and the digestive tract double in size.

clothing budget, as most teens grow no more than another inch or two. Youngsters leave adolescence having attained nearly all of their adult height.

Puberty: Blame It on Hormones

Hormones, chemical messengers produced by the body's glands, travel through the bloodstream to regulate specific cells and organs. They are central to growth, sexual characteristics, procreation, metabolism, personality traits and mood. Some parents would go so far as to say that hormones dictate their teenager's every waking thought.

The initiating event of puberty is one you can't see. For reasons that are not fully understood, sometime between the ages of seven and eleven in girls, and nine and a half to thirteen and a half in boys, the *pituitary gland* at the base of the brain releases two hormones that signal a girl's *ovaries* and a boy's *testi-*

cles to begin producing the female sex hormone, *estrogen,* and the male sex hormone, *testosterone,* respectively.

Each sex hormone then instructs reproductive structures (the *ovaries, uterus, fallopian tubes* and *vagina* in girls; the *testes, penis, vas deferens* and *epididymis* in boys) to develop or mature in preparation for one day being able to bear or father children. Estrogen and testosterone also trigger the development of *secondary sex characteristics,* which encompass other male-female distinctions, such as women's breasts and rounded hips, and men's facial hair and muscle development. The growing ovaries and testicles secrete increasing amounts of sex hormones, further fostering the process of puberty.

Physical Development in Girls: What to Expect

SIGNS OF PUBERTY
BREAST DEVELOPMENT (THELARCHE)

The first visible evidence of puberty in girls is a nickel-sized lump under one or both nipples. *Breast buds,* as these are called, typically occur around age nine or ten, although they may occur much earlier, or somewhat later. In a study of seventeen thousand girls, it was concluded that girls do not need to be evaluated for precocious puberty unless they are Caucasian girls showing breast development before age seven or African American girls with breast development before age six. It is not known why, but in the United States, African American girls generally enter puberty a year before Caucasian girls; they also have nearly a year's head start when it comes to menstruation. No similar pattern has been found among boys.

Regardless of a girl's age, her parents are often unprepared for the emergence of breast buds, and may be particularly concerned because at the onset of puberty, one breast often appears before the other. According to Dr. Suzanne Boulter, a pediatrician and adolescent-medicine specialist in Concord, New Hampshire, "many mistake them for a cyst, a tumor or an abscess." The girl herself may worry that something is wrong, especially since the knob of tissue can feel tender and sore, and make it uncomfortable for her to sleep on her stomach. Parents should stress that these unfamiliar sensations are normal.

> **What Girls Want to Know:** *"Will my breasts get big right away?"*
>
> **What You Can Tell Them:** "Don't worry, it will probably take a couple of years before you finish developing."

What appear to be burgeoning breasts in heavyset prepubescent girls are often nothing more than deposits of fatty tissue. True breast buds are firm to the touch.

TABLE 3.1

Girls' Secondary Sex Characteristics

GIRLS' SECONDARY SEX CHARACTERISTICS	USUAL AGE RANGE
• The breasts begin to develop.	ages 7 to 13
• Pubic hair begins to grow.	ages 8 to 14
• The vagina grows longer, and its outer lips (labia) become more pronounced.	ages 8 to 15
• The body grows taller and heavier.	ages 9 to 14
• Menstruation begins.	ages 9 to 16
• Hair begins to grow under the arms.	ages 11 to 16
• Glands in the skin and scalp begin to produce more oil, which can cause skin blemishes.	ages 11 to 16

Q: "My daughter just started developing breasts. Should she be wearing a training bra?"

A: There's no need for one right now, as long as she's comfortable. But given the sensitivity of early breast tissue, some girls find it more comfortable to wear a soft, gently supportive undergarment like an undershirt or sports bra. Let her decide. Girls' feelings about their first bra are decidedly mixed. Some are thrilled to take this early step toward womanhood, but others are mortified by the thought of wearing a bra to school.

Q: "Why is one of my breasts bigger than the other?"

A: In the early stages of puberty, it is not unusual for one breast to be noticeably larger than the other. Young girls aren't always told this, however, leading many to worry that they're going to be "lopsided" forever. Breast size usually evens out within a year or so, although most adult women's breasts are slightly different in size. Unless the difference is significant, padding the bra cup for the smaller side is frequently considered a satisfactory solution.

TABLE 3.2

What Comes Next?

AGE RANGE	BREAST DEVELOPMENT
8–15	The *areola,* the dark circle around each nipple, widens, and along with the nipple seems to form a separate mound of tissue. After this, the breasts grow in size and assume a more rounded contour.
10–16	The nipples and areolas grow.
11–19	The breasts approach adult dimensions and shape. The areolas blend more into the breast tissue, and the nipples project outward.

However, sometimes the difference in size is very pronounced. This condition, *asymmetrical breasts,* is more common than you might think. The situation occasionally resolves itself, but if not, some young women may want to pursue plastic surgery. However, any such operation should be delayed until at least six to twelve months after breast growth has stopped, usually a minimum of one year following the first menstrual period. The standard approach among physicians is to see young patients every six months for several years, then assess whether the option of surgery should be offered.

SIGNS OF PUBERTY
PUBIC HAIR (PUBARCHE)

For most girls, the second sign of puberty is the appearance of *pubic hair* in the pubic area. (About 10 to 15 percent will develop pubic hair before the breasts begin to bud.) At first the hair is sparse, straight and soft, but as it fills in it becomes darker, curlier and coarser. Over the next few years, the pubic hair grows up the lower abdomen, eventually taking on a triangular shape; finally it spreads to the inner thighs. About two years after the onset of pubarche, hair begins to grow under the arms as well.

SIGNS OF PUBERTY
CHANGING BODY SHAPE

Preadolescent females acquire what, in common language, is often called "baby fat," which may give them a more rounded belly; this development may cause considerable anxiety for these girls. That's hardly surprising in light of our culture's conditioning women, even from an early age, to aspire to thinness. The weight gain of puberty comes at a time when a girl may be comparing herself to the malnourished supermodels she sees worshiped in fashion advertisements or to their plasticized counterpart, the unrealistically proportioned Barbie doll.

These young female patients, and their parents, often worry that baby fat is a harbinger of impending obesity—usually the deposition of *adipose* tissue (connective tissue where fat is stored) around the middle is part of normal development. The body will soon redistribute the fat from the stomach and the waist to the breasts and the hips in order to mold a womanly figure. However, excessive abdominal fat, often characterized by a "D" shape, should be addressed, since obesity predisposes youngsters to diabetes, high blood pressure and other serious health concerns. (See chapter 18, "When Eating Turns into a Problem: Obesity, Dieting and Eating Disorders.")

SIGNS OF PUBERTY
MENSTRUATION (MENSES/MENARCHE)

Girls often have many misconceptions and unfounded fears about menstruation. The time to begin discussing this subject with your daughter is when the breasts start to develop, heralding the arrival of puberty. Typically, one and a half to three years pass before the first menstrual period, or *menarche*.

Here's how a mother or father might go about explaining the concepts of ovulation and menstruation to a twelve-year-old. It's helpful to have on hand a book or pamphlet that includes an illustration of the female reproductive system.

"When you're older, you'll be able to become a mother, if you decide to. Even though that's a long time from now, your body is already getting itself ready for the day when you choose to have a baby.

"Now that you've entered puberty, each month one of your two ovaries will release a ripened egg inside you. A woman becomes pregnant when a man's sperm unites with the egg. If fertilization *takes place, the fertilized egg attaches itself to the inner lining of the* uterus, *which is also called the* womb. *This is where the baby lives while it's growing and waiting to be born. The uterus prepares for this possibility by forming a thick layer of tissue and importing extra blood, just in case.*

> ### *Physiologic Leukorrhea: Prelude to Menstruation*
>
> Frequently, several months before a girl starts menstruating, glands within her vagina discharge a fluid that is clear or milky in color and has a consistency ranging from watery to thick. *Physiologic leukorrhea*, as this perfectly normal phenomenon is called, may persist for several years.

"Most months, though, the egg doesn't meet a sperm. Since the body won't be needing the extra tissue and blood, it discharges the red fluid out your vagina. This is called your menstrual period, and it will happen every three to five weeks or so. During the three to seven days that you're having your period, and for a few days afterward, you need to wear a special absorbent pad in your panties. Or you can use something called a tampon, which is made of soft cotton and goes inside your vagina.

"Menstruation is normal and healthy. It means that you are growing up. It doesn't stop you from doing the things you want to do, like swimming or playing sports. In time, you will begin to ovulate and be capable of getting pregnant."[1]

TEENAGERS' COMMON CONCERNS

Q: "How will I know when I'm going to get my first period?"

A: Although there's no way to pinpoint the day, most girls reach menarche at about the same age as their mothers and older sisters did. Prepare your daughter in advance. Buy her a box of sanitary pads and show her how to wear them.

Explain that her menstruation may be highly irregular at first, with as many as six months passing between periods. Even once a girl becomes regular, any of a number of conditions can cause her to miss a cycle: sickness, stress, excessive exercise, poor nutrition and, of course, pregnancy.

If your daughter has not menstruated by age 16 or 17, or is more than a year older than her mother was at the time of menarche, consult your pediatrician. Although everything is probably normal, it's wise to rule out any medical problems.

Q: "What if I get my period while I'm at school and have an accident?"

A: This is probably every girl's greatest fear. Have your daughter keep a few sanitary pads in her book bag or knapsack at all times, in case of an emergency. Explain that the initial bleeding during a period is usually light, and that she should be able to get to the girls' room or the nurse's office in time.

---

1 For the sequel to this discussion, on how to avoid becoming pregnant, see chapter 12, "Sexuality."

TABLE 3.3

Tampon Safety Tips

- Change tampons at least every three to four hours.

- Know the symptoms of *toxic shock syndrome,* a rare but potentially fatal bacterial infection seen almost exclusively in girls and young women who wear tampons:

Initial Symptoms	Vomiting • Fever of 102° or higher • Watery diarrhea • Headache • Sore throat • Aching muscles
Within 24 Hours	Sunburnlike rash • Bloodshot eyes • Redness under the eyes, inside the mouth, in the vagina
Days 3 and 4	Broken blood vessels may appear on the skin
Other Possible Symptoms	Confusion • Decreased urination • Fatigue • Weakness • Extreme thirst • Weak, rapid pulse • Pale complexion • Cool, moist skin • Rapid breathing

For more on toxic shock syndrome, see page 518, "Gynecologic Conditions."

Q: "Should I use sanitary pads or tampons?"

A: "I usually suggest that girls start out with pads for the first month or so, until they get used to having their period and seeing how heavy the flow is," Dr. Felice explains. "It depends upon when a girl is ready and how comfortable she is with her body." Some girls prefer tampons because they do not like the feeling of wetness or the odor that pads may emit. Other girls may be squeamish about inserting a tampon in their vagina and opt for pads. Buy your daughter some of each type and in absorbencies ranging from light to heavy so she can experiment to find what works best for her.

Q: "Does it hurt to have your period?"

A: The first several periods are almost always painless. Once a girl begins to ovulate, she may experience some discomfort before, during or after her period. Common symptoms include cramping, bloating, sore or swollen breasts, headaches, mood changes and irritability, and depression. Menstrual cramps, probably the most bothersome effect, can range from mild to

---

What Girls Want to Know: *"Won't other kids be able to tell I'm having my period?"*

What You Can Tell Them: "No! Even though you might be able to feel a sanitary pad in your panties or a tampon, no one can see it. There's no 'bulge.' " You can show your daughter how you look, to see if she notices any difference.

---

moderate to severe. If your daughter complains of pain in the lower abdomen or back, talk to her pediatrician, who may recommend exercises and an over-the-counter pain medication such as ibuprofen.

WHEN TO CALL THE DOCTOR

Contact your daughter's pediatrician if she experiences any of the following symptoms, or if there is any concern that there might be a problem:

- a sudden, unexplained change in her periods;
- heavy menstrual bleeding that soaks more than six to eight pads or tampons per day for more than seven to ten days;
- persistent bleeding between periods;
- call your pediatrician immediately if your teen develops severe abdominal pain.

See page 518, "Gynecologic Conditions."

Physical Development in Boys: What to Expect

SIGNS OF PUBERTY
ENLARGEMENT OF THE TESTICLES AND SCROTUM

A near doubling in the size of the testicles and the scrotal sac announces the advent of puberty. As the testicles continue to grow, the skin of the scrotum darkens, enlarges, thins, hangs down from the body and becomes dotted with tiny bumps. These are hair follicles. In most boys, one testicle (usually the left) hangs lower than the other.

SIGNS OF PUBERTY
PUBIC HAIR (PUBARCHE)

Fueled by testosterone, the next changes of puberty come in quick succession. A few light-colored downy hairs materialize at the base of the penis. As

TABLE 3.4

Boys' Secondary Sex Characteristics

BOYS' SECONDARY SEX CHARACTERISTICS	USUAL AGE RANGE
• The testicles begin to enlarge, and the scrotum turns darker and coarser.	ages 10 to 13
• Pubic hair begins to grow.	ages 10 to 15
• The body grows taller and heavier.	ages 10½ to 16
• The penis begins to grow longer and fuller.	ages 11 to 14½
• The voice begins to deepen.	ages 11 to 14½
• Boys become fertile, meaning they are capable of ejaculating semen.	ages 11 to 17
• Hair begins to grow under the arms and on the face.	ages 12 to 17
• Glands in the skin and scalp begin to produce more oil, which can cause skin blemishes.	ages 12 to 17

with girls, the pubic hair soon turns darker, curlier and coarser in texture, but the pattern is more diamond-shaped than triangular. Over the next few years it covers the pubic region, then spreads toward the thighs. A thin line of hair also travels up to the navel. Roughly two years after the appearance of pubic hair, sparse hair begins to sprout on a boy's face, legs, arms and underarms, and later the chest.

SIGNS OF PUBERTY
CHANGING BODY SHAPE

A girl's physical strength virtually equals a boy's until middle adolescence, when the difference between them widens appreciably. During early puberty, both sexes add some fat, lending many boys a chubby appearance. The growth spurt soon offsets that; in fact, the dramatic increase in height often makes them look gangly. Boys continue to fill out with muscle mass long after girls do, so that by the late teens a boy's body composition is only 12 percent fat, less than half that of the average girl's.

SIGNS OF PUBERTY
PENIS GROWTH

A boy may have adult-size genitals as early as age thirteen or as late as eighteen. First the penis grows in length, then in width. Teenage males seem to spend an inordinate amount of time inspecting their penis and covertly (or overtly) comparing themselves to other boys. Their number-one concern? No contest: size.

"Take one hundred boys, and they all feel like their penis isn't as big as it should be," says Dr. Mark Scott Smith, chief of adolescent services at Children's Hospital in Seattle. He recalls examining one young patient who fidgeted anxiously throughout the office visit. When Dr. Smith asked him if he had any concerns or questions, the boy looked down at his lap.

"Well . . ."

Dr. Smith knew to ask, "Are you worried about your penis?"

"Um, yeah." The boy braced for the physician to confirm his fears that his penis was microscopic in size. No: *the smallest penis in the history of humankind.*

"I always say the same thing in that situation," says Dr. Smith. "I told him, 'I examine a lot of kids, and I can tell you that you are entirely normal.' That seemed to reassure him."

Most boys don't realize that sexual function is not dependent on penis size or that the dimensions of the flaccid penis don't necessarily indicate how large it is when erect. Parents can spare their sons needless distress by anticipating these concerns rather than waiting for them to say anything, since that question is always there regardless of whether it is articulated. In the course of a conversation, you might muse aloud, "You know, many boys your age worry that their penis is too small. That almost never turns out to be the case." Consider asking your son's pediatrician to reinforce this point at his next checkup. A doctor's reassurance that a teenager is "all right" sometimes carries more weight than a parent's.

Boys' preoccupation with their penis probably won't end there. They may notice that some of the other guys in gym have a foreskin and they do not, or vice-versa, and might come to you with questions about why they were or weren't circumcised. You can explain that the procedure is performed due to custom, parents' choice or religious beliefs.

"WHAT ARE THESE BUMPS ON MY PENIS?"

About one in three adolescent boys have *penile pink pearly papules* on their penis: pimplelike lesions around the crown, or *corona*. Although the tiny bumps are harmless, a teenager may fear he's picked up a form of venereal disease. The appropriate course of action is none at all. Though usually permanent, the papules are barely noticeable.

SIGNS OF PUBERTY
FERTILITY (SPERMARCHE)

Boys are considered capable of procreation upon their first ejaculation, which occurs about one year after the testicles begin to enlarge. The testicles now produce sperm in addition to testosterone, while the *prostate,* the two *seminal vesicles* and another pair of glands (called Cowper's glands) secrete fluids that combine with the sperm to form *semen.* Each ejaculation, amounting to about one teaspoonful of semen, contains 200 million to 500 million sperm.

NOCTURNAL EMISSIONS AND INVOLUNTARY ERECTIONS

Most boys have stroked or rubbed their penises for pleasure long before they're able to achieve orgasm—in some instances, as far back as infancy. A youngster may consciously masturbate himself to his first ejaculation. Or this pivotal event of sexual maturation may occur at night while he's asleep. He wakes up with damp pajamas and sheets, wondering if he'd wet the bed.

A *nocturnal emission,* or "wet dream," is not necessarily the culmination of a sexually oriented dream. Explain to your son that this phenomenon happens to all boys during puberty and that it will stop as he gets older. Emphasize that a nocturnal emission is nothing to be ashamed of or embarrassed by. While you're at it, you might note that masturbation is normal and harmless, for girls as well as boys.

Erections, too, are unpredictable during pubescence. They may pop up for no apparent reason—and seemingly at the most inconvenient times, like when giving a report in front of the class. Tell your teen there's not much he can do to suppress spontaneous erections (the time-honored technique of concentrating on the most unsexy thought imaginable doesn't really work), and that with the passage of time they will become less frequent.

SIGNS OF PUBERTY
VOICE CHANGE

Just after the peak of the growth spurt, a boy's voice box (*larynx*) enlarges, as do the vocal cords. For a brief period of time, your son's voice may "crack" occasionally as it deepens. Once the larynx reaches adult size, the cracking will stop. Girls' voices lower in pitch too, but the change is not nearly as striking.

SIGNS OF PUBERTY
BREAST DEVELOPMENT

Breast development in boys? Normal? It is, but try telling that to a young man afflicted with *gynecomastia,* which literally means growth of the male mammary glands.

Early in puberty, most boys experience soreness or tenderness around their nipples. Three in four, if not more, will actually have some breast growth, the result of a biochemical reaction that converts some of their testosterone to the female sex hormone estrogen. Most of the time the breast enlargement amounts to less than half an inch and is restricted to the nipples, "but in a lean youngster," says Dr. Norman P. Spack, "gynecomastia can show up quite profoundly."

As you might imagine, this development can be troubling for a youngster who is in the process of trying to establish his masculinity. "They can be teased mercilessly," says Dr. Spack, a pediatrician and adolescent-medicine specialist at Children's Hospital in Boston. If your son suddenly seems self-conscious about changing for gym or refuses to be seen without a shirt, you can reasonably assume that he's noticed some swelling in one or both breasts. (One particularly telltale sign: wearing a shirt to go swimming.)

Boys are greatly relieved to learn that gynecomastia usually resolves in one to two years. "Thanks for telling me! I thought I was turning into a girl!" is a common reaction. There are rare instances where the excess tissue does not subside after several years or the breasts become unacceptably large. Elective plastic surgery may be performed, strictly for the young patient's psychological well-being.

Gynecomastia warrants an evaluation by a pediatrician, especially if it arises prior to puberty or late in adolescence, when the cause is more likely to be organic. A number of medical conditions can cause excessive breast growth, including endocrine tumors, the chromosomal disorder Klinefelter syndrome, thyroid disease and herpes zoster, better known as shingles. Breast development may also be a side effect of various drugs, including certain antidepressants and antianxiety medications, insulin and corticosteroids. Or a boy may not have true gynecomastia after all, but rather *pseudo gyneco-*

mastia, which is common in overweight boys. Fatty tissue, not breast tissue, builds up in the chest area, simulating breasts. "Some of these teenagers can have tremendous amounts of tissue, and it can be extremely embarrassing," says Dr. Spack.

Late Arrivals: Delayed Puberty

The typical adolescent, endowed with the impatience and insecurities of youth, would probably insist that any nanosecond that doesn't bring an increase in height, breast size or beard growth qualifies as *delayed puberty.* Medicine has its own definitions: for boys, no testicular enlargement by the age of thirteen; and for girls, no breast development by thirteen or no menarche by sixteen.

Pubertal delay affects more boys than girls. And it probably affects boys more than girls in terms of how they see themselves. Girls who are slow to develop often seem to acclimate better than boys in similar circumstances. Perhaps that's because girls start the growth spurt earlier. They may be shorter and younger looking than other girls their age, but they blend in just fine with the boys, who are still a year or so away from the countdown to puberty. A girl's main worry, says Dr. Marianne Felice, "is that puberty is never going to come."

Most cases of delayed puberty are simply variants of normal development and not cause for alarm. Generally speaking, the "late bloomers" usually catch up to their peers, and sometimes surpass them. Half of all adolescents who experience such constitutional delays have a parent or sibling whose growth followed a similar pattern.

Nevertheless, when puberty seems overdue, a child should be examined by a pediatrician. Any of a number of medical conditions can slow the process of

> ### Organic Causes of Delayed Puberty
>
> - Severe asthma
> - Congenital diseases, defects or tumors of the central nervous system
> - Long-term effects of prior radiotherapy or chemotherapy to treat cancer
> - Poorly controlled type I diabetes and other endocrine disorders
> - End-stage renal disease requiring kidney dialysis treatments
> - Turner syndrome
> - Klinefelter syndrome
> - Inflammatory bowel disease
> - Sickle-cell anemia
> - Intense physical workouts such as long-distance running, gymnastics, ballet dancing
> - Medications that can curb appetite

maturation. Signs that pubertal delay may be due to a disease include an abrupt change in growth or arrested development, in which puberty starts then stalls. Complaints of headaches, vision problems and other neurological symptoms may indicate a disorder of the central nervous system.

"All my friends in junior high are so much taller than me and more mature-looking than me. Compared to them, I look like I still belong in grade school!"

One of the most common culprits is malnutrition brought on by diseases, medications or eating disorders. Inflammatory bowel disease, a chronic and potentially serious condition, frequently delays puberty and stunts growth in young people by interfering with metabolism: The inflamed intestines cannot adequately absorb the nutrients from food.

According to endocrinologist Dr. Norman Spack, "With the marked increases in the use of stimulants and other medications that, as a side effect, suppress appetite, we're seeing a lot of children whose pubertal delay is indirectly initiated or aggravated by the fact that they're not consuming enough calories." Stimulants are widely prescribed to manage attention deficit hyperactivity disorder, or ADHD.

How Pubertal Delay Is Treated

Unless delayed physical development is found to have an organic cause, reassurance from your pediatrician is the best medicine for your youngster. For instance, the pediatrician can point out to a boy that his testicles have grown in size, the first sign of male puberty but one that is rarely noticed by the boy himself. "Enlargement of the testicles tells us that the system has been switched on and that sexual maturity is going to come," says Dr. Spack. "Very often, parents will bring in a youngster who is upset that he hasn't started to grow yet." The physician can confirm that in fact the process of puberty is under way. "That examination alone usually reassures a child about what is going to happen and at what pace."

SEX HORMONE THERAPY

Under rare circumstances, after a thorough diagnostic workup, a pediatrician might recommend several months of male or female sex hormones, to give a boy or girl a chemical "nudge" through sexual maturity. Candidates for hormonal therapy would include older teens who exhibit early signs of puberty but "haven't gotten going yet," as Dr. Mark Scott Smith puts it. Another consideration is the impact late development is having on a teenager emotionally and socially. "I usually reserve it for the youngster who is truly suffering," says Dr.

Spack. Boys receive injections of testosterone, while girls are prescribed tablets of estrogen and *progesterone,* the other female sex hormone. The dose is comparable to the amount of sex hormone a youngster's body would normally produce. "The hormone therapy gets kids started just enough that we can then back off and let them take off on their own," says Dr. Smith, "without changing where they are going to end up."

GROWTH-HORMONE THERAPY

Another of the chemicals released by the brain's pituitary gland is *growth hormone (GH).* Some youngsters' pituitaries are impaired and secrete too little. This condition, referred to as *hypopituitarism,* severely stunts growth. Injections of synthetic growth hormone have enabled thousands of people to reach the adult height that their heredity intended.

Short stature has many causes other than GH deficiency. Initially it was believed that only people with abnormally low levels of *endogenous* growth hormone—produced by the body—would respond to growth-hormone therapy. But the genetically engineered products have also benefited youngsters on kidney dialysis during the time that they await a kidney transplant as well as those with Turner syndrome. Girls with Turner syndrome make growth hormone, but their bodies appear to be resistant to it.

So what's to prevent anyone who wants to add a few inches to his height from marching on down to the doctor's office and demanding growth hormone? Dr. Stephen LaFranchi, head of pediatric endocrinology at Oregon Health Sciences University in Portland, remarks, "I've had a few experiences where parents requested growth-hormone treatment when it wasn't appropriate for their child. We had to explain that, by and large, growth-hormone treatment is given only to kids who are proven to have pituitary growth-hormone deficiency."

Aside from hypopituitarism, chronic renal failure and Turner syndrome, "all other uses of growth hormone are considered investigational," says Dr. LaFranchi. Insurance companies do not pay for experimental treatments, and at six or seven subcutaneous injections per week for four to five years, GH therapy is prohibitively expensive: approximately $30,000 annually. That factor alone should limit inappropriate use.

Here are two others: Though short-term treatment has produced few, if any, side effects, synthetic growth hormone has been on the market only since the mid-1980s, and nothing is known about what its long-term effects might be, so it seems foolish to use it for any but medically necessary situations. Furthermore, heredity is a more powerful determinant of stature than synthetic growth hormone. So much as a boy might long to be six feet tall, if his parents are short he's likely to be short too. That's the way genetics work!

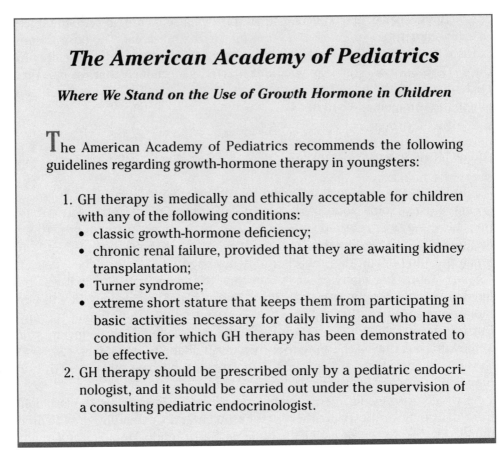

The American Academy of Pediatrics

Where We Stand on the Use of Growth Hormone in Children

The American Academy of Pediatrics recommends the following guidelines regarding growth-hormone therapy in youngsters:

1. GH therapy is medically and ethically acceptable for children with any of the following conditions:
   - classic growth-hormone deficiency;
   - chronic renal failure, provided that they are awaiting kidney transplantation;
   - Turner syndrome;
   - extreme short stature that keeps them from participating in basic activities necessary for daily living and who have a condition for which GH therapy has been demonstrated to be effective.
2. GH therapy should be prescribed only by a pediatric endocrinologist, and it should be carried out under the supervision of a consulting pediatric endocrinologist.

Early Arrivals: Precocious and Pseudoprecocious Puberty

Just as some children will reach physical maturity a little later than their peers, others will develop ahead of the norm. However, pubescence rarely arrives so prematurely that it can be classified as *precocious* puberty, which can be manifested by the appearance of breast buds in a girl under the age of six or seven or an increase in the size of a boy's testicle before he turns nine. The incidence of precocious puberty is roughly the same as that of belated puberty, affecting approximately 1 in 160 otherwise healthy youngsters.

No underlying disease is detected in about 90 percent of girls and 50 percent of boys who experience precocious puberty. Their sexual development, while occurring abnormally early, still falls within the range of normal. As with delayed sexual development, there is often a family pattern. Nonetheless, a youngster who enters puberty unusually early should be evaluated by a pediatrician, who might subsequently refer him or her to a pediatric endocrinologist.

PSEUDOPRECOCIOUS PUBERTY

In *pseudoprecocious puberty,* abnormally high levels of sex hormones prematurely activate the growth process, but only partially: The size and development of the testicles and the ovaries remain at preadolescent levels; boys cannot yet produce sperm, nor can girls make eggs. Believe it or not, the use of hair creams, makeup and other cosmetic products containing estrogen can spur this growth disorder, which is also referred to as *incomplete puberty.*

Organic Causes of Precocious Puberty

- Tumor, cyst or other abnormality of the ovaries or the *thyroid gland*
- Disorder of the central nervous system, such as a *brain tumor, cerebral palsy, tuberous sclerosis, neurofibromatosis*
- Delayed effect of radiation therapy to the brain and/or spinal cord for the treatment of certain childhood cancers
- *McCune-Albright syndrome*
- *Familial male precocious puberty*

HOW PRECOCIOUS PUBERTY IS TREATED

There are circumstances when a pediatric endocrinologist might suggest *hormone-suppression therapy* to treat nonorganic precocious puberty, which manifests itself by causing premature growth.

Suppressive therapy does not permanently stunt growth; what it does is prolong the prepubertal period of childhood. Sexual development begins at a more appropriate age, thus sparing a youngster from the sense of isolation that precocious puberty can bring.

Encouraging Self-Acceptance

Most boys and girls enter puberty with an idealized image of what they hope to look like and an exaggerated sense of their physical flaws. Girls are particularly prone to unhappiness over their appearance. Taken to extremes, a poor self-image can place a youngster at risk for eating disorders and abuse of anabolic steroids, not to mention the emotional and social problems engendered by low self-esteem and self-confidence.

"I'm the only girl in my class who wears a bra. A lot of the boys stare at me and make dirty jokes. Sometimes I wish my chest wasn't so big."

There are many ways that we can help our children to cope with the changes of puberty and learn to be more accepting of themselves. First and foremost, downplay the importance of physical characteristics. Stress to your son or daughter that ultimately what makes a person attractive is a combination of personality, accomplishments and how they treat others. And explain that many of the perfect chiseled faces and bodies they see courtesy of the entertainment and fashion industries benefit considerably from computer-generated images, airbrushing, battalions of hair stylists and makeup artists, lighting that would flatter Quasimodo and plastic surgery. When you come across a picture of a famous beauty sans makeup, show it to your youngster and explain that under the glitz, these are normal people too.

Help your child choose activities based on his abilities and size. A boy who stands five feet three and weighs 110 pounds may find greater success and satisfaction playing soccer or running track than trying out for the freshman football team. On the other hand, you know your son: If he's determined to give it a shot and is realistic about his chances, don't discourage him.

To allay late bloomers' fears that they will never mature, show them pictures of Mom or Dad at the same age. "Then," says Dr. Felice, "they can see what their parent looks like now and know that if they just bide their time, everything is going to fall into place."

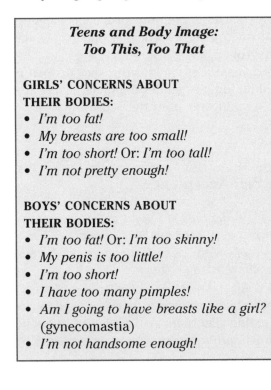

Teens and Body Image: Too This, Too That

GIRLS' CONCERNS ABOUT THEIR BODIES:
- *I'm too fat!*
- *My breasts are too small!*
- *I'm too short! Or: I'm too tall!*
- *I'm not pretty enough!*

BOYS' CONCERNS ABOUT THEIR BODIES:
- *I'm too fat! Or: I'm too skinny!*
- *My penis is too little!*
- *I'm too short!*
- *I have too many pimples!*
- *Am I going to have breasts like a girl?* (gynecomastia)
- *I'm not handsome enough!*

Don't tease kids about their developing bodies. Respect the fact that teens are often highly self-conscious about their "new parts." It is important not to make kidding remarks about a girl's budding breasts or a boy's wisp of a mustache.

Without overemphasizing the importance of physical appearance, tell your teenager over and over how attractive she is. When your daughter moans, "My hair is so hideous," call attention to her elegant hands, her pretty smile, her soulful eyes. She may pretend to be unimpressed ("Of course you think I'm pretty, Dad; it's your *job* to say things like that"), but secretly she'll be pleased by the compliment. Also, encourage youngsters to make the most of their good points by practicing scrupulous personal hygiene and grooming, and maintaining proper posture. If you've got a knack for dressing stylishly and are reasonably familiar with teen fashion trends, help them to pick out clothes that accentuate their best features.

Examine the attitudes you convey about your own body. Do you go from one diet to another and complain chronically about your weight and shape? (Mothers are probably more guilty on this score than fathers are.) "Mom is the most important female figure in a girl's life," points out Dr. Gaggino. "She may think, *If Mom is unhappy with the way she looks, how could* I *possibly look good?* Women have to be careful about what they say about their own bodies, because girls internalize those messages."

Puberty and Parents

Teenagers aren't the only ones who suffer during their adolescence. It is normal to feel a sense of loss as your youngster begins growing up and away from you, looking ever more like an adult with each passing day. As you watch these changes you may also be lamenting, perhaps for the first time, the passage of your own youth, for few events in life force us to acknowledge our aging and ultimately our mortality more than watching our children become young men and women. Parents may share these emotions with other mothers and fathers, but one issue that is rarely spoken about is the discomfort parents often feel about a child's budding sexuality. "Sometimes parents distance themselves from their kids because of these changes," says Dr. Renée Jenkins. "You see this more with fathers and their daughters, perhaps because a girl's physical development is more noticeable. Their little girl is turning into a woman. To make the transition more comfortable, they try to desexualize the child. For example, a father may think it's not appropriate to let his pubescent daughter sit on his lap anymore." The young girl may feel rejected, especially if Dad pulls back emotionally as well. Or she may sense her father's awkwardness, causing her to feel ashamed of her changing body.

Similarly, mothers may be uneasy enough about their sons' sexual maturity that they withdraw emotionally or cease to display physical affection for fear of awakening sexual urges in either themselves or their boys. However, when mothers encounter difficulty adjusting to a child's sexual maturity, usually it's the *daughter,* not the son, who is the object of inappropriate feelings. In a not-uncommon dynamic, a mother may view her daughter's emerging sexuality as a threat to her own attractiveness and begin to "compete" by dressing like her daughter, insisting on not being called "Mom" and flirting with the daughter's boyfriends.

Our society's heightened awareness of sexual abuse involving children undoubtedly has contributed to the confusion some parents feel when it comes to being physically affectionate with their children. What is proper? What isn't? Is it acceptable for parents to continue to kiss their teenagers on the lips, if that's been the family custom over the years? Let a son or daughter sit on their lap? By all means. But if a youngster requests privacy or appears uncomfortable with the level of intimacy, parents should adjust their style accordingly. We must always respect an adolescent's need for privacy and personal space.

Should fathers or mothers share the bathroom with their teens when they are bathing, using the toilet or changing clothes? It is up to each family to develop its own rules in this regard. What is considered proper in your household may not be okay for the family next door, and vice-versa. No guideline, however, can define the exact point at which parental physical affection assumes unhealthy sexual overtones. It is hoped a parent would recognize the difference and seek professional counseling, or the other parent would pick up on the signs and intervene.

4

GROWING INTO ADULTHOOD: YOUR TEENAGER'S DEVELOPING SELF

Unlike physical growth, a youngster's emotional and social development isn't easily measured and charted. Adolescents can act childish one minute, then impress you with their maturity the next.

This chapter provides a glimpse into the inner workings of the teenage psyche, which isn't nearly as mysterious as some adults seem to believe. The behaviors (and misbehaviors) associated with adolescence—such as challenging authority and separating from Mom and Dad—are all signs of the need to create a self-identity and assert one's independence, the primary goals of the teenage years.

Teens may go through these phases at different times and play them out in different ways. But they land on most, if not all, of these stepping-stones at some point on the path to adulthood, just as you probably did when you were your youngster's age. Perhaps that's why so many parents shudder at the thought of a child's impending adolescence: They remember the torment they put *their* mothers and fathers through!

Whether you were a teenage terror, model youth or somewhere in between, being able to reflect honestly on your own adolescence is an indispensable asset now, one that *may* help you to unravel the reasons for your child's behaviors. Periods of rebelliousness, withdrawing and moodiness are all natural, necessary by-products of growing up. Nothing can change that. What you *can* change is the intent and the meaning that you read into these behaviors and how you respond.

A TEENAGER'S DECLARATION OF INDEPENDENCE

Imagine that more than two hundred years after the signing of the Declaration of Independence, a delegation of teenagers convenes to draft a document proclaiming their freedom from the tyranny of the mother-and-fatherland. It begins, "We hold these truths to be self-evident. Whatever." With powdered wigs peeking out from beneath their baseball caps, the framers go on to cite a litany of grievances against the king and queen (". . . kitchen cupboards bereft of potato chips and other snack foods from which to plunder . . .") before concluding with a list of the rights that they will demand from this day forward:

1. *We Shall Spend Less Time with Our Families.*

"My daughter and I have always been extremely close. We'd spend whole afternoons shopping together, or going to the movies, lunch, the beach—like a couple of friends. But lately, anytime I suggest going somewhere, she brushes me off. 'I can't, Mom. Maybe some other time.' I have to admit, it hurts my feelings."

During adolescence, boys and girls typically begin to disengage from their families. They spend less time at home and more time out with their friends. When they *are* at home, they may hibernate in their rooms or generally be more secretive than before. Whereas in the past a youngster might have welcomed his parents' help or input, he may now resist offers of assistance or expressions of concern to the point of becoming irritable: *"I said I don't need any help, okay, Mom? I can bandage my knee myself. It's only a small cut. You're always overreacting."*

"In order to be able to stand on their own two feet," pediatrician Adele Hofmann explains, "teens will reject their dependency on their parents and push away." Typically, this occurs during early to middle adolescence. Moderation is hardly a trait of youth to begin with, but because younger teenagers are particularly prone to seeing the world in black and white, they may push parents farther away than is necessary.

HOW TO RESPOND

"When children start to pull away," observes clinical psychologist Helen Pratt, "parents may get upset . . . they think they're doing something 'wrong,' and they're not." Teenagers *have* to view their parents through a lens of negativity in order to lessen the guilt they feel for withdrawing from them. Of course, this is usually easier to accept in principle than in practice. When your youngster no longer spends as much time with you, acts as if he's ashamed of you, or uses a dismissive tone of voice, it hurts!

Don't be surprised, though, if the teenager who ignored you yesterday clings to you today or vice-versa. Early in adolescence, girls and boys wrestle with conflicting feelings about breaking away. Interestingly, a common pattern is for teenagers to grow closer to the opposite-sex parent during this phase of development. Around ages twelve to fourteen, many daughters clash repeatedly with their mothers. Boys tend not to reject the same-sex parent quite as harshly, although fathers often find their authority being challenged more when their sons are in their middle to late teens.

2. *We Shall Regularly Exercise Our Prerogative to Question or Resist Authority. And Sometimes We'll Argue Just for the Heck of It!*

"Our son deliberately does things to irritate us. Like, I tell him not to drink all the milk. So what does he do? He drinks the last of the milk and doesn't tell anyone. I tell him not to play ball in the house: Yesterday he's bouncing a rubber ball against the wall and breaks my favorite lamp! He's not a bad kid, but he just does not mind!"

In study after study conducted since the mid-1960s, the majority of teenagers have claimed to get along well with their parents. Plenty of mothers and fathers would probably disagree with those findings. With the onset of adolescence, youngsters at times become defiant and argumentative. This is referred to as *oppositional behavior,* or, in plain talk, good old-fashioned rebelliousness. Oppositional behavior is a way for teenagers to serve notice to parents, teachers and society at large that their personal crusade for autonomy has begun. Arguments between teens and parents typically revolve around curfews, dating, friends, household chores and schoolwork.

About four in five children engage in some form of oppositional behavior during adolescence. "It can be difficult for parents to distinguish between what is 'normal' oppositional behavior and what is abnormal," observes Dr. Tomas Silber of Children's National Medical Center in Washington, D.C. Typically, he says, "normal oppositional behavior takes place in settings where the child feels safe to try things out, like at home, but not at school or in other people's homes." The emotional outbursts occur only from time to time and fizzle out relatively quickly. Youngsters who are chronically hostile and disobedient, to the extent that their conduct disrupts the household or the classroom, are said to have *oppositional defiant disorder,* which we discuss in chapter 15 on emotional and behavioral problems.

"Provoking Mom and Dad is how teenagers make home life less comfortable so that it becomes easier to separate from their parents and move toward autonomy," explains Dr. George Comerci, a pediatrician and father of three grown sons. It is also a mechanism for defining their own identity, by contrast-

Red Alert! The Moody Teenager

No, you're not imagining it: Your teenager probably *is* more temperamental than when he was little, as are most adolescents. They can also be unpredictable, irritable, touchy and prone to volcanic mood swings abrupt enough to induce whiplash in their unsuspecting parents, who sometimes feel as though they're walking on eggshells in order to avoid setting off another explosion.

Now for the truly terrifying news: Their behavior is partly beyond their control, a consequence of surging hormones and seesawing emotions. "It is normal for teenagers to be happy one minute and crying the next over the same thing," says Dr. Pratt. However, persistent sadness and crying that lasts two weeks or more may be symptoms of depression and should be called to the attention of your youngster's pediatrician.

ing themselves with the adults around them. Consequently, a teenager may spurn her parents' beliefs and values in dramatic fashion and invest heavily in always seeming to embrace an opposing viewpoint.

In reality, our kids are far more like us than they realize, and the differences narrow the older they get. Researchers at the University of Michigan asked high-school seniors to compare their attitudes to those of their parents on ten selected topics. Roughly three in four teens said that they and their parents held "very similar" or "mostly similar" views on what they should do with their lives: religion, the value of an education, the role of women in society. Two in three agreed with their parents on racial issues and how the kids dressed, while about half saw eye to eye with Mom and Dad on environmental issues, appropriate conduct on dates—even politics. And nobody agrees on politics! The only major difference of opinion revolved around adolescents' handling of money.

From 1975 to 1992, the percentages of seniors who said that they and their parents shared similar beliefs rose, sometimes significantly, in six of the ten categories; stayed the same in two; and declined 1 percent regarding environmental issues and 7 percent on the subject of money. So teenagers aren't really so different from their parents after all. But let's keep this our little secret: They would be absolutely crestfallen if they ever found out.

HOW TO RESPOND

One reason your teen may lash out at you is that you offer a safe target. Spouting off to one of his buddies could cost him a friendship, but a child knows that virtually nothing he says or does will drive you away. Subconsciously, he may be trying to see how hard he can push you without jeopardizing your love. In a sense, you might take it as a backhanded compliment that he evidently feels secure enough to test you.

The most effective response is to *ignore* confrontational behavior, because acknowledging it legitimizes the teenager's challenge to our authority. Example: A father reminds his son to be home by 11 P.M., his normal weekend curfew.

"Eleven o'clock?" the boy protests. "How come I always have to do what you say?" In the gallery of adolescent complaints, this one surely stands as a masterpiece.

"You need to do what I say," replies the father, his voice rising, *"because I'm your dad, and I told you so!"* The ensuing argument only reinforces the son's oppositional behavior. This round goes to the teenager, for seizing control of the conversation.

What the father should have done was to restate the directive—"You need to be home by eleven"—then stipulate the consequence the boy faces should he miss his curfew: "If you're home on time, you get to out again tomorrow night. Come home after eleven, and you're grounded."

Adolescents are certainly entitled to their feelings, including resentment or anger toward their parents. But parents have every right to set boundaries for how emotions and differences of opinion may be expressed, Dr. Pratt emphasizes. "It's okay to say to your child who's screaming at you, 'I hate you!' that she is not allowed to say, 'I hate you, you b——h!' Or maybe you can't tolerate being screamed at, in which case you set your limit there. And if your child crosses that line, you say, 'I refuse to talk to you anymore, because you're being disrespectful.' "

Parents should not respond with name-calling, no matter how much their youngster baits them. The same ground rules apply to arguments between Mom and Dad, too. A kid who cannot offer a different viewpoint without raising his voice and resorting to abusive language may be parroting what he's heard at home.

One way to moderate heated exchanges with your youngster is to respond nonjudgmentally, as in the following examples. Besides setting a civil tone, they encourage teenagers to explore their thoughts:

- "We may not agree on this, but . . ."
- "You have a right to your opinion too . . ."
- "I realize that you have to make your own choices . . ."

3. *We Reserve the Right to Be Someone Different Every Day.*

"Let's see: Since turning twelve, our sixteen-year-old daughter has gone through two major 'image changes,' as my husband and I like to say. First she fell in with a group of what I guess you would call 'slackers.' They were nice kids, but they dressed so sloppily! You couldn't tell the boys from the girls. All of them wore flannel shirts, baggy jeans, boots and baseball caps. Now our daughter says she's bored with the 'grunge scene.' She's gone in the other direction, wearing conservative blouses and skirts to school and trying to act sophisticated."

Forming an identity is a gradual process of trial and error. Younger teens mainly project their evolving self-image externally, adopting new styles in fashion, makeup, music, hobbies and choice of friends. They may reinvent themselves more than once, because an identity that felt comfortable at one time may no longer "fit."

Does a youngster's self-image influence behavior and appearance, or is it the other way around? The answer to that chicken-or-the-egg question is probably both, although there are teens who live up or down to the identity they've chosen. As teens develop intellectually and gain confidence, they may be more likely to let their ideas, talents and interests define them.

Future plans further shape self-image: Many young people find their identity by getting a job, starting a family or joining the military, while those who go to college, with its atmosphere of prolonged adolescence, have more time to refine theirs.

Pediatrician's Perspective

DR. RENÉE JENKINS: *"A mother came to me because her thirteen-year-old daughter wanted to wear her hair in dreadlocks. She and her husband were completely opposed to it, and she wanted to know what I thought. I said, 'If she wears dreadlocks and it looks horrible, she can cut it off. I would give her the chance to make a decision for herself if that's what she wants to do.'"*

HOW TO RESPOND

Trying on different personas, and with them the accompanying uniforms, is generally a safe outlet for teenage self-expression—that is, until years later, when as adults they leaf through old photo albums and wish they'd come of age before the camera was invented.

You may not understand why some teenage boys seem bent on wearing their baseball caps from breakfast until bedtime. And although you've always thought of yourself as reasonably open-minded, perhaps your eighteen-year-old daughter's getting her tongue or other body part pierced is just too . . . too . . . *too.* However, within reason, a child's chosen self-image should not be a battleground.

What is "within reason"? Certainly a youngster's attire must adhere to the school dress code—which to you may seem like no dress code beyond, "No shirt, no socks, no service." As for whether or not to set standards at home, that is up to you. You might want to insist on no hats at the dinner table. On the other hand, if there are more serious conflicts between you and your teenager, this may be an issue to overlook. If your youngster is generally obedient, perhaps you let this slide. Or not.

4. *We Will Spend Vast Quantities of Time Behind Closed Doors.*

"Our son spends so much time alone in his room, we began to worry that he was depressed. But he's reassured us that he's fine. 'I just like to be by myself sometimes, that's all.' "

For a teenager to hole up in her room is not necessarily a sign of depression. Her room is both a haven from the daily pressures she faces as well as a laboratory for testing new identities. "In private," explains Dr. Victor Strasburger, chief of the division of adolescent medicine at the University of New Mexico School of Medicine in Albuquerque, "adolescents can perfect the social masks that they wear." Youngsters also need a quiet place for doing their homework. A teenager should have her own room, unless family finances don't allow for it.

HOW TO RESPOND

Let's respect our children's growing need for privacy. If the door to their room is closed, knock and *wait for permission* before you enter. Siblings should be instructed to observe the same rule. Few things mortify teenagers more than to have a family member barge in and catch them in a state of undress or playing air guitar to a song on the radio. Or perhaps they're practicing their kissing technique with a pillow. You don't know—nor do they want you to know.

Q: I repeatedly tell my son not to lock his bedroom door, but he goes ahead and does it anyway, which makes me suspicious. If he's not doing anything in there that could get him into trouble, why does he need to lock the door?

A: See the reasons noted above. There is no harm in allowing a youngster to lock the door to his room, unless there has been a recent history of substance abuse, sneaking out the window, self-inflicted wounds (known as *cutting*) or suicide attempts.

Yak, Yak, Yak: Teens and the Telephone

Youngsters should be given privacy when they're on the phone. Please: no picking up the extension every ten minutes to bark, "Aren't you done talking yet?!" At the same time, teens should be considerate of other family members and not subject callers to two hours straight of busy signals. If your child gabs on the phone excessively, you might consider imposing restrictions. Or why not insist that she contribute part of her allowance toward the monthly bill? She'll quickly come to appreciate how much public utilities cost, something most young people don't learn until they're on their own.

Teenagers are also entitled to emotional privacy, which we should honor by not badgering them to discuss something they'd clearly prefer not to share. But we should never stop showing an interest in what's going on in their lives. Most of the time, says Dr. Pratt, "kids want their parents to know what's going on." With adolescents, you often have to read between the lines. A seemingly indignant, "Stop always butting into my business!" might in fact *really* mean (deep breath): "You're asking me about something that is too personal or embarrassing for me to discuss with you, but deep down I'm glad you asked, because it shows that you really care about me."

The appropriate response to a terse "I don't want to talk about it" is, "That's fine. But if you ever do want to discuss it—or anything else that's on your mind—please know that I'm always here to listen." In time, she'll probably take you up on your offer and confide in you.

SPYING WITHOUT PRYING

As a parent, it can be difficult to accept that parts of your teen's life have been declared off-limits to you. When he was younger, you probably knew his whereabouts all of the time and were familiar with nearly everyone who made up his universe. Now that he's in middle school or high school, he has friends you know by name only, and he goes to places you know little about except for the few details he dispenses like droplets of water from a slow-leaking faucet.

It is healthy for an adolescent to pursue friendships and activities outside his parents' sphere of influence. The dilemma that parents face is how to avoid trespassing on their teenager's turf yet still be aware of what he's doing.

The best way may be to keep him in your sights as much as possible by opening your home to him and his friends. When you were growing up, wasn't there one house that served as the hub for your social circle more than the other kids' houses? It wasn't so much the house itself—although the pink shag carpet in the family room and the well-stocked refrigerator were indisputable attractions—it was the hospitality of your friend's mother and father. They made you feel welcome. Kids tend not to hang out at houses where they sense that the parents regard their presence a nuisance.

Yes, you'll probably have to put up with some extra noise, and once in a while you'll walk into the kitchen to find your son and his friends wolfing down the last of the homemade cherry pie you had your heart set on, but these are small sacrifices to stay connected to your youngster. Not only will you be privy to his private world, but you'll get to know his friends, whose influence grows stronger during the teen years. As an added bonus, it probably won't hurt your standing with your child to acquire a reputation among his buddies as the coolest parents on the block.

> **Pediatrician's Perspective**
>
> DR. LANI WHEELER: *"I always encourage parents to volunteer for carpools and to listen to the conversations. Every morning for two years, I drove my son and six other middle-school students to band or orchestra rehearsals. Some days they would bring music tapes to share; other days they would talk and almost forget that I was there. Later, with my son, I would then follow up on some of the things they'd discussed."*

5. When Not Closeted by Ourselves, We Will Spend Much of Our Spare Time with Our Friends, So Get Used to It.

"Our daughter Beth is an intelligent, charming girl, but she's easily influenced by what other kids think. If her best friend, Nancy, makes catty remarks about another girl at school, Beth will go along with it, even though I know she doesn't honestly feel that way. These days half her sentences seem to begin, 'But Nancy says . . .' Frankly, it worries me that she's such a follower."

Adolescents rely heavily on friends to help with their separation from the family. Mom and Dad gradually get nudged aside as the standard of behavior and values, because other kids fulfill certain psychological needs in ways that parents cannot. Teenagers, still in the process of finding themselves, look to their pals for approval, acceptance and understanding. Youngsters often feel most comfortable previewing new self-identities and ideas for an audience of their peers.

THE PATTERNS OF TEEN FRIENDSHIPS

In most areas, entering junior high school expands a teenager's social network, introducing her to children from other elementary schools. Younger adolescents, unsure of themselves, often seek the security of a clique. But they usually form an inseparable bond with another youngster of the same sex: "my best friend."

These two confidants will frequently share a loyalty and emotional intimacy that family members might envy. Sometimes, without realizing it, mothers and fathers may resent the young "interloper" and subtly or overtly discourage their son or daughter from seeing so much of him/her. Unless the friend poses a seriously negative influence, a subject we discuss later in this chapter, this is usually a mistake. First, parents have no reason to feel threatened by a child's best friend. Second, friends will probably drift in and out of your youngster's life during adolescence. At each stage of development, he may find that different kids meet his needs. Special friendships, though, will survive teenager-hood and possibly last a lifetime.

By middle adolescence, with the growth spurt more or less completed, youngsters frequently gain confidence and find it easier to socialize. On a practical level, they're also more mobile than they were at twelve or thirteen; friendships are no longer limited to the immediate neighborhood. Ages fourteen to sixteen are when some teens begin to take an interest in the opposite sex, platonically at first. Then may come stirrings of love, which can either enhance the relationship and culminate in romance, or can complicate matters, causing the friendship to collapse.

In late adolescence, teenagers grow still more independent and capable of making friendships last. They may also be dating by this time, if not earlier, and are able to move comfortably among several peer groups, including those made up of both boys and girls. High-school graduation brings one of an adolescent's first brushes with separation and loss, as they leave longtime friends behind—or their friends leave them behind—and have to form new friendships at college or at a job.

Depending on the circumstances, this can be a time of extreme emotional upheaval. Even kids who are counting down the days to graduation like prison inmates serving out their sentences have developed a measure of comfort in school. Most of the faces they pass in the hallways are the same ones they've seen for years, perhaps since they were little. With the end of high school, their familiar social world is often pulled out from under them. They and their fellow classmates scatter around the country, most never to see one another again.

A young adult who goes away to a college or a job far from home has to build a social support system from the ground up. At the same time, he may have to acclimate himself to a drastically different environment, as when relocating from a small rural town to a large city, or vice-versa. He may also be exposed for the first time to young people from different racial, ethnic and cultural backgrounds. On the other hand, a boy or girl from a diverse community may find it equally unsettling to land in a town with a largely homogenous population.

It is *a lot* to absorb at once. Eighteen-year-olds aren't that far removed from the anxiety of wondering where they fit in among their peers. For kids who didn't fare too well socially before, the post-high-school world may present a welcome opportunity to be seen for the person that they are now and to shed a reputation that should have disappeared years ago. For others, the transition will prompt a new identity crisis. They will need their parents' love and attention. Until they adapt to their new surroundings—and most do—family may be their only anchor.

WHEN PARENTS DISAPPROVE OF ONE OF
THEIR TEENAGER'S FRIENDS

Many friends will pass through our child's adolescence. Inevitably, there will be at least one or two we don't like for whatever reason: too loud, too immature, not well mannered, not serious about school. But disliking a child's friend isn't grounds for trying to end the relationship. Choosing friends and judging other people's character are essential life skills that teenagers need to learn—occasionally the hard way.

Sometimes parental disapproval is justified, though, as in the case of a pal who is immersed in the drug culture or sexually promiscuous, and so on. The dilemma is how to express your concerns without angering or alienating your teenager. If he asks your opinion about his friend, be honest, but without sounding like you're attacking the other child. Parents should avoid blurting out unsolicited comments such as, "What are you doing hanging around with that Michael? The whole neighborhood knows he's a bad kid."

A bad kid? That may be precisely Michael's appeal! Subconsciously or deliberately, adolescents sometimes pick friends they know their parents will object to. It's a way of asserting their independence. Teens with "bad" reputations are seductive for other reasons. Through them, a basically good kid can vicariously take a walk on the wild side: joining Johnny Rebel at another friend's house for poker and two cases of beer bootlegged through someone's older brother, but deciding not to drink. Or he can take part without having to accept full responsibility for his actions: If his parents smell the beer on his breath or the police pull him over for driving erratically, he can always deflect some of the blame onto young Mr. Rebel. "I told Johnny we shouldn't be out spraying graffiti, but he wouldn't listen, so I had to go along. I swear!" For still other youngsters, the school troublemakers may be the only social tribe open to them.

Be careful when threatening to put a stop to a friendship. The harsher your criticisms of your child's friend, the more compelled he may feel to run to the boy's defense. The same is often true when parents try to keep young Romeos and Juliets apart. A more sensible approach is to calmly express your reservations about the friendship and encourage her to do the same. It's possible that you're giving voice to thoughts she's had herself.

Q: When our son Eric entered high school last fall, he was befriended by a junior named Michael. This kid comes from a home where there's no supervision, and he's allowed to run wild. He's an aspiring rapper who surrounds himself with younger boys so that he can be the gang leader. Michael picks fights and is constantly getting in trouble at school. Unfortunately, Eric *worships* him and seems to be trying to emulate Michael's mannerisms and behavior. We sat our son down and said that we didn't think his friendship with Michael was a good thing and explained why. We were careful not to sound as if we were attacking the boy, and at that point we didn't forbid Eric from seeing him. Then we heard from some other parents that Michael has been dealing small amounts of pot to kids around the neighborhood. That did it.

We told Eric he could no longer hang around with Michael after school. Much to our surprise, he didn't give us an argument. "Fine. I won't hang around with him anymore." But then we got a phone call from his principal. Eric, Michael and some other boys were caught cutting class and smoking cigarettes behind the big maple tree on school grounds. How do we prevent him from being friends with this boy, when he sees him at school every day?

A: Parents should not be afraid to terminate relationships that are obviously detrimental or potentially dangerous for their youngster. Ideally, the boy or girl agrees to end the friendship. But if not, it is essential to set firm limits and follow through. Eric's parents should inform their son that their trust in him is on the line, and that if they ever find out that he is still defying them by hanging out with Michael they will have no choice but to impose a harsh penalty. Perhaps he must come home directly from school or extracurricular school activities until he regains their trust.

One final point: Do not be afraid to involve legal authorities if you have legitimate reason to believe that one of your youngster's friends is engaged in a harmful or illegal activity, such as drug dealing, shoplifting, truancy, arson, carrying a firearm, defacing or destroying public property and so on.

6. *In Order to Assert Our Individuality, We Need to Follow the Herd.*

"Last year our family moved from Wisconsin to California. My sixteen-year-old son, John, is kind of a straight arrow, at least compared to his friends. He

doesn't curse, drink or use drugs, and he strongly believes in waiting for sex until after marriage. It's how we raised him. John is an outstanding football player. He says that in the locker room, the boys are constantly talking about girls and sex: who's 'done it,' and with whom, in graphic detail. It's like a competition. Their talk makes him uncomfortable, but he told me that he was beginning to feel tremendous pressure to have sex—especially after one of the kids semijokingly called him gay. John said to me, 'Sometimes I think I should go ahead and do it, just to get the guys off my back.' "

Your teenager's world is a melting pot of social groups. Drive past her school in the morning, before the bell/buzzer calls everyone to homeroom, and you'll see each crowd take shape.

Over there, sitting on the steps, are the athletes—the jocks—conspicuous in their varsity jackets. They're clowning around for the benefit of the popular girls, who pretend not to notice as they preen and primp and "casually" toss back their manes of hair. Huddled under a tree by the parking lot, hurriedly puffing down their cigarettes and making wisecracks about the above groups are the stoners. Their hair and dress probably hasn't changed much since you were in high school. Unless *you* were one of the stoners, in which case you wouldn't remember. As for the brains (aka, technonerds, Einsteins), they're inside, dutifully studying at their desks.

Other peer groups are less distinctly identifiable, consisting of five or six close friends or kids who enjoy a common activity. These smaller cliques tend to be open to a wider cross-section of students, whereas the jocks club and the popular-girls club are proudly exclusive. The high-school hoi polloi know better than to bother applying for membership. "*You* want to join *us? As if!*"

Although some kids resist being associated with a specific crowd or clique, this is where most teenage social interactions take place. The lure of a peer group is strongest during early adolescence, when physical appearance and intellectual ability are changing rapidly. The clique is an oasis where youngsters can feel accepted and confirm to themselves that they are "normal." It also provides a model to follow in terms of values, behavior, coping skills—even dress and hairstyles. As adolescents mature, they may leave one clique for another that better reflects their evolving beliefs and interests, or they may circulate among several groups, which later on often include members of the opposite sex.

Each tribe functions like a minisubculture, with its own rules and rituals. Among younger teens, individuality may be tolerated, but conformity is the norm. Their self-identity is shaky enough at this point that a child who was radically different from them might be too threatening. The net result, which adults often find amusing, is a group of "unique individuals" who look alike and act alike as they march down the street in lockstep.

The impact of *negative peer pressure* on young people has probably been overstated somewhat, but it is formidable, especially during the early teens.

According to one survey of youngsters, four in five who had experimented with drugs said they'd been influenced to do so by their friends. (Peer pressure can also be positive; in other studies of adolescents, most claim that their friends are likely to *discourage* them from using drugs or having sex.)

You'll feel better knowing that as kids get older, they become more discriminating in their friendships and are better equipped to resist the peer pressure cooker. But even if your child is at a vulnerable age, don't underestimate your power to offset negative encouragement from other youngsters. Despite the fact that teenagers spend twice as much time with their peers as they do with their mothers and fathers, parents who remain connected to their boy or girl exert roughly equal influence.

HOW TO RESPOND

Short of locking children in their bedrooms and not letting them out until their twenty-first birthday, there is no foolproof way to protect them from friends' negative influences. Now and then most kids allow themselves to get talked into doing things that go against their better judgment.

The teens who are most successful at standing up to peer pressure typically share three main characteristics: self-discipline ("I shouldn't do this, and if my parents find out, I will suffer the consequences"), a strong moral and ethical foundation ("I shouldn't do this because it is wrong") and healthy self-esteem. However, it takes time for a teenager's sense of self to come into focus. Until then, he looks mainly to other youngsters to reflect his self-worth back at him. For better or worse, their acceptance/rejection/ambivalence has much to do with helping him answer the question "Who am I?"

Adolescents with fragile self-esteem—and therefore a greater need for acceptance—are often more easily swayed by negative peer pressure and are likely to develop depression, eating disorders, and problems with drugs and alcohol. Other signs of a poor self-concept are listed in the box on the following page. Most kids will exhibit these behaviors periodically, often in response to a specific situation. A child who acts this way much of the time, though, may see himself in an unflattering light and need help in building his confidence.

WAYS TO BUILD YOUR TEENAGER'S SELF-ESTEEM

Often without thinking about it, parents fortify their youngsters' self-esteem every day, whether it's by complimenting them on a job well done, kissing them good-bye (assuming they still allow it) or disciplining them for breaking a rule. But all of us have days when we inadvertently bruise children's egos or

Signs of Low Self-Esteem

- Avoids tasks or challenges, out of a fear of failure.
- Gives up in games or tasks at the first hint of frustration.
- Cheats or lies when losing at a game or sport.
- Exhibits regressive behavior: acting silly or babyish.
- Is often bossy or inflexible, to compensate for feelings of inadequacy.
- Rationalizes his own mistakes and shortcomings by blaming others, making excuses or downplaying the importance of events.
- Attributes his successes in life to luck or fate, not to his own effort and abilities.
- A decline in school grades or a lack of interest in his usual activities.
- Withdraws socially, losing friends or having less contact with them.
- Experiences mercurial mood swings, marked by sadness, crying, angry outbursts, frustration or quiet detachment.
- Tends to be highly self-critical and given to remarks such as, "I can't do anything right," "Nobody likes me," or, "I'm just stupid."
- Has difficulty accepting either praise or criticism.
- Is excessively concerned and acutely sensitive about what others think of him.
- Is either overly helpful around the house or not helpful at all.

simply miss an opening to make them feel good about themselves. Here are some easy ways to help instill self-esteem.

Be generous with praise. "We don't tell our children often enough what they did *right*," observes Dr. Adele Hofmann. Commend your child not only for accomplishments but for effort—including those times when it fails to bring the desired results. In addition, let's encourage kids to feel proud of themselves. Pride should shine from within, not just in response to external approval.

Teens with low self-esteem may feel awkward accepting praise. If that's true of your youngster, then hand out compliments frugally. Don't slather on the praise so thick that it sounds insincere. Boys and girls have an internal radar that tells them when Mom and Dad are merely trying to make them feel good. If anything, it has an opposite effect.

Criticize when necessary, but constructively, never in a hurtful or demeaning manner.

Instead of saying: "How could you have gotten that answer wrong on your chemistry test?"

Say: "You almost got the answer. With a little extra studying, I'm sure you'll do better next time."

Solicit your youngster's opinions. Teenagers have no shortage of them. Include him in everyday family decisions and implement some of his suggestions. What does he think about the new couch you're considering for the living room? Adolescents love nothing better than to be treated like grown-ups, and they're usually flattered anytime that you invite them into the adult world.

Encourage youngsters to cultivate their talents and interests. Everybody excels at *something.* Everybody *needs* to excel at something. Let your child follow her passion, whatever it may be. Even interests that you may consider frivolous can provide opportunities for success and a safe outlet for peer acceptance. Sports is generally a popular arena for achievement among girls as well as boys. But what if your son's talent is playing bass guitar in his heavy-metal quartet "Marshmallow Bulldozer," which rattles the walls of your basement every Saturday?

Support his hobby, provided that the band, or any other pastime, doesn't interfere with more pressing responsibilities such as schoolwork. "Parents shouldn't just say no to kids," says Dr. Robert Blum of University Hospitals in Minneapolis. "They also have to say yes, to help them find positive ways of building self-esteem and exploring their self-identity."

Performing at school dances could be a boy's ticket to coolness, which just might enable him to avoid going to risky lengths in order to win friends' approval. He may also pick up some valuable skills (musical proficiency not necessarily being one of them), such as how to work as part of a team, how to persuasively present creative ideas to a "committee" and so on.

Just be aware that like boy-girl infatuations, a teenager's enthusiasm for a particular pursuit may be short-lived. Until your child demonstrates a serious commitment, you might want to hold off on buying expensive top-of-the-line equipment or lessons right away, be it ice-hockey gear, a pricey tutor for advanced calculus or an expensive racing bicycle.

Some teens find fulfillment channeling their idealism into volunteer work. A study by the U.S. Department of Education found that of eight thousand students in grades six through twelve, about half had performed volunteer work during the academic year. When schools offered or arranged community service, about nine in ten youngsters took part. In some instances participation was incorporated into the curriculum, and therefore mandatory. But there were nearly as many "volunteens" from schools where community service was optional.

Kids want to feel valued not only by their families but by the greater community. "One way they feel validated is to have social roles that are meaningful and useful," asserts Dr. Blum. "When kids perform community service, they receive positive feedback that makes them feel good about themselves."

Dr. Diane Sacks, a pediatrician from Ontario, Canada, has seen this firsthand. She regularly steers some of her young patients to organizations seeking teenage volunteers. "It started when a center for the handicapped put out a call looking for kids to help lift and transport patients," she says. "Two boys in my practice had told me that they needed to do community service for school credit. I volunteered them, and it was great for them. Many teenagers with low self-esteem find it very difficult to go out and get a job, but if they're directed to a volunteer position, where the expectations may be less demanding and gratitude is expressed more openly, they flower."

To an adult, teenagers' starry-eyed idealism can seem laughably naive, as in "But there shouldn't be *any* wars!" From experience, you probably appreciate that the world and human relations are far more complex than you ever imagined back when you were a youngster. Perhaps you can now see shades of gray where you once saw only black and white. Or maybe the years have had the opposite effect, sharpening the contrast. Whichever side of the political fence you're on, isn't an adolescent's resolve to change the world refreshing in an increasingly cynical age? Let's not stand in his way.

7. We Can't Grow If You Won't Let Go.
Please Allow Us to Make Decisions for Ourselves,
Even If We're Wrong Sometimes.

"I'm having an extremely difficult time learning to let go of my daughter, who is sixteen. Intellectually, I accept that I have to allow her to make her own decisions. And it's not as if I don't trust her, because she's very responsible. But I'm terrified to let her out into the world! The first night that we lent her the car so she could go to a movie with her best friend, I actually got in our van and drove past the theater's parking lot to make sure they got there safely. I don't want to be one of those overprotective, smothering moms—but I guess I am."

Self-esteem and self-determination go hand in hand. Teenagers who are trusted to make decisions for themselves gain confidence as they discover they can meet life's challenges and rebound from mistakes. When kids are kept overly dependent on their parents, however, they may feel less self-assured and be more inclined to follow someone else's lead. Plus, they get less practice making responsible choices and learning essential coping skills. In order to make it on their own, youngsters need opportunities in which to test and develop their abilities to reflect, reason and problem-solve.

The adolescent struggle for autonomy can be likened to a tug of war between parent and child. The outcome is never in doubt, only how the contest will play out. What worries mothers and fathers is the fact that they must relax their grip just when new and dangerous temptations abound. If they let go of the umbilical cord too soon or too abruptly, their child is almost certain to get hurt. But if they hold on too tightly for too long, he may rebel and go seek experiences that make him feel "grown up"—perhaps drug and alcohol use, sex and so on. For him, these represent avenues to freedom.

Now more than at any time of life, the teenager comes to see herself as different, special—and impervious to the laws of biology and physics. *Other girls may get pregnant and other boys might become infected from having sex with an unprotected partner, but not me,* goes the fractured logic. According to a Youth Risk Behavior Survey, conducted by the federal Centers for Disease Control (CDC) and Prevention, approximately two in five sexually active high-school students did not use a condom the last time they had intercourse.

Or: *I don't need to put on my seat belt; nothing's going to happen to me.* About one in five respondents to the CDC poll admitted that they rarely or never wore seat belts. This wishful thinking, coupled with teenagers' narrow band of life experiences, can easily land them in trouble.

HOW TO RESPOND

Since teenagers are hardwired to strive for independence, why resist the inevitable? The more constructive approach, for everyone, is to assist a child's entry into the world. One of chapter 2's essential parenting skills offers pointers on how to coach kids to fend off peer pressure. Moms and dads can further prepare youngsters by helping them exercise their critical-thinking muscles through the following techniques:

Start early, start small. Beginning in the early teens, or even the preteen years, allow children to have a say in decisions that affect them, but where the stakes are low. Instead of buying all of your son's school clothes, why not give him a reasonable budget and accompany him on a shopping expedition for play clothes. If your opinion is sought, give it; if not, suppress the urge to criticize the baggy mustard-yellow nylon track pants and livid-purple sweatshirt that he has his heart set on. However, do remind him that if he has any second thoughts, he should wait before he buys. Maybe your son can return a poorly chosen shirt. But what about that haircut? Or a tattoo?

When it's time to repaint your daughter's bedroom, let her pick out the color. If this would be courting disaster, narrow down the selections to several colors you could live with. As youngsters demonstrate the ability to make sound judgments, we give them increasingly more significant responsibilities.

If your child is faced with having to make a decision and seeks your advice, guide him through these six steps to making responsible choices.

1. Ask him to describe the problem and how he feels about it.

2. Help him to find alternative solutions to the one he may have in mind. Kids don't always realize they have choices.

3. Help him to weigh the pros and cons of each option. How will other people feel about his decision, and how will he deal with that?

4. Talk about "fallback positions." What will he do, for example, when the friend he's decided to exclude from his upcoming party confronts him and asks why?

5. Allow him to reach a decision and implement it.

6. Follow up. Ask him how things turned out and encourage him to reflect upon his choice.

Allow kids to live and learn from their mistakes. The lessons in life that often leave the deepest imprints are those gained from suffering the natural consequences of one's actions. When we see our child heading for trouble, instinct tells us to step in and rescue her. But sometimes a parent's greatest act of love is to resist that impulse and to let her pay the price—again, in safe situations where the cost isn't too high.

"In the sixth grade, my daughter kept putting off some special project that she had to complete for social studies," recalls Dr. Renée Jenkins. "She was up all night trying to get it done and woke me up at four o'clock in the morning because something was wrong with the computer. I got up, I fixed it, I said, 'This is your problem,' and went back to bed.

"She received an *F* in social studies that semester. Now, if this had been the eleventh grade, I wouldn't have let her make that decision, but in sixth grade, I did. By eleventh grade, she knew not to leave projects until the last minute, because she'd been down that road, and it's not a good road."

Parents who get into a habit of bailing out their kids teach them to be rescued, which won't be true later in life.

Anytime a teenager makes a mistake or an ill-advised decision, discuss it with him. Be supportive and explain that setbacks and failure are part of life. Then help him to analyze what went wrong and to figure out how he might have handled the situation differently.

If necessary, don't shy away from helping him face the fact that he may have behaved dishonestly or inappropriately. Not all mistakes are easily forgiven or forgotten. For instance, if your daughter decided to go out with her friends rather than visit her ailing grandfather as she'd promised him she would, she *should* understand the hurt Grandpa may feel. This wasn't something that "just happened," it was a conscious choice that she made, and a selfish one at that. Kids should know that when they make poor choices, other decisions may have to be made for them. You hope that your daughter sees her error and will apologize to her grandfather without any prompting. But if she doesn't, you would be remiss not to encourage her to do so or face other consequences. After all, the world will not be as forgiving of such self-centered behavior.

WHEN WORLDS COLLIDE: ADOLESCENCE VERSUS "MIDLIFE CRISIS"

Ironically, by helping a teenager's progression to adulthood, parents are essentially laying the groundwork for their own demotion, or "temporary parental disablement," as Dr. Adele Hofmann jokingly calls it. (Small consolation, perhaps, but young people's reliance on Mom and Dad's purse strings seems to endure well after the last apron string has been cut.)

When the son or daughter that we love and have protected since birth no longer needs us as much, it is normal for parents' pride to be intermingled with feelings of loss, displacement, even rejection. The timing of a child's adolescence can seem like a cruel trick, coinciding as it frequently does with a parent's "midlife crisis."

You may be going through a life transition and asking yourself some of the same questions that burden teenagers, such as "Who am I?" and "Where do I fit in?" This sudden identity crisis typically affects mothers more than fathers, "especially stay-at-home moms," says Dr. Helen Pratt, "because they've devoted their lives to their children."

Seeing a youngster grow into a man or woman also forces parents to acknowledge the prospect of their own mortality, quite possibly for the very first time. A teenager is at the peak of health and strength and sexuality; life is ripe with possibility. By contrast, Mom and Dad may have peaked in all three departments, and may have reached the summit of their careers as well. Regrets may be piling up next to a dwindling collection of dreams for the future.

Most mothers and fathers adjust well to this strangely unfamiliar dynamic. Those that don't may react in one of two extremes, neither of which is healthy. The resentful parent harbors deep-seated envy or outright hostility toward her blossoming teenager. According to Dr. George Comerci, such emotions "are more common than we'd like to admit."

The eternal-adolescent parent views his teenager as a mirror of himself, or vice-versa. He relives and at the same time perpetuates his own youth through the child's exploits. "Parents who derive vicarious pleasure from their children's achievements create many problems," says Dr. Comerci.

We've all heard the expression "backstage mom," used to describe the overbearing mother who pushes her child-performer to achieve her own unfulfilled showbiz aspirations. The male equivalent is the "football dad." He's so overinvolved with his son's game—pacing the sidelines, shouting encouragement incessantly—that he saps all the fun out of it for the boy. When parents co-opt a teenager's activity, observes Dr. Jellinek, "the kid's risk of seeking dangerous behavior goes up, because that's the only way he can express his autonomy."

According to Dr. Comerci, still other parents overidentify with their adolescent to such a degree, "they gain vicarious pleasure from their children's antisocial or otherwise inappropriate behavior. Parents need to look at themselves and examine their motivation for what they do ostensibly for the 'good' of their child."

During your boy's or girl's adolescence you're likely to experience other emotions that may surprise you. Frankly, there are times when you may not especially *like* your teenager because of his recent behavior. Perhaps in a moment of frustration, you admit to a friend that you're looking forward to the day he goes off to college. Then you feel guilty for saying that. Don't. If you asked around, you would find that virtually all parents have made similar remarks, and worse, on occasion.

PART II

YOUR TEENAGER AT HOME, AT SCHOOL AND IN THE WORLD

5

YOUR FAMILY

Most teenagers genuinely cherish their families. Besides providing an inexhaustible source of love, nurturing, comfort and security, the family bestows upon them a unique identity and history, and a critical sense of belonging and feeling valued. A 1996 poll of twenty-eight hundred high-school students revealed that nothing was more important to them than their relationships at home.

And this is true despite the fact that they spend so little time there. Since you were probably just as involved in activities outside the home when you were a teenager, you should be sympathetic. According to figures from *Youth Indicators 1996,* a statistical compilation from the National Center for Education Statistics, more high-school seniors participated in three or four extracurricular activities in 1972 as compared to 1992, and more sixteen- and seventeen-year-olds were employed in 1970 than in 1993.

What's different today is not teenagers but their parents. Compared to your parents, you almost certainly have less time to devote to your family. Not only are more mothers and fathers working, their jobs are more demanding than ever. That was one finding of the Family and Work Institute's "1997 National Study of the Changing Workforce," which set out to examine work-related trends of the previous twenty years. Researchers from the New York–based organization interviewed three thousand workers. According to the report, full-time employees are averaging forty-seven hours per week on the job, three and a half hours more than in 1977. Many of the participants described a stressful atmosphere that demanded they work "very fast" (68 percent) and "very hard" (88 percent). One in three brought work home at least once a week, also an increase from two decades before.

Strengthening Family Ties

We can't communicate, relate—have fun—as a family if the home is allowed to become a mere docking station where everyone touches down, fuels up and blasts off back out the door. But as a teen's world broadens, it is normal for at least some longstanding household routines to fall away. Daily family meals tend to be one of the early casualties.

Is sharing the dinner table a few times a week really all that important? Yes! Mealtime and other everyday rituals enrich family life and create enduring memories. When your teenager is grown, these simple moments will hold as much meaning for her as they do for you now.

FAMILY MEALS

Between everyone's crowded calendars, though, you'll need to be flexible. For instance, the family meal doesn't *have* to be dinner. In some families, it can't be, because a parent doesn't get home until late or works a night shift.

If everyone's schedules converge in the morning, then coax everyone out of bed half an hour earlier than usual and spend some quality time together over a leisurely breakfast—always a far more enjoyable start to the day than wolfing down a piece of toast while trying to get ready.

Other ideas:

• Have lunch together on the weekend.

• Set aside one night a week where you all go out to a casual dinner. It doesn't have to be expensive. Let a different family member choose the restaurant each week, so long as the menu appeals to all tastes.

• Once everybody is home for the evening, make a time to meet in the kitchen for a nighttime snack.

The number of family meals isn't as important as seeing to it that they happen on a regular basis, although certainly two or three times a week isn't an unreasonable expectation. When you do eat together, ensure that there will be no interruptions. Turn on the telephone-answering machine, turn off the TV and hold off checking e-mail or the fax machine unless it's absolutely necessary. Devote the time to talking and listening to one another. If you notice somebody's being excluded from the conversation, play moderator and draw him in: "So, Josh, tell us all about *your* day at school."

A Dozen Fun Family Rituals

1. *Family video night.* Rent a movie, order in a pizza, make popcorn. The only difficulty may be agreeing on something the whole family wants to watch (and is appropriate for teens and younger children). Again, alternate choices among family members.
2. *After a big snowstorm,* everybody tramp outside to build a snowman or go for a walk together. *Then* shovel.
3. *Sharing the Sunday newspaper over a special breakfast.* This is a ritual with Mom and Dad in mind. Or what about all going out to a restaurant for brunch?
4. *Buy a special dessert to transform dinner into an occasion,* and not just on birthdays, wedding anniversaries and graduations. Celebrate family members' achievements. An unexpected high grade on a test at school or a promotion at work deserves a cake—with candles and an inscription. Be creative!
5. *Spiritual pursuits bring many families together,* whether it's attending services or saying grace together at the dinner table.
6. *Sit around together flipping through old photo albums or watching vintage family videos and home movies.* You'll relive fond memories and give one another hiccups laughing at the sight of certain members' now-outdated hairstyles and assorted fashion faux pas. "Wow, Dad: *Really nice* leisure suit."
7. *Take a car ride.* Where? Anywhere. Take the slow, scenic route and stop off at whatever looks interesting.
8. *Go bowling together.* Golf and miniature golf are two other examples of individual sports that you can do together.
9. *Build a fire in the fireplace,* or at a camping ground, or on the beach, and share stories.
10. *Cook dinner together,* with each member of the family taking part.
11. *Play board games,* cards, dominoes and so on.
12. *Communal chores or collaborating on a household project* can be a lot of fun.

FAMILY OUTINGS AND VACATIONS

Some mothers and fathers like to designate one day of the week Family Togetherness Day. Young children typically look forward to these excursions to the zoo, amusement park, shopping and so on. During adolescence, however, parents may find it harder to sustain the custom. It used to be that your suggestion of a Sunday picnic elicited a delighted "Yippie!" Now the news may be greeted with a groaning, "Do we *have* to?"

It's hard, but try not to take this as a rejection. From the teenager's standpoint, life is regimented enough during the week. Why must he be shackled to the family *every* Sunday? He'd like to see his friends more on the weekend.

Rituals shouldn't be so rigid that they are viewed as yet another obligation. In order to save Family Day from extinction, consider holding it every other week—though if you have other children who enjoy doing things together as a family, give your teenager a furlough for the afternoon while the rest of you head out on your adventure. Or why not plan a family activity on a weeknight? As kids get older, those Saturdays and Sundays quickly fill up with errands and appointments anyway. Another idea is to let your teen invite one of her friends along now and then.

Young people are more likely to be enthusiastic about family outings and holidays if they're given a say in helping to pick the recreational activity or destination instead of feeling like backseat hostages. When planning a vacation, take into account everyone's interests and try to incorporate them into the itinerary. But leave room for flexibility and spontaneity. Family trips that are plotted out to the nanosecond can ultimately prove to be more exhausting and stressful than they are fun. The important thing is for all of you to be together.

Even the most accommodating parents, though, may have to listen to a teenager's grumbling about having been "forced" to go with them to "this boring place." Only an adolescent could be basking in the sun on an island paradise, surrounded by tennis courts, a video arcade and dozens of other activities, and whine, "But there's nothing to *do* here!"

INVITE YOUR TEEN TO YOUR PLACE OF WORK

To teenagers, a parent's occupation and workplace are often as shrouded in mystery as their world can be to adults. That's because many of us don't think to share our work experiences with them. Maybe we're too worn out to discuss it, or we assume kids are too young to understand, but many parents, when asked how their day went, sound no different than your average adolescent: "Ah, it's too complicated to get into. Could you please pass the potatoes?"

TEEN TIP:

Are there summer-employment opportunities for your teenager at your place of work? If so, it could be a wonderful experience for both of you.

Youngsters should have a sense of what their parents do all day. Why not invite your son or daughter to accompany you to work the next time there's a school holiday? Perhaps you've done this already. They're sure to enjoy the attention they'll undoubtedly receive from your colleagues. And seeing you in a context other than *parent* could very well enhance their perception of you. Teens don't always appreciate that a working Dad or Mom has professional responsibilities in addition to parental duties—and some hidden talents too.

We particularly recommend taking your teen to work if work-related commitments have occasionally kept you from attending a school play or other important function. Few employed parents make it through a child's adolescence without hearing the accusation, "You care more about your job than you do about me!"

TEENAGERS AND THEIR SIBLINGS

Adolescence can magnify differences between a teenager and her siblings and *may* lead to less closeness than before, particularly if they're younger. The teen's leaps in physical and intellectual development are one reason. But more than anything else, it's the simple fact that an adolescent spends less time around her family. She's off exploring with her friends, having new experiences that her siblings cannot share.

If your kids have always gotten along well, the preadolescent children may detect this growing distance and feel a sense of loss. Parents whose youngsters squabble constantly may welcome the less intense relationship, because it may lessen the frequency of conflicts.

Friction between siblings tends to peak around ages eight to twelve. In some homes, though, the contest goes extra rounds. As children become increasingly opinionated and physically stronger, they may act more aggressively in order to stake out their place in the family hierarchy.

Contentious relationships are more common between youngsters who are of the same gender, and/or close in age and/or have similar interests. Some

---

Sibs' Night Out?

Amazing, isn't it, how the acquisition of a driver's license instantly enhances a teenager's standing with his younger siblings? To help sustain brotherly and sisterly love during the adolescent years, encourage your kids to go out and have some fun together one night a week.

---

amount of quarreling is to be expected. In fact, it's normal. This is how kids learn to assert, express and defend themselves. With your guidance, it is hoped they'll also learn healthier ways for channeling their anger and resolving whatever problems they have with each other. Competitiveness, too, has its upside in that it can motivate both children to excel.

What you shouldn't allow are insults intended to humiliate, or the use of physical force. Don't underestimate the psychological wounds that a brother's or sister's hurtful comments can inflict. If you regularly have to referee confrontations, the rivalry has gone too far and needs to be controlled.

First, the instigator should be given a time-out. When you're not sure who started the fight or name-calling, *both* children take time-outs, in separate rooms. Future skirmishes demand more severe consequences, as described in chapter 2's section on discipline.

Heightened sensitivity on the part of parents can help to keep simmering hostility from boiling over. Begin by doing your best to treat all the kids fairly and to not show favoritism. In addition:

• Avoid drawing comparisons between your children. Instead, point out each one's strengths. Be especially understanding of the child who is continually outshone by a sibling. Find ways to make him feel special too.

• Be careful not to repeatedly blame one child for all sibling disputes, turning him into the family scapegoat.

• Encourage the children to work out their differences themselves.

• Discourage tattling.

• Set parameters for how *everyone* in the household may express his displeasure with one another. Discussion—even angry discussion—is permitted. Yelling too. But anyone guilty of cruel putdowns or resorting to physical force will receive a stiff punishment.

• Find out what triggered the episode and take appropriate steps to prevent a repeat performance. Example: Your eleven-year-old daughter keeps helping herself to your fifteen-year-old daughter's makeup, CDs, school supplies and other items. Today, without asking permission, she wore the older girl's lucky charm bracelet to school. Now she can't find it. She thinks she may have left it in a gym locker, but she's not sure. When she confessed to your fifteen-year-old what happened, the two volleyed insults back and forth until you intervened.

Be fair but firm: "Audra, if Roxanne's bracelet doesn't turn up in the lost-and-found, you are responsible for paying for a new one out of your allowance. And if you ever take something of hers again without asking first, you will lose a privilege."

- Spend some time alone with each child.

THE IMPORTANCE OF ONE-TO-ONE PARENT-TEEN TIME

Because you enjoy a different rapport with each of your children, one-to-one time is important at any age, but especially during the teen years. Adolescents are striving to assert their individuality, which can be hard to do in a large household or if all family activities take place as a group. Insecure youths may already feel anonymous out in the world; they need to believe that at least their parents and siblings recognize them for who they are. A teenager may also want to use this time to talk to you privately about personal matters that she is not comfortable sharing around the rest of the family.

Household Routines to Keep Things Running Smoothly (Even When You're Running on Empty)

Running the household in a reasonably organized fashion will help to make family life less stressful. So that all members know their responsibilities in terms of chores, curfews and so on, hold an informal family meeting once a week, or as needed. Whose turn is it to walk the new puppy in the morning? What about at night? Who sorts the recyclables this week? If it suits your family's personality, write everyone's assignments on a dry-erase board and post it on the refrigerator.

Next you can open the floor to any gripes, but in the spirit of working together toward a solution, not to assign blame. Mom is tired of washing the dishes from dinner and then finding remnants of snacks in the sink night after night. "The new rule around here," she announces, "is that I will do the dishes from dinner. Otherwise everyone is to clean whatever plates, glasses and utensils he uses." Wisely, no one objects. There's usually no need for such meetings to go beyond twenty to thirty minutes, unless everyone wants to continue.

HOUSEHOLD CHORES

Getting children into the habit of pitching in around the home can begin as young as age two, by having them put away their toys when they're done playing with them. By age twelve, there are few household tasks a teenager shouldn't be expected to master. And once they earn their driver's license, it is appropriate to assign them errands such as going to the grocery store or picking up the dry cleaning.

Helping out at home teaches kids the importance of contributing to a team. It also allows them to feel valued and competent, both of which enhance self-esteem.

A TEENAGER'S BEDROOM: ENTER AT YOUR OWN RISK

Who has jurisdiction over an adolescent's room? This question has divided parents and teenagers going all the way back to the Stone Age, when the first cave teen was reprimanded for always leaving his bear and bison hides on the floor.

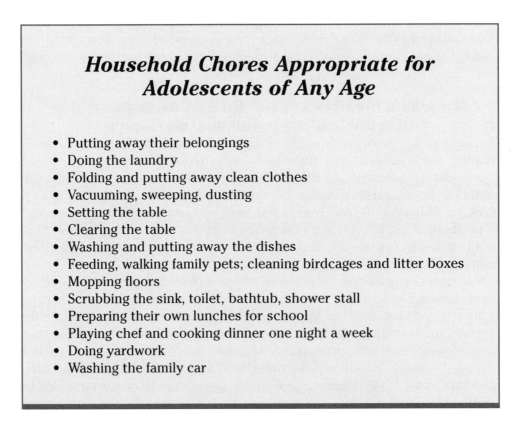

Household Chores Appropriate for Adolescents of Any Age

- Putting away their belongings
- Doing the laundry
- Folding and putting away clean clothes
- Vacuuming, sweeping, dusting
- Setting the table
- Clearing the table
- Washing and putting away the dishes
- Feeding, walking family pets; cleaning birdcages and litter boxes
- Mopping floors
- Scrubbing the sink, toilet, bathtub, shower stall
- Preparing their own lunches for school
- Playing chef and cooking dinner one night a week
- Doing yardwork
- Washing the family car

Let's hear from both sides. Teenagers will insist that it is *their* room, and they should be able to do whatever they want in it. If that includes leaving an obstacle course of junk, clothes and magazines on the floor, that's *their* business. Parents will counter that it may be the teenager's room, but this is *their* house, and what they say goes.

What follows is a compromise: Let your youngster keep his room however messy he wishes, so long as you don't have to call the health department. But there are three conditions:

1. He must keep the door to his bedroom closed whenever he's not at home, so that Mom and Dad don't have to be mortified in front of houseguests.

2. Mom and Dad will not clean his room. "If there's stuff all over the floor," advises Dr. Hofmann, "you don't vacuum. If clothes are not placed in the laundry basket or hamper, they don't get washed. And no picking up after him." That includes throughout the rest of the house too.

3. He must clean his room once a month.

USING AN ALLOWANCE TO TEACH THE VALUE OF MONEY

About three in five teenagers receive an allowance. If your boy or girl isn't among them, consider the benefits. An allowance shouldn't be viewed as a reward but as an opportunity to teach youngsters financial responsibility. It also helps them learn to prioritize (*If I want to buy that pair of boots I've been saving up for, I really can't afford these earrings*) and to weigh their options carefully before making choices (*On second thought, I like the earrings, but I don't* like-*like them. Forget it: I'll wait until I have enough money for the boots*).

As with acquiring any skill, mistakes are part of the learning process. Isn't it preferable for a

> ### *A Teenage Spending Spree*
>
> Young consumers aged thirteen to nineteen spend between $82 billion and $108 billion every year. In 1996 the bulk of that went toward clothing ($36.7 billion), entertainment ($23.4 billion), food ($16.7 billion), personal care ($9.2 billion) and sporting goods ($6.7 billion).

child to mishandle money when the sums and consequences are minimal, as opposed to when he's an adult and possibly flush with credit cards?

There are two schools of thought on whether or not a teenager's allowance should be contingent upon his performing chores at home. Those who oppose the practice say that it sends the wrong message; before long parents could wind up with a sixteen-year-old who drives a hard bargain every time he's asked to put out the garbage. Household tasks are done because every member is expected to contribute to family life. Period. What does he receive in return? Praise and a hug. If allowance is not to be a reward for a job well done, a youngster who is negligent should have a *privilege* rescinded, not his allowance.

The opposite view is that money is no less compelling a motivator for adolescents than it is for adults, and that an allowance is essentially a child's first paycheck. She should know that if she doesn't carry out her responsibilities, part or all of her allowance will be docked.

HOW MUCH ALLOWANCE?

There are several ways to determine the amount of a teenager's allowance. Some parents simply match what other kids in the neighborhood are getting. Others estimate how much money they currently spend on clothes, school supplies, after-school snacks, CDs, videos, going to the movies and other typical teenage expenses and then give all or a portion of that amount directly to the child. Whether you think that is a viable approach will most likely depend on how responsible your teenager is, not to mention your financial situation. Expect to tinker with this system until you hit upon the magic figure that covers your child's expenses without spoiling him.

SOME GUIDELINES TO HELP YOU

• Pay children their allowance on the same day every week. Consistency is important, so that they can practice budgeting their dollars until next payday.

• Try not to interfere with a teenager's money decisions, even if you disapprove. However, feel free to give advice on how to be a savvy consumer. For instance, if your daughter has her heart set on a leather bomber jacket, take her to several stores and point out the differences in price and quality.

• What if your child runs through his allowance too quickly and asks for an advance on next week's payment? Sorry, the bank is presently closed. To lend him money would only foster the buy-now, pay-later spending philosophy that has landed many adults in financial hot oil. No: He must learn to ration his money more conscientiously. A firm position is the proper and loving course.

• Allow your teenager to earn extra money by performing *additional* chores, especially if she's looking to put away money for a pricey item, like a new bicycle. What a terrific lesson in the value of delayed gratification. As for the earlier statement about not linking allowance to chores, this is different. Temporarily think of her as an independent contractor.

MONEY AND VALUES NEEDN'T CLASH

Few parents would probably disagree with the observation that, overall, kids seem more money-oriented and status-conscious than previous generations. They are highly sophisticated (and prolific) consumers with an acute awareness of clothing designers' labels and logos that just didn't exist in your day, at least not to the same degree. Thanks to clothes-crazy girls' magazines, MTV and other media targeted to teenagers—which run scads of fashion ads—many youngsters can tell you which styles are, like, *totally* cool, and which ones will soon be going the way of poodle skirts.

We won't pass judgment on whether this acquisitiveness is a positive or negative development. But by any standard, it is certainly not healthy when a kid must endure cruel taunts from his peers simply because he doesn't own the newest, hippest (read: most expensive) brand of sneakers. We know that adolescents are anxious to fit in with other teens. The clothes they wear often provide an immediately apparent clue.

This can become a recurrent dilemma for families, especially in schools made up of students from varied economic circumstances. If the item in question is beyond your means, be honest but sympathetic: "*Son, I understand that buying this shirt is important to you, but right now our family just can't afford to spend sixty-nine dollars for a shirt.*"

You can help your youngster develop an appreciation for how much things cost by having him sit next to you while you pay the monthly bills—all those hidden expenses of running a household. First show him the bite taken out of each paycheck by taxes and other deductions. He'll probably be shocked.

Explain that your cable-TV bill is approximately equal to the cost of that overpriced shirt you refused to buy him. Ask him to decide if having one shirt is worth giving up cable, for example. Also point out that perhaps two or three of your paychecks per month are already "spoken for" by the mortgage or rent, utilities, groceries and health-care costs, all of which your child may take for granted or not fully understand. The object is to open his eyes to the importance of budgeting and saving.

In fact, many older adolescents would benefit from having their own checking account as well as a savings account. Writing a check feels different from putting a charge on a credit card. And a savings account may actually help encourage saving. If your teenager doesn't yet have a savings account, take him down to the bank to open one. When the monthly statements arrive in the mail, point out how much interest has compounded. He's bound to be impressed. Free money? Without having to work for it? *Cool!*

6

FACING FAMILY DISRUPTIONS AND CRISES TOGETHER

As parents, our natural impulse is to shield our children from anything that threatens the safety and stability of the family, be it the loss of a job, a loved one's death or financial woes. With young boys and girls, that may be appropriate. A teenager, however, is old enough to understand the implications of these and other crises; he deserves to have the situation explained to him and his questions answered.

Let's use as an example a single-income family facing the father's layoff from the aerospace corporation where he has worked as an electrical engineer for nearly twenty years. It is understandable that the parents might want to keep the upsetting news from their teenage son for a while, since the layoff doesn't take effect for another month. "There's nothing he can do it about it anyway," reasons the father.

Nevertheless, it is not fair to the adolescent, who is bound to sense Mom and Dad's anxiety. Denied the truth, he may at first assume that he's done something to upset them. But eventually he is going to piece together clues from snippets of conversations he's overheard, and the scenario he imagines may be far worse than the reality. *Oh no, now we're gonna have to move . . . which means I'll have to leave my school and all my friends . . . and there probably won't be any money to pay for college . . .* While there is cause for concern, meeting the mortgage payments doesn't figure to be a problem for a year, thanks to a generous severance package and the family's savings. The teenager is worrying needlessly about events that aren't going to happen.

How should the parents in this example break the news? Honestly and concisely anticipating as many of his concerns and questions as they can. The mother and father could sit down with him and say something like this:

"Alex, you may have noticed that your mom and I have been a little tense lately."

"Well, yeah, I guess so . . ."

"We want to talk to you about a situation that's going to affect the three of us. You're almost a grown man, you're a member of this family and we feel that you have a right to know.

"Next month they're going to be laying off a lot of people at work, and I'm no longer going to have a job there. We've always been pretty frugal, so you don't have to worry about us losing the house or not having the money for you to go to college in a few years.

"I'm not going to kid you and say that nothing is going to change. Your mom has decided to go back to work until we get back on our feet financially. And we are going to have to budget ourselves much more strictly than we have in the past. Right now, I can't say if we'll be able to afford sending you to tennis camp again next summer. I hope we will, but if not I want to prepare you for that possibility."

The tone is direct and not overly alarming. The parents should ask their son how he feels about what they've just said and if he has any questions. He may be too stunned/confused/upset and reply, "No. Not really." They should assure him that he can talk to them anytime and end by painting a hopeful view of the future:

"This is upsetting for everyone, but we just want you to know that your mom and I love you more than anything, and the three of us are going to work together as a family and get through this. I'm optimistic that I can get a job with another company in the area, so that we don't have to move. Everything is going to be okay."

Parents can use the same approach when introducing other painful subjects, such as a divorce, a loved one's illness or death, and moving. All three are among the major life events that generate the most stress for adolescents, threatening their sense of security or self-esteem.

IF YOUR FAMILY IS PLANNING TO MOVE

Relocating seems to hit teenagers harder than other members of the family. Their roots are deepening at that time so moving often means leaving behind their first true intimate friendships, maybe even a steady boyfriend or girlfriend.

According to a survey of twenty-five hundred children whose families had come to the Denver area, the older the child, the more traumatic the move. Teenage boys generally seem to have greater problems blending in with their new peers than girls do.

There are a number of steps parents can take in advance to help ease a youngster's transition to a new community:

If possible, give your teen three months' notice before an upcoming move, so that she has time to absorb the news and get used to the idea.

Explain the reason for relocating.

Involve your teen in as many decisions as possible about the move—from choosing a home to planning any decorations, etc.

Do your best to minimize other disruptions in her life. For instance, try to schedule the move for the summer instead of during the school year.

Familiarize your child with her new neighborhood or home town ahead of time. If it's within driving distance, give her several grand tours. Drive to the new house or apartment. How far away is the school? Where is the nearest park? Walk around a bit, to get a feel for the community. The trip should dissipate much of her fear of the unknown.

If you're moving far away, help her to gather information about the new location:

• Call the chamber of commerce or town hall and request a map and any printed materials available.

• Check out the area's major newspaper. If there's a community paper, ask to have a sample issue mailed.

• Order a copy of the local Yellow Pages. You can learn *a lot* about a town or city by perusing its phone book.

Emphasize the positive aspects of the move. What does the new location have to offer? Better schools? A larger community center? More activities for young people? Convey the excitement of moving to a new home.

Contact the school your teenager will be attending. If you live nearby, arrange a day and time to visit. Some schools have established a "buddy system" to help newly transferred students adjust socially. From the youth's first day at school, a student volunteer introduces her to other youngsters and joins her at lunch and at recess—two of the more uncomfortable times for children entering a new school.

Let your teen express her feelings. Acknowledge her sadness about leaving friends behind and her nervousness about what lies ahead. Assure your teenager that you will do everything you can to help her get accustomed to the new surroundings.

If you're feeling anxious yourself, you might share this with her. *"You know, honey, I'm going to miss my friends too."* Do be aware, however, that expressing such reservations might only reinforce her negative feelings about the move.

If graduating with her classmates is important to your high-school senior, consider arranging for her to stay behind and live with a trusted relative or family of a friend until the end of the school year.

Once you're settled in your new home, encourage your teenager to involve herself in activities that interest her, as a way of exploring social opportunities. At the same time, assist her in maintaining contact with her old friends, by way of phone calls, sending e-mails and writing letters. Whatever stress your teenager encounters upon moving to an unfamiliar area, in time most adolescents make the adjustment without incurring any long-term psychological problems.

HELPING TEENAGERS COPE WITH DEATH, SERIOUS ILLNESS OR INJURY

Generally speaking an adolescent's first experience with the death of someone close to him will come with the passing of an elderly relative such as a grandparent or a great-aunt or -uncle. (That, or a beloved pet, which can be equally traumatic.) In general, adults may not know what to do or say to help comfort a distraught teenager. When the deceased is a friend, sibling or parent, they are even less prepared to tend adequately to the child's grief.

A Teenager's Understanding of Death

By the age of twelve, a youngster's comprehension of death approaches that of an adult. At five, she may have thought of death as a deep slumber from which the person would eventually awaken, like the princess in *Sleeping Beauty.* Now she realizes that death is permanent. At seven, she may have believed that only grandmas and grandpas and other elderly folks can become ill and die—but not little kids or their parents. Now she understands that death can occur at any age.

Common Reactions

Having the intellectual capacity to grasp the implications of death doesn't necessarily equip teenagers to cope emotionally with the tragedy.

Adolescents typically appear to feel grief more intensely than adults, especially if one of their parents has died. The *Adolescent Life Change Event Scale* (ALCES), which mental-health specialists use to help quantify the events that are the most stress-inducing in teenagers, ranks a parent's death as the number-one cause of adolescent stress. Second is the death of a brother or sister, followed by the death of a friend.

The months or years before the mother or father got sick may have been a rocky period, as often happens when a child becomes a teenager. In this situation, the son or daughter may shoulder tremendous guilt. *"I should have told my father that I loved him, when I had the chance."* A young girl's memory of the night she wished her mother dead following an argument could haunt her for years to come. Angry rages may be directed at everyone from God (for allowing this to happen), to the medical profession (for not being able to prevent it). She may even harbor resentment toward the deceased for, in her eyes, having abandoned her. Bear in mind that the teenager who loses a parent is also subconsciously mourning the end of the childhood she'd led up until now.

Because adolescents are so sensitive about how the world sees them, they may feel self-conscious or outright embarrassed by displays of grief and struggle to suppress their emotions. This can also be a means of protecting themselves or their grieving parents. Try not to take offense if your youngster seems indifferent or makes callous remarks tinged with black humor. There is no "right way" or "wrong way" to mourn. For the time being, her way of coping is to harden her heart. Grief is also frequently expressed in one of the following ways:

- Depression
- Changes in conduct or acting-out behaviors
- "Perfect" behavior
- A decline in academic performance
- Refusing to attend school
- Turning to alcohol or illicit drugs to numb the emotional pain
- Seeking solace through a sexual relationship
- Overeating or undereating
- Sleeping more than usual or not getting enough sleep
- Physical symptoms

"Becoming concerned about physical symptoms is quite common. When someone close to them dies, they may wonder if they too have a medical problem," explains Dr. Morris A. Wessel, a retired Connecticut pediatrician and co-founder of the first hospice facility in the United States.

Dr. Wessel, who continues to work in a child-guidance clinic in New Haven, recalls one teenage patient from many years ago who came to his office specifically for a heart checkup. "She said that her grandfather had recently died of a heart attack. I listened to her chest and took her blood pressure and so forth, and informed her that her heart was in tiptop working order.

"She said quietly, 'I knew there was nothing wrong with my heart. But I needed to hear *you* tell me that.'" According to Dr. Wessel, all physical complaints should be taken seriously. There is evidence to suggest that prolonged sadness and depression can suppress the immune system, and thus lower a youngster's resistance to infection.

Another possible reaction to a loved one's death can mislead parents into assuming their teenager is coping well. That reaction is: no apparent adverse reaction at all. In fact, the youngster may excel in school or perhaps immerse himself in sports or hobbies. What may really be at work here is a defense mechanism known as *sublimation.* The youth is subconsciously attempting to channel his strong emotions into a more socially acceptable outlet. And he may rivet his attention solely to areas where he feels comfortable, as a way of regaining control over a world that has been jolted out of orbit.

The problem is, when we don't confront grief, we postpone indefinitely the day that we are ready to go on with our lives. For some children, months or years may pass before they allow themselves to feel the full impact of a loved one's death.

How You Can Help Your Teenager to Grieve

BEFORE A LOVED ONE DIES—AND AFTERWARD

If death comes as the result of a life-threatening illness, the process of mourning can begin well before the funeral and will help the teenager deal with the impending loss. Consequently, if someone close to the family has been diagnosed with a life-threatening illness, don't hide the person's condition from your children, so that death comes as a shock. Sudden unexpected death tends to be more traumatic for survivors. We'll use the example of an elderly cancer patient whose doctors have determined that her tumor is advanced and beyond therapy.

To a teenager, you might say: "We found out from Grandma's doctors that her breast cancer has come back, in her lung. She's in the hospital right now receiving treatment that will make her much more comfortable."

Be prepared to answer the question: "Is Grandma going to die?" We want to be truthful, yet still hold out some measure of hope. The mother in this instance could reply, "Well, honey, your grandma is very, very sick. But she's getting excellent medical care, and her doctors are doing everything they can to make her better. I know it would cheer her up if you came with me to the hospital to visit her."

In the wake of a serious diagnosis, family members often feel paralyzed with helplessness. If your teenager offers to assist in caring for the ailing person, either at home or when visiting in the hospital, let him. Helping a loved one at the end of her life can be an extraordinarily meaningful experience, one that your teenager will carry with her forever. However, the tasks should always be appropriate to a child's age, maturity and capabilities.

Younger adolescents can read to the patient, adjust her pillows and fetch water and ice when needed. Older teens can perform more intimate nursing skills, if they're willing and able. Important: Never force a youngster to do anything that makes him uncomfortable.

Here's what else you can do during this time:

• Share your own feelings and don't hide your tears. Teenagers often take their cues from us. By showing emotion, we give them permission to do the same.

• Three ways to encourage an uncommunicative youngster to open up after a death:

1. Look through a family photo album together. Though it may very likely bring on the tears, it will also prompt smiles and happy memories.
2. Suggest that he write a letter to the deceased family member. This is a nonthreatening outlet for expressing how he feels.
3. Ask him to tell you of any dreams he's had of the deceased.

• Now is not the moment to make any drastic life-changing decisions; everyone in the family needs time to adjust. Routines and a sense of normalcy are extremely important to a grieving teenager, who may feel more confused than ever about his identity. Suddenly he's gone from being just a regular kid in a regular home to living in a family marked by tragedy. Will his friends see him the same as before? Or from now on will he be known as "the kid whose father died"?

• Remind your child, repeatedly, that she can always come to you to talk or for hugs. However, if it's a family member who has died, remember that you need to heal from the devastating loss too. Realistically, there may be times when your teenager wants your attention and you're submerged in your own sadness. Explain that this is hard on you as well, and that if you sometimes seem distracted, irritable or sad, it's not because of anything he did. Reassure him that your grief does not diminish the depth of your love for him.

Because you may not always be emotionally available to your youngster, recruit other adults who are willing to spend time with him. *"Aunt Jackie asked me to tell you that she'd love to hear from you and that you can pick up the phone and call her anytime."*

• If a child has died, choose your words carefully when speaking about her to the other children in the family. A parent can idealize the deceased to such an extent that the surviving siblings may come to feel inferior by comparison.

• When a teenager has experienced a close loss, inform his school. Ask that his teachers keep you posted about any behavior that is out of character for the youngster and may be an indication that he needs professional counseling.

• Rituals memorializing the dead, such as visiting the grave site, planting flowers there, and so forth, can bring solace to all members of the family. Encourage your youngster to participate, but do not force him.

With the passage of time, you'll probably find that you're able to commemorate your loved one in less formal settings. And—believe in this—there will even be laughter mixed among the tears.

"I always find opportunities to talk to my son about my late father, often when we're in the car together," says Dr. Lani Wheeler, a pediatrician from Annapolis, Maryland. "I'll reminisce about things that my son did together with his grandfather, and he'll share his own memories. I also tell him stories about when his grandfather was a boy, which he really enjoys."

No Timetable for Grief

Most of the emotional turmoil surrounding a death typically surfaces in the first month. However, the mourning process can last anywhere from half a year to two years, and in some cases longer. If months have passed, and you feel that your teenager is not coping well—or you feel that his distress is interfering with his ability to function, at any point—consider enlisting the guidance of a professional counselor experienced in adolescent bereavement issues.

Your child's pediatrician may be able to recommend a practitioner in the area. For additional referrals, call local hospitals and hospices. Grief counseling is a key component of hospice care, while a growing number of hospital chaplains now have bereavement training. Another way to obtain names is to contact a hospital's department of social work or the mental-health association serving your area. They will also know of any nearby bereavement organizations or peer support groups, which can be an excellent complement to therapy.

Before you schedule an appointment, ask the therapist, "Do you regularly counsel bereaved teenagers?" If his or her experience is limited, try someone else. The same advice applies when considering going to a clergyman. Not all priests, rabbis and ministers have training counseling the grief-stricken.

DIVORCE: HOW TO HELP YOUR TEENAGER

By the age of sixteen, close to half of all adolescents will have seen Mom and Dad divorce. An estimated 15 percent will have weathered the ordeal twice, while three in four children of unmarried couples face the prospect of one day living in a single-parent home.

For teens, the demise of their parents' marriage packs nearly the same emotional wallop as a death in the family. Most rebound eventually, but until time heals, they can be expected to mourn the loss of their intact family and with it the end to a way of life. Sad feelings often surface on holidays, birthdays, school events and at other special times when only one parent attends.

The immediate emotional/behavioral repercussions can mirror those typically seen after a family member has died: depression; anger; aggressive behavior; guilt; school problems; frequent stomachaches, headaches and other ailments; a change in eating and/or sleeping habits; and anxiety about being labeled a "child of divorce." Divorce is the fourth-leading cause of stress in adolescents.

> ### Pediatrician's Perspective
>
> DR. ADELE HOFMANN: *"A lovely twelve-year-old girl once came to see me because she had abdominal pain. In talking to her, it quickly became apparent what was going on: Her parents were in the midst of a divorce and a child-custody suit. The mother would say to her, 'If you leave me to go live with your father, I don't know what I'll do. You know I'm not very well; I'll just get sicker. I really need you here.' Meanwhile, the father was promising to buy the girl anything she wanted if she came to live with him. She was utterly torn over which parent would win custody, to the point that it was causing her abdominal pain."*

How well they adjust in the long run appears to be determined by how well the mother's and father's behavior after the divorce aids in the process.

Yes, There Is Such a Thing as a "Good Divorce"

Naturally, dissolving a marriage is a sad time for everyone in the family, particularly the two separating partners. It is normal to feel hurt, depressed, lonely; perhaps angry at your former mate. But although the two of you will no longer live together as husband and wife, your responsibilities as father and mother go on. If children are to emerge from this difficult time emotionally healthy and whole, their parents must do all that they can to transcend negative feelings and cooperate with each other. At times, that may mean giving ground on some points to the ex in order to keep the peace.

It's really this simple: The children come first.

CHILD CUSTODY

Which form of custody is best for the children? That's going to depend almost entirely on the relationship between the mother and father. Sixteen percent of divorcing parents opt for *joint physical custody.* Under this plan, youngsters commute between both residences. By far, the most popular and successful arrangement awards *physical custody* to one parent and *joint legal custody* to both. That means the youngster will live with the *custodial,* or *residential,* parent most of the time, but the two parents share key decisions about education, medical care and religious upbringing. A detailed schedule maps out exactly when the child will spend time with the *noncustodial (nonresidential)* parent.

According to the National Center for Health Statistics, mothers retain physical custody about 72 percent of the time; fathers, in only 9 percent of custody cases. If the husband and wife choose not to *mediate*—negotiating the terms of the divorce with an impartial third party, usually an attorney or mental-

---

TEEN TIP:

Advise your teenager's school about a separation or divorce at home, just as you would following a death in the family. Ask the school psychologist or your child's guidance counselor to pass along any comments from teachers regarding changes in behavior or schoolwork.

TEEN TIP:

Please don't act angry or hurt if your teenager asks to live with the other parent. She feels awkward enough just having to make this decision in the first place.

---

health professional—the case goes to court, and a judge ultimately decides on the living arrangements.

TELLING THE CHILDREN

Ideally, the mother and father should deliver the upsetting news together, no matter how uncomfortable the prospect makes them. Adolescents and even preteens usually understand what it means when adults divorce, so it's best to give it to them straight, minus inappropriate details. Chances are, they're more aware of the crumbling marriage than you would have imagined.

One crucial point to convey is that although you are separating as husband and wife, the two of you will never stop being their parents. *"We both love you very, very much and always will. That never changes."* Another is to reassure them that this is strictly between the two of you and that they are in no way responsible for your decision. You'll be eliminating one frequent seed of anxiety without them having to ask.

Tell them, as lovingly as possible, that they will now have *two* homes. *"We haven't worked out all the details, but most of the time you'll live with your mother right here. Same house, same school. As soon as I get settled, you'll live with me the rest of the time, like on weekends and vacations."* (Say "live with," not "visit.") Volunteer as much information as you can about living arrangements, to ease their fears. If possible, allow at least a few weeks between the announcement and the day one parent moves out of the home.

The conversation will continue to unfold over the next few days or weeks. Expect tears, protestations and a barrage of questions. Topping the list: *"Why are you getting divorced? Didn't you used to love each other?"*

Emphasize the good aspects of your life together. But explain that sometimes even people who were once very much in love can grow apart. Feelings can change over the years. And as much as you've tried to restore your marriage to the way it used to be, you've both come to the sad conclusion that the relationship is beyond repair and that a separation is best for everyone.

In moments of anger and hurt, a youngster may blame one parent—often the residential parent—for the split. *"You could have tried harder to work things out!" "Why did you make Daddy leave?"* It's unfair, but try not to take the accusation to heart or become defensive. In response, you might say: "I understand that you're sad about the divorce. We are, too. You may feel that I am more at fault than your father. But you don't know the full story. There are other ways of looking at what happened. When you're not so angry let's talk more about it."

"Isn't there a chance that you guys'll get back together?"

Could be—you never know. For now, though, don't dangle this fantasy in front of them. Like the identical-twin sisters in the popular film *The Parent Trap,* adolescents need little encouragement to dream about reuniting their estranged parents. One tactic, more common among girls, is to behave like the perfect daughter. The reverse strategy is to get into so much trouble that a concerned Mom and Dad forget their differences and come to the rescue. Either reaction is a form of denial, to avoid facing the painful reality of what has happened to the family.

In some cases, professional guidance and advice may be needed. When necessary, your pediatrician can help you find the appropriate counselor for your child.

THE DIVORCING PARENTS' TEN-POINT PACT FOR MAKING THE BEST OF THE SITUATION

1. *We promise* to let our children know that it is okay to love both of us.

2. *We promise* not to pressure them into taking sides in our disputes.

3. *We promise* to refrain from making disparaging remarks about each other in front of the children.

4. *We promise* not to argue in front of them.

5. *We promise* not to use the children as amateur spies by grilling them for information or gossip about the other parent.

6. *We promise* never to put our youngsters in the position of carrying messages back and forth between us. *"Tell your father I need money to pay the plumber to unclog the upstairs toilet."*

7. *We promise* that our children won't be made to feel self-conscious expressing affection for the other parent or exclaiming how much fun they had during a visit. We will let them know how happy we are for them.

8. *We promise* to try to maintain secondary family relationships, with grandparents, aunts, uncles and cousins. *Too often, children of divorce lose not only the daily presence of the noncustodial parent, but the extended family on his or her side of the family.*

9. *We promise* never to turn the children into scapegoats for the alleged sins of the father (or mother). *Please strike the following sentence from your thoughts: "You're just like your [father/mother]!"*

10. *We promise* to encourage our children's ongoing relationship with the other parent and to not use visitations as a means for punishing the noncustodial parent.

THE VISITING PARENT

The noncustodial parent—usually the father—faces a special challenge to remain a significant presence in his youngsters' lives now that he no longer lives at home.

Probably the most tragic aspect of divorce is that far too many nonresidential parents all but fade from view. Studies show that only one in six children from families of divorce see their father at least once a week, while two in five report not having seen Dad in a year. Ten years after a marriage ends, more than two in three youngsters will not have seen their father for a year.

In defense of divorced fathers, only a minority disappear from the children's lives out of indifference. The majority yearn to maintain a close, loving relationship with their youngsters. But just by virtue of living apart from the children—and essentially being allowed to see them "by appointment only"—even well-intentioned divorced dads find themselves kept at arm's length. They miss many of the ordinary day-to-day interactions that forge the closest bonds between parent and child, like being available to help with homework or deciding on the spur of the moment to pile into the car and go out for ice cream.

The enforced togetherness can be equally confining for the teenager, robbing his life of some spontaneity. Let's say a friend calls on a Saturday: A bunch of the guys are meeting up at the school later in the afternoon to play basketball. Basketball! His passion! If Dad still lived at home, the teen wouldn't think twice about asking him if they could go to the stock-car races tomorrow instead of today, so that he could play. But the father doesn't have visiting privileges on Sunday. "Ah, I wish I could come, but I'm supposed to spend today with my dad."

In this example, unless the last-minute change in plans proved inconvenient for Mom, perhaps she and Dad could switch days. Or the father could accompany his son to the school and watch him play hoops. Forget the stock-car races. Afterward they can go out to dinner or go back to Dad's apartment and watch TV. That's equally special.

Other ways to counter the inherent obstacles imposed on the noncustodial parent include:

• See your child as frequently as everyone's schedules allow. If you ever have to cancel a visit, let the other parent know right away. Never let your teenager hear the news from someone else; get her on the phone and explain the reason for the cancellation.

• Look around your new home: Does it resemble a bachelor pad? Or does it look like a teenager might have set foot in there on occasion? It doesn't matter whether you've moved into a spacious house or a cramped apartment: Add a few personalized touches that will make your daughter feel more at home when she stays over:

1. Stock up on her favorite foods, snacks and beverages.
2. Make sure she has a comfortable, well-lit area for doing homework. A dictionary, encyclopedia and other reference books or computer discs would be helpful too.
3. Purchase bathroom supplies and toiletries, so that she doesn't have to clean out the medicine cabinet at home every time she visits.
4. Encourage her to leave some of her belongings at your place.
5. Let her help you decorate her new room.
6. Ask *her*, "What don't I have here that would make you more comfortable when you come over?"

• Resist the temptation to spoil your teenager with expensive gifts. It is important that she feel loved in the same way as before.

• Noncustodial parents who live out of town can bridge the distance gap by staying in touch between visits. Call, fax or e-mail your teen regularly.

• The custodial parent should routinely apprise the absent parent of upcoming events in your youngsters' lives and encourage him to attend. The absent parent should also be informed of the children's academic progress. If necessary, arrange for separate parent-teacher conferences.

AMID A SEA OF CHANGES, STEADY AT THE HELM

Divorce upends a teenager's world. Not only does one parent depart the home, but financial pressures may force the custodial parent to rejoin the workforce, change jobs or extend her hours. Once Mom and Dad start dating, new adults pass in and out of their lives, and perhaps their children too. Adding to the uncertainty swirling around them: Approximately two in five divorced moms and their children move to a new address within one year of the divorce.

Stability and routines are extremely important to your youngster right now. To the extent that you can, try not to make any major changes in the aftermath of a divorce.

7

OTHER TYPES OF FAMILIES:

Single-Parent, Divorced, Blended
and Gay-Parent Families

Countless articles have decried what has been called the breakdown of the American family. Certainly the stereotypical nuclear family is far less common than it used to be. Probably the most striking change in the family structure in the last thirty years has been the surge in one-parent families: from 9 percent of all families with children in 1960, to 27 percent in 1998. Divorce accounts for about half of the twelve million single-parent families in the United States; out-of-wedlock births account for the other half. One in three babies are born to single mothers, a staggering increase from 1960, when the ratio was one in twenty.

Single-income nuclear households, in which one parent stays home to care for the children, are even rarer than the nuclear family itself. However, the 1950s family model so fondly remembered as the standard against which all families should be measured, was actually something of an anomaly, made possible by a prosperous postwar economy that allowed a family to get ahead on one salary. From colonial days to the present, mothers have held jobs outside the home, particularly during times of war. In 1940, the year before the Japanese attack on Pearl Harbor catapulted the United States into World War II, women comprised one-fifth of the nation's workforce; by 1943, midway through the conflict, one in three U.S. workers were female, many of them married with children. For farm families and minority families, a mother's employment was crucial to their financial survival, in times of peace as well as war.

Today fully half of all families do not meet the definition of a nuclear family. We have stepfamilies, or what are often called *blended* families; single-parent families; families headed by two unmarried partners, either of the opposite sex or the same sex; households that include one or more family members from another generation; adoptive families; foster families; and families where children are raised by their grandparents or other relatives. Each has its distinctive advantages and challenges.

A mounting body of evidence suggests that youngsters who live in nontraditional households—meaning without both natural parents and all biological siblings—are more apt to experience problems while growing up. This flies in

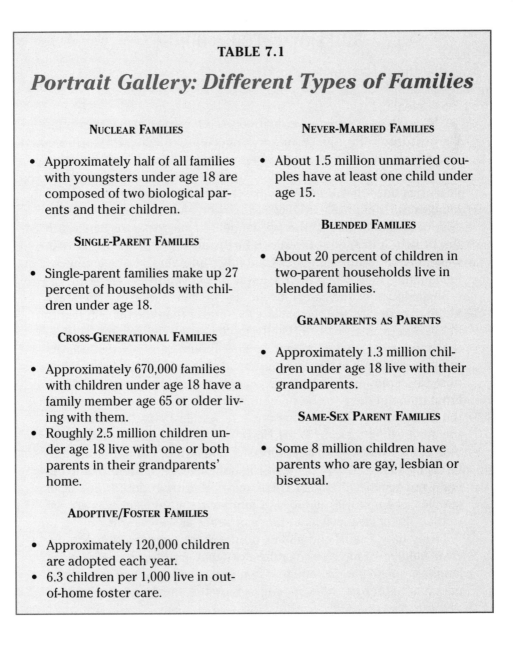

TABLE 7.1

Portrait Gallery: Different Types of Families

NUCLEAR FAMILIES

- Approximately half of all families with youngsters under age 18 are composed of two biological parents and their children.

SINGLE-PARENT FAMILIES

- Single-parent families make up 27 percent of households with children under age 18.

CROSS-GENERATIONAL FAMILIES

- Approximately 670,000 families with children under age 18 have a family member age 65 or older living with them.
- Roughly 2.5 million children under age 18 live with one or both parents in their grandparents' home.

ADOPTIVE/FOSTER FAMILIES

- Approximately 120,000 children are adopted each year.
- 6.3 children per 1,000 live in out-of-home foster care.

NEVER-MARRIED FAMILIES

- About 1.5 million unmarried couples have at least one child under age 15.

BLENDED FAMILIES

- About 20 percent of children in two-parent households live in blended families.

GRANDPARENTS AS PARENTS

- Approximately 1.3 million children under age 18 live with their grandparents.

SAME-SEX PARENT FAMILIES

- Some 8 million children have parents who are gay, lesbian or bisexual.

the face of the conventional wisdom of the 1970s and 1980s, when the incidence of divorce, single parenthood and remarriage was at its height. Many experts, though not all, upheld the view that children were highly adaptable and would adjust to the new family structures. A number of parenting books published during this time exhorted moms and dads to pursue their own bliss. If that led to leaving a marriage that had produced children, or to having a baby out of wedlock, then it must be for the best. *Ultimately the children will thrive,* went this line of reasoning, *because you are happier.* In an era that promoted the credo "Do your own thing," it was a message that many adults were only too eager to embrace.

Now that the smoke has cleared somewhat, we're better able to gauge the impact this shift has had on teenagers. Various studies conducted throughout the 1990s reveal that the overall effect has been detrimental:

• A report from the federal Substance Abuse and Mental Health Services Administration (SAMHSA) concluded that boys and girls who live with two biological or adoptive parents have a considerable advantage in resisting the temptations of adolescence compared to children in other family structures. According to the large study, which was based on the responses of twenty-two thousand youngsters ages twelve through seventeen, they were 50 to 150 percent less likely to use or become addicted to tobacco, alcohol and illicit drugs.

Interestingly, the young people most at risk for substance abuse came from blended families with a biological father and a stepmother—not from single-parent homes, as you might expect. (Children from blended families parented by a biological mother and a stepfather were not as susceptible to substance abuse.) Growing up in a one-parent home does, however, increase the odds that a teenager will engage in substance abuse.

Of the twelve million single-parent families in the United States, ten million are headed by mothers; the other two million by fathers. The SAMHSA study found that the adolescents living with Mom were at lower risk than those who lived with Dad.

• A survey by the National Center for Health Statistics stated that teens in single-parent families were two to three times more likely to develop emotional and behavioral problems. They were also more prone to drop out of high school, become pregnant, abuse drugs and get into trouble with the law.

• Similarly, when researchers from the National Center for Education Statistics contrasted children in two-parent blended families to children in two-parent nuclear families, academic difficulties and unruly behavior were far more prevalent among the youngsters living with the blended families. They were 80 percent more likely to repeat a grade in school, twice as likely to be suspended or expelled, 25 percent more likely to sink to the bottom of their class academically and 50 percent more likely to have their parents contacted about a discipline problem.

The last decade of the twentieth century produced some promising developments that bode well for the future of the family. One is the increased involvement on the part of many fathers in raising their children, although women still shoulder a disproportionate amount of the responsibility—even those who work full time. Employed moms spend 3.2 hours with their youngsters each workday. For working dads, the figure is 2.3 hours; up half an hour per workday from the mid-1970s. What's more, the 1980s and 1990s saw a nearly uninterrupted decline in the divorce rate, while the rise in single-parent families during the 1990s was the lowest of any decade since the 1960s.

Taking Care of Your Family

DISCIPLINE: THE SAME RULES STILL APPLY

Following a family upheaval such as divorce or death, it is not unusual for discipline to begin to break down. One reason is that the custodial parent may now be working outside the home, if she wasn't previously. She may not always enforce household rules because sometimes she's simply too exhausted to summon up the energy. Feeling sorry for the children, and feeling guilty about what they have gone through because of the divorce can also result in an overpermissive atmosphere. *They've been through so much,* the parent reasons. *I don't want to upset them.* But kids will feel more secure and less anxious if the parent continues to set the same limits as before and adheres to familiar household routines. After so much instability, they'll be grateful for the consistency.

Erratic discipline often becomes a charged issue between separated or divorced spouses, especially if they didn't always see eye-to-eye when married. The nonresidential parent has a right to establish his own relationship with the children without interference from the custodial spouse. Maybe you insist that your fourteen-year-old son not sit down to dinner shirtless; your ex, on the other hand, doesn't mind. Let it go. But important rules such as those regarding substance use, sexual activity and car safety must be uniform from home to home.

When one parent is overly lax, it unfairly forces the stricter parent into the role of "Mean Mom" or "Mean Dad." And don't think that your teenager won't use this to his advantage. *"I have to do my homework before dinner? Aw, c'mon, Mom! Dad lets me do it whenever I want."* Kids of divorce have more opportunities to play one parent against the other, as their parents have already demonstrated differences of opinion by separating. It is also more difficult for each parent to know what the other has said to the teen on any subject. It is a way to wrest control of a situation that they've been powerless to prevent.

If you feel that your former mate is too lenient and undermining your authority, discuss the matter with *him, not* with your adolescent. Whenever possible, parents should support each other's decisions. However, if such a conversation is unlikely between the two of you, for whatever reason, seek the advice of your pediatrician or a family counselor.

LET TEENS BE TEENS

In response to the change in family circumstances, a teenager may try to assume an inappropriately adultlike position within the household. For a youngster to want to help out by accepting more responsibility is certainly admirable, and appreciated. But it is unhealthy anytime that children and parents begin to reverse roles. For this reason, *never* refer to an adolescent as the "man of the house" or the "woman of the house," not even in jest.

A boy may emulate his absent father's behavior to such an extent that he begins to act more like a husband than a son. He may remark on his mother's appearance, offer financial advice and become jealous if she begins to date. Similarly, adolescent girls living with their fathers may pattern themselves after their absent mother and function as a sort of surrogate "wife." Girls as young as twelve may essentially run the household while their single father (or mother) is at work. Even if they choose to take on these roles, it shifts their sense of being protected, alters their ability to experiment socially and may undermine the parents' authority in their eyes.

Kids have a right and a need to be kids and to grow up at a normal pace, and single parents need to have reasonable expectations of them. To saddle a teenager with the responsibilities of an adult is often asking too much. Spread the housework around more equitably by involving younger children, grandparents and other relatives. If you can afford it, hire a housecleaning service to come through every few weeks, just to keep things from getting out of hand.

WE ARE FA-MI-LY!

A youngster who has been raised since birth by her mother may yearn for the father figure she's never known. Yet when she looks around the dinner table at Mom and her two siblings, she sees a loving *family*. But what about a teenager who belonged to a traditional nuclear family now splintered by divorce? At first he's likely to view the new arrangement as strangely incomplete—and perhaps a symbol of his family's failure.

It is important to assure kids that their family is whole just the way it is and that they are loved every bit as much as other children. Remind them of this regularly; you can never say it too many times. Another way to impress upon them that divorce or death has not weakened the family bond is to carry on family traditions from the past. In time, you'll establish new ones as well.

FINDING ROLE MODELS FOR YOUR TEEN

As hard as you try, one parent cannot provide all the adult interaction a child needs. Teens whose mother or father has died or dropped out of their lives after a divorce benefit from being surrounded by as many caring, dependable adults as possible. It is particularly important that they spend time with an admired older member of the same sex. Boys "learn" how to be men by patterning themselves after their father or a substitute male role model. The same is true for girls. Receiving the attention of another paternal figure or maternal figure confirms that other people care and that not all adults abandon children.

Look for suitable candidates in your extended family: grandparents, aunts, uncles, cousins. Or contact organizations that run one-to-one mentoring programs, such as Boys & Girls Clubs of America, the YMCA advocacy programs, Black Achievers and the oldest youth-mentoring organization in the country, Big Brothers/Big Sisters of America. These programs pair youngsters with trained volunteers or youth-development professionals. The two meet regularly, giving the teenager someone to talk to and look up to.

BLENDED FAMILIES

The harmonious-sounding euphemism "blended family,"[1] coined around the time that the U.S. divorce rate was peaking, reflects every biological parent and stepparent's secret fantasy: that combining lives could be as easy as mixing an ice-cream soda. A touch of a button and *voilà!* Out pours a new family, with all the ingredients smoothly integrated.

Stepfamily might be the more fitting word, because learning to live together is a step-by-step process. The members have no shared family history or

---

1 "Blended family" is sometimes defined as a household composed of two parents and children from both spouses' previous marriages, whereas "stepfamily" denotes one biological parent, one stepparent and one or more children belonging to the biological parent. We draw no distinction between the two terms and use them interchangeably.

regular routines. On average, it can take two to four years—possibly more—before everyone adjusts to the new situation.

Nothing can fully prepare a mother or father to become a stepparent or the spouse of a stepparent. Prior parenting experience, combined with even the best of intentions, cannot always help new stepparents to see the family as it is. It's too easy to measure this new family against the nuclear family they may have been part of at one time. A stepfamily has to be viewed as a different type of family. Not inherently better or worse, just different.

And certainly more complex. A single-parent home with two children involves three relationships: between the parent and each child, and sibling to sibling. But take a blended family where each partner brings one or more youngsters apiece, and the complexity increases exponentially. Suddenly you have many separate relationships under one roof: parent to parent, each parent to each biological child; each parent to each stepchild; sibling to sibling, on both sides; and each sibling to each of two stepsiblings. Further complicating matters, what if your ex-spouse remarries? What if that union brings into the picture your ex's new stepchildren or if he and his new wife have their own child? The potential for conflict is enormous.

Small wonder that more than half of all remarriages involving children don't last. The higher the number of children, the higher the divorce rate. One way to help your family avoid becoming a statistic is to do exactly what you're doing: gain an understanding of the special challenges that stepfamilies face. Then, it is hoped, you'll be able to identify and sidestep many of the more common pitfalls.

The Stepfamily as Seen through a Teenager's Eyes

When stepfamilies go awry, it's often because one or both partners have unrealistic expectations of what the new family will be like. Or a couple may be so absorbed in their newfound happiness, they don't consider the possibility that their children may not be as thrilled with the new arrangement as they are.

A parent may think:
We're happy together, so the kids should be happy too.

The teenager may think:
I'm happy for Mom—not that anyone cares about my opinion anyway. Just like I didn't have a choice when she and Dad split up.

According to the American Psychological Association, the transition from single-parent household to stepfamily is hardest on youngsters between the ages of ten and fourteen. Older teenagers, in the midst of separating from their families, are building other systems of social support. They have less of an emotional stake in home life and tend to adjust more easily.

But early adolescence is when kids first begin to form their own identities. They accomplish this essential task partly by contrasting themselves with the world around them. With a parent's remarriage, the entire backdrop can change literally overnight: a different atmosphere at home, perhaps a new house, a new school, a new town. If two families with children merge, the oldest child of three can suddenly find herself demoted to middle child of five.

Not only does she lose her status as big sister and the perks that go with it, she must struggle to find a new identity. In a family, a child's identity (the shy one, the most athletic, the one who loves butterscotch) is essential to her sense of self. Imagine how you might feel if your spouse asked you to live with his or her next marriage partner, or if you arrived at work one morning to discover you'd been replaced. Don't underestimate how important it is for your little ballerina or math whiz to be the only one in the family.

A teenager may feel lost and disoriented, like a navigator at sea on a starless night. Worst of all, as she sees it, her life has been upended without her having any say in the matter.

WHAT YOU CAN DO

Give their lives as much continuity as you can. With so much change in the air, make it a point to adhere to long-standing family routines and rituals. For example, if Wednesday night has traditionally been pizza night around your house, let it stay that way. When a new stepparent is joining a household, it's really more incumbent upon him to blend in with the existing rhythm and not attempt to impose his own beat right away.

In the reverse situation—let's say that you and your two children are moving in with your new spouse and her son—implement some of your favorite family customs. You'll also create new customs, of course. Everyone needs to practice flexibility and be willing to accept other members' personal habits and idiosyncrasies.

A parent may think:
Isn't it wonderful to have this good, loving
person in our lives and to be a whole family again?

The teenager may think:
I like my stepmother, but I miss spending time
alone with Dad. Sometimes I feel like an
outsider around here.

Following a separation and divorce, most teenagers live with Mom for an average of five years before she marries again. During that time, points out Dr. Adele Hofmann, "they've had their single parent's undivided attention. Now they have to share her with a new person, and possibly his kids, too, which can be incredibly difficult."

WHAT YOU CAN DO

Spend some one-on-one time with your youngster every day or so. He needs reassurance that although the family composition has changed and you may be less available to him than before, the special closeness and intimacy that the two of you enjoy will never end.

This is also healthy for you. Sometimes when parents in a stepfamily have less time to nurture their natural children, guilt leads them to subconsciously withhold affection and attention from their stepchildren.

A parent may think:
Now that I'm remarried and we've moved to a
new city, we can make a fresh start and
forget about the past.

The teenager may think:
I miss my friends in the old neighborhood.
But most of all, I miss Dad. I wish he
didn't live so far away.

Youngsters need to mourn their old way of life, even if in your opinion it wasn't an especially happy time. "But your father moved out seven years ago. Why are you so sad now?" Remember, until you officially tied the knot with your new spouse, your children may have harbored fantasies of you and your ex reuniting someday. Now that that dream has been dashed, they experience the loss all over again.

WHAT YOU CAN DO

Don't misinterpret a teenager's expressing affection for his other parent as a sign of disrespect to his new stepparent. A stepparent who feels threatened by a teenager's closeness with his biological parent or who frowns whenever the youngster reminisces fondly about an event from the past should seek professional counseling to get more realistic expectations. The family has an entire history that predates the stepparent's arrival. To expect a child to pretend otherwise is unfair, unhealthy and unrealistic. We should never deny kids the right to their feelings, unless we want to incur years of resentment.

One of the most damaging mistakes that a stepparent can make is to try to force an intimate bond with the stepchildren instead of letting feelings of love and attachment grow organically. The biological parent may be equally guilty of pressuring the kids into accepting the stepparent as their parent before they're ready.

Be patient. As you undoubtedly know from your new marriage, love takes time. The same is just as true of the relationship between a stepparent and stepchildren. A stepparent who tries too hard and comes on too strong often alienates a youngster, and it can take a long, long time to win her back.

In a 1998 study of stepfamilies, the largest undertaking of its kind, the teenagers interviewed complained that their stepdads were overly affectionate physically. Not in a sexual way, yet it made many of the kids highly uncomfortable—particularly the girls. What they preferred, they said, was for affection to be expressed verbally.

Never insist an adolescent call the stepparent "Dad" or "Mom." How to define the relationship should be left up to the youngster. Eventually, she may choose to use that term of endearment, or she may continue to refer to him by his first name.

A stepparent's place within a family can vary tremendously, depending on circumstances such as the children's age and their relationship with the non-residential natural parent, assuming there is one. Another variable is, what role does the stepparent see himself playing in the new family structure? In comparison to the typical biological father, stepdads frequently assume a far less hands-on parenting style.

As is true with many things in life, it's best to find a middle ground. New stepparents need to accept the possibility that a teenage stepchild may *never* come to regard them as a father figure or mother figure. But they can fill the rewarding role of an extremely influential mentor and friend—someone the youngster looks to for guidance and an outside perspective. Sometimes kids will confide more in a stepparent than they will in their biological parent.

Discipline in a Stepfamily

For all the unique issues a stepfamily poses for parents, other aspects of parenting remain the same, such as discipline. It is extremely important that Mom and Stepdad regularly discuss and agree upon household rules, then present a united front and support each other's decisions. Disagreements over disciplining the kids are a frequent source of marital strife in stepfamilies.

When the stepparent is the newcomer to the family, it's wise to let the biological parent continue as the primary disciplinarian. If the home were a court of law, think of Mom as judge and jury, and Stepdad as the bailiff, there to maintain order. Teenagers are bound to resent suddenly having to answer to a new authority figure. *"You're not my father! You can't tell me what to do!"*

But whose rules prevail when the stepparent moves in with one or more of her own children? The most sensible approach may be to set all-new regulations that reflect the standards of both families. If Parent A runs a tight ship, but Parent B adopts a more laissez-faire attitude toward household chores and curfews, it would be unfair to hold Parent B's youngsters to all of Parent A's stricter expectations. Both sides will need to compromise.

Once you've settled on prospective ground rules, present them for discussion at a family conference. Further concessions may be made. Then post the finished list in a conspicuous spot for all to see. You'll be glad you took the trouble of drafting a formal "familial unification treaty." Not only does this take some of the heat off the stepparent should he have to penalize one of the children for a rule infraction, it helps promote consistent discipline, which in a household with stepsiblings is as essential as oxygen. Stepsibling rivalries often grow out of one youngster's belief that she is being singled out unfairly by the stepparent or, conversely, that the stepparent is giving preferential treatment to his or her own child.

ADOPTIVE FAMILIES

Between the ages of seven and twelve, many adopted children develop an increasing curiosity about their background and how they came to be adopted. During adolescence, that interest often intensifies. Teenagers sculpt their self-identity largely through studying their parents and siblings. *In what ways am I like them?* they ask themselves. *How am I different?* Adopted teens may not know this information about their birth parents, and this void can add to their usual adolescent struggles.

They are particularly fascinated with their birth parents' physical appearance, as well as many other details that might help them answer the question "Who am I?" But being typically guarded teens, they may not come right out and ask their adoptive parents these and other questions. They may also want to avoid hurting your feelings by being interested. It is hoped you began this ongoing dialogue with your adopted child when she was first old enough to understand (usually between the ages of two and four). The longer parents wait to discuss adoption with their youngster, the harder it will be.

The majority of adopted youngsters deal well with the uncertainty of not knowing their biological origin. Other kids, though, may react in one of three unhealthy ways. The exceptionally obedient child worries that if her biological parents could abandon her, who's to say that her adoptive mother and father won't eventually do the same? She hopes to prevent that through dutiful behavior.

That same fear may prompt another child to misbehave, as a way of testing her adoptive parents' love. The third pattern also involves acting out, but for a different reason. This teen assumes an antisocial role as a sort of birthright, based on his fantasy of what his birth parents might be like. It may be a negative identity, but it's an identity.

Many adopted youngsters may muse aloud about searching for their biological mother and father. Few, though, will act on this impulse. If your teenager expresses a desire to track down her natural mother and father, don't misconstrue this as a rejection of you. Certainly you can appreciate why she might feel compelled to find them. If your teen doesn't bring up the subject on her own, it can be helpful to parents to initiate the discussion. This sends the message that you understand, and are willing to help her work through her feelings.

Unfortunately, that is far easier said than done, unless the child was placed through *open adoption,* in which the birth parents and the adoptive parents are in contact with one another during the adoption process and perhaps even beyond. Many adoptions, however, are confidential. Some states do not allow adoptees to see their original birth certificate containing the names of their biological mother and father. Most states now maintain consult registries, which allow transfer of identifying information if both birth parents and adoptee consent, or allow adoptees full access to birth records outright. Adoptees from other countries may have a more difficult time in this regard.

A private organization called Adoptees' Liberty Movement Association (ALMA) maintains an international Reunion Registry Data Bank. The computer links vital statistics of adoptees and natural parents who wish to get in touch. Frequently, the adopted youngster may know little more than his date of birth and place of birth, but that alone can be enough to make a match. ALMA was founded in 1971 by a woman who spent twenty years before she located her biological mother and father. In its first twenty-five years, the organization reunited more than one hundred thousand families separated by adoption.

GAY- AND LESBIAN-PARENT FAMILIES

Yet another family structure is the household headed by two partners of the same sex. In the United States today, there are two million to eight million gay and lesbian parents of six million to fourteen million sons and daughters. The reason for the broad estimates of numbers is that many homosexual parents are hesitant to reveal their sexual orientation.

In the past, most gay men and lesbian women became parents while part of a heterosexual relationship. Perhaps they discovered their true sexuality after the children were born, or they secretly knew their orientation but didn't acknowledge it. Studies of gay and lesbian parents are scattered, but what little research has emerged seems to contradict claims that growing up in a homosexual household is unhealthy for a child:

• The incidence of homosexuality among teenagers from gay and lesbian families is the same as it is among adolescents with heterosexual parents.

• One frequently voiced criticism of two women raising a child is that the youngster will grow up without a male role model. In fact, several studies show children of lesbian mothers spend more time with their moms' male relatives and friends *and have more contact with their fathers* than do children of single heterosexual mothers.

• According to other studies, children of gay and lesbian parents are *less* likely to be sexually or physically abused at home than kids growing up in other types of families.

If being raised by two members of the same sex is detrimental to an adolescent, it may be due only to the social stigma and isolation that these kids may face should their parents' sexual orientation become known. Early adolescence is often when children of gays or lesbians first become aware that a large segment of society condemns the idea of two men or two women falling in love. They may have to contend with peers' taunts that they, too, are homosexual. This can be extremely upsetting, especially if they are still in the process of discovering their own sexuality.

Teenagers of gay and lesbian parents could benefit from joining a support group of other kids from similar families, either in person or on the Internet. Their moms and moms (or dads and dads) would almost certainly find these organizations useful too.

Explaining Your Sexual Orientation to a Teenager

Before you reveal your sexual orientation to your son or daughter, it is crucial that you can say with confidence, *I am at peace with my homosexuality. I am proud of who I am.* A parent who harbors negative feelings about the fact that he is gay or she is lesbian is likely to *confess* this truth as if it is a source of shame or guilt. You can't expect your teenager to be accepting of your sexuality if you haven't reached that place already. The news should be presented in a positive light and delivered naturally—not quite casually, but not over-wrought with emotion, either.

However, don't wait too long to tell a teenager, who may be old enough to pick up snippets of conversations, clues dropped by the other parent and so forth, and put two and two together. It will be less upsetting if this information comes directly from you. Your child may feel good that you trusted him enough to tell him.

No adolescent wants to hear graphic details about Mom or Dad's sex life, *whatever* the orientation. You might simply say that although most men and women fall in love with members of the opposite sex, not everyone is created the same, and you've come to the realization that you are drawn romantically to other [men/women]. Perhaps this is something you discovered only recently, or perhaps you've known this for some time. If there is someone special in your life, you could mention this, adding, "When you feel you are ready to meet [him/her], I'd like to introduce you. I think the two of you will really hit it off."

Other vital points to emphasize: The time spent with your teenager's other parent was not a "lie." Stress the good points of the relationship. "I respect and love your [mother/father] very much, but not in the way that it's healthy for us to stay together anymore." Change is always difficult for teenagers, so try not to be hurt if your son or daughter reacts negatively; it may be more a response to the fact that his or her life is about to undergo a radical change than it is a rejection of homosexuality. It probably took you a long time to understand that you are gay or lesbian; be prepared to give your youngster time to adjust.

Next, reassure her about the one thing that will never change: "I am still the same [mother/father] I was before, and I love you more than anything in the world."

Once your teen has had an opportunity to absorb the news, expect him or her to have a number of questions, such as:

Q: "Why are you telling me this?"
A: "Because I've always been honest with you in the past and want to continue to be honest with you. This is who I am. My being a [gay man/lesbian woman] is nothing to be ashamed of, and I hope you feel that way about me."

Q: "Does this mean I'm gay too?"
A: "We don't really know why one person is homosexual and another isn't. You will be whatever you were meant to be."

Q: "What do I say if my friends ask me why I have [two moms/two dads]?"

A: "Unfortunately, not everybody understands love between members of the same sex. I would suggest that you tell only your closest friends at first, and see how they react. I hope they'll be accepting of it. Most probably will be. But if not, you may have to put up with some teasing—maybe even some cruel comments. You can talk to me about it anytime you want; I'm always here to listen to you and help you."

8

YOUR TEENAGER
AT SCHOOL

With the start of the intermediate-grade years, school gradually becomes the epicenter of a youngster's life.[1] It is where he hones skills that are every bit as essential to his all-around development and future success as English, math, science and social studies, even if they don't appear on a report card. These include critical thinking, problem solving, respecting authority (and, when appropriate, challenging it), asking questions, defending positions and learning to get along with one's peers.

This chapter focuses on the many ways that parents can help teenagers to succeed both scholastically and emotionally. Studies show that children whose families take an interest in their education earn higher grades and test scores, miss fewer days of school, complete more homework, behave better and enjoy school more, and are more likely to graduate and matriculate to college. Let's get started by taking an overview of the challenges that face your teenager as he moves from grade school to middle or junior high school and on to high school.

TRANSITION NO. 1:
FROM ELEMENTARY SCHOOL TO MIDDLE SCHOOL

This is what the first day of junior high school can feel like to a child:

---

1 "Middle school" typically encompasses grades five or six through eight; "junior high school," grades seven through nine. We use both terms interchangeably.

Imagine arriving at work Monday morning to discover that your company has merged with two others. You settle into your new office, but every forty-five minutes a bell rings, and you get chased out and have to take refuge in another office.

Although you recognize a few familiar faces, who are all of these strangers streaming through the hallways? Say, here comes your boss. And another one, somebody you've never met before. And another one. And another one. This is getting a little nerve-racking.

Well, at least you have your work as a computer programmer to fall back on. You've achieved a level of proficiency and feel reasonably confident that you can handle whatever comes your way. So why are you being handed a welding torch and goggles? You don't know how to weld. Oh. Apparently, you're about to learn.

What's that? You want to go home? But it's not even lunchtime yet.

Advancing from elementary school to middle school can be disorienting at first. Everything seems so drastically different: scholastically, socially—even the structure of the day has changed. Youngsters face many more demands and are often thrown off-balance temporarily. Research compiled since the early 1980s shows that, on average, boys' and girls' grades plunge during their first year of junior high. Most eventually adapt and thrive. Others, however, fall into a rut of failure so deep, they never climb back out. The first step to preventing "middle school malaise" is for mothers and fathers to fully understand just how different this new learning environment is and how much is being asked of their son or daughter. Compared to elementary school, middle school offers fewer opportunities for decision making and classroom discussion, with more rote learning. Grades take on added importance; consequently, teenagers grow increasingly conscious of who is an *A* student and who is a *C* student.

Probably the most striking difference is the amount of homework given. In fourth grade, one in five students spend one to two hours or more per day on homework; roughly half knock off their assignments in under an hour. By eighth grade, one in three students are putting in one to two hours or more per day. Incoming middle schoolers find their adaptability, self-motivation and concentration put to the test like never before.

Adaptability. "In elementary school," observes Dr. Coleman, "a child has the security of one, two, maybe three teachers for all of his subjects. Now he suddenly has a different teacher for each subject. That could mean five, six or seven different teaching styles, personalities and organizational demands.

"Kids also have to make what we call cognitive transitions extremely quickly. They go from, say, math to geography in the course of just a few minutes. The need to be adaptable in each of these settings is dramatic."

Self-motivation. Elementary school is a highly supportive environment for children. Beginning in middle school, students are expected to take more responsibility for themselves, from completing homework assignments, to having their own locker, to perhaps staying after school for an extracurricular activity. From here on, a youngster's academic success will ride largely on his inner desire to do well. No amount of external motivation from parents and teachers can compensate for a lack of industriousness.

Concentration. Teenagers must juggle all of these new demands in an environment buzzing with distractions. Each class fills up with a different set of students. While the possibilities for forming new friendships multiply in a larger, more diverse school, so do the potential opportunities for rejection. And what subject could compete with the daily drama of who's hanging out with whom and its inevitable sequel, who's not speaking to whom? Just finding their way through the hallways of the new building can be overwhelming initially.

The transition to junior high school is often when attention deficits and learning disorders that have gone undetected for years are finally recognized. Some children are intelligent enough or their disabilities mild enough that they can get through third and fourth grade—another critical juncture academically—and graduate from elementary school. But the heightened expectations of middle school may prove to be the proverbial straw that breaks the camel's back. (See chapter 10, "Learning Problems.")

TRANSITION NO. 2:
FROM MIDDLE SCHOOL TO HIGH SCHOOL

"In high school, students encounter a higher level of cognitive demands and achievement than what they were used to in middle school," says Dr. Coleman, a former schoolteacher. The goal of attending college—which two in three high-school graduates will—is no longer a distant dream. Perhaps for the first time, youngsters may feel mounting pressure to achieve in order to get into the college of their choice.

Like the first year of middle school, the freshman year of high school marks a precarious point in a teenager's academic career. According to the U.S. Department of Education, this is around the time that youngsters who've been struggling may drop out. An unhappy ninth-grade experience increases the odds of quitting before graduation.

HELPING YOUR TEEN SUCCEED IN SCHOOL

Helping a teenager get ready for school is not unlike training a boxer, only this bout takes place five times a week from September through June. It's our job to make sure that he is mentally prepared and alert, and takes good care of himself physically. The following strategies will help your child to be at his best come the morning bell.

Creature Comforts

See to it that she gets enough sleep. Feeling groggy lessens our ability to absorb and retain information. Contrary to what many parents believe, older adolescents need *more* sleep than younger teens, not less. But even a full night's slumber may not prevent a boy or girl from nodding off during first or second period.

As with so many other idiosyncrasies of adolescence, biology is to blame. Sleep researchers at the E. P. Bradley Hospital Sleep Research Laboratory in Providence, Rhode Island, discovered that older teenagers' brains secrete the sleep-inducing hormone *melatonin* an hour later than when they were in their early teens. Not only does this forestall the onset of sleep, it robs them of an hour or so of REM (rapid eye movement) sleep, the final and most restful phase of the sleep cycle.

If your child is well organized and willing to prepare for school the night before, consider allowing some extra sleep in the A.M.

Developing Good Homework and Study Habits

The children who endure the rockiest adjustment from elementary school to middle school tend to believe that basic intelligence is unalterable: Either you're born with smarts or you're not. Success or failure is seen as being all but predestined, not a product of hard work.

Teenagers who appreciate the importance of applying themselves have a far easier time, even if they're low on self-confidence. They're more willing to tackle the subjects that give them the most trouble. Parents can help in this regard by pointing out how a diligent effort often spells the difference between success and failure. "An eighty-nine on your geometry test? Way to go! See what you're capable of when you put your mind to it? We're really proud of you."

Create an environment that is conducive to doing homework. Youngsters need a permanent work space in their bedroom or another part of the home that offers privacy. Think minioffice. Buy a desk with drawers for storage and enough space for spreading out homework materials comfortably. Be sure that the entire room is well lit, not just the workstation, that your youngster has a comfortable chair and that all the supplies he needs are right there—a dictionary, thesaurus and any other essential reference books should also be within reach.

When the lure of the TV keeps overpowering the will to work, establish a household rule that the set stays off during homework time. (At least one study has found that the sound of a television, even from another room, interferes with retention of information and skills.) If a member of the family has a particular program she wants to watch, it can always be videotaped for viewing later. There are youngsters who claim they can study to music without losing their concentration. The quality of the work will tell you whether or not to let this practice continue. Although a private area for homework is best for your teen, make sure that any work that needs to be done on a computer is done in a common area of your home. This way, you can monitor his Internet usage.

Set aside ample time for homework. In high school, the late-afternoon hours often fill up with extracurricular activities, sports, part-time jobs and so on. Most days, homework now takes place after dinner. Usually this works out fine since the older teen's changing sleep rhythm allows him to stay alert relatively late at night. But if there aren't enough hours in the night for homework, then you might want to ask the school to include a study hall in your child's day, or, failing that, suggest that he cut back on extracurricular activities or hours spent on a job.

> ### Give 'em a Break— A Study Break
>
> To help alleviate eye fatigue, neck fatigue and *brain* fatigue while studying, it's recommended that youngsters close the books for ten minutes every hour and go do something else. At each break, a teenager should stand up and shake out the muscle tension from his hands, arms and shoulders before hitting the books again.

Be available to answer questions and offer assistance. But never do a child's homework for him. Asking for help isn't a sign of laziness, it's one of the ways that adolescents learn. They have a broad range of subjects to master—a fact that adults don't always appreciate.

Dr. Lia Gaggino, a pediatrician from Kalamazoo, Michigan, says sympathetically, "We expect kids to be good at everything: reading, language, composition, math, spelling, memorization. It's comforting for them to know that they're not totally on their own and that parents are there to assist them. Let's face it: Very few adults get through their day without somebody helping them."

How much homework is too much? It's one thing when a child's procrastinating stretches one hour of homework into three. But if a teenager is burning the midnight oil night after night, the workload being assigned may be excessive.

Homework aids comprehension by reinforcing concepts learned in school and imprinting information in the brain. One guideline sometimes used is ten minutes of homework per day per grade level: an hour for sixth graders, an hour and a half for ninth graders, two hours for high-school seniors and so on. A ten-year study found that anything more than that does not result in significantly higher test scores.

Show That You Value Learning

From an early age, children receive a stream of negative messages about school. How many movies, TV shows and commercials geared toward young people depict classrooms as penitentiaries run by sadistic teachers who delight in tormenting their terminally bored students?

We need to impart to youngsters a love of knowledge. Learning shouldn't be a chore, but an adventure that enriches our lives. Mothers and fathers are in the best position to seize everyday opportunities for opening children's minds to new ideas and experiences. To hear a teenager speak excitedly about something he's just learned or had never considered before is one of the pleasures of parenting.

Let's also instill in our youngsters an appreciation of the value of hard work and the pride that comes with a job well done, whether it's pulling an *A* on a chemistry test or stocking the shelves at the local minimart. One recurrent complaint of employers and managers is that too many young people feel it's "degrading" to start at the bottom and work their way up. Adolescents need to hear that every job, no matter how menial, benefits society in some way and deserves a full effort. A diligent work ethic coupled with the right skills will make your teenager an attractive applicant when it comes time for him to enter the job market.

> ### *Stimulating Young Minds*
>
> - Engage them; ask questions.
> - Get into the habit of routinely pointing out sites and things of interest.
> - Solicit their opinions, or give yours and then ask them what they think.
> - Make history real by framing past events in a present-day context, or conversely, by prompting a teenager to imagine what it might have been like to live in a particular time and place.

Encourage reading. According to a study of approximately thirty-five hundred children and their families, children who read more do better on verbal and math tests. Each week the average boy or girl spends about twelve hours watching television and seventy-five minutes reading. Researchers at the University of Michigan Institute for Social Research found that each additional hour spent reading translated into half a point higher test scores. In contrast, each additional five hours of TV viewing were reflected in math and verbal test scores half a point *lower.*

Consider buying or leasing a computer. Between 1993 and 1997, the percentage of high-school students who had access to a computer at home rose from 29 percent to 49 percent. The computer has become an indispensable tool in our society and a ubiquitous presence both in schools and in the workplace. As youngsters grow older, they play fewer games on the computer and turn to the technology more for learning and word-processing. If you can't afford a computer, schools and public libraries almost always have systems available for use at no charge. (See "Computer Safety" in chapter 14, "Safety and Injury Prevention.")

If your teenager has a part-time job, set a limit on how many hours she can work. About half of all high-school students and college students work part time. Conventional wisdom says that after-school employment teaches responsibility and builds character. While that may be so, the number of hours worked can be a problem. Psychologist Laurence Steinberg of Pennsylvania's Temple University and Elizabeth Cauffman analyzed dozens of studies, including several of Dr. Steinberg's own, and concluded that twenty hours per week appears to be the border line. Cross it, and adolescents are more likely to exhibit emotional distress, school misconduct and alcohol and other drug use.

Academic performance, too, is affected. Students who put in long hours tend to have lower grades, miss more days of school, have difficulty staying awake in class, participate in fewer extracurricular activities and derive less enjoyment from school and less satisfaction in general. Yet one out of every two high-school seniors and one out of every three full-time college students works more than twenty hours per week.

The Child Labor Coalition of the National Consumers League, a private, non-profit consumer-advocacy organization, suggests the following guidelines for hours, late-night hours and supervision:

Fourteen- and fifteen-year-olds:
- no more than three hours per day and fifteen hours per week during the school year
- no more than eight hours per day and forty hours per week during the summer

Sixteen- and seventeen-year-olds:
- no more than four hours per day and twenty hours per week during the school year
- no more than eight hours per day and forty hours per week during the summer
- No working before 7 A.M. or after 10 P.M.

To register a complaint regarding wages, work hours or illegal work by young-sters under eighteen, contact your local wage and hour office. You'll find its tele-phone number under the "Department of Labor" in the "State Offices" section of the White Pages' Government Listings. Each state's department of labor also maintains a Web site. The Web site of the American Federation of State, County and Municipal Employees can link you to any department of labor in the country. Go to www.afscme.org/otherlnk/weblnk29.htm.

Get involved in your teenager's school. When children leave the security of elementary school, parents may assume that their involvement is no longer needed. But it is more important than ever to attend parent-teacher conferences and to contact individual instructors, even if there are no apparent problems. Youngsters perform better in school when their fami-lies are kept apprised of their progress. In addition, parents can gain information about their teens' strengths, which can be important in encouraging their adolescents.

> ### Other Ways to Get Involved in Your Teenager's School
>
> - Attend performances, sporting events, award ceremonies and other functions.
> - Volunteer to chaperone social functions such as school dances and field trips. But alert your teenager before you commit, especially if she's going through that phase where being seen in public with Mom or Dad is grounds for leaving the country.

Nowadays much of the in-teraction between parents and teachers takes place over the telephone. "Teachers are harder to get a hold of than doctors," jokes Dr. Coleman, "because they don't wear beepers!" He suggests that when there's an urgent matter to take up with a teacher, send in a polite note asking her to call you at home in the evening.

Most will be agreeable; they understand that working parents may not have any other occasion to talk. (For that matter, a teacher's responsibilities leave them few breaks for lengthy conversations during the day.) Parents, in turn, shouldn't overlook the fact that many teachers are working moms and dads too. In your note, specify what you wish to discuss, then stick to your point, so that you're not taking up more time than you need to.

About half of all parents of school-age children belong to a parents' group such as the Parent-Teacher Association (PTA) or the smaller Parent-Teacher Organization (PTO). It's a wonderful idea, and not only because the meetings and other functions provide opportunities to help shape school policies. By attending, you get to know the teachers, some of whom may have your youngster in their class. As a recognizable face, and someone who is perhaps perceived as a cooperative, concerned parent, you may be privy to more information about your youngster's in-school performance and behavior than the parent who is rarely if ever seen.

Helping Girls Overcome the Education Gender Gap

Young girls frequently experience a crisis of confidence beginning in early adolescence, when self-esteem is inextricably bound to their changing physical appearance and body image. A survey of seven thousand teenage girls and boys in grades five through twelve found that girls' insecurity tends to intensify as they get older. According to the poll, from the Commonwealth Fund, only two in five high-school girls described themselves as highly self-confident, while one in four claimed they either disliked or hated themselves.

Boys' egos, too, take a bruising during the teen years. But a girl's rickety self-esteem is more likely to contribute to an overall decline in scholastic performance beginning with junior high school. A groundbreaking poll of students ages nine to fifteen contended that both our educational system and our culture unintentionally discourage girls from developing interests in science, math and other academic pursuits. The survey was commissioned by the American Association of University Women (AAUW).

A second AAUW report, made public the following year, expanded on the original findings. "How Schools Shortchange Girls" charged that from kindergarten through grade twelve, girls' educations are inferior to those of boys. The researchers revealed that girls are called on less in class, ask fewer questions, spend less hands-on time in computer labs and science labs, and generally are accorded less attention from teachers. Furthermore, school curricula often underplay women's roles throughout history or promote female stereotypes, while gender bias plagues many standardized tests.

WHAT YOU CAN DO

Teach your daughter not to let gender dictate her interests and aspirations. Why are girls only half as likely as boys to use a computer? Certainly not because they're less capable. The major reason for the discrepancy is that girls aren't encouraged to master technology to the same extent that boys are.

Computer science is still viewed predominantly as a male calling, just as the nursing profession remains largely the domain of females. Although gender gaps have narrowed in medicine, law, and business, only 6 percent of women are in careers that would be considered nontraditional.

To broaden your daughter's opportunities in life, nurture interests that run counter to male-female stereotypes. A girl should be complimented on more than looks; her intellect and athletic prowess deserve no less praise than you would shower on a boy. Below are other ways to create a household free of gender bias:

• Mom, you go cheer on Brother at his next hockey game; Dad, you attend Sis's concert with the middle-school band.

• See to it that sons and daughters have equal access to computers and other forms of technology.

• Put a stop to brothers and sisters hurling insults based on gender. Example: "*You* want to borrow my free weights? But you're a *girl!* You couldn't bench-press twenty pounds!"

• Model equality in your marriage. For instance, on weekends let Dad handle the cooking and cleaning in between his other responsibilities, while Mom gets to do the mowing and other outdoor work. The point is to show children that neither sex has to be confined to rigid husband-wife roles. You're also providing them with a wonderful example of a true partnership.

• Similarly, if you have a teenage son and daughter, assign household chores equitably, not according to sex. There's no reason that he can't baby-sit younger siblings now and then, and she is no less capable of taking out the garbage.

Support your daughter's independence and assertiveness. Long-held sexual stereotypes die hard, evidently, for women still must contend now and then with the lingering perception that assertiveness, independence and intelligence are somehow incompatible with being feminine. In the worlds of junior high and high school, a teenager who is unsure of herself may take this to heart in an effort to fit in among her peers. It can be puzzling to parents and teachers when a girl's competitiveness and self-assurance are replaced by passivity and a reluctance to voice opinions.

You can help your daughter withstand the pressure to suppress her natural intelligence by providing her with opportunities to make decisions, encouraging her to speak her mind, and teaching her how to do things for herself, such as changing the tires on the car.

Counter the mixed messages that girls receive about women's worth in society. The women's liberation movement that took root in the 1970s raised women's expectations of themselves. Yet TV, films and magazines continue to inundate girls (and boys) with narrow images of women—the majority unnaturally shapely and attractive.

"Girls don't get to see many role models of intellectual, achievement-oriented women," observes Dr. William Lord Coleman.

Search for positive women role models—say, a biography of the First Lady, or a female astronaut, comedian or business executive. But also point out possible role models she actually knows, like yourself. Discuss incidents of sexism that you've faced and how you surmounted them. If you went through a phase as a teenager where you tried not to appear "too smart," tell her about it.

Finally, encourage both your sons and daughters to pursue their particular interests. Give them opportunities to try a number of different things and try to avoid pitching them on specific activities just because they fit a stereotype or run counter to it.

PROBLEMS AT SCHOOL

The Problem: Your Teenager Is Gifted

Interestingly, students who are gifted may face many of the same stresses as do teens with learning deficits. In fact, they experience more anxiety and depression than all other social groups of youngsters, while boys and girls with genius-level IQs are at extremely high risk of abusing drugs.

It's really not all that surprising. Intelligence is not as valued during adolescence as it is later in life, which can set these youngsters apart from their peers. Their social skills may be stunted, and not just because they're isolated: Extremely bright children sometimes expend so much energy cultivating their intellect, they neglect their "emotional intelligence." Then there's the practical matter of being out of the social loop much of the time; youngsters who are gifted spend an average of thirteen hours a week honing their talent. Other children who are gifted may have such advanced social skills that they relate better to adults than to their peers.

Parallels between gifted students and those who are learning disabled don't end there. Their potential, as measured by intelligence tests, doesn't always lead to school success, much to their parents' dismay. One reason may be that these youngsters are bored, their curiosity and imaginations untapped; or, desperate to fit in, they may deliberately sabotage their academic success. They'll act dumb, pretend to be stumped by teachers' questions in class and so forth.

If that describes your youngster, you have a right to be concerned. There are a number of ways parents can help a child who is gifted, both at home and at school, such as:

Demand that advanced placement classes be made available in high school, to keep gifted boys and girls stimulated intellectually and to let them get a jump on racking up college-level credits.

Investigate after-school or weekend enrichment programs, either at your child's school or perhaps at a local community college.

Find him a mentoring or tutoring program, in which he assists and befriends younger students who need help with their schoolwork.

Stock your bookshelves at home with reading material that will both challenge and entertain him.

Request that the school district test your child for giftedness. Although children who are gifted do not have protection under federal law as do students with learning disabilities, most states have some form of legislation to serve gifted youngsters. If a school district refuses to assess a child presumed to be gifted, or parents are dissatisfied with the academic program for their son or daughter, they may have their case heard by an impartial hearing officer, in much the same way that parents of learning-disabled children can challenge decisions made regarding an IEP (*individualized education plan*).

As proud as you are of your child's giftedness, never lose sight of the fact that teens need to have friends and to feel reasonably accepted by their peers. At the same time, encourage her love of learning. Remind her that with the start of college, she'll be entering a world where being smart isn't equated with being a dweeb—it's considered cool!

The Problem: Poor School Performance

"It doesn't matter how hard I study, I just can't seem to get the hang of geometry. I guess I must be dumb or somethin'."

At least one in five students will have trouble keeping up academically at some point during junior high and high school. School slumps require our immediate attention, before the damage to self-esteem is irreparable or a youngster develops an aversion to attending school.

While the root of the problem may be school related and nothing more, a drop in grades can be a warning sign of one of the underlying causes below:

- **Physical ailments:** undiagnosed sleep disorders, anemia, infectious mononucleosis, thyroid conditions, impaired vision or hearing, others
- **Emotional disorders:** depression, anxiety, eating disorders, others
- **Learning disabilities/developmental disabilities:** dyslexia, central auditory-processing disorders, attention deficit hyperactivity disorder (ADHD), others
- **Substance abuse:** a drastic decline in grades may be a tipoff that a child is experimenting with alcohol or illicit drugs

WHAT YOU CAN DO

Talk to your teenager. After all, she's the ultimate authority on what's behind her academic difficulties. But this should be a conversation, not a confrontation. Let her know that you're on her side and want to help her get back on track:

"Honey, this is the fourth test in a row that's come back with a C *or a* D. *You're usually a B-plus student. Is there anything going on in school or other areas of your life that you'd like to tell us about? We're concerned and we want to help."*

Arrange a meeting with the teacher(s). Even the most involved parent doesn't truly know what goes on in school. Adolescents sometimes reveal sides of themselves at school that they keep under wraps at home—or vice versa. So a teacher's observations can provide invaluable clues to the cause of a child's academic troubles.

In the days leading up to a parent-teacher conference, write down questions addressing the areas that most concern you. You may not be pleased to hear everything the teacher has to say once you get to the conference. But try to keep in mind that with rare exceptions, less-than-glowing feedback is not a personal attack on your youngster's character or your competence as a parent. If your son's home economics teacher says that he disrupts her class with his wisecracks, accept that what she says contains at least a shred of truth.

Ask her to be more specific and listen politely to what she has to say. For instance: "Could you please give me an example of what you mean? How frequently does he act up in class?" Then work together to come up with a solution. Perhaps you decide to warn your son that any future incidents of misconduct will result in the loss of a privilege, such as one week's allowance or use of the family car.

"And," you can add, "we've asked Mrs. Jackson to call us immediately if you should ever disrupt her class again."

Memo to Mom and Dad: After a conference, always dash off a thank-you note to the teacher.

Consider hiring an after-school tutor. One-on-one sessions with a private tutor can work wonders with students who just weeks ago seemed unable to grasp the subject matter. Learning in a pressure-free environment probably has as much to do with that success as does the one-on-one instruction. Another advantage of letting a tutor work with your child, says Dr. Coleman, is that "it gets parents off their kids' backs."

Private tutors, listed in the Yellow Pages under "Tutoring," generally charge between twenty dollars and forty dollars an hour. If that's beyond your budget, you may be able to locate help through your teen's school. "A lot of high schools," says Dr. Coleman, "have study-buddies programs where teachers assign a peer-aged student or an older student to tutor a child at home or at school." The cost is nominal—four or five dollars an hour—or sometimes free. Local colleges and organizations such as the YMCA may also offer tutoring.

Tutors can also help bridge the gap of time that teens are out of school because of a brief illness, extended family trip, and so on. Instead of falling behind during these short but crucial periods, tutors can make sure students stay caught up and on track until they return to the classroom.

Chronic complaints of feeling either bored or overwhelmed at school may be an indication that a youngster is trudging along on the wrong academic track. The student who yawns at schoolwork that leaves most of his classmates scratching their heads is more likely to thrive if his day includes some more challenging courses, while the perennial *D* student who has never shown much interest in school may be best served by a vocationally oriented program.

In the past, boys and girls belonging to the latter group might have been written off as lost causes destined to drop out. Since the 1970s or so, the educational system has made a greater effort to reach out to these youngsters. Some schools have implemented policies specifically designed for high-school freshmen with histories of academic failure, truancy and misconduct. As we noted earlier, ninth grade is a critical fork in the road for such students, who are considered high risks for quitting before the end of the year. According to the U.S. Department of Education, strategies like those below have been successful at helping them achieve school success:

• Allow students to delay some required courses that may prove too difficult and discourage them to the point of dropping out. In their place they may take more courses that interest them.

- Assemble these students into small groups, who then go from class to class together, offering one another support.

- Establish alternative schools and minischools for alienated students, either within the school building or off-campus. Youngsters who function poorly in a conventional school environment may find the less-structured, less-demanding environment to their liking and be able to graduate.

If you believe that school could be made more enjoyable and fulfilling for your teen, arrange to meet with the guidance counselor or principal. Find out what accommodations could possibly be made in your child's educational plan so that it better meets his or her needs.

The Problem: Conflicts with the Teacher

"I don't know why, but my physics teacher has it in for me. He's always trying to make me look stupid in front of the other kids. I can't stand being in his class."

For the record, we are avid supporters of teachers. Most of them are dedicated professionals who devote themselves to the welfare of children and are deserving of parents' admiration and respect. Years from now, when your youngster reflects back on the adults who most inspired him while he was growing up—aside from Mom and Dad, naturally—one or more teachers will probably rank high on his list.

WHAT YOU CAN DO

The question many mothers and fathers have is, when if ever does a teacher's action warrant parental intervention? Under certain circumstances, it is appropriate to speak up on your youngster's behalf, particularly during the junior-high years. Legitimate gripes include a teacher's humiliating a child in front of the class or not responding to a struggling student's repeated requests for help.

In situations like these, approach the teacher first with your concerns. Explain the problem, refraining from accusatory or insulting language. Then allow the instructor to recount his version of events—which may differ appreciably from your teenager's story. Ideally, a resolution is reached right then and there, but if not, take your complaint up the chain of command. Start with the guidance counselor or assistant principal, who can perhaps act as an intermediary. If this fails to produce a satisfactory solution, your next stop is the principal's office. Rarely is it necessary to go any further.

Now change the setting to high school. At this point, youngsters are old enough to handle minor crises themselves. Offer advice, of course, but resist the urge to dash to the rescue. One of the central lessons of adolescence is coming to the realization that Mom and Dad can't always make everything *okay*. Learning how to deal with disagreeable personalities, overbearing authority figures, small injustices—welcome to Life, kid.

The Problem: Disputes over Grades

"Here it is!" Seventeen-year-old Michelle proudly hands her father her analysis of the use of metaphor in the works of Charles Dickens.

When Dad finishes reading, he lets out a whistle, genuinely impressed. "Wow! You did some terrific job here, honey!" he exclaims. "If any paper deserves an A, this one certainly does."

So he's as stunned as she is when the following week she shows him the returned composition, which bears a B-minus marked in red pencil.

"A B-minus, can you believe it, Daddy?!" Frankly, no, he can't.

"Now I probably won't get an A in English!" she frets. "I absolutely, definitely have to get an A, or how else am I going to get into the English lit program at State University?"

WHAT YOU CAN DO

A parent might be tempted to challenge the grade. But before reaching for a pen or for the telephone, keep in mind that as parents, we're not always in the best position to evaluate the quality of our youngster's work. Not only are we inclined to see it in the best possible light, but we may not have a context in which to judge it. For instance, when the father in the above scenario speaks to the teacher, he's surprised to hear the instructor agree that Michelle's composition on Charles Dickens was extremely well written.

But as the teacher patiently explains, she didn't address the main objective of the assignment, which was to make the case that Dickens was an important commentator on his time. The fact that Michelle slaved over the paper for two weeks is immaterial; her effort was misdirected. Furthermore, she included only eight of the ten required sources, did not follow standard footnote form and overlooked several misspellings and grammatical errors. Hence, her grade of *B*-minus.

The Problem: Nobody Likes Me

"I don't have any friends. At school, everyone's always making fun of me."

Few words are as painful to hear from a child of any age. Being unpopular during adolescence, however, can inflict deep, long-lasting psychological wounds. Youngsters who grow up as social outcasts may be more likely to misbehave, feel depressed and do poorly in school. What's more, the damage to self-esteem can haunt them into adulthood.

When a youngster lacks friends, parents should be concerned regardless of whether she complains about her situation.

WHAT YOU CAN DO

Talk to her. Begin by saying that you've noticed that she spends a lot of time on her own, and ask if this is making her unhappy. Reassure her that many of her classmates probably feel just as uncertain of themselves as she does. It's often effective to share a story about yourself, past or present. Kids generally assume that Mom and Dad glided through adolescence problem-free. This misconception fuels the eternal teenage cry, "You just don't understand!" *Oh yes we do,* more than they'd ever imagine. Want to be a hero? Let them know how much you do understand:

"You know, honey, when I'm at business conventions, I have to make conversation with total strangers. Sometimes it comes easily to me, but other times I can't seem to think of a single thing to say, and I get all nervous and feel like I'm going to pass out."

Your teen may secretly be relieved that you noticed her loneliness. On the other hand, she may feel embarrassed and stubbornly deny that a problem exists. Don't give up. Ask your child's teachers, and any other adults who spend time around her, for their frank assessments of how she relates to others. What are her strengths and weaknesses? Does she tend to be overly shy around her peers, afraid to initiate friendships? Aggressive and bossy? Hostile and defensive? Add their input to your own observations.

Role-play different scenarios with your teen. Kids may act inappropriately in a social situation simply because they don't know how to behave. In role-playing, you set a scene and model socially acceptable alternatives. Concentrate on the areas where he seems to need the most help. Does he tend to stay on the sidelines and avoid group activities? Have a reputation for being a sore loser? Maybe he overreacts to teasing, as in the following example:

"Let's say you drop a pass in touch football, and that smart-mouth kid Kevin who's always bothering you says something sarcastic like, 'Hey, good hands!'

Now, you could get mad and scream at him or take a swing at him, but that's not going to win you any friends or make the other kids want to play with you. Instead, why not disarm Kevin with humor, by poking fun at yourself: 'Yeah, I coat my hands with axle grease before every game.'

"Or you could return the insult, but with a smile on your face: 'Gee, thanks so much for pointing that out, Kev. Love you too, dude.'

"Or you could ignore him. You really want to look cool? Keep your mind on the game and try to catch the next pass. That *would be the sweetest revenge of all.*

"Once you stop reacting to teasing, you take all the fun out of it. After a while, you probably won't get teased as much."

Play several more scenes, this time with you in the antagonist's role and your child starring as himself. See how he does; offer positive feedback. Encourage him to try out these new responses the next time someone teases him. Follow up in a week or two to see if they made a difference.

Help your teenager improve his conversational skills. Most children who don't fare well with peers are sensitive about their social limitations. They're so used to editing themselves (*What do I say to him? What if I sound stupid?*), that they often develop the equivalent of stage fright and say nothing at all.

Few of us are naturally gifted raconteurs, but the art of communication can be learned. The keys to being a good conversationalist are curiosity and generosity—inquiring about other people's lives and interests, then giving them your undivided attention. There's one subject that *everyone* is an authority on and will talk about endlessly: themselves. This is particularly true of adolescents.

Plan structured, pressure-free activities. For a youngster who feels socially inept, just hanging out at home with a friend can be stressful. To ease his anxiety and to help everyone have a better time, his parents will need to supervise these casual get-togethers more closely than is normally necessary.

Ask your teen if he would like to invite a friend over on a weekend afternoon for some structured activity. Dr. Jellinek, a father of four, suggests taking them to a movie, the ballet, the circus, a zoo, a museum, a sporting event—"anything that deflects the one-to-one time between the child and his friend." Sitting side by side as spectators gives kids something to talk about during and afterward, but eliminates the need for constant conversation.

If you're looking for something physical for them to do together, choose a noncompetitive pastime that plays to your child's strengths and promotes sharing and cooperation. Avoid solitary activities or those that involve large groups. Examples include bike riding, ice-skating, in-line skating, rowing or canoeing, skateboarding, snowboarding, skiing, swimming, golf and martial arts.

Err on the side of making the activity too short rather than too long. Right now, the goal is to help your child relax and have fun, and to establish a pattern of successful relationships. "Once your teen begins to feel more comfortable dealing with free time," Dr. Jellinek continues, "you gradually withdraw the structure. For instance, if the movie goes well, you might try giving him money to go to the shopping mall for an hour or two with his friend—not six hours. Then you might suggest that they go out together for a bite to eat. You also gradually encourage them to increase the time that they spend together."

Enlist the cooperation of teachers, coaches, camp counselors and group activity leaders such as scoutmasters. Describe your teenager's difficulties with socializing, and request that they pay a little extra attention to her. If you've discovered some strategies that seem to help your youngster in group situations, let them know, and ask that they keep you apprised of her progress.

Encourage your teen to join a club or group activity that appeals to him, whether it's through the school system or through religious or community organizations. There he's more likely to meet kids who share a common interest or purpose—always a promising foundation for new friendships.

Do not force a child to participate in an activity against his will. The goal is to set him up for success.

Seek the help of a professional. A number of child psychologists, psychotherapists and counselors specialize in social-skills development, with sessions conducted one-on-one or in a small group. Approaches vary somewhat, but most programs employ many of the techniques described here, such as role-playing. One benefit of the group setting is that the youngsters learn from and root for one another. Friendships often bloom, which in itself is therapeutic. For some kids, the social-skills group provides the support and acceptance that's been missing from their lives.

Your child's pediatrician may be able to refer you to professionals trained in this area. Or, call around to local mental-health providers and ask if they offer social-skills instruction. Ideally, the boys and girls in the group should be no more than two years apart in age.

The Problem: Your Teenager Doesn't Want to Go to School

Some youngsters for one reason or another (see box on next page) are afraid to go to school. Although they may pretend to be sick now and then, they may also have psychosomatic symptoms such as headaches, dizziness, nausea, and chest pain, which are triggered by emotions, but real nonetheless. Not surprisingly, aches and pains related to tension tend to vanish over the weekend and during holidays.

WHAT YOU CAN DO

Talk to your teenager about why she doesn't want to go to school. This is a time for compassion; obviously she is hurting. Assure her that you will do everything you can to resolve whatever it is that is causing her so much distress.

Contact the principal, guidance counselor and school nurse, and make them aware of the situation. If you discover that your son or daughter is being harassed or bullied at school, insist that the administration put a stop to it at once.

All students should be able to pursue their education in an atmosphere free of verbal abuse or threats of violence from other children. Can parents legally force a school to take action against the perpetrator? See "Crime and Violence" in chapter 14, "Safety and Injury Prevention."

On days when you do decide to let an anxious youngster stay home from school, do not accord him any special treatment. This shouldn't be misconstrued as a holiday. He is not to receive visitors, and unless he is truly feeling under the weather, some time should be spent on any previously assigned homework.

Situations That Can Contribute to a Teenager's Avoiding School

- fear of failure
- anxiety about growing up
- anxiety over a crisis at home, such as a separation, divorce, illness or death
- entering a new school
- a return to school following a holiday break, summer vacation or an illness
- conflict with a teacher
- teasing, ridicule, sexual harassment, bullying or physical threats from other students
- having been physically harmed at school

After you've taken steps to rectify the upsetting circumstances, insist that your teen return to school immediately. Be sympathetic yet firm. Explain that every member of the family has a job to do, and hers is to attend school. Steel yourself to protests or pleas such as, "I'm not ready to go back yet! Just let me stay home one more day!" Frequently, the feeling of panic seizes youngsters as they walk out the front door; once in school, they usually calm down.

Severe phobias may require a gradual reentry to school. For instance:

- Day one: attending a favorite class or two, then going home.
- Day two: spending half a day in school.
- Day three: back to full days.

Obtain permission for your child to take refuge in the nurse's office or principal's office should the pressure be too overwhelming. A staff member can calm her down and, it is hoped, encourage her to go to her next class.

After five days of anxiety-related absences from school, it's time to visit your pediatrician. He or she can rule out physical illness as the cause of symptoms, as well as refer you to a mental-health professional if necessary.

The Problem: Your Teenager Is Threatening to Drop Out

"I'm thinking of quitting school. I've never been a good student, and it's not like I plan to become a doctor or a lawyer or anything like that. I want to be a master mechanic; maybe open up my own auto-repair shop someday."

Most parents would probably be distraught if their youngster announced that he intended to drop out of high school. In today's job market, not having a *college* degree can be a roadblock to many careers; lacking a high-school diploma closes off even more avenues. Overall, young people seem to understand the financial consequences of leaving school prematurely. From 1960 through 1996, the ratio of high-school dropouts among men and women ages sixteen to twenty-four declined steadily from about one in four to one in ten.

The law mandates that children must attend school until age sixteen. After that, neither parents nor school authorities have any legal recourse to prevent them from quitting. Some youngsters drop out to get married or because they've had a baby; others are eager to get a head start on earning a regular paycheck. However, it's probably accurate to say that the vast majority are relieved to cut short their high-school years, which they often spent adrift, bored and socially isolated. For them, exiting the school doors may very well be the first step toward finding their direction in life. Let's be honest: Not everyone is scholastically minded or meant to work at a so-called white-collar job. Other opportunities await. These youngsters can learn a trade or cultivate a talent in the arts, athletics or some other endeavor, and go on to become as successful and fulfilled as their peers with diplomas.

The parents of a youngster at this crossroads must assess his strengths and weaknesses honestly. If the proper educational program or extra assistance were provided, could he raise his school performance to an acceptable level? Or would pressuring him to stay in school merely prolong a futile, and possibly damaging, situation?

WHAT YOU CAN DO

To the youngster who is considering quitting school, point out the widening gulf between the earnings of high-school dropouts versus high-school graduates, and between high-school graduates and college graduates. According to the U.S. Department of Commerce, the median annual income of men who quit high school was just $13,961 in 1993. High-school graduates earned $20,870; men with some college under their belts, $23,435; and college grads, $32,708. Among women, the gap between median salaries for high-school dropouts and college grads was even wider: $7,674 and $26,043, respectively. Women who only graduated high school earn salaries 5 percent lower than those who graduated from college. What's more, three in five recent high-school graduates not enrolled in college were employed, compared to just two in five recent high-school dropouts.

Work with the school staff to improve your child's school experience. Perhaps your youngster would be interested in a *work-study program,* which allows her to gain practical experience in a field that appeals to her while continuing with school.

To give you an example, the U.S. National Security Agency (NSA), located in Maryland, hires local high-school seniors to work sixteen to twenty-five hours per week in one of four areas, including accounting and clerical work. The students receive salaries, as well as sick leave and an option to participate in the NSA's health- and life-insurance programs. Private companies, too, arrange similar programs with high schools. A member of the guidance-counseling staff should be able to route you to the person in charge of coordinating work-experience programs. Investigate all options *before* a teen drops out of school.

Once a teenager has made up his mind to drop out of school, be supportive—but don't support him financially! If he lives at home, insist that he pay for room and board as well as cover his car insurance and other personal expenses. This is important, even though the average high-school dropout earns just $270 a week.

When parents let a grown child live at home rent-free, they're feeding the adolescent's fantasy that she is independent and self-supporting. They're also smothering any incentive for moving up, not to mention moving *out.* Mom and Dad need to impose a reality check. The realization that her paycheck barely stretches far enough to cover necessities—never mind having money left over for recreation and luxuries—may be the impetus that motivates a dropout to become one of the 750,000 or so adults who earn a *general equivalency diploma (GED)* each year. With rare exception, employers hire GED graduates on the same basis as high-school grads. In fact, one in seven men and women who receive their high-school diploma do so by passing the GED tests, which cover writing skills, social studies, literature and the arts, and mathematics.

That's important for discouraged parents to remember: A teenager's quitting school doesn't necessarily spell the end of her education. Through entering the workforce, she may discover a career that she enjoys, and decide to get her GED *and* a college degree in order to advance herself. According to the American Council on Education, two in three GED test-takers plan to enter a college, university, trade school, technical school or business school the following year.

When the Pressure to Excel Gets Out of Hand

To America's teenagers, adulthood must seem like a comparative vacation. They match us step-for-step during the day, then wade through an hour or two of homework at night. If it seems like youngsters are under fiercer pressures than in your day, you're not imagining things. They are.

"It's a national phenomenon," says Dr. Coleman, who points to two causes. In an increasingly high-tech economy, more will be demanded of tomorrow's workers. As teachers are constantly reminding their classes, they will need superior skills if they expect to land a job. That is, if there are any jobs left, a worry generated by the downsizing trend of recent years.

The pressure to achieve is partly self-imposed, notes Dr. Coleman, but it comes mostly from Mom and Dad. "Teenage patients of mine will complain, 'My parents are putting so much pressure on me to get into a good college that I can't even have fun as a sophomore in high school.' Parents can get very revved up. I've had couples bring in an eight-year-old because she wasn't doing well in spelling. They wanted to know whether or not she'd be able to get into college, be independent and have a good life.

"Some of their concerns are justified," he continues, "but other times they're focused too far ahead and not on keeping their youngster's life balanced *now*."

WHAT YOU CAN DO

Watch carefully for signs of strain. You can't put a number on how many extracurricular commitments are too many. A girl's schedule may resemble the queen of England's social calendar, but if she appears happy and is doing well, then her parents can relax. (Incidentally, research suggests that participating in after-school activities may strengthen students' affection for their schools, which is associated with lower failure rates and dropout rates.)

A youngster who is feeling overwhelmed may seem irritable, depressed or exhausted. Her schoolwork may suffer. "When you notice consistent signs of stress," says clinical psychologist Helen Pratt, a mother of five, "it's time to step in and insist that the teenager give up one or more of her activities."

Examine your expectations for your child. Are they realistic? To demand that a perennial *D* student in science suddenly start pulling *A*'s in eleventh-grade chemistry is not only unreasonable but may very well set her up for failure and discouragement.

A better way is to measure progress in small increments. So although our ultimate aim may be to raise her grade to a *B* by semester's end, we institute short-term goals along the way. Perhaps the first stepping-stone is to help her understand a key concept. Acknowledge this step forward and offer encouragement for the next landmark: a *B* on a forthcoming lab test. And so on. If she falls short, examine why. Was it due to a lack of effort? Or was the bar set too high? If the latter, then the goals need to be reconsidered.

Don't insist on college if your child is determined not to go. You can make a compelling case that attending college will give him a competitive edge, but ultimately the decision is his. Perhaps he's never been academically inclined. Or perhaps he wants to dive directly into the job market, enlist in the armed forces or pursue a field where education is secondary to a particular talent, like acting or athletics.

As long as a youngster has a plan—even if it's short term or not the ambition you would have chosen for him—we'd advise against pressuring him to go to college against his will. All of us progress through life at our own pace and according to our own timetable. Some teenagers know from a young age what they want to do professionally; their career path resembles an arrow's flight, straight and true. Others set their sights on one career but abandon the dream once they achieve it or at some point along the way. Perhaps it was someone *else's* vision for them more so than their own. Eventually they discover that their heart lies somewhere else.

Then there are the many young people who don't come into their own until later in life. They may try their hand at working for a few years, *then* go to college. Maybe they've found their true calling and now want to develop the skills to make a career out of it. Or, their experience in the workforce has taught them to appreciate the advantages of that diploma. Our point is that it's never too late to go back to school. With future generations expected to have two, three or more careers in their lifetime, many adults will no doubt find themselves back in the classroom.

A high-schooler who can't bear the thought of spending four more years in school might consider obtaining an associate of arts degree (A.A.) at a two-year institution. Those armed with an A.A. will find more welcome mats out when looking for a job and higher salaries than if they never went to college at all. Another timesaving option is to enroll in a technical program to obtain the skills and experience sought by employers.

9

PLANNING AHEAD FOR COLLEGE

For teenagers who intend to further their education, the process of choosing and applying to colleges usually doesn't begin in earnest until midway through the cycle of testing, which may have begun as early as the year before.

COLLEGE ENTRANCE EXAMS: PSAT, SAT, ACT AND PLAN

College acceptance or rejection hinges primarily on a student's high-school grade point average (GPA). However, since grading policies are not uniform among the thousands upon thousands of secondary schools in the United States, standardized tests such as the Scholastic Assessment Test (SAT) and the American College Testing Program Assessment (ACT) provide college admission officers with a common yardstick for measuring academic ability and predicting how a boy or girl will fare as a college freshman. The most commonly used tests are described below.

1. Preliminary Scholastic Assessment Test (PSAT): administered in October of tenth or eleventh grade. The test serves as a warmup for the SAT. At slightly more than two hours (shorter than the SAT), it measures verbal, math and writing skills. Colleges are not privy to these scores, but doing well on the PSAT may qualify a student for one of six thousand five hundred National Merit Corporation Scholarships. The awards range from $250 to $2,000 per academic year for up to four years, or a one-time payment of $2,000.

2. Scholastic Assessment Test (SAT): the most widely administered standardized college entrance exam. SAT test dates are scheduled every month during the school year except for September, February and April, with the scores available in about two weeks. Most youngsters take the exam in the spring of eleventh grade or the fall of twelfth grade. The SAT evaluates knowledge and skills in math, vocabulary and reading.

3. American College Testing Program Assessment (ACT): the other major standardized college entrance exam, also given during eleventh or twelfth grade. The ACT differs greatly from the PSAT and the SAT. It is a three-hour multiple-choice exam divided into four parts: English, mathematics, reading and science reasoning, always in that order. Many colleges in the South and Midwest require students to take the ACT test and submit their scores when applying for admission; other institutions accept either the ACT or the SAT. The ACT is growing in popularity: about 1.7 million copies of the test are given annually (in October, December, February, April, June and, in some states, September), as compared to 1.8 million copies of the SAT.

4. PLAN test: The PLAN test, administered in the fall to high-school sophomores, tests the same knowledge and skills as the ACT assessment and provides students with an estimated ACT score. Some schools allow tenth-graders to take both the PLAN test and the PSAT. It can help direct students in their course selection and also functions as a scholastic and vocational aptitude test.

5. Scholastic Assessment Test II Subject Test: Some colleges require applicants to take one or more SAT II Subject Tests, formerly referred to as Achievement Tests. These exams test knowledge in a particular area, such as English, math, a number of sciences, history and foreign languages.

Contrary to what many anxious high-schoolers believe, the exams are not indicative of intelligence. By all means encourage your youngster to study hard, but don't add to the pressure she may already be feeling. Some teens approach these test dates as if their futures hang in the balance. The SAT is just one of several facets that make up a student's profile.

Preparing for the SAT or ACT

Your child's verbal and math scores on the PSAT or the ACT equivalent will indicate where he or she needs improvement. Many teens have benefited from test-preparation courses, offered through a number of companies. While the instructors do review test content, they mainly coach students on test-taking techniques and strategies—for instance, learning how to rule out incorrect answers and knowing how much time to allow before moving on to the next question. If you and your child choose this route, be sure to enroll in a reputable, established program. Many focus on specific areas that are giving a youngster trouble, be it math, vocabulary or reading.

Any practice for the test should be on an authentic PSAT or SAT. The exams are produced by the *College Board,* a national membership association of schools and colleges. Teens can ask their guidance counselors for free copies of its booklets "Taking the SAT I" and "Taking the SAT II." The College Board also publishes *10 Real SATs,* a hefty guide containing full-length exams. You can find it and the SAT II companion (*Real SAT II: Subject Tests*) in bookstores or order it from the College Board directly. The organization's Web site contains many helpful resources for students, including sample PSAT and SAT test questions.

What Else Do Colleges Look for in Students?

If grade point average and standardized test scores were the sole criteria for gaining admission to college, schools could replace their admission-office staffs with a single pocket calculator. Simply add up the numbers, subtract the class ranking and however many seats were available would go to those candidates with the highest totals.

Obviously, the process is far more complicated. In weighing an applicant's qualifications, colleges look to ascertain how well this young man or woman could be expected to handle college-level course work in an environment that demands far more self-sufficiency than high school did.

The transcript, student essay and letters of recommendation that accompany the application also convey an impression of this faceless person's character. A college is a community; some are the size of small cities. Admission officers are seeking newcomers whose presence will enhance campus life in some way. How a teenager spends his time away from class says nearly as much about him as his time in class. So extracurricular high-school activities, recommendations and the essay, when required, are definitely taken into consideration.

Participation in after-school activities indicates that a student is disciplined, has excellent time-management skills and commits herself to a passion, whether it be in the arts, sports or the debating team. Admission departments pay attention to work experience and community-service activities too.

Recommendations, from a current or recent teacher, guidance counselor and/or the high-school principal, give prospective colleges an idea of how the applicant is perceived by her peers and members of the community.

TABLE 9.1

Information Please: Filling Out a College Application

INFORMATION TYPICALLY REQUESTED	EXAMPLES OF ESSAY QUESTIONS
1. *Biographical Info* Name, address, names of parents, siblings, etc.	1. "Write about a significant experience or achievement that has special meaning for you."
2. *Academic Info* Name of secondary school, school advisers, curriculum, years of study in each academic area, any academic honors, senior-year courses.	2. "Describe one of the best conversations you've ever had."
3. *Activities, Hobbies, Experiences* School activities, work experience, community activities, hobbies, travel.	3. "Describe the most challenging obstacle you've had to overcome."
4. *High-School Grades* Some colleges do not require grades from all four years of high school.	4. "Please describe yourself. What quality do you like best in yourself? What quality do you like least?"
5. *Filing Info* • Are you applying as a freshman or as a transfer student? • For which term? (fall, spring, summer) • Will you require campus housing? • Are you applying for a scholarship? • Are you applying for financial aid? • Have you ever applied, attended or interviewed here before? • What is your anticipated career choice, degree, major(s)? • Has anyone else in your family ever attended this college? • Are there any additional comments or statements you would like to make?	5. "What are your reasons for applying to [name of school], and what do you hope to accomplish after you graduate?" 6. "Who is your hero, and why? (This can be someone from your own life or from world history.)" 7. "Discuss some issue of personal, local, national or international concern, and explain why it is important to you." 8. "Discuss a work of art (novel, song, poem, etc.) that encapsulates your personal philosophy." 9. "What do you think the world will be like by the year 2010?"

Mom, Dad: We'd advise reading over your teenager's cover letters, both to prospective colleges and to prospective employers. It's true what they say: First impressions are often lasting impressions.

Finally, the college-application essay not only assesses writing proficiency and analytical ability, it provides a glimpse into the writer's personality, creativity, values, energy and sense of humor. Typically, applicants are asked to describe themselves and their aspirations for the future. Other essay questions are more abstract (see table 9.1 on page 150). Like many amateur wordsmiths, teens tend to freeze up the moment their fingers touch the keyboard. Instead of a personal, engaging voice, the resulting prose is often bloated and stiffly worded, or overly earnest and oozing insincerity. Encourage your youngster to just be *himself.*

HELPING YOUR TEENAGER FIND THE RIGHT COLLEGE

Choosing the "right" college requires as much soul-searching as researching, because this is in large part a subjective decision. The right college is the one that seems most likely to enable a teenager to realize his professional and personal goals. And of course it must also be a school that he can have a reasonable hope of getting into. As you research the different institutions, find out the minimum achievement levels, or cutoff, for college entrance exam scores and grade point averages, if there are such cutoffs.

By the time eleventh grade rolls around, if not sooner, you and your child should be having regular discussions about his future. Many youngsters will not have made up their minds about pursuing further education, much less their career ambitions. They will need our advice and experience in reaching both answers.

Don't be surprised, though, if your teen seems to avoid the subject. He might have every intention of going to college, but you have to appreciate that adolescents often regard this pivotal transition with a combination of excitement and dread.

Q: Our son is entering his senior year in high school. He's upset because several of his friends know what they plan to study in college, and, as he puts it, "I don't have a clue." Michael is an intelligent, creative and very personable boy. He thinks he might like to teach elementary school, but then other times he talks about possibly becoming a newscaster on radio or television. Lately he's been leaning toward going into advertising. Should we be concerned about his indecision?

A: Many students enter college unsure of what career they want to pursue; some don't even declare their in-depth area of study, or *major,* until they are sophomores or juniors. Until then, they take general education classes. A sensible plan for your son might be to attend a *liberal arts* college where he can major in both teaching and communications. Liberal arts programs expose students to a range of courses in the sciences, social sciences and humanities.

A lot of growth takes place during the college years. You can rest reasonably assured that your son will find his direction long before he has to don a cap and gown again.

Picking Priorities: What Is Most Important to Your Youngster?

Many factors enter into selecting one college over another, not just which school has the superior academic reputation. What often sways the vote one way or another are seemingly secondary concerns such as cost, distance, location and size. Learning your youngster's preferences at the outset will help you to focus the search.

Cost. A family that cannot afford privately funded colleges, even if buoyed by financial aid, would want to investigate *public* institutions. Because these schools' budgets are funded mainly by state and local governments, they can charge, on average, less than one-fourth the tuition of *private* schools. At public colleges, state residents pay roughly 33 to 50 percent less in annual tuition than students from out of state. Cost may also be the deciding factor when two colleges are essentially neck and neck in all other respects, and one offers a scholarship and the other does not.

One money-saving option is for your teen to spend her first two years at a community college, then transfer to a four-year school. Based on the national average undergraduate costs for 1996–97, the total savings on tuition by the time she receives her diploma can be substantial: if transferring to a public school, approximately thirty-two hundred dollars; to a private institution, twenty-two thousand dollars. Additional savings are realized during the freshman and sophomore years because most young people attending community colleges live at home.

Distance and location. Perhaps it's important to your youngster to attend a college that is within a few hours' drive from home, in which event your search has been narrowed significantly. Don't feel hurt, though, if she chooses a school far away. For many teenagers, going off to college is the biggest adventure of their lives. It also presents an opportunity to test their newfound independence.

Another consideration is the location. Does your child want to experience urban life, or at least be within close proximity to the diverse culture, entertainment and nightlife that a city has to offer? Or does a small-town environment better suit her personality and interests? If she's interested in marine biology as a course of study, she should probably be near a large body of water.

College size. Here, too, environment matters. Large universities may not be able to provide the personal attention that a smaller college can promise,[1] but schools with greater student populations often boast a broader range of courses and superior libraries and other facilities. Each youngster must determine how she learns best: In a cavernous lecture hall, or in small classes that encourage discussion? In a class where the structure is clearly defined, or in a freer setting?

Types of Colleges

TWO-YEAR SCHOOLS

Community colleges, junior colleges, technical/professional colleges. The sole difference between community colleges and junior colleges is that community schools are supported by state and local funding and mainly serve area residents, while junior colleges are funded privately and therefore may attract students from anywhere in the country. Students can earn several degrees: associate of arts (A.A.), associate of science (A.S.) and associate of applied science (A.A.S.).

Technical schools offer programs geared toward preparing students for specific professions, including accounting, air-conditioning and refrigeration, automotive and diesel mechanics, commercial art and photography, drafting and design, electronics, health care, horticulture, office administration, retail merchandising and welding. Community and junior colleges provide technical training in addition to more general studies. Depending on the vocational program, students can earn an associate degree or a *certificate.* A two-year school may be an end unto itself. Or a graduate may transfer her credits to a four-year institution and resume studying for her bachelor degree there. Be aware, though, that some two-year-school credits may not be transferable. Check with the four-year college about which courses it will accept.

FOUR-YEAR SCHOOLS

Colleges and universities. These institutions confer bachelor of arts (B.A.) and bachelor of science (B.S.) degrees in many fields, including biology, chemistry, economics, English, foreign languages, history, literature, political science and zoology, to name several. Universities differ from colleges in that they usually are larger and encompass one or more colleges of the arts and/or sciences.

---

1 We say *may not,* because some departments within the school may in fact be small.

The size of the school is often reflected in larger classes, which may be taught by grad students instead of professors. What's more, graduates can continue their studies and earn advanced degrees in their chosen field: a *master's degree* (upon completing one to two years of graduate work), a *doctoral degree* (two to three years), or a *professional degree* (one, three, six years, maybe more, depending on the profession and whether the student pursues the degree part time or full time). Some colleges offer graduate programs.

What Teenagers (and Their Parents) Need to Know Before Choosing a College

What educational programs does the college offer? How many students are there in each major, and how many of them graduate? What are the student-teacher ratios, and how available are the instructors and other college staff? There are several ways to gather information about a school.

STEP ONE: RESEARCH AND READ

Bookstore and library shelves are practically sagging from the weight of guides to thousands of colleges. The titles in the box on page 155 are particularly good. The school guidance office may have some of these books on hand for lending to students.

STEP TWO: ASK QUESTIONS

Your child's guidance counselor may be able to fill in some of the gaps about a college; just be advised that counselors' experience varies widely. Other sources of information are alumni of the college in question. A Web site called World Alumni Net (*www.alumni.net*) contains e-mail addresses for school alumni organizations as well as for individual alumni. Feel free to ask the college to put you in touch with current students or recent graduates.

Most colleges now have their own Web sites displaying photos of the campus and accompanying text. Some of the more ambitious sites feature "virtual tours" that take you from building to building. They may incorporate interactive maps, films, sound clips and live Web cameras. For an index to college Web addresses, go to *www.campustours.com*.

STEP THREE: VISIT THE CAMPUS

The best way to get to know a school is to visit the campus. During your teen's sophomore or junior year, drop in at a few local colleges—large and

Recommended College Guides

- *The College Handbook;* publisher: College Entrance Examination Board
- *Complete Book of Colleges,* by Princeton Review; Edward T. Custard, editor; publisher: Princeton Review
- *The Fiske Guide to Colleges,* by Edward R. Fiske; publisher: Times Books
- *Lovejoy's College Guide,* by Charles T. Straughn II and Barbarasue Lovejoy Straughn; publisher: Arco Publishing
- *Peterson's 4-Year Colleges/Peterson's 2-Year Colleges,* by Peterson's; publisher: Peterson's Guides
- *The Insider's Guide to the Colleges,* by Yale Daily News; publisher: Griffin Trade Paperback
- *K&W Guide to Colleges for the Learning Disabled,* by Marybeth Kravets, M.A., and Imy F. Wax, M.S.; publisher, Princeton Review/Random House
- *Peterson's Colleges with Programs for Students with Learning Disabilities or Attention Deficit Disorders,* by Charles T. Mangrum, Stephen S. Strichart and Jon Latimer; publisher: Peterson's Guides
- *College Search,* a free on-line service from the College Board, is a database of more than thirty-two hundred two-year and four-year colleges. You can search a particular school by name or type in your preferences and let the site match you. The information on each school is derived from *The College Handbook.* Go to *www.collegeboard.org/csearch.*

small, if possible—so that she can get a taste of college life. Once she's been accepted at an institution, or two or three, call the admission office and schedule a guided tour. Schools do this all the time, setting up visitors with volunteer student escorts; even arranging overnight stays in a dormitory.

Planning Ahead Financially

Since 1960, the total cost of attending college in the United States has soared ninefold for public four-year colleges and twelvefold for private four-year institutions. But don't rule out a school because it seems too expensive. Financial aid may bring the cost down into an affordable range. Almost half of all college students, from a wide range of economic backgrounds, receive monetary assistance in the form of *grants* and *scholarships, loans* and *work-study programs.* Every year, approximately $50 billion is available, three-fourths of it from the federal government. States contribute, too, as do colleges themselves, and various scholarship organizations and foundations. One of the main jobs of a college financial-aid administrator is to procure funding from these different sources and present eligible candidates with a *financial-aid package.*

When It's Time to Apply to College

Fall, the season of change, is when high-school seniors typically begin mailing their college applications (certified, please; return receipt requested) or filing them via the Internet. Let's say that your teen has decided to apply to six schools, an average number. Guidance counselors generally recommend picking one or two "reaches"—longshots, in other words—and including one or two sure bets. The rest of your child's choices should be colleges where his qualifications seem comparable to those of the average undergrad at each one.

The first of the year is the usual filing deadline for September classes. (Colleges that operate on what's called a *rolling* basis accept applications throughout the year.) Some students, however, elect to apply early, under an *early decision plan* or an *early action plan.* Approximately three hundred institutions offer one or both of these arrangements.

An early decision plan is binding, meaning that the candidate must commit to attending the school if accepted, provided that the financial-aid package offered is adequate. The decision is made quickly; submit your application by November, and you'll receive word sometime in December.

Early action plans are not binding. Notification typically comes in January or February, still well in advance of the usual acceptance date.

Applying early wins applicants the most attractive financial-aid packages and first crack at choosing a dorm room. They also get to enjoy their last six months of high school knowing where they'll be headed come September. However, this process is not recommended for everyone. If your teenager isn't absolutely certain that he wants to attend a particular college, or if he wants to play free agent later in the spring and weigh offers of financial incentives from several schools, he should apply according to the standard schedule.

THE TRANSITION FROM HIGH SCHOOL TO COLLEGE

Academically, the step up from high school to college isn't as steep as previous transitions may have been. Unless a student takes on an unusually heavy course load, the demands aren't markedly different from before.

What *is* different, and what can trip up first-year students, is the atmosphere in which learning and studying take place. College affords young people a level of autonomy they've never experienced before. And if they're attending a college away from home, they don't have Mom and Dad standing sentinel outside their bedroom door to order them back inside to study for tomorrow's midterm exam. Most students have the self-discipline to make the adjustment without too much difficulty, but others get swept up in the social whirl of college life.

"We see it here at the University of North Carolina," says Dr. William Lord Coleman, an associate professor of pediatrics at UNC's School of Medicine in Chapel Hill. "Kids go downhill or drop out because they can't get organized enough to forget about the beer-keg party on a Sunday afternoon and go to the library like they're supposed to."

Colleges, recognizing the potential perils of youngsters living on their own for the first time, usually insist that new undergrads spend their first year or two living in the residential halls. A 1998 study from the Harvard School of Public Health painted a disturbing portrait of alcohol abuse among U.S. college students. Forty-two percent were found to indulge in binge drinking, which is defined as consuming five drinks in one sitting for men, and four drinks for women.

By far, the highest rate of excessive drinking was among fraternity and sorority members: a staggering 84 percent. The second highest rate, 54 percent, was among school athletes. Third highest were students living in coed dorms: 52 percent. Interestingly, the rate of binge drinking among students living in off-campus housing or in single-sex dorms was lower than the overall average: 40 percent and 38 percent, respectively.

You might want to consider steering an impressionable youngster away from schools with reputations for heavy partying. Believe it or not, every year the *Princeton Review* ranks the top ten party colleges in the United States, based on surveys distributed to hundreds of thousands of students.

MONITORING COLLEGE STUDENTS FROM A DISTANCE

Short of secretly taking up residence in an adjacent dorm room, what can parents do to keep tabs on a son or daughter living away from home? Dr. Coleman recommends "the age-old wisdoms: Call regularly, encourage visits home whenever possible and visit your youngster more frequently than just on Parents' Day. Also, if you can, get to know the parents of the roommate or suite mates. If necessary, you can do a little networking together behind the scenes."

If you suspect that your youngster is having difficulty adapting to college (homesickness, for example, is common among students living away from home for the first time), encourage him to speak to a counselor at the student health service. If you're truly worried about his welfare, make the call yourself and ask one of the mental-health professionals there to pay a visit to your youngster or invite him down to talk.

10

LEARNING PROBLEMS

What is a learning disability? Even the experts can't always agree. An important definition is found in the *American Psychiatry Association's Diagnostic and Statistical Manual of Mental Disorders* (*DSM*), the main reference book physicians rely on to help them diagnose these conditions. The most recent edition, the *DSM IV,* identifies three types of learning disabilities: *dyslexia,* the inability to read, spell and write words, but not as a result of faulty eyesight; *dysgraphia,* the inability to write properly; and *dyscalculia,* the inability to perform mathematical calculations.

The federal government takes a broader view. Under the Individuals with Disabilities Education Act (IDEA), all eligible children between the ages of three and twenty-one are guaranteed free and appropriate *special education* and related services in the public schools. IDEA defines "learning disabilities" as follows:

> A disorder in one or more of the basic psychological processes involved in understanding or in using language, spoken or written, which may manifest itself in an imperfect ability to think, speak, read, write, spell, or to do mathematical calculations. The term includes such conditions as perceptual handicaps, brain injury, minimal brain dysfunctions, dyslexia, and developmental aphasia.

That encompasses not only the trio of disorders mentioned above, but also *attention deficit hyperactivity disorder* (ADHD) and *pervasive developmental disorders,* including *autism* and *Asperger's syndrome.* Although the law expressly does not include *mental*

Initials, Initials and More Initials

ADHD: attention deficit
   hyperactivity disorder
AS: Asperger's syndrome
ASD: autism spectrum disorder
CAPD: central auditory
   processing disorder
DD: developmental disabilities
HFA: high-functioning autism
LD: learning disability

MR: mental retardation
OCD: obsessive-compulsive
   disorder
PDD: pervasive developmental
   disorder
PDD-NOS: pervasive
   developmental disorder
   not otherwise specified
SI: speech impairment

retardation, states and individual school districts are free to modify the guidelines. Some do classify mental retardation as a learning disability; others may provide special-education services for students whose academic achievement falls well short of their potential, as measured by test scores.

To add to the confusion, you may hear the same learning problem referred to as a learning disability, a *developmental disability* or yet another term. Ultimately, how these disorders are classified isn't as important as recognizing that each one can seriously interfere with a youngster's ability to learn.

All learning impairments share one thing in common: deviations in processing in one or more locations of the brain. Several studies employing sophisticated brain-imaging technology have been able to observe the workings of brains with learning problems. At Yale University School of Medicine, for example, patients with dyslexia were asked to read while they underwent a magnetic resonance imaging scan. The researchers clearly observed a difference in the parts of the brain that normally handle reading.

Similarly, imaging studies of people with ADHD have found decreased functioning in the areas that enable us to concentrate; and scans of people with autism reveal abnormalities in brain structure, particularly within the shell-shaped *cerebellum* nestled at the base of the brain. Impaired brain development from a variety of causes is also at the root of mental retardation. (These imaging procedures were employed strictly for research purposes, incidentally; they are not part of a routine diagnostic workup.) Learning difficulties are diagnosed in at least four times as many boys as girls. This may be due in part to the fact that boys who have problems academically are more prone to disruptive behavior and to resisting reading and other challenging tasks in school. Therefore they tend to be referred more to specialists and subsequently diagnosed.

Many of these disorders may weave their way through family trees. According to the National Institute of Mental Health, children with ADHD usually have at least one close relative who also has the disorder. Frequently it's the father; at least one in three who have ADHD themselves pass it on genetically to their offspring.

Typically, a learning deficit becomes apparent early in childhood, though not always. If the problems are subtle, a child may compensate sufficiently for quite a while; in fact, some of these boys and girls happen to be extremely bright. It's only after the work in school becomes more complex, beginning around third or fourth grade, that they start to struggle. "This is the time when the curriculum begins to shift from 'learning to read,' to 'reading to learn,' " explains Dr. Mark L. Wolraich, a specialist in learning disabilities. Of the more than 2.4 million children with learning disorders in U.S. schools, about four in five encounter problems with reading and language.

Several of these conditions have overlapping features; consequently, misdiagnoses are not uncommon. For instance: Difficulty concentrating in school characterizes ADHD, but is also a hallmark of Asperger's syndrome, mental retardation or depression. Furthermore, learning difficulties are typically accompanied by secondary problems.

Let's return to the example of ADHD. Some of these children are additionally diagnosed with another learning problem, such as dyslexia. A number develop the behavioral disorder *oppositional defiant disorder*. Their belligerence and fits of temper can be attributed partly to their lack of success in school and other circumstances. "But some of the misconduct," says Dr. Wolraich, "is due to the fact that the two conditions tend to occur together." Less commonly, adolescents or young adults with an attention deficit have or will develop *bipolar disorder,* a serious mood disturbance also referred to as *manic depression.* (See "Bipolar Disorder" in chapter 15, "Emotional and Behavioral Problems.")

LEARNING PROBLEM? IT'S THAT AND MORE

Rarely are the effects of a learning problem confined solely to the classroom. They frequently spill over to other areas of daily life. Making friends can be especially difficult for many of these youngsters, some of whom lack fundamental social skills, such as the ability to understand nuances of language and read facial expressions. A joke that sends others into hysterics may sail right by them. Of course, many boys and girls with learning difficulties get along splendidly with their peers, but for those who are socially awkward, adolescence can be a painful time. Adolescents with learning problems can be screened by their pediatrician or other health professional for other difficulties, such as anxiety or depression.

A child's diagnosis thrusts parents into the role of *advocate:* the person(s) charged with getting her whatever educational, psychological and rehabilitative services she needs. Mothers and fathers are also advocates in the sense of providing constant love and encouragement. Keeping self-esteem aloft and promoting a positive self-image vie in importance with helping a child with a learning problem academically. In short, be your child's number-one fan. Remember: No one will love and support him or her more than you.

If you suspect your teenager might have a learning problem of some kind, consult his pediatrician, who can outline a plan of action. Don't deny your instincts, as parents sometimes do, largely out of fear that a finding of ADHD, or autism or another problem will permanently stigmatize him.

Stigmatize him? With whom? Between increased public awareness and 120,000 new cases of learning disorders among students every year, a learning problem no longer carries the stigma it once did. But, frankly, what other people might think shouldn't even cross a parent's mind. When mothers and fathers ignore the reality of the situation, in a well-intentioned but misguided attempt to protect their child, they are depriving him of the help he needs in learning to live with his disorder. Until then, his schoolwork is likely to suffer, reinforcing a destructive pattern of failure. And without therapy to show him ways to control any alienating behaviors, the more likely it is that he *will* suffer the rejection of his peers.

Approximately two in five boys and girls with ADHD aren't diagnosed until they reach junior high or high school—sometimes not until college. Imagine what it must be like to spend years not understanding why you can't seem to do better in school. How many teens conclude it must be because they're "stupid"? Or "lazy," a frequent accusation. To receive an explanation for why learning has always been hard usually comes as a relief. Although it is preferable for learning problems to be picked up early in childhood, know it is never too late to help a youngster turn things around.

Types of Learning Problems

DYSLEXIA

Dyslexia is defined as difficulty reading. When children are learning to read and write in kindergarten and first grade, it is not uncommon for them to misinterpret a "*b*" as a "*d*," a "*6*" as a "*9*," the word *on* as *no* and so forth. An important distinction is that this is not a vision problem; rather, the brain is reversing, inverting or missequencing the information it receives from the eyes. Most kids outgrow this condition by age seven or so. For *dyslexic* youngsters, however, the reading problems persist.

In another form of dyslexia, the mind accurately identifies a word it "sees" but is slow to connect a meaning to it. These teenagers read extremely slowly and may have to reread material several times before they understand it. Other tasks of communication may pose difficulties as well, such as comprehending spoken language and expressing themselves orally and in writing.

DYSGRAPHIA

Dysgraphia is defined as difficulty writing, as a result of dyslexia, poor motor coordination or problems understanding space. How it is manifested depends upon the cause. A report written by an adolescent with dysgraphia due to dyslexia will contain many illegible and/or misspelled words, whereas motor clumsiness or defective visual-spatial perception affects only handwriting, not spelling.

DYSCALCULIA

Dyscalculia is defined as difficulty performing mathematical calculations. Math is problematic for many students, but dyscalculia may prevent a teenager from grasping even basic math concepts.

AUDITORY MEMORY AND PROCESSING DISABILITIES

Auditory memory and processing disabilities include difficulty understanding and remembering words or sounds. A teen may hear normally yet not remember key facts because her memory is not storing and deciphering them correctly. Or she may hear a phrase but not be able to process it, especially if the language is complex, lengthy or spoken rapidly, or if there is background noise. For youngsters with *central auditory-processing disorders* (CAPD), the hum of a fan or the routine sounds of the classroom may interfere with learning.

ATTENTION DEFICIT/HYPERACTIVITY DISORDER (ADHD)

The American Academy of Pediatrics (AAP) has published recommendations on guidelines for the diagnosis and treatment of ADHD. The guidelines, developed by a panel of medical, mental health and educational experts, are intended for primary-care physicians (and parents as well) to help better understand how to recognize and treat ADHD, the most common childhood neurobehavioral disorder.

Between 4 and 12 percent of all school-age children have ADHD. The first step, diagnosing the condition, cannot usually be done successfully until a child is about age six. The AAP guidelines include the following for diagnosis:

- ADHD evaluations should be initiated by the primary-care clinician for children who show signs of school difficulties, academic underachievement, troublesome relationships with teachers, family members and peers and other behavioral problems. Questions to parents, either directly or through a previsit questionnaire regarding school and behavioral issues, may help alert physicians to possible ADHD.

- In diagnosing ADHD, physicians should use DSM-IV criteria developed by the American Psychiatric Association (symptoms include distractibility, hyperactivity and impulsivity). These guidelines require that ADHD symptoms be present in two or more of a child's settings, and that the symptoms adversely affect the child's academic or social functioning for at least six months.

- The assessment of ADHD should include information obtained directly from parents or caregivers, as well as a classroom teacher or other school professional, regarding the core symptoms of ADHD in various settings, the age of onset, duration of symptoms and degree of functional impairment.

- Evaluation of a child with ADHD should also include assessment for coexisting conditions: learning and language problems, aggression, disruptive behavior, depression or anxiety. As many as one-third of children diagnosed with ADHD also have a coexisting condition.

Treatment guidelines include the following recommendations:

- Primary-care clinicians should establish a treatment program that recognizes ADHD as a chronic condition. This implies the need for education about the condition and a sustained monitoring system to track the effects of treatment and developmental changes in behavior.

- The treating clinician, parents and child, in collaboration with school personnel, should specify appropriate goals to guide management. Goals should relate to the specific problems of the individual child, such as school performance, difficulty finishing tasks and problems with interactions with schoolmates.

- If appropriate, the clinician should recommend behavior therapy and/or stimulant medication to improve specific symptoms in children with ADHD. The guideline provides a review of the scientific evidence for recommending medication and behavior therapy.

- When the treatment for a child with ADHD has not met its goals, clinicians should reevaluate the original diagnosis, all appropriate treatments, adherence to the treatment plan and coexisting conditions, including learning disabilities and mental health conditions.

- The clinician should provide a periodic and systematic follow-up for the child with ADHD. Monitoring should be directed to the child's individual goals and any adverse effects of treatment, with information gathered from parents, teachers and the child. The guidelines recommend areas for future research in treatment options, long-term outcomes and other areas in the management of children with ADHD.

Although ADHD often appears to subside during puberty, "We now know that isn't true," says Dr. Suzanne Boulter, a pediatrician from Concord, New Hampshire. "In reality, hyperactivity may decrease, but the inattention and impulsivity remain unchanged. As these young people navigate their way through high school and college, these problems may stand as their biggest obstacle to academic success."

AUTISTIC SPECTRUM DISORDER (ASD)/PERVASIVE DEVELOPMENTAL DISORDER (PDD)

Autism is a disorder with a variety of symptoms that range from mild to severe. Labels such as classic autism, Asperger's syndrome and pervasive developmental disorder not otherwise specified are often confusing, because youngsters with these conditions share many of the same characteristics, such as deficient social skills, hypersensitivity to sights and sounds, difficulties adapting to change and other idiosyncratic interests. The difference between one child and another is frequently a matter of *degree*. As a result, all of these diagnoses are part of autistic spectrum disorder.

Asperger's and autism occupy opposite ends of the spectrum; in fact, AS is sometimes referred to as "mild" autism. Whereas most children with AS are of average or above-average intelligence, four in five autistic boys and girls exhibit some degree of mental retardation. Another key difference involves speech. Children with autism are frequently speech-delayed; kids with Asperger's syndrome, on the other hand, tend to be verbally precocious. And once they begin talking, it can seem as if a dam has given way. Dr. Hans Asperger, the Austrian pediatrician who discovered the disorder, called his patients "little professors," on account of their penchant for pontificating.

"They're very dependent on their language skills to get by," observes Dr. William Lord Coleman of Duke University Medical Center and the University of North Carolina School of Medicine, "and so they use them excessively, which can overwhelm people." This plays a large part in their difficulties interacting with their peers. Adolescents with Asperger's syndrome spend an inordinate amount of time in their own world—even for teenagers—but they're often lonely and want to make friends. The problem is, they're not sure how to act in social settings. Between that and their eccentricities, they may become victims of teasing and bullying. Parents of a child with AS, or any other disorder, should try their best to stay attuned to their youngster's moods. Rates of anxiety, depression and suicide are unusually high in this group. (See "Helping Teens with Learning Problems Succeed," page 166.)

To distinguish classic autism from Asperger's syndrome, pediatricians and pediatric specialists rely on the diagnostic guidelines from the *Diagnostic and Statistical Manual of Mental Disorders.* Most children fall somewhere in the middle of the spectrum. Only about one in one thousand youngsters is diagnosed with classic autism. The incidence of Asperger's is believed to be double and possibly triple that.

MENTAL RETARDATION

There are about half a million adolescents with mental retardation in the United States. Nine in ten are classified as having *mild* retardation,[1] with an intellectual-functioning level, or *IQ,* between 50 and 69—some fifty-five points below average. (An IQ of 35 to 49 places a person in the category of *moderate* mental retardation; 20 to 34, *severe* mental retardation; and *under* 20, *profound* mental retardation.)

Cognitively, many mildly retarded boys and girls function not that far below their nondisabled classmates. They absorb new information and skills, only more slowly. The problems they do have may be related to memory, problem-solving skills, logical thought, perception and attention span.

Like parents of other adolescents with special needs, mothers and fathers are probably as concerned about their child's social development as they are with his academic progress. Adolescence, of course, is a time when being dif-

---

1 A diagnosis of mental retardation is based on IQ and two other standards: (1) significant limitations in two or more essential skills of daily living (communication, self-care, reading, writing and so on) and (2) the condition must be present before the age of eighteen.

ferent can set one up as an object of teasing. Youngsters who are mentally retarded, in addition to their intellectual limitations, may possess physical and/or mental health problems that also make them stand out. They are often keenly aware of feeling set apart from their peers without learning deficits. Understandably, they are susceptible to feelings of frustration and depression.

Helping Teens with Learning Problems Succeed

Urge your youngster to tell you if another student is giving her a hard time. Then take appropriate action to see that it stops. (See "Putting an End to Bullying" in chapter 14, "Safety and Injury Prevention.")

Facilitate friendships. Perhaps this means that your child and his friends get together at your house more than at other youngsters' homes, or that you take on additional chauffeuring duty. To see your teenager enjoying himself with his peers will more than make up for the extra effort and mileage.

Heighten teachers' awareness. Teachers can have a hand in easing these teens' way socially by showing sensitivity to the obstacles they face.

Encourage your teen to join activities and recreational programs for boys and girls with special needs. As much as it is beneficial for children who have difficulty learning and socializing to be placed in mainstream classes, they also need opportunities to compete on a more level playing field—or to simply be among others where their disability isn't so "special." In addition to local educational programs and sports programs, there are also summer camps geared specifically for youngsters with autistic spectrum disorder, attention deficit hyperactivity disorder, impaired speech and hearing, impaired vision and physical disabilities. (See Table 19.3 in chapter 19, "Physical Activity and Sports.")

If You Think Your Teen Might Have a Learning Problem

The scene: *Twelve-year-old Nicholas has never been a standout student, but two semesters into middle school, he's getting C's, D's—even a couple of F's. The teen complains that he feels "lost" in class much of the time, and his worried mother can see his self-confidence eroding. She confides to a friend that she's concerned Nicholas might have a learning disability.*

"I've had my head in the sand the last year or two, hoping that Nick would catch on in school, but he's doing worse and worse," she says. "I've finally accepted that we need to have him tested; I just don't know where to go from here."

Under the Individuals with Disabilities Education Act, school districts are obligated to test students suspected of having a learning problem. This may be carried out by school personnel or referred to an educational psychologist or health-care professional, at the district's expense. To request an evaluation, you must write to the school principal or the district's office of special education. Under most state statutes, districts are required to arrange the testing within a certain number of weeks. We suggest that you send your letter via certified mail, return receipt requested.

Some parents choose to have the testing done privately, then submit the results to the school. Insurance may or may not cover this service, though, so you might want to consider letting the school conduct the evaluation. "If the parents are dissatisfied with the results," says Dr. Wolraich, "parents may be able to insist that the school obtain a second evaluation, without them having to pay for it." One advantage to letting the school order the assessment, he adds, is that "there is a clear set of rules and regulations that they have to follow." Too, the district may be less likely to challenge or disregard its own findings should the testing indeed confirm a disability.

The exact number and types of tests used varies. But typically, a battery of *psychological, educational* and *social* tests will be performed to evaluate IQ, language skills, perceptual and cognitive abilities, social skills and academic level. Additional exams may be necessary to rule out medical conditions that could be causing or contributing to the problem, such as vision loss, hearing loss, mental disorders or behavioral disturbances. The evaluation must be repeated a minimum of every three years.

Parents play an integral role in helping to pinpoint the nature of a learning problem, as do teachers, coaches and others who know the youngster well. You may be asked to fill out a lengthy questionnaire about your teenager's medical history and her past and present behavior. Dig out old report cards and other mementos to prod your memory. Often, when mothers and fathers think back on their son's or daughter's early childhood, they may see a trail of clues that were overlooked at the time.

How Learning Problems Are Managed

Learning problems can often be managed very successfully, even though they cannot be cured. The goal of therapy is to enable youngsters to live with their limitations as productively as possible. Treatment is usually waged on four fronts:

1. **Psycho-social-behavioral therapies:** teaching children strategies for maximizing their strengths and compensating for their weaknesses.

2. **Other interventions:** Specialized language instruction, taught by a teacher or therapist who has received special training, is used to teach dyslexic teenagers to read, write and spell. Comparable programs exist for children with dysgraphia and dyscalculia.

3. **Medication therapy:** using medications to improve concentration problems and other conditions such as depression.

4. **Special education:** a school environment tailored to the unique needs of each child with a learning disability. Until such time as it is determined that a teen no longer needs special services, once a year the school and parents work together on formulating an appropriate *individualized education plan,* or *IEP,* for the following academic year.

With so many differences among adolescents who have learning deficits, treatment must be individually tailored. Anticipate frequent lane changes on the road to improvement, as one medication gets substituted for another, or you switch therapies midstream because the behavioral technique you were hoping would help your son or daughter fell short of expectations.

This is a field where even the experts freely admit that no one has all the answers. Like rest stops on the interstate, useful advice and tips come along sporadically, assembled from physicians, therapists, special-ed teachers, other moms and dads, support groups, on-line chat rooms and so on. The members of your team may include the pediatrician, a private pediatric psychologist or psychiatrist, and the school psychologist or social worker. Whomever you choose, make sure that they treat children with *your teenager's disability* on a regular basis. You want people who have a broad and long-term overview of your child's ongoing saga.

PSYCHO-SOCIAL-BEHAVIORAL THERAPIES

• **Cognitive-behavioral therapy:** teaches children techniques to change their behavior. For example, children may be taught to place their hands on their stomach and relax when they feel upset, or be taught to think through tasks step by step when problem solving.

• **Behavior modification:** a technique for modifying behavior through reinforcement. Desirable behaviors are explained to the youngster, as are the small rewards for complying and the mild penalties for when he doesn't. If this sounds like the method of discipline described in chapter 2, "Essential Parenting Skills," you're right, only boys and girls with learning difficulties may need more frequent reinforcement.

- **Social skills training:** teaches youngsters fundamental social skills such as making eye contact when talking to someone else and how to read people's facial expressions. Typically held in a group setting.

- **Psychotherapy:** is talk therapy intended to help patients reverse defeatist attitudes and also to understand and accept their disabilities.

- **Support groups:** gatherings of adolescents who have learning disorders or their parents. Support groups bring together people in similar circumstances to share their experiences and feelings in a supportive, nonjudgmental atmosphere. Meetings, typically sponsored by patient-support organizations, hospitals and other health-related agencies, are often more productive when they're led by a social worker, nurse or other health-care professional. Members take away the knowledge that they are not alone—always comforting—as well as practical advice, referrals to specialists and local services, and other valuable information.

- **Family counseling:** Destructive family patterns can become so deeply ingrained that they persist even after a youngster with a learning deficiency begins to make progress. Family counseling can be a useful forum for airing intrafamily conflicts, reexamining issues through the eyes of an impartial third party and discovering new solutions for breaking an unhealthy cycle.

Medication Treatment

Stimulants (see table 10.1; ask your teen's pediatrician for specific brand names) are the most widely used pharmaceutical treatment for attention deficit hyperactivity disorder. At least 1.5 million young people take the stimulants three or four times a day. "Stimulant medication can have a very dramatic effect," concludes Dr. Wolraich. "Most kids benefit from being on it."

Why, then, have stimulants sometimes received a black eye in the popular press? Several criticisms have been leveled against the drugs: They are irresponsibly prescribed as a performance enhancer, a by-product of our success-obsessed culture; they are likely to be abused by the same teens they are supposed to help; they stunt growth and may produce other unwanted long-term side effects.

Not true.

The American Medical Association publicly repudiated the claim that doctors were overwriting prescriptions, while studies show that teens who use stimulants to manage their ADHD are less likely to engage in substance abuse and other risky behaviors. As for side effects, says Dr. Wolraich, "I usually tell parents that stimulants have fewer side effects than aspirin and no known severe long-term consequences."

TEEN TIP:

No teenager is thrilled to be diagnosed with a condition that might make him feel different from his peers. Sometimes youngsters refuse to take their medication. They may claim that the drug isn't helping them or, conversely, fret that swallowing a pill to improve their school performance somehow constitutes "cheating." This second line of reasoning can drain the satisfaction out of any subsequent success.

You could respond by saying, "The stimulant isn't turning you into someone that you're not. It's just allowing you to tune out distractions and focus better, so that you can perform up to your natural abilities. You wouldn't say it's 'cheating' to wear glasses, would you? This is no different." As pediatric psychopharmacologist Dr. Timothy Wilens tells his young patients at Massachusetts General Hospital in Boston, "I've never seen a stimulant do somebody's homework for them."

If your teen is still insistent on discontinuing his medication for an ADHD disorder, ask the doctor about the possibility of forgoing the drug for several weeks. The youngster who still needs his medicine to help him concentrate will undoubtedly experience a return of his symptoms, at which point he may volunteer to resume treatment.

SPECIAL EDUCATION

Having a learning problem doesn't by itself qualify a student for special-education services. It's the gap between her current school performance and her academic and intellectual potential, as determined by the testing, that decides eligibility. A significant discrepancy between the two would warrant special services. Now the question is, which services?

One of the cornerstones of the Individuals with Disabilities Act is that students with disabilities be educated alongside their nondisabled peers to the maximum extent possible. By that standard, the ideal situation is *inclusion:* being taught in a regular classroom in the regular school building, but with additional services provided as needed. One teen's schedule might include weekly speech therapy and time in a resource room; another might require sessions with a school psychologist.

In general, fewer options exist in junior high and high school than at the elementary-school level, where special education often takes place in separate, self-contained classrooms. As early as kindergarten, a student may spend one or two periods in a regular classroom, with an eye toward full *mainstreaming* before going on to middle school. In U.S. public schools, four in five youngsters with learning disabilities and nearly two in five boys and girls who are mentally retarded are taught in regular classes.

By the time of junior high, only those adolescents who have been diagnosed with severe learning problems are likely to be placed in alternative sites, which typically offer small class sizes and a curriculum that blends both academic and vocational skills. Students with mild or moderate disabilities are almost always mainstreamed. However, they may receive special *accommodations* in

---

TABLE 10.1

Commonly Prescribed Medications for Treating ADHD

CATEGORIES

Psychostimulants

- methylphenidate
- dextroamphetamine
- amphetamine compounds

Used to treat symptoms of attention deficit hyperactivity disorder.

Antidepressants (Selective Serotonin Reuptake Inhibitors, or SSRIs)

- fluoxetine
- citalopram
- sertraline
- fluvoxamine
- paroxetine

Used to treat depression, anxiety and obsessive-compulsive behavior. Not used if only ADHD is present.

Antidepressants (Tricyclics)

- imipramine
- desipramine
- nortriptyline

Improve attention, help control depression, other conditions.

Antihypertensives

- clonidine
- others

Clonidine calms, improves frustration tolerance and reduces aggression.

Consistency Is Key

Accommodations made at school will be more effective if they are duplicated at home.

---

classroom environment or instruction to help them learn, depending on their needs. Below are some examples of special measures that might be implemented in a regular classroom:

• Having the student sit front center, near the teacher's desk and away from windows, doors, air conditioners, radiators and other potential distractions.

• Simplifying instructions and avoiding multiple commands.

• Allowing the student to take exams in a small, quiet room.

• Allowing the student extra time to finish tests and other classroom assignments.

• Reviewing test instructions or homework assignments on the blackboard.

• Allowing a student with an auditory-processing problem to wear earplugs, to block out extraneous noise. Or alternately, having her wear a wireless device that transmits the teacher's voice directly to an earpiece while blocking out ambient noise.

• Ordering a second set of books to keep at home, in the event that a student leaves his books in his locker—a not-uncommon occurrence.

• For dyslexic, dysgraphic students who have difficulty spelling and poor penmanship, grading papers primarily on content rather than on spelling and neatness.

• Allowing students with learning disabilities to use word processors, calculators, audiobooks, tape recorders, spellers and other *assistive technology*.

There Ought to Be a Law? There Is! The Individuals with Disabilities Education Act (IDEA)

Each child in a public school who receives special education and related services must have an individualized education plan (IEP). Whatever special services and classroom accommodations a student is to receive should be entered in his or her IEP. IDEA, originally passed as Public Law 94-142 and updated in 1997 as Public Law 105-17, clearly states that parents are entitled to participate *as equal partners* in developing an effective IEP, which is a binding legal document.

The process goes through the following steps:

Either the school will contact you about the need for an IEP, or you may request a conference at any time. The school district will then notify you of the date, time and location of the meeting. Let the school district know as soon as possible whether you're available that day. If not, the meeting can be rescheduled.

IDEA requires that parents be present, along with the student's teacher, a district specialist or supervisor in special education and other personnel involved in the student's education. In some instances, the student is invited to participate. It is essential that parents attend. Although the plan cannot be put into effect without parents' written consent, failing to appear gives the school district the right to make decisions in their absence. We recommend that parents go together. With such vitally important decisions at stake, the responsibility of advocating for a child shouldn't fall to one parent.

IDEA asserts that all children receive a free, appropriate public education irrespective of the level or severity of their disability. However, appropriate doesn't guarantee optimal. The caliber of programs can vary dramatically from one district to the next. You should know that schools receive funding from the federal or state government for each student who requires special-ed services. Because this is the case, the economic makeup of the community may play a smaller role in determining the quality of a special-ed program than its overriding philosophy toward special education and how much of a priority it is given.

However, the appropriateness of your teenager's IEP is probably going to turn on your role as his advocate.

How to Be an Effective Advocate

1. *Know the law!* You can obtain a copy of the Individuals with Disabilities Education Act from the Government Printing Office.

Since the IDEA was not written with public consumption in mind, it makes for demanding reading. There is a *general information* section on the Web site, which provides helpful information such as an overview of the history of IDEA and frequently asked questions and answers. If you have questions about your educational rights, try contacting the Office of Special Education Programs (OSEP), or your state's director of special education or Parent Training and Information Center (PTIC). Parent centers were established to serve parents of special-needs children. Besides answering questions, they present informative workshops about changes in education laws, how to be an effective advocate and other pertinent topics.

2. *Learn everything you can about your youngster's disability and the services that would benefit her most.* Read the evaluation report, which details your teen's strengths and weaknesses, and their impact on her school performance. If you need help interpreting the results, consult the diagnostician who wrote the report.

3. *Keep impeccable records.* Start a file for any and all written correspondence and phone notes for every related call you make. The Learning Disabilities Association recommends also holding on to samples of homework, tests, quizzes and classwork. Not only will this keep you abreast of your son's or daughter's progress, it may prove useful as documentation later on.

4. *Put away the vinegar and take out the honey.* In advocating for their youngster, parents sometimes mistake hostility for assertiveness. Staking out an adversarial position is rarely productive in any situation. You're more likely to win cooperation by presenting yourself as a parent who is committed to obtaining the best services for her youngster, is well informed, courteous and diplomatic, and who views education as a cooperative effort between school and home. Try to be someone who asks, "What can we do to help our son/daughter improve academically?"

A final word: Anytime someone is helpful, be sure to say the two words that educators don't hear nearly enough: *thank you.*

5. *Don't neglect your own needs.* As rewarding as it is to see your youngster's progress, parenting a child with a learning disorder can be emotionally draining at times. Lonely, too. A physical disability is readily apparent; mothers and fathers of children with learning disorders frequently find themselves having to explain the condition over and over again, or having to defend behavior that others don't understand may be beyond their teenager's control.

We highly recommend joining a parents' support organization. Being able to unload on other mothers and fathers who *understand* may help you to preserve the infinite patience demanded of you. Plus, you'll pick up invaluable recommendations and skills for improving family life.

Constructing the Perfect (or Close to Perfect) IEP

Make certain that the following issues are discussed at the IEP meeting and are ultimately included in the plan:

• A statement of your student's current educational performance, in language arts, communication, social studies, mathematics and other areas.

• A statement of the educational goals for the coming academic year.

The objectives should be clearly defined. Not "Vic will demonstrate improvement in reading," which is subject to interpretation, but "Vic will read at grade nine level."

• A statement of how special education and related services will be provided.

• The starting and termination dates of these services.

• If your student is age sixteen or older, a *transition plan* outlining his progression to college or into the workforce must be included.

• A statement of how the school intends to enable your student to meet these educational objectives and how his performance is to be measured.

• A statement addressing whether or not the previous year's goals were achieved.

Regulation 300.16 of the Individuals with Disabilities Education Act states that students with disabilities have a right to "related services," which consist of "transportation and such developmental, corrective and other support services as are required to assist a child with a disability to benefit from special education." Will your student require any of the following:

• assistive technology?
• speech pathology and audiology?
• occupational therapy?
• physical therapy?
• psychological therapy?
• therapeutic recreation?
• social-skills training?
• school health services?
• counseling with a social worker?
• a specific classroom environment?
• a classroom aide?
• an outside tutor?
• transportation?

If You Are Dissatisfied with the IEP

If you agree with the IEP, it goes into effect for the coming academic year. If you disapprove, *do not sign it.* The law provides parents with several approaches to resolving the stalemate. The first is to request an IEP review. At this point, you might want to consider retaining a volunteer parent advocate or an attorney to accompany you.

A parent advocate is a layperson like yourself who has been trained through his or her state or local Parent Training and Information (PTI) Center to understand and interpret federal and state education laws, as well as local guidelines. Advocates do not take an exam, but the staff at the center will be able to recommend someone capable, either to counsel you over the phone or to attend the IEP meeting with you. (You can also take this seminar yourself, incidentally.) Generally, advocates do not charge a fee.

The PTI can also refer you to attorneys who specialize in special-education issues. Granted, no parent welcomes the added expense, but your willingness to retain a lawyer sends a message that will be heard loud and clear. More often than not, conflicts are settled then and there and don't have to be taken to the next step in the complaint process: a legal hearing presided over by an impartial hearing officer. However, if it does progress that far and the officer rules in your favor, the district is required to reimburse you for your legal fees.

What Will the Future Hold?

For the parents of a youngster with a learning problem, the adolescent years can awaken anxieties and fears as they contemplate his future. Will he be able to go to college or hold a job?

In most instances, the answer is yes. There will be challenges ahead, for everyone, but doesn't that describe all families? As teenagers who have learning problems mature and their adaptive skills develop, they often find their niche socially and professionally. For example, a person with attention deficit hyperactivity disorder may flourish in many fields. So parents have legitimate cause for optimism.

Whichever direction your youngster takes following high school, she will enjoy advantages and opportunities that did not exist for previous generations of people with learning problems. Under the Individuals with Disabilities Education Act, the high-school transition-planning team (typically the same individuals involved in formulating IEPs) begins working with youngsters to help them assess their strengths, needs and interests, and match them with a college or occupation.

DIRECTION: EMPLOYMENT

The Americans with Disabilities Act protects men and women who are mentally retarded and those with specific learning problems against discrimination in the workplace. The law, enacted in 1990, applies to employers of fifteen workers or more. Its goal is to level the playing field for people with special needs—not by lowering standards, as detractors claimed at the time, but by modifying the work environment or restructuring the job description so that *qualified* applicants or employees with a disability have the same rights and privileges in employment as the nondisabled.

The term for this is *reasonable accommodation.* For the employer of an office worker with mild dyslexia who additionally suffers from a mild hearing impairment, "reasonable accommodation" might consist of nothing more than installing a flashing light on the telephone, furnishing her with a spell checker and seeing to it that instructions are conveyed through visual cues as well as verbally.

> ### *Pediatrician's Perspective*
>
> DR. MARK WOLRAICH: *"There are some aspects of having attention deficit hyperactivity disorder that can actually work to people's benefits. They can be creative and have lots of energy. To give you an example, the father of one of my patients was an airline pilot, also with ADHD. He said that it's an asset for him professionally because if anything happens in the cockpit, he notices it right away, being easily distractable."*

If your teenager believes that he's been denied employment or unjustly fired due to a learning problem, he can send a complaint to the federal *Equal Employment Opportunity Commission (EEOC)*. Call 800-669-3362 for information on how to file a claim. Another agency that can help redress job discrimination is the *local human rights commission;* consult the "Government Listings" section of the White Pages for the telephone number.

DIRECTION: COLLEGE

Hundreds of colleges now offer many of the same services and accommodations found in high-school special-ed programs: tutorial services, extended time for taking exams, note-taking services, reduced course loads, assistive technology and more. When it's time to begin researching postsecondary schools, purchase or borrow copies of the *K&W Guide to Colleges for the Learning Disabled,* by Marybeth Kravets, M.A., and Imy F. Wax, M.S.

(Princeton Review/Random House), and *Peterson's Colleges with Programs for Students with Learning Disabilities or Attention Deficit Disorders,* by Charles T. Mangrum, Stephen S. Strichart and Jon Latimer (Peterson's Guides). Both books list each school's learning-disability services, entrance requirements and much more.

11

TUNED-IN TEENS:

TV, Movies, the Internet, Video Games, Radio, Rock and Rap

From the late 1940s through the mid-1960s, one American household after another was welcoming a new arrival, and not just as a result of the postwar baby boom.

This boxy, rabbit-eared newcomer immediately was insinuated into family life like an out-of-town guest who wouldn't leave. Space was cleared in the den or living room. Before long, Mom, Dad and the kids were spending more and more time there, because television was a gifted storyteller and a constant companion.

All these years later, television is still here. It's everywhere. In 1946 there were only six thousand sets in the entire country. Within five years that figure had swelled to twelve million. By the mid-1960s, 93 percent of U.S. homes had at least one TV. Today there are more households with televisions than there are with telephones or indoor plumbing.

The box is a lot wider in the middle than it used to be and requires an infusion of cable channels to sustain interest. Three in five households have it hooked up to a cable or satellite service. Some have it wired into its most recent rival, the home computer. While it can still spin an engrossing yarn, it's acquired a caustic edge and tends to shout a lot. In its younger days, it kept its jokes clean and shied away from controversy, but nowadays its monologues are full of foul language and sophomoric sexual innuendos.

Even back when TVs were being adopted by the millions, critics raised concerns about the medium's effect on children. Now that television seems bent on pushing the boundaries, more and more parents are wishing that their teenagers didn't spend so much time in its company. We readily acknowledge the influence wielded by a teenager's peers. Television constitutes a super peer, with the

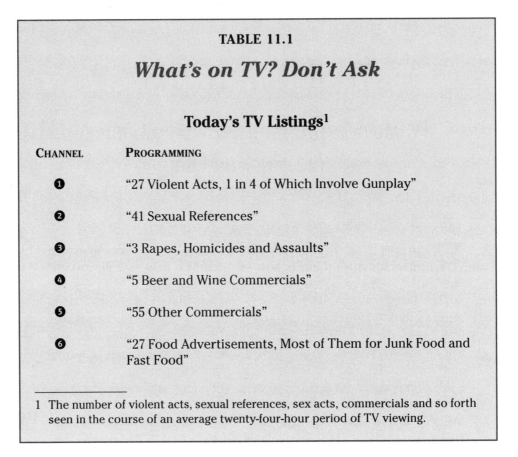

TABLE 11.1

What's on TV? Don't Ask

Today's TV Listings[1]

CHANNEL	PROGRAMMING
❶	"27 Violent Acts, 1 in 4 of Which Involve Gunplay"
❷	"41 Sexual References"
❸	"3 Rapes, Homicides and Assaults"
❹	"5 Beer and Wine Commercials"
❺	"55 Other Commercials"
❻	"27 Food Advertisements, Most of Them for Junk Food and Fast Food"

1 The number of violent acts, sexual references, sex acts, commercials and so forth seen in the course of an average twenty-four-hour period of TV viewing.

power to tell our kids what's cool, what's sexy, what's acceptable behavior and what to buy.

THE MEDIA AND ITS EFFECT ON OUR TEENAGERS

Television: Stranger in the House

In 1961, at the height of what is referred to as television's "golden age," Newton Minow, chairman of the Federal Communications Commission (FCC), declared the medium "a vast wasteland." With the explosion of cable companies and satellite services, television has become a vast*er* wasteland. Hundreds of channels compete for a narrow share of an increasingly fragmented audience and the advertisers' dollars that follow. To lure viewers, many feature heavy helpings of sex, violence and language far raunchier than the shows you might remember from your youth. For instance, the programs that fill today's "family hour" (8 P.M. to 9 P.M.) contain four times as many sexual incidents than were seen during the same time slot in 1976.

When it comes to teen violence, smoking and drug use, however, there is sufficient research to establish that TV influences youthful behavior. Since 1955, more than one thousand studies have substantiated that for some adolescents, frequent exposure to television violence contributes to overly aggressive behavior.

Many other factors, such as violence in the home, are accountable too, but experts estimate that TV's impact, on average, ranges from 5 to 15 percent, which is significant. One study, conducted by psychologists Leonard Eron and L. Rowell Huesmann, followed males from age eight to age thirty. The third-graders who immersed themselves in programs depicting violence were more likely to grow up to be aggressive teenagers than were the participants who did not watch excessive amounts of TV violence. As adults, they were more likely to have criminal records.

Another study by Dr. Huesmann disproved the assumption that TV violence had a less-pronounced effect on girls. In the late 1970s, he and his team of researchers interviewed nearly four hundred girls in grades one through five about their viewing habits. About fifteen years later, they checked in on their

Mom Was Right: Too Much TV Is Bad for You

Excessive television viewing has been implicated as one possible cause of teenage obesity and as an obstacle to academic success. Numerous studies have documented that youngsters who watch more than one to two hours a day see their schoolwork suffer, especially their reading ability. The more hours they waste in front of the tube, the poorer their reading skills.

The association between television viewing and weight gain is twofold. Besides the fact that TV takes time away from physical activity, what is it that couch potatoes like to do while staring at the screen? Snack. And the string of commercials for this sugary cereal and those fat-laden chips are more likely to send them scurrying to the kitchen in search of something other than a carrot stick, setting the pattern for an unhealthy, sedentary lifestyle.

subjects, who by then were in their twenties. Three in five of those who had professed to be avid fans of such combative TV heroines as *Charlie's Angels* and *Wonder Woman* (at the time, relatively novel role models for women) were involved in a higher-than-average incidence of violent confrontations, including shoving matches, chokings and knifings compared to the women who'd watched few or none of these shows during grade school.

Besides glamorizing and normalizing aggression, TV violence numbs youngsters to the horror of violence. The 1990s saw the proliferation of so-called reality-based "shockumentaries," which treat viewers to full half-hours of nothing but horrific car wrecks, police shoot-outs and rampaging animals. Imagine: Now you can rubberneck from the comfort of your living-room sofa. These programs, shot on videotape, may have a greater impact than most because of the audience's belief that the on-screen action is real and unpredictable.

WHAT YOU CAN DO

Limit TV time. Restrict TV viewing to the recommended one to two hours of quality programming a day—for everyone in the family over two years of age—and you'll all discover more constructive ways to fill the time, separately and together. Some examples include reading, exercising, taking part in outdoor activities and talking more to one another, the most valuable family activity.

Expect to encounter resistance at first. After all, change is never easy. If yours is a household where the TV regularly blares for five, six or seven hours a day, wean the family gradually. Try cutting down by an hour a week or go cold turkey. The two-hour maximum includes time spent in front of *any* screen, including the computer and video games.

Make TV viewing an active choice, as if you were picking a movie from the newspaper. "How about if we watch _____ at seven-thirty?"

Hide the remote! Eliminate channel surfing, which encourages passive viewing. When family members have to get up to change the channel, they may be more selective about the programs they watch. If nothing else, at least they'll be getting *some* exercise.

When the show you wanted to watch is over, turn off the set. Also, if the program you choose isn't compelling enough to watch actively, it's not worth keeping on as background noise.

Make a household rule: no TV in your youngster's bedroom. Although adolescents deserve their privacy, they hardly need another reason to isolate themselves from the rest of the family. Children should watch their favorite shows in a central area of the home. Even if you're not sitting down with them,

Too Much TV Spells Trouble

- Between viewing TV, playing video games and watching videocassettes, some teenagers spend thirty-five to fifty-five hours per week in front of the tube; that's more time than any other activity except for sleeping.
- The average adolescent watches approximately twenty-three hours of television per week.
- The problem of excessive TV viewing is usually at its worst during early adolescence. One in eight thirteen-year-olds watches six or more hours of TV per day. By age seventeen, only one in fourteen boys and girls watches that much television.
- In one study, students reported spending four times as many hours each week watching television as doing homework.
- More than half of all fifteen- and sixteen-year-olds have seen most of the popular R-rated films.
- The average teenager spends nearly two hours on-line per day.
- With so many choices of media, why pick just one? We're referring to the youngster who watches TV with the volume off while chatting on-line *and* listening to music over headphones, like a multimedia one-man band.

this allows for conversation when you're passing through *and* enables you to keep closer tabs on what they're watching.

Whenever possible, videotape programs and watch them later. Fast-forwarding through commercials will shave ten minutes off every hour of TV viewing, not to mention help your youngster hold on to her allowance longer. (When watching TV in "real time," mute the sound during the breaks.) Taping shows ahead of time also allows you to hit the PAUSE button when you want to make a point or have a family discussion about something you've just seen on-screen.

Discourage repeated viewings of the same video. The graphic language, violence and sexual content of movies rated PG-13 and R can have a cumulative effect on a child if they're watched over and over again.

Harness the power of television in a positive way. For all its flaws, TV can be a valuable tool for learning and expanding one's awareness of the world.

Here's what you can do to help your teenager get the most enjoyment out of the experience:

- Peruse the TV listings for programs, specials, documentaries and other films that explore areas of interest to him.
- Use events in the news and subjects of fictitious programs as spring-boards for discussion.
- Encourage your youngster to broaden her horizons by watching programs that transport her to other times and places, or that expose her to different perspectives or philosophies.

Make use of ratings systems to know whether or not a program or movie is appropriate for your child. The National Association of Broadcasters (NAB), the National Cable Television Association (NCTA) and the Motion Picture Association of America (MPAA) jointly developed the "TV Parental Guidelines," similar to the movie-rating system adopted by the MPAA in 1966.

Did You Know?

- Most graphic violence is seen on cable TV.
- Children with access to cable TV or a videocassette recorder have seen more R-rated films than their peers whose families do not have cable or a VCR.

Talk back to your TV! Parents are rightfully perturbed about the seemingly endless stream of violence and sex in television programs and films, including those aimed at young people. We should be equally concerned about what they *don't* show: namely, the real-life consequences of such actions. For example, 75 percent of the violent scenes on TV fail to show the perpetrator expressing remorse, or being criticized or penalized for his actions. Similarly, a study from the Henry J. Kaiser Family Foundation found that over a one-week period, roughly 90 percent of the television programs containing sex scenes did not include a single reference to the risk of pregnancy or acquiring a sexually transmitted disease from unprotected sex.

What's Wrong with This Picture?
Points to Make to Your Teenager

VIOLENCE IN THE MEDIA

- "Did you ever notice how on TV and in the movies, the 'good guys' are often shown committing acts of violence? By making these characters attractive and likable, don't you think that glamorizes violence?"

- *On television, two in five violent incidents are instigated by characters with positive qualities that make them appealing role models.*

- "In real life, victims of violence may be affected physically and emotionally for years. But in the movies and on television, you rarely if ever see the aftermath of violence."

Did You Know?

Even in the era of AIDS, casual sex is more the rule than the exception on television. According to "Sex on TV: Content and Context," a 1999 study from the Kaiser Family Foundation, only about half the scenes depicting or implying intercourse are between partners in a romantic relationship.

- *Only about one in eight violent TV programs depict the long-term suffering caused by violence.*

SEX IN THE MEDIA

- "Don't you think it's hypocritical that more than half the programs on television contain sex scenes or references to sex, yet the major networks generally refuse to air commercials for condoms and other birth-control products?"

- *Of the various types of TV programs, soap operas are the worst offenders. More than eight in ten contain steamy scenes.*

BODY IMAGE IN THE MEDIA

- "It's a shame that so many kids, especially girls, are starving themselves to be thin based on the idealized images of women's bodies they see in the media. Nearly half the women on television are thin or very thin. In reality, the average woman wears a size fourteen dress, and more than one-third of all adult women are overweight—partly because they probably watch too much TV!"

Did You Know?

The media promotes different standards of attractiveness for men and women. Another study by the Kaiser Family Foundation analyzed how women were portrayed in six media: television and TV commercials, film, teen magazines and magazine ads, and music videos. If you combine the figures for each, about one in three of the female performers or models is thin or very thin, as opposed to just one in twelve of their male counterparts.

- *A 1996 study reported that the more teenagers watched soap operas, movies and music videos, the more dissatisfied they were with their bodies and the more they wanted to be thin.*

Did You Know?

To watch most media, you'd hardly know the women's liberation movement ever happened. Teenage girls are stereotypically portrayed as boy-obsessed shopaholics. Seldom do you see them discussing their academic interests or career goals. In films, for example, about twice as many of the male characters are shown on the job as are the female characters. Yet in 1997 sixty-three million women were employed, compared to seventy-three million men. That gap is expected to narrow further during the first decade of the twenty-first century.

Another study, from the Harvard Eating Disorders Center, demonstrated that television's influence apparently transcends cultures. In 1995, TV came to the Fiji Islands, where heaviness has traditionally been accepted as normal and healthy. In fact, among the Fijian people, conspicuous weight loss is regarded as a worrisome sign of illness.

At the time of television's arrival, only 3 percent of girls in Fiji were bulimic (vomiting after meals as a way to control their weight). But after three years of a steady diet of programs from the United States, Australia and England, there were five times as many bulimics. The girls were trying to emulate Western culture's standards of beauty—or should we say false standards of beauty?

MALE-FEMALE STEREOTYPES IN THE MEDIA

- "Why is it that so much emphasis is placed on women's physical appearance? In the movies, television and TV commercials, girls' and women's looks are commented on two to three times more frequently than the male characters' appearance. Does that seem fair to you? Imagine if the roles were reversed!"

- *The facts, from the Kaiser Family Foundation study "A Content Analysis: Reflections of Girls in the Media," are these:*

1. *Fifty-six percent of TV commercials directed at teenage girls use promises of enhanced beauty to sell the product; only 3 percent of commercials aimed at teenage boys employ a similar strategy.*
2. *Female actresses are far more likely than male actors to be shown clad only in their underwear: on TV, by a ratio of three to one, and in the movies, by a ratio of nearly four to one.*

RACIAL AND ETHNIC STEREOTYPES IN THE MEDIA

- "Negative racial or ethnic stereotypes in the media are damaging on two levels. Not only can they prejudice other people's perceptions about a particular group, but eventually the group being stereotyped may come to adopt the attitudes and behaviors that have been attributed to it."

- "The media are more sensitive to avoiding insulting portrayals of minority groups than they used to be. But minorities remain sorely underrepresented on prime-time TV. And why is it that the criminals on so many police dramas are predominantly from minority groups?"

Parents who belong to a minority group will want to counter unflattering depictions in the media. They should seek out books and films that call attention to the many accomplishments of their race or ethnic group. For instance, African American parents might encourage their teens to read about important figures such as Supreme Court Justice Thurgood Marshall, Baseball Hall of Famer Jackie Robinson, civil rights leaders Dr. Martin Luther King and Malcolm X, jazz legend Miles Davis—the list goes on and on.

All youngsters could benefit from learning about admirable role models from other races and ethnic backgrounds. An appreciation of how it would feel to be the object of a stereotype is also important. Here are two exercises parents can practice with their adolescents:

> ### *Did You Know?*
>
> One famous study from the 1950s demonstrated how victims of negative stereotypes can come to internalize the stereotype themselves. A group of black children was shown a pair of dolls, identical in all respects except skin color. When asked which doll was "pretty," "clean," "nice" and "smart," most of the children pointed to the white doll. Negative characteristics—"ugly," "dumb," "dirty," "evil"—were associated almost exclusively with the dark-skinned doll.

1. Have your child compare the images of race/ethnicity/physical or mental handicaps/old age he sees on TV with people he knows in real life. How accurate or inaccurate is that image?
2. Let's say your teen is Caucasian. You're watching a crime drama on which the majority of the muggers, drug dealers and so on are played by African American actors, while most of the victims are white. Ask her how she would feel if the roles were reversed. "This show makes it look like all white people are violent criminals!" Unfair, isn't it? Now imagine being barraged with these and other unfavorable images on a regular basis.

TOBACCO, ALCOHOL AND ILLICIT DRUGS IN THE MEDIA

• "The tobacco and alcohol companies insist that they're not trying to target minors with their advertisements. But several ad campaigns have clearly been directed at children. Even though you cannot legally smoke or drink, they're hoping to plant the seeds for when you become an adult.

"The companies *know* that their ads reach young people. Listen to this: The brands of cigarettes that are most popular with teens just happen to be the brands that advertise most heavily in magazines read by teenagers. And many sixteen-year-olds list advertisements for alcohol among their favorite commercials."

• "Think about the impressions that tobacco and alcohol advertisements try to convey about smoking and drinking. How truthful are they? What *don't* they tell you about the products?"

Movies: More of the Same—And Then Some

Scenes of sex, violence and drug use in motion pictures are magnified many times over what is shown on television, and not just because the silver screen dwarfs the small screen in size. The depictions are considerably more graphic, and if it's quantity you're after, grab some popcorn and take your seat. It's *show time!*

The film genres most popular with young people—horror flicks, action/ adventure, sci-fi and suspense thrillers—routinely feature so much bloodshed, you need a calculator to tally up the carnage. The average science-fiction film contains fifty-five killings; horror films, thirty-seven; action/ adventure, thirty-six; and suspense thrillers, thirty-two.[2]

The movies also surpass all other media when it comes to portrayals of substance use. A study by Dr. George Gerbner, a professor of communications at Pennsylvania's Temple University, compared TV programs, music videos and the twenty top-grossing U.S. pictures in 1994 and 1995. The forty films averaged 6.3 scenes of tobacco, alcohol and illicit drug use per hour; music videos on MTV, 5.6; music videos on BET, 4.7; prime-time dramatic shows, 4.4; and daytime serials, 2.5.

---

2 Based on 107 sci-fi films from 1996 to 1999, according to SCMS (Some Career Movie Statistics), a Web site that ranks films according to their body counts. As for the other three categories: horror films, 147 movies from 1996 to 1999; action/adventure films, 102 movies from 1996 to 1999; and suspense thrillers, 66 movies from 1996 to 1999.

As they do with television, parents need to make use of the ratings system devised by the Motion Picture Association of America. Read movie reviews too. Many newspapers and magazines now include information specifically for moms and dads who insist on knowing the content of a film before they give their teenager permission to go to the movies or rent a videocassette for home viewing.

The Internet: Surf's Up

The *Internet*'s rising wave of popularity has attracted millions of young people eager to get out their boards (keyboards, that is) and surf the Net. In 1996, one in six adolescents had access to cyberspace; in 1998, one in three. In 2002, three in four U.S. teenagers were on-line, a higher proportion than any other age group. Already, more than four in five college freshmen use the Internet for research or homework.

Did You Know?

- Hollywood apparently longs for a return to the days when the stars of the big screen couldn't seem to utter a line of dialogue without first taking a seductive drag on a cigarette and letting the smoke hang in the air. Since the 1964 Surgeon General's report that linked smoking to several types of cancer, Americans have cut their tobacco use by nearly half. Yet today's films continue to show actors and actresses with cigarettes in hand, as if they'd been glued there. According to one study, lead movie characters are 65 percent more likely to smoke than the folks sitting in the audience.
- Teenage smokers are influenced by cigarette advertising twice as much as by peer pressure to smoke.
- Music videos show performers singing about or using alcohol every fifteen minutes; and tobacco, every thirty minutes.

TEEN TIP:

If you walk in on your youngster and find him sitting in front of a blank screen, there's a chance that he was somewhere he shouldn't be on the Net and hurriedly switched off the screen or hit the computer's RESET button when he heard your footsteps.

SPIDER'S WEB: HELPING TEENS STAY OUT OF
TROUBLE ON THE INTERNET

Whether you are computer literate or a certified technophobe who's never gotten the hang of an Etch-A-Sketch, parental involvement and guidance are critical in ensuring that a youngster's experience in cyberspace is safe, productive and fun.

WHAT YOU CAN DO

Keep the computer in a central location of the home. You'll be better able to monitor your child's on-line activities this way than if he's holed up in his room with the door shut. The fear of being discovered may also deter him from trespassing into regions of the Net that you've declared off-limits.

Set limits on the amount of time your child is allowed on-line per day. Adolescents and adults alike can quickly become addicted to the Internet. In either case, this is not healthy, but with teens, the time spent in isolation would be better invested in developing their social skills or engaging in physical activity.

Specify which types of sites your teen may visit and those that are prohibited.

Review the Internet safety guidelines with your teen, then post them near the computer.

Install a Web-filtering program. Parental-control tools are programmed to scan and block addresses containing sexually explicit, obscene, hateful or violent content, as well as sites and features deemed inappropriate for children: unsupervised chat rooms and newsgroups, private messages, Web-page advertisements and so forth.

Most computer stores carry Web-filtering software programs. Popular brands include Surf Watch, Cyber Patrol, Cybersitter, NetGuardian, Net Nanny and Net Shepherd. In addition, Internet providers and commercial services like America Online usually offer their own control features (frequently for free), as do certain Web browsers.

However, with tens of thousands of adult sites and more than forty million sites in all, some unwanted material inevitably slips through. In the Times Square of cyberspace, hundreds of new porn peddlers open shop every week, while existing adult-oriented sites change their addresses periodically in order to outsmart the Web filters. According to a *Consumer Reports* review of fil-

Teens, the Internet and the Law

The *Protection of Children From Predators Act of 1998* made it a federal crime to use the Internet ("any means of interstate or foreign commerce") to attempt to transfer obscene material to a child under age sixteen; or to transmit the name, address, telephone number, social security number or e-mail address of someone under age sixteen "with the intent to entice, encourage, offer, or solicit any person to engage in illegal sexual activity." The bill also toughened the penalties for attempting to use the Internet to coerce or entice minors to engage in criminal sexual activity. In addition, several states have enacted their own laws prohibiting the use of a computer for luring minors into committing unlawful sex acts.

tering devices, the highest-rated product weeded out only about two-thirds of adult sites, while several blocked *none.*

What's more, "teenagers can easily learn to overcome the blocking devices," says Dr. Marjorie Hogan, former chair of the American Academy of Pediatrics' Committee on Communications. The filters should be regarded as helpful allies in protecting children from inappropriate material, but they in no way absolve us of our responsibility to keep tabs on where our youngsters venture on-line.

Instruct your teenager on what to do if she is ever harassed or threatened via e-mail or instant messages while on-line. The most effective response is for her to ignore the person, write down identifying information such as a screen name or e-mail address, exit the Net and tell you or another trusted adult what happened.

Next, report the incident immediately to your service provider. Most treat complaints of on-line harassment seriously, especially when the victim is underage. Offenders may have their Internet accounts canceled, and if there is the possibility that a crime was committed, parents can usually depend on the provider to cooperate with authorities.

Make a second call to the CyberTipline of the National Center for Missing and Exploited Children, which forwards all reports to the appropriate law-enforcement agencies. The NCMEC works in conjunction with the Federal Bureau of Investigation (FBI), the U.S. Customs Services and the U.S. Postal

Inspection Service. While its primary purpose is to assist in locating and recovering missing children, the nonprofit organization also handles leads reporting the on-line enticement of children for sexual acts.

Video Games: Violence Taken to Extremes

By today's standards, the first video game, the sedate Pong, introduced in the early 1970s, seems like a quaint round of lawn bowling played on the old village green. Two opponents each used a control unit to bump a small white ball back and forth onscreen, the object being to get it past the other player. With each hit, the television emitted a meek electronic *beep!* that made any room sound like an intensive-care unit.

Now games incorporate ultrarealistic graphics and sound effects that deposit the player in the middle of the fast-paced action. If only the content would advance as impressively as the technology. While there are many fun, challenging titles for youngsters, four in five of the most popular video games feature violence or aggression. Often it is directed against women. In one game, for example, players earn points for inducing a stripper to take off her clothes. Then they win bonus points for *killing* her. Thanks to the sophisticated new technology, the scenes of blood and gore are often chillingly lifelike.

In the late 1990s, a rash of shootings at schools around the country focused national attention on excessively violent video/computer games and the possible impact they might have had on some of the teenagers who brought guns to school and opened fire. Because the medium is still relatively new, the body of research is small. But early claims that video-game violence actually defuses destructive impulses by providing an outlet for aggression have been dismissed. Based on the studies conducted to date, it appears that young children and preteens act more aggressively immediately after playing or merely watching video games with violent themes. In fact, many mental-health experts believe that because the interactive games place weapons in the player's hands, they contribute more to aggressive behavior than the passive act of watching similar fare on TV.

The effect on adolescents is less clear. Youngsters who play these games will tell you that we adults are getting all worked up over nothing, as usual. They insist that they can distinguish fantasy from reality, and that shooting imaginary weapons at imaginary targets isn't going to trigger deadly rampages in real life. The video-game industry, which generates more than $6 billion in sales annually, trots out this argument whenever the issue of excessively violent themes and imagery is raised. But if violent TV and movies can desensitize teens, isn't it logical to presume that interactive videos can, too?

WHAT YOU CAN DO

Familiarize yourself with a video game's content before allowing a teen to buy it or download it from the Internet. According to the National Institute on Media and the Family, most mothers and fathers don't realize how offensive some of these titles are. In a survey of five hundred parents, fewer than one in twenty had ever heard of one popular game, much less knew its content, compared to four in five junior-high-school students.

With thousands of videos on the market, it is impossible to know the content of each one. Fortunately, three major ratings systems have been devised to help parents and youngsters make wise choices. After Congress threatened to regulate the industry, most major game manufacturers voluntarily began labeling their products through the independent Entertainment Software Rating Board.

Limit game-playing time to a maximum of one hour per day.

Encourage your teenager to play games that involve two players. The trend in video games has been toward games that are played alone. A typical scenario pits our young hero against a horde of hostile foes. Too much time spent absorbed in violent fantasy may foster social isolation.

Ask your store to enforce policies prohibiting the sale or rental of "T" (teen) or "M" (mature) videos to underage children. A National Institute on Media and the Family survey of video stores across the country found that more than four in five sold or rented "T" videos to children younger than age thirteen, and "M" videos to those not yet seventeen.

Video games that are at odds with your family's values should not be allowed in your home. Explain to your youngster that she cannot play a new video game until you've had an opportunity to look the product over and determine whether or not it is suitable. If you decide no, it goes back in the rack

---

TEEN TIP:

The best way to know the contents of a video game is to rent it and play it with your youngster before you commit to buying it.

or back to the store. It is parents' prerogative and responsibility to impose their personal rating system, no matter what games are played at friends' or neighbors' houses.

The World According to Teen Magazines

"Getting Him to Notice You!"
"Shedding Those X-tra Pounds!"
"Shedding Those X-tra Pounds So He'll Notice You!"

"Teen magazines" is for all intents a synonym for "girls' magazines." Boys really don't have anything comparable to these publications, which have changed surprisingly little in the years since your or your sister's subscription expired. On the whole, they still convey a two-dimensional impression of adolescent girls as boy-crazy clotheshorses who are obsessed with how they look. A study by the Kaiser Family Foundation analyzed the top-four teen magazines. Forty-four percent of the articles focused on dating or sex, and 37 percent on appearance. A mere 12 percent of the articles were reserved for advice about school or careers.

The accent on physical appearance spills over into the advertisements, four in five of which are for clothing and beauty products. Models predominate the ads and the photos used to accompany the articles. With rare exception, the faces are strikingly pretty and the bodies, well toned. You've probably suspected that repeated exposure to such images would influence

---

A Well-Rounded Girl?

Sample Articles from Popular Teen Magazines

- "The Ultimate Get-a-Guy Guide"
- "Get a Bikini Butt"
- "Six Star Couples' Secrets for Everlasting Love"
- "Dude Snagging Do's and Don'ts"
- "Love Clues: Fifteen Ways to Make Him Want You Bad"
- "Get Gorgeous: A Survey of One Thousand Teens Reveals Seventy-five Favorite Beauty Products"
- "Find True Love: Twenty-four Crucial Clues to Snag Your Crush"

young female readers, but you may be surprised just how strong an impression they make.

Teens also read fashion-oriented magazines for adults, which present a similar mix of clothing ads and articles about relationships and sex. A study published in a 1999 edition of *Pediatrics,* the official journal of the American Academy of Pediatrics, distributed a questionnaire to approximately 550 girls in grades five through twelve. Nearly half the participants reported that magazine pictures convinced them they needed to lose weight. Disturbingly, while 66 percent overall said that they wanted to shed some pounds, more than half of those girls were not overweight at all. According to the researchers, from medical institutions in Massachusetts and Virginia, girls who frequently read fashion magazines were two to three times more likely to diet than occasional readers.

WHAT YOU CAN DO

Flip through each month's issue and use the articles as catalysts for discussion. You may gain some insights into your teenager's views and values.

Example: "I picked up your latest issue of *Go Girl!* magazine and started reading the article about that poor boy who was nearly killed in a college-fraternity hazing ritual. I couldn't put it down. When I went to college, fraternities and sororities were considered *un*cool. Now they're back in a big way. Would you ever consider joining a college sorority? What do you think about these initiation ceremonies where kids are humiliated, or beaten, or made to drink until they pass out?"

Counter the magazines' undue emphasis on beauty and celebrity by handing your daughter interesting articles and books about women who are famous for accomplishments other than being a fashion model or an MTV veejay. (See "Encouraging Self-Acceptance" in chapter 3, "Your Teenager's Physical Development.")

From the Sound of Young America to the Sound of Corporate America

Rock and roll, once regarded with suspicion as a musical manifesto for social revolution, ingratiated itself into the cultural mainstream long ago. Today, buzzsaw guitars and cannoning drums provide the sonic backdrop for TV commercials pitching everything from professional sports to sports cars, while some of the most meaningful songs from rock's past have been processed into Muzak or used to hawk beer, burgers and countless other products.

Just as television and film have repeatedly knocked down the fences of good taste, the relatively small percentage of music lyrics that contain objectionable language are far more graphic than years ago when network censors wouldn't let the Rolling Stones perform their song "Let's Spend the Night Together" on TV's *The Ed Sullivan Show* unless they sang, "Let's spend *some time* together." Research has not found that listening to music filled with violent imagery, sexually explicit lyrics or pro-drug sentiments adversely affects adolescent behavior.

Defenders of the music note that the words aren't intended to stand alone as if they were poetry. While adults wring their hands over obscene lyrics, the youngsters who buy the CDs are largely oblivious. Only about one in three even know the words to their favorite songs. What grabs them isn't any one element, it's the recording as a whole—the way the melody, the rhythm, the emotion in the singer's voice, and the lyrics combine to create a certain sound, feel, spirit.

"Even if they know the lyrics, they may not have the knowledge or experience to comprehend their meaning," notes Dr. Victor Strasburger. For that reason, he points out, it may be counterproductive to print the song lyrics on the insert to every CD, as was proposed at the 1985 U.S. Senate hearings on rock music.

The hearings, which pressured the Recording Industry Association of America (RIAA) into placing "Parental Advisory Explicit Content" labels on all recordings that contain strong language or depictions of violence, sex or substance abuse, created the impression that rock music was awash in filth. But according to the RIAA, only about one in two hundred CDs meet the criteria to warrant the black-and-white warning labels. Many of those belong to the genre known as "gangsta rap," which is notorious for themes of violence, misogyny and glorification of drug use.

ENTER THE MUSIC VIDEO

Adding sound to motion pictures, beginning with *The Jazz Singer* in 1927, elevated the medium creatively. Few would probably make the same claim about music videos, which came to the fore as a music marketing tool with the birth of MTV in 1981.

Initially, the clips simply trained cameras on the performers as they lip-synched and mimed their way through their latest single. The pendulum quickly swung to elaborate and costly "concept" videos—minifilms that often have little or nothing to do with the lyrical content of the song. Because the early crop of directors had backgrounds in television and advertising, music videos, too, are marred by excessive violence and portrayals of sex and eroticism. One in four rock-music videos depict weapons being carried,

15 percent contain violent scenes and one in four show tobacco, alcohol or illicit drugs being used.

WHAT YOU CAN DO

Keep your ears open. A teenager's musical tastes can sometimes provide a glimpse into her state of mind. This is hardly an exact science, of course. Sometimes we put on music that reflects our innermost feelings; other times we use it for the express purpose of transforming our mood.

Nevertheless, certain genres, such as heavy metal, hardcore, goth, punk and gangsta rap, do tend to be associated more with rebellious, antisocial behavior, substance abuse, self-harm and thoughts of suicide than jazz, country and show tunes, to cite three examples. That's not to say you won't find model youths slamming into one another in the mosh pit at the foot of the stage, or that every young fan of the latest outwardly wholesome teen idol is chaste and pure. But paying attention to the music a youngster likes may be a way to learn more about the social group he or she belongs to at school. Some cliques come together based on a mutual interest in a particular style of music. The songs become their anthems. Each genre has its own dress code and attitude, which adolescents will adopt as a way of borrowing a self-identity. It's been that way ever since rock and roll came along and gave young people an art form they could call their own, says Dr. Francis Palumbo, a pediatrician from Washington, D.C.

"When I was a teenager in the 1960s," he recalls, "basically there were the kids who listened to folk music and those who listened to rock and roll. And the distinctions between them were very clear." If a child seems depressed and isolated and listens to little else besides music laden with themes of death and despair, "that should send up a red flag that the situation needs to be addressed," he says. The music is symptomatic of the youngster's state of mind, not the other way around.

However, there is no evidence to link teenage suicide and rock lyrics, no matter how bleak and unsettling they may be. According to Dr. Palumbo, "Suicide does not occur in a vacuum. If listening to a song lyric or watching a video can push a child to that point, other events almost certainly led up to it. I don't think that you can hold a recording artist responsible for that kind of action. It's part of the overall picture, but no one factor is going to be singularly responsible for a youngster's suicide."

If your child is listening to music that contains ideas or words that you feel are inappropriate for him or her, "it is always a parent's place to censor it," says Dr. Palumbo. "But do so in a gentle, thoughtful way and do your homework first, so you know what you're objecting to."

Caution children not to listen to music at excessively high volume, especially through earphones or headphones. According to the National Institutes of Health, one in three cases of hearing loss derive at least in part from the noise pollution of daily life, including rock music.

Any loud noise eighty decibels or higher can potentially cause permanent ear damage. The louder the sound, the less time it takes to impair your hearing. A typical rock concert or stereo headset played at maximum volume—about 110 decibels—can damage a youngster's ears in just thirty minutes. (See box on Noises and Decibel Levels in chapter 20, "Common Medical Conditions During the Teen Years," page 495.

PART III

THE HURDLES OF ADOLESCENCE: SAFEGUARDING YOUR TEENAGER

12

SEXUALITY

It was a decade of unbridled teenage sexual activity, distinguished by the highest rate of adolescent childbearing of the twentieth century. More than half of all girls and boys lost their virginity while still in their teens, and the number of illegitimate babies placed for adoption rose sharply. The decade? The 1950s.

Yes, it was the teens of the 1950s who went wild back in the days of pleated skirts worn below the knee, saddle shoes and blue jeans with cuffs deep enough for storing school supplies—in a time so remote that they didn't even have the birth control pill. Which helps to explain why, in 1957, ninety-six out of every one thousand American girls aged fifteen to nineteen were having babies—nearly double the teen birth rate in 1997.

It's helpful to keep such facts in mind if it seems to you that today's adolescents can't think about anything but sex. You were probably the same way when you were a teenager—consumed by your interest in the opposite sex (or same sex). That's because the desire for companionship, love and, yes, physical intimacy is normal and healthy at this age.

None of which means that you shouldn't be concerned—you should. As adults, we know that a single act of sexually irresponsible behavior can have life-altering consequences: an unintended pregnancy, a sexually transmitted and possibly fatal disease, and let's not forget the pain of a broken heart. How could a child's budding sexuality not be a source of concern for parents?

Some mothers and fathers might disagree, but the aim of educating youngsters about sex is not to suppress their sexuality; adolescence is a time of sexual experimentation. A more realistic expectation is to impress upon boys and girls the many compelling reasons for abstaining from sexual intercourse *at least* until they're responsible enough to protect themselves against pregnancy and disease and emotionally mature enough to handle the new, intense feelings stirred by their first romantic experiences.

In addition, most parents would probably wish that when their sons and daughters do decide to have sex, it's in the context of a loving relationship. Judging by the declining rates of teenage intercourse and teen pregnancies, this is what increasing numbers of young people appear to want for themselves. From 1991 to 1998, the number of births per one thousand girls aged fifteen to nineteen tumbled from sixty-two to fifty-one. Rates of abortions, second births and babies born out of wedlock are also down.

The dramatic increase in the use of contraceptives by teenagers accounts for much of that drop; according to the Centers for Disease Control and Prevention, condom use rose from 11 percent in 1983 to 58 percent in 1999. But also, more adolescents are choosing to wait until adulthood before "going all the way." From 1991 to 1999, the percentage of high-school students who engaged in intercourse fell from 59 to 50 percent. These are all encouraging trends, and they reflect the value of sex education at home and at school. But parents and teachers have to keep driving home the message. The United States still has the highest teenage pregnancy rate among Western nations—twice as high as Canada and England, and nine times as high as Japan and the Netherlands.

TALKING TO YOUR TEENAGER ABOUT SEX

Parents are a teenager's primary source of information and guidance in matters of sex, sexuality, dating and love. It's probably fair to assume that most of us are more comfortable talking about sex than our mothers and fathers were. But there are still plenty of parents who are so uncomfortable that they avoid raising the subject with their children. If you are among them—the following pointers should help to ease your anxiety.

Admit to your youngster that you feel awkward. You could start off by saying, "Talking about sex isn't easy for me. But I love you and think it's important that you hear this information from me." Remember that your teenager probably feels just as embarrassed as you do, and you don't want your discomfort with the subject to convey the impression that lovemaking between two people is somehow "dirty" or "wrong."

If you can't utter words like "penis," "vagina," "erection" and "orgasm" without turning crimson, practice saying them over and over until they come naturally for you. Reminding yourself that these are merely body parts and natural biological functions will also help you to transcend any inhibitions.

When discussing sex with an adolescent, always use adult language, not slang or baby talk. "Penis" may sound clinical, but that's the word.

"Rehearse" beforehand. You say you haven't felt this jittery since the time you portrayed a sturdy oak tree in the second-grade school play? Then recruit your spouse or someone else, and brush up on what you plan to say.

If you don't feel sure of your command of the facts of life, consult a book about teenage sexuality and share it with your youngster. "But buying a book doesn't let parents off the hook," emphasizes Dr. Renée Jenkins of Howard University Hospital in Washington, D.C. "A book is a facilitator for talking to their teenager about sex, not a substitute."

If you absolutely ***cannot bring yourself to talk to your son or daughter about sex,*** consider asking your teen's pediatrician to pinch-hit for you. "I have parents call me all the time and ask me to discuss menstruation or other sexual issues with their teenager when he or she comes in for a checkup," says Dr. Hoyle. Most adolescents feel at ease talking about sex with their trusted doctor.

Some parents justify not educating their children about sex with the rationale that to do so will only encourage them to become sexually active. But the opposite is true, says Dr. Claire Brindis, executive director of the National Adolescent Health Information Center at the University of California at San Francisco. "Research shows that teenagers who come from homes where the parents talked to them about sex tend to delay having sex until later. And once they do have sex, they tend to be more responsible about using contraceptives." Furthermore, the earlier you have this talk with your teenager—or preteen—the better.

Having "The Talk" at age twelve is on the late side. With the arrival of puberty, the hormones that flood a teenager's body and brain stimulate an irresistible curiosity and interest in sexual matters.

According to one study, nine in ten adolescents do not reveal to their parents the full extent of their sexual knowledge or activity.

Incidentally, a curiosity about sex doesn't necessarily indicate

---

Sex Stats

- Average age of first intercourse: sixteen.
- One in twelve youngsters have had sexual intercourse before age thirteen: among African American youth, one in five.
- One in six high-school girls have had four or more sex partners during their lifetime.

Source: Youth Risk Behavior Surveillance, United States, 1999

that a teen is having sex or planning to have it; and conversely, the fact that a youngster does not ask questions shouldn't be taken as "proof" that he is not yet sexually active.

You've Worked Up Your Courage, You're Ready to Have "The Talk." Now What Do You Talk About?

In reality, "The Talk" is an ongoing series of discussions (not lectures) that take place whenever your teenager has a question concerning sex or whenever a "teachable moment" presents itself. Dr. Richard Brookman, chairman of the division of adolescent medicine at the Medical College of Virginia, observes, "A parent can't expect to teach a child about sexuality just once and then go, 'Whew! Thank goodness that's over with!' The message takes a lot of repeating and really should be reinforced at every opportunity." Once the basics have been covered—the names and functions of the male and female reproductive organs, the physical changes that will take place during puberty and the process of human reproduction, from sexual intercourse, to conception, pregnancy and birth—there is still plenty to talk about. Following are some guidelines for what to talk about with your teen and when. But if your son or daughter seems to be maturing early, the timetable may need to be speeded up.

AGES TWELVE TO FOURTEEN
KEY TOPIC FOR EARLY TEENS

MASTURBATION

Masturbation marks a young person's sexual awakening. A boy may experience nocturnal emissions before he learns to masturbate, but "wet dreams," as they're known, occur involuntarily while he is asleep. Masturbation is a conscious act of self-stimulation for the purpose of achieving sexual pleasure.

Centuries-old myths about the allegedly harmful effects of masturbation have long since been discounted. Nevertheless, jokes about it causing everything from insanity to blindness remain a staple of locker-room humor. How do you know if your son has discovered genital self-gratification? Two giveaways are stained pajamas and bedsheets, and holing up in the bathroom with the door locked for unusually long periods of time.

In one study of fifteen- and sixteen-year-olds, three-fourths of the boys and more than half the girls admitted to masturbating. Dr. Mark Scott Smith, a pediatrician from Seattle, reckons that the real figures are substantially higher, particularly for boys. "There's an old joke that 99 percent of teenage boys masturbate and the other 1 percent lie about it," he says. "That's probably closer to the truth."

Nevertheless, youngsters can feel conflicted about the practice. On the one hand, they know that it feels good, but for boys the sight of semen is often unnerving at first, especially early ejaculations, which may be tinged with blood. Children who grow up in religions and/or cultures where masturbation is still regarded as wrong may feel guilty that they enjoy doing it. Parents can spare their child needless anxiety by bringing up the subject of masturbation, but discreetly and indirectly:

"You're at an age where many boys discover that it feels good to rub their penis with their hand or against the sheets while they're lying in bed." (For girls: *". . . to stroke their clitoris with their fingers . . ."* or *"to insert their fingers or an object in their vagina."*)

To avoid embarrassing your teen, feign ignorance of his or her habits:

"I don't know if that's ever happened to you, but you should know that masturbating is normal and nothing to be ashamed of. By the way, not *masturbating is normal too."*

Besides serving as a release for tension, sexual and otherwise, it's through genital self-stimulation that youngsters get in tune with the sexual side of their bodies, by discovering which sensations bring them pleasure. A cause for concern would be if self-gratification became a compulsion or a substitute for forming relationships. Other than that, you can assure your child that any of the allegedly dreadful consequences he or she hears attributed to masturbation are pure bunk.

AGES FIFTEEN AND UP
KEY TOPICS FOR OLDER TEENS

Now the focus of discussions shifts from the mechanics of sex and human reproduction to the social and emotional aspects of sex and human relationships. There are many complex questions your son or daughter will need help in answering, such as:

- "When should I start dating?"
- "When is it okay to kiss a boy [or a girl]?"
- "What qualities should I look for in a boyfriend [or a girlfriend]?"
- "How do you know when you're in love?"
- "How far is too far?"
- "How will I know when I'm ready to have sex?"

The guidance you offer on these kinds of questions should be based on your personal code of ethics, even if your values are considered old-fashioned by today's standards. "Parents can talk about sex without having to modify their views," says Dr. Hoyle. "If, for example, a parent believes that premarital sex is wrong, she should say so, but," he adds, "with the understanding that teenagers will ultimately draw their own conclusions and make their own decisions."

Abstinence until marriage has long been the yardstick for measuring sexual morality. Claims that previous generations adhered to higher standards fail to take into account the fact that people are marrying later in life than at any time in U.S. history. Currently the average first-time bride is twenty-six years old; the groom, twenty-seven. Compare that to the 1950s and the 1960s, when the median age for walking down the aisle was twenty-one and twenty-three; many newlyweds were still in their teens or barely out of them.

If your son or daughter seems to be maturing early, these topics may need to be discussed sooner.

WHEN YOUR TEENAGER STARTS DATING

Dating customs have changed since you were a teenager. The most striking difference is the young age at which children now begin dating: on average, twelve and a half for girls, and thirteen and a half for boys.

However, you might not recognize it as dating per se. The recent trend among early adolescents is for boys and girls to socialize as part of a group. They march off en masse to the mall or to the movies, or join a gang tossing a Frisbee on the beach.

Don't confuse group dating with double-dating or triple-dating. While there may be the occasional romantic twosome among the members, the majority are unattached. If anything, youngsters in the group spend as much time interacting with their same-sex friends as they do with members of the opposite sex.

Dr. Ron Eagar, a pediatrician at Denver Health Medical Center, views group dating as a healthy way for adolescents to ease into the dating pool rather than dive in. "The number-one benefit is safety," says the father of two grown children. Going out in mixed groups also gives boys and girls an opportunity to just enjoy one another's company, without the awkwardness and sexual tension that can intrude upon a one-to-one date.

One-to-One Dating

At what age are children old enough to date "solo"?

Not before they're thirty-five. Preferably forty.

Many of us feel that way when we imagine our son or daughter disappearing into the night arm in arm with a young lady or a young man.

As a general guideline, Dr. Eagar advises not allowing single dating before age sixteen. "There's an enormous difference between a fourteen- or fifteen-year-old and a sixteen- or seventeen-year-old in terms of life experience," he says. You might add or subtract a year depending on how mature and responsible your youngster is. Community standards might be a consideration. Are other parents letting their teens date yet?

Love and Relationships

While parent-teen conversations must encompass the hormones, hydraulics and other biological aspects of love and attraction, equal time should be devoted to thoughtful discussions about love as the most powerful and heartfelt of all human emotions.

Love is a subject of unending fascination for adolescents. Topping their list of questions is, "How do you know when you're in love with somebody?" They are also genuinely curious about their parents' courtship and marriage ("Mom, did you fall in love with Dad at first sight?") and, if applicable, divorce ("Dad, how can two people love each other for years and years, then stop being in love?").

Having an imperfect romantic résumé yourself does not disqualify you from initiating this conversation. You might say, "I haven't always made the wisest decisions when it comes to love, but I've promised myself that the next time I become involved with someone special, I won't settle for anything less than a healthy, honest relationship. When you're older and ready to start dating, I hope that you will do the same. We both deserve the best, right?"

CALL IT PUPPY LOVE, IT'S STILL LOVE

Adults generally take a cynical view of teenage romance, as if it were a chemical imbalance in need of correction. "It's all about sex," they say. "You know what they're like when their hormones start raging." A boy and a girl float down the street holding hands, dizzy in love, and all parents see is testosterone and estrogen out on a date.

Just look at the words used to describe affection between two young people: "infatuation," "crush," "puppy love." If it feels like love to the two puppies, isn't it love? To reiterate a point made earlier, it wasn't all that long ago that many couples got married in their teens.

"Parents should never minimize or ridicule a first love," says Tucson pediatrician Dr. George Comerci. "It is a very important relationship to teenagers, and it's important for another reason, in that it is their first intimate relationship with someone outside their family."

When "going out" evolves into "going steady," it is natural to worry that things are getting too serious too soon. If you see schoolwork start to suffer and friendships fall by the wayside, it is reasonable to restrict the number of times Romeo and Juliet can rendezvous during the school week. High-school romances tend to have limited life spans. Those that endure until graduation day rarely survive the post-high-school years. If one or both young people leave home, the physical distance has a way of opening an emotional distance between them, and eventually the relationship coasts to a halt.

FIRST HEARTBREAK: HELPING YOUR TEENAGER COPE

The breakup of a romance can be painful at any stage of life. Still, when an adult relationship ends badly, at least the wounded party knows from having weathered other disappointments that the all-too-familiar hollow feeling and veil of depression will inevitably lift.

Teenagers haven't yet learned how resilient the heart is. The first time they experience romantic rejection, the sadness can seem bottomless. Parents need to treat a brokenhearted youngster's feelings seriously.

"Breakups are one of the major precipitators of suicidal gestures in young people," says Dr. Eagar. The vast majority of kids, though, will get over their hurt and be fine. Moms and dads can aid the healing process by being generous with their time, patience and hugs. A little extra sensitivity helps, too, for in this situation, knowing what *not* to say is as important as choosing the right words.

Acknowledge your teen's pain but assure her that she will be happy again. "I understand how upset you are, and I know you may feel like your sadness is never going to go away. But it will, and probably sooner than you think."

Do not *use this opportunity to reveal how you never liked the newly insignificant significant other in the first place.* Your son may be venting his rage at the girl who dumped him, but don't be fooled. It will probably be some time before he abandons the hope that she'll realize her mistake and come crawling back. Remember, too, that teen relationships on the wane frequently flicker on again.

Allow your child to feel sad. To tell someone who is upset, "Hey, cheer up! It's not that bad!" (or words to that effect) essentially implies that she does not have a right to her emotions. However, blues that linger for more than a few weeks may warrant professional counseling.

Encourage him to get together with friends—but don't nag. When he's ready to socialize, he'll do so without any prompting.

Share a story from your own adolescence. "My first year in college, I fell madly in love with this girl named Elyse. We spent every moment together. I couldn't imagine ever being with anyone else, and I thought she felt the same way about me.

"One day, out of the blue, she told me that our relationship was getting too serious, and that she wanted to date other people. I was crushed! I moped for *weeks*. I used to spy on her around campus; some nights I'd stand outside her dorm just to see if she walked in the front door with anybody. My friends couldn't stand to be around me, and I don't blame them! I'd get all morose and moan about Elyse, Elyse, Elyse.

"Now I'm thankful that she broke up with me. Because if she hadn't, I'd never have met your mother!"

HANDLING SEXUAL PRESSURE

Abstinence: A Positive Approach

When teaching your child about sexuality, why not accentuate the advantages of delaying sexual intercourse instead of harping on the potentially adverse consequences? It's the same message, only framed in a more positive light. You might begin by acknowledging that physical intimacy between two loving adult partners is beautiful and joyful, while also warning about the perils of experience that comes too early.

"When young people have sex before they're ready, they usually end up regretting it. I'd hate to see that happen to you." Then you can continue with some of the other good reasons that many dating couples offer for their decision to practice abstinence.

Why wait? It's the only fool-proof way to avoid an unplanned pregnancy. If you don't have sexual intercourse, a girl can't get pregnant.

Why wait? It's the best way to avoid contracting a sexually transmitted disease (STD). (See "Sexually Transmitted Diseases" in chapter 20: "Common Medical Conditions During the Teen Years.")

Teens Are More Likely to Have Sex if They . . .

- entered puberty early
- socialize with youngsters who approve of and encourage sexual activity
- place little value on education
- have a poor relationship with their parents, particularly their father
- rarely attend religious instruction or services

Why wait? Because later on, girls who didn't often wish that they had. Researchers in New Zealand interviewed nearly one thousand young people, all in their midtwenties, about their first sexual experiences. On average, the men had become sexually active when they were seventeen; the women, at age sixteen. Looking back, more than half the women admitted that they now wished they'd held onto their virginity longer, a sentiment seconded by 70 percent of the women who had been fifteen or younger the first time they had intercourse.

Helping Teens Resist Sexual Pressure

"The pressure on teenagers to have sex is enormous," says Denver pediatrician Dr. Ron Eagar, adding that kids often feel as if they're caught in a vise. Not only do they have to contend with the direct pressure to "do it" from their date or steady boyfriend/girlfriend, there's the peer pressure applied by friends who want to know (elbow jab, wink wink) "didja do it?" They may also feel the internal pressure to keep pace with their friends, as if competing in a marathon to lose their virginity. One way of helping them resist these pressures is to anticipate them and discuss them.

Let's say that you have a daughter who's just beginning to date. Describe a scenario such as this one:

A sixteen-year-old girl is trying to fend off an overamorous date who's had too much to drink at a party and is clumsily trying to slip his hand under her bra as they kiss in the front seat of his father's car. She likes this boy and has known him for years, but she's uncomfortable with the direction the evening is taking and wants to stop things from going further—yet without hurting his feelings unnecessarily.

Then ask your daughter: *"What could the girl do or say to regain control of the situation? Is she being too timid? Should she be more forceful?"*

Another variation of this exercise is to ask your teenager to picture herself in a given situation and imagine how she might react, as if watching herself in a movie frame by frame. For example: *"If I was invited to a boy's house and discovered after I got there that his parents were out of town, what would I do?"* Athletes and performers often use visualization to help them prepare for upcoming challenges, including those they're encountering for the first time.

Let's encourage youngsters to think ahead, anticipate potential trouble and be alert to warning signs. Perhaps the girl in our example saw her date drink two beers at the party. Though he wasn't staggering around drunk or slurring his words, she should have registered this as a warning that trouble might lie ahead. Then she could have decided not to take any chances and caught a ride home from the party with some other kids, thus avoiding the awkward situation in the car.

TABLE 12.1

Hook, Line and Sinker

Giving Teens the Words for Fending Off Unwanted Sexual Advances

HOOK AND LINE	SINKER
"Aw c'mon, everybody does it!"	"I don't care, I'm not everybody. And besides, not everybody 'does it,' including some of the kids who say they do."
"If you loved me, you'd go to bed with me."	"If *you* loved *me,* you wouldn't pressure me into doing something that I'm not ready to do."
"If you don't have sex with me, I'll break up with you."	"If being your girlfriend means that I have to sleep with you, then I guess I don't want to be your girlfriend."
"Why won't you have sex with me?"	"Because I don't want to." No further explanation needed.
"We had sex before; why are you turning me down now?"	"I'm entitled to change my mind. It's my body and my life, and I want to wait until I'm older before I have sex again."
"Yo, let's do it. You know you want to!"	"No. No. *No!* What part of 'no' don't you understand?"
"Your parents are out all night; let's go back to your house."	Use your ace in the hole: blame your folks. "Go back to my house? We can't. My parents won't let me have boys over when they're not home."

Date Rape

Every girl, whether she's in secondary school, college or on her own, should know how to protect herself against *date rape,* also known as *acquaintance rape.* Although the incidence of sexual assaults against young men is under-reported to police, date rape is overwhelmingly committed by males against females, and so this section is addressed to parents of teenage daughters.

Words Worth Knowing

Rape: the legal term for nonconsensual sexual intercourse, involving the use of force, fear or fraud. ***Statutory rape*** refers to consensual *or* nonconsensual intercourse with a minor. Both acts are sex crimes and are punishable by law.

In a national poll conducted by the Kaiser Permanante health-maintenance organization, one in seven girls aged fourteen to seventeen said that a date had tried to force them to have sex. Two in five reported knowing at least one girl who'd been hit or beaten by her boyfriend. Rape is an act of violence, not sexual desire.

What can make acquaintance rape doubly traumatizing is that it is difficult to prove in a court of law. The sexual assault almost always takes place in private, with no eyewitnesses—and, many times, no signs of physical force. Rather, the rapist uses his physical advantage and the threat of violence to intimidate the woman into submission. If the victim presses charges, and many do not, the case turns on the word of the accuser versus the word of the accused. She says, I was raped against my will. He says, no, the sex was consensual.

This is a nightmarish scenario to have to contemplate. If you heeded your protective instinct, you'd probably chaperone every date or at least follow several car lengths back in an inconspicuous rental. Alas, you can't; you're learning to let go, remember?

The best that parents can do to ensure their daughter's safety is to talk to her about the types of dating situations that are most likely to snowball out of control and therefore should be avoided. Review with her the fol-

---

Gender Benders

"It's rarely talked about, but some sexually aggressive girls will take advantage of boys. Seven percent of the boys in a recent poll claim to have been on the receiving end of harassment. You see this most often in junior high school, when girls are much older than boys in terms of biological age," says Dr. Jim Hoyle. "I would remind parents to watch the interest in boys from either girls or boys during that time, especially older kids."

lowing tips for making wise decisions about the people she dates, the places she goes, and how she behaves.

BE SMART ABOUT WHOM YOU DATE

Do not go out alone with someone you barely know. In a study of more than one hundred teenage rape victims, many of the girls' stories sounded a similar theme: They'd foolishly agreed to accompany a young man they had known for less than twenty-four hours back to his home or car, which is where the sexual assault occurred.

Explain to your daughter that before she goes anywhere with a new suitor, he must come inside and meet Mom and Dad. When he does, ask him for his parents' names, address and telephone number. If he has a cell phone or beeper with him, take down that number too. "Just in case of an emergency," you say while he squirms ever-so-slightly. You're sending a message that you are concerned, involved parents who expect proper behavior on the date.

Be cautious when dating someone significantly older. According to a study by the Alan Guttmacher Institute, three in ten adolescent girls' sexual partners are three to five years older. That may not seem like a huge difference, but just picture a nineteen-year-old boy—*man*—with his arm around a fourteen-year-old girl. "The differences in cognitive abilities and life experience are enormous," observes Dr. Eagar. "They're on a different playing field."

Not surprisingly, the older half of the couple typically wields the power in the relationship, "and the chances that the girl will be victimized escalate." A telling statistic is that while only one in fourteen girls date substantially older men (six years their senior or more), they account for one in five teen pregnancies.

Pick up on any clues that might hint at a controlling or abusive personality, such as: overly possessive, jealous behavior; frequent and inappropriate explosions of temper; expressing anger by punching walls, breaking objects; verbally abusive language; or a history of violence toward others. Any of these is grounds for breaking off the relationship at once.

BE SMART: ABOUT WHERE YOU— AND THE SITUATION—ARE HEADED

Avoid compromising situations. Again, a girl should rely on her intuition. If she senses that the boy is trying to get her alone for sexual purposes, and that is not what she wants, she should turn down suggestions to go somewhere secluded, like parking in a car or going to a residence where no adults are present. More than three-fourths of all first-time sexual encounters occur at a teenager's home, usually the boy's.

Always have a way out. Parents can help in this regard. *In the boy's presence,* instruct your daughter that you expect her to call home at some point during the evening and any time the itinerary for the date changes. Remind her to take change for a pay phone; better still, if you own a cellular phone, loan it to her for the night.

Finally, all teens should be told that if they find themselves in a jam, Mom or Dad will pick them up anytime, anywhere, no questions asked until the next day.

Consider going Dutch treat. Surveys of teenagers have revealed some shockingly Neanderthal attitudes. For instance, surprisingly high numbers of boys *and girls* concur that it is acceptable for a boy to force sex upon his date if he has spent money on her. By paying her own way, a girl restores some of the psychological balance of power in the relationship.

Do not drink alcohol or use substances, and don't date anyone who does. Drugs and alcohol contribute to date rape by impairing judgment and loosening inhibitions. It's regrettable that a young woman who gets drunk or stoned may be considered fair game for nonconsensual sex, but in a poll of high-school students, that was the viewpoint of 39 percent of the boys and—again, incredibly—18 percent of the girls. Thus a teenager is putting herself in danger by drinking or drugging. (See chapter 13, "Tobacco, Alcohol and Other Drugs of Abuse," page 251.)

BE SMART ABOUT THE MESSAGES YOU COMMUNICATE

Say what you mean, mean what you say. If you are uncomfortable with the direction a date is taking, say so directly and forcefully. Example: "I don't like what you're doing, and I want you to stop now." Otherwise, a boy is likely to interpret your passivity as tacit approval for him to continue.

Be conscious of the subliminal messages you send. We communicate volumes without saying a word, through our body language, tone of voice and so on. Although it is unfair that the onus is on women to worry about how men may misinterpret these silent signals, they need to accept that as an unfortunate fact of life.

"If a girl dresses a certain way," says Dr. Margaret Blythe, "there's this idea that she is 'asking for it.' She 'wants it.' " Parents need to explain to their daughter that one way to help protect herself from sexual harassment and abuse is not to dress too provocatively. When getting ready to go out, she should ask herself what image will her appearance project to others?

BE SMART ABOUT DANGER

In the same way that we drill our children on what to do in the event of a house fire, teenagers should be instructed on how to react if they ever feel threatened physically or sexually by a date or a steady boyfriend/girlfriend.

• Trust your instincts. If your companion's behavior frightens you, act on the feeling.

• Protest loudly. If there are other people nearby, don't hesitate to create a scene; you *want* to draw attention to yourself.

• Leave immediately. Get out of the car. Walk out of the house.

• Flag down a bystander or telephone the police for help.

• Report the assault to your parents, who will then contact the appropriate authorities.

• If you can't get away, size up the danger. How safe is it to resist? Does the person have a weapon? Generally speaking, a woman who screams and fights back has a better chance of thwarting the rape than a woman who pleads or tries to reason with her attacker.

ASSISTING A YOUNG VICTIM OF RAPE

In your parent-child discussions about dating safety, emphasize that if your daughter is ever victimized sexually, she should come to you immediately. Reassure her that you would *never* blame her for what happened. It wouldn't matter if she'd been someplace she shouldn't have been. Your sole concern would be to get her help as soon as possible. In order to prevent pregnancy and to preserve evidence that could possibly lead to the rapist's conviction, the following steps must be carried out *within seventy-two hours of a rape.*

1. The girl should not urinate, shower, change her clothes or disturb the scene where the sexual assault took place.

2. Call your local rape-crisis center. You'll find it listed in the Community Service Numbers section of the White Pages, or call information. You will be advised to go to the hospital emergency room. A counselor from the crisis center may meet you there, to help you and your child through the process.

3. Go to the local emergency department for a rape examination. Typically, these procedures are performed:

• A physical examination, to treat any cuts, bruises, trauma and internal injuries.

• A rape kit is used to collect any forensic evidence that might be necessary in a criminal investigation, including specimens for diagnosing sexually transmitted diseases.

• Blood would be drawn and tested for specific sexually transmitted diseases.

• *The incidence of STDs acquired from sexual assaults is not known, but it is becoming standard procedure to offer preventive antibiotics. The girl will be asked to return in six weeks for a follow-up examination and blood tests for the human immunodeficiency virus, hepatitis B and syphilis. The HIV test should then be repeated in three to six months.*

• A urine pregnancy test is performed, then repeated two to three weeks later.

• *The risk of conception following a rape is 2 to 4 percent. If the girl was not using birth control, she should be offered emergency hormonal contraception.*

4. Call your pediatrician and explain what happened. He or she may want to meet you at the emergency department or see your daughter for a follow-up exam.

5. Report the crime to the police. You don't need to decide right now whether or not to prosecute. If the rape occurred on a college campus or by a student at the college, report the assault to campus authorities.

6. It is essential that the girl receive psychological counseling, even if she appears to have bounced back from the assault emotionally. Denying the seriousness of what happened is a common reaction. Months or years may pass before the girl fully recovers.

"Boys Will Be Boys"? Why Not "Boys Will Be Gentlemen"?

While we're advising our daughters to be mindful of how they dress and act around boys, let's strive to eliminate the sexual comments and unwanted advances that too many of our sons seem to think is acceptable behavior. In a poll of adolescents, 29 percent of the girls surveyed said they had been sexually harassed; among those who held a part-time job, 36 percent.

> ### *Teenagers and the Law*
>
> A 1999 Supreme Court decision ruled that a school district can be sued for damages if it fails to stop a student from subjecting another student to "severe and pervasive sexual harassment."

And given what is portrayed in the popular media, such figures should come as no surprise. In a typical hour of watching music videos, a boy can count on catching an eyeful of half-naked women writhing for the camera; they're little more than props, and usually submissive to the male performers. Rap music, with its frequent derogatory references to girls as "bitches" and "ho's," hasn't done much to advance respect for women, either.

We should try to counteract those ugly influences and not dismiss sexist talk as merely boys being boys. If you overhear your son and his friends making offensive comments about a girl, challenge them. "How would you like it if another group of boys was saying the same things about your sister? Or your mother?"

An essential lesson to impart is that when it comes to sexual activity, a young woman's "no" means no. Any time a girl says "stop," even if the tone of her voice suggests a mixed signal, the boy should apply the brakes at once.

EDUCATING YOUNG PEOPLE ABOUT BIRTH CONTROL

To teach teenagers about birth control might seem inconsistent with promoting abstinence. By doing so, aren't parents waving the white flag? Resigning themselves to the idea that teenagers are going to have sex, and nothing adults say or do is going to change that?

No, they're being pragmatic. Nine in ten adolescents have had intercourse by the time they turn twenty.

The consequences of unprotected sex are too devastating and affect too many lives for parents not to inform boys and girls about methods of birth control other than continuous abstinence. School sex-education programs cannot be depended on to present this information. In 1996, Congress passed a federal-entitlement program that rewards states for deliberately omitting any mention of contraception or STD prevention in school sex-ed classes. In order to receive their share of $250 million in federal money, states must implement a curriculum teaching abstinence until marriage "as its exclusive purpose."

Studies show that fewer than one in ten U.S. students receive a comprehensive sex education that promotes abstinence but also addresses the use of contraception for sexually active young men and women. Critics of such programs typically assert that if youngsters learn about birth control, they'll soon want to put this knowledge to practical use.

Studies indicate otherwise. The division of HIV/AIDS prevention at the U.S. Centers for Disease Control and Prevention states: "Research has clearly shown that the most effective programs are comprehensive ones that include a focus on delaying sexual behavior *and* provide information on how sexually active young people can protect themselves." Our best hope that youngsters will choose to delay sexual activity lies with education, because there is no stronger case for abstinence than to candidly discuss the risks of having sex too early.

In the Netherlands, as in other European countries, sex education routinely incorporates such topics. Yet the adolescent birth rate there is thirteen times lower than in the United States; the abortion rate, seven times lower. In addition, the average Netherlands teen waits more than a year longer than his or her American counterpart before becoming sexually active.

Teenagers' "Mythconceptions" about Sex

For all their seeming sophistication, adolescents can harbor some astoundingly inaccurate ideas about sex. These fallacies then get passed along to their fellow teens. Your job as your child's primary sex educator is not just to teach him about sex, it's to "unteach" all the misinformation he's heard that may get him into trouble.

What Your Teenager May Believe: A girl can't get pregnant the first time she has sexual intercourse.

The Facts: Oh yes she can! In fact, pregnancy can occur even *before* a girl's first menstruation.

What Your Teenager May Believe: A girl can't get pregnant during her menstrual period.

The Facts: Wrong again. No time of the month is completely safe for unprotected vaginal intercourse, although there are approximately seven or eight days when a girl is *most likely* to become pregnant: five days prior to ovulation, the day of ovulation and one or two days afterward.

What Your Teenager May Believe: One way to avoid pregnancy without using contraception is for the boy to withdraw his penis from the vagina before he ejaculates. The medical term for this maneuver is *coitus interruptus* (pronounced coe-*iy*-tus in-ter-*rupt*-us).

The Facts: Not necessarily. Prior to orgasm, the penis leaks drops of semen containing thousands of sperm. It takes only one to wiggle up the uterus and into the fallopian tube to fertilize the ovum.

What Your Teenager May Believe: Oral sex (mouth-to-genital contact) "doesn't count" as sex.

The Facts: That was the response of six in ten college students polled by the Kinsey Institute in 1991. At the time, the study drew little attention.

Other results of the Kinsey report are equally disturbing: 85 percent of the college men and women said that they did not consider hand-genital stimulation to be sex, and, somewhat remarkably, 20 percent did not regard anal intercourse as sex. Why, then, should their attitudes toward intercourse be any different?

For the record, "sex" is any intimate physical act between two people, not solely penis-vagina intercourse. That most definitely includes oral sex, manual sex and anal sex.

What Your Teenager May Believe: All teenagers are having sex nowadays.

The Facts: It may *seem* that way, especially if you're prone to believing what you see on TV, but the truth is that slightly more than half of all high-school students are still virgins when they graduate.

Methods of Birth Control

- **Abstinence:** the starting point of any discussion about birth control. Refraining from sexual intercourse is the surest way to avoid pregnancy and sexually transmitted diseases.

- **"Outercourse":** In the field of teenage sexuality, contact that does not involve intercourse is referred to tongue-in-cheek as "outercourse." Dr. Donna Futterman, director of the adolescent AIDS program at New York's Montefiore Medical Center, encourages parents to talk to their youngsters about these other forms of sexual expression. "Kids should know that they don't need to have intercourse to be fulfilled," she says.

There are many safe ways to enjoy sexual pleasure without penis-vagina or penis-anus penetration. To date, there have been no reported cases of pregnancy through kissing, hugging or caressing.

Methods of Birth Control for Sexually Active Teens

Table 12.2 provides information about both over-the-counter and prescription forms of birth control. However, many mothers and fathers will not feel comfortable having sexually blunt conversations or discussing contraception with their teen. If you're nodding your head in recognition, call your youngster's pediatrician. He or she regularly counsels young patients about sexual behavior, birth-control methods and techniques for preventing STDs. Many times, your son's or daughter's doctor can provide or prescribe a suitable form of contraception right there in the office, or refer an adolescent to an appropriate facility in your community.

Teenagers and the Law

Obtaining Contraception: Their Rights, Your Rights

Adolescents in any of the fifty states can receive family planning services confidentially, without having to obtain their parents' notification or consent. However, no laws prohibit physicians from contacting parents when necessary. For example, says Dr. Robert Brown, "If a doctor felt that a teenager was behaving in a way that was harmful to himself or herself, he could revoke that privilege and notify the parents."

Parents needn't worry that open access to family planning will spur teenage sexual activity, says Dr. Brown, chief of the section of adolescent health at Children's Hospital in Columbus, Ohio. "In other countries that provide *free* confidential contraceptive services, the rates of adolescent sexual intercourse are no higher than they are in the United States," he points out, "but the teen-pregnancy rates are significantly lower."

TABLE 12.2

Methods of Birth Control for Sexually Active Teens

METHOD EFFECTIVENESS	WHAT IS IT?	ADVANTAGES	DISADVANTAGES
General Methods			
Rhythm Method Consistent Use: 80%–90% Typical Teen Use: Ineffective	A woman is most likely to conceive starting approximately five days before she ovulates and ending a day or two afterward. During this time, she should refrain from having vaginal intercourse. To follow the rhythm method, women may be taught three techniques for predicting ovulation: (1) keeping records of what day of the month her menstrual cycle starts, (2) taking her temperature before getting out of bed in the morning, and (3) inspecting her cervical mucus for color and texture, also every morning.	• No side effects. • No devices. • Free.	• Requires a level of diligence that is well beyond most teens and many adults. In addition, at this age girls' menstrual cycles are unpredictable. Not usually recommended for teens, on account of its high failure rate.
Withdrawal Method Consistent Use: 81%–96% Typical Teen Use: Ineffective	Withdrawing the penis from the vagina just prior to ejaculation.	• No side effects, apart from both partners' anxiety over whether or not the boy will pull out in time. • No devices. • Free.	• *Not* pulling out in time. Even when the man withdraws before reaching orgasm, his penis has leaked semen containing thousands of sperm and possibly bacteria, viruses and other germs into the vagina. • High failure rate.

METHOD Effectiveness	WHAT IS IT?	ADVANTAGES	DISADVANTAGES
Barrier Methods			
Latex Condom Consistent Use: 88%–98% Typical Teen Use: 65%	A thin sheath of rubber that slips over the penis and is tipped with a small nipplelike reservoir for catching semen. Condoms are also made of other materials, like polyurethane and lambskin, but only latex prophylactics have been proved to safeguard against STDs. Condoms' effectiveness can be improved upon by using them in combination with a spermicide. Some brands come prelubricated with the spermicide nonoxynol-9.	• Available without a prescription. • Easy to use. • Inexpensive. • Protects against sexually transmitted diseases.	• Needs to be used each time. • Can break or slip off during sex. • Some people are allergic to latex. • Needs to be used properly.
Female Condom (Vaginal Pouch) Consistent Use: 94%–95% Typical Teen Use: Not known	A prelubricated polyurethane sheath similar in design to its male counterpart. When the bulky device is inserted into the vagina, the closed end shields the cervix, the sheath lines the vaginal walls, and the ringed open end hangs outside the vagina to cover the labia. For maximum protection, should be used with a spermicide.	• Available without a prescription. • The only female contraceptive that defends against STDs.	• Difficult to insert. • Outer ring may slip into the vagina during intercourse. • Diminished sexual sensation. • More expensive than the male condom.

Diaphragm Consistent Use: 94% Typical Teen Use: 82% **Cervical Cap** Consistent Use: 91% for girls who've never had a child; 74% for those who have Typical Teen Use: 82% for girls who've never had a child; 64% for those who have	The diaphragm is a dome-shaped soft rubber barrier, worn internally, that blocks sperm from coming into contact with it. Up to six hours before intercourse, a girl inserts the flexible device into her vagina and pushes it all the way back. The *cap*, which resembles a thimble, fits firmly onto the opening of the cervix. Both contraceptives must be used with a spermicide jelly or cream and both must remain inside for at least eight hours after intercourse. A girl should visit her gynecologist anytime she gains or loses ten or more pounds to see if she needs to be fitted for a larger or smaller diaphragm.	• No side effects. • Inexpensive. • Neither method is popular with teens. Many girls are turned off by the thought of having a foreign object inside them during and after intercourse. • Not all young women can be fitted for cervical caps, which come in only four sizes. • Can lead to increases in urinary-tract infections, yeast infections and bacterial vaginosis. • Requires doctor's appointment for fitting.
Spermicide Consistent Use: 94% Typical Teen Use: 70%	Spermicide, in the form of over-the-counter contraceptive foams, jellies, gels, creams, suppositories and absorbable films, immobilizes and kills sperm. Shortly before sexual intercourse, the girl inserts the product deep into her vagina. Body heat causes the spermicide to melt, forming a protective coating.	• No prescription necessary. • Messy, less effective than other methods. • Can be used with condoms to provide additional protection in case condom breaks or slips off.

METHOD EFFECTIVENESS	WHAT IS IT?	ADVANTAGES	DISADVANTAGES
Contraceptive Sponge Consistent Use: 94% Typical Use (Adults): 75%	The round foam device is presaturated with spermicide. Once inserted into the vagina, it blocks and kills sperm for up to twenty-four hours.	• Convenient and easy to use. • OTC.	• Teenagers can have difficulty positioning the sponge, which occasionally will dislodge during intercourse.

Hormonal Methods

METHOD EFFECTIVENESS	WHAT IS IT?	ADVANTAGES	DISADVANTAGES
Birth-Control Pill Consistent Use: 97%–99.9% Typical Teen Use: 64%–75%	The only oral contraceptive, and the most widely used form among women. There are two types: The *combination pill* consists of synthetic estrogen and progesterone, the two female sex hormones that share control of the menstrual cycle. The *progestin-only pill*, rarely prescribed for teenagers, contains just progesterone. They prevent pregnancy in different ways and at different points in the reproductive process. The combination pill is now available in a "patch" form as well. *The clinician prescribing the pill will explain what the teen should do if she misses a dose.*	• Convenient and highly effective at preventing pregnancy. • Young patients are often surprised to learn that oral contraceptives confer several impressive health benefits, including reduced risks of ovarian and endometrial cancers, benign breast tumors, ovarian cysts, pelvic inflammatory disease, tubal (ectopic) pregnancy and iron-deficiency anemia. Also used to treat acne, irregular menstruation, menstrual cramps and other conditions.	• Irregular vaginal bleeding is common for the first two to three months. This indicates that the body is adapting to the hormonal drug and is not a cause for worry. • Serious side effects, though rare, include blood clots, stroke, hypertension, migraine headaches. • Requires doctor's visit, but does not require pelvic exam. • Must be taken consistently every day.

Depo-Provera

Consistent Use: 99.7%

Typical Teen Use: 62%–80%

Because not all teenagers are able to take oral contraceptives faithfully every day, this long-acting injectable progesterone-like drug (medroxyprogesterone) has been gaining on the birth-control pill in popularity. One shot of Depo-Provera in the arm or buttock prevents conception for approximately three months. A monthly shot is also available that contains both an estrogen and a progestin.

- A girl's only responsibility is to return to the doctor's office in 12 weeks for her next injection. "The Shot" also protects against endometrial cancer and iron-deficiency anemia.
- Weight gain and irregular menstrual bleeding.
- Once the hormone is discontinued, fertility may take up to two years to return to normal (usually within one year).

Norplant

Consistent Use: 99.7%

The most effective and longest-acting reversible method of birth control developed to date. The Norplant system consists of six flexible rod-shaped capsules about the size of matchsticks, each containing the synthetic progesterone levonorgestel. Once implanted under the skin in a simple office procedure, the sealed containers continually release the hormone into the body for up to five years, then must be surgically removed.

- Provides up to five years of worry-free birth control, plus protection against endometrial cancer and iron-deficiency anemia.
- Before committing to using Norplant, a young woman should be reasonably certain that she doesn't foresee wanting children in the near future, although the capsules can be removed at any time.
- Potential side effects include irregular menstruation, headaches, weight gain, acne, depression, hair loss.
- Doctor's visit required for insertion and removal.

(continued)

TABLE 12.2

METHOD EFFECTIVENESS	WHAT IS IT?	ADVANTAGES	DISADVANTAGES
Other Types of Birth Control			
IUD (Intrauterine Device) 97.4%–99.2%	A physician inserts this small soft-plastic birth-control device into the uterus, where it remains for one year up to several years, depending on the type.	• Provides safe, effective and inexpensive long-term birth control.	• IUDs were once believed to increase the risk of incurring a sexually transmitted infection. Though this has never been proved conclusively, safety concerns persist. Since adolescents have high rates of STDs, intrauterine devices are rarely recommended for them. • Side effects: menstrual cramps, heavy periods.

Which Forms of Contraception Are Preferable for Teenagers?

"The best method of contraception is whichever one a teenager will comply with," Dr. Richard Brookman says simply. "If a girl at our clinic says that she will use only the rhythm method, then we teach her how to do it the best way possible. But we make sure she understands that she is taking a risk."

TEACHING TEENS TO USE CONDOMS *FAITHFULLY*

The latex condom is the only form of birth control that provides protection against both pregnancy and sexually transmitted diseases. While not infallible, using a prophylactic correctly is much safer than not using one. *The optimal safety strategy, if abstinence is not chosen, calls for the male to wear a condom, while his female partner uses any of the three hormonal methods: the pill, Depo-Provera or Norplant.*

One of the most heartening changes in young people's sexual habits, says Dr. Claire Brindis, is that boys have begun to share responsibility for birth control. "The pendulum has shifted," she observes. "Contraception no longer falls solely to the young woman."

Even so, too many boys try to squirm their way out of donning a prophylactic before sexual activity. You're probably familiar with some of the reasons (excuses) typically given:

"It ruins the spontaneity."

"It dulls the sensation."

Girls, too, may have an aversion to condoms, though the reasons typically have less to do with physical pleasure than with the stigma often associated with this much-maligned form of contraception. Some young women, for example, say that using rubbers makes them feel "cheap," when in fact they should congratulate themselves for being sexually responsible. Others worry that to keep a few condoms in their purse or backpack, just in case, might be misconstrued as a sign that they're easily coaxed into bed or that seduction was on their agenda all along. It's been found that adolescents who carry condoms are nearly three times more likely to use them for protection during intercourse.

When discussing birth control with teenagers, the message is the same for sons as it is for daughters: to have intercourse without a prophylactic, even once, could potentially derail their future and possibly even cost them their lives. They need to inform any and all sexual partners that no condom means no sex—no excuses, no exceptions.

"Teenagers still believe they can 'tell' who has HIV and who doesn't," observes Dr. Donna Futterman. "The line I hear from boys and girls is, 'I can look in a person's eyes and know.'" The fact is, we can't confirm anyone's monogamy but our own. We trust our romantic partner to be both true and truthful, but a study that surveyed about two hundred HIV-positive patients at a pair of New England hospitals revealed that four in ten of the infected men and women admitted they'd never informed their partners of their condition. Furthermore, nearly two-thirds of them did not always wear a condom.

Arming our sons and daughters with this information can help them face down the pressure to have sex without condoms—or to have sex at all. If they're ever in a situation where someone is trying to plead/cajole/insist/coerce them into foregoing a prophylactic, they might try responding with one of the comebacks in Table 12.3.

WHAT TEENS SHOULD KNOW ABOUT BUYING AND USING CONDOMS CORRECTLY[1,2]

Check the expiration date on the package before purchasing a condom. Never buy outdated prophylactics or those about to expire.

Heat can damage condoms, so store them in a cool, dry place. They can be carried around in a purse or wallet, but not for long periods of time, which shortens their shelf life.

When tearing open the aluminum foil or plastic package, be careful that you don't rip the latex. The condom comes rolled into a ring shape.

If one partner is allergic to latex, be sure to buy a polyurethane condom.

To enhance sensation, place a drop or two of lubricant inside the lips of the condom. Never use oil-based products like petroleum jelly, skin lotions or vegetable oil on latex condoms, because such products can damage them. Polyurethane prophylactics, stronger and thinner than the latex brands, are not damaged by oil-based lubricants.

How to put on a condom:
- Place the rolled condom over the tip of the penis when it is erect, making sure to leave a quarter-inch to half-inch at the tip.
- Holding the tip with one hand, press out the air. Most condom ruptures are caused by friction against air bubbles.
- With the other hand, unroll the condom over the penis shaft, down to the base.

---

1 Girls as well as boys; nearly as many condoms are bought by women as by men.
2 Condoms are not foolproof—only abstinence guarantees the absence of pregnancy and STDs.

TABLE 12.3

No Condom, No Sex

If One Partner Says:	The Other Partner Might Reply:
"Don't you trust me?"	"It's not a question of trust. A person can be infected with a sexually transmitted disease and not know it."
"Come on, just this once."	"No. Once is all it takes to become pregnant or to contract a disease."
"I can't believe you think I sleep around! You've really hurt my feelings."	"I never said that. But I'd feel better if we used a condom."
"I hate using condoms; it interrupts everything."	"It doesn't have to, if we have them on hand."
"But I'm a virgin."	"I'm not. Using condoms will protect us both."
"I forgot to bring condoms with me."	"I have some right here." Or: "We can please each other without having intercourse."
"It's not as sensitive when I wear a condom."	"Maybe you'll last longer and the sex will be even better."
"It's such a turn-off to use a condom."	"Not if I help you put it on . . ."
"But I love you!"	"I love you too. Protecting each other is what people in love do."
"I'm not using a rubber, and that's final."	"Suit yourself. Either we have fun another way, or we don't have sex at all."
All-Time Favorites Barely Worthy of a Response: "But I'm too big!" "But I'm sterile!" "Obviously you don't care about me!" "If you get pregnant, I'll help you care for the baby." *Right. And the check is in the mail . . .*	**All-Purpose Rejoinder:** "You know what they call couples who don't use condoms?" "No, what?" "Parents." And: "Patients at the STD clinic."

- Smooth out air bubbles, if possible.
- Now lubricate the outside of the latex.

Sexually active girls should learn this maneuver, not just boys, so that putting on a condom becomes a seamless element of lovemaking instead of an interruption.

How to take off a condom:
- While the penis is still hard, hold the condom against the base of the penis and withdraw from the vagina.
- Dispose of the condom. Prophylactics are never to be reused.
- Wash the penis with soap and water before any postcoital cuddling.

If the condom splits during sexual intercourse, the penis should be pulled out immediately.
- If semen seeps out, wash it away with soap and water.
- If semen appears to enter the woman's vagina, contact her pediatrician or gynecologist and ask about emergency contraception.

Emergency Contraception

In the event that a girl has unprotected vaginal intercourse, or a condom breaks or ruptures, there is still a narrow window of time in which to prevent conception *postcoitally.* Yet surprisingly few parents and adolescents are aware of this option, which has been available since the 1960s, when it was offered solely to victims of rape. In a survey taken by the Kaiser Family Foundation, only one in ten health professionals said that they routinely informed their patients about "morning-after" contraception. With approximately three million unintended pregnancies in the United States each year, more must be done to get the word out.

The most common method of emergency contraception consists of two higher-than-normal doses of birth-control pills. The first dose must be taken within seventy-two hours of intercourse; the second dose, twelve hours after the first.

In 1999, the Food and Drug Administration approved the first synthetic progesterone intended specifically for emergency contraception. Treatment with levonorgestrol, sold under the name Plan B, requires ingesting two tablets twelve hours apart.

A follow-up appointment with a physician should be made to confirm that the emergency contraception was effective and to discuss birth control options.

As much as it's a relief to know that therapies exist to undo the potential consequences of having unprotected sex, teenagers need to understand that emergency contraception provides a smaller safety net than regular birth control does and should not be viewed as a substitute for responsible reproductive behavior.

WHERE TO OBTAIN EMERGENCY CONTRACEPTION

Your pediatrician may prescribe emergency contraception. You can also locate this service at women's health centers, hospital emergency departments, and other facilities in your community. The toll-free Emergency Contraception Hotline gives callers the names and telephone numbers of local health-care practitioners who provide emergency contraception. Call 888-668-2528 (888-NOT-2-LATE) twenty-four hours a day, seven days a week.

TEENAGE PREGNANCY

Even with a steadily declining adolescent birth rate, two in five young women will become pregnant before age twenty, and four out of five of those pregnancies will be unintended, including about half of those among married teenage girls.

Whatever their circumstances, though, the news that they are pregnant usually comes as a shock, and often not a welcome one.

The unforeseen development typically throws young lives into turmoil, at least for a time, forcing the girl to make perhaps the most agonizing decision of her life. Does she carry the baby to term, as 50 percent of pregnant teenagers elect to do? Or does she terminate the pregnancy?

It is hoped she knows she can count on her mother and father for guidance and support as she confronts these choices. Youngsters who fear meeting with rejection or abuse at home may try to keep the pregnancy a secret as long as possible. As a result, they often don't receive adequate prenatal care and counseling during the crucial early months of fetal development.

One-third of girls aged fifteen to nineteen, and one-half of girls under fifteen receive no prenatal care at all during their first trimester. The lack of medical attention can lead to problems

> **Teenagers and Miscarriage**
>
> About 14 percent of adolescent pregnancies end in *spontaneous abortions*, or *miscarriages*. They typically occur between the sixth and twelfth weeks after the last menstrual period. A very early miscarriage sometimes goes unrecognized, appearing to be nothing more than a late menstrual period.

later on. If they go forward with the pregnancy, the pregnancy could be complicated with an increased risk for mother and baby. And if they choose to abort, the earlier the procedure is performed the safer it will be.

However, anxiety over Mom and Dad's reaction isn't the only reason a girl may hide the fact that she is pregnant. "Young women can be in terrible denial," explains Dr. Claire Brindis, "simply refusing to accept the reality of their condition." Psychologists call this *dissociation.* Since today's baggy fashions make it easier for a girl to go for months, or perhaps through her entire pregnancy, without anyone noticing her expanding abdomen, don't go by appearances alone. If you suspect that your daughter might be pregnant but is trying to hide it, act on your intuition—but tactfully, perhaps with words like these: "Honey, you've been complaining of feeling tired and nauseous the last week or so, and you're going to the bathroom a lot. Are you all right? You remind me of what I felt like when I was pregnant."

Parents' Common Reactions

A tearful "I'm pregnant!" isn't easy for any mother or father to hear. Worry, disappointment, anger—all are understandable responses. Most likely this isn't what you had in mind for your daughter. Meanwhile, a similar scene is probably being played out at the home of the boy involved (if the boy even tells his parents).

Give yourself and your spouse permission to be upset for a day or two. Talk things over together. If you blurt out an incredulous "What on earth were you thinking?!" or "How could you be so irresponsible?!" so be it; you're human. But then shut the door on anger and lock it away. Hurling blame at your teenager isn't going to change anything; it's time to sit down as a family and calmly discuss what to do next.

"A parent's most important role is to listen to the young woman or the young couple as they sort through their options," says Denver pediatrician Dr. Roberta Beach. "We know that in the long run teenagers usually feel satisfied with whatever choice they made, as long as they feel that the decision was theirs and that their family supported them."

First Things First: Verify the Diagnosis

A skipped period and a positive result on a home pregnancy test are usually what prompt a young woman to believe she's pregnant. The home test, while generally accurate, isn't as reliable as the laboratory test the doctors do to confirm a pregnancy. So the first step is to make an appointment with your daughter's pediatrician or gynecologist.

Next Step: Reaching a Decision

The doctor's office just called: The pregnancy test came back positive. Now where do we go from here? There are three options: abort, give birth and raise the baby or give birth and place the child up for adoption. Parents certainly have a right to voice their opinions; if circumstances allow, the young man and his family should be invited to take part in the decision-making process too. But legally, the ultimate verdict belongs to the expectant mother.

For some young women, the decision about what to do is never in doubt. Perhaps they are personally opposed to abortion. Or they know deep in their hearts that they are not ready to have a child this early in life and therefore wish to have an abortion.

> **Teenagers and the Law**
>
> No state laws mandate that parents be notified when their underage child receives prenatal medical care. Legislation in more than half the states and the District of Columbia grants minors the right to obtain prenatal care and delivery services without parental notification or consent.

Most girls, though, agonize over this difficult decision, which is further complicated by the fact that abortion is one of the most politically and emotionally charged issues of our times.

Depending on where she lives, she may face the harrowing prospect of having to travel dozens or even hundreds of miles just to find an abortion provider and once there she may need to wind her way through a gauntlet of taunts and threats by antiabortion demonstrators.

If you and your daughter feel that you might benefit from hearing an objective viewpoint, arrange a consultation with the pediatrician. In a nonjudgmental fashion, he or she can help you to evaluate the pros and cons of each option. Once the young woman has made up her mind, most pediatricians can refer her to health-care practitioners who provide abortion services, or to an obstetrician or adolescent clinic to begin prenatal care.

OPTIONS
CARRYING A PREGNANCY TO TERM

A girl who has decided to have her baby should be under the care of an obstetrician, preferably someone with experience in working with adolescents. Visits to the doctor's office will be scheduled every two to four weeks through week number thirty-three. Then they double in frequency until the baby's arrival.

According to Dr. Richard Brookman, the optimal health-care setting for pregnant teens combines medical care with nutritional counseling and psychosocial services, "to address some of a teenager's other needs." Ask your pediatrician if she knows of any comprehensive adolescent prenatal programs or *multidisciplinary* obstetrics practices in your community.

One of the staff's top priorities, besides being alert to potential medical problems, is to impress upon the young woman the importance of keeping herself healthy. "Medically, most pregnant adolescents do just as well as adults," says Dr. Brookman. "The increased risk of complications in teen pregnancies is due to behavioral factors such as smoking and substance abuse, or a girl being found to have a sexually transmitted infection at the time her pregnancy is diagnosed. Late entry into perinatal care may also increase the risks."

Tobacco's detrimental effect on the fetus is well documented, having been linked to increased risks of spontaneous abortion and fetal death, and babies born with low birth weight and developmental delays. One in seven premature deliveries can be blamed on maternal smoking. Yet the mid-1990s witnessed a rise in the percentage of teenagers who smoked throughout their pregnancy—one in six, at last count. Parents of the parent-to-be play an important role in ensuring the unborn child's well-being. Keep an eye out for signs of tobacco use, drinking, taking drugs and reckless sexual behavior. If you have reason to believe the mother isn't acting in her baby's best interest, alert the obstetrician.

The First Prenatal Visit
THESE TESTS SHOULD BE PERFORMED

- Pelvic exam and Pap smear
- Complete blood count
- Complete urinalysis
- Blood type and group
- Blood-test screenings for sexually transmitted infections, including HIV, chlamydia, gonorrhea and syphilis
- Blood-test screenings for sickle-cell anemia and rubella

At each appointment, girls receive counseling on other aspects of pregnancy, such as contraception, infant care and diet. Contrary to popular belief, most teenage girls have little difficulty eating for two. But compared to adults, adolescents are more likely to lack sufficient stores of iron and other nutrients. During pregnancy, those nutrients go selectively to the baby. That's why taking prenatal vitamins and iron is so important.

PREPARING TEENS FOR PARENTHOOD

Fears about the future are common among new mothers—and pregnant teens too. Even before the birth, they may begin to feel isolated from their peers, and frustrated by the many restrictions that pregnancy imposes. While they're lying on an examining table at the doctor's or attending a Lamaze class, their friends are out partying and having fun. "A great deal of envy and resentment often emerges," says Dr. Brindis.

Indications of emotional conflicts should be brought to the obstetrician's attention no less promptly than you would report a physical ailment. A full-service practice might have a mental-health counselor available. If not, an anxious or depressed patient would be referred out to the appropriate professional.

It's now, before the baby is born, that someone in the family should start investigating what support services the community offers to young couples or single parents with children. Naturally the number of programs will vary widely, depending on where they live. But compared to a generation ago, you're liable to be happily surprised at how much help may be waiting.

If there's a social worker on staff, you're in luck. Social workers act as case managers; their job is to link eligible patient-clients with available support services. Usually, though, this task falls to a parent or other family member. A good place to start your search is at your teenager's school. In response to the epidemic of adolescent pregnancies, a number of districts have established programs geared toward improving the quality of life for teen parents and their children. Here are some examples:

- child-care programs, so that the parents can continue to attend school
- classes in parenting skills and child development
- child health care
- counseling in life skills such as problem solving, decision making and interpersonal relationships
- job-training programs
- assistance in finding employment
- bus transportation to and from school
- tuition and child care during summer school
- tutorial assistance
- baby-sitting services

Few school programs offer all of these features. Many districts may fund none at all. You'll most likely wind up cobbling together several services from a variety of government and private resources, such as:

- your state, county or city department of social services

> ### *You Should Know*
>
> In order to be eligible for financial assistance under the Federal Assistance for Needy Families (FANF) program, unmarried teenage parents are required to live with a responsible adult or in an adult-supervised setting. They must also participate in educational and training activities.

- the U.S. Department of Health and Human Services
- Catholic Charities USA, the largest private network of social-services organizations in the United States
- United Way of America, a national network of local charity organizations

GETTING YOUNG FATHERS INVOLVED

You may have noticed someone's conspicuous absence from this discussion so far: namely, the young man who is equally responsible for bringing a new life into the world.

When a baby is born out of wedlock and it is clear that the parents have no intention of marrying, too often the father is instantly absolved of his obligations toward both mother and child. Other times a teenager will want to be involved in raising the child, but he gets nudged aside—if not actively pushed away, then never invited in. Either way, his exclusion becomes a self-fulfilling prophecy.

Some boys may feel too frightened or too guilty to make their interest and concern known. It is sometimes overlooked that this can be a traumatic time for the prospective father as well as for the pregnant girl. He, too, will need his parents' love and support during this crisis.

Many times it's the baby's grandparents, not the mother, who seek to cut the teen father out of the picture. "There can be a strong sense of anger and resentment on the grandparents' part for his having gotten the girl pregnant," says Dr. Brindis. "But they have to recognize that the child will benefit from having both parents involved, as well as both sets of grandparents."

No one is advocating that we pressure expectant couples to marry when the two teens involved clearly have no future together. That would merely be compounding one mistake with another. "But even if the father isn't in a position to help support the baby economically," suggests Dr. Brindis, "he can provide emotional support and physical support, in terms of changing diapers and taking care of the child. That's extremely important."

WHAT WILL THE FUTURE HOLD?

If the general tone of the last dozen pages or so has seemed discouraging, the statistics ominous, take heart in the fact that success stories abound. There are single teenage mothers who complete their educations and go on to carve out happy lives rich with accomplishments, just as there are young marrieds who buck the odds and not only survive but thrive together.

You can lend support by helping your youngster avoid the pitfalls that trip up other teenagers. The first and foremost priority is to avoid having more children before having entered into a stable marriage—and a steady source of income. Encourage him or her to get a high-school diploma, then a college degree. Assist in accessing the support services described earlier, to ease their load now, when it's at its heaviest. With you behind them, your child and your grandchild can look forward to brighter prospects than many other teens in similar straits could. They're lucky to have you!

OPTIONS
ADOPTION

Fewer unmarried adolescents are choosing to put their babies up for adoption, largely because bearing a child out of wedlock doesn't carry the same social stigma it once did. Around 1950, roughly one in every twelve premarital births were placed for adoption; that number had fallen to one in every one hundred by century's end. For teenagers who feel unable to parent a child successfully right now but who do not want to consider abortion, adoption is a very loving option to best meet everyone's needs.

If your teenager is considering adoption, here is what she needs to know.

First, placing a baby with an adoptive family is a *permanent* measure. Most states allow the birth mother anywhere from several days to several months after the child is born to change her mind. But once the deadline for *withdrawing consent* passes, the agreement is legal and binding.

In a *public adoption,* the child is placed in a home by an agency that is either operated by the state or contracted by the state.

In a *private adoption,* placement is made by a nonprofit or for-private agency.

An *independent adoption* may be carried out by any of the following: the birth parents, an attorney, a medical doctor, a member of the clergy, or a licensed or unlicensed facilitator.

Under an independent adoption, the birth parent can decide at the outset whether or not she

> ### *Teenagers and the Law*
> #### THE ADOPTION OPTION: THEIR RIGHTS, YOUR RIGHTS
>
> In all but a few states, minors may place their babies for adoption without their parents' consent.

wishes to personally select the adoptive parents, meet with them, even maintain an ongoing relationship, if she so chooses. That is called an *open adoption.* In a *closed adoption,* the names of the birth mother and the adoptive parents are kept secret from each other.

OPTIONS
ABORTION

Preferably, an abortion should be carried out during the first trimester of pregnancy, which means the first twelve weeks, when 90 percent of abortions are performed. An early abortion usually takes place in a reproductive-health clinic, a doctor's private office or the department of outpatient surgery at a hospital.

Teenagers and the Law

Their Right to an Abortion, Your Right to Know

Only a handful of states grant minors access to abortion without their parents' knowledge or permission. The majority of state laws mandate that one or both parents be notified or give their consent prior to the procedure.

Most teenagers who intend to have an abortion voluntarily inform their parents. Studies have shown that when girls make up their minds not to tell, they often do so out of self-protection. On average, one in three come from families with histories of violence. The young women fear that telling the truth may get them thrown out of the house or bring them physical harm.

An adolescent living in one of the states that legislate parental involvement would have one of two choices. She could travel to a state with less stringent laws or she could file a petition requesting a judge's approval, called a *judicial bypass.* Both are tall orders for any teenager, much less one who is probably anxious and scared. Her pediatrician should be able to advise her on how to go about petitioning the court.

Few young women are turned down. But the legal route is time-consuming. According to the American Civil Liberties Union, the court proceedings routinely delay a girl's abortion by more than one week and sometimes by as much as three weeks. The result is a riskier and more expensive procedure. After the state of Minnesota enacted a parental-notification law, the proportion of second-trimester abortions among adolescents rose 18 percent.

Abortions are illegal during the third trimester (anytime after the twenty-fourth week), except when deemed medically necessary.

THE AFTERMATH OF ABORTION

The initial relief that some girls feel following an abortion can give way to temporary pangs of sadness, anger, regret or grief. Adolescents who suffer miscarriages several weeks into an unplanned pregnancy frequently experience similar emotions.

Loved ones aren't always as sensitive as they should be toward the young woman. They may not understand why she seems sad and upset. *After all, the abortion was her choice.* Or: *She just found out she was pregnant a week ago. It's not like she was in her ninth month.*

Your daughter needs empathy and, above all, patience right now. Abrupt hormonal changes may be contributing to her shifting emotions as well. The blues rarely linger for too long. In fact, severe, protracted emotional problems are more common after having a child, in the form of *postpartum depression.*

GAY AND LESBIAN TEENAGERS

Adolescence is a time for exploring one's sexuality. It starts with socializing and flirting. Perhaps a boy and a girl are in the same ninth-grade Spanish class, and they find themselves talking and laughing together every morning until the teacher calls everyone to attention. They exchange shy smiles during the lesson, then part company in the hallway to go to their next classes. The chemistry between them is unmistakable, to them and to their friends.

Gay or lesbian adolescents may have those same feelings, but to express them openly would be unimaginable to most of them, even if they live in relatively tolerant communities. Homosexual youth often have to conduct their sexual exploration in secret from their peers and their families—most of all their families. In a survey of students in public high schools, 97 percent said they regularly heard other teens make antigay (*homophobic*) remarks. Fearing ostracism, or physical harm, many gay and lesbian teenagers try to keep their *sexual orientation* a secret or suppress it altogether.

What Determines Sexual Orientation?

An estimated 2 to 5 percent of adolescents are homosexual, the same percentage as among adults. Scientists generally agree that several factors converge

Dispelling Myths About Homosexuality

Homosexuality is not a mental disorder, as was once believed. In 1973 the American Psychiatric Association reclassified it as a normal form of sexual orientation.

Gays and lesbians are no more likely to sexually abuse children than heterosexuals are.

Homosexuals cannot "indoctrinate" young people into adopting a gay lifestyle. There is no evidence that being around gays and lesbians has any influence on a person's sexual orientation.

to form a person's sexual orientation. But there is increasing evidence that human beings may be genetically predisposed toward heterosexuality or homosexuality. These tendencies may even be established prior to birth, just as gender, hair color and complexion are all preprogrammed. Contrary to what some believe, we do not *choose* to be straight or gay. Come adolescence, a person is innately drawn toward one sex or the other.

During early and middle adolescence, a youngster's sexuality may be in a state of flux. In a survey of thirteen-to-nineteen-year-olds, approximately one in ten boys and one in seventeen girls acknowledged having had at least one homosexual experience. Yet that doesn't mean every one of them is gay, for experimentation is normal at this age. Some later came to the realization that they were straight. Similarly, gay youths may engage in sexual activities with members of the opposite sex. Or, in an attempt to deny their homosexuality, they may try to convince themselves that same-sex encounters were merely part of a "phase."

The Four Stages of Coming Out

STAGE ONE
"I FEEL DIFFERENT FROM OTHER KIDS . . ."

In retrospect, many gay and lesbian teens say they sensed something "different" about themselves early in life, sometimes as far back as age five. A boy may have been inclined to play house instead of sports, and vice-versa for a girl. Patterns of social isolation from peers frequently start here.

STAGE TWO
"I THINK I MIGHT BE GAY, BUT I'M NOT SURE.
AND IF I AM, I'M NOT SURE THAT I WANT TO BE . . ."

Puberty is when many homosexual youngsters first realize that they are attracted to members of their own sex. A common response is to try to bury those feelings. "Young gay people often go through a stage where they label themselves bisexual," says Dr. Donna Futterman, "as a way to give themselves more options."

Relatively few gay adolescents declare their homosexuality, or *come out,* during this stage of identity confusion. They may isolate themselves from other teens for fear of being exposed, or "outed." Loneliness is frequently a way of life, especially if they live in a community that doesn't have an active gay-youth subculture. Imagine growing up unable to confide in your own parents or to truly be yourself when among friends.

STAGE THREE
"I ACCEPT THE FACT THAT I'M GAY, BUT WHAT'S MY FAMILY
GOING TO SAY?"

Studies of homosexual men and women found that most did not come to accept their sexual orientation until they were in their late teens or their twenties. As societal prejudice against gays and lesbians abates, albeit slowly, a youngster may arrive at this point somewhat earlier.

STAGE FOUR
"I FINALLY TOLD MY PARENTS I'M GAY."

In a study, there was an on-line survey of nearly two thousand gay and bisexual young people aged twenty-five or under. On average, the respondents were sixteen the first time they revealed their sexuality to anyone. Homosexual teens often don't begin to date in earnest until they're out of high school and on their own—possibly in a city with a sizable gay population. Feeling free to explore their sexuality for perhaps the first time, they may become romantically involved with a number of partners. You could almost say they're going through a delayed adolescence, having experiences that straight kids may encounter earlier in their sexual development.

Parents Go through Stages Too

When a youngster acknowledges his or her homosexuality, parents' initial reaction is often one of shock. If they are truly honest with themselves, one or both may have suspected as much for some time. It's common, though, for family members to deny the obvious, not only long before a gay youth's coming out but afterward too.

According to Dr. Futterman of Montefiore Medical Center, a mother or father may seize on a gay teen's sexual confusion as proof that he's merely going through a stage. "Parents will say, 'We can help you change, if only you'd try.'" Some religious organizations have financed advertising campaigns promoting so-called "conversion therapy," which purports to be able to transform homosexuals into heterosexuals. Since sexual orientation is neither a disease nor an ideology, their claims of success are dubious at best, says Dr. Futterman, adding, "There is fairly substantial evidence that such programs can harm people." Professional counseling may be helpful for someone who is uncertain about her sexual identity or how to express it, but the goal is to foster self-acceptance, not to change the person's orientation. Professional counseling may also be helpful for the parents and family to accept and understand the adolescent's sexual orientation.

Sadly, in one study of gay and lesbian high-school students, half claimed to have been rejected by their parents after they disclosed their homosexuality. In another study, one in four adolescent gay males said that family friction over their sexuality grew so heated that they had to leave home. Sometimes the estrangement between parent and child is never bridged. Dr. Futterman, offering advice that applies to any teen, says, "Parents don't have to approve of everything their kids do to be loving and supportive of them."

Perhaps the biggest adjustment for mothers and fathers is the need to revise some of their hopes and dreams for their son or daughter. One of the first thoughts that might cross a parent's mind is, *Now we'll never get to have grandchildren.* That's not necessarily true, because as Dr. Futterman points out, "More and more gay people are having children. But parents do have to allow themselves to go through the process of accepting that some expectations might not come to pass."

Interestingly, when a young person reveals a gay orientation, some mothers and fathers trade places with him. They go into social hibernation, unsure of how relatives, friends and coworkers will react. But keeping secrets is exhausting work and disloyal to your child. Be honest with as many people as you can. Most people will surprise you with their support. If you were proud of him before he disclosed his homosexuality, you should continue to be proud of him now.

A Parent's Support: Educate and Advocate

"All youngsters need their parents' love and involvement," observes Dr. Futterman, "but for gay and lesbian kids, having the guidance and support of their parents can literally be life saving." Rates of AIDS, substance abuse and attempted suicides are considerably higher among homosexual youths than among their heterosexual peers. Ensuring a youngster's safety requires educating and advocating. Educate by giving your child the facts about how he can keep himself healthy; advocate by getting involved in the fight to end discrimination against gay people.

When discussing sexual responsibility with a gay teenager, make sure that he understands the dangers of unprotected anal sex. In contrast to the previous generation of gay men, which was decimated by the HIV virus, a homosexual teenager might not know anyone with AIDS—or might not know he knows anyone, since drugs now can keep people alive for many years. To him the disease is abstract and not an immediate threat.

The importance of using contraception, including condoms, should be impressed upon adolescent girls regardless of their orientation. According to a study from Minneapolis's University of Minnesota, one in five gay and bisexual women have frequent heterosexual intercourse and consequently may be exposed to the HIV virus as well as other STD microbes.

Help your youngster find opportunities for socializing with other gay teenagers. Some communities have gay and lesbian youth centers where youngsters can come just to hang out or to participate in social events, discussion groups, and other services. State departments of health may fund crisis centers and hot lines exclusively for gay youngsters. Such services are most likely to be found in the Yellow Pages under "Social and Human Services"; in the White Pages' Business Listings, under "Gay"; or by searching on-line.

Stand up to prejudice, discrimination and violence against homosexuals. Lesbians and gays are the most frequent victims of hate crimes in the United States—hate crimes being acts perpetrated because of a person's sexual orientation, race, religion or other defining characteristic. You can help to make the world safer for your youngster. For example:

• Refuse to tolerate homophobic remarks or jokes.

• In one survey, more than half the young people polled said that their teachers portrayed homosexuality in a negative light. If that describes your child's school, suggest to the administration that it present a community-education assembly, to enlighten students about antigay harassment and violence. Gay and lesbian community centers and crisis centers often have speakers available to address schools and youth organizations.

13

TOBACCO, ALCOHOL AND OTHER DRUGS OF ABUSE

O f all the potential pitfalls that can trap young people, the one that probably worries parents the most is substance abuse. Happily, the 1980s and 1990s witnessed a considerable downturn in substance use—confirmation of the positive influence that years of antitobacco and antidrug public-awareness campaigns have had on youngsters' attitudes. Since the drug epidemic peaked at the end of the 1970s, regular illicit drug use among twelve-to-seventeen-year-olds has declined by nearly 50 percent.[1] In 1977, when disco music still pulsated from car radios as drivers waited in gas lines, just under one in six teenagers were current users, compared to about one in ten in 1998. Over that same period, alcohol use plummeted by more than half, from one in two adolescents to one in five. The year 1998 also brought a record low in the proportion of teens who had smoked cigarettes in the past month: fewer than one in five.

Nevertheless, substance abuse remains a major national problem. After rates of drug use reached lows in the early 1990s, the latter half of the decade saw an alarming increase in the percentages of young people that experimented with drugs. From 1992 to 1998 regular usage nearly doubled among twelve-to-seventeen-year-olds, from 5.3 to 9.9 percent. The most disturbing trend: Those adolescents who do use substances are trying them at younger ages than

---

1 In the National Household Survey on Drug Abuse, which we cite throughout this chapter, "illicit drugs" encompasses marijuana/hashish, cocaine/crack, inhalants, hallucinogens, heroin or any mind-altering prescription drug that is used nonmedically. The term does not include cigarettes, smokeless tobacco or alcohol.

their counterparts did at the height of the drug revolution. That is a crucial difference to bear in mind, especially if a parent holds the opinion that to smoke a little grass and drink a little beer on occasion is a teenager's rite of passage and nothing to get worked up about.

"I did my share of getting stoned in college, and it didn't turn me into a drug casualty," the parent might say. "Same for most people I knew back then." Perhaps. But in the mid-1960s, the typical first-time pot-smoker was twenty years old, not *fourteen,* as in the mid-1990s.

It is believed that one of the keys to helping prevent boys and girls from experimenting with substances is to begin drug education prior to adolescence. According to a 1999 survey from Columbia University's National Center on Addiction and Substance Abuse, the most dramatic leap in drug awareness comes between the ages of twelve and thirteen. Thirteen-year-olds are three times more likely than twelve-year-olds to know how to buy drugs and to know a student who used so-called "hard" drugs. Middle school is also when attitudes toward drugs are formed. In the Columbia University poll of one thousand teenagers, more than three times as many thirteen-year-olds said that they would not report a kid they observed doing drugs.

We want our messages about the hazards of tobacco, alcohol and other drugs to reach them before then. Studies clearly show that if children can be strongly discouraged from experimenting with substances during adolescence, they will be unlikely to do so as adults. The earlier drug use begins, the greater the chances that a teenager will develop a serious abuse problem.

PREVENTION STRATEGIES

Talk to Your Youngster About Drugs—And *Keep* Talking

"Are you listening to me?" Sometimes it seems as if half of what parents say to teenagers skips off their consciousness like rocks skimmed across the surface of a lake. When discussing the subject of drugs, however, you're liable to have an unusually attentive audience. The Partnership for a Drug-Free America's annual "Partnership Attitude Tracking Study," the largest survey on drug-related attitudes in the United States, sampled the opinions of approximately nine thousand youngsters aged nine to eighteen. Three-quarters of the fourth-graders said that they wanted *more* information about drugs from their parents.

Your words carry weight, too. According to the 1998 survey, the stronger and more frequent the antidrug messages at home, the less likely a child is to become a user. Only 26 percent of adolescents who said their parents had taught them "a lot" about the dangers of drugs had smoked marijuana. But

TABLE 13.1

Parental Involvement Related to Drug Use

"HOW MUCH HAVE YOU LEARNED AT HOME ABOUT THE DANGERS OF DRUGS?"	PERCENTAGES OF TEENS TO HAVE USED:		
	INHALANTS	*LSD*	*COCAINE/CRACK*
A Lot	14%	7%	7%
A Little	22%	11%	9%
Nothing	28%	20%	16%

Source: 1998 Partnership Attitude Tracking Study

among youngsters who claimed to have learned "a little" or "nothing" from their families, the rates of pot use were progressively higher: 33 percent and 45 percent, respectively. That pattern remained consistent for other drugs, too. Overall, boys and girls whose parents ignored the issue were about two times as likely to use drugs than kids who learned "a lot" at home.

A mere one in four teens felt that they were receiving adequate parental guidance. Clearly, more of us have to broach the subject with our youngsters, and on a regular basis. On the following pages, we present some ideas of what to say.

TIPS FOR TALKING TO YOUR CHILD ABOUT SUBSTANCE USE

Leave no doubt as to where you stand. *"You are not to use any drug, including tobacco or alcohol, under any circumstances."* Then explain why:

- Because we love you.
- Because drugs are dangerous, and we don't want to see you harm yourself.
- Because it is against the law.

As when setting any limit, clearly spell out the consequences for defying the rules: what the punishment will be and how it will be implemented. Later in this chapter we suggest plans of action for parents who discover that their child is smoking, drinking and/or using illicit drugs. (See "Making Discipline Work" in chapter 2, "Essential Parenting Skills.")

Don't hesitate to aim for the emotional jugular. Remind your teen that you would be deeply disappointed in his behavior if he were to disobey you on this matter. Research shows that when a child is deciding whether or not to indulge, a key consideration is, *What will my parents think?*

When discussing the dangers of drugs, emphasize the immediate consequences. "Parents have to keep in mind where their children are at developmentally," notes Dr. Richard Heyman, a pediatrician from Cincinnati and former chair of the American Academy of Pediatrics's Committee on Substance Abuse.

"Younger teens tend to think mainly in terms of today, tomorrow and the next day," he explains. "It's not until much later in adolescence that kids begin to contemplate how their actions could impact on their lives down the line." They're also still at a stage of thinking that they are invincible. Therefore, warnings that cigarette smokers are more than ten times as likely to die of lung cancer than nonsmokers are probably going to elicit little more than a shrug from a thirteen-year-old. Or a twenty-year-old, for that matter.

Instead, stress how smoking tobacco causes bad breath, hoarseness and a hacking cough; stains teeth yellow; impairs athletic performance; and in general makes other people not want to be around the smoker. In an American Cancer Society survey, eight in ten boys and seven in ten girls aged twelve to seventeen said they wouldn't date someone who smoked.

Remind your teenager that smoking, drinking and drugging aren't just harmful, they're expensive. A youngster with a pack-a-day cigarette habit sees close to a thousand dollars a year go up in smoke. Surely your son or daughter could find better ways to spend all that money, whether it's buying CDs and clothing or saving up for a car and college.

Appeal to an adolescent's natural independent streak by praising his determination to avoid using drugs. "I admire the way you've stuck to your principles and refused to use drugs. It takes courage to not always go along with the crowd, and I'm proud of you."

Explain to your child that once people start using drugs, they may not be able to stop. *Addiction* is poorly understood, by both substance abusers themselves and those who care about them. The young person with an addiction tells himself and everyone around him that he can quit whenever he wants.

But with prolonged use, the addictive substance triggers long-lasting changes in the chemical composition of the brain. At that point professional treatment is required to cure him of his compulsive behavior. Even then, many tobacco users, alcoholics and drug abusers will relapse and revert to their old ways.

Which Teens Are Most Vulnerable to Substance Abuse?

One in four illicit-drug users between the ages of twelve and seventeen develops dependency, a rate significantly higher than that of any other age group. In talking to your youngster about tobacco, alcohol and *controlled substances* (drugs regulated under federal law), make the point that no one who begins using drugs ever imagines that he or she will become hooked. It's still unclear why our bodies react to drugs differently; why one teenager can flirt with alcohol or pot and then break off the engagement cleanly, while another rushes headlong into commitment.

Heredity appears to play a large role in determining a person's susceptibility to drugs' effects. For instance, the rate of alcoholism among sons of alcoholic parents is four to five times higher than among children of nonalcoholics. If there is a history of substance abuse in your family, tell your child this. Perhaps knowing that she might have inherited a gene predisposing her to addiction will serve as a deterrent.

In addition to genetic traits, certain social and environmental factors raise the odds that a boy or girl may be drawn to alcohol and controlled substances. Do any of the characteristics below apply to your child? The greater the number of risk factors, the greater an adolescent's vulnerability.

- Untreated psychological conditions such as depression, anxiety, conduct disorder, oppositional defiant disorder and personality disorder. For these youngsters, as well as for those with untreated attention deficit hyperactivity disorder (ADHD) and other learning problems that interfere with academic and social success, taking illicit drugs may be their way of self-medicating.

- Temperament: thrill-seeking behavior, inability to delay gratification and so forth.

- An eating disorder.

- Associating with known drug users.

- Lack of parental supervision and setting of consistent limits.

- Living in a family where substance abuse is accepted.

- Living in a home scarred by recurrent conflicts, verbal abuse and physical abuse.

Know the facts. Coming to this discussion well informed will enhance your credibility with your teenager. You'll also be better able to spot problems in the early stages, when they're most treatable. The U.S. Department of Education recommends that, at a minimum, parents should know:

- The different types of drugs and their street names.
- What each drug and any associated paraphernalia look like.
- The physical and behavioral signs of drug abuse.
- How to get a child help if you suspect that he or she has a substance-abuse problem. (See "Teenagers' Drugs of Choice," on page 254.)

Helping Teens Resist Pressure to Try Drugs

The peer pressure to try drugs is no less intense than the sexual pressure that so many adolescents face. As with any situation that could conceivably lead to trouble, we need to prepare our kids to refuse offers of alcohol and other drugs—preferably without alienating their peers, although sometimes that isn't possible. The strategies below mirror those in chapter 12, "Sexuality," for rebuffing sexual advances.

Give them the words to avoid temptation. "Just say no"? It's a start, but few teens bent on enticing a peer to try drugs will let the matter rest there. In fact, substance abusers tend to view converting the "straight" kid as an irresistible challenge, if not their civic duty, and they can be exasperatingly persistent.

"C'mon, dude, you'll love the buzz from this stuff! It's kickin'."

Role-play this scene with your youngster. The repertoire of possible replies includes:

- A firm but friendly "No thanks!" There's no need for self-righteousness, along the lines of "Getting drunk? That's for losers." Let's encourage teens not to label other people as good or bad, only their behavior. Using drugs is wrong, but that doesn't necessarily make the drug abuser a bad person.

- Change the subject. "No thanks. Hey, what did you think of that test yesterday in social studies?"

- Suggest a change of plan. "I was hoping to get you guys to shoot some hoops down at the school. How about it?"

- Say no repeatedly.

"Wanna party with us? This weed rocks!"

"No thanks."

"Aw, c'mon, man! It's killer stuff!"

"Sorry, not interested."

"Not even one toke?"

"Not even one."

- Teach your child respect for her body. "No thanks, I don't drink. Besides, the girls' swim team has a meet tomorrow, and I need to be in top shape."

- Then there's always this standby: "My parents would kill me if they found out that I got high, and they *always* manage to find out!"

Warn your child about the dangers of "date-rape" drugs. In particular, the odorless, colorless drug benzodiazepine flunitrazepam (Rohypnol) has been linked to thousands of rapes in which youngsters secretly drop it into their unsuspecting dates' drinks, alcoholic or otherwise. It quickly causes them to be dizzy, disoriented and to black out.

Share the following tips with your daughter. Reading them could spare her from having to experience one of the most traumatic events of her life, and maybe even save her life.

- Never leave your drink unattended at a party, dance club, restaurant or other gathering. If you have to use the rest room, take it with you or ask a trusted friend to keep an eye on it until you return.

- Don't accept open-container drinks from anyone you don't know well (excluding servers and bartenders).

- Although these substances are difficult to detect in a beverage, be aware of the taste, texture and appearance of your drink. For instance, GHB has a salty taste, while Rohypnol has been described as slightly bitter when sprinkled into alcohol. The new green tablets make light-colored liquids assume a bluish hue; darker liquids turn cloudy.

- Friends look out for friends. If you suspect that another girl has ingested any drug—*including alcohol, the most abused depressant of all*—that could leave her defenseless against a possible rape attempt, get her out of the situation.

A young woman who believes she may have been drugged and sexually abused should go to a rape crisis center or hospital at once and alert the staff.

Among other tests, a urine sample will be analyzed for evidence of any of these substances, which usually remain detectable for about three days. (See "Assisting a Young Victim of Rape" in chapter 12, page 215.)

Examine Your Own Attitudes and Behaviors Toward Tobacco, Alcohol and Other Drugs

Mothers and fathers communicate their most powerful messages about substance abuse through their attitudes and behavior. Youngsters whose parents use tobacco, alcohol or illicit drugs are more likely to imitate those habits themselves. But those of us who smoke or drink can still be good role models.

Eliminate "I need" from your vocabulary. To groan, "I *need* a drink!" (or a cigarette or a headache medication), perhaps after a hard day, implies that the way to solve problems or remedy unhappiness is to reach for a drug.

Consume alcohol responsibly and in moderation. If your son or daughter asks why you drink, emphasize that you enjoy the taste of certain alcoholic beverages—for instance, a glass of wine to complement a fine meal—and that you never drink to deliberately alter your mood. Should you ever overdo it, the next day explain to your children that even experienced drinkers don't always realize when they've had too much.

Don't involve children in your smoking or drinking. No letting them light your cigar, fetch a beer from the refrigerator, help mix a cocktail and so on.

Skip the alcohol the next time you're celebrating a holiday or other festive occasion. Let's show teenagers that people don't need alcohol in order to have a good time.

Never express approval of someone's ability to "hold his liquor," not even in jest. But do point out examples of irresponsible drinking and the consequences. An evening of TV viewing or a night out at the movies should provide more than enough fodder.

If you've attempted to give up tobacco but haven't been successful thus far, take advantage of this opportunity to make your children aware of how habit-forming it is. *"When I started smoking as a teenager, I thought I could quit anytime I wanted. But cigarettes contain a highly addictive chemical called nicotine, which convinces the brain and body that they can't function without it. Once you become dependent on tobacco, like I am, it is tremendously difficult to stop. I hope you'll be smarter than I was at your age and never smoke."*

Abusing alcohol or a controlled substance is incompatible with being a parent. An estimated 12.8 million U.S. children under the age of eighteen live in households with a parent who has used an illicit drug in the past year. That's about one in every six boys and girls. Some 6.6 million children live with one or two alcoholic parents.[2] According to the National Institute on Drug Abuse, these figures are probably on the *conservative* side.

Parents who drink to excess or use illegal drugs undermine their children's sense of safety and stability, for few things are more disconcerting to a youngster than to see Mom or Dad out of control. What's more, their disregard for the law shatters their credibility as moral authorities. This can leave its imprint on a teenager's developing set of values.

If you or your partner have a substance-abuse problem, please get help immediately, either through a peer support group or at a drug-treatment facility. Children of substance abusers, too, can benefit greatly from professional counseling and from attending support groups formed especially for them.

> ### *Four Things You Can Do to Help Reduce Teenage Drug Use in Your Community*
>
> - Lobby the schools to develop extracurricular programs—in academics, the arts, recreation—that will entice students into staying later, so that fewer go home to an empty house. Teens are most likely to experiment with alcohol and other drugs during the hours between school and dinner.
> - Neighborhood parents agree to ensure that all teen parties are supervised and drug-free.
> - Parents volunteer to chaperone student parties, school functions and other activities.
> - Parents agree to alert one another and the police about any local merchants that are known to sell alcohol to underage boys and girls. (Approximately two-thirds of teenage drinkers report being able to purchase their own alcohol.) Until the practice stops, take your business elsewhere.

Get Involved in School and Community Drug-Prevention Efforts

Of sixty-five hundred teenagers interviewed for a U.S. government study, about one in three reported easy access to alcohol and marijuana at school; one in

---

2 These figures probably overlap somewhat, since substance abusers frequently use alcohol *and* illicit drugs.

five said that other drugs, too, were readily obtainable. Approximately 30 percent of the students, in grades six through twelve, claimed to have seen other youngsters attend school obviously impaired by alcohol or other substances.

What does your child say about the infiltration of drugs in her school, and what do you hear from other parents? Does the security on and around campus seem adequate? A good way to learn what is going on is to attend meetings of your Parent-Teacher Association. If enough parents express dissatisfaction with student safety, they should raise their concerns with the administration. Depending on the magnitude of a school's drug problems, there is much that can be done to protect the majority of pupils.

Officials at one school might only need to step up supervision of the hallways and grounds and require students to carry hall passes. At a school plagued by rampant drug use, however, administrators might hire security personnel to closely monitor school property and bar nonstudents from the grounds, and ask local police to patrol the neighboring area for drug dealers.

TEENAGERS' DRUGS OF CHOICE

Tobacco: The First Choice

It took more than thirty years, but in the 1990s the tobacco industry finally conceded that Luther L. Terry had been right all along. Terry was the U.S. surgeon general who in 1964 released the first government report to officially recognize that cigarette smoking was a cause of cancer, chronic bronchitis and other serious diseases.

The tobacco manufacturers' belated admission couldn't have been less startling had they publicly announced that the earth was round; even most teenagers are aware that cigarette use is the leading cause of death from cancer. Whether or not that's enough to dissuade them from smoking is another matter, because what teenagers *don't* understand is the power of addiction.

But the most sinister constituent in tobacco would have to be *nicotine,* the addictive mind-altering drug that keeps smokers coming back for more. Adolescents can become hooked on cigarettes after smoking only a few packs. One national study asked young tobacco users if they thought they would be smoking in five years. Those who replied no were contacted five years later. Three in four were still addicted, still puffing away. Seventy percent of teenage smokers wish they'd never taken up the habit in the first place.

Selling cigarettes to minors is against the law in all fifty states plus the District of Columbia, yet each year children under the age of eighteen purchase more than 947 million packs. The illegal peddling of tobacco products to kids nets $221 million in profits annually.

Fortunately, America's teenagers have largely resisted the tobacco manufac-

Smoking-Cessation Strategies That Work

Most youngsters who smoke heavily attempt to quit tobacco at least once while still in their teens, but only about one in eight do so successfully. Stopping abruptly, or going "cold turkey," rarely works with adolescents; the symptoms of nicotine withdrawal (in order of frequency: nervousness, drowsiness, anxiety, light-headedness, headaches, fatigue) usually send them back to the pack.

One sound strategy combines *behavioral therapy* and *nicotine replacement therapy*. The former consists of short-term counseling from the pediatrician or a nurse, or joining a smoking-cessation support group. Smokers learn how to get along without their cigarettes. While they're cutting down, the nicotine substitute eases withdrawal by delivering a low, even dose.

In Dr. Richard Heyman's experience, young smokers often prefer the nicotine skin patch over other nicotine products (nicotine gum, nasal spray and inhaler), because it is discreet. "They can wear the patch hidden underneath their clothes," he explains. The oral antidepressant Wellbutrin (bupropion) has also been shown to reduce withdrawal symptoms and the urge to smoke, although just how is not known.

turers' overtures. From 1985 to 1998, cigarette use among twelve-to-seventeen-year-olds fell by more than one-third. One alarming trend has been the increase in the number of young female smokers, which now exceeds the number of boys who smoke. Dr. Richard Heyman attributes this to girls' growing obsession with staying slim. "They learn from their friends that nicotine is a potent appetite suppressant," he observes. "Plus, cigarette ads portray girls who smoke as sexy, assertive and independent."

WHAT EVERY PARENT AND TEEN SHOULD KNOW ABOUT TOBACCO

SIGNS OF TOBACCO USE

- dizziness
- burning of the eyes, nose, throat

TABLE 13.2

Drugs of Choice for Twelve-to-Seventeen-Year-Olds

SUBSTANCE	USED IN PAST 30 DAYS	USED IN PAST YEAR	USED IN LIFETIME
1. Alcohol	19.1%	31.8%	37.3%
2. Cigarettes	18.2%	23.8%	35.8%
3. Marijuana and Hashish	8.3%	14.1%	17%
4. Hallucinogens	1.8%	3.8%	5.3%
5. Analgesics (Painkillers)	1.3%	3.1%	4.6%
6. Smokeless Tobacco	1.2%	3.7%	8.9%
7. Inhalants	1.1%	2.9%	6.1%
8. Cocaine and Crack	1.0%	2.2%	2.9%
9. Stimulants	0.6%	1.2%	1.7%
10. Depressants	0.5%	1.7%	2.7%
11. Heroin	0.2%	0.3%	0.4%

Source: 1998 National Drug Household Survey, U.S. Department of Health and Human Services, Substance Abuse and Mental Health Services

- bad breath
- stained teeth and fingertips
- hoarseness
- shortness of breath
- smoker's cough, a hacking cough caused by inflammation of the respiratory tract from tobacco smoke
- tremors
- decreased appetite
- hair and clothes that reek of tobacco smoke

POSSIBLE LONG-TERM EFFECTS OF TOBACCO USE

- cancers of the lung, larynx, oral cavity, esophagus, kidney, bladder and pancreas
- heart disease
- asthma, chronic bronchitis, emphysema and other respiratory illnesses
- increased health risks to others, by way of the *sidestream* cigarette smoke that curls into the air; the Environmental Protection Agency (EPA) has declared secondhand smoke a class-A carcinogen capable of triggering cancer in humans

TOBACCO: A GATEWAY DRUG

The most serious *immediate* effect of smoking is that it introduces a youngster to the subculture of substance abuse. Granted, not all tobacco users graduate to addiction, but according to the Centers for Disease Control and Prevention, adolescents who smoke are three times more likely to drink alcohol, eight times more likely to smoke marijuana and twenty-two times more likely to use cocaine. For that reason, tobacco has been dubbed a "gateway" drug.

Dr. Heyman compares smoking cigarettes to on-the-job training for other substances. "Through smoking," he explains, "kids learn a number of skills that they will need if they're going to become regular drinkers, marijuana users and users of other drugs. To begin with, they learn how to obtain an illegal product, how to hide it and how to con their parents into thinking they don't smoke. Then they learn how to smoke and how to use a mind-altering drug; they figure out how to sense its effects, how large a dose they need and how to 'pace' themselves.

"So the choice to use cigarettes is really the opening of Pandora's box."

OTHER FORMS OF TOBACCO

- **Smokeless Tobacco.** Twenty-six million containers of *chewing tobacco* and *snuff* are illegally sold each year to young people under the age of eighteen, virtually all of whom are boys, no doubt trying to emulate their favorite major league baseball stars or to look like a rough, tough cowboy.

Most probably equate "smokeless" with "harmless," which isn't the case at all. Tobacco dippers face a much higher risk of cancer than nonusers. Within just three years of their first chaw, more than half develop *leukoplakia*, a premalignant condition marked by thick, white patches in the mouth. Unless surgically removed, the lesions will grow larger, and they can become quite painful. Roughly one in twenty will progress to oral cancer.

As for immediate effects, warn your teenager that chewing tobacco is almost certain to dim a user's social prospects. Cigarettes, in spite of their well-known dangers, still enjoy an inexplicable association with sophistication and sensuality. Not smokeless tobacco. It does, however, permanently stain teeth reddish-brown, and it also dulls the senses of smell and taste, promotes tooth and gum decay and produces breath that is extremely foul.

Contrary to what many young people believe, smokeless products are more addicting than cigarettes, particularly snuff. According to the National Clearinghouse of Alcohol and Drug Information, an average-sized pinch held in the cheek for just thirty minutes releases the nicotine equivalent of two to three cigarettes. Former tobacco users who've given up both habits will often attest that discarding their cigarettes was easier compared to quitting smokeless tobacco.

- **Cigars.** In a most radical image change, the cigar has undergone a resurgence in acceptance. Once scorned as a token of antiquated values and a crassly capitalistic society, the cigar has again come to symbolize success, wealth and status. From 1993 to 1998, sales in the United States doubled.

The trend has filtered down to adolescents, unfortunately, with one in four high-school students having lit up. Cigar packages, unlike those for cigarettes, do not bear the surgeon general's warning, which might lead youngsters to assume that cigars are less hazardous to your health. In fact, cigar smokers are twice as susceptible to cancers of the respiratory tract as nonsmokers. The swallowed tobacco juice also bathes the digestive tract, giving rise to tumors of the esophagus, stomach and other gastrointestinal organs. Furthermore, cigars contain higher nicotine levels than cigarettes.

Memo to Mom and Dad: Sometimes a cigar is just a cigar, sometimes it's not. Resourceful drug users buy blunt-shaped brands to make *blunts.* They scrape out most of the tobacco and pack the leaf or paper wrapper with marijuana. The result: an immense joint that looks like a legal cigar.

- **Bidis.** These exotic-looking, greenish-brown unfiltered cigarettes from India are growing in popularity with adolescents. The main attraction of *bidis* (pronounced "*bi*-dees" or "*bee*-dees") is their price, about half that of regular cigarettes. They also resemble marijuana joints, which undoubtedly adds to their appeal.

Because bidis are often sold in health-food stores and rarely contain health warnings, kids often assume they're smoking an herbal product, when in fact these not-so-itty bidis contain pure tobacco. They come in flavors such as chocolate, vanilla and grape; the sweet scents mask the pungent taste of the tobacco. A federal study conducted by the Centers for Disease Control and

Prevention in 1999 found that bidis produced five times the tar of cigarettes and more than three times the carbon monoxide and nicotine.

Alcohol: The Most Popular Choice

Try explaining *this* to a teenager:

Alcohol is by far the most widely used psychoactive drug in the United States. Four in five men and women over the age of twelve have tried it, two and a half times the number to have experimented with marijuana. There are approximately 18.3 million alcohol abusers and alcoholics in the United States[3]; every year 3.4 million Americans aged twelve and older undergo treatment for alcoholism and alcohol-related problems. Alcohol contributes to one hundred thousand deaths annually, including nearly two in five traffic fatalities. Similar proportions of drownings, boating deaths, fatal falls, fire-related deaths and industrial fatalities also can be traced to alcohol abuse. The financial cost to society from alcohol abuse is approximately $166.5 billion a year, for medical treatment, rehabilitation therapy, lost earnings, car crashes and so forth. That's $55 billion more than the cost from all other drugs combined.[4]

Yet while the possession, use or sale of those other drugs is against the law, alcohol is legal for those aged twenty-one or older.

"We have a double standard in this country," observes Dr. Peter Rogers, a pediatrician and specialist in addiction medicine at Children's Hospital in Columbus, Ohio. "Parents will say, 'My kid may be drinking, but at least he's not doing drugs.' "

An adolescent may employ similar logic to gain permission to drink alcohol. *"C'mon, Dad, the three of us are just gonna split a six-pack while watching the playoffs at Andy's house. How come you and your friends get to do it and we can't? Besides, it's not like I'm smoking weed or shooting up heroin. It's just beer."*

In discussing alcohol use with a teenager, address the glaring contradictions in our societal views about drinking. Your candor will be appreciated. Here is an example of what you might say:

"It does seem hypocritical, doesn't it, that we say it's okay for adults to drink

---

3 In the particular study from which these figures are taken, "alcohol abuser" is defined as a drinker who during the past year experienced at least one severe or moderately severe consequence of alcohol abuse, such as job loss, arrest or illness; "alcoholic" is defined as a drinker who during the past year exhibited one or more symptoms of alcohol dependence, such as loss of control or a symptom of alcohol withdrawal.

4 Not including tobacco.

but not to smoke marijuana. Maybe nobody should use alcohol at all, but it's such a part of our culture that I don't see us going back to the days of Prohibition anytime soon.

"Until you turn twenty-one, our rule on alcohol is simple: You are not to drink, if for no other reason than it is against the law. Once you're of legal age, then it will be your decision whether or not to use alcohol. Illicit drugs, you are never to take; I don't care how old you are."

WHAT EVERY PARENT AND TEEN SHOULD KNOW ABOUT ALCOHOL

Adolescents who drink usually start with beer, wine or wine coolers, a sweet-tasting blend of wine and carbonated fruit juice, which many youngsters tend to guzzle like soda pop. Although many teenagers mistakenly believe that these drinks are "safer" than hard liquor, it's the amount of alcohol you drink, not what you drink, that matters. Fact is, a twelve-ounce can of beer and a four-ounce glass of wine each has the same amount of alcohol as a shot of eighty-proof whiskey, and wine coolers have the same amount of alcohol as many beers. *Proof* is twice the percentage of *ethanol,* the active ingredient in alcohol. Thus an eighty-proof drink contains 40 percent alcohol.

There is no generalization we can make about how much alcohol it takes to get drunk. Everyone is different in his or her ability to metabolize alcohol, and women metabolize it less efficiently than men. However, we do have a legal definition of drunkenness—the *blood alcohol content,* or BAC, in each state has been established for drivers and the means to assess BAC, which can be done through a *Breathalyzer test,* which measures the weight of alcohol in a volume of breath, or a blood test. BAC is expressed as a percentage.

The legal limit varies from one state to another, ranging from .05 to .09 (grams per 210 liters of breath or 100 milliliters of blood). You can see from the table below surprisingly little alcohol is necessary to render a young person legally drunk and unfit to drive. In 1998, drunk drivers between the ages of sixteen to twenty were responsible for 7,755 fatal car crashes, a decline of one-third from ten years before. (See "Automobile Safety" in chapter 14, "Safety and Injury Prevention.")

Perhaps Pass on That Party Punch . . .

Party punches spiked with substantial amounts of alcohol can taste deceptively mild, because fruit juices disguise the flavor. When your youngster attends a teenager's party, remind her to ask if the punch contains any alcohol before she ladles herself a cup.

TABLE 13.3

Calculating Blood Alcohol Content

He weighs	160 pounds	**She weighs**	120 pounds
He drinks	8-ounce glass of wine (10% alcohol content)	**She drinks**	8-ounce glass of wine (10% alcohol content)
Number of drinks	3	**Number of drinks**	3
Time elapsed since first drink	2 hours	**Time elapsed since first drink**	2 hours
His estimated blood alcohol content (BAC)	0.08 BAC	**Her estimated blood alcohol content (BAC)**	0.13 BAC

SIGNS OF ALCOHOL USE

- slurred speech
- impaired judgment and motor skills
- poor coordination
- confusion
- tremors
- drowsiness
- agitation
- combative behavior
- nausea and vomiting
- depression
- weight gain
- possession of a false ID card
- smell of alcohol on breath

POSSIBLE LONG-TERM EFFECTS

- blackouts and memory loss
- vitamin deficiencies
- malnutrition
- suppression of the immune system, which leaves a person open to infectious diseases such as pneumonia and tuberculosis

- hormonal deficiencies, sexual dysfunction, infertility
- inflammation of the pancreas (pancreatitis)
- alcoholic hepatitis
- alcoholic cirrhosis
- cardiovascular disease and stroke
- alcohol-withdrawal delirium, or *delirium tremens,* which can range in intensity from mild irritability and sleeplessness, to frightening hallucinations and delusions

While the most serious physical effects of excessive drinking typically take many years to develop, alcohol abuse can exact a terrible toll on adolescents' lives.

Car crashes are just the most obvious of the adverse consequences of getting drunk. Statistics from the National Council on Alcoholism and Drug Dependence implicate alcohol use in about half of all sexual assaults involving adolescents and college students, including date rape. A frighteningly high proportion of teens—one in six—admit to having experienced alcohol-induced blackouts, where they could not recall the events of the previous evening.

Sexually active teens who overindulge are also less likely to protect themselves against pregnancy and sexually transmitted diseases, for the simple reason that they're too besotted to take the necessary precautions before having intercourse. The fact that heavy drinking wears down the immune system adds to their risk of contracting a sexually transmitted disease (STD).

A point to impress upon boys and girls: It isn't just confirmed alcoholics who suffer the more harrowing repercussions of alcohol abuse. A single episode of reckless drinking can end in tragedy, as when a boy slides behind the steering wheel of a car while under the influence, or when an intoxicated young woman accepts a bar acquaintance's offer to continue partying back at his apartment.

NO UNDERAGE DRINKING EVER! ANY QUESTIONS?

Some genuinely caring mothers and fathers not only allow their teenagers to drink, but encourage it—so long as it's done at home. The rationale? "I'd rather have him drink here at home, where I know what's going on, than to have him out drinking at a friend's house or who knows where, and maybe get arrested or crash the car." It's hard to fault such logic, at least in theory.

In reality, it's a poor idea. As Dr. Rogers notes, "The parents who say they're going to let their teenager drink at home are sending a clear message that it's okay to use alcohol. Most teenagers growing up in a household where that's the attitude are extremely likely to drink." And not just at home, he adds.

Once this genie is out of the bottle, so to speak, parent and child may both regret having removed the cork. Whereas it takes adults anywhere from eight to twelve years to progress from first drink to alcoholism, young people can streak there in a matter of months, because their bodies and minds aren't fully mature.

"I've worked with many fifteen-year-old alcoholics," says Dr. Rogers. "They haven't damaged their brains and bodies as much as older alcoholics, who've subjected themselves to years of abuse. But they exhibit the hallmark of the disease, which is the continued use of alcohol despite negative consequences. If a kid is getting into fights, or getting into trouble with the law, or has blackouts, and yet he continues to drink, that's an alcoholic. The criteria is the same whether he's thirteen or thirty."

BINGE DRINKING: COLLEGE TREND WITH A SORRY END

The National Minimum Drinking Age Act of 1984, the centerpiece of efforts to reduce young people's alcohol consumption by raising the drinking age from eighteen to twenty-one, has yielded impressive results. One lingering storm cloud in this otherwise brightening sky has been the increase in binge drinking among eighteen-to-twenty-five-year-olds. At the start of the 1980s, 75 percent of college-age men and women used alcohol; by the end of the 1990s, that figure had fallen to 60 percent. Yet the rate of bingeing has hovered above 30 percent, meaning that about one in three members of this age group knocked back five or more drinks in one sitting (four or more for women) in the past month; nearly one in seven had binged *five times* in the past month. (On an encouraging note, binge drinking has declined significantly among younger teens, from one in five in 1985 to one in thirteen in 1998.)

Bingeing has become so prevalent on college campuses, it's a wonder that schools don't station bouncers at dormitory entrances to conduct ID checks. A Harvard School of Public Health survey of college students found that 50 percent of the men and 39 percent of the women binged regularly. And they're teetotalers compared to residents of fraternity or sorority houses, who are four times as likely to be binge drinkers as other students.

Every person's physical tolerance for alcohol differs; therefore it's impossible to state categorically that drinking *x* amount induces *alcohol poisoning,* the severe and potentially fatal reaction to an alcohol overdose. But with a blood alcohol content (BAC) between 0.20 and 0.29, a youngster might exhibit poor coordination and feel nauseated; a BAC between 0.30 and 0.39 could cause him to pass out and bring about memory loss. For the BAC to exceed 0.40, a person would have to consume the equivalent of *sixteen* drinks. At that level, the portion of the brain that regulates breathing becomes depressed. If treatment isn't initiated promptly, the person may sink into a coma or die; the odds of surviving are about fifty-fifty.

Alcohol and Other Drugs:

Terrible Twosome

Combining alcohol and depressants or marijuana or other drugs produces *synergism,* whereupon the effects of each chemical are intensified. Naturally this increases the threat of an overdose.

When a teenager takes hits off a joint in between gulps of alcohol, the pot disarms the portion of the brain that ordinarily would put an end to the evening's carousing by inducing vomiting. But marijuana switches off this "vomit control," which under normal circumstances instructs the valve at the bottom of the stomach to close, sealing off the entrance to the rest of the digestive tract. Instead, the toxic alcohol is allowed to proceed into the small intestine, then pass into the liver. The adolescent continues drinking, oblivious to his body's distress—until it refuses to be ignored any longer.

Colleges are justifiably concerned over the prevalence of bingeing. Some have taken steps to reduce the availability of alcohol and to encourage alcohol-free rock concerts and other dry events. If you have a child who has battled any addiction in the past, you might want to steer him away from colleges with reputations as "party" schools. Or maybe you insist that he not join a fraternity during his freshman year. The idea, as with any recovering substance abuser, is to minimize temptation as much as possible. A particularly vulnerable young person might do well to initially attend a local college and commute from home. This way, his parents can continue to monitor his progress until everyone feels he's ready to possibly transfer to a school out of town. (See "The Transition from High School to College" in chapter 9, "Planning Ahead for College.")

Controlled Substances: Out of Control

The Controlled Substances Act (CSA), part of the Comprehensive Drug Abuse Prevention and Control Act of 1970, is the legal cornerstone of the government's war against drug abuse. The U.S. Drug Enforcement Administration (DEA) has divided these substances into five categories, called "schedules," based on each drug's (1) potential for abuse, (2) safety, (3) addictive potential and (4) whether or not it has any legitimate medical applications.

Schedule I includes marijuana, heroin and other narcotics, and hallucinogens such as LSD and psilocybin. All are street drugs, with no accepted therapeutic uses. But there's a good chance that your medicine cabinet contains one or more potent highs from one of the other categories. For example, if someone in the family recently underwent major surgery, there might be a vial of the powerful narcotic painkiller Demerol, a schedule II medication, sitting next to the dental floss. Methylphenidate, which goes under the brand name Ritalin, is commonly prescribed to treat attention deficit hyperactivity disorder (ADHD) in children and adults, as are two other schedule II drugs, Adderall and Dexedrine.

Benzodiazepines, a family of sedatives, muscle relaxants and more, belong to schedule IV. They rank among the most widely used pharmaceuticals in the country—and also among the most abused. Finally, what household doesn't have a bottle of cough syrup stored somewhere under the bathroom sink? Many brands are laced with the ubiquitous narcotic analgesic/cough suppressant codeine. Swigging a bottle of that is enough to zonk out a youngster, not to mention make him good and sick. The fact that as many as one in four adolescents have tried inhalants—sniffing the vapors of ordinary household products like glue, nail-polish remover and cleaning fluid—tells us the lengths some teenagers will go to alter their consciousness.

CANNABIS (MARIJUANA)

Marijuana's psychoactive potency is measured chiefly by the amount of *Delta-9-tetrahydrocannabinol (THC)* it contains. The THC content of domestic marijuana used to average just 1 percent. But improvements in the way the *cannabis* plant is selected and cultivated have increased the strength fivefold. And sinsemilla, which is derived from the buds and flowering tops of the unpollinated female plant, may have a THC content of up to 17 percent. So marijuana is not only at least five times stronger than what was available in the 1970s and 1980s, but, "At least 40 percent of this potent marijuana is now homegrown, making it much easier to obtain," explains Dr. Richard Schwartz.

Although a person cannot overdose on marijuana, regular use can lead to dependency. Chronic pot smokers may exhibit signs of what is called *amotivational syndrome*. As the term implies, they act listless and apathetic and no longer seem to care about their personal appearance, activities they'd once enjoyed or their future. A study of college students demonstrated that heavy marijuana use impairs critical skills related to attention, memory and learning even after the drug had been discontinued for a minimum of twenty-four hours.

Researchers contrasted two groups of undergrads: One group had smoked marijuana approximately twenty-nine out of the past thirty days; the other group had smoked only one day during that time. Following a day of abstinence from marijuana and other illicit drugs and alcohol, the study's subjects were given several standard tests measuring aspects of attention, memory and learning. Compared to the light users, the heavy marijuana users made more errors and experienced more difficulty sustaining their attention, shifting their attention to undertake new tasks, and registering, processing and using information.

RELATED PARAPHERNALIA

- cigarette rolling papers
- wooden, metal and glass pipes
- bongs (water pipes)
- alligator clips ("roach clips")
- scales
- razor blades
- resealable plastic bags
- butane lighters
- matches
- foil-wrapped cakes of hashish

LEGAL OR ILLEGAL

Illegal. Aside from Marinol, a prescription drug containing THC and used as an appetite stimulant for people suffering weight loss for a variety of reasons, no approved medical uses.

SIGNS OF MARIJUANA USE

- a sweet burnt scent on clothes, breath, in youngster's bedroom
- mood swings
- euphoria
- giddiness and inappropriate laughter
- difficulty concentrating
- lapses in short-term memory
- slowed reflexes and loss of coordination
- glassy, red eyes
- increased appetite ("the munchies")
- dry mouth

- increased heart rate
- delusions
- hallucinations
- anxiety
- irritability
- combativeness
- drowsiness

POSSIBLE LONG-TERM EFFECTS

- amotivational syndrome
- weight gain
- increased risk of cancer, particularly lung cancer and cancers of the head and neck
- with heavy use, delayed or arrested sexual development
- lower sperm counts and lower testosterone levels for men; increased risk of infertility for women
- irregular menstruation

INHALANTS

Many kids' first drug experience comes from inhaling chemical fumes to get high. This practice, called "huffing," "sniffing," "snorting" and "bagging," has continued to climb steadily among younger teens. By age fourteen, one in five boys and girls have tried inhalants at least once; fortunately, the incidence begins to flag after eighth grade or so.

Inhalants are easy to buy, inexpensive and unlikely to arouse suspicion. If Mom does inquire what happened to the half-full aerosol container of dessert topping in the refrigerator, a youngster can lie that she loves eating whipped cream out of the can—not that she was holding it up to her nose, depressing the nozzle *just so,* then breathing in the intoxicating nitrous-oxide propellant. The effects usually last only a few minutes.

With the exception of amyl nitrite and butyl nitrite, inhalants are legal, although most states have passed laws banning the sale of commonly abused products to minors. Still, in almost any home, a child's search is bound to turn up at least one of the legal highs in the box on the following page. It's impractical to think that you can banish all *one thousand* potential inhalants from your household or that you could remember to always keep them locked up in a utility closet when not in use.

Kids need to hear that snorting inhalants can decimate brain cells permanently. The chemicals can also send the heart into cardiac arrest, causing

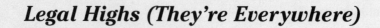

Legal Highs (They're Everywhere)

Kitchen: Cooking spray, disinfectants, fabric protectors, felt-tip markers, furniture polish and wax, oven cleaners, vegetable cooking sprays, whipped cream in aerosol cans, spot remover

Bathroom: Air fresheners, spray deodorants, hair sprays, nail-polish removers

Garage/Workshop: Pressurized aerosol sprays, butane, gasoline, glues and adhesives, lighter fluid, paint, paint thinner, paint remover, propane, refrigerants (Freon), rust removers, spray paints

Miscellaneous: Shoe polish, rubber cement, asthma spray, typewriter correction fluid

instantaneous death. *Sudden sniffing death,* as this is called, is responsible for more than half the fatalities from inhalant abuse. Other overdose victims typically asphyxiate. Ominously, no one can predict from one time to the next how much of an inhalant it would take to cost a youngster her life.

RELATED PARAPHERNALIA

- handkerchiefs and paper bags reeking of inhalants
- aerosol cans
- small metal cylinders with an attached pipe or balloon, for sniffing nitrous oxide (buzz bombs)

LEGAL OR ILLEGAL

Most of these products are readily available in any store, with two exceptions: amyl nitrite, which requires a prescription, and butyl nitrite, which is an illegal substance. Nitrous oxide is used medically for anesthesia.

SIGNS OF INHALANT USE

- an unusual number of spray cans in the trash
- chemical-like smell on breath, clothing and skin
- sores or rashes around the nose and mouth, known as "glue sniffer's rash"
- paint or stains on body or clothing
- drunk, dazed or glassy-eyed expression
- nausea
- appetite loss
- anxiety, excitability, irritability
- slurred speech
- impaired coordination
- suppressed breathing
- wheezing
- numbness and tingling of the hands and feet
- headaches

POSSIBLE LONG-TERM EFFECTS

- brain damage
- pains in chest, muscles, joints
- heart trouble
- deep depression
- toxic psychosis
- nerve damage
- fatigue
- appetite loss
- impaired sense of smell
- hearing loss
- irregular heartbeat
- bronchial-tube spasming, similar to an asthma attack
- nosebleeds
- diarrhea
- nausea
- bizarre, reckless or violent behavior
- asphyxiation
- damage to the bone marrow, liver and/or kidneys
- brain damage
- irregular menstruation

HALLUCINOGENS

Hallucinogenic drugs, on the wane throughout the 1980s, found a receptive constituency in 1990s adolescents. By the end of the decade, annual use of LSD (lysergic acid diethylamide) by high-school seniors was the highest it had ever been: one in twelve.

The effects of most hallucinogens are unpredictable. They depend on the amount taken; the user's personality, mood and expectations; and the surroundings in which the drug is used. Usually, a teenager begins to feel the initial effects of the drug within thirty to ninety minutes. In addition to producing physical symptoms, psychedelics can bring about rapid mood swings, delusions, visual hallucinations, distortions of time and a phenomenon called *synesthesia,* in which the user "tastes" sounds or "hears" colors.

Hallucinogenic "trips" range from less than an hour on DMT, to six hours on psilocybin, to twelve hours on LSD and peyote. On a bad trip, which can happen the first time the drug is taken or anytime thereafter, users are entombed in terrifying thoughts and feelings, panic, fear of going insane or dying and despair that they'll be trapped in this state forever like passengers on an endless ride through an amusement-park house of horrors.

According to the U.S. Drug Enforcement Administration, today's acid is about one-third as strong as it was during the drug's original heyday in the late 1960s. The lower dose, or *tab,* produces milder effects and fewer horrific trips. Many LSD users experience what are called *flashbacks,* in which their minds briefly replay the visual hallucinations of a previous trip. A flashback comes on without warning and may occur a few days or many months after their last psychedelic excursion. It may never recur again or happen repeatedly. It's not known why some people are tormented more than others, but stress, fatigue and drug abuse are all believed to trigger episodes.

RELATED PARAPHERNALIA

- vials
- resealable plastic bags and bottles of pills, powder, liquid
- syringes
- eyedroppers

LEGAL OR ILLEGAL

Illegal. No medical uses.

SIGNS OF HALLUCINOGEN USE

- delusions
- hallucinations
- "seeing" sounds and "hearing" colors
- a trancelike state
- excitation
- euphoria
- seesawing emotions or feeling several emotions at the same time
- distortions of time, space, body image
- increased heart rate, blood pressure and body temperature
- sleeplessness
- dilated pupils
- tremors
- appetite loss
- profuse sweating
- dry mouth
- slurred speech
- bizarre, irrational, paranoid and/or aggressive behavior
- detachment from others

Effects of PCP (phencyclidine)

At low to moderate doses:

- shallow, rapid breathing
- elevated blood pressure and heart rate, flushed skin
- profuse sweating
- numbness of the arms and legs
- lack of coordination
- feeling of detachment, estrangement

At high doses:

- drop in blood pressure, pulse rate and respiration
- nausea, vomiting
- blurred vision
- rapid, involuntary eye movements
- drooling
- garbled, incoherent speech
- dizziness, loss of balance
- seizures
- coma

- hallucinations
- auditory hallucinations
- distorted images
- amnesia
- delusions
- paranoid, violent behavior
- enhanced muscle strength and lowered pain perception, a dangerous combination
- jumbled thinking
- time and body movements seem to occur in slow motion

POSSIBLE LONG-TERM EFFECTS

- unpredictable flashbacks to a previous "trip"
- schizophrenia
- severe depression
- memory loss
- impaired speech
- weight loss
- irregular menstruation

In teenagers, chronic PCP use may interfere with hormones related to normal growth and development, and impair their ability to learn.

HEROIN AND OTHER NARCOTIC ANALGESICS (PAIN RELIEVERS)

Heroin use, while rare, has seen a major resurgence among teenagers. One in one hundred have tried the highly addictive narcotic, which is processed from the potent painkiller *morphine,* the major active component in *opium.* The bitter dried juice of the Asian poppy plant has been used to relieve pain for centuries. Other narcotic analgesics, like Demerol and methadone, are synthesized in the laboratory.

The heroin sold on the street today bears little resemblance to the heroin that was available in 1980, when the average bag was 4 percent pure. "Now people can buy heroin that is 40 percent pure," says Dr. Schwartz, "or even 66 percent pure." Yet as the quality has risen, prices have gone down, due to increased competition from a number of foreign countries.

That purer heroin could lead to more overdoses is troubling enough. But in addition, it's so strong that users can get high by snorting or smoking the powder instead of having to inject themselves under the skin or in a vein.

Because of this, the younger generation doesn't necessarily associate heroin only with strung-out junkies shooting up in a garbage-strewn basement. To them, ingesting the pure powder may seem glamorous, like having a toot of cocaine, and not know how dangerous it really is.

> ### *Words Worth Knowing*
>
> **Bag:** glassine envelope containing 200 to 400 milligrams of heroin. A *nickel bag* sells for $5; a *dime bag* sells for $10, and so on.
> **Spoon:** equal to four bags.

Heroin activates the brain's pleasure center, producing a transcendent high. Users describe feeling a wave of euphoria wash over them. *The rush.* Then the undertow gently pulls them into an alternately wakeful and drowsy state. With regular use, greater amounts are needed to achieve the same intensity, and physical dependence and addiction develop. Reducing the dosage or quitting "cold turkey" will bring on days of agonizing withdrawal symptoms. Addicts ultimately depend on heroin not to feel good but to avoid feeling bad.

RELATED PARAPHERNALIA

- syringes
- burnt spoons
- bottle caps and other cooking implements
- glass pipes
- razor blades
- cotton balls
- tourniquets
- glassine envelopes
- resealable plastic bags
- eyedroppers
- bottles
- aluminum foil packets
- rolled-up dollar bills and straws, for snorting
- pipes
- butane lighters
- matches

LEGAL OR ILLEGAL

Some, such as codeine, are available by prescription only; heroin is illegal.

SIGNS OF NARCOTICS USE

- needle marks, skin infections and/or abscesses
- lethargy
- drowsiness ("nodding off")
- euphoria
- coughing and sniffling
- nausea
- constipation
- contracted pupils
- pupils unresponsive to light
- slowed breathing
- slurred speech
- slow gait
- droopy eyelids
- dry skin, itching
- profuse sweating
- twitching
- appetite loss

POSSIBLE LONG-TERM EFFECTS

- heart or respiratory problems
- mood swings
- tremors
- chronic constipation
- toxic psychosis
- appetite loss
- collapsed veins from repeated injections
- blood-borne infections, including HIV/AIDS and hepatitis, from contaminated needles
- track marks
- irregular menstruation

STIMULANTS

COCAINE AND CRACK

The use of cocaine, the scourge of the prosperous 1980s, crashed resoundingly by the end of the decade, as did a number of those who abused it. Ironically, when the stimulant first attracted the attention of the baby boomer generation, it had been touted as harmless and non-habit-forming. A *recreational* drug.

Hardly. Even now, with cocaine use less than half of what it once was, addiction to the drug accounts for more admissions to publicly funded rehabilitation programs than any other form of substance abuse, with the exception of alcohol.

At the height of the mid-1980s surge in cocaine abuse, roughly one in eight high-school seniors had used the drug in the previous year. Another one in twenty-five had tried the new smokable permutation *crack,* which is made by mixing the powdered "salt" cocaine with a dangerously flammable chemical to convert it back to its original "freebase" form. Smoking the small rocks of hardened paste produces an immediate, more intense high. (The name refers to the crackling sound the drug makes when freebased.) Crack is more addictive than powdered cocaine and also more affordable. However, the effect is short-lived: five to ten minutes, as opposed to the fifteen-to-thirty-minute high from cocaine. Thus teenagers who are dependent on crack need hits more frequently.

The hazards of coke and crack received massive news coverage. Presumably, the reports scared off a sizable portion of young substance abusers, because both drugs took a tumble in popularity.

Use of other stimulants has also dipped sharply from the 1981 high of one in four twelfth-graders. In 1998, only one in ten admitted to having taken uppers.

MDMA (ECSTASY)

Sometimes a substance arrives linked to a cultural phenomenon, as with Ecstasy, also called "Adam" or "XTC" on the street. The amphetamine is frequently taken in preparation for attending large late-night dances called raves, supposedly to enhance the experience. Ecstasy is an *analog,* one of the "designer drugs" synthesized by underground chemists in an attempt to evade the Controlled Substance Acts.

An analog closely resembles another chemical structurally, but the clandestine laboratories alter the formula just enough to render it a different compound and thus not covered under the law. The Drug Enforcement Administration (DEA) began adding these modified drugs to its list of controlled substances in 1984, but new analogs promise to keep materializing on the street.

Disciples of Ecstasy, a synthetic amphetamine with hallucinogen-like properties, insist that it breaks down barriers of communication, enhances music and promotes warm, tranquil vibes—echoing the claims once made about LSD.

Ecstasy is a dangerous chemical (see "Effects of Ecstasy," page 278), and should not be used. However, one in twelve high-school seniors who responded to the 1999 Monitoring the Future Study (a national survey that tracks drug-use trends among America's adolescents) admitted to having tried MDMA, an increase of nearly 40 percent over the year before.

Some young people have gravitated toward herbal ecstasy, which is marketed as a "natural" alternative and is available over the counter in most states. "Many of the herbal ecstasy products are junk," Dr. Schwartz says bluntly. "They have no effect.

"Other brands, though, contain an ancient Chinese herb called ephedra, or *ma huang*. The active chemical in ephedra is ephedrine, a stimulant. It can elevate blood pressure, but it also dries you out by preventing sweating and salivation. That combination can cause heat stroke and a number of other problems." Ephedrine-laced dietary supplements have been implicated in seventeen deaths and hundreds of adverse reactions, leading several states to ban the products.

METHAMPHETAMINE

Methamphetamine is the only other stimulant besides Esctasy to have widened its hold on young people. It has been approved for attention deficit hyperactivity disorder in children, though it is often difficult to obtain. Physicians prescribe the powdered form sparingly, though, because meth, or "speed," is extraordinarily addictive.

Like cocaine, the drug can be processed illegally into smokable crystal-like chunks sold on the street as "ice." Either form propels users on an intense high lasting anywhere from two to twenty-four hours. But once the effects wear off, they come crashing down into an oppressive psychological low that can linger for days. Chronic methamphetamine abusers may experience hallucinations and emotional disturbances virtually indistinguishable from schizophrenia, a major mental disorder.

RELATED PARAPHERNALIA

- vials
- resealable plastic bags
- syringes
- cotton balls
- matches
- butane lighters
- spoons, bottle caps and other implements for "cooking" the drug over a flame
- straws, rolled-up dollar bills, for snorting

Cocaine/Crack

- mirrors
- razor blades
- straws, small plastic tubes, rolled-up dollar bills, for snorting
- scales
- "snow seals" (folded pieces of white paper) and foil strips, for storing
- tiny plastic bags
- syringes
- matches
- butane lighters
- glass vials
- glass pipes
- bottles of ether, sodium bicarbonate or ammonia, used in freebasing
- ceramic mortar and pestle, for crushing rock cocaine

LEGAL OR ILLEGAL

Cocaine, amphetamines and methamphetamine are available only with a written prescription.

SIGNS OF STIMULANT USE

- excitability
- mental clarity
- euphoria
- talkativeness
- restlessness
- aggressive behavior
- following the high, a "crash," or depression, marked by irritability, anxiety, paranoia, agitation
- dilated pupils
- visual and auditory hallucinations
- rapid, irregular heart rate
- elevated blood pressure
- fever
- convulsions
- dry nose and mouth
- stuffy nose and sniffing, from snorting cocaine

Effects of Ecstasy

- confusion
- depression
- sleep disturbances
- drug craving
- severe anxiety and paranoia during and sometimes weeks after taking MDMA (psychotic episodes have been reported)
- muscle tension
- involuntary teeth-clenching
- nausea
- blurred vision
- rapid eye movement
- faintness
- chills or sweating
- increased heart rate and blood pressure

POSSIBLE LONG-TERM EFFECTS OF STIMULANTS

- violent or erratic behavior
- hallucinations
- drug-induced psychosis
- appetite loss
- insomnia
- impaired sexual performance
- chronic respiratory problems
- nosebleeds, ulceration of the mucous membrane of the nose and perforation of the nasal septum, from snorting cocaine
- blockage of the tear ducts from snorting cocaine, leading to serious eye infections and eventually the destruction of the bone in the eye sockets
- cardiac or respiratory arrest
- irregular menstruation

DEPRESSANTS

Depressants encompass several large groups of drugs that slow down the central nervous system. In small doses, they affect sections of the brain responsible for our conscious, voluntary actions, while large doses act on areas that govern automatic functions like breathing and heart rate.

Hypnotics are prescribed as sleeping aids.

Tranquilizers are divided into two categories. "Major" tranquilizers are used to treat mental illness. You may hear them referred to as *neuroleptics* or *antipsychotics.* "Minor" tranquilizers, also called *anxiolytics,* ease anxiety without slowing down the body.

Sedatives exert a calming effect on the mind and body. In higher doses, many also induce sleep. Some see double duty as *anticonvulsants,* for controlling seizures, and as muscle *relaxants.*

Teenage abuse of depressants tapered off in the 1980s and remained relatively stable in the 1990s. Only about one in eighteen adolescents have experimented with these drugs, despite their presence in millions of home medicine cabinets. An estimated four million prescriptions are written for tranquilizers each year. But that number is dwarfed by the number for sedatives. One type of sedative, *benzodiazepines,* accounts for 30 percent of controlled substances prescribed by U.S. doctors.

The potential for addiction is high. *Barbiturates,* the forerunner to benzodiazepines, quickly lead to tolerance. When that happens, the margin of safety between an effective dose and a lethal dose narrows dangerously. It's akin to driving a car along a treacherous mountain ridge, with a breathtaking view on one side and a precipitous drop on the other. A young person under the influence may be too heavily sedated to remember how much of the drug he or she has taken, and inadvertently overdose.

Barbiturates still make up one-fifth of all prescriptions for depressants, but serious side effects and the high incidence of fatalities eventually led to the development of benzodiazepines in the 1960s. While these medications are safer overall, chronic use can progress to dependence, and to ingest them with alcohol may be courting death.

A benzodiazepine called flunitrazepam (brand name: Rohypnol) began infiltrating American dance clubs in the 1990s. Though illegal here, "roofies" are smuggled in from the dozens of foreign countries where they are routinely prescribed to treat severe insomnia and psychiatric disorders. Just one of the inexpensive white tablets induces intoxication equivalent to two six-packs of beer and is ten times more powerful than another sedative, Valium. Taking Rohypnol and alcohol together heightens the effects.

In response to this growing problem, Congress passed the Drug-Induced Rape Prevention and Punishment Act of 1996. Now anyone who uses Rohypnol or another drug to aid in committing a sexual attack can be sentenced to up to twenty years in prison. What's more, although flunitrazepam remains a schedule IV controlled substance, the penalties for manufacturing, smuggling or distributing it were increased to those of schedule I depressants.

The drug's manufacturer also took steps to make the product more detectable in beverages and thus thwart would-be rapists. First it colored the tablets green and reformulated them so that they take longer to dissolve. Then the company phased in a new Rohypnol that is half the dose of the now-discontinued original. However, it may take years before the less potent roofies receive approval in every one of the many countries in which they are marketed.

Not only that, but Rohypnol is just one of several so-called "date-rape drugs." The others, GHB (gamma hydroxybutyrate), GBL (gamma butyrolactone, a precursor of GHB) and the hallucinogen ketamine (an animal tranquilizer) are also being used to spike girls' drinks for the purpose of sexually assaulting them. At high doses, these chemicals can send a young woman into a deep comalike sleep lasting anywhere from one to eight hours.

SIGNS OF DEPRESSANT USE

- slurred speech
- inability to speak
- depressed breathing and heart rate
- sluggishness, drowsiness
- dilated pupils
- dizziness, confusion, disorientation
- poor concentration
- poor coordination
- blackouts
- sleeping for long periods of time
- amnesia
- nausea
- vomiting
- skin rashes
- large swollen areas of skin, sometimes with open sores, at injection sites
- tremors
- seizures
- lack of inhibitions
- delusions
- hallucinations, especially when taken with alcohol

POSSIBLE LONG-TERM EFFECTS

- aggressive behavior
- profound depression
- irregular menstruation

ANABOLIC STEROIDS

The word *anabolic* means growing or building. Anabolic steroids, synthetic versions of the male sex-hormone testosterone, promote the growth of muscles, bones and skin. Steroid users who exercise and eat a high-protein diet will usually see significant increases in their lean muscle mass.

In 1975 the International Olympics Committee banned steroid use by all participants. The National Football League and other professional sports organizations soon followed suit. By then, however, the drugs had begun filtering down into high schools, and not just the gym locker rooms. With teen media force-feeding youngsters idealized images of muscle-bound boys and perfectly proportioned girls, more and more adolescents started turning to steroids purely for cosmetic reasons.

"Many of them aren't athletes," observes Dr. Gene Luckstead, a sports-medicine specialist in Amarillo, Texas. "They just want to 'look better,' bulk up, strut around the beach. Until adolescents decide that the price tag is too high, it is likely to continue."

You would think that unwanted side effects such as shrunken testicles and breast growth (gynecomastia) for boys and facial hair and deep, masculine voices for girls would deter kids from these drugs, but three-fourths of all steroid users are teenagers. Because their bodies are still developing, the synthetic hormone can stunt a youngster's growth permanently.

A lucrative black market has made it easy for teenagers of either sex to procure illegal steroids over the Internet, through mail-order businesses, at the gym, from friends "and sometimes from their coaches," Dr. Luckstead says disapprovingly. There are roughly a dozen different brands available, in both oral and injectable forms. Abusers typically combine multiple steroid preparations, in a practice known as "stacking," for six to fourteen weeks. Then they temporarily reduce the dosage or stop altogether before beginning another cycle. To "pyramid" is to slowly escalate the number of drugs taken, or the dose and frequency of one or more steroids; reach a peak amount midway through the cycle; and gradually taper the dose. Adherents claim that pyramiding maximizes muscle-building and minimizes adverse side effects, though this is difficult to prove scientifically. Perhaps the greater incentive for stacking and pyramiding is that the two practices help abusers outfox drug tests.

Anabolic steroids should not be confused with corticosteroids, a family of synthetic hormonal drugs frequently prescribed to treat asthma and other common conditions.

OTHER PERFORMANCE-ENHANCING DRUGS

The ban on anabolic steroids has also created a market for substances that are purported to provide the same benefits as anabolic steroids, but without the undesirable side effects and at a fraction of the cost. Because products such as creatine and androstenedione are classified as dietary supplements, they do not fall under the regulatory power of the U.S. Food and Drug Administration. Therefore, children can purchase them without a prescription and without their parents' knowledge or consent.

Creatine monohydrate is a synthetic version of a natural substance in the body that powers muscle contractions. At doses of 5 to 20 grams per day, the powdered supplement does appear to increase adult athletes' muscle strength and energy for short periods of repetitive, high-intensity exercise. However, we don't know much about its effects, positive and negative, on adolescents, or its long-term impact on the body.

As for androstenedione, once ingested, a natural enzyme in the body converts it to testosterone. There was sufficient belief that the supplement enhanced athletic performance and could possibly be harmful that the National Football League, the International Olympic Committee and the National Collegiate Athletic Association all prohibited its use. Professional baseball, however, still allows its players to take the tablets.

RELATED PARAPHERNALIA

- vials
- resealable plastic bags
- hypodermic needles, for injecting drugs into muscle tissue

LEGAL OR ILLEGAL

Many steroids have legitimate medical uses in humans and animals. They are available by prescription only.

SIGNS OF STEROID USE

- severe acne
- wild mood swings and angry, combative behavior known as "roid rages"
- delusions
- feelings of invincibility

In Teenagers

- premature halt in physical growth

In Men

- shrunken testicles
- hair loss
- breast development (gynecomastia)
- impotence
- reduced sperm count
- painful or difficult urination

In Women

- growth of facial hair
- irregular menstruation
- cessation of menstruation
- enlarged clitoris
- breast reduction
- deep-pitched voice

POSSIBLE LONG-TERM EFFECTS

- liver damage
- primary liver cancer
- jaundice
- fluid retention
- high blood pressure
- trembling
- bad breath
- swollen feet or ankles
- aching joints
- increased chance of injury to muscles, tendons and ligaments
- in men, lowered sperm count and infertility

INTERVENTION STRATEGIES

Adolescents who abuse alcohol or other drugs can be as secretive as undercover agents, leading double lives. In the Partnership for a Drug-Free America's 1998 Partnership Attitude Tracking Study, only 14 percent of the parents surveyed acknowledged the possibility that their children had tried marijuana. Then the youngsters were polled. Three times as many—42 percent—admitted to having smoked pot.

When Parents Believe a Teenager
May Be Experimenting with Drugs

According to studies of young people in drug treatment, some were abusing alcohol and other substances for more than two years without their mothers or fathers knowing. We suspect that many times it's more a question of not *wanting* to know, because when a child is on drugs, the household may be beset by other problems—faulty communication, for starters.

To parents who may already be feeling inadequate or guilty, admitting that a son or daughter is using drugs may be too hard to face. We would certainly encourage moms and dads to honestly appraise the state of family life and to make improvements wherever necessary. But adolescent substance abuse doesn't affect just delinquent youth from neglectful homes. Plenty of "good kids" get mixed up in drugs, much to the dismay of their conscientious, loving parents.

The first step in addressing any problem is to acknowledge it. If you've been carrying around the nagging feeling that your teenager may be doing drugs, please don't ignore it. Communicate your concerns to your child. Having physical evidence in hand can help to force the issue, which raises the question: Is it ethical to search an adolescent's room?

When all signs point to substance abuse, says Dr. Adele Hofmann, "a parent has every right to violate a kid's privacy and look for drugs. I wouldn't make a habit of it," she emphasizes, "but teenagers are not autonomous adults living in their parents' houses. Sometimes, in order to protect them, this is what's necessary."

GETTING TO THE TRUTH

Raging at a suspected substance abuser is not likely to elicit a confession, and even if it does, what then? Parents need to be able to present a plan of action, so that the youngster understands their main concern isn't to be punitive but to help him get off drugs. Likewise, never confront an adolescent who is intoxicated. Wait until he has sobered up.

Before you talk to your youngster, take time to figure out a strategy to approach him or her. If you're at all unsure of what the next step should be, call your child's pediatrician for advice. Next, select a time when interruptions will be minimal. Take the phone off the hook and send other kids in the family outside or to a movie. Then abide by these rules of fair play:

Avoid direct accusations of drug involvement until you have all the facts.
After all, you could be wrong. Some behaviors that suggest substance abuse,

like a flat affect and acting distant, could also be symptomatic of depression. Or perhaps the teen is having a hard time in school but hasn't confided all the details.

Don't belittle or heap on the guilt, as in, "You keep this up, mister, and you'll kill your father!" Substance abusers are usually well acquainted with self-loathing and may already feel remorseful for the heartache they've caused. Ratcheting up their feelings of worthlessness and shame probably will not motivate them to stop. If anything, it might compel them to get high, in order to mute their pain.

You might try stating your concerns this way: "We've noticed some changes in you lately." Name them. "We love you and sense that something may be troubling you. Sometimes people act differently because they experiment with drinking or other drugs and then realize that they've gotten in over their heads.

"Should we be concerned about that? If so, we hope you will be honest with us and tell us so that we can help you to stop, because drugs are too big a problem for any kid to have to handle all by himself."

Pediatrician's Perspective

DR. PETER ROGERS: *"I had one case where two parents were very frustrated because they couldn't get their teenage son to talk to them about his drinking problem. Fortunately, I have some experience in this, so I had them bring the boy in to see me.*

"The four of us talked together for a while. Then, before the parents left the room, I explained to everyone that whatever the boy told me was confidential. 'Unless it involves something life-threatening,' I told the parents. 'Then I'll tell you.'

"I started talking to this teenager, and he trusted me. It turned out that he was drinking a whole lot more than his parents realized. He was also doing cocaine. I told him that by using cocaine and alcohol together, he was endangering his life, and that his parents had a right to know. He finally agreed. Before the family left my office, he told his parents the truth."

POSSIBLE REACTIONS

Your teenager may admit everything to you right then and there. But probably not. Drug users are usually virtuoso con artists. They have to be. Spinning a web of lies is how they manage to shuttle back and forth between their two worlds. By the time their behavior is finally drawing suspicion, they've deceived Mom and Dad so many times that who can blame them for thinking they can get away with it once again?

So expect to hear:

"Drugs? I've never used drugs. I swear. Not even once!" *(The look-you-in-the-eye-and-feign-innocence con.)*

"I can't believe you have so little faith in me!" *(The I'm-deeply-insulted-that-my-own-parents-would-think-I-could-do-such-a-thing con.)*

"All right, so me and some friends have gotten drunk once in a while. I don't have a *drinking problem,* okay? It's not a big deal. I'll stop, I promise." *(The let-me-tell-you-what-you-want-to-hear-and-get-you-off-my-back con.)*

Taking Appropriate Action

Assessing how to handle an adolescent's substance abuse is a decision that few parents are prepared to make alone. We suggest consulting a mental-health professional who specializes in this field. Your youngster's pediatrician may be able to begin intervention himself, then refer you to an experienced local practitioner. Other sources for recommendations include:

- the psychiatry/psychology departments at area hospitals
- your state or county department of mental health
- state or county chapters of professional organizations such as the American Psychiatric Association, the American Psychological Association and the National Association of Social Workers
- the American Medical Association
- any of the following three national help lines:
  1. DrugHelp, a service of the American Council for Drug Education (ACDE)
  2. National Council on Alcoholism and Drug Dependence (NCADD)
  3. National Drug and Alcohol Treatment Referral Routing Service of the Center for Substance Abuse Treatment (CSAT)

The direction therapy will take depends on the extent of a youngster's involvement with drugs. Typically, the problem is more serious and goes back farther than the parents imagined and the teenager is willing to admit. According to Dr. Schwartz, the types of substances and paraphernalia used reveal a great deal about an adolescent's stage of chemical dependency.

"Let's say that you find a bag of marijuana in your kid's room," he says. "It's almost always going to be his, even though he may claim that he's 'holding' it for someone else. This tells you that the teenager has gone beyond the passive acceptance of marijuana at a party once or twice and has actively made a purchase. Also, he wants the drug badly enough that he's willing to risk storing it at home.

"If you find a good-sized bong," he continues, "you know that he's had experience with high-grade marijuana, because he knows how to concentrate the marijuana smoke by using one of these large water pipes." Based on the evidence, you'd have to place the young person in this example at stage two on a scale of one to four.

General behavior, too, will influence which intervention is most suitable. "Is this kid cooperative at school and at home?" Dr. Schwartz asks rhetorically. "Has he been reasonably honest and responsible? Or is he rebellious and untrustworthy, and disruptive to the household? If it's the latter, then treatment probably needs to be more restrictive," which might include inpatient care in a hospital program rather than an outpatient program. Taking him out of the home temporarily might be best for the family, too, especially if the household includes impressionable younger brothers and sisters. Never lose sight of the fact that one member's addiction becomes everyone's problem; their needs also require attention.

The following overview of treatment strategies is intended to introduce you to the various approaches to helping abusers straighten out their lives. These are general guidelines, not recipes for sobriety. Every adolescent's situation is unique, and therapy must be tailored accordingly.

Treatment Options for First-Time Offenders at Stage One:
Occasional Use of Tobacco, Alcohol and Marijuana

Impose stricter limits at home. At stage one, drugs have not yet hijacked an adolescent's life or corrupted her values. Parents may be able to discourage future use through stricter discipline alone. The goal of imposing measures like those below isn't so much to penalize as it is to keep the youngster out of situations where drugs are likely to be present.

We recommend putting the terms in writing, as part of a formal agreement between parents and child. From the outset, it should be understood that a second violation of the no-alcohol, no-controlled-substances policy will result in immediate placement in a drug-treatment program.

For every month that the teen adheres to the "contract," standards can be relaxed; perhaps you extend weekend curfew by an hour, restore his full allowance, and so on. But if he breaks a rule, the restrictions are tightened. Responsibility is rewarded, noncompliance is penalized.

SAMPLE FAMILY AGREEMENT

I _____ [*teenager's name*], promise to observe the following rules:

1. No using alcohol or controlled substances.
2. No using tobacco.
3. No associating with friends who are known to use drugs or who have gotten me in trouble in the past.
4. No leaving school grounds during the day.
5. On school days, coming straight home from class or from extracurricular activities.
6. No going out on school nights, unless to an activity or function okayed by Mom or Dad.
7. No attending parties without adult supervision.
8. All callers must identify themselves to Mom or Dad, or they will not be put through.
9. When friends are over, the door to my room must be kept open at all times.
10. Obeying weekend curfew.
11. Responsible for same number of chores as before, but for less allowance—just enough to cover a teenager's necessities.
12. Car use is restricted to approved activities only.
13. Mom and Dad reserve the right to search my room for cigarettes, alcohol and other drugs.

Date effective:

Signed:

_____
[*Teenager's Name*]

_____
[*Parent's Name*]

_____
[*Parent's Name*]

After six months to a year, whenever you feel it's time, you can discuss whether or not the agreement should remain in effect. If your teenager has earned back your trust, wonderful! Return to your normal household rules. Oh yes: Do allow him the satisfaction of ripping this contract to shreds.

Home Drug Testing?
Not a Wise Idea

Some addiction experts advocate that adolescent substance abusers be randomly screened at home for traces of drugs. Urine-testing kits, similar to home pregnancy tests, are widely available.

The American Academy of Pediatrics opposes the idea of parents demanding urine specimens from their son or daughter, primarily on the grounds that it creates an antagonistic atmosphere when the family should be focused on mending and moving forward.

Furthermore, the test kits are not foolproof; a positive result must be verified at a second laboratory. And truly cunning youngsters know they can purchase additives, detoxification formulas—even powdered urine—that will ensure a negative finding.

Treatment Options for First-Time Offenders at Stage Two:
Frequent Use (Four or Five Times per Week) of Alcohol, Marijuana, Inhalants, Stimulants and Depressants— Has Purchased Drugs

Impose stricter limits at home.
Insist on attendance at a peer-support twelve-step program.

PEER-SUPPORT GROUPS

Peer-support groups such as Cocaine Anonymous, Marijuana Anonymous and Narcotics Anonymous are modeled after Alcoholics Anonymous (AA), the fellowship that was founded in 1935 by two chronic drinkers. During their lifetimes, they were known only as "Bill W." and "Dr. Bob S.," for anonymity is one of the cornerstones of "self-help" organizations, in which substance abusers help one another maintain abstinence.

"Group" meets once a week or more, usually in public libraries, houses of worship and community centers, and members are free to attend other chapters' meetings if they wish. The average AA member takes in two meetings per week; some people go daily. What do they get out of it? Mainly, the knowledge that they are not alone, and strength from listening to former drug users talk openly about how they continue to battle their addictions. To help abusers keep up their resolve between meetings, each one chooses a "sponsor"—a veteran member of the same sex who has stayed sober. This person agrees to be available by phone twenty-four hours a day to lend encouragement and a sympathetic ear.

According to AA, nearly half its membership has maintained sobriety for more than five years. All groups are open to teenagers, although boys and girls under the age of twenty-one make up just 2 percent of the organization. (Eleven percent of Narcotics Anonymous members are under age twenty.) Since young people may not be comfortable sharing personal stories with a room full of adults, check around for adolescent-only groups.

We recommend that parents sit in on the first few meetings open to non-members, then gradually let the youngster attend on her own. If this makes you uneasy, consider dropping her off and waiting in the car or outside the room.

Treatment Options for First-Time Offenders at Stage Three:
Daily Use of Aforementioned Substances Plus Cocaine
and Hallucinogens—Involved in Selling Drugs
First-Time Offenders at Stage Four:
Chemically Dependent—Needs More Drugs to Achieve Desired
Effect and to Avoid Withdrawal Symptoms
First-Time Offenders at Stage Five:
Addicted—Needs Drugs to Feel Normal and to Avoid Withdrawal
Second-Time Offenders at Any Stage:

Impose stricter limits at home.
Drug abuse treatment program.

DRUG ABUSE REHABILITATION PROGRAMS

Substance abuse is treatable. But as with any rehabilitative therapy, the prospects for recovery brighten when the intensity of therapy and the setting for therapy closely match the extent of the person's problem.

For drug users who are not yet addicted, treatment typically consists of *behavioral therapies:* individual psychotherapy and counseling, group therapy and peer-support groups like those described above. The goal is to show youngsters new ways of living drug-free. One technique is *contingency management,* a system of rewards and punishments intended to present abstinence as more appealing than substance abuse. Family therapy, too, is an essential component of treatment, to repair the damage that is all but inevitable when a member of the household is using drugs.

For young people who are addicted to narcotics or sedatives, treatment often combines behavioral therapies and drug therapy. Methadone and levomethadyl (LAAM), used to wean patients off heroin and other opioids, block the physiological craving and silence the withdrawal symptoms. They are employed one of two ways. For *detoxification,* or *medically assisted withdrawal,* the addict receives just enough of the substitute drug to suppress the most severe effects of withdrawal. Methadone is taken daily; levomethadyl, three times a week. Over the course of two days to two weeks, the dose is tapered under strict medical supervision. A similar approach can be utilized for withdrawal from sedatives, using long-acting sedatives, which are then gradually reduced.

Maintenance therapy attempts to achieve the same result, but over a period of months, and using a higher dose than for detox. Not only does the surrogate drug put an end to withdrawal symptoms and the hunger for narcotics, but if the addict reverts to his old behavior and uses again, he won't experience the high. A third, less-commonplace drug, naltrexone (ReVia), prevents the high but not the craving. It does, however, diminish the desire for alcohol and is used in alcoholism treatment.

Critics of maintenance therapy contend that it merely substitutes one addictive substance for another. Proponents would counter that the treatment's objectives are not only to cure people of narcotics addiction but to reduce the number of overdoses and stem the spread of AIDS by way of contaminated needles. According to researchers at the National Institute on Drug Abuse, it has succeeded on both counts.

TYPES OF TREATMENT PROGRAMS

Short-Term Outpatient Therapy

Of the approximately seventy-five thousand adolescents admitted to substance-abuse treatment programs each year, four in five are seen as outpatients. They go to school during the day, then report to a drug-rehab clinic, which may be a freestanding facility or within a hospital or mental-health center.

These programs are typically for kids whose lives are relatively under control and who do not require medical therapy to stop them from using. Treatment involves a full range of behavioral therapies. After roughly four to six months, the staff reevaluates the young patient. If she is pronounced recovered, she enters the *aftercare* phase of treatment. Once a week for the next six months to a year, she either returns to the clinic for counseling or participates in a peer-support group.

Short-Term Residential Therapy

Many of these programs, often referred to as *chemical-dependency units,* base themselves on Minnesota's world-renowned Hazelden rehabilitation center. Four weeks of inpatient care, on average, are followed by six to twelve months of aftercare as an outpatient. When necessary, detox is carried out on the premises or at an affiliated hospital or clinic.

Long-Term Outpatient Maintenance Therapy

Drug abusers receive their doses of methadone or levomethadyl as outpatients, and return to the center for counseling, also on an outpatient basis.

Long-Term Residential Therapy (Therapeutic Communities)

When an adolescent has been using drugs for a long time, not only does he need to be set free from substance abuse, he must be redirected toward a new lifestyle. This may not be possible if every day he returns to the same environment as before.

Therapeutic communities are just that: residential communities of recovering substance abusers. They may be located in a cramped city building or on sprawling estatelike grounds. Whatever the setting, the daily routine is usually a highly structured blend of academic classes, therapy sessions, exercise, social-skills training and chores. If it sounds a bit like boot camp, it is, except that your drill sergeant is likely to possess a degree in social work or psychology.

After six to nine months, the youngster is transferred to a separate dormitory, called a *halfway house,* as part of his preparing to rejoin society. While in the reentry phase, which lasts another three to six months, he attends school or works at a job. The final phase is outpatient aftercare, for an unspecified amount of time. In all, treatment can take anywhere from nine months to two years.

The American Academy of Pediatrics recommends inpatient drug treatment under any of the following circumstances:

1. When previous attempts at sobriety have failed.
2. When the child has become a danger to himself or to others.
3. When the child has run away from home or seems suicidal.
4. When the child's physical and emotional health have deteriorated to a point that is life-threatening.

As a general rule, the longer the treatment, the more favorable the outlook. Studies show that patients who remain in therapy for more than three months usually fare better than those who don't reach that landmark. Likewise, inpatient programs tend to be more successful than outpatient care. One to two years following treatment in a therapeutic community, 60 percent of all admissions showed significant improvement, while more than 33 percent could be declared success stories.

HOW TO FIND A DRUG TREATMENT PROGRAM

When calling or visiting a prospective drug treatment center, don't hesitate to ask as many questions as necessary about its staff and services. A program that meets the following guidelines should inspire reasonable confidence in its caliber of care.

1. The program adheres to an abstinence-only policy. No nonmedical drug use is tolerated.

2. The program includes a comprehensive evaluation by an experienced physician to diagnose and treat any associated medical, emotional or behavioral problems.

3. The staff includes a psychiatrist or a clinical psychologist with expertise in adolescent behavior and development and in treating chemical dependency.

4. The facility maintains a low ratio of patients to staff.

5. Support groups led by a professional facilitator and self-help groups are integral components of treatment.

6. If the center treats both minors and adults, the adolescent unit should be separate from the adult unit.

7. The program must include family therapy.

8. The program must include an aftercare phase, typically consisting of outpatient counseling or attending a peer-support group for up to one year or more.

9. Depending on the youngster's needs, the program should include academic classes, vocational training, social-skills training, physical education and other services intended to aid his reentry into society.

10. The program's administrators should be willing to discuss financial arrangements.

11. *Inpatient programs and hospital-based outpatient programs should be approved by the Joint Commission for the Accreditation of Healthcare Organizations, the largest accreditation organization of its kind. To find out if a treatment center is accredited, call the JCAHO at 630-792-5000.*

Aftershocks: When Treatment Ends

Once a teenager completes substance-abuse treatment, family members sometimes fool themselves into believing that the crisis is over. But to prevent history from repeating itself, everyone in the household needs to understand that the former drug abuser is entering perhaps the most trying time of her recovery.

With the end of aftercare, the final line tethering them to a sober lifestyle having been snipped, recovering substance abusers often shoulder tremendous pressure and feel as if they are under surveillance—which, truth be told, they probably are. They themselves are most likely worried about how they'll react the first time someone offers them a drink or a hit off a marijuana joint.

Although this phase of therapy is called reentry, it is actually a step into a different world. Former drug users have to learn to enjoy themselves and find excitement without the aid of chemicals and the lifestyle they built around it. They have to find a new self-identity, a new daily narrative. What's more, they may have to learn to fill this void in their lives without much help from friends. As Dr. Schwartz explains, "On the one hand, they're not supposed to hang around with their old friends—the kids who use drugs. But other cliques may not accept them.

"Also, kids who have done drugs for a long time miss out on some of the tools they need to grow up." They may be lacking in social skills, he notes, "and still may act as if the world revolves around them. It's a lot for them to deal with."

Their parents probably feel as if they've been through the emotional wringer; several cycles' worth, in fact. But their recovering teen needs them more than ever. Here are several things that mothers and fathers can do to bolster their youngster's commitment to staying straight:

1. Praise your teen when appropriate.

2. Help him to cultivate new interests through structured and unstructured activities.

3. Encourage him to learn alternative techniques for handling stress, like relaxation exercises.

4. Be tolerant of his attempts to find new ways of expressing his individuality.

5. Work with him on polishing his refusal skills.

6. Suggest he join a self-help group or continue to attend his meetings. Studies show that former substance abusers who become involved in these groups are less likely to use drugs after treatment. Researchers from the Stanford University School of Medicine found that the major benefit of self-help groups is simple: They provide a pool of new friends who encourage sobriety.

7. If he should backslide and use drugs, explain to him that this one mistake doesn't equal failure. Two in three adolescents who go through drug rehabilitation relapse at least once.

8. Above all else, reassure your teen that he can always confide in you and that he always has your love.

DRUG APPENDIX

Types of Cannabinoids

MARIJUANA (SCHEDULE I CONTROLLED SUBSTANCE)

- *The most commonly used illicit drug in the United States.*

- *Slang terms include:* pot, grass, weed, loco weed, tea, Thai sticks, reefer, joint, herb, others.

- *Looks like:* a green, brown or gray tobacco-like mixture of dried, shredded flowers and leaves of the hemp plant, *Cannabis sativa.*

- *How it is used:* rolled in cigarette paper (*joint*) or stuffed into a hollowed-out cigar (*blunt*) and smoked; can also be mixed into foods—brownies, for instance—and used to brew tea. Produces a high lasting two to three hours.

DELTA-9-TETRAHYDROCANNABINOL
(SCHEDULE I CONTROLLED SUBSTANCE)

- *The main psychoactive ingredient in* Cannabis sativa.

- *Slang terms include:* THC.

- *Looks like:* soft gelatin capsules.

- *How it is used:* ingested orally.

HASHISH (SCHEDULE I CONTROLLED SUBSTANCE)

- *The resinous material of the* Cannabis *plant, which is dried and then formed into cakes, balls and other shapes. It is five to ten times more powerful than marijuana, with a THC content of around 6 percent.*

- *Slang terms include:* hash, black Russian.

- *Looks like:* brown or black cakes or balls.

- *How it is used:* placed in a pipe or water pipe (*bong*) and smoked.

HASH OIL (SCHEDULE I CONTROLLED SUBSTANCE)

- *Neither hashish nor oil. What resembles oil is in fact one of several solvents that can be used to extract the mind-altering chemicals from the* Cannabis *plant. THC content: 15 percent, on average.*

- *Looks like:* a syrupy liquid, varying in color from amber to dark brown.

- *How it is used:* added to a cigarette and smoked. A drop or two of hash oil produces the same psychoactive effect as a single marijuana joint.

DRONABINOL (SCHEDULE II CONTROLLED SUBSTANCE)

- *Synthetic THC, used to stimulate appetite and control nausea and vomiting in people with cancer and other serious illnesses.*

- *Brand name:* Marinol.

- *Looks like:* tablets.

- *How it is used:* ingested orally.

Types of Inhalants

AMYL NITRITE/BUTYL NITRITE (UNREGULATED)

- *Amyl nitrite is a flammable liquid once used to treat the heart condition angina pectoris; butyl nitrite is a vasodilator similar to amyl nitrite, but less potent.*

- *Brand names:* ram, thrust, liquid gold, others.

- *Slang terms for amyl nitrite include:* poppers, snappers, pearls, amies, ames, boppers.

- *Slang terms for butyl nitrite include:* rush, snappers, rush snappers, bolt, others.

- *Looks like:* clear, yellowish liquids sold in tiny glass ampules or bottles. Both have a pungent, etherlike odor.

- *How it is used:* Users place the container up to their nose and inhale the vapors. The ampules are snapped in half with the fingers, producing the pop! or snap! sound that gave these drugs their street names.

GASES (NITROUS OXIDE AND THOSE USED IN HAIR SPRAY, SPRAY PAINT AND OTHER PRESSURIZED AEROSOL SPRAYS) (UNREGULATED)

- *Nitrous oxide, found in whipped-cream cans and car fuel, is used medically as a general anesthetic.*

- *Slang terms for nitrous oxide include:* laughing gas, whippets, shoot the breeze, buzz, grocery-store high, nitro.

- *Looks like:* nitrous oxide is sold in small metal cylinders with balloons.

- *How it is used:* huffed directly from the can, bottle or container; from balloons; or from paper bags or a piece of clothing or cloth.

LIQUID SOLVENTS (UNREGULATED)

• *Glues, paints, nail-polish remover and other liquid solvents found in many household and industrial products.*

• *Slang terms for liquid solvents include:* air blast, Oz, spray.

• *How it is used:* huffed directly from the can, bottle or container; or from paper bags or a piece of clothing or cloth.

Types of Hallucinogens

LYSERGIC ACID DIETHYLAMIDE (LSD) (SCHEDULE I CONTROLLED SUBSTANCE)

• *One of the most potent mood-altering chemicals, manufactured from an acid found in the fungus ergot.*

• *Slang terms include:* acid, barrels, window pane, blotter acid, cube, microdot, white dust, purple haze, sugar cubes, others.

• *Looks like:* colored tablets, capsules; thin squares of gelatin; blotter paper impregnated with the colorless, odorless chemical and divided into small decorated squares. LSD is occasionally sold in liquid form.

• *How it is used:* ingested orally; licked off the absorbent paper; the liquid and gelatin can be put in the eyes.

MESCALINE/PEYOTE (SCHEDULE I CONTROLLED SUBSTANCES)

• *Mescaline is the principal active ingredient in peyote, a small, spineless cactus plant indigenous to the southwestern United States and northern Mexico. Mescaline can also be manufactured synthetically.*
• *Slang terms include:* mescal, cactus buttons, cactus head, mesc, blue caps, moon, others.

PSILOCYBIN/PSILOCIN (SCHEDULE I CONTROLLED SUBSTANCES)

• *A pair of chemicals derived from wild mushrooms found in Mexico and Central America; can also be produced in the laboratory.*

- *Slang terms include:* psychedelic mushrooms, 'shrooms, purple passion, mushies, sacred mushrooms.

DIETHYLTRYPTAMINE (DET); NN-DIMETHYLTRYPTAMINE (DMT); ALPHA-ETHYLTRYPTAMINE (AET) (ALL SCHEDULE I CONTROLLED SUBSTANCES)

- *A family of hallucinogens, all closely related to one another in chemical structure and effects.*

KETAMINE (SCHEDULE I CONTROLLED SUBSTANCE)

- *An anesthetic closely related to PCP; used by veterinarians primarily to immobilize cats and monkeys.*

- Brand names: Ketaset, Vetalar.

- *Slang terms include:* K, special K, ket, kit kat, cat Valium, super acid, super C, bump.

- *Looks like:* white crystalline powder, liquid, capsules.

- *How it is used:* The liquid is injected, applied to marijuana or another smokable substance, or mixed into drinks. The powder, too, can be consumed as part of a drink, smoked or snorted.

PHENCYCLIDINE (PCP) (SCHEDULE II CONTROLLED SUBSTANCE)

- *PCP was once used by veterinarians as an anesthetic for animals. So many young people abused the drug, though, that in 1978 the Drug Enforcement Administration reclassified Sernalyn, as it was known, as a schedule II drug. Its manufacturer discontinued phencyclidine shortly thereafter. Use among high-school seniors plummeted from about 12.8 percent in 1979 to 2.4 percent by 1992. PCP, considered one of the most dangerous drugs of abuse, can make users hostile and violent toward others or suicidal.*

- *Slang terms include:* angel dust, hog, animal trank, elephant, belladonna, DOA, magic dust, others.

- PCP combined with marijuana: killer joints, supergrass.

- PCP combined with crack: space blasting, star dust, white powder.

- *Looks like:* crystalline powder ranging in color from white to tan to brown; also turns up on the market in the forms of tablets, capsules, liquids.

- *How it is used:* ingested orally, injected, but most often applied to a leafy substance such as mint, parsley, oregano or marijuana, and smoked.

Selected Types of Narcotics

HEROIN (SCHEDULE I CONTROLLED SUBSTANCE)

- *Diacetylmorphine, a highly addictive narcotic derived from opium.*

- *Slang terms include:* smack, H, Big H, scag, scat, junk, black tar, China white, chiva, dope, others.

- *Looks like:* white to dark-brown bitter powder, or tarlike or coal-like substance.

- *How it is used:* injected just beneath the skin ("skin popping"), into a vein ("mainlining") or into a nasal passage ("shabanging"); smoked; snorted; heated on aluminum foil and inhaled ("chasing the dragon"); or dissolved in lemon juice and administered through a nose dropper.

MORPHINE (SCHEDULE II CONTROLLED SUBSTANCE)

- *The major active substance in opium, and the source of its analgesic properties.*

- *Brand names:* Duramorph, M S Contin, MSIR, Oramorph, Roxanol.

- *Slang terms include:* M, Miss Emma, Mister Blue, morph, dreamer, monkey.

- *Looks like:* white crystals, tablets, injectable solution.

- *How it is used:* ingested orally, injected or smoked.

METHADONE (SCHEDULE II CONTROLLED SUBSTANCE)

• *Synthetic morphine. Originally introduced as a painkiller, it is now used primarily in heroin-detoxification programs, to wean patients off heroin. Methadone is habit-forming, too.*

• *Brand names:* Dolophine, Methadose.

• *Slang terms include:* junk, jungle juice, dolls, dollies, fizzies.

• *Looks like:* tablets, oral solution.

• *How it is used:* ingested orally.

HYDROMORPHONE (SCHEDULE II CONTROLLED SUBSTANCE)

• *A highly potent painkiller that is two to eight times stronger than morphine.*

• *Brand name:* Dilaudid.

• *Slang terms include:* Lords, Little D.

• *Looks like:* tablets, injectable solution, oral solution, white powder, cough syrup, rectal suppositories.

• *How it is used:* ingested orally, inserted rectally; the tablets are also dissolved and injected as a substitute for heroin.

FENTANYL (SCHEDULE II CONTROLLED SUBSTANCE)

• *Originally introduced in the 1960s as an intravenous anesthetic called Sublimaze. Now used in pain control too. More than one dozen analogs of fentanyl have been produced illegally.*

• *Slang terms include:* apache, friend, great bear, he-man, jackpot, king ivory, TNT, poison.

MEPERIDINE (SCHEDULE II CONTROLLED SUBSTANCE)

• *A synthetic opioid that produces effects similar to morphine.*

• *Brand name:* Demerol.

• *Slang terms include:* Demmies.

CODEINE (SCHEDULE II, III, AND IV CONTROLLED SUBSTANCE)

• *The most widely used naturally occurring opioid in medicine. Found in many pain relievers and cough medicines, either alone or in combination with aspirin or acetaminophen.*

• *Slang terms include:* schoolboy.

DIHYDROCODEINE (SCHEDULE III CONTROLLED SUBSTANCE)

• *Combines a narcotic analgesic with aspirin and caffeine.*

PENTAZOCINE (SCHEDULE IV CONTROLLED SUBSTANCE)

• *A pain reliever consisting of an opioid analgesic (Talwin); also combined with acetaminophen (Talacen) or naloxone (Talwin NX).*

PROPOXYPHENE (SCHEDULE IV CONTROLLED SUBSTANCE)

• *An opioid manufactured alone or in combination with acetaminophen or aspirin.*

Selected Types of Stimulants

METHYLENE DIOXYMETHAMPHETAMINE (MDMA) (ECSTASY)
METHYLENE DIOXYAMPHETAMINE (MDA)
METHYL-DIMETHOXYAMPHETAMINE (DOM)
(ALL SCHEDULE I CONTROLLED SUBSTANCES)

• *Chemicals similar to mescaline and amphetamine, with both hallucinogenic and stimulant-like properties.*

• *Slang terms for MDMA include:* ecstasy, XTC, Adam, love drug, decadence, essence.

• *Slang terms for DOM include:* STP.

- *Looks like:* white powder, tablets, capsules.

- *How it is used:* ingested orally, inhaled, injected.

COCAINE/CRACK (SCHEDULE II CONTROLLED SUBSTANCE)

- *A highly addictive stimulant derived from the leaves of the South American cocoa bush. In the 1980s, as prices for powdered cocaine were soaring, crack cocaine rose in popularity.*

- *Slang terms for cocaine include:* coke, blow, flake, snow, happy powder, gold dust, nose powder, nose candy, toot, white lady, Big C, Peruvian flake, Bolivian marching powder.

- *Slang terms for crack include:* rock, base, baseball, bazooka, piece, kibbles and bits, gravel, one-fifty-one, teeth.

- *Cocaine combined with amphetamine:* snow seals.

- *Crack combined with heroin:* goofball, speedball, Belushi, whiz, bang, wings, witch.

- *Crack combined with marijuana:* banano, bush, coca puff, hooter, woolah.

- *Crack smoked with PCP:* parachute.

- *Looks like:* cocaine: a snowy white powder; crack cocaine: small white to tan nuggets or crystalline rocks that resemble soap.

- *How it is used:* Cocaine is snorted, or diluted in water and injected. Crack is smoked in a pipe or in a cigarette.

AMPHETAMINES (SCHEDULE II CONTROLLED SUBSTANCES)

- *"Amphetamines" is the collective name for three central-nervous-system stimulants: amphetamine, dextroamphetamine and methamphetamine. They are prescribed for attention deficit hyperactivity disorder (ADHD) and the sleeping disorder narcolepsy.*

• *Brand names:* Adderall (amphetamine); Dexedrine, DextroStat (dextro-amphetamine); Desoxyn (methamphetamine); Biphetamine (amphetamine and dextroamphetamine).

• *Slang terms for amphetamines include:* uppers, amies, amp, bennies, dexies, dominoes, pep pills, others.

• *Slang terms for methamphetamine include:* meth, chalk, crystal meth, speed, crank, crypto, crystal, glass, ice.

• *Looks like:* pills, capsules, tablets. "Ice," a smokable form of methamphetamine, is a clear, crystalline substance that resembles tiny chunks of ice.

• *How it is used:* Amphetamines are ingested orally, snorted or injected. Ice can be snorted or injected too, but it is typically smoked in a glass pipe.

METHYLPHENIDATE (SCHEDULE II CONTROLLED SUBSTANCE)

• *An amphetamine-like psychostimulant used to treat attention deficit hyperactivity disorder. When abused, it produces the same effects as amphetamines.*

• *Brand names:* Ritalin, Concerta, Metadate, Methylin.

• *Slang terms when combined with heroin:* pineapple.

• *Looks like:* tablets.

• *How it is used:* ingested orally. However, some narcotics addicts dissolve the tablets in water and inject the mixture. This practice can be highly dangerous, because the drug's fillers may block small blood vessels, seriously damaging the lungs and the retinas of the eyes.

Types of Depressants

METHAQUALONE (SCHEDULE I CONTROLLED SUBSTANCE)

• *Introduced in 1965 as a safe substitute for barbiturates, Quaaludes quickly caught on with young people. "Luding out"—taking methaqualone with wine—became a popular practice during the 1970s. As it turned out, overdoses from Quaaludes were more difficult to treat than barbiturate overdoses. Although the drug was discontinued in the United States, methaqualone manufactured in other countries can occasionally be found on the street.*

- *Brand names:* Quaalude, Sopor.

- *Slang terms include:* ludes, disco biscuits, lemmon 714s, love drug, Mandrax, vitamin Q.

- *Looks like:* tablets.

- *How it is used:* ingested orally.

GAMMA HYDROXYBUTYRATE (GHB); GAMMA BUTYROLACTONE (GBL) (SCHEDULE I CONTROLLED SUBSTANCES)

- *Two of the so-called "date-rape" drugs, along with flunitrazepam (Rohypnol). GHB and GBL have also been abused by bodybuilders as alternatives to anabolic steroids, although there is no evidence that they increase muscle mass or reduce body fat.*

- *Slang terms include:* cherry meth, easy lay, liquid ecstasy, grievous bodily harm.

- *Looks like:* grainy white-colored or sandy-colored powder; a clear liquid sold in small bottles or vials.

- *How it is used:* ingested orally by the capful or teaspoonful or mixed into a drink.

BENZODIAZEPINES (SCHEDULE IV CONTROLLED SUBSTANCES)

- *Benzodiazepines are one of the most widely prescribed medications in the United States today, and also one of the most frequently abused.*

- *Brand names for short-acting benzodiazepines:* estazolam (brand name: ProSom), flurazepam (Dalmane), quazepam (Doral), temazepam (Restoril) and triazolam (Halcion).

- *Brand names for intermediate-acting benzodiazepines:* alprazolam (Xanax), chlordiazepoxide (Librium), clorazepate (Tranxene), diazepam

(Valium), flunitrazepam (Rohypnol), lorazepam (Ativan), and oxazepam (Serax). Clonazepam (Klonopin) is prescribed to treat seizures.

- *Slang terms for Rohypnol include:* roofies, rophies, R-2, row-shay, ruffies, rib, rope, ruffles, ro, Roachies, date-rape drug, forget-me drug, Rochas dos, La Rocha, Mexican valium.

- *Slang terms for Librium include:* L, lib.

- *Slang terms for Valium include:* V, blues, drunk pills.

- *Looks like:* tablets, capsules.

- *How it is used:* ingested orally.

Types of Anabolic Steroids

ANABOLIC STEROIDS (SCHEDULE III CONTROLLED SUBSTANCE)

- *Brand names:* Android, Oreton Methyl, Testred, Virilon (methyltestosterone); Anadrol (oxymetholone); Anavar (oxandrolone), Delatestryl, Depo-Testosterone, Testoderm (testosterone); Dianabol (methandrostenolone); Durabolin, Deca-Durabolin (nandrolone); Equipoise (boldenone); Finajet (trenbolone); Halotestin (fluoxymesterone); Maxibolin (ethlestrenol); Winstrol (stanozolol).

- *Slang terms include:* juice.

- *Looks like:* tablets, capsules.

- *How it is used:* ingested orally, injected, patch worn on skin.

14

SAFETY AND INJURY PREVENTION

A child's push toward independence can be measured partly by tire size, as she progresses from stroller to tricycle to bicycle to car. Each new set of wheels expands the boundaries of a young person's world, so that by late adolescence much of her time is spent beyond the range of her parents' protection.

Realistically, the best any adult can do to safeguard teenagers is to make safety a way of life and to instill in their sons and daughters respect for firearms, motor vehicles and other potential hazards. Then they have to trust them to go out into the world and observe the same standards practiced at home.

Judging by statistics from the National Center for Injury Prevention and Control, parents are preparing their children well. Today's teenagers are more safety-conscious than their predecessors. In the late 1970s, unintentional injuries claimed roughly twenty thousand young lives annually. Two decades later, the number had fallen to a record low of about thirteen thousand. Even so, that's more deaths than from all childhood illnesses combined. Every year another six million adolescents suffer injuries requiring hospitalization, while sixteen and a half million more hurt themselves badly enough to warrant emergency-department care.

This chapter examines the most frequent causes of serious injuries to teenagers—some of which will surprise you—and suggests ways to protect your youngster. (Sports-related injuries, which send more than one million teens and young adults to the ER per year, are discussed in chapter 19, "Physical Activity and Sports." Suicide is discussed in chapter 15, page 353.)

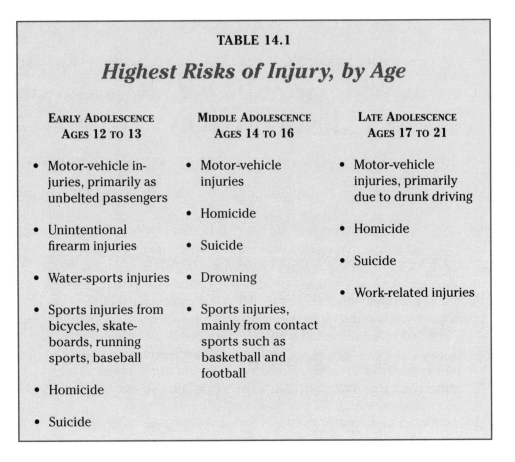

TABLE 14.1

Highest Risks of Injury, by Age

EARLY ADOLESCENCE AGES 12 TO 13	MIDDLE ADOLESCENCE AGES 14 TO 16	LATE ADOLESCENCE AGES 17 TO 21
• Motor-vehicle injuries, primarily as unbelted passengers	• Motor-vehicle injuries	• Motor-vehicle injuries, primarily due to drunk driving
• Unintentional firearm injuries	• Homicide	• Homicide
• Water-sports injuries	• Suicide	• Suicide
• Sports injuries from bicycles, skateboards, running sports, baseball	• Drowning	• Work-related injuries
• Homicide	• Sports injuries, mainly from contact sports such as basketball and football	
• Suicide		

AUTOMOBILE SAFETY

There is no underestimating the significance of a driver's license to teenagers. The arrival of that laminated card opens up a world of possibilities, symbolizing freedom and a growing independence from adults.

As far as boys and girls are concerned, the day they pass their road test can't come too soon. But from a developmental standpoint, the license may indeed come too soon. Hence the disproportionately high rates of automobile-related injuries and fatalities among this age group. Youngsters aged sixteen through nineteen make up just one in twenty motorists, yet they are behind the wheel in one in seven accidents that kill either the driver or passengers. Sixteen-year-old drivers are more than *twenty* times as likely to have a car crash than other motorists; seventeen-year-olds, more than six times as likely.

The chief reason for adolescents' poor safety record is their lack of experience in handling a car and sizing up and reacting appropriately to hazardous circumstances like merging onto a highway, making a left-hand turn at a crowded intersection or driving in poor weather conditions.

Inexperience aside, teenagers may lack some of the motor coordination and judgment needed to perform many of the complex physical maneuvers of ordinary driving. According to Dr. Richard Schieber, a child-injury specialist at the Centers for Disease Control and Prevention in Atlanta, "Teens are relatively clumsy compared to how they will be as adults. Driving may be one of the first skills where they have to coordinate their eyes, hands and feet. They're also more likely to miscalculate a traffic situation and are more easily distracted than older drivers." Immaturity and the adolescent propensity for taking risks—by speeding, tailgating, cutting off other cars and so forth—frequently endanger lives as well.

What You Can Do

Give your youngster extra practice behind the wheel. School driver's-ed programs and private driving instruction typically provide a total of six hours on-the-road training when the number actually needed to become reasonably proficient is closer to fifty hours, however—or about two hours a week spread over six months.

Once a teen acquires a *learner's permit,* by passing a vision test and taking a written exam, she may drive when accompanied by a licensed driver aged twenty-one or older. "Parents should give kids as much time in the driver's seat as possible," advises Dr. Schieber, "in as many situations as possible. You start with basic skills, then introduce other scenarios," such as driving at night, on country roads, in bumper-to-bumper traffic, on freeways, at dusk, in rainy weather and so on. It's a good idea to ask your youngster's driver's-ed instructor which areas have been mastered and which ones need work. In addition, get into the habit of

Leading Causes of Death from Unintentional Injury Among Boys and Girls Aged Ten to Nineteen, 1997	
CAUSE	DEATHS
1. Motor Vehicle Accidents	6,346
–as occupant	3,999
–as pedestrian	497
–while bicycling	199
–while motorcycling	132
2. Homicides	2,883
3. Suffocations	857
4. Drownings	590
5. Poisonings	444
6. Unintentional Shootings	258
7. Fires	212
8. Falls	163

Source: National Center for Injury Prevention and Control.

handing your teen the car keys when you're out running errands together. There is no substitute for experience.

Teaching a Teen to Drive
(WITHOUT DRIVING THE TWO OF YOU CRAZY)

The Allstate Insurance Company suggests these valuable tips for productive driving lessons:

1. Before getting started, discuss the route you'll be taking and the skills you'll be practicing.
2. In an even tone of voice (please, no barking like a drill sergeant), give clear, simple instructions: "Turn right at this corner." "Brake." "Pull over to the curb."
3. If your teen makes a mistake, ask him to pull over, then calmly discuss what he did wrong.
4. Encourage your teen to talk aloud about what he's observing while driving.
5. After each session, ask, "How do you think you drove today?" Let him point out any lapses in judgment or other gaffes. Then evaluate his progress together. Be sure to offer praise where appropriate.
6. Keep a log in which you enter the route taken and your critique of each skill practiced.

Institute a graduated licensing program. Although many states allow boys and girls as young as sixteen to obtain a license, the American Academy of Pediatrics recommends that youngsters not receive an unrestricted license until age eighteen or until they have been driving under adult supervision for at least two years.

A number of states have added a middle step as part of a graduated licensing system. Passing the road test gains novice drivers aged sixteen or older (the minimum age varies according to state, as do the restrictions) a *provisional license.* For the next year, they may take the wheel independently during the day. But after dark, they must have one licensed adult in the vehicle with them. At the end of their probationary period, they are awarded a full license, provided that their record is free of moving violations and car crashes.

Florida was the first state to adopt a graduated system for motorists under eighteen, in 1996. The following year, its rate of automobile injuries and fatalities among fifteen-, sixteen-, and seventeen-year-olds dipped by 9 percent. Other states that have joined this growing movement have reported similar reductions.

You don't need to wait for your state to pass a graduated-licensing law to institute a program of your own devising. Perhaps you will choose to set the probation period at six months instead of twelve; or, conversely, you could prolong the learner's-permit stage from the usual period of six months to twelve months, as Georgia and North Carolina have done. Extend driving privileges at a pace that you feel your teenager can handle.

Spend an afternoon teaching your youngster how to perform routine car maintenance such as checking the air pressure in the tires, the water level in the battery, oil and transmission fluid and the windshield-wiper fluid. Also show her how to change a flat tire. *If you can afford it, consider enrolling in an automobile club that provides road service.*

See to it that your adolescent's car meets all safety standards. While it's an admirable goal for a teenager to want to save up to buy his own car, newer models with modern safety features are beyond most young people's budgets.

Ideally, youngsters should be driving midsize or full-size cars equipped with air bags. In fact, a big ol' clunker is preferable to a spanking-new compact, because it offers more crash protection. The Insurance Institute for Highway Safety suggests avoiding sleek, high-performance vehicles, which may tempt teens to speed. Sport utility vehicles are generally frowned upon for teens as well; their higher centers of gravity make them less stable and more likely to roll over. Having a heavy-duty roll bar installed will greatly enhance their safety.

Set a good example for your kids. As a parent, you are a powerful role model. No speeding, no weaving in and out of traffic, no drinking and driving, no fiddling about for a compact disk to put in the CD player, no chatting on the cell phone, no fits of road rage because the car in front of us is poking along, and seat belts at all times.

Rules of the Road

Even after a young person receives her license, she's still in the process of learning how to drive. A number of clear safety guidelines and appropriate penalties should be developed with her input before she starts to drive. These "rules of the road" can include:

- No driving or riding with others under the influence of alcohol or other drugs.

- Because teens are easily distracted, insist that they have no more than two friends in the car at a time. Consider implementing a no-friends rule for the first few months of licensed driving.

• No eating or drinking while driving.

• Music must be kept at low to moderate volume.

• Everyone in the vehicle must wear a seat belt at all times. Failure to use seat belts more than triples the risk of injury in a serious crash.

• No nighttime driving. Driving when it's dark is inherently more demanding, especially for adolescents, who are four times as likely to die in a car crash at night than during daylight hours. In cities that have instituted curfews for young people, the teenage fatality rate has gone down by one-fourth.

• No driving when tired or upset.

• No driving beyond a certain distance from home. If your youngster wants to travel beyond the boundaries you've established, he must ask permission.

• No talking on a cellular phone when the vehicle is in motion.

• No picking up hitchhikers, unless it is someone they know well, and no hitchhiking themselves.

Breaking any of these rules constitutes grounds for some form of penalty. Minor offenses call for a stern warning. Repeated violations and serious infractions will cost him the keys. For how long is up to you.

"Teens need to understand that driving the family car is a privilege not a birthright," says Dr. Schieber, a pediatrician since 1981. He encourages parents to stand firm on issues of automobile safety. "If it means that a kid has to take the bus to school or can't borrow the car for a date, maybe he'll think twice about committing the infraction in the future. Parents have the obligation *and the liability* to help their child grow, in this case by stepping in and teaching them responsibility when driving."

TEEN TIP:

More than thirty states give parents the authority to request that the department of motor vehicles revoke their child's license if he or she is a minor.

Substance Abuse and Driving

Mind-altering substances are implicated in nearly half of all fatal auto crashes involving adolescents. The rule regarding drugs and driving is simple: Never drink or do any drugs and drive, and never accept a ride from someone who has been indulging. Tell your youngster that contrary to popular myth, the only remedy for sobering up is *time,* so that if a friend has a couple of drinks and insists that he's alert enough to drive ("I pumped myself full of coffee; I'm okay now"), she is to refuse to get in that car. Families should have a standing agreement that in an emergency a teen can call home for a ride *at any time,* and Mom or Dad will pick her up, no questions asked until the next day. If no one is going to be available, she should have money to call a taxicab.

At the same time, a true friend doesn't let a pal jeopardize his and other people's lives by driving while intoxicated. Each year, alcohol-related traffic deaths claim the lives of nearly three thousand six hundred young people between the ages of sixteen and twenty-four. Every effort should be made to get the keys from the driver, whether it's by gently coaxing him, using force to disarm him or announcing assertively, "I am your friend, and I will not let you drive drunk; I am taking your keys"—whatever it takes.

That Other Set of Wheels: Bicycle Safety

Teenagers may fantasize about the day they're old enough to drive, but for most of adolescence it's the humble bicycle that whisks them from here to there. Bicycling is an excellent form of aerobic exercise. It is also far more dangerous, per mile, than riding in a car. Every year a quarter-million bicyclists between the ages of ten and nineteen are treated in the emergency department, mainly for bruises, broken bones and head trauma. According to the U.S. Consumer Product Safety Commission, the highest death rates are seen among boys and girls between the ages of eleven and sixteen.

The most important safety measure for youngsters is to wear a helmet, which can reduce the odds of sustaining a head injury by 85 percent. Of the approximately eight hundred bicycle riders who were killed in 1997, all but a few dozen of them were not using protective headgear.

Just as you insist that your teen buckle up in the car, declare headgear use mandatory for riding the bike and observe that rule yourself if you're a biker. Your youngster might be more inclined to put on a helmet if it's a professional-looking model that makes him feel like a competitor in the Tour de France. Or suggest he use paint and decals to transform an otherwise plain helmet into a work of art.

When purchasing a helmet, be sure that it bears a sticker or label indicating that the product meets the U.S. Consumer Product Safety Commission's mandatory safety standards for head protection. Headgear should fit securely and be worn level on the head, not tilted back or pulled down low. Here are other safety tips for bicyclists:

- Never assume that drivers see you.
  - Wear bright clothing during the day.
  - Make eye contact with motorists.
  - Avoid biking after dark. But if you are out at night, wear neon or reflective clothing and equip your bike with a white headlight, a red taillight and at least one red rear reflector.
  - Reflective material should also be worn on the helmet, back, wrists and ankles.
  - Bicycles should also be outfitted with a horn or bell that is audible at least one hundred feet away.

- Always use hand signals before turning or stopping.

- Stay alert. Watch the road ahead for potholes, puddles, gravel, wet paint stripes, and other hazards.

- Cross railroad tracks at a ninety-degree angle and proceed slowly.

- Attach a carrier to the back of the bicycle, not the front.

- Should you have to brake suddenly, apply more pressure on the front handbrake while you lean down and shift your weight back to keep yourself from being hurled over the handlebars.

- Observe all safety rules.
  - Ride with traffic, as close to the edge of the road as you can, never against traffic.
  - All traffic signals, signs and pavement markings apply to cyclists as well as to motorists.

- Keep your bike in good working condition.
  - Before riding, check brakes and air in tires, and make sure wheels are securely fastened.

Motorized Recreational Vehicles and Watercrafts

Operating or riding in any motorized recreational vehicle or watercraft may be dangerous. Youngsters who may have immature judgment and motor skills

TABLE 14.2

Potential Hazards and Precautions for Motorized Recreational Vehicles and Watercraft

All-Terrain Vehicles (ATVs)
Approximately 20,000 injuries and 75 deaths per year (ages 15 and under)

POTENTIAL HAZARDS	PRECAUTIONS TO TAKE
• Drivers losing control and crashing into trees or other solid objects or being thrown from the vehicle. • Injuries: to the head, spinal cord and/or abdomen.	• The U.S. Consumer Product Safety Commission warns that adolescents under age 16 should not drive these four-wheel off-road vehicles, which can attain speeds of up to fifty miles per hour but have poor stability. • Have your youngster take a hands-on training course offered by certified instructors. • Riders should wear protective clothing, including boots, goggles and a helmet. • Never carry passengers. • Never ride on paved roads.

Motorcycles
Approximately 10,000 injuries and 350 deaths per year (ages 21 and under)

POTENTIAL HAZARDS	PRECAUTIONS TO TAKE
• Compared to car passengers, per mile, motorcyclists are twenty times more likely to die on the road as car passengers. • Injuries: About half of all motorcycle incidents involve collisions with other motor vehicles. Adolescents should not operate motorcycles until they receive their driver's license.	• A helmet, while only partially effective for preventing fatalities, should be worn at all times. • Aspiring teenage motorcyclists must apply for a Class M junior learner's permit; while practicing, they must be supervised by an adult with a valid motorcycle operator's license. Before youngsters take the state road test, it is recommended that they receive *at least* thirty hours of

(continued)

TABLE 14.2

professional instruction, including ten hours of driving in moderate to heavy traffic.
- We recommend discouraging youngsters from riding motorcycles.

Motorscooters, Mopeds, Minibikes, Minicycles, Trail Bikes
23,000 injuries per year (ages 19 and under)

POTENTIAL HAZARDS	PRECAUTIONS TO TAKE
• Motorscooters and mopeds are on-road vehicles with a top speed of about 30 miles per hour. However, a moped's acceleration is not sufficient for mixing with city traffic. • Minibikes, minicycles and trail bikes are all intended for off-road use. Their design, sluggish acceleration and inadequate brakes make them particularly dangerous. • Injuries: typically occur as a result of being struck by other motorists who have poor visibility, hitting a rock, bump, hole in the road, causing the driver to lose control.	• Many states classify mopeds as bicycles and therefore do not require licensing or helmet use; riders of any of these vehicles should *always* wear protective headgear. Other states set minimum ages of 14 to 16. • The American Academy of Pediatrics recommends that young people who do not know how to drive a car should not be allowed to operate other motorized vehicles. • Off-road vehicles are never to be used on the street.

Ride-On Lawnmowers
Approximately 4,800 injuries and 25 deaths per year (ages 5 to 15)

POTENTIAL HAZARDS	PRECAUTIONS TO TAKE
• Mainly a hazard for younger teens when riding on the mower as a passenger or playing in the vicinity of the mower while it is in operation; some youngsters, though, are injured while operating the machine. • Injuries: lacerations, amputations and/or fractures, often to the fingers, hands, feet, head, chest.	• Teenagers should be at least 16 years old and receive the same degree of training as for an all-terrain vehicle before being allowed to mow the lawn with one of these machines. The complexities of operating the gears, clutch, brakes and mower blade make ride-on mowers potentially dangerous.

Riding in the Backs of Pickup Trucks
Approximately 1,000 injuries and 127 deaths per year (ages 19 and under)

POTENTIAL HAZARDS	PRECAUTIONS TO TAKE
• Injuries occur when a passenger riding in the bed of a pickup truck falls off, frequently while standing, sitting on the rail, changing position or fooling around. • One in three youngsters injured this way suffers severe head trauma. • Camper shells offer no protection and may even cause additional injury.	• No one, regardless of age, should ever ride in the back of a pickup truck or anywhere else in a vehicle not equipped with a seat or seat belt.

Snowmobiles
Approximately 5,700 injuries per year (ages 15 to 24) and 62 deaths per year (all ages)

POTENTIAL HAZARDS	PRECAUTIONS TO TAKE
• Teenage boys and young male adults are the victims in three-fourths of all snowmobile crashes. Alcohol use frequently plays a role in the mishap. • Injuries: head injuries; drowning; fractures of the lower legs; frostbite and/or hypothermia, from the cold.	• Adolescents under age 16 should not operate snowmobiles. Those old enough to drive one should receive adequate instruction, specifically about snowmobiles, from an adult. • Wear protective clothing, including boots, goggles and a helmet • Travel only on designated trails and avoid roads, railroads, waterways and pedestrians.

Personal Watercraft (Jet Skis/Water Scooters)
Approximately 12,000 injuries and 83 deaths per year (all ages)

POTENTIAL HAZARDS	PRECAUTIONS TO TAKE
• During the 1990s, the number of Jet Ski–type craft on U.S. waters quadrupled, as did the number of related injuries. Today's models are capable of carrying three people and racing along at speeds up to sixty miles per hour. Users are eight times more likely to be injured than those on motorboats.	• No one under sixteen should operate a personal watercraft. That is the position not only of the American Academy of Pediatrics but the Personal Watercraft Industry Association, which represents the *manufacturers* of these recreational craft.

(continued)

TABLE 14.2

- Injuries: lacerations, contusions, fractures and blunt trauma, mostly from collisions with other jet-skiers; wave jumping is a leading cause of fatal jet-ski accidents.

- Everyone aboard should wear U.S. Coast Guard–approved flotation devices.
- Do not jump waves created by the wakes of motorboats.
- Never operate while under the influence of alcohol.
- Never operate in swimming areas.

---

may be placed at risk of injury, and even death. Crashes can occur when drivers lose control and hit objects, when drivers or passengers are thrown from the vehicle or when there are collisions with other motor vehicles. Precautions should be taken to prevent injuries, especially involving the head, neck, and back. See Table 14.2 for a list of potential hazards and precautions concerning motorized recreational vehicles and watercrafts.

CRIME AND VIOLENCE

Although a spate of senseless killings in schools and other public buildings around the country have captured the attention of the news media, schools have actually become safer over the past decade. A study from the U.S. Centers for Disease Control and Prevention showed a 30 percent reduction in the number of students who carried weapons to school (from 26 percent in 1991 to 18 percent in 1997) and a 14 percent reduction in the number who'd been involved in physical altercations within the last year (from 43 to 37 percent).

Many guns fall into the hands of young people. According to several studies from the U.S. Office of Juvenile Justice and Delinquency Prevention, the tripling of juvenile homicides from 1986 to 1993 can be attributed to increased access to handguns—and not to a new breed of ruthless adolescent criminal, as some have theorized. Once police departments started aggressively confiscating guns from teenagers, the wave of homicides began to recede. Youth between the ages of ten and nineteen committed 4,002 murders in 1993, an all-time high. The year 1997 marked the fourth year in a row the homicide toll fell substantially, to 2,883. Of those killings, four in five involved guns.

The American Academy of Pediatrics

Where We Stand on Firearm Safety

The American Academy of Pediatrics (AAP) believes that firearm regulation, to include bans of handguns and assault weapons, is the most effective way to reduce firearm-related injuries. It also recommends that handgun ammunition be regulated, that the number of privately owned handguns be reduced, until such time as they are banned altogether, and that restrictions such as waiting periods and background checks be placed on handgun ownership. In addition, the AAP supports product-liability legal actions aimed at firearm manufacturers, trigger locks and safe-storage legislation.

Safety in Our Schools

Overall, our educational system deserves high marks for providing a safe environment in which to learn, though certainly more needs to be done. Youngsters worry less about the threat of violence infiltrating their schools and communities than they did in the mid-1990s. In a 1999 *New York Times*/CBS poll of approximately one thousand teens, nearly 90 percent said that they felt safe at school.

Though most schools have managed to improve security without resorting to measures like installing metal detectors and stationing guards out front, sometimes these measures are necessary. Other measures that may sometimes be warranted include a schoolwide sweep for weapons or an isolated search. The Supreme Court holds that students suspected of possessing weapons on school grounds may be searched, as well as their personal property and their lockers. School officials, unlike the police, don't need a warrant to conduct a search; nor must they prove there was reasonable cause to believe that the suspect had violated the law.

Under the federal Gun-Free Schools Act of 1994, students who bring firearms to school face a mandatory suspension of at least one year. Furthermore, they are reported to the criminal-justice system or the juvenile-delinquency system.

TABLE 14.3

Safety Measures Implemented by Schools

SAFETY MEASURE	PERCENTAGE OF SCHOOLS TO INSTITUTE THIS MEASURE
• Visitors required to sign in before entering the building	96%
• Controlling access to the school grounds	24% (49% of large schools)
• Controlling access to the school building	53%
• Students prohibited from leaving campus during lunch	80%
• Daily use of metal detectors	1%
• Random metal-detector checks	(Large schools) 15% (Medium-sized schools) 4% (Small schools) Less than 1%
• Police or other law-enforcement personnel stationed at school	(Available as needed) 12% (1 to 9 hours per week) 3% (10 to 29 hours) 1% (30 hours or more) 6% (Total) 22%

Source: U.S. Department of Education

PUTTING AN END TO BULLYING

The outbreak of school shootings brought to light another form of teen-on-teen violence that has been allowed to go virtually unchecked: bullying. It turns out that many of these adolescent gunmen had been ostracized or actively bullied by their fellow students for much of their young lives. The killings awakened adults' sensitivity to the torment that many kids are subjected to at the hands of their peers and the possible measures children may take if they are in deep emotional pain (for whatever reason) and have access to firearms.

According to one 1999 survey of a midwestern junior high school, four in five students admitted to some form of bullying behavior at least once a month, ranging from name-calling, to verbal threats, to physical violence. Another 1999 study, of children aged fourteen to sixteen, found that schoolyard bullies were prone to psychological problems such as depression and thoughts of suicide, just like the kids they pick on. As many as half also find themselves on the receiving end of taunts from other children.

WHAT YOU CAN DO

The first step is for adults to dispense with the conventional wisdom that teasing is a harmless ritual of youth. Mild teasing may be harmless, but ridicule should not be tolerated.

Let's teach our children that it is wrong to hurt other people's feelings. Ask them to remember an incident where someone made fun of them and how it made them feel.

Encourage youngsters to defend those who get picked on. If more bystanders had the courage to intervene ("Why don't you leave him alone? No one thinks this is 'cool.' "), most tormenters would probably slink off down the hallway, their deflated ego dragging behind them. At the very least, the right thing to do is to inform a teacher of the harassment and let him or her deal with the matter.

Look for the silent signs that a teenager is being bullied. A youngster may be too embarrassed to admit to Mom and Dad that someone is badgering him. Among the behaviors that often indicate a problem are a sudden lack of interest in school; a drop in grades; not wanting to go to school; and morning-time complaints of psychosomatic symptoms such as stomachaches and headaches. Unexplained bruises and other physical injuries should also nab a parent's attention. These symptoms are important, because they may also indicate depression or other significant problems.

If you suspect that your teen is being victimized, coach him on how to assert himself without resorting to violence. Anytime a confrontation seems potentially dangerous, he should walk away and alert a school official.

What if the bullying continues? Let's say that a sophomore boy repeatedly makes pig grunts and assorted hurtful comments to an overweight girl whenever she walks into homeroom. The situation should be brought to the administrative office's attention right away. The girl's mother and father can offer to either contact the principal or advise their daughter on how to handle the situation herself if their involvement would make her uncomfortable. Always give youngsters that option.

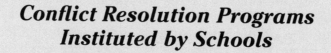

Conflict Resolution Programs Instituted by Schools

Peer Mediation—Specially trained student mediators serve as impartial third parties to help their peers work out problems nonviolently, without the need for extensive teacher involvement.

Process Curriculum—a course or daily lesson devoted to problem-solving techniques.

Peaceable Classroom—teachers are instructed on how to integrate conflict-resolution techniques into the day-to-day management of the classroom, including discipline. The emphasis is on practicing cooperation and effective communication, and learning to appreciate diversity.

Peaceable School—incorporates all of these approaches.

The National Parent-Teacher Association recommends that victims of bullying (or their parents) keep written records of each incident, including names, date, time, place and circumstances. Then submit a copy of the report to the principal.

Sometimes merely separating the two adversaries puts an end to the matter. Perhaps the boy in the above example is transferred to another homeroom. He and the girl rarely cross paths for the rest of the term. By their junior year, he's matured and is no longer given to making cruel remarks. More severe measures include suspension and expulsion.

A number of schools have instituted counseling programs intended to help antisocial students control their anger and learn to resolve conflicts peacefully. The four most popular approaches are *peer mediation, process curriculum, peaceable classroom* and *peaceable school,* all of which are described in the box above.

If your attempts to get the school to take action fail, keep your teenager home while you pursue a hearing with the school board addressing his safety. Yes, this is a drastic step, but it may be necessary to force school administrators to understand the seriousness of the situation. Some parents have had to resort to legal measures in order to protect their youngster from being victimized, although usually these problems are resolved long before anyone is considering litigation.

Finally, throughout this process, explain to your teenager that she has done nothing wrong; it's the other person who is at fault. Give her your patience and full support. Her self-esteem could probably use a boost, so remind her how terrific she is in so many ways.

TEENAGERS AND GANGS

During the first half of the 1990s, the number of gangs in the United States multiplied more than sixfold, from 4,881 in 1992 to an estimated 31,000 in 1996. Beginning in 1995, the Office of Juvenile Justice and Delinquency Prevention's National Youth Gang Center has conducted an annual poll of some three thousand police departments and sheriff departments, asking them about local gang activity. In the first survey, 58 percent of the law-enforcement agencies reported the existence of youth gangs in their communities. Since then, the numbers have fallen slightly, to 53 percent in 1996, and to 51 percent in 1997.

The results contradict the long-standing perception that gangs are primarily an inner-city phenomenon. Granted, the prevalence is highest in large cities, with 74 percent of those jurisdictions acknowledging the presence of gangs. But suburban counties aren't far behind, at 57 percent, which is considerably higher than small cities (34 percent). As for rural counties, rarely thought of as hotbeds of gang activity, 25 percent have gang members prowling the streets. What's more, the number of gangs has been on the rise in our small cities, suburbs and rural areas, while our large urban centers have seen the opposite pattern develop.

Another surprising trend has been the influx of female members. Girls are believed to make up as much as one-quarter to one-third of all urban gangs, whereas males used to outnumber females twenty to one. Nearly three in four gang members are between the ages of fifteen and twenty-four; one in six is fourteen or younger.

Parents have good reason to be concerned if their teenager joins a gang. Older members are often involved in drug-dealing and criminal activity. Gang involvement increases the likelihood that a boy or girl will become entangled in drugs, gunplay, vandalism and theft. For one thing, gangs attract kids who want to belong and tend to be highly susceptible to peer pressure. But also, the combination of security and anonymity that membership in any group confers sometimes exerts a strange power over people, leading them to do things they would never consider on their own.

"Mores change when someone is part of a gang," observes Dr. Kenneth Sladkin. A child and adolescent psychiatrist in the Fort Lauderdale area, he has worked with gang members over the years. "Once you belong to a gang long enough," he continues, "it's easy to lose your moral foundation and adopt the group's standards."

Not every kid in a gang turns to crime. In fact, many don't. Of the estimated eight hundred thousand gang members in the United States, a fair number undoubtedly could be described as gang "wanna-bes"—kids whom Dr. Sladkin describes as "not the backbone of the gangs but more on the periphery."

Being in a gang appeals to some adolescents' fantasies of rebellion and desire for high drama. They're also drawn to the camaraderie and the "colors" and hand signs that distinguish one bunch from another.

"For these kids, the gangs are almost like social clubs," says Dr. Sladkin. "They meet in school and talk about who's in this gang or that gang. They're not the youngsters who are staying out all night and getting mixed up in crime and turf wars."

PROTECTING TEENS FROM GANGS

The National Parent-Teacher Association recommends that parents contact their local police department to get a sense of the extent of gang activity, if any, in their community and schools. Teenagers who are most vulnerable to the lure of gangs include those on the fringes of the social hierarchy. Low self-esteem and a history of academic failure also drive young people to gangs.

Among the tip-offs that a teen may be fraternizing with a gang:

- change in friends
- wearing the same color combination repeatedly
- flashing hand signs
- secrecy about his whereabouts and activities
- suddenly having money, with no known resources
- loss of interest in school
- symptoms of substance abuse
- tattoos, either self-drawn in ink or professionally executed

The best way for keeping a young person from getting caught up in the gang lifestyle is to follow the same principles stressed throughout this book: Spend time with him, show him affection and stay in touch with him and his world, even when he seems to be shutting you out. It's a sad commentary that for some young people, gangs function as surrogate families. Making a teenager feel loved and accepted for who he is at home eliminates much of the lure of a gang in the first place.

PUTTING A HALT TO HAZING

In the early 1970s, at the height of the counterculture, college fraternities had all but vanished from most U.S. campuses. Since then, membership has more than tripled to approximately half a million students; the incidence of deaths and injuries from the tradition known as hazing has risen accordingly. On average, four students die each year and many more are injured while pledging for a fraternity or sorority, or seeking to ingratiate themselves with their fellow athletes on a college sports team. The practice has filtered down to high schools as well.

Hazing is hardly new. All manner of clubs, societies and organizations have held induction ceremonies as a way to foster a communal bond among their members. Too often, what is supposed to be prankish fun gives way to initiation rites intended to humiliate and degrade; for example, forcing pledges to parade naked around campus, guzzle swill-like alcoholic concoctions and serve as other students' personal slaves. Other activities are merely an excuse for committing physical violence; witness the custom of "Bringing the Knowledge," in which members take turns slamming a dictionary on prospective inductees' heads. That the participants are willing doesn't make the practice any less reprehensible.

Alcohol use is involved in about half of all hazing rituals, according to a 1999 survey conducted by New York's Alfred University—where two decades earlier a twenty-year-old male pledge died of acute alcohol poisoning and exposure to the cold after being locked in the trunk of a car in freezing weather and forced to drink a lethal cocktail of beer, wine and bourbon. At the time, only three states had enacted antihazing legislation. Now all but a handful of states have similar laws on the books, yet hazing goes on.

If parents can't dissuade their sons and daughters from joining a fraternity or sorority, they should explain how dangerous hazing can be and forbid their participation in any hazing activity that crosses the line, either as perpetrator, victim or onlooker. Common sense dictates where that line is drawn. If they are at an induction ceremony and things get out of hand, they are to leave. Many colleges, in an effort to clamp down on hazing brutality, hold eyewitnesses just as accountable as those actively involved in meting out the abuse. As punishment, students have been expelled, fraternities have been disbanded and sports teams have had their seasons canceled. There are better ways to make new friends.

Safety in the Home

The two main safety concerns for teens at home are poisonous substances and firearms. Both must be locked securely away, if not disposed of altogether.

POISON PREVENTION

At least four in five childhood poisonings occur in the home. The annual Toxic Exposure Surveillance System, compiled by the American Association of Poison Control Centers, recorded approximately 160,000 cases of poisoning among thirteen-to-nineteen-year-olds in 1997. Forty-four percent were the result of suicide attempts, deliberate abuse of the product in an effort to get high or experimental misuse for other purposes.

WHAT YOU CAN DO

Inspect your home for medicinal and nonpharmaceutical products that an adolescent could conceivably be exposed to or could use to harm herself. Go from room to room, and put away, throw away or lock up as many of the items below as is feasible. If you have any reason to fear that a teenager might be a suicide risk, rid your house of any poisonous products, including alcohol, while you get him the professional help he needs.

FIREARM SAFETY

One in three handguns is kept unlocked and loaded at home. In the more than 35 percent of U.S. households where firearms are present, the risk of

---

TABLE 14.4

Products That Poison

MOST COMMON CAUSES	NUMBER OF CASES AMONG CHILDREN AGED 6 TO 19
Household cleaning substances	19,555
Plants	16,621
Hydrocarbons	9,628
Chemicals	9,040
Insecticides/Pesticides	8,102
Adhesives/Glues	4,308

Source: 1997 Toxic Exposure Surveillance System

homicide is three times greater than in homes that do not have weapons. The risk of a family member committing suicide is five times higher. Meanwhile, in fewer than 2 percent of home break-ins are guns actually fired for protection; as a matter of fact, guns are twenty-two times more likely to be used to kill someone the residents know than to kill an intruder in self-defense.

In 1997, 258 teenagers were unintentionally shot and killed; about three in five of those fatal shootings occurred in or near the home. But mishaps involving firearms account for perhaps one-tenth of adolescent deaths from weapons. "The bigger problem," points out Dr. Katherine Kaufer Christoffel, "is that teenagers get into guns and use them for committing homicides as well as for suicide."

WHAT YOU CAN DO

"The safest action that parents can take is to not keep any guns at home," says Dr. Christoffel, medical director of the violence and injury prevention center at Children's Memorial Hospital in Chicago. But if your household does contain weapons, we urge you to observe these safety measures:

* Unload guns before you store them.

* Put on the trigger lock and place the weapon—uncocked—in a securely locked case. Then put the container in a locked drawer or closet. Only Mom and Dad should know where guns have been hidden. Ammunition should be kept in a separate location, also locked.

* When cleaning a firearm, never leave it unattended; keep it in view at all times.

With so many guns in circulation, it is possible that your teen spends time at friends' homes where weapons can be found. Adolescents should never touch a firearm without adult supervision. All too often we read in the news stories about a pair of pals who are handling a parent's gun, perhaps for the first time. *"Don't worry; it doesn't have any bullets in it."* The weapon discharges, and one boy winds up wounded or dead, and the other one emotionally scarred for years to come.

Instruct your youngster that if he is in somebody else's home when no adults are present, and a gun is brought out, he is to leave at once. As always, let's suggest ways of finessing the situation so that he doesn't have to lose face in front of his friend(s). He could either make an excuse ("I just remembered: My mom needs me to pick up the dry cleaning; I'd better get there before they close.") or try to convince the others to go do something else.

WHAT ABOUT AIR GUNS, AIR RIFLES, PELLET GUNS AND BB GUNS?

Parents should recognize that these *nonpowder firearms* aren't toys. Some boast muzzle velocities greater than seven hundred feet per second—impact at half that speed can penetrate skin and bone. Teens have lost their eyesight and have even been killed playing with air rifles and their ilk.

Toy guns that fire projectiles can cause very real injuries—according to the U.S. Consumer Product Safety Commission's count, about 750 per year. Parents should not let teenagers outside with realistic-looking plastic rifles and handguns, even for seemingly harmless purposes. With the amount of guns on our streets, law-enforcement officers can't always distinguish the replicas from the genuine articles, particularly at night. Youngsters bearing these toys have been shot at by the police. It's only after the youth is lying on the ground dead or wounded that the menacing "weapon" is seen to be a fake.

NOW SHOWING FIVE DAYS A WEEK: HOME ALONE

Teen-proofing the household becomes essential once a child is old enough to be left alone. On school days, one in three adolescents come home to a house with no adult present. Police departments have an expression for the hours between 2 P.M. and 8 P.M.: "crime time." More than half of all youthful law violations are crammed into those six hours.

Child experts generally agree that eleven or twelve is the age at which parents can consider allowing their boy or girl to become a so-called "latchkey kid," provided that it is during the day and for no more than approximately three hours. Before you do, there are several factors to take into account. For instance, is the neighborhood generally a safe one? Are there neighbors around during the day who could lend a hand in an emergency?

The most crucial question is whether or not your son or daughter is ready to handle this major responsibility. Studies have found that latchkey kids exhibit higher levels of fear, stress, loneliness and boredom; miss more days of school; and have lower academic scores. They are also more likely to experiment with sex and drugs than kids who aren't left by themselves for long periods of time. After all, part of what kept earlier generations of adolescents safe from temptation was lack of opportunity. Women were more likely to be stay-at-home parents, and households often included members of the extended family.

Before you crown a youngster the afternoon keeper of the castle, she should be able to perform the following routine household tasks:

☐ Knows how to properly answer the telephone. *Kids should never disclose to an unfamiliar voice that they are alone. An appropriate response would be: "My mom's not able to come to the phone right now; can I take your number and have her get back to you?"*

☐ Knows what to do and who to call in the event of a fire, a medical crisis, a suspicious stranger at the door or other emergency. *Coach teens on how to respond to each of these situations. Conspicuously post emergency telephone numbers on the refrigerator and by every phone in the house, and be sure they know at least two escape routes from the home.*

☐ Knows where to find the first-aid supplies and how to handle basic first aid (or whom to call) for cuts, scrapes, nosebleeds, minor burns and so on.

☐ Knows how to switch on a shutoff electrical circuit breaker or replace a fuse.

☐ Knows where to find the shutoff valves on all toilets and sinks, as well as the main water valve, in the event of a leak or overflowing toilet.

☐ Knows how to put out a cooking fire. *Keep baking soda, flour or a fire extinguisher in the kitchen. Teens should know never to throw water on a grease fire.*

☐ Knows how to contact you in an emergency.

☐ Knows the names of her pediatrician, the preferred hospital and the family medical-insurance plan and type of coverage.

Decide on the prevailing rules and responsibilities during the hours your son or daughter is home without supervision. To eliminate confusion, we suggest you put them down in writing. Among the points to bear in mind:

• Is she allowed to have friends over? How many? Same-sex friends only?

• Under what circumstances is she to answer the door? Or is she not to open the door at all?

• Which activities are off-limits? For example, if your home is wired for cable television, are there channels she is prohibited from watching? Parents who are not home in the afternoon might want to investigate purchasing parental-control tools for TVs and for computers linked to the Internet. Though by no means infallible, the "V-chip" and Web filters do enable you to choose the types of programming that come into your home. (See chapter 11, "Tuned-In Teens.")

- Is she expected to complete her homework and/or certain chores before you get home?

Try your best to contact your teenager on afternoons when she's home alone, even if it's only a brief conversation to find out how her day went. Kids should always be able to reach you *or another responsible adult,* either by phone, fax, e-mail, pager or beeper.

If you're out for the evening or away, leave your itinerary, including when you expect to be home.

Mom, Dad: You're late! If you're going to be home late, let your youngster know. Kids worry too!

ALTERNATIVES FOR AFTER-SCHOOL HOURS

The increase in single-parent and double-income families has prompted more and more public and private schools to provide child-care programs to fill the afternoon hours constructively. The federal government, recognizing the need for aftercare, doubled its appropriation to $450 million in 1999, but the programs are funded primarily through the modest fees paid by parents.

Before- and after-school services are generally intended for and appeal to children in prekindergarten through eighth grade, though some older boys and girls do attend. Based on the results of two national studies, these programs can be beneficial on a number of levels.

Early adolescence is a time of increased sociability, so many youngsters thrive on the extra hours of being around their peers. Programs often offer board games, sports, free time, homework time and tutoring. Two in five of the school principals surveyed for one of the studies noted that the children enrolled in their school-age child care were exhibiting fewer behavioral problems; half observed that the children also seemed more cooperative with adults.

The YMCA of the USA is the country's largest provider of school-age child care. More than one in ten children in school-age care attends a YMCA program at some eight thousand sites nationwide. Other private organizations that offer this service to some extent include Boys Clubs of America, Camp Fire Girls and the Association for Retarded Citizens (for developmentally delayed children).

15

EMOTIONAL AND BEHAVIORAL PROBLEMS

Some parents, having spent a year or two trying to work around their teenager's roller-coaster mood swings, will insist that adolescence itself constitutes an emotional disorder. After all, the same behaviors that may signal a psychological disturbance could describe any teenage boy or girl at a given moment. The difference is a matter of duration and frequency.

Truth be told, our kids are remarkably stable and resilient. According to the Office of the U.S. Surgeon General, nine out of ten traverse the teen and preteen years without any major emotional and behavioral problems. But an estimated six million youth do suffer from mental illnesses such as depression and obsessive-compulsive disorder. Unfortunately, only one in five of them receive treatment.

Signs that a child may be suffering severe psychological problems include being alienated from family and friends, an abrupt and persistent decline in academic performance, a loss of interest in activities that once brought pleasure and a disturbing new group of friends. Mental disorders can also reveal themselves in the guise of physical symptoms.

"We'll see kids who have headaches, stomachaches or acute viruses that never seem to go away," says Dr. Charles Irwin, director of the division of adolescent medicine at San Francisco's Moffitt University of California Hospital. "In talking to them, over time we often find out that they're actually deeply depressed."

CAUSES OF EMOTIONAL AND BEHAVIORAL PROBLEMS

By and large, psychological problems result from an interaction between our internal human biochemistry and our environment.

During a Mental Health Evaluation

- A description of the teen's current problems and symptoms
- A full medical history, including past illnesses and treatments
- A full psychosocial history: Has he ever had emotional/behavioral problems? If so, did he require treatment? Does he frequently get into fights? Has he ever carried a weapon?
- Is there any history of physical abuse, sexual abuse, substance abuse?
- Parent and family mental health histories
- Information about the young person's development, school performance, friends, family relationships

---

Just as emotional stress can wreak havoc on the body, certain physiological changes have the ability to influence emotions and even our perceptions of the world around us. You might also be wondering about the role of genes in psychological disorders. Are some people simply "born" depressed? Or anxious? Not quite. However, there are sometimes genetically inherited predispositions to many of the disorders discussed in this chapter. Thus, mothers and fathers with personal histories (and/or family histories) of mental illness would be wise to observe their children closely for any signs of susceptibility to particular emotional disorders. Whenever a child's behavior becomes a source of concern, the first stop should be the pediatrician's office, to identify or rule out possible organic as well as psychological causes. If necessary, the pediatrician can refer you to therapists who specialize in adolescent emotional and behavioral problems. For information about the testing and referral processes and the mental health professionals who you may need to consult see "Getting Youngsters the Help They Need," on page 344.

TYPES OF EMOTIONAL/BEHAVIORAL PROBLEMS

Mood Disorders

DEPRESSION

As many as one in thirteen adolescents experience symptoms of depression at some time. The condition can be deceptively difficult for parents to recognize, however, and not only because teens often adhere to a don't-ask, don't-tell policy when it comes to expressing their emotions. While some kids become depressed for reasons that are obvious to you, such as a romantic breakup, a death in the family or academic failure or disappointment, others can sink into profound depression without any apparent cause—just as adults do.

Yet another confounding feature of depression in teenagers: Unlike adults, they may not act sad at all. Some children seem high-strung, and they frequently get into trouble. The misbehavior often leads to misdiagnoses of attention deficit hyperactivity disorder, a learning disorder or a conduct disorder.

Depression is classified as major or minor. The definitive diagnosis of major depression is based on a patient's exhibiting deep despair and at least four of six other classic symptoms (page 334) for two weeks or more. *Minor depression,* or *dysthymia* (pronounced *dis*-thim-*ee-uh*), on the other hand, can persist for some time, without producing overt symptoms or interfering too much with the person's daily functioning. A child may become so used to this background hum of depression that she comes to accept her blue mood as normal. According to several studies, many kids mired in mild depression eventually experience an episode of major depression typically lasting seven to nine months.

DEPRESSION AND GENDER: IF BOYS ARE THE WARRIORS,
GIRLS ARE THE WORRIERS

Rates of depression among boys and girls are relatively equal up until age eleven or so. During adolescence, though, girls become twice as likely as boys to experience bouts of depression. Why? Probably for the same reason that depression is twice as common among adult women than adult men: They're conditioned to be more reflective about themselves and their lives. In a poll of 615 California teens, the boys out-fretted the girls on only one issue: excelling at sports and other activities. The girls felt more anxious about virtually every other matter listed on the questionnaire: appearance, popularity, personal problems, safety, friendships, romance, family problems and whether or not they were a good person.

BIPOLAR DISORDER

Manic depression, no longer the preferred medical term for this mental illness, neatly describes its effects. *Bipolar disorder* sends a person's mood seesawing up and down, from euphoric highs (the manic phase) to oppressive lows (the depressive phase), with normal periods in between (see box, page 335).

At least two million Americans and perhaps one in one hundred teenagers are afflicted with bipolar disorder or a milder form called *cyclothymia.* "People with bipolar disorder can be delightful when they're manic," says Dr. Charles Irwin, recalling one patient in particular. "He was incredibly successful: president of his high-school class, attended an Ivy League university, graduated in less than four years. The life of the party. But when he crashed, he crashed very badly." The young man, who never sought treatment, later killed himself. Suicide is a very real concern with adolescents suffering from manic-depressive disorder.

Two other patterns may be seen. In *bipolar II disorder,* one mood state is dominant: either frequent depression and occasional mania, or vice-versa. Depression and mania occurring together is referred to as a *mixed bipolar state.*

Anxiety Disorders

Feeling anxious is as much a part of adolescence as first dates, final exams and acne, to name just three perennial sources of teenage anxiety. In a 1999 survey of eight thousand young people, conducted by researchers at the University of Michigan, two-thirds claimed they felt stressed out at least once a week; one-third reported being on edge at least once a day.

Anxiety is a normal reaction to the stresses of life. A case of the jitters isn't necessarily harmful; in fact, it can spur us to be at our best. Ordinarily, stressful situations prompt a flurry of brain and hormonal activities, in what is called the fight-or-flight response. Body systems mobilize to meet the challenge, and a person feels more alert, focused and energetic.

Know the Signs of Major Depression

CLASSIC SYMPTOMS:

1. Sadness, anxiety, crying
2. Sleeps too much or too little; wakes up early in the morning and can't get back to sleep
3. Poor appetite or excessive appetite
4. Chronic fatigue and lack of energy
5. Feelings of guilt, worthlessness, helplessness, hopelessness
6. Difficulty concentrating or making decisions
7. Thoughts of death or suicide, or a suicide attempt

OTHER SYMPTOMS:

- Sudden decline in school performance
- Loss of interest or pleasure in activities, hobbies
- Withdraws socially from family and friends; spends large blocks of time alone in room or bathroom
- Restlessness, boredom
- Irritability leading to aggressive behavior, violent outbursts
- Highly self-critical
- Abuse of alcohol or other drugs
- Neglects personal appearance
- Complains frequently of psychosomatic symptoms such as headaches, dizziness, stomach pains
- Forgetfulness
- Self-mutilation, or "scarring"

An *anxiety disorder,* by contrast, can be incapacitating. It is an illness, one that frequently runs in families. The anxiety may be overwhelming—and at times terrifying—or it may be relatively mild but incessant, often with no apparent cause. A young person has nearly a one-in-seven chance of developing an anxiety disorder, which is the most common mental health condition among all age groups. Below we describe the six major types.

> ### *Know the Signs of Mania*
>
> * Euphoria
> * Friendly, sociable behavior
> * Extreme irritability
> * Grandiose ideas and an inflated sense of self
> * Excessive, rapid-fire talking in a loud voice
> * Racing thoughts and distractibility
> * Heightened energy level; can go for days with little or no sleep
> * Increased sex drive
> * Poor judgment that leads to reckless behavior
> * Obnoxious or provocative behavior

GENERALIZED ANXIETY DISORDER (GAD)

Description: excessive worry and fears lasting six months or more. Teenagers with generalized anxiety disorder may be perfectly competent, fine students and so forth, yet they'll worry inordinately about *everything,* or so it seems: Will I be late for school? I hope I don't blow my lines in the one-act-play contest and make a jerk out of myself in front of the whole school. I have to take my driver's test next year; how will I know what to do? What am I going to wear tomorrow?

The undercurrent of apprehension often leads to insecurity, perfectionism or overly conformist behavior. Unlike other anxiety disorders, however, generalized anxiety disorder rarely affects youngsters to the point where they avoid uncomfortable situations. The condition follows about half of all children with GAD into adulthood; for others, it fades as they mature.

SIGNS OF GENERALIZED ANXIETY DISORDER

* restlessness
* headaches
* lightheadedness
* difficulty concentrating
* irritability
* muscle tension
* sleep disturbance

- frequent fatigue
- trembling or twitching
- nausea
- lump in the throat
- profuse sweating
- hot flashes
- difficulty catching breath
- easily startled

SEPARATION ANXIETY DISORDER

Description: abnormal anxiety about becoming separated from parents or other significant people in one's life, lasting at least one month.

A teenager with this condition will often refuse to go to school and complain of physical symptoms. No cause has been identified, though we do know that separation anxiety is more common in girls than in boys; that it tends to affect children from large, close-knit families; and that it may arise following an illness or death in the family.

SIGNS OF SEPARATION ANXIETY DISORDER

- when separated from her parents, the teenager becomes deeply distressed, and/or fears that her parents will meet with harm or become lost, and/or fears becoming separated from her parents
- fear of going to school and/or other places
- fear of being alone or without parents
- fear of going to sleep without parents nearby
- recurrent nightmares featuring themes of separation
- recurrent stomachaches, headaches and other maladies when separated from parents or in anticipation of a separation

PANIC DISORDER

Description: a condition marked by recurrent episodes of paralyzing fear, known as *panic attacks.*

Panic disorder, which affects three million to six million Americans, typically surfaces between ages fifteen and nineteen. Panic attacks may be precipitated by specific events, but they can also come crashing down without warning, even during sleep.

The average attack lasts about five to ten minutes. "It can be very scary for kids," says Dr. Charles Irwin. "They usually come into the emergency room terrified that either they're going crazy or they're having a heart attack." Some of the features of a panic attack do in fact mimic those of a heart attack: palpitations, chest pain, shortness of breath, sweating, dizziness and nausea. A child having these symptoms should be evaluated carefully to determine the underlying cause.

Many youngsters never have another panic attack, which tells us they don't suffer from panic disorder. However, those afflicted with the condition usually develop deep-seated anxieties about when and where the next one will occur. They avoid so many places and situations, their world often becomes progressively smaller. For instance, if they were driving during their last panic attack, they may become phobic about being in a car.

SIGNS OF PANIC DISORDER

At least four of the following symptoms:
- palpitations
- sweating
- trembling and shaking
- shortness of breath
- choking sensation
- chest pain or discomfort
- nausea or abdominal distress
- dizziness, lightheadedness
- feeling detached from oneself (*depersonalization*)
- feeling unreal (*derealization*)
- fear of losing control or going crazy
- fear of dying
- sensation of numbness or tingling
- chills or hot flashes
- worrying about future panic attacks

PHOBIAS

Description: persistent, irrational fears about certain objects or situations.

Teenagers suffering from a phobia are usually mature enough to recognize that their intense fear defies logic, but they are unable to control it. The phobias seen most frequently during adolescence are *agoraphobia,* fear of leaving a familiar setting, such as one's home, *social phobia,* a painful fear of humiliating oneself in public; and *specific phobia,* a chronic fear of a single thing or event. Among the more common phobias to prey upon teens are fears of snakes, heights, needle injections, flying in airplanes and getting low grades.

As long as the object of the phobia can generally be avoided and not disrupt a child's day-to-day life, treatment may not be necessary. Social phobia, though, almost always gets in the way of normal functioning. Young people with social phobia may be too intimidated to speak up in the classroom or present a speech. (Fear of speaking in public is the most common manifestation of social phobia.)

This is *not* the same thing as shyness. Plenty of people with social phobia are outgoing and completely at ease around others much of the time. But the thought of attending a party, walking into class late or any number of situations can send them into a panic. With some teens, social phobia takes the form of school avoidance. They wake up in the morning complaining of various physical ailments, which not-so-mysteriously vanish once they're pardoned from having to attend school. (See "The Problem: Your Teenager Doesn't Want to Go to School," in chapter 8, "Your Teenager at School.")

SIGNS OF A PHOBIA

One or more of the following symptoms when exposed to or thinking about the source of the phobia:

- palpitations
- sweating
- trembling and shaking
- nausea
- diarrhea
- flushed face
- disturbing thoughts and images

OBSESSIVE-COMPULSIVE DISORDER (OCD)

Description: chronic anxiety-provoking thoughts and repetitive rituals that the person cannot control.

Obsessive-compulsive disorder (OCD), which affects an estimated one in fifty people, frequently arises during the teen years. It can be the most disabling of the anxiety disorders. In OCD, the mind torments youngsters by replaying the same distressing or pointless thoughts, called *obsessions.* Imaging studies have revealed that people with obsessive-compulsive disorder have a brain chemical imbalance.

No matter how hard the patient tries to tune out the intrusive, unwelcome thought, it repeats itself dozens or hundreds of times a day. The classic obsession is a preoccupation with cleanliness. *My hands must be dirty.* To banish the thought—and with the hope of preventing it from recurring—he feels driven to carry out a routine, or *compulsion;* in this case, washing his hands over and over. The ritual, which can be painstakingly elaborate, brings temporary relief but not pleasure. If it isn't performed exactly or a certain number of times, some people with OCD can become extremely anxious and upset. Most of them realize that these thoughts and behaviors are irrational and alienating to others. They will go to great lengths to hide their symptoms, and that in itself becomes an enormous strain.

These teenagers are often haunted by multiple obsessions and compulsions, the most common being the fear of germs and subsequent cleaning rituals. Other examples of obsession/compulsion tandems include the nagging thought that you've left the lights on or forgotten to lock a door, coupled with the need to check it again and again. Such senseless activities typically consume at least an hour of an OCD patient's day and may eventually interfere with his education, career, and social life. For that reason, obsessive-compulsive disorder is one of the conditions covered under the Americans with Disabilities Act (ADA), the landmark federal law that prohibits discrimination against people with physical or mental impairments.

SIGNS OF OBSESSIVE-COMPULSIVE DISORDER

Obsessions:

- fear of contamination
- thoughts of harming oneself or committing violence against others

Compulsions:

- excessive hand washing
- checking behavior (locks, windows, doors, the stove, the iron)
- the need to constantly touch or rearrange objects
- excessive housecleaning
- hoarding
- incessant counting, praying, mentally repeating words or phrases
- making endless series of lists

POST-TRAUMATIC STRESS DISORDER (PTSD)

Description: recurrent disturbing memories of a traumatic experience.
Post-traumatic stress disorder (PTSD) forces people to relive ordeals such as murder, rape, war, accidents and natural disasters. The recollections come

in the form of persistent memories and nightmares, as well as *flashbacks*—memories so vivid that the person feels transported back to the horrific event for a matter of seconds or hours. Some patients become so immersed in the scene that they lose touch with reality; the imaginary sights, sounds, smells and emotions seem real to them. Afterward, they usually display phobic reactions to whatever situations or activities triggered the awful memories.

Not every victim or witness to a crime, accident or other form of disaster develops PTSD. In those that do, the symptoms typically appear within three months and linger for a period of several months. Researchers at Children's Hospital of Philadelphia studied approximately one hundred children and teenagers who'd been injured in car crashes. One in four met the diagnostic criteria for post-traumatic stress disorder, including youngsters with only minor injuries.

SIGNS OF POST-TRAUMATIC STRESS DISORDER

Two or more of the following symptoms when reminded of the traumatic experience:

- insomnia
- irritability or angry outbursts
- poor concentration
- memory impairment
- startles easily
- feeling of detachment, numbness
- always seems to be watching out for danger

ANTISOCIAL PERSONALITY DISORDER

Description: pervasive indifference toward other people's rights and needs. Teenagers with true antisocial personality disorder usually have exhibited this pattern of behavior from before the age of fifteen, although the diagnosis cannot be officially made until age eighteen. Without professional help and a supportive family, they may grow up to become immature, irresponsible adults with an alarming lack of conscience.

SIGNS OF ANTISOCIAL PERSONALITY DISORDER

- irritability and aggressiveness
- frequent fighting

- lying, cheating and other deceitful behavior
- impulsivity
- reckless disregard for personal safety or the safety of others
- lack of remorse for hurtful acts
- failure to apply oneself in school
- history of truancy, delinquency, vandalism, theft, unlawful acts

Psychotic Disorders

A *psychotic* person is out of touch with reality. He may cling to irrational beliefs; for instance, insisting that someone or something is planting thoughts in his head or that people are whispering about him. Additional symptoms of *psychosis* include extreme stubbornness, paranoia, visual hallucinations, hearing voices, social isolation, deteriorating personal hygiene, a need to carry out specific rituals and delusions of grandeur. Psychosis can be triggered by substance abuse; it may also arise out of other mental illnesses, like depression and bipolar disorder.

> ### *Words Worth Knowing*
>
> ***Delusions:*** irrational beliefs. Examples include delusions of grandeur, delusions of being talked about and delusions that someone is planting ideas in their head.

SCHIZOPHRENIA

Description: the most chronic and debilitating of all psychiatric conditions, and the most widespread form of psychosis.

"Schizophrenia," which literally means "split mind," is frequently confused with a separate disorder, "split personality or multiple personality disorder." Schizophrenia causes people to waver between reality and their own distorted perception of reality. Early intervention may improve a youngster's prognosis. Unfortunately, the subtle warning signs are apt to be attributed to the normal growing pains of adolescence.

SIGNS OF SCHIZOPHRENIA

- impaired concentration
- bizarre thoughts, ideas, statements (delusions)
- seeing imaginary objects or people; hearing voices that do not exist (hallucinations)

- severe depression
- jumbled thinking and incoherent speech
- lack of emotion, or "flat affect"
- withdrawing socially from others
- paralyzing anxiety and fear
- immature behavior

Behavioral and Disruptive Disorders

OPPOSITIONAL DEFIANT DISORDER (ODD) AND CONDUCT DISORDER (CD)

Oppositional behavior, discussed in chapter 4, "Growing into Adulthood," is part and parcel of adolescence, but it is not all the same as oppositional defiant disorder, in part because it is a much milder form of behavior, and in part because teenagers engaging in typically rebellious behavior are also prone to moments of spontaneous affection and warmth.

> ### Know the Signs of Oppositional Defiant Disorder
>
> - Consistent pattern of defiance, disobedience, belligerence, irritability
> - Frequently gets into arguments and fights
> - Easily loses temper
> - Blames others for his mistakes or misconduct
> - Often annoys others intentionally
> - Often behaves vindictively or spitefully toward others
> - Always seems angry, resentful

Oppositional defiant disorder, a pattern of persistently negative behavior with a hostile edge, is decidedly outside the range of normal adolescent development. In this behavioral disturbance, a consistent pattern of disobedience and disrespect toward parents may be directed at other adult authority figures too, such as teachers. Exhibiting four or more of the features in the box above for a minimum of six months meets the criteria for making the diagnosis. Oppositional defiant disorder sometimes leads to more disruptive behavior, or *conduct disorder.*

Verbal and physical aggression toward people and animals are the hallmarks of conduct disorder. The diagnosis is established when a child has committed three or more of the acts listed on page 343 within the past year, and one in the past six months. Without treatment, most young people with this condition face a dim future. Studies of juveniles in prison found that approximately nine in ten had conduct disorder.

Identifying the Problem

Adolescent emotional disorders can be difficult to diagnose definitively. First, to determine whether a youngster's behavior warrants treatment or not, a pediatrician or a mental health professional needs to assess his intellectual, psychological and social development, and the ways in which these may interact to produce problems common to a number of disorders.

For example, young people with attention deficit hyperactivity disorder may display the belligerent behavior and quick temper that characterize oppositional defiant disorder, while the eating disorder, bulimia, is often accompanied by obsessive-compulsive behavior. Learning disabilities, substance use and depression in particular may be seen in any emotional/behavioral disturbance. The medical term for coexisting conditions is *comorbidities.*

Further complicating the diagnostician's job, teenagers may not be able—or willing—to verbalize their thoughts and feelings. You will be asked for your observations about your child,

> ### *Know the Signs of Conduct Disorder*
>
> - Frequently bullies, threatens or intimidates others
> - Frequently starts fights
> - Cruelty to people or animals
> - Has wielded a gun, knife, broken bottle, bat or other weapon
> - Has confronted and robbed another person
> - Has committed a sexual assault
> - Has set fire to public or private property with the intention of causing serious damage
> - Has used other means to deliberately destroy other people's property
> - Has burglarized a home, building or car
> - Frequently cons others into lending him money, possessions and so on
> - Has shoplifted
> - Has used forgery to illegally obtain money
> - Has run away from home overnight at least twice, or has run away for an extended period once
>
> **BEGINNING BEFORE AGE 13:**
>
> - Frequently disobeys parents by staying out at night
> - Frequently cuts school

typically through a detailed questionnaire and an office interview. With your permission, relatives, teachers and your pediatrician may also be asked to take part in the evaluation process.

According to the American Academy of Child and Adolescent Psychiatry, you can expect a comprehensive mental health evaluation to take several hours over the course of one or more office visits. Besides gathering information, the clinician will spend time talking to the young patient. Special tests assessing cognitive ability, speech and language, and so forth, may be ordered.

In addition, blood tests, X rays and other diagnostic procedures may be carried out by the adolescent's pediatrician or other medical clinician, to look for evidence of a biological cause to the behavior.

GETTING YOUNGSTERS THE HELP THEY NEED

Your pediatrician can help you find one of the mental health professionals, any of whom can diagnose and treat adolescent emotional/behavioral problems. Dr. Helen Pratt, a clinical psychologist in Kalamazoo, Michigan, observes that the top consideration in choosing a practitioner shouldn't be the set of initials after his or her name, "it's how much experience the person has treating psychological disorders in teenagers."

Also try contacting your community mental health services agency. Each state's office of mental health funds nonprofit mental health programs. One advantage of these public clinics over private practitioners is that they may offer a broad range of therapies under one roof, and at *sliding scale* fees, based on the ability to pay. You'll find the telephone number in the government listings section of the white pages.

Let's say that your research has turned up the names of three known therapists. How do you know whom to choose? Spend a few minutes on the telephone with each one and be sure to ask how long they have been seeing teenage patients and how much of their practice is made up of adolescents.

Naturally, the therapist will want to hear a capsule history of your son's or daughter's situation. Describe the symptoms, what most concerns you and what you hope therapy will accomplish, both in the short term and over time. Next inquire about the practitioner's general approach to treatment. The most effective strategy for treating adolescent mental health disorders often combines talk therapy and psychopharmaceutical medications. Talk therapy for many of the adolescent psychological problems discussed here may involve short-term *behavioral therapy* or *cognitive therapy,* and sometimes both. *Psychoanalysis,* the intensive long-term therapy fathered by Sigmund Freud, is rarely employed with young people. (See "Finding the Right Pediatrician for Your Teen" in chapter 16, "Medical Checkups and Immunizations.")

HOW EMOTIONAL AND BEHAVIORAL DISORDERS ARE TREATED

Parental cooperation is crucial to the success of treatment. You'll want to communicate regularly with the therapist to keep abreast of what progress is being made. If you and your youngster are just starting down this road, take

Mental Health Care: Who's Who

Psychiatrist: an M.D. (doctor of medicine) or D.O. (doctor of osteopathy) who specializes in diagnosing and treating mental disorders, and the only practitioner listed here who can prescribe medication. (Your child's pediatrician can also write prescriptions, while some states additionally permit selected psychologists to order pharmaceutical treatment.) The psychiatrist diagnoses and prescribes medication and therapy. He may also refer the patient and/or family to others for ongoing talk therapy while he focuses on the medications.

Licensed Psychologist: a counselor with a master's degree or doctoral degree in psychology (Psy.D.), philosophy (Ph.D.) or education (Ed.D.). Trained to make diagnoses and conduct individual and group therapy. Only psychologists are able to administer many of the tests used to measure a young person's intellect and psychological health.

All of the mental health counselors listed below are also trained to make diagnoses and provide individual and group counseling. What's the difference, then? Their degrees and perhaps their area of specialty.

Clinical Social Worker: master's degree in social work (M.S.W.); Licensed Clinical Social Workers (L.C.S.W.) have additional supervised training and clinical work experience.

Licensed Professional Counselor: master's degree in psychology, counseling or a related field.

Mental Health Counselor: master's degree and several years of supervised clinical work experience.

Marital and Family Therapist: master's degree, with special education and training in marital and family therapy. May also have a doctorate degree.

Psychiatric Nurse: registered nurse (R.N.) with specialized training in psychological disorders.

heart in the fact that the prognosis is usually bright. As many as 60 to 80 percent of patients with severe disorders such as schizophrenia, major depression and bipolar disorder demonstrate a positive response to treatment.

Talk Therapy

The most widely practiced one-to-one talk therapies for teenagers are cognitive therapy and behavioral therapy. Both are results-oriented, short-term in-

Health Uninsurance and Mental Health Care

Even though many emotional/behavioral problems have a biological origin, health insurers often draw a distinction between physical illness and mental illness, particularly where children are concerned.

With the mass exodus from traditional fee-for-service policies to managed-care plans, families in crisis may be surprised to learn they're entitled to relatively little in the way of mental health coverage. Before you choose a therapist, read your policy or call your insurer and ask the following questions:

1. What are my benefits for psychotherapy? What percentage of the practitioner's fees are covered, and is there a limit on the number of visits per year? Over the life of the policy?
2. Are psychological evaluations and tests covered?
3. What about psychiatric medications?
4. *If you're insured by a health-maintenance organization (HMO), a preferred-provider organization (PPO) or a point-of-service plan (POS):*

   - Who are the mental health providers in my area? Do any of them specialize in treating adolescents?
   - Do I need to get a referral from my primary care physician first?
   - What happens if I wish to use a therapist from outside the network of approved clinicians?

terventions, consisting of anywhere from ten to thirty-five weekly sessions. Many times the two approaches are merged into *cognitive-behavioral therapy.*

Briefly, cognitive therapy seeks to free patients from the negative thought patterns that often weigh them down when they're feeling low, like the tendency to overgeneralize ("I can't do anything right!"), catastrophize ("My new perm looks *gross!* I can't let anybody see me until it grows out!") or to view each unhappy experience as further proof of a preordained conspiracy to thwart their enjoyment of life ("Nothing good ever happens to me!"). It's not as simple as exhorting youngsters to "think positive!" In fact, studies show that the power of positive thinking is a rather feeble weapon against depression. Cognitive therapy teaches patients not to dwell in negativity and to exercise mind control over how they perceive situations.

The goal of behavioral therapy is to "unlearn" self-defeating attitudes and behavior. With young children, behavior modification often incorporates a reward system, like gold stars in school. With teenagers and adults, desirable behaviors are reinforced through the general improvement in the patient's mental outlook.

Cognitive-behavioral therapy may include *social-skills training,* because youngsters who are anxious or despondent frequently feel awkward in social situations. They're probably not nearly as inept as they believe themselves to be, but their self-consciousness gets in the way of making eye contact, initiating conversation and so on. Socialization training allows them to practice being more self-assertive, approachable and communicative.

Individual therapy is usually complemented by *family counseling* and possibly *group therapy.* Dr. Pratt, director of behavioral and developmental pediatrics at Michigan State University's Kalamazoo Center for Medical Studies, highly recommends a combination of all three.

"The whole family should always be treated along with the adolescent," she asserts. "The child in therapy obviously is unable to handle what is going on in his or her environment, and that environment includes home and school." In family therapy, the counselor guides the members in airing their feelings and helps them work toward resolving household conflicts.

Group therapy, attended by five to ten teenagers and led by a trained counselor, provides opportunities to learn with and from one another. Youngsters realize that they are not alone. What's more, sometimes examining other people's behavioral patterns can shed light on our own problems. The group doubles as a socialization group, helping kids to refine their social skills.

MAKING THERAPY WORK

If you find that you have conflicted feelings about your child's starting therapy, you're not alone. But why do mothers and fathers sometimes regard a youngster's need for counseling as a mark against their competence as parents? You wouldn't fault yourself for not being able to fix a broken bone! Confronting a serious problem also requires professional help and you should take pride in having the courage to deal with it.

But kids can be equally sensitive about seeing a therapist; it confirms their fears that there's something "wrong" with them. We must respect those feelings. One ironclad rule throughout therapy is to never badger your child to tell you what she talked about with the therapist.

"I know why you won't tell me. It's because you were going on about what a mean mother I am, right?"

In all honesty, at some point during therapy you might very well be spoken about unflatteringly. Regardless, a child's right to privacy must be honored. The only times a therapist will break the code of doctor-patient confidentiality are when a teenager expresses a desire to harm herself or others, has been the victim of sexual or physical abuse, or admits to substance abuse serious enough to warrant professional treatment.

The idea that our youngster is confiding in a stranger can be threatening at first. We need to accept that sometimes it takes an outsider's objectivity to help young patients (and Mom and Dad) arrive at solutions, especially if one of the issues being worked on happens to be parent-teen conflicts.

Psychiatric Medications (Psychopharmaceuticals)

If a teenager developed diabetes, few parents would reject a physician's recommendation that she needs insulin injections to stabilize her condition and allow her to lead a normal life. But when a psychiatric disorder is the culprit—and symptoms are mental rather than physical—the idea of having a psychoactive drug prescribed is more likely to meet with resistance.

> ### Words Worth Knowing
>
> **Psychoactive drugs:** medications that act on the central nervous system. Also referred to as *psychotropic* medications.

"As with many things, this area is surrounded a lot more by myth than by fact," says Dr. Timothy Wilens. A pediatric psychopharmacologist at Boston's Massachusetts General Hospital, he's heard all the reservations that parents express about incorporating medication into their child's treatment. But as Dr. Wilens points out, "Most emotional and behavioral disorders in kids are probably biological insomuch as they begin with an adverse experience that leads to biochemical changes in the brain. Therefore it doesn't surprise us that medications can control a number of the different symptoms."

Medication should not be looked to as a substitute for psychotherapy, nor should it be looked down upon as a measure of last resort. In appropriate cases, it is a complement to talk therapy, which is intended to hone self-awareness and teach coping skills that will help patients to function out in the world. But results from counseling can be slow in coming. Medication, carefully prescribed by a psychiatrist or pediatrician familiar with teenage psychological conditions, can usually lighten symptoms *now* and give boys and girls back their adolescence.

Two and a half million young people in the United States use psychotropic drugs. However, the frequently heard accusation that doctors are too quick to prescribe psychoactive medications is not supported by the facts. A 1999 study from Yale University suggests that as many as nine in ten people suffering from depression go unmedicated.

Parents' resistance to the idea of drug therapy is often based on outdated information and images of the stupefying effects of psychiatric drugs. "We're much more selective about the medicines we use now," says Dr. Wilens, "and there's a broader repertoire of drugs available to us."

> ### *"I'm Worried About the Side Effects"*
>
> As with any medication, bothersome side effects from psychotropic drugs can vary considerably from one person to another, depending on the patient's age, sex, size, body chemistry, diet, and other variables. We note potential side effects to make you aware of what *could* happen. Your youngster might experience no ill effects at all.
>
> Other considerations may influence a doctor's choice of medication(s), such as:
>
> - Whether or not the teenager has another condition requiring medication.
> - Whether or not the teenager has a history of substance abuse or is considered at risk for a possible suicide attempt by way of an overdose.
> - The physician's prior experience prescribing the drug.

Admittedly, these medications have not been evaluated extensively in children, and some not at all, but according to Dr. Wilens, the studies conducted to date and years of experience prescribing the drugs "strongly suggest that the new generation of medications are safe and effective, with far fewer downsides than the older generation.

"The other point that parents need to know is that we usually start psychotropic medications at inordinately low doses and increase them over time, so that the body and brain can get used to them. But in doing so," he adds, "it takes longer for the full therapeutic effects to be seen. Selective serotonin reuptake inhibitors (SSRIs) sometimes have to build up in the brain for two to six weeks before bringing relief.

Because conditions wax and wane, after a year or so the doctor may suggest taking a "drug holiday" to get a sense of where the young patient stands without medication. He might fare just fine. Or he might require a reduction or an increase in dosage, or to be switched to another drug. Patients should *never* discontinue a psychopharmaceutical without a doctor's supervision; several of these drugs require that the dosage be tapered gradually in order to avoid withdrawal side effects. (See "Questions to Ask the Pediatrician Before a Teenager Starts Any New Medication" and "Storing Medications Safely" in chapter 20, "Common Medical Conditions During the Teen Years.")

CATEGORIES OF PSYCHIATRIC MEDICATIONS

ANTIDEPRESSANTS

There are three major categories of antidepressants: SSRIs, *tricyclic antidepressants* (TCAs), and *monoamine oxidase inhibitors* (MAOIs). While chemically unrelated to one another, all alter mood by affecting the central nervous system's levels of *neurotransmitters*—substances that bridge the gaps (*synapses*) between the nerve cells (*neurons*) in our brains and enable them to talk to one another. Neurons in different parts of the brain rely on different neurotransmitters to facilitate this communication.

Depression is associated with deficiencies of the neurotransmitters such as *serotonin, norepinephrine* and, to a lesser degree, *dopamine.* Each of the three groups of drugs goes about its job in unique fashion. Normally, the nerve cells absorb and recycle "used" neurotransmitters for future use. Tricyclics prevent the serotonin neurons and the norepinephrine neurons from taking the two substances out of circulation, so to speak. SSRIs are more selective (hence their name); they block only the nerve cells for serotonin. As for MAOIs, their strategy is to inhibit an enzyme that would otherwise destroy all three neurotransmitters. MAOIs are not used as much as the others in teenagers, due to possible severe side effects.

Since the introduction of the first SSRI, fluoxetine (brand name: Prozac), in 1988, selective serotonin reuptake inhibitors have overtaken the older tricyclics as the drug of choice for lifting adolescent depression. SSRIs are prescribed for both adolescents and adults, though most of the research is with adults. Studies have shown SSRIs to be just as effective as the tricyclics, but with fewer unwanted side effects, like drowsiness. There is also less chance of a youngster dying from an intentional overdose of an SSRI compared to other drugs—a realistic concern anytime someone is depressed. Most ado-

EMOTIONAL AND BEHAVIORAL PROBLEMS

lescents experience no unpleasant side effects from SSRIs, but if they do, side effects may include nausea, vomiting, diarrhea, headaches, insomnia, nervousness and sexual dysfunction. Most of these subside in a week to two weeks. If they persist, another SSRI can be tried. Besides Prozac, examples include sertraline (Zoloft), paroxetine (Paxil), fluvoxamine (Luvox) and citalopram (Celexa).

ANTIANXIETY AGENTS (ANXIOLYTICS)

SSRIs also play a major role in treating anxiety disorders, including obsessive-compulsive disorders and post-traumatic stress disorders. Benzodiazepines, the most widely prescribed *anxiolytics* for adults, are used sparingly in adolescents, partly because of their potential for abuse and dependence. Nor have they proved highly effective. The same is true of tricyclic antidepressants.

A relative newcomer among anxiolytics, buspirone (BuSpar) is finding favor with pediatricians and child psychiatrists. The drug doesn't have the sedating and disinhibiting effects of benzodiazepines. "Buspirone also doesn't have nearly as much addictive potential," explains Dr. Wilens. However, whereas benzodiazepines work immediately, BuSpar must be taken for two to three weeks before patients feel its antianxiety effect.

MAJOR TRANQUILIZERS (NEUROLEPTICS AND ANTIPSYCHOTICS)

Traditional *neuroleptics* such as chlorpromazine (Thorazine, the first psychiatric agent to be marketed commercially) and thioridazine (Mellaril) are used to treat a wide range of serious psychiatric disorders in adolescents: schizophrenia, manic behavior, autistic spectrum disorder, conduct disorder and psychosis.

Neuroleptic drugs have a calming and stabilizing effect, and control aggression and agitation. They can also temper if not eliminate hallucinations and delusions. Antipsychotics are prescribed judiciously, however, because of their adverse side effects. Most alarming of all is a rare complication called *tardive dyskinesia,* in which the person develops involuntary, almost Parkinson's-like movements of the facial muscles and possibly the arms and legs. Tardive dyskinesia usually goes away within a few months after the neuroleptic agent is discontinued, but in some cases it continues indefinitely.

To reduce the chances of tardive dyskinesia and other unwanted side effects, the doctor prescribes the minimal dose possible and monitors the patient closely. Every six months he will order blood tests to assess liver function and the levels of red cells, white cells and platelet cells. Fortunately, recent years have seen the introduction of several so-called "atypical" neuroleptics, beginning with clozapine (Clorazil). The incidence of tardive dyskinesia and other muscle-related effects from these drugs appears to be extremely low.

ANTIMANIC MEDICATIONS (MOOD STABILIZERS)

For decades, manic behavior has been brought under control with the *mood stabilizer* lithium. It is also prescribed as maintenance therapy to prevent future manic-depressive episodes. Youngsters require careful monitoring on this medication, including periodic blood tests and electrocardiograms. Lithium is associated with birth defects; therefore, sexually active girls may undergo a pregnancy test at the doctor's visit. Anticonvulsants (as carbamazepine) can serve as mood stabilizers as well.

PSYCHOSTIMULANTS

Methylphenidate (Ritalin, Concerta, Metadate CD, others), amphetamines (Dexedrine, Adderal) and pemoline (Cylert) are used to treat attention deficit hyperactivity disorder. (See "How Learning Problems Are Managed" in chapter 10, "Learning Problems.")

"Since children often have multiple psychiatric disorders at one time," says Dr. Wilens, "sometimes we use two or even three medications at lower doses, so that we don't get as many side effects or problems with tolerance. To treat anxiety, for example, it's not uncommon to prescribe an anxiolytic with an antidepressant." *Tolerance* means that the dosage must be increased in order to maintain the same response as before.

Memo to Mom and Dad: Don't be discouraged if a medication fails to manage the symptoms adequately. Explain this to your youngster too. A teenager whose disorder is impervious to one drug may respond beautifully to another. Or perhaps the physician merely needs to adjust the dosage or go to a multi-drug regimen. When your child is in emotional distress, it's not easy to be patient waiting for medication to work. But reassure your teen (and yourself) that in most cases, relief does come.

TALKING TO TEENS ABOUT PSYCHOACTIVE MEDICATIONS

"Will taking this pill turn me into a different person?"
"Because I need this medicine, does it mean I'm crazy?"

When medication has been prescribed, these are the types of thoughts that may go through a young person's mind. For insight into how to respond to such questions, here is what Dr. Wilens generally tells his adolescent patients:

First I'll talk to the teen about what seems to be the problem. He's depressed, or irritable, or he has a negative self-image. Then I'll say, "We don't think you purposely brought this on yourself. You have a deficiency or imbalance of chemicals in the brain, and it's affecting your life.

"We have ways to improve that. One way is talk therapy. But we also have medications that help to subtly change some of the chemistry in the brain. Not 'turbo-charging' it, but *normalizing* the brain chemistry. Now, we want the medication to agree with your body and your mind, so that you'll feel better but without feeling like you're 'on' something. If you should react to the drug to the point where you don't feel right, then we know that's probably not the right medicine for you, and we'll find something that does fit with you. You will still be *you.*"

When you address these points, compliance increases dramatically. When you don't, and you give kids something that doesn't feel natural to them, they won't take it.

In Dr. Wilens's experience, "probably the number-one reason psychiatric medications cease to be effective is that kids stop taking them. I strongly advise parents to monitor children who are on a medication, to make sure that they're using it as directed."

What to Do If You Think Your Child Is Suicidal

To read the newspapers or watch the television news-magazine programs, you would assume that the United States is in the midst of an epidemic of adolescent suicides.

It *is* true that the suicide rate per one hundred thousand fifteen-to-twenty-four-year-olds more than tripled between 1950 and 1994, from 4.5 to 13.8. However, the ostensibly higher incidence of suicides may partly reflect more accurate identification by local coroners. And the good news is that even if we accept those figures at face value, from 1994 to 1997 the rate fell steadily to 11.4 suicides per one hundred thousand, the lowest number recorded since the 1970s.

In the National Longitudinal Study on Adolescent Health, which polled some twelve thousand middle-school and high-school students, nearly nine in ten reported never having so much as entertained the thought of suicide in the past year. Still, mothers and fathers should never let these comforting statistics lull them into a false sense of security. Approximately 250,000 U.S. teenagers attempted to end their lives, with twenty-one hundred boys and girls between the ages of ten and nineteen completing the act.

WHICH KIDS ARE AT HEIGHTENED RISK FOR SUICIDE?

No child is immune, but statistics tell us that some adolescents are more vulnerable than others and may require closer parental attention:

Teenage boys suffering from an emotional or behavioral disorder. Although girls are more prone to depression, the suicide rate among teenage boys is four times higher. One theory as to why is that girls generally have more intimate friendships than boys do. In times of stress, girls can often lean on one another for emotional support, whereas boys tend to internalize their feelings.

Gay or lesbian youth. Many adolescents who take their own lives are homosexual. Depression and substance abuse are prevalent among these young men and women, who often face rejection and ridicule due to their sexuality identity.

Teenagers with substance-abuse problems. "Many suicides occur on the spur of the moment in association with alcohol or other drugs," explains Dr. Robert W. Blum, director of the division of pediatrics and adolescent health at University Hospitals in Minneapolis. "The drugs are disinhibiting and allow the person's underlying distress to surface."

Teenagers with easy access to potentially lethal medications. Another scenario involving substances is when a young person underestimates the toxic effects of medications found at home. A girl desperately seeking to numb her unhappiness, *not* end her life, accidentally overdoses on just a few pills. The re-

---

Know the Warning Signs of Violent Behavior

- Quick to anger
- Low tolerance for frustration
- Extreme irritability
- Extreme impulsivity
- Consistently ignores authority figures
- Insensitivity to the feelings or rights of others
- Cruelty to animals
- An unnatural preoccupation with firearms and with violent movies and video games; imitating violent scenes from films and TV
- Fantasizes aloud of harming others, exacting revenge
- Frequently gets into fights or threatens physical violence
- Blames others for his problems
- Poor performance in school
- Frequent truancy
- Gets suspended from school or drops out of school
- Joins a gang, gets involved in fighting, stealing or destroying property
- Drug use

verse can happen to a boy intent on going to sleep and never waking up swallowing a smorgasbord of drugs, only to regain consciousness in the hospital.

"Teenagers aren't pharmacologists," notes Dr. John Kulig, director of adolescent medicine at Boston's New England Medical Center. "So they can look in the medicine cabinet and think that taking two antibiotics, three acetaminophen and four vitamin C tablets would be lethal [highly unlikely] but not understand that as few as three or four tricyclic antidepressants could very well prove deadly."

Youngsters with a history of suicidal behavior. One in three suicide victims has tried to kill themselves in the past. A history of violence may be seen. (See box on page 354.)

Boys and girls who have lost a friend or relative to suicide. Studies show that a considerable number of youth suicides and suicide attempts occur in the wake of the self-inflicted death or injury of someone else. The person may be known to them, or he may be a stranger whose suicide was reported by the media. Plano, Texas, is one of several towns plagued by a "suicide cluster," where one youngster's death touches off a chain reaction among teenagers.

According to Dr. William Lord Coleman of the University of North Carolina School of Medicine, "Anytime there is a suicide in the community, parents need to be extra vigilant about how that may be affecting their child." Don't be afraid to raise the subject with a teenager, for fear that by bringing it out into the open you're planting thoughts that will one day be acted upon. To the contrary, you can use this opportunity to point out that the victim probably didn't realize that there were many people and resources available to help him overcome his mental illness.

PREVENTING THE WORST: TEN THINGS THAT PARENTS CAN DO

1. ***Don't let a teenager's depression or anxiety snowball.*** Maybe your child is merely having a bad day, but maybe it's something more. Nine in ten adolescents who take their own lives were previously diagnosed with a psychiatric disorder—more than half of them with a mood disorder such as depression. Depressed people often retreat into themselves, when secretly they're crying out to be rescued. Many times they're too embarrassed to reveal their unhappiness to others, including Mom and Dad. Boys in particular may try to hide their emotions, in the misguided belief that displaying vulnerability is a fifty-foot-high neon sign of weakness.

Let's not wait for youngsters to come to us with their problems. Knock on the door, park yourself on the bed, and say, "You seem sad. Would you like to talk about it? Maybe I can help."

2. *Listen to your teenager—even when she's not talking.* Not all, but most kids who are contemplating suicide (this is called suicidal *ideation*) tip off their troubled state of mind through behaviors like those in the box on the next page. Studies have found that one trait common to families shattered by a son's or daughter's suicide is poor communication between parents and child.

If your instinct tells you that a teenager might be a danger to himself, heed your instincts and don't allow him to be left alone. In this situation, it is better to overreact than to underreact.

3. *Never shrug off threats of suicide as typical teenage melodrama.* "Any written or verbal statement of 'I want to die' or 'I don't care anymore' should be treated seriously," says psychologist Helen Pratt. "Often, children who attempt suicide had been telling their parents *repeatedly* that they intended to kill themselves." Conventional wisdom holds that people who openly threaten suicide don't really intend to take their own lives; the threat is a desperate plea for help. While that is true much of the time, what mother or father would want to risk being wrong?

Any of these other red flags warrants your immediate attention:

> "Nothing matters."
> "I wonder how many people would come to my funeral?"
> "Sometimes I wish I could just go to sleep and never wake up."
> "Everyone would be better off without me."
> "You won't have to worry about me much longer."

When a teenager starts dropping thinly veiled comments like that or comes right out and admits to feeling suicidal, try not to react with shock ("What are you, crazy?!") or scorn ("That's a ridiculous thing to say!"). Above all, don't tell her, "You don't mean that!"—though you'd probably be right. Be willing to listen nonjudgmentally to what he's *really* saying, which is: "*I need your love and attention because I'm in tremendous pain, and I can't seem to stop it on my own.*"

To see your child so distraught would tear at the heart of any parent. Nevertheless, the immediate focus has to be on consoling him; you'll tend to your feelings later. In a calm voice, you might say, "I see. You must really, really be hurting inside.

"Honey, plenty of people feel that way at one time or another. They may really mean it at that moment, but that's because they're depressed. Depression is an illness of the mind. Not only does it make you sadder than you've ever felt before, it takes control of your thoughts so that you can't see any way out of your sadness. I know that right now it probably seems like it will last forever. But it won't. We love you so much. Please let us get you the right help that will make your sadness go away."

4. ***Seek professional help right away.*** If your teenager's behavior has you concerned, don't wait to contact your pediatrician.

5. ***Share your feelings.*** Let your teen know he's not alone and that everyone feels sad or depressed now and then, including moms and dads. Without minimizing his anguish, reassure him that these bad times won't last forever. Things truly *will* get better.

6. ***Encourage him not to isolate himself*** from family and friends. It's usually better to be around other people than to be alone. But don't push if he says no.

7. ***Recommend exercise.*** Physical activity as simple as walking or as vigorous as pumping iron can put the brakes on mild to moderate depression. There are several theories why. One is that working out causes a gland in the brain to release *endorphins,* a substance believed to improve mood and ease pain. Endorphins also lower the amount of *cortisol* in the circulation. Cortisol, a hormone, has been linked to depression.

Two other benefits of exercise: It distracts people from their problems and makes them feel better about themselves. Experts recommend working out for thirty to forty

---

Know the Signs of Potentially Suicidal Behavior

- Depression
- Sudden decline in school performance
- Suddenly acts cheerful after a period of depression
- Difficulty eating or sleeping
- Unexplained or unusually extreme violent or rebellious behavior
- Withdrawing from family or friends
- Taking unnecessary risks, such as driving recklessly or overdosing on drugs "accidentally on purpose"
- Purchasing a gun or taking a sudden interest in firearms
- Running away from home
- Uncharacteristically neglects hygiene and appearance
- Drastic change in personality
- Complaints of imagined physical problems
- Preoccupation with death and dying
- Giving away or throwing out prized possessions, as if putting his or her affairs in order
- Talking about suicide, even jokingly
- Threats of suicide
- Suicide attempts

minutes a day, two to five times per week. Any form of exercise will do; what matters most is that youngsters enjoy the activity.

8. *Urge your teen not to demand too much of herself right now.* Until therapy begins to take effect, this is probably not the time to assume responsibilities that could prove overwhelming. Suggest that she divide large tasks into smaller, more manageable ones whenever possible and participate in favorite, low-stress activities. The goal is to rebuild confidence and self-esteem.

9. *Remind a teenager undergoing treatment not to expect immediate results.* Talk therapy and/or medication usually take time to improve mood, so he shouldn't become discouraged or blame himself if he doesn't feel better right away.

10. *If you keep guns at home, store them safely* or move all firearms elsewhere until the crisis has passed. In 1997 there were 4,186 suicides among young people aged fifteen to twenty-four, three in five of which involved guns. Most of the victims were male. Whereas men typically end their lives through violent means, women generally choose the less reliable method of overdosing on drugs. If you suspect your son or daughter might be suicidal, it would be wise to keep all alcohol and medications under lock and key—even nonprescription drugs. (See "Firearm Safety" in chapter 14, "Safety and Injury Prevention.")

PREVENTING THE WORST: EFFECTIVE INTERVENTIONS

A teenager who has tried to commit suicide should be taken at once to a hospital emergency department for treatment of physical consequences as well as a psychological or psychiatric evaluation. If she is presently under the care of a mental health professional, that person should be alerted, so that he can meet the family at the hospital or consult over the phone with the mental health staff.

The desire to take one's own life typically fades within a few hours or several days. Provided that the youngster is judged emotionally stable enough to be discharged, she returns home. The parents pledge to watch her around the clock until the crisis has passed. In this intervention, dubbed "24-7" by Dr. Pratt, "a child is not even allowed to go to the bathroom unsupervised.

"What this does is to illustrate dramatically to a youngster how important she is to her family, the fact that everyone is willing to rearrange their entire lives to protect her. The adolescent also realizes how much independence she really had, when she probably thought that she didn't have *any* freedom."

Teenagers and the Law

Mental Health Care: Their Rights, Your Rights

There is little consistency in state statutes governing a minor's right to confidential mental health care. A number of states allow youngsters aged twelve to seventeen to commit themselves to a mental institution without having to obtain their parents' permission, while other states permit teenagers to arrange outpatient therapy on their own, but not inpatient treatment. In the many states that have no such legislation, federal law applies. Under a U.S. Supreme Court ruling, parents may commit a minor against his will. However, the statute contains legal checkpoints, to prevent parents from unjustly institutionalizing a disruptive child merely to remove him from the family home.

Most families are able to return to their normal routines after two or three days.

Follow-up outpatient treatment, in the form of one-to-one counseling, family therapy and possibly medication, should begin promptly. Talk therapy aims to improve the teen's problem-solving skills, interpersonal relationships and tolerance for stress, while the goal of family therapy is to enhance communication and in general make for a more harmonious household.

According to Dr. Pratt, the intensity of treatment depends on the seriousness of the suicide attempt. Outpatient therapy is appropriate for a child with no prior history of harming himself and who let's say gulped down a handful of aspirin. He might have needed his stomach pumped, but he was never in any genuine danger of dying. "However," she says, "when a child seems to have no hope or has used stronger means, such as cutting themselves, taking a combination of drugs or using a gun, they need to be admitted to a psychiatric ward or facility." Inpatient care would also be recommended for a youngster who did not have a stable home life or if it seemed apparent that he would not cooperate with an outpatient counseling program.

Inpatient treatment in a hospital is the most restrictive setting for mental health care. Other programs include *partial hospitalization* (provides the same services as a psychiatric facility, except that patients return home at night), *residential treatment* (patients live with other youngsters in a campuslike environment for anywhere from one month to one year), *crisis residential treatment* (short-term crisis intervention consisting of twenty-four-hour supervision), *therapeutic group-home care* (six to ten young people reside in a home under the supervision of a trained staff) and *home-based treatment* (specially trained staff go to patients' homes and develop a treatment plan designed to aid both the teenager and the family as a whole).

WHEN A TEENAGER IS OUT OF CONTROL

None of the crises discussed in this chapter have a simple solution. Sometimes, though, a teenager's misconduct is so extreme or has been an ongoing problem for so long that his parents can no longer manage him and feel they have no recourse but to order him out of the home. Examples would include chronic substance abuse, drug dealing, incidents of violence toward family members, continued defiance and disobedience, repeatedly running away, habitual truancy from school and regularly stealing money and possessions.

No parent takes a step like that without a good deal of agonizing and soul-searching. Most do so out of the sincere belief that it is in the best interest of the family, particularly siblings, and ultimately may serve as the impetus for the troubled youth to receive the professional help he needs—be it psychiatric care, a drug-rehabilitation program or some other form of treatment—and turn around his life.

What Is a PINS Petition?

A minor cannot simply be thrown out of the house. His parents would have to go to their state's family court to file what is called a PINS petition. "PINS" stands for "Persons in Need of Supervision"; in other states it may be known as Children in Need of Supervision, or CHINS.

The process may vary somewhat from one state to another. Typically, before filing, the parents and child must meet with a representative of a government social-service agency, who attempts to resolve the family crisis and keep the case out of court. This step, called *diversion,* can last ninety days. If reconciliation proves unsuccessful, the parents may then file the petition asking the court to order supervision or treatment for the child. (Legal guardians, school districts or social-service agencies charged with looking after a child may also file a PINS petition.)

The court will appoint an attorney for the young person and for the parents as well, if they cannot afford one. While the case is under consideration, the youth will continue to live with his parents, unless the court decides that is an unwise arrangement. In that event, the adolescent may be released to the temporary care of a relative, foster care or possibly a group home. A hearing is then held. The family may place the youngster in either a treatment facility or in foster care.

What Is Emancipation?

Teenagers are not without legal rights. A youth who wishes to live on his own legally, without running away from home, can appeal to the family court for a declaration of *emancipation*. "This doesn't mean that he wouldn't receive money from his parents, but they would not be in a position to tell him how to spend it," explains Dr. Robert Brown, chief of the division of adolescent medicine at Ohio State University College of Medicine and Public Health.

The criteria for emancipation varies according to jurisdiction. Most states do not allow youngsters under eighteen to initiate such a contract, but in some, children as young as age fourteen may seek legal independence. Having graduated from high school may qualify a minor for emancipation, depending upon where he lives. Other criteria frequently includes marriage, parenthood or enlistment in the armed forces. Emancipation is also sometimes granted if the parents give their permission.

Teenagers and the Juvenile Justice System

"In order to be prosecuted for a crime, a person has to be deemed an independent adult," explains Dr. Brown. "If a person commits a crime while still a dependent minor, then it is considered not a criminal act but a delinquent act." Accordingly, the case is heard in family court or juvenile court rather than in criminal court. Exceptions may be made, however, for minors who have perpetrated particularly serious or violent crimes, called *designated felonies*. They may be treated as juvenile offenders in a criminal court, although the criminal court may return the case to family court.

The process is similar to that of filing for a PINS petition. The youngster is entitled to legal representation, and if he cannot afford an attorney, one will be appointed by the court. An initial hearing is held to determine whether or not the teenager should be released to his parents' custody and allowed to go home. With minor or first-time offenses, that's usually what happens. But if he is felt to be a danger to the community or unlikely to return to court, he can be detained in a locked or nonlocked facility until his day in court.

A minor found guilty of a delinquent act may be sent to a detention center, a shelter, even a boot camp. But the growing trend, says Dr. Brown, is to place teenagers in the least restrictive environment possible, such as a nonsecured group home. "Ideally, the kid can eventually come back home and return to school. The goal of the court is not to punish, it's to rehabilitate and create a productive adult capable of functioning in society."

A delinquent act does not become part of a minor's criminal record; a designated felony, however, does.

WHAT TO DO IF A TEENAGER RUNS AWAY FROM HOME

Every year, one million teenagers run away from home, typically after a heated family quarrel. The majority stay at a friend's house for a day or two, then sheepishly return home. Statistics show that nine in ten adolescent runaways come home voluntarily or are brought home by the police within one month.

But the potential seriousness of a child's absence needs to be acknowledged. Too often, when a child is missing, mothers and fathers mistakenly hold off contacting the police. Contrary to what many believe, you do not have to wait twenty-four hours before filing a runaway report or a missing-persons report for anyone under eighteen years old. Most runaways do not leave behind notes announcing that they have run away from home. As a parent, you know your child. If your normally responsible daughter was due home hours ago from a nighttime outing with friends, and your intuition is telling you that something is wrong, don't hesitate to make the call.

When a youngster has run away or, worse, has been abducted, the sooner parents contact law-enforcement officials, the greater the likelihood that he or she is still in the area and will be returned home safely. According to the National Center for Missing and Exploited Children, mothers and fathers have the right to ask local investigators to enter their child into the National Crime Information Center Missing-Persons Files and to put out a be-on-the-lookout (BOLO) bulletin.

Once you've called the police, here is a suggested plan of action:

- Call your teenager's friends and their parents. Have they seen your child?

- If the young person has left behind an address book, get in touch with anyone that you believe might know her whereabouts.

- Also contact relatives, employers, coaches, youth-group members, school administrators, teachers and school security guards. When was the last time they saw your teenager?

- If your bank uses automated-teller machines, check ATM transactions.

TEEN TIP:

Has your teenager been emotionally distressed? Has she threatened to run away, perhaps in the heat of a family argument? Ask trusted friends and relatives if they wouldn't mind opening their door to your youngster should she ever feel the need to leave the house for a while. Both of you will probably feel relieved to know that she always has a safe place to go to calm down, collect her thoughts and speak with someone else.

Credit-card transactions, too, might provide clues as to a young person's whereabouts.

• Peruse recent phone bills. Does it list repeat calls to an out-of-town telephone number you don't recognize? That could possibly be helpful to authorities in establishing a trail. If your teenager has access to the Internet, check her e-mails. Most Web browsers have a "History" feature listing which Web sites were recently visited. This, too, might yield useful information.

• Call the National Runaway Switchboard (NRS) (800-621-4000), a nonprofit organization that operates a free, confidential switchboard twenty-four hours a day, seven days a week. The Chicago-based NRS is linked to more than twelve thousand state and local agencies around the country. The switchboard provides the following services free of charge:

—*Message Delivery.* Runaways who aren't ready to call home yet but want to let their parents know they are safe can leave a message with the switchboard, which then conveys this to the parents. Parents, too, can leave messages for their child. It is recommended that they inform all of their youngster's friends that a message is waiting for their child at the NRS.

The National Runaway Switchboard will also arrange for conference calls between parents and runaways, with a volunteer counselor on the line to moderate the conversation and make it as productive as possible. It is hoped the end result will be reconciliation, followed shortly by a reunion.

—*Home Free Program.* Runaways who meet certain eligibility requirements can receive free bus transportation home.

—*Referrals* to organizations that can assist with poster or photo distribution, runaway shelters, counseling centers, support groups and many other resources.

• Call the National Center for Missing and Exploited Children hot line (800-843-5678). Founded in 1984, the NCMEC assists parents and law-enforcement agencies in recovering missing children. The organization will post a color photo of the missing teen on its Web site and print up fliers for you to distribute in your community.

OVERCOMING THE CRISIS

Few things tear at a parent's heart more than reading the pain etched on her youngster's face and feeling powerless to take away his unhappiness. It was so much easier when he was little, though it may not have seemed that way at the time. Back then, he ran to you with his problems, knowing there was virtually nothing Mom or Dad couldn't fix with a few well-chosen words and a reassuring hug. Now his world is far more complicated; so are his problems. But as part of a teen's growing independence, he may be less inclined to ask you for advice or even to volunteer when something is bothering him.

Maybe we can't make everything better for kids like we used to, but we *can* make some things better. The biggest obstacle to successful outcomes for emotionally troubled adolescents is their parents' failure to acknowledge when a son or daughter seems to be experiencing more than the usual difficulties of growing up. Let's be honest: That's a painful admission for any mother or father to have to make.

But once you clear that hurdle, you're on your way toward a solution—if not a perfect solution, then certainly an improvement over the way things were. As we've stressed throughout this chapter, the vast majority of young people diagnosed with a psychological disorder can be treated and go on to face the future as emotionally healthy adults.

PART IV

GOOD HEALTH: SETTING THE PATTERNS FOR A LIFETIME

16

MEDICAL CHECKUPS AND IMMUNIZATIONS

Once a boy or girl reaches adolescence, most pediatricians explain to the family that it is time for his primary relationship to be with the young patient rather than with Mom and Dad, for part of a child's journey to adulthood includes learning to take care of himself and becoming a discerning medical consumer.

Until now, one or both parents have probably been at their youngster's side for every medical examination since the first time they brought him to the pediatrician's office in his infant carrier. From this point on, part of each doctor's visit may be conducted in private. Your input is just as essential as before, and afterward your pediatrician will apprise you of your teen's health, especially if a condition requires medication or special care. But in keeping with the policy of physician-patient privilege, doctors are allowed by law to keep certain medical information confidential at the adolescent's request, if they feel it is in the best interests of their patients.

TEENAGE CONFIDENTIAL: A YOUNG PERSON'S RIGHT TO PRIVACY

Federal and state statutes legislating a minor's right to medical confidentiality are often vague, and many times the decision whether or not to disclose medical information is left to the doctor's discretion. According to Dr. Joe Sanders Jr., executive director of the American Academy of Pediatrics (AAP), most pediatricians make a verbal "contract" with the parents and the teenager regarding confidentiality. It is mutually understood that any information the young patient shares with the physician remains in strict confidence *unless* in the doctor's judgment the teen poses a danger to himself or to others or has been abused.

"For instance," says Dr. Sanders, "if a teenager tells me, 'I'm really depressed and I've been thinking of killing myself,' I cannot hold that information in confidence, because I've got to get this kid the proper help. But if an adolescent tells me that he is sexually involved with his girlfriend, and he doesn't want his parents to find out, I won't share that information. I will work with him to minimize the risk of contracting a sexually transmitted disease or having an unintended pregnancy."

Teenagers' concerns about confidentiality can be a major barrier to obtaining health care. In a Louis Harris/Commonwealth Fund poll of more than six thousand five hundred teens, nearly one in three high-school girls and nearly one in four high-school boys admitted to at least one occasion when they needed medical care but did not see a doctor. The number-one reason given: They did not want their parents to know. So it is important to remember that "the pediatrician serves both generations," in the words of Dr. Morris Wessel, now retired after nearly half a century of practicing pediatrics.

What Is Informed Consent?

Since the 1970s, the U.S. Supreme Court and many state legislatures have expanded the rights of minors to make health-care decisions for themselves. These laws were enacted not to undermine parents' authority, but in recognition of the reality that harmony and open communication do not reign in every family. In cases where notifying a parent would pose an obstacle to an adolescent's receiving needed medical care, the boy's or girl's right to privacy supersedes the parent's right to know.

Examples include abortion, obtaining birth control and screening for the HIV virus, as well as treatment for AIDS and other sexually transmitted diseases; mental health problems; substance abuse; and rape, incest or sexual abuse. The majority of teenagers who test positive for HIV or who desire an abortion do tell their moms and dads. It's not surprising; they're usually scared and upset, and desperately want their parents' love and support. When kids choose to keep their condition a secret, it's frequently because they fear their parents will react violently, or throw them out of the house.

Minors do not have unrestricted access to health care, however. A concept known as the Mature Minor Doctrine provides physicians with general guidelines for determining when to provide medical treatment based on an adolescent's consent. (Some states have adopted the doctrine as law; in other states, it is not on the books, but the courts acknowledge that the principle exists.)

One requirement is that the young patient must be sufficiently mature to fully understand the nature of the proposed treatment, including its benefits

You Give the Okay, You Pay

Legally, parents cannot be held financially accountable for medical services that their minor child authorized; the patient is responsible for footing the bill. But realistically, it's the rare teenager who has the monetary means to afford quality health care. Mom and Dad's insurance generally will not cover the costs, since the claim can't be processed without the parents' involvement, and some plans require that the policyholder contact them for preauthorization prior to medical procedures. As part of the verbal agreement regarding the teenage patient's confidentiality, your pediatrician may ask you to make arrangements authorizing your insurance company to be billed for medical care that is provided without your knowledge.

and risks. The rather subjective decision as to whether or not consent is informed rests with the physician. According to Dr. Robert Brown of Children's Hospital in Columbus, Ohio, few pediatricians would allow a thirteen-year-old to authorize her own medical care, "because it isn't until later that youngsters have the cognitive ability to think in an adultlike manner."

Another major consideration is whether or not trying to secure a mother's or father's consent would delay the treatment, and if so, would deferring therapy endanger the young person's health? In a medical emergency, the treating physician usually may institute treatment without the consent of the family *or* the patient. (See "Teenagers and the Law: Obtaining Contraception—Their Rights, Your Rights," box on page 233 and "Teenagers and the Law: Their Right to an Abortion, Your Right to Know," in chapter 12, "Sexuality.")

FINDING THE RIGHT PEDIATRICIAN FOR YOUR TEEN

Some teens will happily remain with their pediatrician through the college years. Others will want to change doctors—perhaps as a way of proclaiming their autonomy and maturity. A number of pediatricians have created separate waiting areas for their older patients, decorated with posters giving important health messages to youth. You may also find yourself in the market for a new pediatrician because your employer has switched insurance companies

---

TEEN TIP:

Let your teenager participate in the process. After all, this will be her doctor. Many adolescents, girls in particular, prefer to see a doctor of the same sex.

---

or your current doctor is leaving a managed-care plan that requires members to stay within its network of approved practitioners.

Whatever the reason, if you're looking, a good place to start is the American Academy of Pediatrics. For the names of qualified pediatricians in your area, visit the AAP Web site at *www.aap.org*. Other potential sources of recommendations include the department of pediatrics at nearby medical centers, your state's medical society, the school nurse, physicians and of course family, friends, neighbors and coworkers.

Once you've assembled a list of names, call each prospective pediatrician's office to schedule a get-acquainted session. Invite your teen to accompany you. Meeting face to face gives you insight into the pediatrician's overall philosophy and manner. We'd suggest preparing a list of questions beforehand, such as:

- How long have you been a pediatrician?
- Are you board certified through the American Board of Pediatrics?
- Are you a member of the group that subspecializes, or has an interest in, adolescent medicine?
- Approximately what proportion of your practice consists of teenagers?
- What is your policy regarding confidentiality?
- Is there anything that you would like to know about my family?

Don't hesitate to address any other concerns that come to mind. Afterward, discuss your impressions with your spouse (and your teenager, if she was present). Did the pediatrician answer your questions clearly, thoughtfully and thoroughly? Was she a good listener? Above all, did you feel comfortable talking to her, and can you imagine her establishing a rapport with your son or daughter?

THE ANNUAL MEDICAL CHECKUP

The American Academy of Pediatrics recommends that all young people aged eleven to twenty-one be seen annually by their pediatrician; the evaluation includes a history of what is going on in the teen's life. When necessary, there will be a physical examination, screening for vision and hearing and laboratory tests (such as blood work or a urinalysis). The pediatrician decides what needs to be done at each annual visit depending on what has been happening in your teen's life and what tests have been done in the past.

The Physical Exam

After your pediatrician has reviewed your teenager's medical history, she begins the full-screening physical examination, which will most likely include the following:

- Height and weight measured.

- Blood pressure and pulse taken.

- Discussion of important health and safety issues such as sexuality and the prevention of sexually transmitted diseases, the dangers of experimenting with alcohol and other drugs, dietary and exercise habits, driving safety and so on.

- Vision is tested and if your pediatrician detects any sign of injury or disease, or suspects that your teen might need glasses, you'll be referred to an eye care specialist.

- The doctor uses her fingers to feel the neck for swollen lymph nodes or an enlarged thyroid gland. She also touches and presses on the abdomen to feel for any problems with the spleen, liver and kidneys.

- Placing a stethoscope to your youngster's chest and back, the pediatrician assesses respiration and listens for any abnormal sounds from the heart.

- Posture is checked. Any apparent abnormality of the spine may warrant X rays, because adolescents are prime candidates for developing progressive curvature of the spine, such as *scoliosis.*

- The pediatrician tests joint flexibility and muscle strength.

- Both girls and boys have their breasts felt, or *palpated,* for lumps. At this age, a mass in a girl's breast is almost certainly benign. As for boys, early in puberty, many will develop excess breast tissue. This condition, *gynecomastia,* is usually temporary and more distressing than it is serious.

• The pediatrician may conduct a full-body skin inspection, checking for acne and suspicious looking moles.

• Pediatricians often inspect the genitals last, knowing that this is the part of the exam that many teenagers, self-conscious about their bodies, dread the most. (See "The Gynecologic Exam," below, and "The Testicular Exam," page 379.

Immunizations and Laboratory Screening Tests

Vaccinations? Still? With his last inoculation several years behind him, your teenager may have assumed he was all through with having to get shots. One in five adolescents and young adults are not adequately immunized against preventable diseases such as measles and mumps. As you can see from tables 16.1 and 16.2, early adolescence is the time for several important shots and laboratory tests to prevent or screen for various diseases. *If you don't have a pediatrician, call your local health department. Public health clinics may provide immunizations at reduced cost.*

The Gynecologic Exam

A young woman should have a full gynecologic exam that includes a pelvic exam and a Pap smear as soon as she becomes sexually active, or at the first sign of a possible gynecologic disorder. It is normal for a girl to be nervous beforehand. A parent's taking the time to patiently describe the procedure should help relieve her anxiety. This is what she can most likely expect.

THE INTERVIEW

First a doctor or nurse will ask the young woman questions about her reproductive health, such as, "When did your last period start? How regular are your periods? How long do they last?" She may also inquire about the patient's sexual history and discuss methods of protection against sexually transmitted diseases and unintended pregnancies. Then the patient is escorted to the exam room, where she's asked to take off her clothes and put on a gown.

THE BREAST EXAM

In examining the breast, the pediatrician looks for lumps and other abnormalities, such as signs of infection. The pediatrician may use this opportunity

TABLE 16.1

Immunization Schedule during Adolescence

VACCINE	FOR WHOM? AT WHAT AGE?	WHY?
Hepatitis B	• Any adolescent who has not been immunized against the hepatitis B virus. A second dose is administered 1 to 2 months later, followed by a third shot at least 6 months after the first.	• Of the approximately 125,000 patients diagnosed with the liver disease hepatitis B each year, 7 in 10 are adolescents or young adults.
Tetanus-Diphtheria Booster	• Ages 11 to 12 (and every 10 years thereafter) if at least 5 years have passed since the last tetanus-diphtheria or tetanus-diphtheria-pertussis (whooping cough) vaccination.	• Although the highly contagious childhood disease diphtheria is rare in the United States, 1 in 10 cases are fatal.
Measles, Mumps, Rubella	• Any youngster aged 11 to 12 who (1) never received two doses of the measles vaccine; (2) was immunized before turning 1 year old; (3) received the "dead" measles vaccine.	• Measles are no longer the nuisance they were when you were a kid, but roughly 200 youngsters aged 11 through 19 are infected each year. • *Pregnant girls should not receive the measles-mumps-rubella vaccine.* • *Sexually active girls should take steps to avoid becoming pregnant for at least 1 month after an MMR vaccination.*
Varicella (Chickenpox)	• Any youngster aged 11 to 12 who has never had chickenpox and never been vaccinated against the varicella virus.	• Approximately 1 in 5 11-to-12-year-olds have never had chickenpox. Serious complications are possible.

(continued)

TABLE 16.1

VACCINE	FOR WHOM? AT WHAT AGE?	WHY?
Varicella (Chickenpox) (continued)	A second shot follows 4 to 6 weeks later if the child is 13 years of age or older. If under 13, only one shot is recommended.	• *Pregnant girls should not receive the varicella vaccine.* • *Sexually active girls should take steps to avoid becoming pregnant for 1 month after a varicella immunization.*
Hepatitis A	• Any teenager living in a high-risk state. Check with your pediatrician. • Any teenager who plans to travel to a country known to have a high rate of hepatitis A. • Any teenager with chronic liver disease or a clotting-factor disorder, or who abuses drugs or has anal intercourse with other males. • Any teenager who is at risk of occupational exposure (e.g., handling of non-human primates and persons working with hepatitis A virus in a research/ laboratory setting).	• Hepatitis A, a highly contagious viral disease of the liver, infects as many as 200,000 Americans per year, including approximately 60,000 boys and girls under the age of 16.
Influenza	• Any teenager with one of the following ailments: chronic conditions affecting the heart, kidneys or lungs; diabetes; sickle-cell anemia and other blood disorders; cancer; HIV/ AIDS and any other illness that compromises immunity against infection.	• Youngsters with any of these conditions are at risk for developing complications such as pneumonia, the fourth leading killer among diseases.

Vaccine	For Whom? At What Age?	Why?
Pneumococcus	• Any teenager who is receiving cancer chemotherapy or who has one of the following ailments: kidney disease, sickle-cell anemia, HIV/AIDS and any other illness that compromises immunity against infection; Hodgkin's disease; and any teenager whose spleen is either malfunctioning or has been surgically removed.	• Any of these conditions elevate a youngster's risk of developing a pneumococcal infection, such as bacterial pneumonia.
Meningococcal Disease (Meningitis and Meningococcemia)	• The federal Advisory Committee on Immunization Practices (ACIP) recommends that college freshmen consider getting vaccinated against bacterial meningitis, an inflammation of the membrane that surrounds the brain and spinal cord. In meningococcemia, the bacteria infiltrates the blood. (See "Neurological Conditions," in chapter 20, "Common Medical Conditions During the Teen Years.") This is one type of bacterial meningitis.	• Meningitis, while rare, can be deadly. Of the approximately 150 college students stricken each year, 1 in 8 die, while 1 in 7 survivors sustain permanent brain damage. Studies show that college freshmen who live in dormitories are 6 times more likely than other college students to develop the contagious disease, probably from living in such close proximity to other young men and women. Use of tobacco and alcohol increases the risks in crowded dorms.

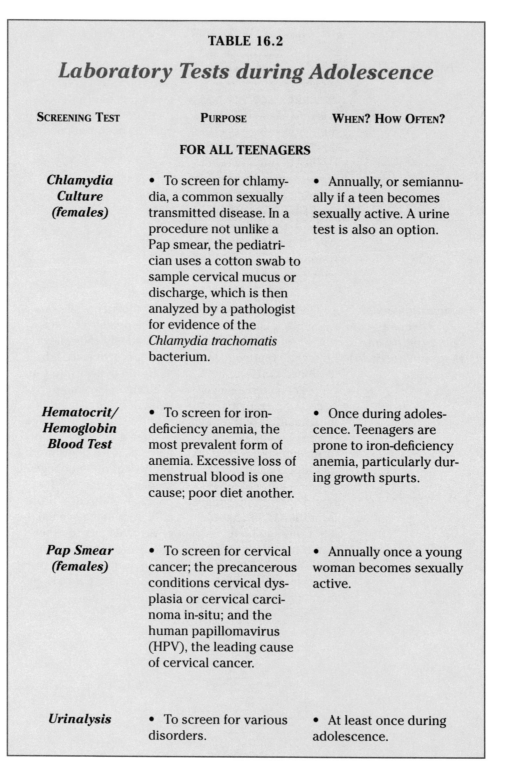

TABLE 16.2

Laboratory Tests during Adolescence

SCREENING TEST	PURPOSE	WHEN? HOW OFTEN?
FOR ALL TEENAGERS		
Chlamydia Culture (females)	• To screen for chlamydia, a common sexually transmitted disease. In a procedure not unlike a Pap smear, the pediatrician uses a cotton swab to sample cervical mucus or discharge, which is then analyzed by a pathologist for evidence of the *Chlamydia trachomatis* bacterium.	• Annually, or semiannually if a teen becomes sexually active. A urine test is also an option.
Hematocrit/ Hemoglobin Blood Test	• To screen for iron-deficiency anemia, the most prevalent form of anemia. Excessive loss of menstrual blood is one cause; poor diet another.	• Once during adolescence. Teenagers are prone to iron-deficiency anemia, particularly during growth spurts.
Pap Smear (females)	• To screen for cervical cancer; the precancerous conditions cervical dysplasia or cervical carcinoma in-situ; and the human papillomavirus (HPV), the leading cause of cervical cancer.	• Annually once a young woman becomes sexually active.
Urinalysis	• To screen for various disorders.	• At least once during adolescence.

Screening Test	Purpose	When? How Often?

OPTIONAL SCREENING TESTS FOR TEENAGERS CONSIDERED AT RISK FOR SPECIFIC CONDITIONS

Screening Test	Purpose	When? How Often?
HIV-Antibody Blood Test	• To screen for the human immunodeficiency virus (HIV) *antibody,* which the immune system produces in response to the presence of the virus. A positive result dictates a second, more accurate blood test called the Western blot. Two positive findings are considered definitive.	• Periodically for all sexually active teens. Counseling is given before and after testing.
Cholesterol Blood Test	• To screen for high cholesterol and high blood lipids, which increases the risk of developing cardiovascular disease.	• Once during adolescence for youngsters with any of the following risk factors: chronically high blood pressure (hypertension); obesity; diabetes; family history of hyperlipidemia, an elevated concentration of fatty substances (lipids) in the blood; family history of premature heart attacks.
Gonorrhea Culture	• To test for suspected gonorrhea, by analyzing mucus or discharge for evidence of the bacterium *Neisseria gonorrhoeae.* In girls, the specimen is usually taken from the cervix; in boys, from the penis. A urine test is also available.	• Annually or semiannually in sexually active teens. • The test would be performed if a teenager had reason to believe a sexual partner was infected or if symptoms arose. Symptoms are far more common in men; 4 in 5 women with gonorrhea experience none at all.

(continued)

TABLE 16.2

SCREENING TEST	PURPOSE	WHEN? HOW OFTEN?
Sickle-Cell Screen Blood Test	• To screen for sickle-cell anemia, a hereditary disease that particularly affects African Americans, causing chronic fatigue and episodes of bone pain.	• Once during adolescence for African American youths not previously tested.
Syphilis Blood Test	• To test for suspected syphilis, either by examining pus from a genital sore or by analyzing a blood sample for the *Treponema pallidum* bacterium that causes the disease.	• Periodically in any sexually active teenager. • The test would be performed if a teenager had reason to believe a sexual partner was infected or if symptoms arose.
Tuberculosis Screening Skin Test	• To screen for exposure to the tuberculosis bacterium.	• Periodically, if at risk. Your pediatrician can advise you on specific recommendations.

to instruct the patient how to examine her own breasts. Periodic breast self-exam (BSE) is often recommended for young women.

THE PELVIC EXAM AND PAP SMEAR

For the pelvic exam, the young woman lies down on the table with her knees apart and her feet placed in a pair of metal stirrups. A sheet is draped over her legs and stomach for added modesty. Throughout the procedure, the pediatrician will describe and explain what she is doing, which greatly helps to put patients at ease.

The examination has three parts. First the pediatrician uses a light to inspect the anatomy of the outer vagina and surrounding areas. Next an instrument called a *speculum* is gently inserted into the vagina. Made of plastic or metal, it widens the vaginal opening just enough so that the physician can view the vaginal canal and the cervix. Most patients say they feel pressure, but not pain. If your daughter feels nervous or uncomfortable, she should take several slow, deep breaths, to relax the vaginal muscles.

Some girls who have never had sexual intercourse worry that the procedure will tear the hymen and rob them of their biological virginity, or that the doctor won't be able to place the speculum. There is no cause for concern; the vaginal opening is large enough to accommodate the device. Also, the teen should always feel that she has a right to discontinue the exam once it has begun.

A pelvic exam includes a Pap smear, one of the most effective screening tests in medical history. First the doctor takes a long-handled brush and gently obtains a small sampling of cells from the outer and inner linings of the cervix. The cells are placed on a slide and sent to a laboratory, which will test for cancer and other diseases.

In the third part of the exam, the pediatrician removes the speculum and inserts one or two fingers in the vagina. She feels the uterus and the ovaries, checking for size and cysts, while pressing on the abdomen with her other hand. Usually, a pelvic exam for an adolescent does not require a rectal exam. With that, the exam is over, and the young woman can get dressed. The internal exam is a limited part of the gynecologic exam. "For a girl's first visit," says Dr. Marianne Felice of the University of Massachusetts Medical Center in Worcester, "we spend a lot more time with her, getting her ready for the initial exam."

The Testicular Exam

As part of a teenage boy's annual physical, he will be asked to lower his pants and underwear so that the pediatrician can examine the testicles for cancer and for hernia. In a hernia, part of the intestine protrudes downward until eventually it descends into the scrotum. Some hernias cause a bulge that the doctor can feel. The condition is corrected with surgery.

As the physician palpates each testicle for possible tumors, he's also explaining to his patient the importance of practicing testicular self-examination (TSE) at home on a monthly basis. Testicular cancer, while rare in teenagers (approximately thirty cases a year), is the leading malignancy among young males aged fifteen to thirty-nine. It is also one of the most curable of all cancers.

"While I'm examining a boy, I'll describe what I'm doing and what I'm looking for," says Dr. Mark Scott Smith, chief of adolescent services at the Children's Hospital in Seattle. "It's a good idea for boys to learn how to check

> ### That Other Doctor: The Dentist
>
> Teenagers should have regular dental checkups twice annually or as determined by the dentist.

themselves, just so they know what's normal and what's abnormal."

Memo to Mom and Dad: Mention to your son ahead of time that it is not uncommon for an adolescent to reflexively develop an erection during a testicular exam. Assure him that this is a normal (although inconvenient) reaction.

HELPING COLLEGE-BOUND TEENS STAY HEALTHY

Throughout adolescence, it's wise to encourage self-sufficiency wherever you can. That applies to health care. Before your teens leave for college, help them prepare to stay healthy while living away from home. Here are some ideas:

Select a health-care provider. The student health services on campuses are often good sources of health care. However, some students, especially those with chronic medical conditions such as asthma and diabetes, may want to form a relationship with a doctor in the community. The student health service can refer you to local physicians; or you can follow the steps for finding a practitioner outlined earlier in this chapter.

Make sure that your teen has insurance and her insurance card. Whether she's going to continue on your family health plan or purchase low-cost health insurance through the college, review the policy with her. Remember, what is familiar and routine to you will in all probability be completely new to her. Does the insurer require preauthorization for all medical procedures or notification within twenty-four hours of a trip to the hospital emergency department? She will also need to know how to get prescriptions filled based on insurance plan specifics. These are points she should know.

List all pertinent medical information on a wallet-sized card. Be sure to note:

- any medications that your youngster takes regularly, including the dosage and strength.
- any allergies or other existing medical conditions.
- any past medical problems, mental-health problems, hospitalizations, surgeries.

- relevant family medical history.
- pack your youngster a first aid kit.

Encourage him to take care of himself. College freshmen are notorious for falling into poor health habits. It's their first time living on their own, and the combination of freedom and temptation can lead to nights of cold pizza washed down with gallons of soda and trying to get by on five hours or less of sleep. That lifestyle will grind down anyone's resistance to disease. Do what you can via long-distance phone calls and/or e-mail to remind your son or daughter to get enough rest and eat properly.

17

GOOD NUTRITION DURING THE TEEN YEARS

Eating habits are often a problem for teenagers. A report from the Federal Agency Forum on Child and Family Statistics found that fewer than one in fifteen youths consume a nourishing diet. The rate among younger children, while well below where it should be, is four times higher. Why the decline in healthy eating during adolescence?

To begin with, they spend less time at home and more time out with their friends. One in three twelve-year-olds eats just one daily meal with their family, while half of all seventeen-year-olds are unaccounted for at *two* out of the three major daily meals. So instead of raiding the refrigerator when they get hungry, they feast on candy, snack cakes and other vending-machine staples. Not to be overlooked is the fact that one of the first ways teenagers assert their independence is by making their own food choices. An eighth-grade boy may be years away from earning a driver's license or a salary, but he can feel grown up by ambling into the local burger emporium, plunking his allowance down on the counter and declaring in his manliest voice: *"Couldja please gimme extra cheese on those fries?"*

Mary Story, a registered dietitian and associate professor of public-health nutrition at the University of Minnesota, cites another reason why teenagers seem to subsist on little more than soda and junk food. "There are so many issues to deal with during a child's adolescence that parents sometimes become lax about nutrition. They also feel like they no longer can control what their kids eat. They may not have *as much* control as they used to," says Story, the mother of two teenage boys, "but unless the kids are doing the grocery shopping and the cooking, it's the parents who ultimately decide which foods are and aren't allowed in the home."

The family that eats together generally has a healthier diet than the family whose members fend for themselves. Researchers at Harvard Medical School studied the eating habits of sixteen thousand boys and girls aged nine to fourteen. Those who ate with their parents frequently were one and a half times as likely to eat the recommended five servings of fruits and vegetables every day as those who rarely joined Mom and Dad for meals. "When you sit down together as a family, there are usually more food choices available," dietitian Mary Story observes. "Your boy or girl is less likely to have just a bowl of ramen noodles or a bag of popcorn and call it dinner." Eating together also allows parents to monitor their children's nutrition.

A TEENAGER'S NUTRITIONAL NEEDS

Calories

A surge in appetite around the age of ten in girls and twelve in boys foreshadows the growth spurt of puberty. How much of a surge? Let's just say that Mom and Dad might want to oil the hinges on the refrigerator door and start stockpiling a small cache of their own favorite snacks underneath the bed.

"Adolescents seem like they're hungry *all* the time," says Mary Story, "especially boys." *Calories* are the measurement used to express the energy delivered by food. The body demands more calories during early adolescence than at any other time of life. On average, boys require about two thousand eight hundred calories per day; and girls, two thousand two hundred calories per day. Typically, the ravenous hunger starts to wane once a child has stopped growing, though not always, says the dietitian. "Kids who are big and tall or who participate in physical activity will still need increased amounts of energy into late adolescence." During middle and late adolescence, girls eat roughly 25 percent fewer calories per day than boys do; consequently, they are more likely to be deficient in vitamins and minerals.

Nutrients

The nutrients *protein, carbohydrates* and *fats* in food serve as the body's energy sources. Each gram of protein and carbohydrate supplies four calories, or units of energy, whereas fat contributes more than twice as much: nine calories per gram.

PROTEIN

Of the three nutrients, we're least concerned about protein. Not because it isn't important—50 percent of our body weight is made up of protein—but because "adolescents in the United States get twice as much protein as they need," Story explains. The densest sources of protein include teenage favorites such as beef, chicken, turkey, pork, fish, eggs and cheese.

CARBOHYDRATES

Carbohydrates, found in starches and sugars, get converted into the body's main fuel: the simple sugar *glucose*. Not all carbs are created equal, however. In planning meals, we want to push *complex-carbohydrate* foods (see box on next page) and go easy on *simple carbohydrates*. Complex carbs provide sustained energy; that's why you often see marathon runners and other athletes downing big bowls of pasta before competing. As a bonus, many starches deliver fiber and assorted nutrients too. They are truly foods of substance: filling yet low in fat. Most nutritionists recommend that complex carbohydrates

---

TABLE 17.1

How Much Protein Does My Teenager Need Per Day?

MALES

11–14 years	15–18 years	19–24 years
45 grams	59 grams	58 grams

FEMALES

11–14 years	15–18 years	19–24 years
46 grams	44 grams	46 grams

make up 50 to 60 percent of a teenager's caloric intake. Simple carbs, on the other hand, seduce us with their sweet taste and a brief burst of energy but have little else to offer and should be minimized in the diet.

> ### Carbohydrates: So Simple, Yet So Complex
>
> **Complex carbohydrates:** Breads, cereals, rice, pastas, nuts, seeds, beans, barley, all vegetables and fruits.
>
> **Simple carbohydrates:** Candy, cakes, pies, cookies, soft drinks, fruit drinks, canned fruits in heavy syrup, sugary cereals.

DIETARY FAT

Nutrition experts recommend that fat make up no more than 30 percent of the diet. While Americans have trimmed their fat consumption in recent years, as a nation we're still about 4 percentage points above the suggested level.

Let's give dietary fat its due. Fat supplies energy and assists the body in absorbing the *fat-soluble* vitamins: A, D, E and K. But these benefits must be considered next to its many adverse effects on health. A teenager who indulges in a fat-heavy diet is going to put on weight, even if he's active. It would take a workout befitting an Olympic athlete to burn off excess fat calories day after day.

Fatty foods contain *cholesterol,* a waxy substance that can clog an artery and eventually cause it to harden. The danger of *atherosclerosis* is that the blockage will affect one of the blood vessels leading to the heart or the brain, setting off a heart attack or a stroke. Although these life-threatening events usually don't strike until later in adult life, the time to start practicing prevention is now, by reducing the amount of fat in your family's diet. Researchers studying the eating habits of approximately two hundred California high-school students were dismayed to find that more than one-third had abnormally high levels of blood cholesterol. Ultrasound scans of their carotid arteries revealed evidence of atherosclerosis already. The carotids, a pair of large vessels located in the neck, serve the brain. One of the doctors involved in the study commented that some of the teenagers' arteries resembled those normally seen in a person twice their age. Fortunately, at this early stage, the condition is still reversible.

THE THREE TYPES OF FAT

Dietary fat contains varying proportions of *monounsaturated fat, polyunsaturated fat* and *saturated fat.* The last type—found in meat and dairy products like beef, pork, lamb, butter, cheese, cream, egg yolks, coconut oil and palm

The "Nutrition Facts" Label

How do you know how much fat is in a particular food? The "Nutrition Facts" label on most canned and packaged products lists the amounts of saturated fat and total fat per serving and also tells you what other kinds of fat are present, including partially hydrogenated fats. In addition, it tells you what percentage of your child's total recommended daily fat intake (called the "daily value") will be expended by eating one serving of this item, based on a diet of 2,000 calories per day and a recommended serving size. Consult the label for the same information regarding protein, carbohydrates, sodium, potassium, fiber, sugar and cholesterol. The label also tells you calories and the daily values of various vitamins and other minerals per serving.

oil—is the most cholesterol-laden of the three. You want to limit your family's intake of saturated fat to no more than 10 percent of your total daily calories.

The other 20 percent of daily calories from dietary fat should come equally from the two *unsat*urated kinds of fat, both of which are contained mainly in plant oils. Corn oil, safflower oil, sunflower oil, soybean oil, cottonseed oil and sesame-seed oil are predominantly polyunsaturated. So are the oils in fish and almonds. Foods high in monounsaturated fat, the healthiest kind, include olives and olive oil; peanuts, peanut oil and peanut butter; cashews; walnuts and walnut oils; and canola oil. You'll want to avoid the partially hydrogenated oils in most margarines and vegetable shortenings.

If your family eats a lot of packaged and processed foods, you should make a habit of reading the "nutrition facts" food labels. You may be surprised to see how much fat, not to mention sugar and salt (sodium), is in the foods you eat every day. And almost all packaged goods that contain fat are likely to have partially hydrogenated fat, because it has a longer shelf life.

Vitamins and Minerals

A well-rounded diet based on the USDA guidelines should deliver sufficient amounts of all the essential vitamins and minerals. Adolescents tend to most often fall short of their daily quotas of calcium, iron and zinc. Unless blood tests and a pediatrician's evaluation reveal a specific deficiency, it's preferable to obtain nutrients from food instead of from dietary supplements, because unlike supplements vegetables, fruits and grains contain *phytochemicals*—natural substances that are believed to help safeguard us from disease.

CALCIUM: THE BONE BUILDER

Adolescence provides a window of opportunity for avoiding *osteoporosis* later in life. The disease silently depletes the bones of calcium, typically over the course of decades. Eventually the bones lose their density and weaken; half of all fractures in women over age fifty are due to osteoporosis.

During the teenage years, the growing bones absorb more calcium from the blood than at any other time of life. By early adulthood, our bones stop accepting deposits. Not long after that, the gradual loss of calcium begins. In women, it accelerates following *menopause,* when the ovaries cease producing estrogen. "Girls who don't consume enough calcium as adolescents start out at a deficit, with a lower bone mass," Mary Story explains. In a clinical study sponsored by the National Institute of Child Health and Human Development, one group of teenage girls received daily supplements containing an extra five hundred milligrams of calcium; the other group's calcium came strictly from food with no supplement. The girls who were given supplements saw their bone density improve by 14 percent. Each 5 percent increase in bone mass reduces the risk of suffering a bone fracture by a remarkable 40 percent.

Milk and milk products provide three-fourths of the calcium in the American diet. You can see from the box above that other foods contain calcium too, like broccoli and collard greens. However, these vegetables also contain substances that impair the body's ability to absorb calcium. "You'd have to eat approximately nine cups of broccoli a day to meet the recommended intake for calcium," says Story. Boys and girls aged nine to eighteen are advised to consume one thousand three hundred milligrams of calcium per day. That's equivalent to about four and a half eight-ounce glasses of low-fat milk.

Unfortunately, two-thirds of adolescent girls in the United States fail to meet this requirement, something that Story and other dietitians call a serious public-health problem. According to a survey from the U.S. Department of

---

Calcium Sources

- Most foods in the milk group: milk and dishes made with milk, such as puddings and soups.
- Cheeses: mozzarella, cheddar, Swiss, Parmesan, cottage cheese.
- Yogurt.
- Canned fish with soft bones, including sardines, anchovies, salmon.
- Dark-green leafy vegetables, such as kale, mustard greens, turnip greens, bok-choy.
- Tofu, if processed with calcium sulfate.
- Tortillas made from lime-processed corn.
- Calcium-fortified juice, bread, cereal.

Agriculture, more and more teenagers are giving up milk in favor of other drinks—mostly soft drinks. Little more than half the teenagers in the poll said they drank milk regularly, as opposed to three-fourths of 1970s youngsters.

The National Institutes of Health supports the use of supplements for young people who don't get sufficient calcium through their diet. For optimal absorption, no more than five hundred milligrams should be taken at one time. Your pediatrician can guide you as to the appropriate dosage and dosing schedule. Because adolescents utilize calcium relatively efficiently, they may be best off ingesting the tablets between meals.

OTHER WAYS FOR TEENS TO BUILD STRONG BONES

Eat dairy products and other foods fortified with vitamin D. Vitamin D supports bone development by increasing the body's absorption of calcium from food. Most of us get all the vitamin D we need from everyday exposure to the sun; the rays trigger an internal chemical reaction, producing vitamin D.

For kids who aren't getting enough calcium, make use of calcium-fortified milk, orange juice, cereals and granola bars. Some of these products contain so much calcium that a single serving takes a youngster halfway to her recommended daily value.

Read cartons and labels carefully when shopping. The terms used may seem interchangeable—"High in Calcium," "Calcium Enriched," and so forth—but they actually indicate the amounts of calcium inside:

"HIGH IN CALCIUM" "EXCELLENT SOURCE OF CALCIUM" "RICH IN CALCIUM"	The product contains 20 percent or more of the daily value
"CONTAINS CALCIUM" "GOOD SOURCE OF CALCIUM"	The product contains 10 to 19 percent of the daily value
"CALCIUM ENRICHED" "MORE CALCIUM" "PROVIDES CALCIUM"	The product contains up to 10 percent of the daily value

Your teen isn't a milk drinker? There are other ways to obtain calcium through the diet. "Many adolescents don't like milk, especially girls," says dietitian Mary Story. Try tempting your son or daughter with chocolate-flavored skim milk. You can also disguise milk by adding it to soups, puddings, baked products, sauces and stews.

TABLE 17.2

Foods Rich in Calcium

	IN MILLIGRAMS
BREAD-CEREAL-RICE-PASTA GROUP	
Cooked cereal, rice, pasta, unsalted, ½ cup	Trace amounts
Ready-to-eat cereal, 1 oz.	100–360
Bread, 1 slice	110–175
VEGETABLE GROUP	
Fresh or frozen, cooked without salt, ½ cup	Less than 70
Canned or frozen, with sauce, ½ cup	140–460
Tomato juice, canned, ¾ cup	660
Vegetable soup, canned, 1 cup	820
FRUIT GROUP	
Fresh, frozen, canned, ½ cup	Trace amounts
MILK-YOGURT-CHEESE GROUP	
Milk, 1 cup	120
Yogurt, 8 oz.	160
Natural cheeses, 1½ oz.	110–450
Processed cheeses, 2 oz.	800
MEAT-POULTRY-FISH-DRY BEANS-EGGS-NUTS GROUP	
Fresh meat, poultry, fish, 3 oz.	Less than 90
Tuna, canned, water pack, 3 oz.	300
Bologna, 2 oz.	580
Ham, lean, roasted, 3 oz.	1,020
OTHER	
Salad dressing, 1 tbsp.	75–220
Ketchup, mustard, steak sauce, 1 tbsp.	130–230
Soy sauce, 1 tbsp.	1,030
Dill pickle, 1 medium	930
Potato chips, salted, 1 oz.	130
Corn chips, salted, 1 oz.	235

Source: U.S. Department of Agriculture

Alternatives to milk include cheese and yogurt. Eight ounces of yogurt and two ounces of cheese contains about the same amount of calcium as eight ounces of milk and therefore each would equal one serving. Half a cup of cottage cheese, however, is lower in the mineral and counts as half a serving.

Go easy on the salt. Besides its association with high blood pressure (hypertension), which is a risk factor in heart disease, kidney disease and stroke, a diet high in salt may deprive the body of calcium by increasing the amount excreted in the urine. Since about 75 percent of the salt we eat has already been added to the various processed foods in our diet, this means not just holding back on the use of the salt shaker, but also cutting down on fast foods and other processed foods, as well as high sodium seasonings like soy sauce, bouillon cubes, meat tenderizer, tamari sauce and Worcestershire sauce.

Stay physically active. Adolescents' bones respond to weight-bearing exercise by growing stronger and denser. Any activity that gets your teenager up and moving will do, whether it's jogging, dancing, walking the dog, bowling or jumping jacks.

Don't smoke tobacco or drink alcohol. In addition to their many other detrimental effects, cigarettes and alcohol decrease bone mass.

PUMPING UP IRON

Iron is a major component of *hemoglobin,* the pigment in red blood cells that transports oxygen to all the body's tissues. According to a national survey conducted by the USDA, three in four teenage girls' diets are deficient in this essential mineral, as compared to just one in five of their male counterparts.

Adolescent girls are prone to iron-poor blood for reasons other than nutrition. Their iron tends to be low after unusually heavy menstrual periods and during growth spurts. The latter is true of boys as well. When the hemoglobin (HGB) count sags severely, a person is said to have *iron-deficiency anemia,* the leading nutritional disorder in the United States. Since the body is being deprived of oxygen, your teen may complain of feeling exhausted, weak and short of breath. Milder forms, however, may not produce symptoms.

Iron supplements, prescribed by your pediatrician, typically return hemoglobin levels to normal in a matter of weeks or months. A word of caution: Keep iron tablets out of reach of younger siblings, for iron toxicity is a major cause of poisonings in young children.

OTHER WAYS TO IMPROVE
YOUR TEEN'S IRON INTAKE

Include beans, grains and fresh or frozen vegetables with meals. The iron in meat, poultry and fish is readily absorbed by the body, unlike the iron in vegetables, beans and grains. Serve them together, however, and suddenly the body is as much as ten times more receptive to the less-potent iron-laden foods.

Finish off meals with fresh fruit. The vitamin C in fruits, as well as the citric acid in citrus fruits, promote absorption of iron that normally would not find its way into the body. If serving fruit juice, make sure the label says "100 percent pure fruit juice," because anything less than 100 percent does not pass muster as a serving of fruit. Punches, "ades," and most so-called fruit drinks contain plenty of added sugars but precious little juice. Similarly, orange soda, grape soda, and other fruit-flavored carbonated beverages do not count as fruit juice—no matter how strenuously your teenager may attempt to argue otherwise.

Suggest that your teen limit tea. Tannins, the chemical compounds that give tea its acidic quality, interfere with the body's metabolism of iron from nonmeat sources.

Use iron pots and pans to cook vegetables, beans, potatoes and other foods with poorly absorbed iron. Doing so can boost a meal's content of usable iron considerably.

> **Foods Rich in Iron**
>
> - Meats: lean beef, pork, lamb, liver and other organ meats.
> - Poultry: chicken, duck, turkey—especially dark meat.
> - Fish: sardines, codfish, shellfish, anchovies.
> - Dark-green leafy vegetables, such as kale, mustard greens, turnip greens, collards, broccoli.
> - Legumes, such as lima beans, green peas, dry beans and peas, canned baked beans.
> - Dried fruits such as prunes, apricots, raisins.
> - Potatoes, with skin.
> - Seeds: sunflower, pumpkin, squash.
> - Egg yolk.
> - Yeast-leavened whole-wheat breads and bread products.

ZINC: GOOD FOR GROWTH

Neither sex fares well when it comes to eating enough foods rich in zinc, a mineral that is integral to normal growth and sexual development. Two in

> ### *Foods Rich in Zinc*
>
> - Meats: lean beef, pork, liver.
> - Dairy products: nonfat dry milk, cheese.
> - Poultry: dark-meat chicken, turkey.
> - Eggs.
> - Shellfish, particularly oysters.
> - Seeds: pumpkin, sunflower, squash, watermelon, lentils.
> - Nuts: peanuts, pecans, Brazil nuts, pine nuts.
> - Yeast-leavened whole-wheat breads and bread products.
> - Wheat germ, whole-grain cereals.
> - Dry beans.

three teenage boys and three in four teenage girls fail to meet the recommended dietary allowance of 15 milligrams and 12 milligrams a day, respectively. A shortage of zinc weakens immunity, so that youngsters may develop more infections than usual; minor cuts may take longer to heal, too.

It's best to replenish the body through the diet.

Vegetarians, however, may be particularly prone to zinc deficiency. Much of the zinc in fruits, vegetables and bread is not always fully absorbed. Lean red meat is an ideal source of zinc, as are chicken and fish. A multi-vitamin with zinc provides the daily requirements for this mineral.

FOLIC ACID

Various experts, including the American Academy of Pediatrics and the United Public Health Service, recommend that all females of child bearing age and who are capable of becoming pregnant take 0.4 mg of folic acid each day. This will lower the risk for spinal cord defects (called neural tube defects) in babies whose mothers did not take supplemental folic acid during pregnancy. A higher dose is taken if there is an increased risk for these defects.

Fiber

Fiber, while not an essential nutrient, performs several vital functions. A natural laxative, it keeps traffic moving through the intestinal tract and may also lower the concentration of cholesterol in the blood. Yet parents are often reluctant to implement a low-fat, high-fiber diet, out of concern that their teenagers won't get enough calories and nutrients to satisfy the demands of their growing bodies. According to a study from the department of food and nutrition at North Dakota State University in Fargo, consuming more than twenty grams of fiber a day appears to exert the opposite effect. For the study, 319 fifteen-year-olds were divided into four groups, based on their eating habits: low-fat, low-fiber; high-fat, high-fiber; low-fat, high-fiber; and high fat, low-fiber. The students who ate plenty of fiber-rich foods obtained just as many calories as the students in the low-fiber groups. ("Low fiber" is defined as less than fifteen grams of fiber a day.) A high-fiber intake also supplied greater amounts of vitamins A, B_6, B_{12}, C, niacin, thiamin, riboflavin and folate, as well as the minerals magnesium, iron, zinc, calcium and phosphorus.

Foods Rich in Fiber

- Grains: wheat germ, wheat bran, whole-wheat bread and bread products, oat bran, rice bran, brown rice, barley.
- Legumes: kidney beans, navy beans, pinto beans, black beans, lima beans, lentils, chickpeas.
- Vegetables: cauliflower, broccoli, celery, potatoes, peas, beans, carrots, asparagus, artichokes, cucumbers, summer squash, parsley, Brussels sprouts.
- Fruits: apples, oranges, grapefruits, blackberries, tomatoes, dates, raisins.

WAYS TO FIT FIBER INTO YOUR TEEN'S DIET

Serve uncooked vegetables as snacks and toss them into salads. Raw carrots, broccoli and other vegetables contain more fiber than cooked vegetables.

Substitute whole-grain bread for white bread.

Don't overcook vegetables. Vegetables should be served while still crisp. Steaming them until they're mushy destroys much of their fiber.

Garnish salads with seeds (poppy, pumpkin, sunflower, sesame) and sprouts. Bean sprouts and alfalfa sprouts lend a unique flavor to sandwiches, too.

Add dates and raisins to snacks and cereals.

Don't peel apples, cucumbers, potatoes and other fruits and vegetables with edible skins. They're excellent sources of fiber.

Popcorn is the perfect snack for anyone looking to bone up on fiber. But use only a small amount of butter and salt.

Eat dried beans, peas and legumes, such as lentils, kidney beans, black beans, white beans, chickpeas, split peas and the like. They are brimming with fiber as well as vitamins, minerals and both complex carbohydrates and proteins, yet low in fat.

BUILDING THE PYRAMID: HOW TO MAKE THE DIETARY GUIDELINES WORK FOR YOUR FAMILY

The Food Guide Pyramid is not a bland, rigid meal prescription. While you want to incorporate all five food groups in your menus as often as possible, variety within each category is essential for achieving nutritional balance, because foods differ in the kinds and amounts of nutrients they provide.

Tips for Menu Planning

Mom/Dad (whoever does most of the cooking): Be gentle. Eating habits develop over many years and can be hard to change. To help your family adjust to a healthier diet, start small; for instance, use a low-fat salad dressing or sneak in an extra serving of vegetables.

Don't ambush your family with too many unfamiliar dishes at once. Not unless you're inordinately fond of leftovers. Introduce new foods one at a time, accompanied by time-tested favorites.

Keep in mind that no set of menus can satisfy everyone. Nor can you always eat exactly as planned. It's how you eat over the long run that adds up to good nutritional health.

Number of Servings

The pyramid gives a range of servings for each major food group. The number of servings that are right for your teenager hinges on how many calories he or she needs—which is based on age, sex, size and activity level. Most youngsters (and adults) should eat *at least* the minimum amount of servings in the ranges.

You might wonder how you'll ever get your teenager to eat the recommended several servings of fruits and vegetables. But if you look at table 17.4, you'll see that many of the recommended serving sizes are actually quite small. For example, a recommended serving of ready-to-eat cereal—just one ounce—would barely cover the bottom of the bowl, when it wouldn't be unusual for a growing boy to scarf down a cupful or more at breakfast. That's at least three servings from the bread-cereal-rice-pasta group before he's even left for school. Send your daughter out the door with a good-sized turkey-lettuce-tomato sandwich and an apple for lunch, and she's got two more servings from her bread group, two from the meat group and nearly three servings of fruits and vegetables.

TABLE 17.3

Numbers of Servings Per Day for Teenagers

FOOD GROUP	NUMBER OF SERVINGS PER DAY	
	FEMALES AGED 11–24 TOTAL CALORIES: 2,200	MALES AGED 11–14 TOTAL CALORIES: 2,500 AGED 15–18 TOTAL CALORIES: 3,000 AGED 19–24 TOTAL CALORIES: 2,900
Bread, Cereal, Rice and Pasta Group *6–11 servings*	9 servings	11 servings
Milk, Yogurt and Cheese Group *4–5 servings*	4 or 5 servings	Aged 11–18 Aged 19–24 4 or 5 2–3 servings servings
Vegetable Group *3–5 servings*	4 servings	5 servings
Fruit Group *2–4 servings*	3 servings	4 servings
Meat, Poultry, Fish, Dry Beans, Eggs and Nuts *2–3 servings*	6 ounces total	7 ounces total
Total Fat	73 grams	Aged 11–14 Total grams: 83 Ages 15–18 Total grams: 1,000
Total Added Sugar	12 teaspoons	18 teaspoons

Source: U.S. Department of Agriculture

TABLE 17.4

Selected Serving Sizes, by Food Group

Bread, Cereal, Rice and Pasta Group	Milk, Yogurt and Cheese Group	Vegetable Group	Fruit Group	Meat, Poultry, Fish, Dry Beans, Eggs and Nuts Group
1 slice of bread	1 cup of milk or yogurt	1 cup of raw, leafy vegetables	1 medium apple, banana, orange	2–3 ounces of cooked lean meat, poultry or fish
½ cup of cooked cereal, rice or pasta	1½ ounces of natural cheese	½ cup of other vegetables	½ cup of chopped, cooked or canned fruit	½ cup of cooked dry beans or 1 egg counts as 1 ounce of lean meat
1 ounce (dry weight) of ready-to-eat cereal	2 ounces of processed cheese	¾ cup of vegetable juice	¾ cup of fruit juice	2 tablespoons of peanut butter or ⅓ cup of nuts counts as 1 ounce of meat

Source: U.S. Department of Agriculture

THE FOUR MOST FREQUENT FOOD FAUX PAS OF ADOLESCENCE: WHERE TEENS USUALLY GO ASTRAY DIETARILY AND WHAT TO DO ABOUT IT

Food Faux Pas Number One: **Skipping Meals, Beginning with Breakfast**

In a Gallup poll of more than four hundred boys and girls aged nine to fifteen, fully half claimed to skip breakfast on school mornings. Many youngsters just aren't hungry at that hour, but the major obstacle to a sound morning meal seems to be a lack of time. By the time they finally sit down to lunch in the school cafeteria, they may have gone twelve, fourteen hours or more without eating.

In doing so, they're depriving their brains of essential nutrients needed for concentration, short-term memory, problem solving and processing information. Missing any of the three traditional square meals also reduces by one-third their chance of meeting the daily required intake (DRI) for calcium.

WHAT YOU CAN DO

Fix breakfast the night before. In the time it takes to pour the orange juice, you can be warming up the plastic-wrapped plate of precooked eggs and lean bacon, or whatever appeals to your teen's taste buds. A nutritious breakfast should provide a minimum of three hundred calories.

If time is tight, fresh fruit and low-fat or no-fat yogurt make for a perfectly healthy breakfast. Or drop some fruit in the blender, add skim milk and mix up a filling morning shake. This, too, can be prepared the day before and kept chilled in the refrigerator.

Whole-grain english muffins, toaster pastries, breakfast bars and bagels are easily munched on while getting ready for school. For spreads, consider peanut butter instead of cream cheese. While equal in calories, peanut butter contains more nutrients but with four times less saturated fat and twenty-seven times less sodium than cream cheese.

Think beyond traditional breakfast fare. "Leftover pizza or chicken are perfectly acceptable for kids to eat in the morning," says Mary Story. Other possibilities: fresh fruit with cheese, cottage cheese or yogurt.

When a sit-down breakfast is out of the question, pack a breakfast-to-go. Taste may be less of a priority here than portability; if a food can fit in a jacket pocket or a backpack without creating a mess, you're in business. Here are several examples: bananas, apples, tangerines and other portable fruits; hard-boiled eggs; sandwiches; resealable plastic bags filled with nuts and raisins; and breakfast bars.

Food Faux Pas Number Two: Eating on the Run

Much of the food teenagers eat comes served on trays. Two in three of them purchase lunch at school, where they're at least assured a nutritionally balanced, if not always appetizing, meal. They also spend a lot of time crammed together in booths at fast-food restaurants. The popularity of these establishments has less to do with the quality of cuisine than the fact that they provide an informal and inexpensive venue for socializing.

In response to Americans' growing interest in healthy eating, the fast-food industry has expanded its menus to include less fattening options like salads, low-calorie dressing and grilled-chicken sandwiches. Some chains now cook their french fries in vegetable oil instead of animal fat and offer meatless soy-based veggie burgers. Despite these commendable innovations, the fact remains that 40 to 50 percent of the calories in the average fast-food meal comes from fat.

WHAT YOU CAN DO

Share with your teenager the following tips, which will allow her to minimize the fat and salt she consumes when joining her friends at the local burger mecca or sub shop. In the end, though, parents have to accept that they have no control over what their children eat when they're out and about—all the more reason for seeing to it that they eat sensibly at home!

Un-*supersize it*. Teenagers don't have to give up the fast foods they've always enjoyed, but it's wise to scale down the portion size. For example, *don't* order the giant triple-decker deluxe cheeseburger; pick a regular hamburger instead.

Would you care for something else with that?

Yes: a *small* order of fries and a *small* juice or milk.

If a portion is too big, don't feel obligated to eat it all in one sitting; take it home in a doggie bag.

Have it your way—with as few fattening condiments as possible.
- Order burgers minus cheese, ketchup, mayonnaise and the ever-mysterious "secret sauce."
- Instead of ordering the burger, try the grilled chicken sandwich with no mayo.
- Top pizza with vegetables instead of sausage, pepperoni and other fatty meats.
- Ask for salad dressings to be served on the side, so that you can determine how much to put on.
- Coolly resist the subtle pressure from the counterperson to dress up your simple baked potato in layers of sour cream, melted cheese, chives and bacon.

- Hungry for a sub? Choose lean deli meats such as turkey instead of fat-heavy cold cuts.
- Don't slather bread, rolls and biscuits in butter. Use only a little or eat them plain.

Food Faux Pas Number Three:
Snacking, Snacking, Snacking

Teenagers derive nearly a quarter of their daily calories from snack foods. This is an area of diet that parents can control, by not bringing salty, fattening chips, nuts and so forth home from the grocery store.

WHAT YOU CAN DO

Have healthy snacks on hand. Much of the time, kids snack out of habit, not because they're genuinely hungry. When a youngster comes sliding into the kitchen during the commercial break and has two minutes and twenty seconds to decide upon a snack and hustle back to the TV, convenience is as important as taste.

If the pantry is stocked with plenty of low-fat, low-sugar, low-salt snacks, that's what he'll grab. These days the good-for-you convenience foods don't taste all that different from the unhealthy ones. So do away with the nonnutritious products, such as candy, cake, and soft drinks. You might have to put up with a day or two of protest—*"Hey, what happened to the glazed donuts?! Where'd all the cookies go?!"*—but once it's understood that from now on those items will be occasional treats (and once his sugar withdrawal subsides), peace will return to the household.

Now, are you ready to get *really* radical? Keep cleaned and

Healthy Convenience Foods
• Salt-free crackers
• Graham crackers
• Baked potato chips
• Low-salt or no-salt pretzels
• Bagels
• Popcorn (without butter)
• Applesauce
• Gelatin
• Granola
• Hard-boiled eggs
• Yogurt
• Frozen yogurt
• Juices
• Unsalted nuts
• Sugar-free cereals
• Low-fat cheeses
• Dried raisins, prunes, apricots
• Sunflower seeds
• Soybeans

ready-to-eat celery stalks, carrot sticks, fresh strawberries, melon wedges and other favorite fruits and veggies in your refrigerator, and see what happens.

"I know with my own kids that they would never dream of taking the time to peel an orange or cut up a cantaloupe, which they love," says Mary Story. "But if I set down a platter of cut-up fruit or vegetables, it's devoured in no time at all."

Food Faux Pas Number Four:
The Freshman Fifteen

The "freshman fifteen" refers to the fifteen pounds that neophyte college students have been known to put on their first year away from home. It's not surprising, given the academic pressure and the stress of a new environment—perhaps a bout of homesickness—coupled with unlimited access to food. There's the cafeteria and several other eateries on campus, as well as nearby pizzerias willing to deliver at all hours. Another reason freshmen can fall into poor eating habits: Mom and Dad aren't around to nag them.

WHAT YOU CAN DO

Not much, aside from offering encouragement to eat right and exercise faithfully. For teens who need motivation to improve their diets, consider sending "care packages" of healthy snack foods and other items.

TEENAGERS WITH SPECIAL DIETARY NEEDS

Vegetarians

Vegetarian diets are consistent with the dietary guidelines for Americans and can meet the recommended dietary allowance (RDA) and daily required intake (DRI) for nutrients. The only difference is in the meat, poultry, fish, dry beans, eggs and nuts group, where meat, poultry and fish are supplanted by tofu, legumes, nuts (avoid these if allergies exist), seeds and other meat alternatives. As long as they eat a variety of foods in sufficient amounts, they can obtain enough protein and enjoy excellent health.

Most vegetarians consume milk, dairy products and eggs. However, strict vegetarians, known as "vegans" (pronounced *vee*-gans), believe in excluding all animal products from their diet. This places them at possible risk for deficiencies of several nutrients, particularly vitamins D and B_{12}. In the United

States, milk fortified with vitamin D serves as the primary dietary source of this vitamin. Unless your son or daughter has ample exposure to sunlight, a supplement may be recommended. As for getting enough vitamin B_{12}, the most reliable method is to take a supplement containing *cyanocobalamin,* the most usable form of B_{12}. You can also find cyanocobalamin in vegetarian speciality foods such as soy milk, cereals and veggie-burger patties.

Athletes

All athletes, it seems, are constantly looking for anything that could conceivably give them a competitive edge, whether it's a new batting stance, a change in their exercise regimen or insisting on wearing their "lucky cap" until their luck runs out. Many times that search leads them to dietary fads. At best, these supposed winning formulas are ineffective, as in the case of "carbohydrate loading" before events. At worst, they can be downright dangerous, such as the misguided advice to forego water prior to a marathon run.

One of the myths to circulate among prepubescent boys is that consuming large amounts of protein, or taking protein supplements, increases muscle mass. Not true, says dietitian Mary Story, who goes on to explain that except for vitamins A, D, E and K, which are stored in fatty tissue, the body swiftly excretes all nutrients. "There's an old saying," she adds with a laugh, "that athletes who take vitamin supplements have the most expensive urine in the world!"

Adolescent athletes can usually obtain all the protein they need—15 percent of their caloric intake—simply by following the dietary guidelines. The same is true for vitamins and minerals, with one exception: Female athletes and long-distance runners tend to lose iron over the course of the sports season. As a general rule, they should have their iron status assessed beforehand and rechecked periodically. Iron loss can usually be rectified simply by eating more iron-rich foods, although some pediatricians will recommend a daily iron supplement.

If your teenager participates in intensive athletic training and competition, he'll almost undoubtedly lose water, sodium and potassium, particularly during hot weather. Remind him to eat generous amounts of citrus fruits, bananas and other potassium-laden foods throughout the season, and to *always* stay well hydrated. It's best to drink lots of water before an event, then take in smaller amounts during the activity.

Memo to Mom and Dad: To make weight before wrestling matches, some youngsters ill-advisedly turn to diuretics or even force themselves to vomit in order to drop the extra pounds. This can severely deplete a teenager of potassium and other essential electrolytes and should be unequivocally prohibited, to the point of not letting him participate in the sport should the practice continue.

Pregnant Young Women and Nursing Mothers

Pregnant teenagers need to increase their intake of calories, protein and all vitamins and minerals except for vitamins A and D, and phosphorus. As the saying goes, they must now "eat for two." Should they decide to nurse their newborn, their bodies demand still more nutrition. Many physicians will prescribe young women a special prenatal multivitamin supplement. (See "Teenage Pregnancy" in chapter 12, "Sexuality.")

18

WHEN EATING TURNS INTO A PROBLEM

Obesity, Dieting and Eating Disorders

More and more teenagers seem to be following in their parents' footsteps: wearing a path from the TV to the refrigerator and back again. According to the Centers for Disease Control and Prevention (CDC), over 50 percent of the U.S. adult population is overweight, while one in five are heavy enough to be considered obese. The rates of overweight and obese teenagers are believed to be about the same as the adult population. That is almost double what they were at the beginning of the 1980s.

Dr. William H. Dietz, director of the CDC's Division of Nutrition and Physical Activity, holds television largely responsible for the ballooning of adolescent America. Several studies support his claim. Based on a large national poll of boys and girls aged twelve to seventeen, researchers implicated TV viewing as the second most pivotal predictor of teenage obesity. The number-one predictor of teenage obesity was a history of excessive weight during childhood. The more hours youngsters spent slumped in front of the set—instead of being physically active—the greater their risk of becoming obese.

Conversely, television bears some of the blame for the growing number of girls who starve themselves in the hope of looking as unnaturally thin as their favorite actresses, pop singers and supermodels. If TV programs aimed at adolescents and young adults provided your sole window into their world, you would assume that every overweight person under the age of thirty had been exiled to some South Pacific atoll, leaving behind a society populated almost exclusively by goddesses with flat tummies and exposed navels and their hard-bodied boyfriends.

"The mass media at large deluges kids with messages equating thinness with popularity, attractiveness and success," says Dr. Neville H. Golden, codirector of the Eating Disorders Center at

Schneider Children's Hospital in New Hyde Park, Long Island. The unspoken inference, of course, is that people who aren't thin stand less of a chance of enjoying any of the three. Just the fact that heavyset characters are a minority on TV, introduced mainly for comic relief, reinforces this perception. How many times have you seen the following stereotype: the overweight, inherently wise young woman who cracks self-deprecating jokes about her weight. While she may serve as a boy's confidante/best friend, she knows not to expect him to ask her out on a date.

What adolescents may not realize is that the culturally imposed image of the ideal female body borders on unhealthy. It is also unattainable for the overwhelming majority of women—even many of the celebrities idolized by millions of girls. Those seemingly flawless features are frequently the handiwork of photo retouchers, makeup artists and plastic surgeons, in addition to heredity and personal hard work.

The preponderance of svelte, impossibly proportioned beauties on TV and in movies, music videos and magazines shapes boys' perceptions of female attractiveness, which in turn compounds the pressure on girls to conform to these absurd standards. Not that young males are immune from anxiety about their own bodies. In a survey conducted at California's Stanford University School of Medicine, the percentages of teens to express dissatisfaction with their weight hovered around 50 percent for boys as well as for girls. The young men, however, wished they were *heavier* and more muscular.

More than twice as many girls go on diets: three in five versus one in four. They are also far more prone to developing eating disorders such as *anorexia nervosa* and *bulimia nervosa*. An estimated five million to ten million young women suffer from an eating disorder, as compared to one million young men.

One worrisome trend is that even preteens are getting caught up in the national obsession with thinness. Forty percent of nine- and ten-year-old girls who took part in a government-sponsored study admitted to having tried to lose weight at least once. Not too long ago, that would have been unthinkable, says Dr. Dean Lasseter. "Now I begin screening girls for indications of distorted body image at around age ten, by asking if they are trying to gain weight, lose weight or stay the same," says the Warsaw, Indiana, pediatrician. "If they tell me they're trying to lose weight, further questioning often reveals altered dietary habits."

TEENAGE WAISTLAND: THE INCREASE IN OVERWEIGHT AND OBESE ADOLESCENTS

Some twenty-nine million men and women joined the ranks of overweight Americans on a single day, June 17, 1998, and not from gorging on cheeseburgers. That was when the National Heart, Lung and Blood Institute (NHLBI) officially unveiled its new guidelines for determining healthy and unhealthy body weights. The major change was replacing the venerable height-weight table with a measurement called *body-mass index* (*BMI*), which describes body weight relative to height and better reflects a person's state of health:

- Below 19   = Underweight

- 19 to 24.9   = Normal weight

- 25 to 29.9   = Overweight

- 30 to 39.9   = Obesity

- 40 and Over = Morbid Obesity

Previously, a body-mass index of 25 or 26 was deemed normal. But under the revised guidelines, they now classify a person as overweight by approximately ten pounds. A BMI of 30 would put someone about thirty pounds over his or her ideal weight. Calculate your teen's BMI using the formula in the box below.

The body-mass index is an imperfect system, because it doesn't differentiate between fat and muscle. According to the NHLBI, the BMI is meant to be complemented by a second key measurement, *waist circumference,* which is determined by wrapping a measuring tape snugly around the waist, just above the navel. A waist circumference of over forty inches in males and over thirty-five inches in females signals excess upper-body fat, or an "apple" shape.

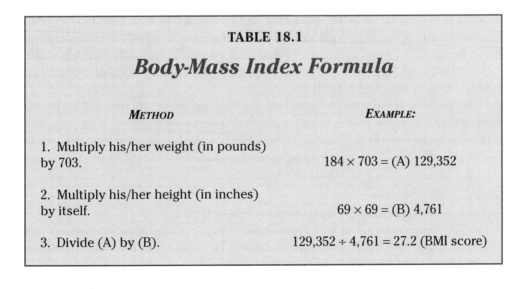

TABLE 18.1

Body-Mass Index Formula

METHOD	*EXAMPLE:*
1. Multiply his/her weight (in pounds) by 703.	$184 \times 703 =$ (A) 129,352
2. Multiply his/her height (in inches) by itself.	$69 \times 69 =$ (B) 4,761
3. Divide (A) by (B).	$129,352 \div 4,761 = 27.2$ (BMI score)

These overweight people face a greater danger of developing heart disease and diabetes than those who are said to be "pear shaped," with the body fat distributed mainly below the waist.[1]

Organic Causes of Weight Gain and Obesity

The most harmful misconception about obesity is that overweight people have only themselves to blame for their extra pounds. They're often presumed to be self-indulgent and weak-willed, which explains the lack of support and understanding accorded many large children and adults.

If overeating and underexercising were the sole causes of this chronic condition, the rate of long-term dieting success stories wouldn't be an abysmal one in fifty. A number of factors contribute to obesity, beginning with genetic inheritance. Doctors at New York's Columbia University College of Physicians and Surgeons studied 132 twins, aged three to seventeen. In every one of the sixty-six pairs, both youngsters had similar body-mass indexes and percentages of body fat, leading the researchers to conclude that a child's body composition is 80 percent preprogrammed at conception.

Playing devil's advocate for a moment, it stands to reason that twins would have similar body types. After all, they live in the same household and probably have adopted the family's eating habits. But other studies have found that even siblings raised in *different* homes usually shared near-identical body-mass indexes. One landmark Danish study compared the BMIs of adult adoptees with those of their birth parents and those of the couples who adopted them. Most of the adopted men's and women's body composition mirrored those of their biological parents, not their adoptive parents.

Heredity also determines to a large extent a person's *metabolism:* the process by which the body converts the nutrients in our diet into energy (*calories*). The *basal metabolic rate* (*BMR*) is the pace at which we burn energy while resting. Sixty to 75 percent of our total energy is expended in this state, to maintain vital functions such as breathing, circulation, body temperature, digestion and glandular activity.

One person's metabolic "tempo" may be as much as 20 percent faster or slower than someone else's. That amounts to a difference of four hundred calories per day. So two teenagers can go bike riding together and eat the same number of calories, but the one with the naturally lower BMR is going to burn fewer

---

[1]   This calculation is inexact also because children's body fatness changes as they mature. The interpretation of BMI depends on the child's age. Additionally, girls and boys differ in their body fatness. For more precise data, refer to the CDC's BMI-for-Age growth charts found online at *www.cdc.gov.*

calories. When more calories are taken in than are expended, the surplus gets stored for future use in the form of body fat. Obese adolescents frequently had lower than normal resting metabolic rates as children, *before* they became heavy.

Still other organic factors partly determine which kids can eat anything they want and never seem to gain an ounce, and which kids face a lifelong struggle to keep their weight in check.

Insulin resistance. Ordinarily, the hormone insulin binds to tissue cells and assists them in absorbing blood sugar (*glucose*), the body's fuel. In youngsters who are resistant, the insulin fails to work effectively. Instead of being burned for energy, the sugar builds up in the body. Insulin resistance can eventually lead to *noninsulin-dependent diabetes,* also known as *type II diabetes.*

Low leptin levels. Some people are deficient in leptin, a hormone that appears to regulate weight in two ways. The substance, produced by the fat cells, essentially signals the brain when the body has had its fill of food. It also inhibits the production of an enzyme crucial to fat production. In studies of heavy men and women, blood tests consistently revealed extremely low concentrations of leptin. The substance is currently being tested in volunteers as a potential weight-loss drug.

Chromosomal abnormalities and endocrine abnormalities. A very few adolescents are obese due to a birth defect or a disorder of the endocrine (hormonal) system, such as hypothyroidism.

The Impact on Health

At least three in four obese teens grow up to become obese adults, which predisposes them to serious ailments such as degenerative arthritis, heart disease, stroke and several forms of cancer. Although these illnesses usually don't strike until much later in life, other medical problems can emerge during the teen years for youngsters who are morbidly obese:

- hypercholesterolemia and hypertriglyceridemia
- skin infections, from fungi trapped in folds of skin and hard-to-clean areas, and bacteria
- pseudogynecomastia, in which excess fatty tissue gives boys the appearance of breasts
- back pain
- pain in the knee, hip or thigh from *slipped capital femoral epiphysis* (see box on page 408)
- ankle fracture

- chronically high blood pressure (hypertension), a risk factor for cardiovascular disease and kidney disease
- gallstones
- inflammation of the pancreas (pancreatitis)
- excessive insulin secretion (hyperinsulinism)
- insulin resistance, diabetes
- obstructive sleep apnea, a blockage of the upper airway that disrupts normal breathing during sleep

Even a moderate, sustained weight loss of approximately 10 percent can return elevated levels of blood pressure, insulin and blood sugar to normal, and all but eliminate the threat of gallstones, pancreatitis and the other conditions listed above.

However, the emotional damage accruing to being overweight in adolescence can be considerable and long lasting. To be sure, plenty of heavyset teenagers rank high in popularity with their peers. But in our thin-obsessed culture, the social stigma associated with obesity is too deeply ingrained for many large boys and girls to escape.

"It starts long before adolescence," says Dr. Garry Sigman, director of the division of adolescent medicine at Advocate Lutheran General Children's Hospital in Park Ridge, Illinois. "Studies show that children as young as age five begin to consider an overweight person as somehow 'bad' or less desirable than someone who's thinner, based on the derogatory images and messages they've received." The pervasive societal prejudice against heavy people has been called one of the last acceptable forms of bigotry; in fact, several studies have shown striking similarities between the psychological characteristics of obese teenage girls and victims of racism.

Taunts and ridicule, feeling excluded from the social whirl of junior high and high school, inevitably leave their mark. "One of the normal developmental tasks of adolescence is to become comfortable with your body and your self-identity," explains Dr. Sigman. Overweight youngsters are more likely to have a negative body image and low self-esteem, which may make them withdraw socially and possibly turn more than ever to food as a source of comfort. Parents should be aware that they are also prone to anxiety and depression.

Words Worth Knowing

Slipped Capital Femoral Epiphysis: (SCFE): displacement of the head of the *femur,* the long bone that fits into the hip socket(s). This rare but serious condition, which typically appears around the time of puberty, is seen most frequently in overweight teens. Initial symptoms include limping and pain in the thigh or knee; the hip often becomes painful too. Surgery is necessary to prevent permanent damage to the joint(s).

Losing Weight Safely, Sensibly, Successfully

Boys and girls who weigh 10 percent or more above their healthy weight may be candidates for a weight-management program. The teen years are a crucial time to slim down: Statistics show that for every twenty youths who are obese upon exiting adolescence, all but *one* will wear that excess weight for the rest of their lives.

HOW MUCH WEIGHT SHOULD MY TEENAGER LOSE?

Dr. Sigman advises targeting a healthy weight *range* as opposed to an exact figure. To begin with, our weight fluctuates naturally by anywhere from five to twenty pounds. But, too, "The ultimate goal is to get kids into the habit of eating nutritious foods and exercising regularly," he says, "and letting their weight drift down to a level that is comfortable and realistically attainable."

Dangerous Diets

Teenagers should not follow any of these diets unless they are enrolled in a research project at a medical center and are thoroughly informed of the risks involved.

- Very low-calorie diets of fewer than 800 calories per day
- Ketogenic diets
- Low-carbohydrate diets such as the Atkins Diet, the Scarsdale Diet, the Woman Doctor's Diet and Dr. Stillman's Quick Weight Loss Diet
- High-carbohydrate diets such as the Pritikin Diet and Dr. Stillman's Quick Inches Off Diet
- Liquid diets
- The Grapefruit Diet, the all-juice Beverly Hills Diet and other unbalanced diets emphasizing a particular food

---

HOW MANY CALORIES SHOULD MY TEENAGER EAT?

Low-calorie diets, which promise a weight reduction of three to four pounds per week, are doomed to failure, and not just because the majority of adolescents find them too restrictive to stick with for any length of time. At a mere 400 to 800 calories per day, these crash-diet programs provide less than one-fourth the caloric requirements of the average teenage boy and less than one-third the calories needed by the average teenage girl.

In response to this threat, the brain seeks to return the body to its ideal biologic weight, or *set point*. It acts like a thermostat, slowing down metabolism and increasing the proportion of excess calories stored as fat. The brain also sends hunger messages to its owner. That is why diets often seem to get off to a promising start, then soon plateau. Most dieters, in fact, actually gain back *more* pounds than they lost.

A sensible diet plan seeks a gradual weight loss of no more than one to two pounds per week. Most youngsters should be able to reach this goal without having to drastically modify their diets. Fully grown teens need trim only five hundred calories a day; boys and girls who are still in puberty can reduce their caloric intake by half that amount and shed pounds without stunting their growth. The focus, though, should always be on developing healthy eating habits, not on weight loss per se.

DIETARY MEASURES

We direct these suggestions to parents, since you probably do most of the shopping and cooking for the household—and also because if a youngster's diet is to succeed, other members of the family need to abide by the same dietary rules.

"You can't tell a kid, 'These potato chips are not for you, they're for your brothers,' " says Dr. Reginald Washington, a pediatric cardiologist from Denver. A heavy teenager may feel like an outsider around his peers; he doesn't need to feel excluded from his family, too. Besides, being forced to watch others eat forbidden foods would push any dieter's willpower to its limit. Many teenagers, just like adults, munch on fattening snacks for the same reason that mountain climbers scale tall peaks: because they're there. For everyone's benefit, bring fewer of those items into the home.

Count calories, not just fat. How is it that grocery-store shelves are brimming with low-fat and fat-free foods, yet America's collective waistline keeps expanding year after year? Unfortunately, many of us have mistakenly assumed that if something is labeled fat-free, we can eat as much of it as we want, when in fact many reduced-fat products harbor nearly as many calories as their full-fat versions—thanks to the fact that they are very often loaded with sugar.

Despite the increased emphasis on fat content, the mathematics of weight

---

Binge Eating

Obesity itself is not an eating disorder. However, approximately three in ten obese adolescent girls who seek treatment have gone on eating sprees where they gorge themselves whether hungry or not, then feel guilty and depressed afterward. "Bingeing," as this is called when severe and persistent, may fit the definition of an eating disorder by the American Psychiatric Association. See "Binge-Eating Disorder," page 421.

loss and weight gain remains unchanged: Take in more energy than you expend, and the balance gets stored as body fat, regardless of whether the calories came primarily from fat, protein or carbohydrate.

The same guidelines that help adults cut back on calories will work for their children. Here are some of the most important:

Monitor portion size. As the fat content of many foods has gone down, portion sizes have been growing steadily larger without anyone seeming to notice. Today's "supersized" order of french fries would have fed three hungry teens when you were a kid!

In a survey commissioned by the American Institute for Cancer Research, only 1 percent of more than one thousand men and women were able to correctly estimate the standard serving sizes for potatoes, pasta and six other major foods. One of the biggest misconceptions among the public is that a single food item equals a single serving. Not necessarily. A youngster biting into one of those eight-ounce bran muffins the size of a small head of lettuce probably doesn't realize that he's eating the equivalent of *four* servings.

Home is where we have the most control over what kids eat. Instead of placing serving dishes on the table and letting everyone help themselves, prepare their plates for them. For just one week, use the Food Guide Pyramid guidelines, which specify the numbers as well as the size of servings to help you measure out appropriate portions. For example, give your teenage daughter six ounces of chicken, which constitute two servings from the meat, poultry and fish group that a teenage girl is supposed to have each day. Measuring food portions for a week will educate you about what appropriate serving sizes look like. After a week of doing this, you will be able to restrict portions to that size.

Tricky, Tricky

To prevent overweight adolescents from overeating:

- Don't overstock the fridge and pantry with high-calorie food.
- Cook only enough food for one serving per person, so that there are no leftovers.
- Consider using smaller plates, to make portions appear larger!

Eat slowly, eat less. Youngsters will feel more satiated if they eat at a leisurely pace, take smaller bites and chew their food thoroughly, and swallow one mouthful at a time. Warm foods, too, tend to be more filling than cold items.

Learn to read the nutrition facts labels. Direct your teenager's attention to serving sizes, the number of servings per package, and the amount of calories per serving. Expect to hear this exclamation more than once: "Wow, I had no idea _____ was so fattening!"

Add fiber to meals. Vegetables, fruits, grains and other fibrous foods are filling yet low in calories.

Drink ice water instead of soft drinks, which make up 8 percent of the average youngster's daily caloric intake. Sports drinks, fruit drinks—even fruit juice—also bring little of nutritional value to the table.

Snack healthfully. All teenagers snack to some degree; it is unrealistic to completely eliminate that aspect of their eating habits. However, keeping a supply of low-calorie snack food in the house, as suggested in chapter 17, will help in this area.

Scale back on fast foods. A dieter can squander an entire day's calories on a single fast-food meal. For example, one double burger with the works plus a supersized order of french fries and a large soda totals 1,410 calories (and 50 grams of fat, almost the whole daily allotment of 60 grams). What's more, boys and girls who regularly dine on burgers, fries, shakes and the like develop what the American Dietetic Association (ADA) calls "fast-food palate." According to the ADA, most fast-food items are so intensely flavored that they desensitize youngsters' taste buds. As a result, they're less likely to find vegetables or a piece of fruit satisfying.

Allow for occasional indulgences. "For a dieting teen to decide that she's never going to eat sweets or fatty foods again is unrealistic," says Dr. Sigman, adding that it is also a recipe for failure. "Those foods can be permitted every so often, like for special occasions or eating out at a restaurant." (See "The Four Most Frequent Food Faux Pas of Adolescence" in chapter 17, "Good Nutrition During the Teen Years," for more tips on how to promote a healthy diet.)

Q: *My sixteen-year-old daughter is on a one thousand five hundred-calorie-a-day diet. I'm worried that she's not getting enough vitamins and minerals. Should she be taking any supplements?*

A: As long as a teen eats one thousand two hundred or more calories per day, including five servings of fruits and vegetables, supplements should not be necessary. However, adolescents' favorite foods tend to shortchange them of calcium, zinc, iron, magnesium and folic acid. Your pediatrician can advise you whether or not supplementing any of these vitamins or minerals is warranted. All teenage girls need at least four hundred milligrams of folic acid per day and most need a supplement to ensure reaching this level. See chapter 17.

BEHAVIORAL MEASURES

Get moving. When youngsters take off weight through dieting alone, 80 percent of the loss is from fatty tissue and 20 percent is from muscle. Adding weight-resistance training to an exercise routine preserves the muscle tissue. Virtually every ounce dropped comes from fat. Once an adolescent meets her goal, regular exercise is essential for maintaining the desired weight. (See chapter 19, "Physical Activity and Sports.")

Limit TV viewing to one hour per day. Not only does television promote snacking and take up time that could better be spent exercising, it turns out to have another pernicious effect on weight. Researchers at Tennessee's Memphis State University have discovered watching television contributes to weight gain by slowing down metabolism. They assigned children of normal weight to one group, obese boys and girls to another group. All the youngsters had their metabolic rates measured twice: once while resting and once while watching TV. The findings clearly showed that participants expended significantly more energy while resting than while sitting mesmerized by the tube.

Avoid temptation. Watching television is just one activity that may trigger an urge to eat. Help your teen eliminate as many of those situations as he can. For example, if his morning walk to school takes him past Donut Galaxy, *severely* taxing his resistance, suggest that he travel an alternate route.

One way to identify unhealthy eating triggers is for the overweight youngster to keep a journal, in which he writes down the food he ate, where he ate it, the time of day and—extremely important—his reasons for eating. Did he devour two slices of meatball pizza after school because he was truly hungry or because he simply wanted to hang out at the pizza parlor with his friends? If he gives the latter reason, perhaps next time he and his buddies split a pizza, he could consciously choose to "nurse" a single slice, even if everyone else grabs two.

Give positive reinforcement. When goals are reached, reward your teen with a small present, tickets to a show—whatever would elicit a proud grin—and, of course, plenty of compliments. In addition, help your teen set realistic, short-term goals that allow for more chance for success.

Look for help if you and your teen can't manage his weight problem on your own. There are several types of programs designed specifically for adolescents. "You're likely to find them available through local hospitals, schools, community centers and YMCA/YWCAs," says Dr. Sigman. "They're worth seeking out."

MEDICALLY SUPERVISED, MULTIDISCIPLINARY PROGRAMS

In recognition of the fact that obese adolescents often have to radically change their lifestyles in order to *keep* the weight off, this type of program features a team approach, with a physician, a registered dietitian, an exercise specialist and a mental health professional all involved in each case. Psychological counseling might address issues that may have preceded or in some way contributed to a young person's gaining weight. For example, food can be a source of love and comfort to a child who feels emotionally deprived.

PEER SUPPORT GROUPS

These "self-help" groups, led by an adult facilitator, give overweight youngsters an opportunity to share their feelings in front of other kids who truly understand. Members swap suggestions for losing weight and support one another's progress.

COMMERCIAL WEIGHT-LOSS PROGRAMS

Commercial chains generally attract an adult clientele, which may not appeal to teens. It's difficult to state definitively how effective these programs are, since they rarely make such statistics public. Attrition rates, though, tend to be high. In one independent study, half the attendees in a particular weight-loss regimen dropped out after just six weeks; by week twelve, fewer than one-third remained.

WEIGHT-LOSS SUMMER CAMPS

These camps combine summer fun with education on how to eat healthy, and how to *keep* eating that way when it's time to return home. The meals, planned by a dietitian/nutritionist, are low in fat and calories but not drastically different from those served at regular camps, and the physical activity level is very high. Typically, camps report weight losses on the order of fifteen to fifty pounds. The boost to a teen's confidence, though, can be immeasurable.

MEDICAL MEASURES

PRESCRIPTION WEIGHT-LOSS MEDICATIONS

Pharmaceutical interventions are rarely considered for adolescents and then *only* for morbidly obese boys and girls who have not been able to lose weight after several months of dieting and exercise.

NONPRESCRIPTION APPETITE SUPPRESSANTS AND DIETARY SUPPLEMENTS

Teenagers should not be taking over-the-counter oral appetite suppressants, although some do. In addition to lack of evidence for inducing weight loss, herbal supplements cannot be assumed to be safe.

SURGICAL MEASURES

GASTROPLASTY AND GASTRIC BYPASS

Abdominal surgery is reserved for morbidly obese youths suffering from serious complications such as sleep apnea and elevated blood pressure. In a *gastroplasty,* also referred to as "stomach stapling," the surgeon uses a row of staples to reduce the size of the stomach so that it can hold no more than two to four ounces of food or liquid. Normally the stomach can accommodate as much as one and a half quarts. A *gastric bypass* decreases the intestine's absorption of dietary fat. Here the surgeon staples across the upper stomach, closing off the remainder. Then he joins the open portion to the lower small intestine, thus bypassing 90 percent of the small bowel. Both procedures have high rates of future complications. Still, for a dangerously overweight young person with no other options, the potential results may be worth the risk. On average, patients slim down by about half.

SETBACKS DO NOT SPELL FAILURE

Both parents and the teen have to accept that she's going to veer off course now and then. Maybe she doesn't get around to her aerobic exercises for a couple of days; or a personal crisis sends her reaching out for two old friends: vanilla ice cream and chocolate syrup. Don't let her be too hard on herself. And if she starts grumbling about giving up—*"I'm never going to lose weight; this dieting business is hopeless!"*—remind her that a slipup is a temporary setback, not a defeat.

"Sometimes a teen's weight becomes a source of conflict between her and her parents," observes Dr. Sigman. Mom and Dad, meaning well, believe they're helping their daughter when one of them arches an eyebrow and says to her at the dinner table: "Are you *sure* you should be eating that?"

"The teen just sees that as nagging," Dr. Sigman continues, "then the parents feel ineffectual in helping her to make changes." You'll need a tightrope-walker's skills to negotiate this one. You want to encourage her to eat right and stay active, but without hounding her. Ironically, when parents place too much emphasis on a child's weight and obsess about the calorie content of every morsel she puts in her mouth, it could be setting the stage for an eating disorder.

EATING DISORDERS

Our eating habits can reveal a great deal about our emotional state. Favorite foods comfort us when we're feeling sad or lonely; they're also an integral part of celebrations and other joyous occasions. Although we refer to *anorexia* and *bulimia* as eating disorders, the destructive food patterns are merely the most visible manifestation of the turmoil within. These are mental illnesses.

An estimated one in twenty adolescents suffer from an eating disorder; on college campuses, the incidence may be as high as one in fourteen. Nine in ten of them are girls. The National Institute of Mental Health estimates that 0.5 to 1 percent of female adolescents and young women are affected by anorexia; 1 to 3 percent, by bulimia; and 0.7 to 4 percent, by compulsive overeating. The characteristics of each vary, but in all three conditions the young person's weight and the act of eating become the central focuses of her life. It typically takes years for girls to escape its clutches. Sadly, not all do before the damage to their bodies proves fatal. Intervening early, before these behaviors have become entrenched, can shorten the road to recovery. Therefore it's important for parents to familiarize themselves with the physical and behavioral signs of eating disorders—which can be harder to detect than you might think.

"Parents need to be aware that lying and deceit are a part of this illness," says Dr. Suzanne Boulter, a pediatrician and adolescent-medicine specialist in Concord, New Hampshire. "In my practice, I've had anorexic patients sew rocks into their underwear, hide weights inside their bras, conceal rolls of coins in hair 'scrunchies' and load up on water to the point of vomiting to make it appear that they weigh more than they do."

Anorexia Nervosa

The term *anorexia,* which means "lack of appetite," is really a misnomer. Girls who are *anorexic* don't lose their sense of hunger. Rather, they suppress it and consciously starve themselves, out of an illogical/pathological fear of becoming heavy. To be diagnosed with anorexia, a youngster must weigh less than 85 percent of the normal weight for her height or fail to gain weight at a time when weight gain is expected (puberty).

Although anorexics eat little at meals, they devote uncommon attention to their food: cutting it up into tiny pieces; arranging and rearranging it on their plate; and chewing each bite of food twenty, thirty times before swallowing, in order to eat less. Over time, their body image grows distorted. An anorexic can be gaunt and emaciated, yet the girl she sees in the mirror is still "too fat."

Anorexia Nervosa

A diagnosis of anorexia nervosa is based on these four criteria:

1. A relentless pursuit of thinness.
2. The teen harbors an intense fear of becoming heavy yet in reality is severely underweight through self starvation.
3. Body-image disturbance: The teen believes herself to be overweight when she clearly is not.
4. The teen has missed at least three menstrual periods—although this may be normal in young adolescent girls.

BEHAVIORAL SIGNS

- Preoccupation with food and weight
- Distorted body image
- Eats primarily low-fat, low-calorie foods
- Buys, prepares and cooks food for others but not for herself
- Obsessive-compulsive behavior at meals, as described above (excessive cutting, chewing and other rituals)
- Exercises compulsively, and becomes upset when she is not able to work out or if her routine is disrupted
- Wears baggy clothing to camouflage her thinness
- Complains that clothing is too tight
- Spends less time with family and friends; becomes more isolated, withdrawn, secretive
- Excitability, difficulty sitting still, easily distracted
- Depression
- Anxiety
- Abuse of diet pills

- Prone to irritability and outbursts of anger
- Loss of sexual desire
- Denies feeling hungry yet never seems to eat
- Denies having an eating disorder
- Strongly resists treatment
- Bingeing and purging (bulimia)

PHYSICAL SIGNS

- Excessive weight loss
- Dehydration
- A constant sensation of coldness, especially in the hands and feet, because the body has lost its "overcoat" of fat and muscle; may also be symptomatic of abnormally low activity of the *thyroid* gland (*hypothyroidism*), a potential complication of anorexia
- The appearance of fine, downy hair (called *lanugo* hair) on the face, limbs and torso. Interestingly, this is the body's attempt to compensate for the lack of warmth normally provided by the body tissue
- Hair loss
- Dull, brittle hair
- Brittle fingernails
- Dry, scaly, yellow or gray skin
- Hollow, vacant eyes
- Protruding bones and shrunken skin, creating the appearance of a "pot belly"
- Swollen joints
- Menstruation stops (*amenorrhea*) or is delayed if a girl becomes anorexic prior to reaching menarche
- Dizziness and light-headedness
- Indigestion, bloating, constipation
- In youngsters who are still developing, stunted growth and delayed sexual maturation
- Fatigue, pallor, difficulty catching breath and other signs of anemia
- Impaired immune function, leading to frequent colds and infections
- Unexplained bruises and black-and-blue marks, due to impaired blood clotting
- Muscle cramps, tremors

An anorexic's appearance gradually deteriorates until it becomes apparent that something is terribly wrong, although weight loss, the most glaring sign, may go undetected for a while. "Mothers and fathers will often notice it in the spring, when their child starts wearing shorts and T-shirts," says Dr. Golden, "or the first time she puts on her bathing suit."

The most serious complications, however, may not be evident to even a parent's discerning eye. An anorexic experiences many of the same medical problems as someone suffering from starvation and malnutrition. The body, in an effort to protect itself, slows down heartbeat and pulse, respiration, blood pressure, metabolism and many other functions as the disease progresses. Laboratory tests may reveal deficiencies of crucial vitamins, minerals and electrolytes, as well as hormonal imbalances. Those who die from anorexia usually succumb to cardiac arrest or kidney failure, or they take their own lives.

Bulimia Nervosa

In a survey of approximately three thousand five hundred girls, one in five ninth graders and two in five high-school seniors admitted to stuffing themselves with food and then forcing themselves to vomit at least once. Up to one in four U.S. teenagers *binge and purge* regularly. If the practice continues for three months, the young person is said to be *bulimic.*

Half of all anorexics have episodes of bulimia at one time or another. Like the girl who starves herself, the bulimic is dissatisfied with her body and obsessed with slimming down.

> ### *Bulimia Nervosa*
>
> *A diagnosis of bulimia is based on these four criteria:*
>
> 1. Recurrent episodes of binge eating.
> 2. Regularly purging in order to control weight, through self-induced vomiting; abuse of laxatives, diuretics, enemas, ipecac or other medications; fasting; or exercising obsessively.
> 3. Bingeing and purging at least twice a week for three months.
> 4. Excessive concern over weight and figure.

She starts to diet and may also go on an exercise campaign, but eventually surrenders to her cravings for food. Stress or strong emotions can set off a binge, in which a bulimic will devour whatever food she can lay her hands on, often starchy junk foods. It is not unheard of for girls with this eating disorder to put away three thousand to seven thousand calories in a couple of hours, stopping only after they're too full to take another bite. In a cruel irony, bulimics barely derive any pleasure from eating; as if possessed, they chew and swallow almost mechanically.

Afterward, feeling guilty and ashamed, the teenager attempts to rid her body of the food before it is digested. Inducing vomiting by sticking her fingers down the throat is one method. Girls have also been known to take excessive doses of *laxatives, diuretics* or *emetics,* drugs that promote bowel movements, urination or vomiting, respectively. Bulimics plan their secret binges in advance—usually for times when nobody else will be home.

BEHAVIORAL SIGNS

- Preoccupation with food and weight
- Distorted body image
- Long periods of time spent in the bathroom—sometimes with the faucet running, to mask the sound of vomiting
- Depression
- Anxious about eating, especially dining out in public
- Abuse of laxatives, enemas, emetics, diuretics
- Spends less time with family and friends; becomes more isolated, withdrawn, secretive
- Stealing food and hoarding it in unusual places, such as in the closet or under the bed
- Excitability, difficulty sitting still, easily distracted

PHYSICAL SIGNS

- Dramatic fluctuations in weight, from alternately dieting and bingeing
- Puffy face and throat from swollen salivary glands
- Burst blood vessels in the face
- Bags under the eyes
- Indigestion, bloating, constipation, gas pains, abdominal cramps
- Dehydration
- Eroded tooth enamel from the gastric acid in vomit; discolored teeth
- Cavities
- Inflamed, bleeding gums (gingivitis)
- Calluses on fingers and knuckles, from self-induced vomiting
- Swelling (edema) of the feet or hands
- Sore throat
- Tremors
- Dizziness, light-headedness, fainting spells
- Stiff, achy muscles
- Muscle weakness
- Muscle cramps
- Irregular menstruation
- Extreme thirst, frequent urination

- A constant sensation of coldness, especially in the hands and feet, because the body has lost its "overcoat" of fat and muscle (if underweight)
- Hair loss
- Blurred vision

Because a bulimic's weight generally hovers around average or above-average, she can often hide her condition for years. Despite her outwardly healthy appearance, bingeing and purging exacts a heavy toll on vital organs such as the liver, kidneys, intestines and heart. Potassium deficiency can bring about an irregular heart rhythm and possibly cardiac arrest. As in anorexia, the other major cause of death is suicide.

Binge-Eating Disorder (*Compulsive Overeating*)

Like bulimics, binge eaters polish off enormous quantities of food in a short amount of time, then regret having done so. However, they do not purge themselves afterward, or fast, or exercise or attempt in any way to compensate for the thousands of calories they've just ingested.

Roughly one in three obese adolescent girls who seek treatment for their weight are compulsive overeaters. Compared to other overly heavy teens, those diagnosed with binge-eating disorder are more concerned about their weight and figure. Yet they are more likely to fail at diets. Low-calorie meals leave them hungry, and they are prone to overeating when angry, sad, bored, anxious or depressed. Binge-eating disorder affects far more boys than either anorexia or bulimia; more than one-third of compulsive overeaters are men.

BEHAVIORAL SIGNS

- Preoccupation with food
- Depression
- Feelings of failure

Binge-Eating Disorder

A diagnosis of possible binge-eating disorder is based on these seven criteria:

1. Recurrent food-bingeing at least twice a week for six months or more.
2. During binges, the teen feels unable to control her overeating.
3. Eats despite not feeling hungry.
4. Often eats until uncomfortably full.
5. Tends to eat alone out of embarrassment over the amount of food in front of her.
6. After bingeing, the teen feels guilty, depressed or upset with herself.
7. The teen is distressed by her behavior, but unable to stop it.

- Spends less time with family and friends; becomes more isolated, withdrawn, secretive

PHYSICAL SIGNS

- Typically overweight or obese
- Following binges: indigestion, bloating, diarrhea, gas pains, abdominal cramps
- Often sleeps for many hours after binge-eating

The compulsive overeater faces fewer immediate health consequences than do anorexics and bulimics, but unless he seeks treatment for his obesity, he may be setting himself up for a future of diabetes, cardiovascular disease, gallbladder disease and certain cancers.

Eating Disorder Not Otherwise Specified (EDNOS)

More than half the teenagers treated in eating-disorder programs don't meet all the criteria for anorexia, bulimia or binge eating. Nevertheless, they exhibit enough features of dysfunctional eating to warrant professional treatment under the diagnosis *Eating Disorder Not Otherwise Specified.*

What Causes an Eating Disorder?

Eating disorders are believed to stem from a confluence of genetic, biologic, psychological and social/cultural factors. Even asking a young teenager if she is gaining weight can send a vulnerable person off on the start of an eating disorder.

Research funded by the National Institute of Mental Health has found that anorexics and bulimics seem to have abnormally low levels of the brain chemical serotonin, which regulates mood and appetite. According to Dr. Golden, it's no coincidence that most of these illnesses take hold during the teen years.

"The eating disorder becomes a way of coping," he explains. "Take anorexia nervosa as an example: You have a young girl who is doing well at life. Then all of a sudden, things become a little confusing for her. She has to deal with a changing body, changing feelings and changing expectations. Should she go to this college or that college? Go out with this boy or that boy? One way to deal with all that—or to *not* deal with it—is to focus inward on other issues, such as how much she's eating and exercising. The eating disorder is a form of self-protection.

"In the case of anorexia," he continues, "it affords a teenager *control*. The more the anorexic controls what she eats or how many times she chews her food, the less out of control she feels." Disordered eating can serve as an outlet for rechanneling or burying uncomfortably strong feelings such as anger, shame and sexual desire. In addition, it can lend an identity to a youngster who is floundering in her attempt to discover herself.

The other major contributor to eating disorders is the societal pressure on teens to conform their bodies to the idealized images perpetuated by the media and fashion industries. Pollsters conducting a survey of U.S. adolescents asked respondents to name the one thing they would most like to change about themselves. About one-third of the girls (and one-quarter of the boys) replied, "my looks" or "my body."

Another study, from California's Stanford Center on Adolescence, observed that girls begin to worry about their bodies even before they've reached puberty. The findings also illustrated the importance that kids place on physical appearance and the disturbing degree to which it towers over other attributes, in their minds. Of 150 or so girls aged ten to thirteen, those who had been teased or ignored by their peers were more likely to voice unhappiness with their bodies, regardless of their actual weight or stage of development. The girls apparently believed that if they were prettier or skinnier, they wouldn't be picked on as much.

Is Your Teen at Risk for Developing an Eating Disorder?

Poor self-esteem and body image are two traits common to adolescents with eating disorders, as is depression. Thereafter, the profiles of youngsters suffering from anorexia, bulimia or compulsive overeating begin to diverge.

THE ANOREXIC

"These girls frequently come from high-striving families where one or both parents may be overprotective and somewhat smothering," says Dr. Golden. "They are usually overachievers who excel in a number of spheres, such as academics and sports."

To an outsider, they appear to be totally in control of their lives. "Yet no matter how well they do," he explains, "they don't feel satisfied. They tend to be self-critical and perfectionistic." A desire to please others and a need to be liked is another hallmark of the anorexic personality. She sees controlling her weight as a way to master her body while gaining approval from others.

THE BULIMIC

"In bulimia," says Dr. Golden, "there is often a family history of depression or substance abuse." Young people prone to bulimia may themselves wrestle with addictions to alcohol and other drugs. They have difficulty handling stress and exerting impulse control. Compared to the typical anorexic, the bulimic girl is more outgoing but less anchored emotionally. Psychiatric illnesses such as obsessive-compulsive disorder are more prevalent in this group than in the other two.

THE COMPULSIVE OVEREATER

As many as half of all binge eaters have suffered from depression in the past. Anxiety and stress, too, are frequent tormentors. Previous efforts at dieting have usually ended in failure.

How Eating Disorders Are Treated

Because adolescents with eating disorders rarely seek help on their own, it is important that parents act on their suspicions quickly and not retreat behind a wall of denial. Often, the teenager's school nurse, teacher or pediatrician may be the first to alert the parents to the possibility of an eating disorder and that help is necessary.

Parents who raise the issue with their teenager should expect a heated denial of any problem. Unless the youngster appears to be in immediate medical danger, this conversation may need to be repeated many times before she admits to her illness and consents to treatment. You might begin by telling your daughter that you believe she is suffering from an eating disorder that is beyond her control and that you are extremely worried about her.

Next, calmly relate the observations that have aroused your concern. It could be your accidental discovery of cupcakes and other foods stashed under the bed, or having found laxatives and diet pills lying around on more than one occasion. This can have a sobering effect: A young person with an eating disorder, like a substance abuser, often assumes that she's been outsmarting the entire world; no one, least of all Mom and Dad, could possibly be wise to her.

Allow her to respond. Listen carefully and nonjudgmentally. Do not criticize her behavior or try to shame her, which will only further isolate her from the rest of the family. It is best not to tell an anorexic or a bulimic she's too thin. That's precisely what she wants to hear.

Finally, present a plan of action. Discuss with your pediatrician how to proceed with an evaluation and treatment.

FIRST: STABILIZING THE PATIENT

"The purpose of the medical intervention is to treat the young person for complications, if necessary," he explains. This may warrant admission to a hospital. Severe malnutrition, defined as less than 75 percent ideal body weight, is one indication for inpatient care. Others include dehydration, electrolyte disturbances, low blood pressure, low body temperature, slow heartbeat, pancreatitis and cardiac failure. A teenager who steadfastly refuses to eat or who is behaving erratically would also be admitted.

"Stabilizing the patient medically can usually be done relatively quickly," says Dr. Golden. "The difficult part is trying to get someone who hasn't been eating to eat. At first, these patients don't want to comply. There's also an art to it. You can't just start feeding a two thousand four hundred calorie diet to a malnourished person weighing eighty pounds; patients have died unexpectedly that way."

The medical term for this phenomenon is the *refeeding syndrome.* "It was first described in concentration-camp survivors, who were living in starvation at the time they were freed," he explains. "After being fed, a number of these men and women died. The syndrome is thought to be related to disturbances in phosphorus and other electrolytes that occur when you refeed someone too rapidly.

"So we start off very slowly, maybe at one thousand calories. Then, in a very structured way, we increase the intake by two hundred calories every two or three days, based on the patient's weight and metabolism." The goal in anorexia, to get the person back up to 90 percent of her ideal weight and correct all nutritional deficiencies, can take some time. (Bulimics, who generally weigh within a normal range, rarely require the aggressive measures that might be necessary with an anorexic.) Some do well with partial hospitalization, where patients spend their days at the hospital, but go home at night.

MANAGEMENT

BEHAVIORAL THERAPY

One or more mental health professionals work with patients to help them identify the psychological aspects of their illness. Youngsters also learn how to change self-destructive reactions to stress. For example, a compulsive overeater might be taught a technique called "pausing": Whenever she feels the urge to binge, she forces herself to switch to another activity; perhaps calling a friend on the phone, going for a walk and so on.

In addition to individual therapy, kids often take part in group counseling as well as family therapy. The entire family must make some adjustments as treatment continues. At home, parents need to resist the temptation to constantly scrutinize the recovering teen's dietary habits. Mealtime should be an occasion for enjoyable family conversation, not charged with tension over how much or how little one member may be eating.

Parents can help to prevent relapses by monitoring their own attitudes toward weight and diet and the subliminal messages they send. For example, a young preadolescent may worry she is getting heavy, not realizing this tissue will, in due course, shift to the hips and breasts. A comment by the parents about this weight, even if meant in a positive or playful way, can help lead to the start of an eating disorder. Also, parents can be too concerned with their own weight and should be careful about what is said to their children in this regard.

MEDICATIONS

Since depression is a common companion to bulimia, antidepressant medications may be prescribed in combination with various behavioral therapies.

Pediatrician's Perspective

DR. DEAN LASSETER, WARSAW, INDIANA: *"In my practice, I've come across cliques of girls who've formed friendships based on their eating habits and altered body image. These children will talk about little else besides dating and weight control. Peer pressure, of course, exerts a powerful influence on teenage behavior, and the results of this can be devastating. I've had cases of adolescents whose eating disorders improved only after they had changed schools in order to remove themselves from these unhealthy peer groups."*

NUTRITION COUNSELING

Nutrition counseling is a key component of recovery from an eating disorder. The dietitian educates the young person about how to eat in a way that is healthy yet takes into account her past behaviors. For instance, bulimics often have difficulty deciphering the signals that the body transmits to the brain when it's hungry or full. Youngsters with a history of bingeing and purging may worry that they're overeating and be tempted to either starve themselves or return to their old habits. Eating small, frequent meals instead of the conventional three squares a day keeps both their hunger and their anxiety at bay.

The nutritionist may suggest that your teen keep a food journal, jotting down what she's eaten, when, as well as her emotions and reasons for eating. However, this practice should be discontinued if it seems to promote a preoccupation with food and diet.

OUTLOOK FOR THE FUTURE

The recovery rates for adolescents are more encouraging than they are for adults with eating disorders. About half of all bulimics and anorexics can be said to recover fully, while around 30 percent experience occasional relapses. A complete reversal is typically measured in years.

Even those who reach the point where they can say with confidence that their illness is behind them stumble from time to time, especially in the beginning. Again, parallels can be drawn between disordered eating and substance abuse, in that it becomes a lifestyle and colors a teenager's thinking.

19

PHYSICAL ACTIVITY AND SPORTS

Remember how as children our kids practically lived outside? They could spend hours frolicking on a playground or running under the sprinkler. That often changes during adolescence. According to a 1999 report from the Office of the U.S. Surgeon General, the average eighteen-year-old boy gets 24 percent less exercise than he did at age six. For girls, the decline over the same period amounts to 36 percent. Another study of young females, this one sponsored by the American Heart Association, reported an *88 percent* plunge in overall physical activity between the ages of nine to ten and sixteen to seventeen.

Where did all that boundless energy go? Adolescents' increasingly sedentary lives are attributable to most of the same factors that have contributed to the expanding girth of the American adult: less time for recreation, on account of greater demands at school, and a growing array of leisure-time pursuits that exercise little else besides the finger muscles required to work a video-game joystick, peck out messages to fellow denizens of on-line chat rooms or wield the television remote control.

Getting teenagers into the routine of exercising increases the likelihood that they will grow up to value healthy living and stay active. It will take the concerted efforts of parents, schools and communities, however, to counter the many diversions vying for a youngster's time and attention. Here is what you can do.

Limit television viewing to one to two hours per day.

Organize fun family activities that promote fitness, such as bicycling, hiking, neighborhood strolls, Frisbee tossing, three-man football and so on.

Make it happen! Assist your child in finding a sport or exercise class that interests him. If transportation is necessary, drive him yourself or make other arrangements. Not having a ride is one of the main reasons that kids drop out of fitness-related activities.

When extolling the benefits of physical activity, stress the short-term effects. Informing a teenager that regular exercise will reduce her future risk of diabetes, hypertension, cardiovascular disease and several cancers probably isn't going to impress her as much as explaining that it helps to build strong bones and lean muscle, control weight and generally enhance a person's sense of well-being, both physically and mentally.

Extracurricular athletic programs, like nighttime basketball leagues, are popular with teens. Some schools have attempted to entice adolescents to exercise by establishing "health clubs." If funding isn't available through the school, county or state, perhaps your district's Parent Teacher Association can raise the money through donations from local businesses, bake sales and so forth.

The American Academy of Pediatrics recommends that school physical education programs emphasize lifetime sports or physical activities that are not just for athletes. Team sports and physical education classes should always enhance physical fitness, working within the short amount of time allotted for gym. Some do not. For example, baseball, our national pastime, may involve more passing the time than action. Researchers at San Diego State University found that in an average thirty-minute physical education period, students spent a mere five minutes in motion. They mostly stood or sat while listening to instructions or waiting their turn.

Gym class should keep students moving around and working their muscles as much as possible. It should also be fun and free of pressure. Parents can encourage schools to be sure that both physical education and organized sports emphasize the joy of exercise, not just winning.

A SENSIBLE PHYSICAL FITNESS PLAN

Early adolescence is when the differences in youngsters' size, strength and coordination are the most pronounced. Not coincidentally, this is also the stage that separates the athletes from the nonathletes.

Often teens, regardless of their physical development or athletic prowess, lose interest in sports—at least school sports—around this time. They might be turned off by the more competitive atmosphere or the strict discipline that many coaches demand. Or perhaps they aren't passionate enough about any one sport to commit themselves to daily practices after school. Fifty percent of high-school students choose not to join a team.

All boys and girls, whether they play a sport or not, can keep themselves in shape by following the national fitness plan devised by the U.S. Department of Health and Human Services. "Healthy People 2010" calls for thirty minutes of moderate exercise a day. What type of exercise? That's up to your son or daughter. "The best exercise," says pediatric cardiologist Dr. Gene Luckstead, "is one that a teenager enjoys enough to stick with." The only prerequisite is that the activity burn approximately 150 calories per day, or 1,000 calories per week.

"I encourage kids to take up 'lifetime sports,' " continues Dr. Luckstead, who is also a sports medicine specialist who has been a team physician for twenty-

---

TABLE 19.1

Physical Activities: Intensity and Duration

- Washing and waxing a car for 45 to 60 minutes
- Washing windows or floors for 45 to 60 minutes
- Playing volleyball for 45 minutes
- Playing touch football for 30 to 45 minutes
- Gardening for 30 to 45 minutes
- Walking 1¾ miles in 35 minutes
- Shooting baskets for 30 minutes
- Bicycling 5 miles in 30 minutes
- Dancing fast for 30 minutes
- Raking leaves for 30 minutes
- Walking 2 miles in 30 minutes
- Performing water aerobics for 30 minutes
- Swimming laps for 20 minutes
- Playing a game of basketball for 15 to 20 minutes
- Bicycling 4 miles in 15 minutes
- Jumping rope for 15 minutes
- Running 1½ miles in 15 minutes
- Shoveling snow for 15 minutes
- Stair climbing for 15 minutes

five years at the junior-high, high-school and college levels. "Lifetime sports" include walking, jogging, bicycling, skiing, skating, swimming, golf, tennis, racquetball, martial arts—recreational activities that, for the most part, can be performed alone or with just one partner. Many people find that it is more fun to exercise with someone else.

Shooting hoops is one example of a moderately intense exercise. More demanding pursuits, like rumbling up and down the court in a game of basketball, can achieve the desired results in shorter sessions. Table 19.1 lists various activities and their suggested durations, from least vigorous to most vigorous.

Any activity involving movement qualifies as exercise. That includes *household chores.*

Types of Exercise

AEROBIC EXERCISE

A teen's fitness program should include *aerobic* exercise such as brisk walking, basketball, bicycling, swimming, in-line skating, soccer, jogging—any continuous activity that increases heart rate and breathing. Regular workouts improve the efficiency of the *cardiorespiratory system,* so that the heart and lungs don't have to work as hard to meet the body's increased demands for freshly oxygenated blood.

> ### *The Four Components of Physical Fitness*
>
> 1. Cardiorespiratory endurance (aerobic fitness)
> 2. Body composition (percentage of body fat)
> 3. Muscle strength and endurance
> 4. Flexibility

Aerobic exercise also affects *body weight composition,* by burning excess calories that would otherwise get converted to fat. In general, the more aerobic an activity, the more calories are expended. For instance, if a teenager weighing 132 pounds walks at a moderate pace for ten minutes, he burns forty-three calories. Running instead of walking more than doubles the amount of energy spent, to ninety calories.

Low-intensity workouts burn a higher *percentage* of calories from fat than high-intensity workouts do. However, the more taxing aerobic exercises ultimately burn more fat calories overall. One study compared the burn rates for a thirty-minute walk at three and a half miles per hour and a thirty-minute run at seven miles per hour. The walking group expended an average of 240 calories. Two-fifths came from fat, and three-fifths came from carbohydrates, for a total of ninety-six fat calories. In the running group, the ratio of fat energy burned versus carbohydrate energy burned was significantly less: one to four.

Yet overall, the runners consumed 450 calories. Total number of fat calories burned: 108.

WEIGHT TRAINING

Under the guidance of well-trained adults, children aged eight or older can safely incorporate *weight training* (also called strength training and resistance training) into their workouts to increase muscle strength and muscle endurance. Muscle strength refers to the ability to displace a given load or resistance, while muscle endurance is the ability to sustain less-intense force over an extended period of time. Males will not be able to develop large muscles until after puberty. Females generally are not able to develop large muscle mass. They do not have to worry about getting too muscular.

THE PROPER TECHNIQUE: LESS WEIGHT, MORE REPS

Multiple studies show that young people gain strength and endurance faster by lifting moderately heavy weights many times rather than straining to hoist unwieldy loads for just a few repetitions.

Teens should always be supervised by a qualified adult, who can help them and demonstrate the proper technique. For that reason, it's safer to work out at school or at a health club than on home exercise equipment. Other precautions to take include the following:

See your pediatrician for a physical and medical checkup before your youngster starts training.

Remember that resistance training is a small part of a well-rounded fitness program. Experts generally recommend that adolescents exercise with weights no more than three times a week.

Don't overdo it (part 1): Excessive physical activity can lead to injuries and cause menstrual abnormalities. Your teenager may be exercising too much if her weight falls below normal or her muscles ache. Complaints of pain warrant a phone call to your pediatrician.

Don't overdo it (part 2): Teens should be reminded not to step up the weight resistance and number of repetitions before they're physically ready. Getting in shape takes time.

Drink plenty of fluids when exercising. Young people are more susceptible to the effects of heat and humidity than adults. Teens' ability to dissipate heat through sweating is not as efficient as adults. The Centers for Disease Control and Prevention recommends that teens drink at least two six-ounce glasses of water before, during and after working out in steamy conditions.

Always warm up and cool down with stretching exercises before and after training. Stretching the muscles increases their *flexibility:* the ability to move joints and stretch muscles through a full range of motion, and the fourth component of physical fitness. It also helps safeguard against injury.

PLAYING SPORTS

On weekday afternoons, around six million boys and girls of high-school age take to the gym floor, the track, the baseball diamond, the swimming pool and so on, for school-based sports. Another twenty million head off to athletic programs offered outside of school.

Participating in a sport, in addition to promoting fitness, can bolster self-confidence and impart life skills that will be employed both on and off the playing field for years to come. That's no less true for a youngster of modest ability as it is for the gifted athlete, provided that the activity suits his personality, skills, and, especially, interest. For all the physical, psychological, and social benefits athletics has to offer, this is supposed to be *fun*.

Adolescents should be allowed to choose which sport(s) they'd like to play, unless they have a medical condition that would preclude them from taking part. Most young athletes naturally gravitate toward one or two activities. Perhaps they've displayed a talent for a particular sport, or they're rabid fans of a professional team and dream of emulating their favorite players.

For a youngster who can't decide which sport to pursue, if any, a discussion with Mom and Dad can provide direction. Among the points to bear in mind: What are the teen's abilities, and how closely do they match those needed to play a particular activity? Physical strength, an advantage for a wrestler or football player, is not as essential for success in baseball, swimming or running, while speed and stamina are certainly key assets for playing lacrosse. Also, height is an advantage for basketball or volleyball, but is less important in sports such as soccer, gymnastics and tennis.

Sometimes, though, boys and girls get steered toward a sport because of their height or build, and the result can be a setup for failure. The classic example is the early developer who towers over the other kids and is typecast as a future basketball star—until it becomes apparent that he lacks the necessary coordination and quickness. "I worry about the single-sport adolescent who may be in the 'wrong' sport," observes Dr. Luckstead. For that reason, he recommends exposing young people to a variety of activities from an early age. The advice applies as well to teenagers who excel at a sport, to prevent their enthusiasm from burning out.

A child's emotional makeup should also be taken into account when picking an activity. Would your youngster prefer an individual sport to a team sport? Is a fast-moving sport such as basketball more his speed than a game that proceeds at a more deliberate pace, like baseball? These may seem like trivial details, but they're really not. For instance, youths diagnosed with attention deficit hyperactivity disorder (ADHD), autistic-spectrum disorder and other conditions that often impair concentration tend to do best in structured, individualized activities; these teens tend to be better in soccer, hockey, lacrosse and basketball, but may have trouble in baseball, gymnastics and golf.

Two other considerations are the intensity of the competition and the amount of time involved. Many teenagers, including those who enjoy sports, don't want to commit to an interscholastic sport, with its after-school practices, or to a local, regional or national sports program. But they can still keep active through school intramural programs, community recreational centers or others, which get together once or twice a week and are geared more toward the recreational athlete.

Or they can organize games on their own. Put the word out to a half-dozen or more friends to meet at the park for some basketball, baseball, football or soccer. No leagues, no umpires, no adult supervision at all. The fading of informal sports play from the American landscape is one of the sadder casualties of modern life, agrees Dr. Luckstead. "When I was growing up in the forties and fifties," he recalls nostalgically, "there was nothing more fun than to get together a pickup game of baseball. You don't see that nearly as much anymore."

Fortunately, bowling, biking, jogging, martial arts, swimming and the other lifetime sports referred to earlier provide exercise without having to assemble a dozen kids. These activities are ideal for youngsters who shy away from organized athletics; here they compete against no one but themselves.

Sports Injuries

Young adolescents, both athletes and nonathletes, are prone to injuries because their bodies are still developing. Some of these injuries are the same as those suffered by adults, others are specific to adolescence.

ACUTE SOFT-TISSUE INJURIES

Soft-tissue injuries involve muscles and the bands of connective tissue known as *tendons* and *ligaments*. Tendons connect muscle to bone, while ligaments connect bone and bone, providing joint stability.

STRAINS

A strain occurs when a muscle or tendon is torn or stretched. In severe cases, muscle fibers can tear, or the tendon can detach from the muscle or bony attachment.

SPRAINS

A sprain is an injury to a ligament. Sprains usually occur when a joint is forced to move beyond its normal range of motion. Ligament sprains are graded according to the resultant joint instability. A grade 1 or "mild" sprain causes pain and tenderness along the ligament, but not increased joint instability. A grade 2 or "moderate" sprain results in a partial tear of a ligament, and a grade 3 or "severe" sprain is a complete tear or disruption of a ligament to the point where the ligament does not provide any stability to the joint.

CONTUSIONS

A contusion is a muscle bruise usually brought on by a jarring blow, as when a defensive linesman rams helmet-first into an opposing running back's thigh muscle (quadriceps) while making a tackle. Bleeding in this muscle may result in swelling, pain, spasm and restricted motion in the muscle. In some situations, a deep muscle contusion can result in the muscle becoming warm, tender and firm to the touch. This calcification of muscle contusion is known as *myositis ossificans traumatica.*

ACUTE BONE INJURIES

Broken bones account for only one in twenty sports injuries overall. The rate for young people is lower still, as their skeletons are more resilient than adults' and less susceptible to *fracture. Growth-plate injuries* and *avulsion fractures,* explained below, are unique to the teenage years.

GROWTH-PLATE INJURIES

Through late puberty, the ends of the long bones continue to lengthen, widen and change shape. An *epiphysis* is a growth plate that contributes to the growth of long bones and the formation of a joint surface. An *apophysis* is a growth plate that serves as an attachment site for a tendon or ligament. During growth, the epiphysis and the apophysis may be more susceptible to injury than the related ligament or tendon. Because of this, growth-plate injuries are easily confused with sprains or strains. A youngster with a suspected sprain should always be evaluated for possible epiphyseal or apophyseal injury.

AVULSION FRACTURES

In teens, muscle-tendon units are often stronger than the growth centers (apophyses) to which they are connected. An avulsion fracture occurs when the muscle and tendon exert so much force that they tear away (avulse) the apophysis. Apophyseal avulsions commonly occur around the knee and the pelvis.

OVERUSE SYNDROMES

Overuse syndromes, the other major category of injuries among young sports enthusiasts, are so subtle that they usually go unnoticed at first. Over time, though, repeated damage to the same anatomic area can culminate in tendinitis, bursitis and other injuries, such as stress fractures. Overuse injuries are more common in repetitive motion, as noted in swimming, running or dance. This is in contrast to acute injuries, which are more common in contact or collision sports, such as football or hockey.

OSGOOD-SCHLATTER DISEASE (OSD)

In this condition, there is inflammation of the site where the tendon from the thigh muscle meets the shin bone. Adolescents are predisposed to injury in this area (*tibial tubercle*) because it is still growing. OSD is associated with running and jumping sports such as basketball, soccer, volleyball, gymnastics and ice-skating. The symptoms of swelling and mild pain over the tibial tubercle usually go away on their own within one to two years if the condition is recognized and properly managed. Complications are limited to a localized bump.

ANTERIOR KNEE PAIN

Normally the kneecap glides smoothly over the end of the femur or thigh bone. Sometimes, though, it shifts slightly and grates against the bone. A youngster may find it painful to sit for long periods of time, as when riding in a car or watching a movie.

SEVER'S DISEASE

This is inflammation of one or both heel bones, producing mild pain. Running and jumping exacerbate this condition, seen primarily in young basketball and soccer players.

SHIN SPLINTS

This common injury involves the muscles or tendons that surround the *tibia,* better known as the shin bone. Pain can be noted in the muscle-tendon units of the tibia and a stress fracture of the leg bones may develop. The pain may improve with resting the leg, use of pain medications, a change in the exercise that is causing the condition and other measures.

CHRONIC EXERTIONAL COMPARTMENT SYNDROME

The leg muscles are housed within four separate compartments. When we run, the muscles expand in size and strain against the tough outer tissue that encases each compartment. The built-up pressure can impinge on blood vessels, causing muscle pain, and on nerves, leading to tingling in the foot.

TENDINITIS

This condition is a painful inflammation of a tendon due to excessive, repeated strain. Among the body parts affected are the elbow (dubbed "tennis elbow"), knee ("jumper's knee"), the back of the heel and ankle (Achilles' tendinitis) and the shoulder (Biceps tendinitis).

HOW SPORTS INJURIES OF THE BONES AND
SOFT TISSUES ARE MANAGED

Complaints of pain or stiffness should be brought to your pediatrician's attention right away, for timely treatment can often prevent minor injuries from becoming worse or causing permanent damage. Never allow a teenager to "play through" pain.

The National Athletic Trainers' Association (NATA), a professional organization with over twenty-three thousand members, studied trends in high-school sports injuries over a three-year period. Only one in eleven injuries are classified as "major," which NATA defines as any mishap that sidelines an athlete for more than three weeks. Basic treatment frequently consists of "RICE" (see box, page 438), an acronym that comes from rest, ice, compression and eleva-

> ### RICE: Home Care for Minor Injuries
>
> 1. **Rest:** the first step to permit healing.
> 2. **Ice:** Place an ice pack or a plastic bag full of ice over the injured area. Caution: Never apply ice for more than 20 minutes at a time; can also use chemical ice packs (blue ice).
> 3. **Compression:** Compression should be maintained even when ice is not being applied. Wrap an elastic bandage around the swollen joint or extremity.
> 4. **Elevation:** Place pillows or cushions beneath the injured arm or leg and keep it elevated until the pain or swelling subsides. Try to raise the limb above the level of the heart to prevent blood from pooling in the area.
>
> *To relieve pain and swelling, the pediatrician may prescribe a mild analgesic or an antiinflammatory medication—sometimes both.*

tion. The pediatrician may additionally recommend a regimen of home exercises for improving muscle strength and flexibility. Consultation with other experts, such as sports medicine clinicians or orthopedists, may occur as well.

HEAD INJURIES

The annual number of mild head injuries among high-school varsity athletes approaches sixty-three thousand, according to the National Athletic Trainers' Association. By far, the most common sports-related brain injury is a *concussion.* The term refers to any blow to the skull that alters mental functioning. In a departure from the long-standing medical definition, a person can have a concussion without being rendered unconscious.

A study from Detroit's Henry Ford Health System found that one in three college football players had suffered a concussion during the course of their career. One in five had suffered multiple concussions. The rate of multiple mild concussions among high-school football athletes was lower: one in thirteen. These repeated injuries can impair teenagers' cognitive abilities for years.

Football accounts for six in ten mild brain injuries, with wrestling (one in ten) a distant second. The leading cause of concussions among high-school girls' sports was soccer; but overall, young women sustain fewer than one-fifth the number of concussions than their male counterparts.

HOW SPORTS INJURIES OF THE BRAIN AND SKULL ARE MANAGED

Although there is no consensus on the proper medical protocol following a mild concussion, the American Academy of Neurology has developed a set of recommendations based on the severity (*grade*) of concussion, from one to three.

SPINAL INJURIES/SPINAL CORD INJURIES

Coaches, parents *and teens* should know what to do in the event of an apparent spinal injury. First and foremost, never move the person yourself; doing so could lead to permanent paralysis. Summon emergency medical assistance. Among the signs that point to possible damage of the spine or spinal cord:

- complaints of severe pain in the neck or back
- complaints of weakness, numbness, paralysis in extremities
- lack of control of the bladder, bowel or the limbs
- the injured person sustained a massive blow to the head, the neck or the back
- the neck or back appears twisted or out of position

PREVENTION *IS* THE BEST MEDICINE: SPORTS SAFETY GUIDELINES

Common Symptoms of a Concussion Include:

- Vacant stare
- Slurred or incoherent speech
- Momentary confusion and lack of focus
- Impaired coordination and balance
- Amplified emotions, such as crying for no apparent reason
- Delayed responses to questions
- Headache
- Dizziness
- Blurred or double vision
- Nausea
- Sensitivity to light
- Altered mental state (one or more of the following features):
  - *Disorientation* as to awareness of own name, date, time, and place
  - *Lack of concentration;* for example, can't recite the months of the year backward
  - *Transient memory loss;* for example, can't recall the names of the two competing teams, details of the game, recent newsworthy events

One of the most telling signs of a serious concussion is retrograde amnesia; an inability to recall events prior to the injury.

No sport is 100 percent safe. But there is much that parents, players and coaches can do to minimize young athletes' risk of injury.

The frequency and the type of injury will vary according to the nature and the demand of the sport. Contact and collision sports such as basketball, ice hockey and soccer are associated with a greater risk of acute injuries such as sprains, strains, contusions, fractures and dislocations. Endurance sports may have lower injury rates, but may have a higher proportion of overuse injuries such as tendinitis, apophysitis and stress fractures. Following are some suggestions for minimizing injuries.

TABLE 19.2

Steps to Take When a Teenager Suffers a Concussion

	GRADE 1	GRADE 2	GRADE 3
Symptoms	• Temporary confusion	• Temporary confusion	• Loss of consciousness for any length of time
	• No loss of consciousness	• No loss of consciousness	
	• Concussion symptoms resolve and/or mental state returns to normal within 15 minutes	• Concussion symptoms and/or altered mental state persist for more than 15 minutes	
Immediate Precautions	• The young athlete should go to the sidelines and be evaluated immediately and at 5-minute intervals by a coach, trainer or others experienced in handling head injuries.		• Call the local emergency medical service immediately.
	• After 15 minutes with no improvement, the young athlete should be kept from returning to the game.		• The young athlete should be taken by ambulance to the nearest hospital emergency department for a thorough neurologic examination.
	• The young athlete should see a physician the next day or that day if symptoms persist.		
	• In order to be cleared to return to play, the young athlete should undergo a neurologic exam 1 full week after the symptoms subside.		

(continued)

TABLE 19.2

	GRADE 1	GRADE 2	GRADE 3
Return to Action	• Minimum of 15 minutes. Most experts feel a child should not return to play on the same day if he has any level of concussion, including grade 1.	• 1 week, with physician's clearance	• 2 weeks, with physician's clearance
	For multiple concussions: • 1 week, with physician's clearance	*If this is not the young athlete's first grade 2 concussion:* • 2 weeks, with physician's clearance	*If this is not the young athlete's first grade 3 concussion:* • *1 month or longer, as determined by the evaluating physician*

Be sure that your youngster is competing against players of comparable size and development. Young athletes can be the same age yet vary considerably in height, weight and physical maturity. This can place the less-developed child at a competitive disadvantage and jeopardize his safety, particularly when players of varying strength and size are competing in contact or collision sports. "Even at the high-school level," observes Dr. Luckstead, "there are differences in size between a sophomore and a senior."

Encourage young athletes to train for their sport rather than rely on the sport to whip them into shape. Proper physical conditioning can go a long way toward keeping a player off the disabled list and on top of his game. Ask your teen's coach to help design a suitable exercise regimen.

Don't abuse or overuse arms and legs. In recent years, an epidemic of recurrent elbow pain from overuse led Little League Baseball, Inc., to limit pitchers under the age of thirteen to six innings per week; thirteen-to-sixteen-

Boxing: Down for the Count

The American Academy of Pediatrics opposes the sport of boxing for teenagers and young adults. Although other collision sports have higher rates of injury, boxing is the only athletic event that rewards participants for causing brain injury in opponents.

Boxers are at risk for serious eye injuries as well as *dementia pugilistica,* a potentially devastating brain disorder brought on by the repeated blows to the skull.

year-olds are allowed to pitch a maximum of nine innings. The organization also instituted mandatory rest between mound appearances. Since then, the incidence of recurrent elbow pain has decreased dramatically.

Runners can prevent overuse injuries by running on soft, flat terrain, and alternating days of strenuous running with less demanding workouts. They should gradually build up to their training goal. It has been suggested that increases of more than 20 percent per week should be avoided. For example, if the total mileage for a week is twenty miles, the maximum mileage for the next week should be no more than twenty-four miles.

Stretching and warm-up before practice and competition potentially help improve performance and decrease injuries. To gain flexibility, it may also be helpful to stretch after activity. Whether before or after a workout, the muscles should be warmed up before stretching.

Water breaks should be scheduled at least every twenty minutes to prevent dehydration. Inadequate fluid replacement can decrease muscle strength and endurance and can increase the risk of heat-related injury. Plain water is usually adequate to replenish fluid losses, but athletes may be inclined to drink more if the fluid is flavored and contains glucose and electrolytes.

Use the right equipment the right way. Teens often use "hand-me-down" equipment that may not be the correct size or fit for their particular use. A racket or club that is a poor fit can lead to undesirable compensations in technique, or the frustration of suboptimal performance. The same can be said for protective equipment such as helmets and pads. If the equipment is not properly fitted or maintained, the efficacy will be compromised. And be sure to replace athletic footwear when the soles of the shoe begin to show wear and tear.

When practicing or playing in hot weather, steps should be taken to avoid heat-induced illnesses such as heat cramps, heat exhaustion and heatstroke. Exercising in dry, mildly warm weather generally poses no problem for teenagers unless there is high humidity. In high-temperature, high-humidity conditions, young people take longer to adjust than adults do. Teenagers have less sweating capacity than adults and may generate more heat during activity. With the proper precautions, heat injury and dehydration are preventable in nearly all cases.

• At the start of a heat wave or a vigorous exercise program, workouts should be shorter and less taxing. Gradually, the duration and intensity can be increased over a period of ten to fourteen days.

• Practices and games can be held in the morning or the late afternoon, when the heat is less oppressive.

• Drink up! Teenagers should drink 10 to 15 ounces of cool water before exercise; and 8 to 10 ounces every twenty to thirty minutes while working up a sweat. Sports drinks become necessary only for prolonged activities (marathons). Neither fruit juices nor soft drinks rank among the beverages of champions; in fact, both can upset youngsters' stomachs and interfere with the absorption of fluid.

• Boys and girls should be outfitted in a single layer of lightweight, absorbent clothing, in order to facilitate sweat evaporation and to expose as much skin as possible. Perspiration-soaked garments should be replaced by dry ones.

HEAT-RELATED ILLNESSES

Heat Cramps

Muscle pains or spasms, usually in the abdomen, arms or legs, may arise during strenuous activity. Heat cramps mostly affects youngsters who perspire freely, depleting their bodies of fluid.

What to do:

1. Usher the teen to a cool place, indoors or outdoors.
2. Give him water or a sports beverage to drink.
3. Gently massage the affected muscle to bring relief.
4. Insist that he wait several hours after the cramping subsides before he resumes any physical activity; further exertion may lead to heat exhaustion or heat stroke.
5. *If cramping continues after one hour, seek medical attention.*

Heat Exhaustion

This is the body's response to an excessive loss of water and salt contained in sweat. Warning signs include: profuse perspiration; cold, pale, clammy skin; muscle cramps; fatigue; weakness; headache; nausea or vomiting; dizziness; fainting; rapid, shallow breathing; rapid, weak pulse.
What to do:

1. Use a thermometer to take body temperature (preferably rectal). If the body temperature is elevated to 103.1 degrees F or higher, proceed to recommendations for heatstroke listed below.
2. Same steps as for heat cramps.
3. In addition, prepare a cool bath, shower or sponge bath.
4. *If symptoms worsen or continue after one hour, seek medical attention, for untreated heat exhaustion can progress to heatstroke. Severe symptoms warrant an immediate trip to the hospital emergency department.*

Heatstroke

This is a potentially deadly condition in which the body's thermostat malfunctions. It is not unusual for body temperature to soar to 105 degrees F or higher within ten to fifteen minutes. Compounding the danger, the person is unable to perspire adequately, so body heat is retained rather than released. Symptoms include: oral temperature of 103.1 degrees F or higher; red, hot, dry skin; rapid, strong pulse; throbbing headache; nausea; dizziness; confusion; unconsciousness.
What to do:

1. Have someone call for emergency medical assistance while you begin to cool the young victim.
2. Move her inside or to a shady area outdoors.
3. Remove as much clothing as possible.
4. Get cool water on her skin, either by immersing her in a bathtub or shower; giving a sponge bath; or spraying her with a garden hose. In low humidity, you can also wrap the teen in a cool, wet sheet.
5. Aim a fan or air-conditioner at her.
6. Take her body temperature every five minutes and continue your cooling efforts until the thermometer reads 102 degrees F or less.
7. Important: Do not give the youngster anything to drink. In her state, she could inadvertently inhale the liquid into her lungs, bringing about *aspiration pneumonia.*
8. *If emergency medical personnel are delayed, call the hospital emergency department for further instructions.*

9. *Heatstroke victims sometimes begin to twitch uncontrollably. In the event of a seizure, make sure that the young person doesn't injure himself on furniture. Never try to insert a spoon or other hard object in his mouth to prevent him from swallowing his tongue; simply turning his head to the side will suffice. The same advice applies if the teenager is vomiting, to keep his airway open.*

Before letting your teenager play in an athletic program, find out if the school or league has a medical-emergency plan in place. The National Athletic Trainers' Association suggests asking these questions:

- Who will provide emergency first aid?
- Who will summon emergency medical services (EMS), and how?
- How will parents be notified in the event of an emergency?
- Is the coaching staff trained to administer first aid and cardiopulmonary resuscitation (CPR)?
- Are emergency medical devices readily available at all times?
- Is there a qualified health-care provider available to school athletes on a daily basis?
- Does the school or league consult with a physician experienced in sports medicine?

Teenagers should see their pediatrician for an annual medical screening at least six weeks prior to the start of the athletic season. More than two-thirds of the fifty states require yearly physicals to screen youngsters for any health condition(s) that could preclude their taking part in athletics. The *preparticipation evaluation* (*PPE* for short) is not intended as a substitute for the annual medical checkup described in chapter 16, "Medical Checkups and Immunizations." However, studies show that it winds up serving that purpose for about four in five teens.

The sports evaluation should preferably be performed on an individual basis at the pediatrician's office. The exam is designed to look at medical issues and injury risk factors relevant to sports participation. Height and weight are measured. Then the doctor examines the eyes, ears, nose, oral cavity, lungs, cardiovascular system, abdomen, genitals and skin. Strength, flexibility and joint stability are also assessed.

A thorough medical history alone picks up 75 percent of all medical problems that could affect adolescent athletes. Particular attention is paid to any familial patterns of heart disease, the leading cause of sudden cardiac death in young athletes. Fortunately, *sudden cardiac death* (SCD) is extremely rare in teenagers. "In the United States," says pediatric cardiologist Dr. Luckstead, "perhaps fifteen kids a year might fit into that category. The difficulty is in picking it up." Most victims of SCD exhibited no signs of illness prior to the fatal collapse.

"What we try to do is to look for red flags that will tip us off," he explains. "For instance: Does the teenager pass out sometimes when he runs or get dizzy sometimes while exercising? Did he have a relative who died suddenly of heart failure at a relatively young age? If we suspect that the teenager may have a risk factor, we usually order an electrocardiogram at the time of the examination. And if we're extremely suspicious, we get a more costly test called an echocardiogram." By measuring the thickness of the heart wall, as seen on the ECHO, doctors can predict which patients are in danger of suffering fatal cardiac arrest.

Only about 3.3 percent of boys and girls who undergo the PPE have medical problems that could restrict their athletic involvement, but many more have conditions or effects from prior injuries that could, without attention, lead to further injury. Following additional evaluation, all but approximately 0.3 percent of kids will be cleared to play. If a teen is found to have a disqualifying condition, a second opinion is in order, given how disappointing it can be for a child to learn that she is medically ineligible to pursue a favorite activity. It is also worthwhile to examine other options for safe physical activity. For example, if a spine disorder makes football unsafe, the athlete may still be eligible to participate in a noncontact sport such as swimming, tennis or track.

Sportsmanship Isn't Everything, It's the Only Thing

We look to sports to build young people's character, self-esteem and self-discipline, not just muscle. Research indicates that competing in athletic activities benefits adolescents emotionally and socially. They learn to be part of a team, to respond to pressure and to motivate themselves—all valuable skills, whether put to the test on the ballfield or in the classroom. They also develop their ability to cope with adversity and to bounce back from defeat, two more essential tools for life.

Ultimately, the values that sports instill in young people reflect the attitudes of the adults in charge. When the desire to win corrupts the principles of sportsmanship, it turns what should be a positive experience into a negative one. A win-at-all-costs atmosphere can also lead to injuries by leading youths to feel pressured into playing when hurt.

Sometimes it seems as if kids maintain a healthier perspective on the importance of winning than their parents and coaches. Let's never lose sight of the purpose of amateur athletics: to help boys and girls grow and to have fun. Below are tips for helping your son or daughter get the most out of sports participation.

Attend as many games and practices as you can. Teenagers may not always admit it, but they get a charge out of seeing Mom wave to them from the bleachers with a proud smile on her face.

TABLE 19.3

Medical Conditions That May Rule Out Sports Involvement

CONDITION DESCRIPTION	IS PARTICIPATION PERMITTED?	RECOMMENDATIONS
Atlantoaxial Instability *Instability of the joint between the two uppermost vertebrae in the neck*	Conditional yes	Teen needs evaluation to assess risk of spinal cord injury during sports participation. For example, some teens with Down's syndrome may have atlantoaxial instability and be at increased risk for neck injury.
Bleeding Disorders, *including hemophilia*	Conditional yes	Evaluation needed. *As a rule, hemophiliacs are counseled not to play contact/collision sports.*
Cancer	Conditional yes	Evaluation needed.
Cardiovascular Diseases		
CARDITIS *Inflammation of the heart*	No	Exertion may result in sudden death.
HYPERTENSION *Chronically high blood pressure*	Conditional yes	Teens with significant essential (unexplained) hypertension should avoid weight and power lifting, body building and strength training. Secondary hypertension (caused by a previously identified disease) or severe essential hypertension warrant a medical evaluation.

(continued)

TABLE 19.3

Condition Description	Is Participation Permitted?	Recommendations
CONGENITAL HEART DISEASE *Structural heart defects present at birth*	Conditional yes	Teens with mild forms may participate fully; those with moderate or severe forms, or who have undergone surgery, need evaluation.
DYSRHYTHMIA *Irregular heart rhythm*	Conditional yes	Evaluation needed, because some dysrhythmias require treatment and/or make certain sports participation dangerous.
MITRAL VALVE PROLAPSE *Malfunctioning heart valve*	Conditional yes	Teens with symptoms (chest pain, symptoms of possible dysrhythmia) or evidence of mitral regurgitation (leaking) on physical examination need evaluation. All others may participate fully.
HEART MURMUR	Conditional yes	If the murmur is "innocent"—that is, does not indicate heart disease—full participation is permitted. Otherwise, evaluation needed.
Cerebral Palsy	Conditional yes	Evaluation needed.
Diabetes Mellitus	Yes	All sports can be played with proper attention to diet, hydration and insulin therapy (if necessary). Particular attention is needed for activities that last 30 minutes or more.
Diarrhea	No	Unless mild, the youngster is not allowed to play, because of the risk of dehydration and heat-related illness.

Condition Description	Is Participation Permitted?	Recommendations
Eating Disorders (anorexia nervosa, bulimia nervosa)	Conditional yes	These teens need both medical and psychiatric assessments before participation.
Eye Disorders (functionally one-eyed, loss of an eye, detached retina, prior eye surgery, serious eye injury)	Conditional yes	A functionally one-eyed teen has a best corrected visual acuity of 20/40 in the worse eye. These athletes would suffer significant disability if the healthier eye were seriously injured, as would those who have lost an eye. Some young people who have previously undergone eye surgery or had a serious eye injury may have an increased risk of injury because of weakened eye tissue. Availability of eye guards approved by the American Society for Testing Materials (ASTM) and other protective equipment may allow participation in most sports, but this must be judged on an individual basis.
Fever	No	Fever adds to the workload of the heart and lungs, and increases the chances of suffering heat exhaustion or heatstroke.
Heat Illness, *history of*	Conditional yes	Because of the increased likelihood of recurrence, the athlete needs individual assessment to determine the presence of predisposing conditions and to establish a prevention strategy.

(continued)

TABLE 19.3

Condition Description	Is Participation Permitted?	Recommendations
Hepatitis B (HBV) *Hepatitis C (HCV)* *Human Immunodeficiency Virus (HIV)*	Conditional yes	The risk of these viruses being transmitted through sports participation is believed to be extremely low. Therefore, all sports should be open to athletes infected with HIV or with hepatitis B or C. However, sensible precautions must be taken, such as making sure that cuts, abrasions, wounds or other areas of broken skin are covered with a protective dressing before and during events.
Kidney, loss of one, due to injury or disease	Conditional yes	Evaluation needed for contact/collision and limited-contact sports.
Liver, enlarged (hepatomegaly)	Conditional yes	If the liver is acutely enlarged, participation should be avoided because of risk of rupture. If the liver is chronically enlarged, evaluation needed before collision/contact or limited contact sports are played.
Musculoskeletal Disorders	Conditional yes	Evaluation needed.
Neurologic Disorders HISTORY OF (1) SERIOUS HEAD OR SPINAL TRAUMA, (2) SEVERE OR REPEATED CONCUSSIONS, (3) BRAIN SURGERY	Conditional yes	Evaluation needed for collision/contact or limited-contact sports, and also for non-contact sports if there are deficits in judgment or cognition. Recent research supports a conservative approach to management of concussion.

Condition Description	Is Participation Permitted?	Recommendations
CONVULSIVE DISORDER	Yes, if well controlled	If disorder is well controlled, the teen faces little risk of having a seizure while participating in sports.
	Conditional yes, if poorly controlled	If disorder is poorly controlled, evaluation needed for collision/contact or limited-contact sports. The teen should avoid the following noncontact sports: archery, riflery, swimming, weight or power lifting, strength training, sports involving heights. In these sports, a convulsion, though unlikely, could pose a risk to the patient or to others.
Obesity	Conditional yes	Because of the risk of heat illness, obese teens need careful acclimatization and hydration.
Organ Transplant Recipient	Conditional yes	Evaluation needed.
Ovary, loss of one, due to disease	Yes	The risk of severe injury to the remaining ovary is minimal.
Respiratory Disorders		
ACUTE UPPER-RESPIRATORY INFECTION	Conditional yes	Upper-respiratory obstruction may affect pulmonary function. Evaluation needed for all but mild disease.
ASTHMA	Yes	With proper medication and education, only teens with severe asthma will have to modify participation.

(continued)

TABLE 19.3

CONDITION DESCRIPTION	IS PARTICIPATION PERMITTED?	RECOMMENDATIONS
COMPROMISED PULMONARY FUNCTION, *including from cystic fibrosis*	Conditional yes	Evaluation needed, but, generally, all sports may be played if the teen's oxygenation remains satisfactory during a graded exercise test. Youngsters with cystic fibrosis need acclimatization and proper hydration to reduce the risk of heat illness.
Sickle-Cell Anemia	Conditional yes	Evaluation needed. In general, if the teen is asymptomatic, all but high-exertion, collision/contact sports may be played. Steps should be taken to prevent overheating, dehydration and chilling.
Sickle-Cell Trait	Yes	It is unlikely that teens with sickle-cell trait (AS) have an increased risk of sudden death or other medical problems during athletic participation except under *extreme* heat, humidity and possibly increased altitude. These young people, like all athletes, should be carefully conditioned, acclimatized and hydrated to reduce any possible risk.
Skin Conditions (boils, herpes simplex, impetigo, scabies, molluscum contagiosum)	Conditional yes	While the patient is contagious, participation in gymnastics with mats, martial arts, wrestling or other collision/contact or limited-contact sports is not allowed. The herpes simplex virus probably is not transmitted via mats.

Condition Description	Is Participation Permitted?	Recommendations
Spleen, *enlarged (splenomegaly)*	Conditional yes	A teen with an acutely enlarged spleen should avoid all sports because of risk of rupture. Those with chronically enlarged spleens need evaluation before playing collision/contact or limited-contact sports.
Testicle, undescended or missing	Yes	Certain sports may require a protective cup.

Extreme Sports, Extreme Consequences

"Extreme" sports, a phenomenon that began around 1990, would appear to be tailor-made for the thrill-seeking adolescent years. The term encompasses various daredevil pursuits such as bungee jumping (diving off a bridge or other high perch while attached to a long, stretchable secured cord that yanks the person back up into the air shortly before he hits the ground), and adrenaline-pumping variations on existing sports. There's barefoot water-skiing, gravity-defying skateboarding tricks, snowboarding (riding a fiberglass board down a steep slope), sky surfing (a hybrid of skydiving and surfing) and other activities guaranteed to heighten a parent's anxiety.

With good reason. Although national statistics on injuries and fatalities from these pastimes have yet to be compiled, reports from around the country tell us that young people *are* getting hurt. Extreme sports may be popular with the teenage set partly for their free-spirited, livin'-on-the-edge appeal, but the safety measures are no different than they are for any other recreational activity: Wear the proper protective gear, learn and practice the necessary skills and always know your limits.

Work with teens on improving their skills. Your six-foot-four eighteen-year-old will never forget the evening Dad or Mom donned a catcher's mitt and let him practice hurling his eighty-mile-per-hour curve ball the day before he was to start in the division championships. Judging by Dad's/Mom's bruised shins and throbbing hand, the memory will stay with them for some time too.

Measure your child's performance by the yardstick of effort. Adolescents respond better to positive encouragement for trying hard than to criticism for their shortcomings. In a survey of 658 coaches from 43 sports, many noted that the most damaging aspect of sports on young athletes was constant negative feedback from parents (and coaches). Occasionally a teen may need a psychological nudge ("I know you can hustle harder than that"), but before you do, be certain of two things: (1) that your expectations are realistic and (2) that you make it clear that you love her whether she succeeds or fails.

"Kids need their parents most of all when things *don't* go well," observes Dr. Luckstead. "Some mothers and fathers—and I've been guilty of this myself—are their child's best buddy when they win, but when the child loses, the parents take out their frustrations on the child. That's obviously not the right thing to do."

Don't be one of those parents who berate officials from the stands. A key lesson that sports imparts to kids is respect for the rules of the game and those whose job it is to enforce them. If you don't agree with a referee's call or a coach's benching your teen in favor of another player, keep it to yourself. Learning how to accept seemingly unfair decisions is useful preparation for everyday life.

Monitor your teenager for evidence of sports-related stress. Some amount of stress is inevitable prior to an important athletic event. But if you see your youngster placing undue pressure on herself to excel or taking losses too hard, it's time for a talk.

Help her to view defeats in the proper light. Point out that even the best hitters in baseball fail to reach base roughly seven out of every ten times at bat, future Hall of Fame quarterbacks connect only 60 percent of the time, and so on.

Be alert to signs of unhealthy weight-control practices or use of performance-enhancing drugs. The quest for excellence can be carried too far, as when athletes attempt to improve their production with stimulants or bulk up with anabolic steroids or legal substances that act similarly on the body.

Extreme weight-loss measures are associated mainly with sports where "making weight" is deemed crucial to success: bodybuilding, cheerleading, distance running, diving, figure skating, gymnastics, rowing, swimming, weight-class football and wrestling. Methods of rapid weight loss include overexercising; prolonged fasting; self-induced vomiting; repeated episodes of bingeing and purging; taking laxatives, diuretics, diet pills, other licit or illicit drugs and/or nicotine; wearing rubber suits; and immersing oneself in steam baths and saunas.

In two surveys of 208 female collegiate athletes, 32 percent and 62 percent admitted to engaging in at least one unhealthy weight-loss behavior. Male athletes, too, sometimes go to drastic lengths to drop a few pounds. Of 171 collegiate wrestlers taking part in another study, 82 percent revealed that back in high school they'd fasted for more than twenty-four hours.

Though these teens may not fully meet the diagnostic criteria for anorexia nervosa and bulimia nervosa, they risk making themselves seriously ill. If you suspect your child may be malnourished or secretly abusing substances, notify your pediatrician immediately. (See "Anabolic Steroids" and "Other Performance-Enhancing Drugs" in chapter 13, "Tobacco, Alcohol and Other Drugs of Abuse," and chapter 18, "When Eating Turns into a Problem.")

What if your youngster reports a conflict with a sports coach? Two sample scenarios:

"Coach keeps riding me in front of the whole team. You'd think it was all *my* fault that we're 0–3."

"I haven't gotten in a single game, and the football season is half over. Yesterday we were up 35–7 in the fourth quarter, and Coach still didn't let me play. I think he has it in for me."

In either situation, the advice is no different than for addressing clashes with teachers. First, let your teen try to reason with the coach on his own. (It's fine to help him construct a coherent case for why he feels he's being treated unfairly.) If that doesn't prove productive, speak to the coach yourself, but privately. This is not a discussion to have in front of your child or anyone else's child.

And if the problem persists? In a community-based league, you might request in writing that the organizers transfer your son or daughter to another team. In extracurricular athletics, however, appealing to school administrators probably is not going to resolve the issue—unless the coach is verbally or physically abusive, in which event, the chances are that other team members might have similar complaints. Your child's options essentially boil down to (a) tolerate the coach for the remainder of the season or (b) leave the team. Separate your child from a coach who is abusive to your child and report the coach to the proper authorities.

IF A CHILD WANTS TO QUIT

According to the American Psychological Association, two in five youngsters drop out of a sports program. The reasons voiced most often include:

- conflicts with the coach
- lack of enjoyment
- loss of interest in the sport
- insufficient playing time
- would rather play another sport
- too much else to do
- an overly competitive atmosphere
- too much stress and pressure
- not performing up to the standards they've set for themselves

It is a teenager's right to share in the decision to end involvement in a sport. If your child comes to you with a desire to quit an athletic program, gather as many facts as you can. Listen to and discuss her reasons. If there is a way to rectify the situation, perhaps by speaking to the coach, offer to do so. However, while we don't want to see children fall into a pattern of avoiding difficult situations, sometimes dropping out is the most reasonable course of action.

IF SPORTS PARTICIPATION INTERFERES WITH SCHOOLWORK

Youngsters must understand from the outset that academics take precedence over athletics. Dreams of college athletic scholarships and multimillion-dollar professional sports contracts can blind parents and teens alike to the reality that fewer than 1 percent of athletes qualify for a sports scholarship, and a mere fraction of those young men and women go on to make sports their career.

Nevertheless, poor grades shouldn't necessarily keep an adolescent from participating in sports. A child who is struggling in the classroom still needs the benefits of exercise, competition and a sense of accomplishment. Sports may be his or her only avenue of success.

Dr. Luckstead believes in using athletic involvement as the carrot at the end of the stick. "I think that kids work harder at hitting the books if sports is the payoff," he says. "Take away that incentive, and you can lose them." Too, the self-confidence derived from sports may carry over to other areas of life, including academics. Instead of eliminating sports participation, why not look for other ways to bolster school performance? Perhaps he has to give up a part-time job or sacrifice TV viewing to carve out more time for schoolwork. Ask your youngster what you can do to help him improve his grades.

20

COMMON MEDICAL CONDITIONS DURING THE TEEN YEARS

When faced with health problems, teenagers often seem to be guided by the same mercurial thought processes that influence their actions in other areas of life. On the one hand, they tend to be preoccupied with their changing bodies and prone to high drama, so that minor complaints may get inflated to Mom-I-think-I'm-dying proportions. Yet the invincibility of youth can blind them to the potential seriousness of an ailment. Consequently, they may fail to seek medical attention or even inform their parents that they're not feeling well.

This chapter examines the disorders common to adolescents, with an emphasis on those that either first appear or peak in frequency during the teen years, such as acne, type II diabetes and sexually transmitted diseases. We *don't* discuss what to do when your child has a cold or traipses through poison ivy, on the assumption that by now you probably know the drill as well as any doctor.

Several aspects of illness are unique to this age group. One is that the hormonal changes of puberty can spur the development of certain medical conditions, like acne, breast disorders, menstrual problems and pelvic inflammatory disease. Conversely, chronic kidney failure and thyroid disease are just two disorders that affect the timing of puberty itself.

In addition, teenagers' infirmities can sometimes be traced to stress or other emotions. The medical term for this phenomenon is *psychosomatic* (*psycho* meaning "mind"; *soma,* "body"). A youngster gripped by anxiety over family problems, academic pressure and so forth may experience fatigue, dizziness, headaches, chest pain or abdominal distress. The fact that an ailment is psychological in origin doesn't mean the symptoms are a figment of the imagination. They are quite real and may respond to medical treatment.

A small percentage of adolescents, though, will complain repeatedly of symptoms like those noted above, yet medical exams and/or tests will reveal little or no evidence of any abnormality. For the most part, these teens are not hypochondriacs or attention seekers; they suffer from depression or anxiety. All it usually takes for the aches and pains to subside is a doctor's reassurance that they're in good health, says Dr. John Kulig, director of adolescent medicine at Boston's New England Medical Center, "because teenagers are highly sensitive to somatic symptoms and tend to fear the worst." However, should this pattern of behavior begin to disrupt a youngster's daily life, he would most likely be referred to a mental-health professional for counseling and possibly psychiatric mediation. (See "How Emotional and Behavioral Disorders Are Treated" in chapter 15, "Emotional and Behavioral Problems.")

ENCOURAGING TEENS TO TAKE RESPONSIBILITY FOR THEIR OWN HEALTH CARE

As children mature, they may become increasingly reluctant to share health concerns with Mom and Dad; partly out of modesty and partly to assert their independence. That is why teenagers need a pediatrician in whom they can confide. Chapter 16, "Medical Checkups and Immunizations," explains how to go about finding your son or daughter a physician who is both experienced in adolescent health issues and sensitive to young people's emotional needs.

Now is also the time for teens to learn to become savvy medical consumers. They should be encouraged to schedule their own doctors' visits and to ask questions anytime they don't understand something the pediatrician has said. Where health matters are concerned, there is no such thing as a "dumb" question. Every patient, regardless of age, is entitled to clear explanations of her condition and the recommended treatment plan.

Above all, adolescents need to be coached on the importance of taking medications as directed. If there is one source of frustration for pediatricians, it's their young patients' lack of compliance (although as Dr. Kulig points out, "compliance among adults isn't much better"). In one study of children suffering from throat infections, more than 80 percent failed to finish their antibiotics, which had been prescribed for ten days. Presumably, most of them started to feel better after several days and figured they could stop taking the medicine. But we know that the entire course of antibiotics must be completed in order to fully eradicate the infection. Otherwise, the bacteria regain a foothold, stronger than ever, and the symptoms return.

Teens may also resist following doctors' orders as a display of rebellion. Dr. Kulig advises that parents monitor their youngster's compliance, but without assuming the mantle of responsibility. The most successful strategy, he's found, "is to solicit kids' input about how to best stick to medication schedules, rather than demanding, '*You must take this medicine.*' " He offers several tips:

To eliminate confusion, post a calendar on the refrigerator and place a check mark in the appropriate box each time the medication is taken. Or purchase an inexpensive plastic pill holder, in which oral drugs are stored according to the day of the week and daily Sunday through Saturday, and dose (morning, afternoon, evening).

Have the teenager take the medicine at the same time as one of his daily rituals, like brushing his teeth. "It becomes a cue for compliance," explains Dr. Kulig. "When they brush their teeth in the morning and at night, they remember they need to take their medicine."

Practice positive reinforcement. Praise your adolescent each time he adheres to the medication schedule.

Remind young men and women why a medication has been prescribed. "Adolescents should understand the purpose of the therapy as well as the potential consequences of noncompliance," says Dr. Kulig. "They should also be aware of how long they may have to be on the medication before they can expect to see optimum results.

"For instance, some acne medications can take upward of twelve weeks to start working. If a teen gets discouraged and discontinues the drug, obviously the acne won't get better. Likewise, if he grows impatient and overuses it, he may irritate and dry out the skin."

Another reason for supervising young people's consumption of medicines is that some drugs have the potential for abuse, whether they're prescribed or over-the-counter. "Tylenol is a good example," says Dr. Kulig. "Too high a dose can basically destroy the liver." Most overdoses of nonprescription agents are taken intentionally, as part of suicide attempts, but excessive amounts can be ingested accidentally. "Teenagers," he stresses, "are not aware of how toxic these products can be."

As a precaution, it's wise to never leave a family member's medication out where it can fall into the hands of an inquisitive child or a teenage pal looking for a "legal" high. According to Dr. Timothy Wilens, a pediatric psychiatrist at Massachusetts General Hospital, also in Boston: "Most prescription drugs are abused not by the kids for whom they're prescribed, but by *other* children. All containers should be stored away, with each dose administered individually."

Questions to Ask the Pediatrician Before a Teenager Starts Any New Medication

- What are the medication's generic name and trade name?
- What is the purpose of using this medication?
- How often should the medication be taken, and at what time(s) of day?
- What is the dosage?
- Is it necessary to swallow this medication with food or milk?
- *If your youngster has difficulty ingesting pills, ask if the medication can be crushed, or if it comes in the form of a liquid, skin patch, rectal suppository, inhaler or nose spray.*
- Are there any foods or beverages to avoid while on this medication?
- Will the drug interfere with other medications my child is taking, or vice-versa?
- *List for the pediatrician all medications your teenager takes, including over-the-counter agents, nutritional supplements and "natural" herbal remedies.*
- What should we do if we miss a dose?
- For how long must the medicine be taken? Does my child have to finish the entire prescription?
- Does the prescription include refills? If so, how many? What should we do if we need a new prescription ordered?
- What are the potential side effects of this drug, and which ones should we report to you?
- If side effects occur, how will they be managed?
- When will we be able to tell if the medicine is working?
- How much does the prescription cost?
- Is there any written information available about the medication?

CANCERS IN ADOLESCENCE

Description

Cancer is a group of diseases in which the genetic controls that regulate the normal proliferation of the body's cells become disabled, and the cells begin to divide chaotically, at an accelerated pace. In time, they amass into a lump of excess tissue called a *tumor*. A tumor that does not invade normal tissue is said to be *benign*. It is not cancerous. Aside from tumors embedded in the brain, most benign growths can be removed surgically without incident.

Invasive tumors *are* cancerous. If not treated successfully, these *malignant* masses will continue to enlarge and possibly spread to other parts of the body.

The tumor can extend through one organ and into another, or a colony of cells from the *primary* tumor may break off and travel the circulatory system to seed a *secondary* tumor a distance away. The medical term for this is *metastasis.*

It is important to keep in mind that cancer is identified according to the original location and cell type. A colon tumor that *metastasizes* to the liver is not the same disease as primary liver cancer, nor is it treated the same way. In this example, the new malignancy would be referred to as *colon cancer metastatic to the liver.* Its cells, though found in the liver, are colon-cancer cells. Early detection is crucial to a cancer patient's prognosis, because tumors that remain *localized* to the original site are generally more easily controlled or cured than tumors that have metastasized.

WHAT IS STAGING?

Once cancer is definitively diagnosed, the *oncologist* orders additional tests to establish the size and extent of the tumor. *Staging,* as this is called, is really just a universal language for expressing this information. A commonly used staging system assigns each tumor a number from 0 to 4. Generally, stage 1 and stage 2 disease are still confined near the original site, while stage 3 tells the doctor that the cancer has invaded neighboring sites or has spread to nearby *lymph nodes.* Stage 4 is defined by spread to distant lymph nodes or organs. Not all cancers are staged using numbers; some are simply classified as localized or disseminated.

TYPES OF CHILDHOOD CANCERS

Although cancer is the most deadly disease of childhood and adolescence, it strikes just nine thousand youngsters a year, as compared to approximately 1.2 million adults. Nine in ten adult cancers are *carcinomas,* malignancies that take hold in the cells lining the inner or outer surfaces of organs such as the lung, breast, prostate, colon and bladder. Cancers of children and adolescents belong mainly to four other groups: *leukemias, lymphomas, sarcomas* and *gliomas.*

Cancers of childhood tend to be more curable than adult tumors.[1] While the five-year survival rate for adults has struggled to exceed the 50 percent mark, about 70 percent of young patients—nearly three in four—can expect to enjoy a normal life span. That is a dramatic increase from the mid-1970s, when nearly half of all youngsters with cancer died.

---

1 Oncologists employ the word "cure" judiciously, probably because it wasn't too long ago that relatively few patients survived the disease. Being cancer-free five years from the time of diagnosis is the yardstick generally used to measure a cure.

TABLE 20.1

Common Cancers of Childhood and Adolescence

TYPE	PERCENTAGE OCCURRENCE
Leukemias	25%
Lymphomas	15%
Hodgkin's Disease, 9%	
Non-Hodgkin's Lymphomas, 6%	
Brain cancers	17%
Gonadal cancers	5%
Neuroblastoma (a cancer of the nervous system)*	5%
Wilms' tumor (a cancer of the kidney)*	4%
Rhabdomyosarcoma*	3%
Thyroid cancers	3%
Malignant melanoma	3%
Osteosarcoma (bone cancer)	3%
Ewing's sarcoma (bone cancer)	2%
Retinoblastoma*	2%
Others	13%

* Rare in teenagers

Leukemia

This is cancer of the *bone marrow,* which manufactures the three types of blood cells. *White blood cells (leukocytes)* serve as the body's defense system against infection. In leukemia, the marrow produces an overabundance of cancerous white cells. Eventually they crowd out the healthy, infection-fighting mature leukocytes in the marrow and the bloodstream, opening the door to viruses, bacteria and other microorganisms. At the same time, the impaired marrow grinds out fewer oxygen-toting *red blood cells* and fewer *platelets,* the clotting cells responsible for stopping bleeding.

Leukemias are classified as *acute* or *chronic.* Young leukemia patients usually develop the acute forms. *Acute lymphocytic leukemia* (ALL) affects white blood cells called *lymphocytes,* while *acute myelogenous leukemia* (AML) affects other white blood cells called *granulocytes* and *monocytes.* You may hear leukemia referred to as a "liquid" tumor. Because it floods the circulation with malignant white cells, the disease is by nature *systemic,* or system-wide. When the cancer spreads outside the bone marrow, the blood vessels may whisk it to the brain and spinal cord, the testicles, the ovaries, the kidneys and other organs.

Hodgkin's Disease and Non-Hodgkin's Lymphoma

These are cancers of the lymphatic system. Intertwined among the blood vessels is a network of thin *lymphatic vessels,* which collect straw-colored *lymph fluid* from the body's tissues and return it to a pair of veins in the upper chest so that it can repeat its excursion through the body as the liquid portion of the blood.

En route, lymph passes through pea-sized organs called *lymph nodes,* which filter out and destroy infectious agents and toxic substances. The nodes are scattered through the lymphatic system but can be found in large clusters in the neck, pelvis, abdomen, chest and armpits.

Because there is so much lymph tissue in the body, Hodgkin's lymphoma and non-Hodgkin's lymphoma can occur and spread virtually anywhere. When these cancers metastasize, it's often to the liver, the bone marrow or the *spleen.* Hodgkin's disease usually progresses at a slow but predictable rate and is extremely responsive to treatment. With a five-year survival rate exceeding 90 percent, it is one of the most curable cancers of adolescence.

The three major types of childhood non-Hodgkin's lymphomas are more aggressive and harder to control, although the overall cure rate is still a promising 75 percent. Doctors can determine whether a youngster has *small-cell noncleaved lymphoma* (the most common type), *lymphoblastic lymphoma,* or *large-cell lymphoma* (the least common type) by the appearance of the cells under the microscope and other more sophisticated tests. Combined, lymphomas and leukemias account for almost half of all pediatric cancers.

Brain Cancers

Pediatric brain tumors fall into one of four categories: *astrocytomas, primitive neuroectodermal tumors* (*PNET,* for short), *brain-stem gliomas,* and *ependymomas.* Their names reflect the types of cells in which these tumors arise.

The brain is a frequent site of metastatic tumors from other parts of the body; primary brain lesions, however, rarely spread beyond the central nervous system. Therefore, doctors look at the tumor's *grade* rather than its stage to help them determine the most appropriate treatment. The grade, expressed as low or high, rates the cancer cells' appearance. Do they resemble normal cells? Or do they have the disorganized structure of malignant cells? Grade provides a profile of the cancer's behavior. Low-grade astrocytomas, which look similar to healthy astrocytes, grow slowly and rarely spread to other parts of the brain, whereas high-grade brain tumors are much more aggressive.

Primitive neuroectodermal tumors, which include *medulloblastomas,* spring from primitive nerve cells and are rarely seen in adolescents. Brain-stem gliomas develop in the bundle of nerve tissue at the base of the brain, where crucial functions such as heart rate, breathing, and swallowing are regulated.

Ependymomas usually arise in the membranous lining of the *ventricles,* the four interconnected hollow pockets within the brain. The ventricles produce the *cerebrospinal fluid* that surrounds and cushions the brain and the spinal cord. Consequently, the fluid often disseminates malignant cells up and down the central nervous system.

Rhabdomyosarcoma

This is a cancer of muscle tissue. There are two main types of pediatric rhabdomyosarcoma: the rarer form, *alveolar rhabdomyosarcoma,* which involves large muscles of the trunk, arms and legs is more likely to occur in teenagers; *embryonal rhabdomyosarcoma,* seen in infants and young children, occurs in the head and neck, bladder, prostate, testicles and vagina. Most youngsters are diagnosed with the disease still limited to the original site. When rhabdomyosarcoma does spread, it typically creates new lesions in the lymph nodes, bone, bone marrow or lung.

Osteosarcoma and Ewing's Sarcoma

These are cancers of the bone. Osteosarcoma, the more common of the two, often strikes during the growth spurt of puberty. Boys and girls who sprout up rapidly can possibly be at greater risk of developing the disease than are youngsters whose growth rate is average or less than average, although a growth spurt should not be cause for alarm.

About half of osteosarcomas develop in the region of the knee, whereas Ewing's sarcomas frequently target the pelvis, ribs and the long bones in the upper legs and arms. Both cancers may spread to the lungs, as well as to other bones and soft tissue. Ewing's sarcoma sometimes spreads to the bone marrow, the body's production center for blood cells, thus giving rise to abnormal blood counts.

Symptoms of Childhood Cancers

As you can see from Table 20.2, the location of a tumor greatly determines the local effects. But the disease also takes its toll on the body at large. Most patients, young or old, go through periods of extreme fatigue as the body expends extra energy healing itself from the cancer and the side effects of treatment.

The malignant cells also interfere with the process of metabolism, depriving their healthy counterparts of essential nutrients. Compounding matters, during treatment, patients often see their appetites wane. Now add to this the countless other reasons why a youngster with cancer might feel exhausted: anemia, inadequately controlled pain, not to mention the wearing effect from the daily stress of coping with a life-threatening illness.

TABLE 20.2

Symptoms of Pediatric Cancers

TYPE OF CANCER	SYMPTOMS MAY INCLUDE:
Acute Leukemias	Fever • chills • appetite loss • aching bones or joints • swollen lymph nodes • weakness, fatigue, shortness of breath, pale complexion and other symptoms of *anemia* • unexplained bleeding, bruising and other symptoms of a blood-clotting disorder • bone pain • joint pain • a swollen abdomen due to enlargement of the spleen and liver
Hodgkin's Disease and Non-Hodgkin's Lymphoma	Persistent fever • night sweats • unexplained weight loss • fatigue • appetite loss • itching • painless swelling of the lymph nodes in the neck or armpit • distended stomach, from swelling of lymphoid tissue in the abdomen • constipation or urinary retention, from swelling of lymphoid tissue near the intestines or the kidneys • coughing or shortness of breath, from swelling of the *thymus,* a lymphoid gland in the upper chest
Brain Cancers	Symptoms depend on the tumor's location within the brain—and increased pressure within the skull: dizziness • seizures • changes in behavior and personality • memory loss • confusion • gradual weakness or paralysis • impaired vision, hearing, speech, smell, balance, motor skills • persistent headaches, morning vomiting and blurred vision
Sarcomas of the Soft Tissues and Bones	*Rhabdomyosarcoma* Painless mass or swelling • tumors located in the abdomen or pelvis can cause vomiting, pain and constipation *Osteosarcoma and Ewing's Sarcoma* Bone pain • swelling • a palpable mass

How Cancer Is Diagnosed

As with symptoms, the tests used to detect cancer vary according to the suspected type of tumor. However, a diagnostic workup usually consists of a physical examination followed by several procedures from one or more of the categories below:

• **Laboratory/specimen tests:** to analyze blood and other bodily fluids for the presence of malignant cells or *tumor markers*. These are substances produced by the cancer itself or the body in response to the tumor.
Examples: complete blood count (CBC); lumbar puncture (spinal tap).

• **Imaging studies:** to view internal organs for signs of a tumor.
Examples: X rays; computed tomography (CT scan); magnetic resonance imaging (MRI scan); radionuclide scans; ultrasound.

• **Endoscopic exams:** to examine internal organs directly through a flexible lighted *endoscope,* which the doctor inserts through an opening such as the nose, mouth, vagina, urethra or anus.
Examples: gastroscopy of the stomach; colonoscopy of a lower bowel.

• **Biopsy:** The only way to conclusively diagnose cancer is for the physician to biopsy a specimen of tissue from the questionable area. This is obtained using either a needle or a surgical knife. A medical specialist called a *pathologist* then studies the sample under the microscope, looking for the telltale signs of cancer. In addition to identifying whether a mass is benign or malignant, the biopsy reveals other essential information that may influence the proposed treatment plan.
An *incisional biopsy* cuts out a small portion of tumor. If the pathology report comes back positive for cancer, a second surgery may be scheduled. In an *excisional biopsy,* the surgeon removes the entire growth and a rim of normal tissue on all sides. This is called a *margin.* Depending on the type and stage of cancer, no further therapy may be necessary. However, most often the patient will require additional treatment with anticancer medicine (chemotherapy) and/or radiation therapy.

How Childhood Cancer Is Treated

The incidence of cancer in the United States is second only to that of heart disease. Yet when you consider that there are more than one hundred different forms of cancer, you begin to appreciate how rare the majority of them are,

TABLE 20.3

Tests Used to Diagnose Pediatric Cancers

TYPE OF CANCER	DIAGNOSTIC AND STAGING PROCEDURES MAY INCLUDE:
Acute Leukemias	Physical examination • complete blood count (CBC) • bone-marrow biopsy • lumbar puncture (spinal tap) • tumor-cell chromosome analysis • liver-function and kidney-function blood tests • imaging studies such as X rays, radionuclide bone scan, ultrasonography, computed tomography (CT scan) and/or magnetic resonance imaging (MRI scan)
Hodgkin's Disease and Non-Hodgkin's Lymphoma	Physical examination • imaging studies such as X rays, computed tomography (CT scan) and/or magnetic resonance imaging (MRI scan) • lymph-node biopsy • bone-marrow biopsy
Brain Cancers	Physical examination • neurological exam • lumbar puncture (spinal tap) • electroencephalogram (EEG) • imaging studies such as magnetic resonance imaging (MRI scan), computed tomography (CT scan), positron emission tomography (PET scan), angiography • brain tumor biopsy
Sarcomas of the Soft Tissues and Bones	*Rhabdomyosarcoma* Physical examination • soft-tissue imaging, tumor biopsy *Osteosarcoma* Physical examination • imaging studies such as X rays, computed tomography (CT scan), magnetic resonance imaging (MRI scan) and/or radionuclide bone scan • bone biopsy *Ewing's Sarcoma* Physical examination • imaging studies such as X rays, computed tomography (CT scan), magnetic resonance imaging (MRI scan) and/or radionuclide bone scan • bone biopsy • complete blood count (CBC)

pediatric cancers in particular. Childhood leukemia, the most common form, strikes a mere two thousand two hundred youngsters a year. Consequently, a general adult oncologist may go for years without seeing a case of cancer in an adolescent. Although research in cancer therapy hasn't produced any major breakthroughs since the early 1980s, enough small victories have been won that the overall cancer survival rate has crept from 51 percent of patients in 1982 to 60 percent in 1994. Unless a cancer specialist treats a particular cancer regularly, he may not be aware of the latest treatment guidelines. A lengthy 1999 report from the National Cancer Policy Board concluded that a "substantial" number of cancer patients "do not receive care known to be effective for their condition."

THE BENEFITS OF A PEDIATRIC CANCER PROGRAM

Both the American Academy of Pediatrics and the National Cancer Institute recommend that children and adolescents receive diagnosis, staging and treatment at one of the more than two hundred medical centers that specialize in pediatric cancers. According to several studies, young patients' survival rates are *20 to 40 percent higher* when their care is coordinated by pediatric oncologists and is carried out at comprehensive, multidisciplinary cancer centers.

The term *multidisciplinary* means that although your teenager will have one or possibly two attending physicians orchestrating her care, her case will be reviewed by specialists in various treatment disciplines. In this comprehensive approach, the health-care team might consist of a *pediatric surgeon;* a *pediatric oncologist,* or chemotherapist; a *radiation oncologist;* a *pathologist;* and other specialists as needed.

Increasingly, cancer therapy incorporates several modalities, in an effort to improve not only the cure rates but patients' quality of life. It is now routine to follow many surgeries with chemotherapy or radiation therapy—sometimes both—to treat any remaining tumor cells (whether visible or not) and seek to prevent a future return of the disease, or *relapse.* Another trend in cancer medicine is to administer these treatments preoperatively; perhaps to whittle a previously inoperable tumor to a surgically resectable size or to spare a patient from having to undergo an amputation or other mutilating surgery. With so many variables in terms of sequencing treatment, it is essential that all the specialists be assembled at the time of diagnosis. This occurs in a multidisciplinary cancer center. A team of specialists reaches a consensus on what it believes is the most appropriate course of treatment, or *protocol,* for your child.

What Are Clinical Trials?

For all the progress made in cancer treatment, there is still a long way to go. It is through conducting *clinical trials* that new drugs, improved methods of de-

How to Find a Pediatric Cancer Center of Excellence

The **National Cancer Institute's Cancer Information Service** and the National Childhood Cancer Foundation (NCCF) can refer you to the more than two hundred children's cancer centers that belong to the Children's Oncology Group (COG—this is a merger of various former pediatric cancer groups, such as the Children's Cancer Group, Pediatric Oncology Group and others). In order to participate in this network, funded by the NCCF, an institution must meet strict standards of excellence for childhood cancer care. For information, call 800-422-6237 (4-CANCER).

The *National Childhood Cancer Foundation (NCCF) funds pediatric-cancer research by the Children's Oncology Group. For a list of COG institutions, call 800-458-6223 or 626-447-1674.*

livering radiation, and multimodality protocols find their way into practice. About seven in ten children who are treated at pediatric cancer centers participate in investigational studies. They receive treatments that earlier studies have found to be effective and that researchers believe will prove superior to existing therapies. These are usually modifications of standard treatments, so there is little risk of receiving inferior therapy. In what's called a phase 2 clinical trial, the new treatment is given to a large group of similarly diagnosed patients (the study group), while another large group with the same disease (the control group) receives the current standard treatment. The National Cancer Institute is involved with these drugs at all levels of development, before approval is given.

One other consideration when deciding on a treatment center: As parents of a child with a potentially life-threatening illness, you're seeking not only medical expertise but experience in treating young cancer patients. Dr. Gerald Gilchrist, a pediatric hematologist-oncologist at the Mayo Clinic Comprehensive Cancer Center in Rochester, Minnesota, observes, "With teenagers, the emotional and developmental issues that come up in the course of a catastrophic disease are very different from the issues adults often face. The average internist or oncologist is not trained to deal with these issues and may not be *comfortable* dealing with them."

At a multidisciplinary pediatric cancer center, it is understood that quality cancer care encompasses the whole patient; maintaining his sense of well-being as well as his physical health. The medical team routinely includes an *oncology social worker* sensitive to the concerns and anxieties of adolescents diagnosed with cancer. (See chapter 21, "When a Teenager Has a Chronic Illness or Disability.")

TYPES OF CANCER THERAPIES

• **Surgery:** The objective of surgery is to completely remove the cancer and a margin of tumor-free tissue; or, if the tumor cannot be totally removed or a clear margin achieved, to eliminate as much of it as possible, so that subsequent measures such as chemotherapy and/or radiation therapy might be more effective.

• **Radiation therapy:** External-beam radiation therapy destroys tumor cells using a narrow beam of high-energy X rays from a special machine.

• **Chemotherapy:** The word *chemotherapy* literally means "drug therapy," but it has become synonymous with cancer treatment. Surgery and radiation therapy treat cancer locally; chemotherapy is usually a systemic therapy. Ingested orally or injected, the chemicals hunt down vagrant tumor cells anywhere in the body and stop them from proliferating. Your youngster may be prescribed a single medication, but more likely she'll receive *combination chemotherapy* of two, three, perhaps more drugs. One regimen used for advanced lymphoblastic lymphoma consists of no fewer than ten drugs.

Anticancer agents owe their effectiveness to the fact that they zero in on rapidly dividing cells. While malignant cells sustain the most damage, normal cells in the lining of the digestive tract, the white blood cells and the hair also happen to be highly active, and they too incur the wrath of the chemo agents. Consequently, symptoms such as nausea, lowered resistance against infection, mouth sores, diarrhea and hair loss may accompany treatments. Radiation also targets rapidly dividing cells, but the adverse effects tend to be confined to the treatment area, or *field*.

If defined loosely, chemotherapy can be said to include *hormonal* drugs and *immunologic* agents. This latter group, long regarded in some quarters as the future of cancer treatment, has been slow in fulfilling its promise. The principle behind *immunotherapy* is to beef up the body's immune system against the intruders, or to direct antibodies (with or without a drug attached) to the surface of cancer cells. For the time being, immunologics have yet to assume their place as front-line treatments.

- **Bone-marrow transplantation (BMT):** Bone-marrow transplantation has two roles in cancer treatment. In leukemia, it may be curative therapy, replacing the diseased marrow with new marrow withdrawn from the hip bone of a family member or a matched unrelated donor, then infused into the patient's bloodstream.

In other pediatric cancers, BMT makes it possible for youngsters to receive higher-than-normal doses of chemotherapy and/or radiation therapy. The increased amounts of drugs wipe out more cancer cells but also destroy the bone marrow, which then must be replenished with healthy marrow cells—often the patient's own. You may hear this procedure referred to as *high-dose chemotherapy with stem-cell support. Stem cells* are the undeveloped cells in the marrow that mature into blood cells. They are also found, in lesser numbers, in the bloodstream. Half the transplants performed in the United States now use *peripheral-blood stem cells (PBSCs)* in place of bone marrow.

There are two main types of bone-marrow transplants: *allogeneic* and *autologous.* In an allogeneic transplant, the stem cells are harvested from another person with genetically compatible cells. A perfect match improves the chances that the body will accept the transplanted marrow, or *graft,* and that the graft will take to its new home. The most-likely matched donor is a brother or sister, followed by a parent. However, two in three BMT candidates do not have an immediate family member with matching cells. In that event, the patient's doctor might arrange for him to be registered with the National Marrow Donor Program, which attempts to match patients with volunteer donors from its ever-expanding data base.

In autologous stem-cell transplantation, the patient's own marrow is aspirated through a needle during a period of remission, frozen, then given back to him later. (If the person never enters remission, the marrow can be treated with chemotherapy in the laboratory until it tests negative for cancer cells.) This technique, which has been used in relapsed Hodgkin's disease and non-Hodgkin's lymphomas, and experimentally for several other resistant pediatric cancers, is less dangerous and less costly. It is now the front-line treatment for neuroblastoma. Since the patient is receiving his own stem cells, there is no chance of the body rejecting the graft and

---

Words Worth Knowing

Oncologist: a physician who specializes in diagnosing and treating cancer. A *pediatric oncologist* cares for children with cancer.

Refractory: refers to a cancer that does not respond to treatment.

Remission: the absence of an identifiable tumor. As a general rule, the longer the disease stays in remission, the less likely it is to recur.

TABLE 20.4

Treatment Options for Childhood Cancers

TYPE OF CANCER	TREATMENT OPTIONS MAY INCLUDE ONE OR MORE OF THE FOLLOWING:
Leukemia	• Combination chemotherapy • CNS prophylaxis: injecting chemotherapy into the cerebrospinal fluid (intrathecally) as a preventive measure against the leukemia spreading to the central nervous system • Radiation therapy to the head in selected cases • Allogeneic bone-marrow transplantation in first or second remission, depending on the type of leukemia • Investigational therapies
Hodgkin's Disease	• Chemotherapy • Radiation therapy • Investigational therapies
Non-Hodgkin's Lymphomas	• Chemotherapy • CNS prophylaxis: injecting chemotherapy into the cerebrospinal fluid (intrathecally) as a preventive measure against the lymphoma spreading to the central nervous system • Radiation therapy to the chest is sometimes given to shrink a lymphoblastic lymphoma that is obstructing breathing or circulation • Allogeneic bone-marrow transplantation (after relapse) • High-dose chemotherapy followed by autologous bone-marrow transplantation (usually after relapse) • Investigational therapies
Brain Tumors	• Surgery to remove the tumor from the brain • Radiation therapy to the brain (and to the spine, if the cancer is disseminated) • Chemotherapy • Investigational therapies
Rhabdomyo-sarcoma	• Surgery to remove the tumor • Chemotherapy • Radiation therapy

TYPE OF CANCER	TREATMENT OPTIONS MAY INCLUDE ONE OR MORE OF THE FOLLOWING:
	• High-dose chemotherapy followed by autologous bone-marrow transplantation (usually after relapse) • Investigational therapies
Osteosarcoma	• Preoperative chemotherapy • Limb-salvage surgery, to preserve the limb, or amputation • Chemotherapy • Surgery to remove any metastatic tumors that remain following chemotherapy • Investigational therapies
Ewing's Sarcoma	• Preoperative chemotherapy • Surgery to remove the tumor • Radiation therapy (if the tumor is not completely resected) • Surgery, to remove metastases to the lungs • High-dose chemotherapy followed by autologous bone-marrow transplantation (after relapse) • Investigational therapies

avoids the chance that the graft will mistake its old haunt for a foreign invader and go on the attack. *Graft-versus-host disease* (GVHD), as this is called, is a common and potentially serious side effect of allogeneic BMT and is a particularly severe problem when unrelated donors are used.

SIDE EFFECTS OF CANCER TREATMENT

If your teenager should require chemotherapy, radiation therapy and/or bone-marrow transplantation, and so on, her oncologist will undoubtedly discuss with you the possible side effects that may occur during treatment. While it is important to be aware of the possibilities, don't jump to conclusions that your teenager is going to be racked with nausea and diarrhea and lose all of her hair. There is no way to predict how a patient's body will respond to the drugs or the radioactive rays. Some youngsters sail through their treatments, barely missing a day of school.

It is hoped that will be your son's or daughter's story too. But it's wise to be aware of potential problems. One of the first questions to ask the doctor in the wake of a cancer diagnosis is, "What steps can be taken to relieve any symptoms and side effects?" You and your teenager will probably be heartened by his answer, for some of the most striking progress in cancer care has come in the area of symptom management. For instance, we now have such effective antinausea drugs that many chemotherapy patients never spend a day feeling sick to their stomachs. The key to success is to have the doctor prescribe them *prophylactically*, to be taken just prior to treatments. This is a point to take up with the pediatric oncologist.

CARDIAC CONDITIONS

Teenagers frequently experience chest pain. Rarely, though, is the symptom related to the heart. Nevertheless, such complaints should be brought to the attention of your pediatrician, who will diagnose the problem through process of elimination.

"Usually, just asking the patient questions points us to the source of the pain," says Dr. Reginald L. Washington, a pediatric cardiologist from Denver. Among the red flags he looks for are chest pain upon physical exertion and chest pain accompanied by dizziness. "Those situations would warrant further evaluation," he says, "but most of the time the cause turns out to be anxiety, too much caffeine, asthma, muscle strain or *costochondritis*." The latter condition, an inflammation of the chest wall, is treated with rest, over-the-counter anti-inflammatory medications and heat.

High Blood Pressure (Hypertension) and High Blood Cholesterol (Hypercholesteremia)

Doctors once believed that virtually all high blood pressure in youngsters was a complication of another medical condition, such as kidney disease. We now know that even infants can develop *primary hypertension*, also referred to as *essential hypertension*. Abnormally elevated levels of the fatlike substance *cholesterol* in the circulation are also sometimes seen in teenagers. Either problem can pave the way for a future heart attack, cerebral stroke, renal failure, or blindness, among other conditions.

SYMPTOMS THAT SUGGEST PRIMARY HYPERTENSION OR HYPERCHOLESTEREMIA INCLUDE:

- Dizziness and/or headache from high blood pressure
- High cholesterol does not cause symptoms in teenagers

HOW HYPERTENSION AND HYPERCHOLESTEREMIA ARE DIAGNOSED

Diagnostic measures include physical examination and thorough medical history, plus one or more of the following procedures: (1) multiple blood-pressure readings (2) cholesterol blood test.

In teenagers, an abnormally high blood-pressure measurement calls for a second reading, then several additional readings over the course of other office visits before a definitive diagnosis is made. The first number represents the *systolic* pressure: the peak pressure within the blood vessels when the heart contracts. The second number expresses the *diastolic* blood pressure reached when the heart relaxes between beats. If the blood pressure remains elevated, more extensive laboratory tests would be ordered, along with an electrocardiogram (EKG).

Memo to Mom and Dad: Stress can contribute to hypertension. As parents of a teenager, have you had *your* blood pressure taken lately?

Too Much of a Bad Thing

A cholesterol level of 200 mm/100 ml (milligrams per 100 milliliters of blood) or a blood-pressure reading over 130/90 to 140/90 Hg/mm (millimeters of mercury) places a young person in the danger zone.

HOW HYPERTENSION AND HYPERCHOLESTEREMIA ARE TREATED

• **Improved diet and exercise:** Both hypertension and *hypercholesteremia* are uncommon among teenagers. Often, studying the family tree reveals a genetic thread entwined throughout its branches. About half of all youngsters diagnosed with hypertension and two-thirds of those with high cholesterol have a hereditary predisposition to the disorder.

"The rest of the cases are due to poor dietary practices and a lack of physical activity," says Dr. Washington. "In general, those are the easiest to treat. If they learn to eat healthily and engage in aerobic exercise, almost all of them can get their blood pressure and cholesterol down into a normal range." Even if your youngster's blood pressure and cholesterol level are normal, we advise following the sensible eating plan outlined in chapter 17, "Good Nutrition During the Teen Years." Getting into the habit of choosing foods that are low in saturated fat, cholesterol and salt may help prevent cardiovascular disease later in life.

• **Drug therapy:** Adolescents who fall into the high-risk categories for hypertension or hypercholesteremia may require medication in addition to modifying their diet and lifestyle. Agents typically used to bring down the concentration of cholesterol in the blood include cholestyramine, clofibrate and statins.

To lower blood pressure, a pediatrician might prescribe a *diuretic* in combination with an agent from one of four families: *beta-blockers, angiotensin-converting-enzyme inhibitors* or *ACE* inhibitors; *calcium-channel blockers;* and *alpha-beta blockers.* Diuretics, also known as "water pills," act on the kidneys to flush excess water and sodium (salt) from the body. The other medications reduce blood pressure through various mechanisms.

HELPING TEENAGERS TO HELP THEMSELVES

Youngsters with or without hypertension or hypercholesteremia should be encouraged to:

- Maintain a healthy weight.

- Engage in aerobic exercise for at least thirty minutes per day.

- Abstain from using tobacco or alcohol.

- Learn techniques for relieving stress, be it exercise, deep breathing or meditation.

- Consult the pediatrician if considering taking birth-control pills. Although neither condition is common in healthy teens, oral contraceptives can worsen both high blood pressure and high blood cholesterol.

Mitral Valve Prolapse (*MVP*)

Four flaplike valves regulate the flow of blood through the heart's four chambers. The *mitral valve* is situated in the left side of the heart, the side that receives freshly oxygenated blood from the lung, then pumps it out to the circulation. Under normal circumstances, the valve opens to let blood pass from the upper left chamber (the *left atrium*) into the lower left chamber (the *left ventricle*).

Approximately one in eight otherwise healthy adolescents and young adults are found to have *mitral valve prolapse.* For reasons that remain unclear, one or both flippers billows out (*prolapses*) into the upper chamber instead of snapping shut. This can produce a clicking sound, audible through the pediatrician's stethoscope. Occasionally, blood may leak backward into the atrium, causing a murmur (see box below). "The sounds usually come and go," says Dr. Washington. Some youngsters with mitral valve prolapse have both a click *and* a murmur, while others have no abnormal heart noises at all.

SYMPTOMS THAT SUGGEST MITRAL VALVE PROLAPSE MAY INCLUDE:

- Abnormal heart murmur
- Fluttering sensation in the chest, as if the heart were racing or skipping a beat
- Shortness of breath
- Headache
- Sharp, fleeting chest pain

Nineteen out of twenty people with mitral valve prolapse do not exhibit any symptoms; the condition is discovered during a routine physical.

Heart Murmur: Language of the Heart

"A heart murmur," explains Dr. Washington, "is merely the sound of the heart vibrating slightly or valves opening and closing as blood flows through it. There are probably fifty different types, each with its own distinctive sound. Most of them," he emphasizes, "are perfectly normal." As many as four in five young people have these "innocent" murmurs now and then. Unless the murmur occurs during a doctor's visit, it generally goes undetected.

An abnormal murmur, which a pediatrician can identify with a stethoscope, indicates a heart condition that may require further diagnostic testing, possibly by a pediatric cardiologist. Possible causes include infections of the heart (*endocarditis, myocarditis*), faulty valves and cardiac defects that had been present since birth.

Normal heart murmurs don't call for limits on activities. With abnormal murmurs, says Dr. Washington, "the underlying cause will determine whether restrictions are necessary."

HOW MITRAL VALVE PROLAPSE IS DIAGNOSED

Physical examination and thorough medical history, plus one or more of the following procedures: (1) Stethoscopic exam (2) echocardiogram (3) chest X ray

HOW MITRAL VALVE PROLAPSE IS TREATED

"The vast majority of people with mitral valve prolapse can go about their lives without having to worry about the condition or restrict athletic activities," explains Dr. Washington. Under certain circumstances, however, a leaky mitral valve can become infected. To reduce the risk of *endocarditis,* rare though it may be, the current recommendation is for antibiotics to be taken just prior to dental appointments and surgical procedures.

HELPING TEENAGERS TO HELP THEMSELVES

Reducing caffeine consumption can help alleviate heart palpitations. Remember that caffeine is present not only in coffee but in soda, chocolate and tea.

DENTAL HEALTH

Twin studies conducted by the Centers for Disease Control and Prevention show that the average U.S. adolescent of the 1970s had six or seven cavities; his 1990s counterpart, just three. Today's teenagers are twice as likely to return from the dentist and report, "Look, Ma, no cavities!"—to quote a famous toothpaste commercial of yesteryear.

Dr. Jim Steiner, director of pediatric dentistry at Children's Hospital in Cincinnati, Ohio, attributes the improvement in young people's dental health primarily to increased access to fluoridation. "Fluoride reduces tooth decay as well as slows down the decaying process," he explains. "More than 95 percent of all toothpastes now have fluoride in them, and about 65 percent of our population drinks fluoridated water."

A related advance is the use of *dental sealants,* clear or white thin plastic coatings that can be painted onto permanent teeth. As Dr. Steiner explains, "Fluoride protects the areas between the teeth. But it can't always reach the chewing surfaces of the back molars." Sealants fill the tiny pits and grooves of those teeth, the site of most cavities. *Second molars* typically arrive around age twelve. One sealant application costs roughly half the price of a filling.

Teens who do develop cavities have less reason to dread the dentist's chair than you might have when you were their age. New dental instruments such as the *laser* and the *air abrasion unit* make getting fillings virtually painless. Laser therapy doesn't require anesthesia. Nor do many treatments with the air abrasion handpiece, which resembles a tiny sandblaster. However, the devices can't be used in all situations, so don't expect to see the high-speed drill become obsolete anytime soon.

Another advance of interest to young patients is cosmetic. Beside the traditional silver-colored metal alloy used to fill cavities, a composite material can be used so that the color can be tinted to match the teeth.

Orthodontic Problems

Crooked teeth, overbites and underbites are best corrected with braces during puberty, while the facial bones are still growing. These are usually inherited traits, although some orthodontic problems stem from injuries, years of thumb-sucking or losing one's baby teeth earlier or later than normal.

HOW ORTHODONTIC PROBLEMS ARE DIAGNOSED

- Oral examination and thorough medical/dental history
- X rays of mouth and head
- Photos of face and teeth
- Plaster models of the teeth are made

HOW ORTHODONTIC PROBLEMS ARE TREATED

If you were a "metal mouth" as a teenager, you'll immediately notice that modern dental appliances are less conspicuous than the braces you wore. "Years ago," says Dr. Steiner, "the silver bands that hold the wires had to be placed around all the teeth. That's no longer done. Nowadays we might band only the first and second molars, and bond brackets directly to the rest of the teeth." The brackets can be colored to match the teeth. They also come in a clear material, as well as metal. Some patients may be candidates for "invisible braces," which are worn on the inside of the teeth.

On average, youngsters can expect to wear the appliances for about two years. During that time, they return to the orthodontist on a monthly basis. The doctor will usually tighten the wires at these appointments, in order to increase the tension on the teeth. Any discomfort or soreness afterward can usually be alleviated with an over-the-counter pain reliever.

When braces alone aren't sufficient to straighten the teeth, a child may have to wear a *night brace* to bed, to apply pressure externally. Two prongs on the headgear are inserted into a pair of cylinder-shaped metal receptacles constructed on the outer surface of the back molars. Then an elastic band wraps around the back of the head to keep the apparatus in place. Understandably, teens usually aren't too happy about having to put on the night brace, but parents can reassure them that this is a temporary measure.

After the orthodontist removes the braces, the young person is given a removable *retainer* to wear for the next six to twelve months in order to maintain the alignment of the teeth. The simple device consists of a metal wire attached to a plastic plate that has been conformed to fit against the roof of the mouth.

You and the orthodontist will want to impress upon your youngster the importance of wearing the retainer as instructed. "I usually explain that the supporting structures around the teeth have an elastic memory," says Dr. Steiner. "If the teeth aren't given time to 'settle in,' they may revert to their previous positions. That reaches some kids, while others don't seem to care." Moms and dads who've invested several thousand dollars in their teen's smile usually care *plenty* and have no compunctions about seeing to it that the retainer is used properly.

DENTAL HYGIENE WHILE WEARING BRACES

Braces are virtual traps for food and plaque. "If kids don't brush carefully," says Dr. Steiner, "the plaque builds up around the appliances. Then when the brackets are popped off, they're left with white circles on their perfectly straight teeth." The stains, which indicate demineralized areas, can be permanent. Cavities form around the brackets too.

"The problem," he continues, "is that it's hard to brush your teeth well when you have braces, because the bristles are always getting caught in the hardware." To help compensate, he advises his young patients to use both a fluoride toothpaste and a fluoride rinse. Oral-irrigation devices, when used in conjunction with brushing, "do a very good job of keeping teeth clean."

Impacted Wisdom Teeth

Boys and girls typically have their full complement of twenty-eight teeth by their early teens. Sometime between ages fifteen to twenty-five, the *third molars* begin to erupt at the rear of the mouth; two on top and two on the bottom. You probably know them as *wisdom teeth.* Their name refers to the time of life when they appear: the "age of wisdom."

Most of the time, the four new teeth become trapped, or *impacted,* in the jawbone and gum. They either emerge partially and grow in crooked or never surface at all. Evolution is to blame. Prehistoric teenagers "did a lot more chewing," explains Dr. Steiner. "They needed those teeth to grind and tear apart raw meat and other uncooked foods."

Their faces were also much longer than ours, from front to back. It is theorized that as humans learned to cook food and invented cutting tools, their jaws became progressively smaller. Modern man's mouths simply aren't large enough to accommodate third molars. Left untreated, impacted wisdom teeth can damage neighboring teeth, nerves and the jawbone.

SYMPTOMS THAT MAY SUGGEST IMPACTION INCLUDE:

- Swelling
- Infection
- Pain
- Difficulty opening the mouth wide

HOW IMPACTION IS DIAGNOSED

- Oral examination
- X rays of mouth and head

HOW IMPACTION IS TREATED

- **Oral surgery:** Third molars pose no problems if they grow in properly. However, nine in ten people have at least one wisdom tooth that remains embedded in the gum. As a general rule, all four teeth are removed by a dentist or an *oral and maxillofacial surgeon*—a specialist in diagnosing and treating medical conditions of the mouth and jaw.

The surgical procedure, performed on an outpatient basis at the doctor's office or a hospital, is performed using what's called *conscious sedation.* Patients are administered both an anesthetic and a mild, short-acting sedative through an intravenous tube inserted in the arm.

Once the patient is asleep, the doctor makes an incision into the gum and carefully cuts away any overlying bone. Then the impacted tooth is extracted whole or in sections. The tissue is sutured closed, and the patient can be taken home. Expect your youngster to feel groggy for several hours. The tips below will help you to ease discomfort and promote healing:

• Swelling typically persists for several days. Place an ice pack on the affected cheek(s) every other thirty minutes.

• Bleeding, too, is a common postoperative side effect. To stanch the bleeding, take a piece of clean gauze and gently apply pressure to the surgical site.

• Serve soft foods and soups, and encourage your teen to drink plenty of fluids.

• Brush teeth the day following surgery, but *carefully.*

• Complications, while rare, can occur. Alert your physician or oral surgeon at once should your child experience fever, swelling, and pain—evidence of a possible infection—or excessive bleeding.

TIMING IS EVERYTHING

Impacted wisdom teeth should be extracted immediately if they are causing pain, swelling or infection. For youngsters who are asymptomatic, it's preferable to schedule the surgery during adolescence, as younger patients heal faster and suffer fewer complications. In one study of nine thousand five hundred patients aged twelve to eighty-three, the rate of complications was four times higher among those aged twenty-four and older. "I usually encourage patients to get them removed before they go to college," says Dr. Steiner.

HELPING TEENAGERS TO HELP THEMSELVES

Youngsters should be encouraged to:

• see their dentist twice a year.

• brush regularly to reduce the buildup of *plaque:* a colorless substance consisting of food particles, acids and bacteria, and the cause of tooth decay. Teens should clean their teeth thoroughly for at least two minutes each time. The American Dental Association recommends changing toothbrushes every three to four months.

• use a toothpaste that contains fluoride.

• floss at least once a day, especially after eating popcorn, potato chips and other foods that embed themselves between teeth. Flossing cleans areas a toothbrush can't easily reach and prevents plaque from infecting the gums. *Gingivitis,* as this is called, "is common in adolescents," says Dr. Steiner. "If it's not brought under control, by middle age gingivitis can give way to *periodontitis,* an infection of the bone that supports the teeth. The teeth start to loosen and are often beyond saving, all because of poor oral hygiene."

• forgo sugary foods. The bacteria in plaque convert sugar to acid, which eats away tooth enamel. Caramels, taffy and other sticky, gooey treats that cling to teeth should especially be avoided.

• drink less soda, which exposes the teeth to sugar, sugar and more sugar. Teenagers' consumption of soft drinks has more than doubled since the 1970s. Boys, who guzzle four times as much as girls, ingest *fifteen* teaspoons of sugar a day, on average, from soda pop alone.

• confine eating and drinking to five times per day—breakfast, snack, lunch, snack and dinner. Drink only water between meals. This strategy reduces the amount of acid produced by oral bacteria.

DIGESTIVE DISORDERS

A pediatrician trying to solve a case of chronic abdominal pain has many potential culprits to pursue. "The conditions that usually come to mind are gastritis, irritable bowel syndrome and inflammatory bowel disease," says Dr. Alan Lake, a pediatrician and pediatric gastroenterologist at Baltimore's Johns Hopkins University School of Medicine. But conditions such as anxiety disorder, endometriosis, pelvic inflammatory disease and other gynecologic concerns may also be the cause of a significant percent of chronic abdominal pain.

Irritable Bowel Syndrome (*IBS*) and Inflammatory Bowel Disease (*IBD; Crohn's Disease and Ulcerative Colitis*)

Irritable bowel syndrome (IBS) is often referred to inaccurately as "colitis" and "mucous colitis." But the suffix "*itis*" in a medical condition's name denotes inflammation, which is not a hallmark of IBS. Rather than inflaming the colon, IBS sensitizes the nerves responsible for the contractions (called *peristalsis*) that propel partially digested food through the organ. As a result, the muscular inner wall overreacts to mild stimuli like milk products and emotional stress, and goes into spasm. Irritable bowel syndrome produces cramplike pains and bouts of diarrhea and/or constipation.

The more serious disorders, Crohn's disease and ulcerative colitis, are both forms of *inflammatory bowel disease.* IBD damages the tissue of the small bowel and the large bowel, respectively, through the process of inflammation. As the body's response to injury, inflammation is characterized by blood-carrying, infection-fighting white blood cells that rush to the site of the injury. Their presence accounts for the painful swelling, warmth and redness associated with an inflammatory reaction.

Among teenagers, Crohn's is two times more prevalent than ulcerative colitis. Whereas ulcerative colitis affects only the inner lining of the intestine and is confined to one section, "Crohn's disease can penetrate the full thickness of the bowel and tends to occur in more than one area," explains Dr. Lake. In colitis, however, *ulcers* form where inflammation has destroyed the tissue. The open sores ooze blood, mucus and pus.

The cause of inflammatory bowel disease has yet to be discovered, although theories abound. Heredity is a factor: 15 to 30 percent of IBD sufferers have a relative with either disorder.

SYMPTOMS THAT SUGGEST IRRITABLE BOWEL SYNDROME MAY INCLUDE:

- Cramplike pain and spasms in the lower abdomen
- Nausea
- Bloating and gas
- Headache
- Rectal pain
- Backache
- Appetite loss
- Alternating bouts of diarrhea and constipation
- Fatigue
- Depression
- Anxiety
- Difficulty concentrating

SYMPTOMS THAT SUGGEST INFLAMMATORY BOWEL DISEASE MAY INCLUDE:

CROHN'S DISEASE

- Cramping abdominal pain and tenderness, particularly after meals
- Nausea

- Diarrhea
- General ill feeling
- Fever
- Appetite loss possibly leading to weight loss
- Bloody stool
- Swelling, pain, stiffness in the knees and ankles
- Cankerlike sores in the mouth
- Eye inflammation
- Irritation or swelling around the rectum
- Fatigue
- Depression
- Anxiety
- Difficulty concentrating
- Delayed growth and sexual development in younger teens, due to lack of nutrition

ULCERATIVE COLITIS

- Pain and cramping in the left side of the abdomen
- Intermittent episodes of bloody, mucuslike stool
- Swelling, pain, stiffness in the knees and ankles
- Cankerlike sores in the mouth
- Fatigue
- Depression
- Anxiety
- Difficulty concentrating
- Growth retardation in younger teens, due to lack of nutrition

Acute attacks may include:
- Up to twenty bloody, loose bowel movements a day
- Urgent need to move bowels
- Severe cramps and rectal pain
- Profuse sweating
- Dehydration
- Nausea
- Appetite loss
- Weight loss
- Abdominal bloating
- Fever up to 104 degrees F

You can see that many of the symptoms overlap, making diagnosis complicated at times. In general, says Dr. Lake, "the patient with ulcerative colitis has more bloody bowel movements, and the patient with Crohn's disease experiences more pain." He goes on to say that while ulcerative colitis is usually picked up quickly, "with Crohn's disease, many months can pass between the onset of symptoms and the time of diagnosis. Not only are the symptoms subtle, but they can be minimized by cutting back on eating. So it can be difficult for parents to recognize that something is the matter.

"Frequently, kids are diagnosed because they develop inflammation elsewhere, like the eyes, the mouth and the rectum. If your child has irritation or swelling around the rectum," he advises, "never assume that it is hemorrhoids, which is all but unheard of in teenagers. The concern should be that he or she has Crohn's disease."

HOW IRRITABLE BOWEL SYNDROME IS DIAGNOSED:

Physical examination and thorough medical history, plus one or more of the following procedures:

- Urinalysis
- Urine culture
- Complete blood count
- Erythrocyte sedimentation rate (sed rate) blood test
- Stool blood test
- Sigmoidoscopy

HOW INFLAMMATORY BOWEL DISEASE IS DIAGNOSED:

Physical examination and thorough medical history, plus one or more of the following procedures:

- Complete blood count
- Prothrombin time blood test
- Erythrocyte sedimentation rate (sed rate) blood test
- Stool blood test
- Urinalysis
- Sigmoidoscopy or colonoscopy
- Upper gastrointestinal (GI) series (also known as a barium swallow)

Still other laboratory tests may be ordered.

HOW IRRITABLE BOWEL SYNDROME (IBS) AND INFLAMMATORY BOWEL DISEASE (IBD) ARE TREATED

All of these chronic conditions are incurable but treatable, meaning that steps can be taken on several fronts to reduce the frequency and severity of symptoms.

- **Changes in diet:** Boys and girls with IBS or IBD are able to eat relatively normally when the disease is in remission, which is much of the time. During flareups, though, they need to be conscientious about avoiding certain foods. Your pediatrician will work with a nutritionist or a GI specialist to tailor an eating plan for your youngster.

In irritable bowel syndrome, adding roughage to the diet may be all that's necessary to ease cramping and soften hardened stool or eliminate diarrhea. However, high-fiber foods induce the opposite effect in a teen with Crohn's disease or ulcerative colitis, who should stick to easy-to-digest low-residue items like broth, gelatin, skinless poultry, fish, rice, eggs and pasta. Fried foods and dairy are also taboo when the disease is active.

Memo to Mom and Dad: Help spare your son or daughter some of the unwelcome consequences of IBD by serving five or six small meals a day instead of the customary big three.

- **Drug therapy:** If diet alone doesn't bring relief from an irritable bowel, occasionally a pediatrician will prescribe an *antispasmodic* agent to slow down its activity. Medication is usually indicated in Crohn's disease or ulcerative colitis, where the favored drugs include *corticosteroids* such as prednisone ("the cornerstone of treatment," according to Dr. Lake), and the *5-ASA* agents sulfasalazine, olsalazine and mesalamine. Should these fail to stem the inflammation, your pediatrician might prescribe one of the following *immunomodulators:* azathioprine, cyclosporine, methotrexate or 6-mercaptopurine. They work by altering the body's immune response. An IBD patient's medicine cabinet often contains *antibiotics* and *antidiarrheal* medicines as well.

- **Dietary supplements:** From a teenager's perspective, one of the most upsetting effects of inflammatory bowel disease is its suppression of growth and sexual maturity. Large doses of prednisone can decelerate physical development; accordingly, pediatricians lower the dose or gradually take young people off the drug once it has controlled the inflammation.

The main cause of poor growth, however, is insufficient nutrition. Adolescents with IBD sometimes fall into the habit of skimping on breakfast and lunch in order to avoid repeated trips to the bathroom while at school. As a result, they may be lacking in calories, nutrients, vitamins and minerals. Protein is especially crucial for growth.

Your pediatrician will monitor your child's eating patterns. Most nutritional deficiencies can be corrected by tinkering with the diet. If necessary, though, she can prescribe oral supplements and/or high-calorie liquid formulas.

• **Surgery:** Cases of inflammatory bowel disease that resist drug therapy or develop complications may require an operation to remove part or all of the colon. This route is rarely taken during the teen years.

• **Mental health care:** Emotional stress does not cause IBS or IBD, but it can aggravate either condition. Therefore, patients may benefit a great deal from seeing a mental health professional who can teach them stress-reduction techniques such as progressive muscle relaxation and progressive guided imagery.

As with other chronic ailments, inflammatory bowel disease can be frustrating for teenagers. Flareups often leave them more dependent on their parents than they want to be and make them feel different from their friends. They may feel as though their body has betrayed them. If you suspect that your son or daughter is having a hard time coping, ask your pediatrician for a referral to a suitable counselor.

Peptic Ulcers (Duodenal Ulcers and Gastric Ulcers)

The highly acidic digestive juices in the stomach and bowel can erode the delicate lining of the gastrointestinal tract, causing sores known as *ulcers.* The most common site is the *duodenum:* the portion of the small intestine that receives the soupy mixture of semidigested food from the stomach. Both duodenal ulcers and gastric (stomach) ulcers are referred to as "peptic" ulcers. The name alludes to *pepsin,* the digestive enzyme responsible for breaking down the protein in food.

Doctors used to believe that all ulcers were caused by diet and stress. We now know that a bacterium known as *Helicobacter pylori* is behind many adult ulcers. The percentage of adolescent ulcer patients infected with *H. pylori* may be in the neighborhood of 25 percent. Scientists believe that this common microorganism enters our bodies via food and water, and possibly through kissing. Half of all men and women over sixty carry the bacteria. Why the majority of them never develop peptic ulcer disease is a question still in search of an answer.

SYMPTOMS THAT SUGGEST PEPTIC ULCERS MAY INCLUDE:

• Sharp, burning or gnawing pain in the upper abdomen that lasts anywhere from thirty minutes to three hours and comes and goes
• Appetite loss

- Weight loss
- Weight gain
- Nausea and vomiting
- Blood-tinged vomit
- Bloody stool
- Bloating
- Belching
- Anemia

HOW ULCERS ARE DIAGNOSED

Physical examination and thorough medical history, plus one or more of the following procedures:

- Endoscopic exam of the stomach (*gastroscopy*) or the upper bowel (*esophagogastroduodenoscopy*), including tissue biopsy, to detect *H. pylori* bacteria

To locate the source of gastrointestinal bleeding, the doctor may order one or more of the following:

- Stool blood test
- Complete blood count
- Prothrombin time blood test
- Angiogram
- Sigmoidoscopy or colonoscopy
- Scintigraphic studies
- CAT (CT) scan
- Magnetic resonance imaging (MRI) scan

HOW ULCERS ARE TREATED

- **Drug therapy:** "When I started in gastroenterology in the 1970s," says Dr. Lake, "I was subjecting six to eight teenagers a year to partial removal of their stomachs to treat chronic peptic ulcer disease. But since the mid 1980s, I haven't sent a single patient to surgery. The medication options that are now available have virtually eliminated the need for an operation."

Several types of drugs are typically incorporated into treatment:

- Nonprescription *antacids,* taken intermittently to neutralize excess stomach acid and relieve abdominal pain.

- *H_2 blockers* (cimetidine, rantidine, famotidine), which reduce acid production in the digestive tract.
- *Antibiotics,* if diagnostic tests reveal the presence of *H. pylori.*
- *Acid pump inhibitors* (omeprazole).
- *Mucosal protective agents* (sucralfate, misoprostol).

Youngsters taking H_2 blockers should begin to feel significantly better after several weeks. The medication can then be discontinued. Your teen can also resume eating normally; the bland diet of old has not been found to help treat or prevent ulcers. Should the disease recur—as happens in half to four-fifths of all cases—most pediatricians would recommend staying on the drug for six months to two years.

Appendicitis

Early adolescence is prime time for *appendicitis,* a potentially serious inflammation of the appendix. The small appendage, located on the right side of the lower abdomen, sticks out from the colon like a protruding tongue. Should it become inflamed and need to be surgically removed—the sole treatment for appendicitis—the appendix is hardly missed, for it has no known function.

SYMPTOMS THAT SUGGEST APPENDICITIS MAY INCLUDE:

- Persistent abdominal pain that migrates from the midsection to the right lower abdomen
- Nausea and vomiting
- Constipation
- Gas pain
- Diarrhea
- Low fever, beginning after other symptoms
- Tenderness in the right lower abdomen
- Abdominal swelling
- Elevated white blood cell count
- Appetite loss

"Anybody who's had appendicitis will tell you that pain is unlike any other kind of pain," says Dr. Lake. "In adolescents, it begins as a vague stomachache near the navel. Then patients feel it in the lower part of the right side of the abdomen." He describes the sensation as a peculiar combination of pressure and fullness.

The distinctive symptom should be heeded *very* seriously; should the appendix rupture, it may infect the double-layer *peritoneal* membrane that lines the abdominal cavity. The medical term for this is *peritonitis*. Notify your pediatrician at once or contact a local hospital emergency department. While you wait to see the doctor, instruct your teen to lie down and be still. Any kind of movement, including coughing or taking a deep breath, can exacerbate the pain. Don't offer water, food, laxatives, aspirin or a heating pad.

HOW APPENDICITIS IS DIAGNOSED

Physical examination and thorough medical history, plus one or more of the following procedures:

- White blood cell count
- Urinalysis, to rule out a urinary-tract infection
- Ultrasound
- Lower GI series (*barium enema*)
- CT scan
- Exploratory laparoscopic surgery

HOW APPENDICITIS IS TREATED

- Surgery: Appendicitis can be difficult to diagnose definitely. Therefore, your physician may not schedule the *appendectomy* until the symptoms have progressed somewhat. Conventional "open" surgery usually requires a two-day hospital stay, barring complications, and leaves youngsters with a small scar, but completely cured.

HELPING TEENS TO HELP THEMSELVES

Youngsters should be encouraged to follow these basic guidelines for a healthy digestive tract:

- Eat at regular hours.
- Drink lots of water (at least eight cups of water or other liquid every day).
- Keep physically active.
- Chew food slowly and thoroughly before swallowing.
- Use aspirin and nonsteroidal anti-inflammatory medications sparingly; these drugs can irritate the fragile gastrointestinal lining.
- Don't smoke; cigarettes, too, contribute to ulcers.
- Listen to your body! Don't suppress the urge to move your bowels.
- Try not to strain during bowel movements.

- And most important, even with a busy schedule regular meals should be taken daily. Attempts should be made to have at least some of these meals sitting around a table preferably allowing time to talk, chew and digest. This will not only help your teens' gut, but help the whole family stay connected.

CONDITIONS OF THE EARS, NOSE AND THROAT

The Ears

SWIMMER'S EAR (*EXTERNAL OTITIS*)

Infancy and early childhood are the peak years for middle-ear infections (*otitis media*). Adolescents are more prone to infections of the outer ear (*otitis externa*). They may contract the bacteria or fungus while swimming in polluted lakes and ponds—although frequent dips in chlorinated swimming pools can also lead to external otitis. Teens who don't swim can also develop swimmer's ear by cleaning their ears too roughly.

SYMPTOMS THAT SUGGEST SWIMMER'S EAR MAY INCLUDE:

- Severe ear pain that worsens whenever the ear is touched or tugged
- Itching in the ear canal
- Greenish-yellowish discharge
- Temporary hearing loss in the affected ear, due to the canal's becoming swollen or filled with pus
- Redness around the canal opening

HOW SWIMMER'S EAR IS DIAGNOSED

- A thorough medical history and physical examination, including an ear exam using an *otoscope*
- Laboratory analysis of the ear drainage may also sometimes be of help

HOW SWIMMER'S EAR IS TREATED

- **Drug therapy:** After cleaning the infected ear, your doctor will begin treatment with eardrops. These drops contain medicines that kill certain bacteria and fungus, as well as treat inflammation. The average course of treatment runs approximately one week. Occasionally, the external otitis is severe enough to warrant the additional use of an oral antibiotic. Most cases of swimmer's ear are caused by either of two bacteria: *Pseudomonas aeruginosa* and *Staphylococcus aureus* or a fungal infection called "*Aspergillus.*" Be forewarned that it is not uncommon for the ear pain from external otitis to intensify for a day or two before the drops take effect.

- **Additional therapy:** Teenagers must keep their ears dry and continue taking their medication *for two to three weeks after the symptoms fade.* When showering or washing their hair, they should cover their head with a plastic cap or protect their ear canals with a soft earplug such as a cotton ball covered with vaseline or commercially available ear putty. Placing a warm compress or heating pad against the ear will help reduce pain. Analgesics such as acetaminophen or nonsteroidal anti-inflammatory drugs will also help.

HELPING TEENAGERS HELP THEMSELVES

Adolescents prone to developing swimmer's ear should:

- Stay out of polluted water.
- Clean the ears gently with a cotton swab, never anything hard like a bobby pin, and don't probe too deeply.
- Avoid getting hair spray and other hair products inside the ear canal.
- Use preventive drops, prescribed by the doctor, after swimming. Often a few drops at bedtime will help.

ACOUSTIC TRAUMA/HEARING LOSS

All parents complain at one time or another that their teenagers seem to hardly hear a word they say. An estimated fifteen in one thousand young people under the age of eighteen, however, do in fact have some degree of hearing loss. According to the National Institutes of Health, one-third of those cases can be blamed partly on our environment. Our ears are assaulted by excessive noise day in and day out: the teeth-grinding whir of a neighbor's leaf blower; a temperamental car alarm shrieking in the distance; a jet airliner roaring overhead.

Sound volume is measured in units called *decibels* (*dB*). Sudden or extended exposure to lower sounds (85 dB or more) can potentially cause temporary or permanent hearing loss. This is called *acoustic trauma.* How loud is 85 decibels? Surprisingly, not very loud, about equivalent to the bleating of city traffic as heard from inside your car. The Occupational Safety and Health Administration (OSHA), which regulates hearing safety in the workplace, mandates that employees should not be subjected to more than 90 dB over a period of eight hours, and never more than 115 dB.

Each 5-decibel increase in intensity reduces the safe-exposure time by half, so that the average rock-music performance (110 dB) begins to take its toll on kids' hearing after just half an hour. Teenagers exposed to such high-intensity sound can and do experience transient hearing loss characterized by ear ringing. The effects of such brief duration acoustic trauma usually resolves in several days.

However, years of repeated exposure to hazardous levels of noise may lead to irreversible hearing damage, by destroying the tiny hair cells in the inner ear. With the loss of those cells, a person begins to experience difficulty hearing high-pitched sounds. In addition, the nerve fibers that transmit sound messages to the brain begin to degenerate, as do the corresponding nerves within the central nervous system. Eventually, the lower frequencies, where a good deal of speech is deciphered, become affected too. Although the symptoms of hearing loss may not emerge until later in life, the damage is already underway.

SYMPTOMS THAT SUGGEST HEARING LOSS MAY INCLUDE:

- Loss of hearing sensitivity, first to high-pitched (high-frequency) sounds, then eventually to lower pitches
- Difficulty hearing conversation, especially when other people are talking or there is significant background noise
- Temporary or permanent ringing in the ears
- A sense of fullness in the ears
- Voices and other noises sound muffled and/or distorted

HOW HEARING LOSS IS DIAGNOSED

A thorough medical history and a physical examination, including an ear exam with an otoscope. *Impedance testing,* a hearing assessment for evaluating the functioning of the middle ear, and *pure-tone audiometry,* to test the softest level at which a young patient can hear various frequencies of sound.

HELPING TEENS PREVENT ACOUSTIC TRAUMA

"Turn down that music!!!" Now where have we heard *that* before? It was "sound" advice when imparted by your parents however many years ago and

Huh?! Ranges of What?!

Noises and Decibel Levels

Decibel levels and assorted noises, by category:

Faint
30 dB   Whisper

Moderate
40 dB   Moderate rainfall
50 dB   Quiet room

Very Loud
60 dB   Conversation, dishwasher
70 dB   Busy traffic, vacuum
80 dB   Alarm clock

Extremely Loud
85 dB   City traffic while sitting in a car
90 dB   Lawnmower, train whistle
100 dB   Snowmobile, chain saw
110 dB   Rock music, both recorded and live

Painful
120 dB   Jet plane taking off
125 dB   Nightclub music
130 dB   Jackhammer
140 dB   Air-raid siren

Sources: Food and Drug Administration (FDA), others

remains so today. Recorded music should never be played so loud that other sounds can't be heard above the din. Likewise, when listening to music over headphones, the volume should be kept low enough so that only the young music aficionado can make out the lyrics (*maybe*), not everyone within several yards.

Wear ear protection in situations where hazardously loud noises can't be avoided such as:

- attending a rock concert or car-racing event
- operating a lawnmower, chain saw, or other noisy tool/machinery/appliance
- riding a motorbike, motorcycle or tractor
- performing as part of a music group
- working on a construction site
- discharging a firearm, as when hunting or target-shooting

Simply stuffing cotton in the ears does not block out the sound. Foam-rubber or soft-plastic earplugs and heavy-duty earmuff-type protectors are available at musical instrument dealers, sporting-goods stores, hardware stores and drugstores. Make sure that whatever ear protection product you or your teen buys reduces noise sufficiently to bring it into a safe range, at the very least below 85 dB. Each product's label bears a noise-reduction rating from the U.S. Environmental Protection Agency.

ENDOCRINE DISORDERS

The *endocrine system* consists of *glands* and groups of cells that release substances called *hormones* into the circulation. Each hormone influences the functioning of another gland or organ. This section looks at the two most common endocrine disorders of adolescence: thyroid disease and diabetes.

The *thyroid,* a butterfly-shaped gland that is located just below the voice box, is the largest of the endocrine glands and secretes *thyroxine.* This hormone affects such key functions as heart rate, energy, weight, linear growth, mood, skin condition and, in women, fertility and menstruation. If the concentration of thyroid hormone falls too low, the *hypothalamus* at the base of the brain secretes *Thyrotrophin-releasing hormone* (TRH). In response, the nearby *pituitary gland* releases *thyroid-stimulating hormone* (TSH). As its name implies, TSH prompts the thyroid to produce more hormone until the level stabilizes. Conversely, when the hypothalamus detects excess thyroid hormone in the blood, the pituitary temporarily cuts off its supply of TSH until the level stabilizes.

Diabetes is a disease affecting the *islets of Langerhans,* which reside within the *pancreas* and are among the smallest of the endocrine glands. These tiny, round clusters of *alpha cells* and *beta cells* control the amount of simple sugar (*glucose*) in the blood. When the level rises—say, after a meal—the beta cells discharge *insulin,* a hormone that spurs body tissue to *metabolize,* or burn, the glucose. Meanwhile, excess sugar gets stored primarily in the liver. When the level of blood glucose falls to a certain point, alpha cells emit *glucagon,* which instructs the liver to discharge the glucose into the bloodstream. But in people with diabetes, this regulatory mechanism malfunctions.

Diabetes Mellitus

Prior to a meal, the blood normally contains 80 to 110 milligrams of glucose per 100 milliliters; after eating, 100 to 140 mg/ml. Because persons with diabetes cannot utilize sugar efficiently, it builds up in the circulation. Two generally accepted definitions of diabetes (and of *hyperglycemia,* which means "high blood sugar") are:

1. 200 mg/ml or higher
    or
2. 126 mg/ml or higher after fasting for eight hours

There are two types of diabetes, type 1 and type 2, which were once thought to affect distinctly different populations. Until the 1970s, type 1 was thought to be exclusive to children and adolescents and thus, it was called "juvenile diabetes"; type 2 was referred to as "adult-onset diabetes" because it rarely developed before middle age. Of the sixteen million Americans of all ages now with diabetes, type 2 accounts for nine in ten cases.

Most people with type 2 diabetes still make the hormone—but not in sufficient amounts. In type 1, however, the body's immune system mistakes the beta cells for foreign invaders and destroys them. Accordingly, type 1 is also referred to as *immune-mediated diabetes.* The rise in obesity in the population of all ages has led to an increase in type 2 diabetes, including adolescents, over the past decade.

SYMPTOMS THAT SUGGEST DIABETES MAY INCLUDE:

- Frequent urination
- Excessive thirst and hunger
- Unexplained weight loss
- Dehydration, from increased urination
- Recurrent infections
- Sores and cuts that are slow to heal
- Irritability
- Weakness and fatigue
- Drowsiness

- Blurry vision
- Dry mouth
- Dry, itchy skin
- Tingling or numbness in the feet or hands
- Nausea
- Severe yeast infections in young women

"The three classic features of diabetes," says Dr. Stephen LaFranchi, head of pediatric endocrinology at Portland's Oregon Health Sciences University, "are increased urination, increased thirst and weight loss that develop over a period of two to four weeks."

Type 2 diabetes can be asymptomatic and thus evade detection for many

---

TABLE 20.5

*Diagnostic Tests for Diabetes**

	FASTING BLOOD-GLUCOSE TEST	RANDOM BLOOD-GLUCOSE TEST	TWO-HOUR (POSTLOAD) BLOOD-GLUCOSE TEST
Preparation	• Patient must fast beforehand	• No fasting necessary; can be performed any time of day	• Patient must fast beforehand
Description	• Blood sample is drawn and analyzed	• Blood sample is drawn and analyzed	• Blood sample is drawn and analyzed • Patient eats a meal or drinks a sweet glucose syrup • After 2 hours, blood is drawn again and analyzed
Results Confirming Diabetes	126 mg/ml or higher	200 mg/ml or higher, accompanied by diabetic symptoms	200 mg/ml or higher

* To definitively diagnose diabetes, a positive result must be repeated on a separate day.

years. All the while, the disorder is silently wreaking havoc on small and large blood vessels. The American Diabetes Association recommends that overweight youngsters be tested for diabetes mellitus at puberty or at age ten if they have two out of three additional risk factors: (1) signs of insulin resistance (as determined by your pediatrician), (2) a family history of diabetes and (3) belonging to an ethnic group with a high rate of diabetes, such as African Americans, Hispanics, Asian Americans and Native American Indians.

HOW DIABETES IS DIAGNOSED

Physical examination and thorough medical history, plus one of the following laboratory procedures measuring the concentration of glucose in the blood:

- Fasting blood-glucose test
- Random blood-glucose test
- Two-hour (postload) blood-glucose test
- Urinalysis

The fasting blood-glucose test is almost universally preferred over the other two. According to Dr. LaFranchi, type 1 diabetes is detected largely on the basis of symptoms. "Kids with type 1 diabetes will almost always have blood sugars ranging from two hundred to one thousand," he says, "and they'll be sick enough that there is little question they have the disease." Urinalysis will also show the presence of glucose and ketones in teens with type 1 diabetes.

HOW DIABETES IS TREATED

Although diabetes is incurable at present, blood-sugar levels can be managed through diligent monitoring, exercise and balancing medication along with diet. In the wake of a diagnosis, parents need to impress upon their youngster that adhering to the four-prong program will help him to sidestep not only acute adverse effects like elevated blood sugar (hyperglycemia) and ketoacidosis but serious long-term consequences. Ketoacidosis may occur when there is not enough insulin to handle the glucose that is present; fats and proteins are used and there is a rise in fatty acid metabolites, called ketones, which may be detected in the blood and in urine. Ketoacidosis can be a life-threatening condition that must be corrected immediately.

Diabetes is the sixth most fatal illness in the United States. Years of elevated blood sugar damage blood vessels; later in life, that may come back to haunt patients in the forms of cardiovascular disease, kidney failure, vision problems (*diabetic retinopathy,* the leading cause of acquired blindness in this

---

Preventing Diabetes

Kids bordering on type 2 diabetes may spare themselves from getting the disease, or at least delay its onset, simply by improving their diets, exercising regularly and losing weight. In a 2000 Finnish study, volunteers who took these steps exhibited less than half the incidence of diabetes than their counterparts in the other group.

---

country), lack of sensation (*diabetic neuropathy*) and poor blood flow to the lower legs.

Conversely, diabetics who keep their glucose levels within a normal range as much as possible significantly reduce their odds of developing life-threatening complications. In a government-funded study called the Diabetes Control and Complications Trial (DCCT), patients with type 1 disease received either standard management or more aggressive care. At the end of nine years, the latter group had a 62 percent lower risk of eye disease than those treated less aggressively; their progression of kidney impairment and nerve damage was approximately 60 percent lower as well. A few years later, a British study of type 2 diabetics yielded similar results.

- **Hormone therapy:** All adolescents with type 1 must learn to give themselves *subcutaneous* injections (in the fatty tissue beneath the skin) of insulin two, three or more times a day. Type 2 patients, on the other hand, control their disease through diet and exercise, and possibly the oral medications described below. Although formerly referred to as "*non*-insulin-dependent diabetes," type 2 diabetes may eventually require insulin because the pills used to control blood sugar may eventually lose their effectiveness in about one-third of all patients.

Insulin administration must be timed with eating, so that the hormone reaches the circulation around the same time that glucose from food makes its arrival. This task has been simplified somewhat by the introduction of different types of insulin programmed to commence working, achieve their maximum effect, and then subside at various times. Standard therapy calls for two shots a day. In the more aggressive approach, patients self-administer three or four doses of various insulins.

Most insulin-dependent youngsters soon become quite proficient at wielding the needle syringe. However, many are now switching to an *external insulin pump,* which administers a continuous dose of the hormone at the same rate

TABLE 20.6

Types of Insulin

TYPE	ONSET OF ACTION	PEAK ACTION	DURATION OF ACTION
Short-acting (Regular)	Within 30–60 minutes	2–3 hours	4–6 hours
Rapid-acting (Humalog, Novolog)	Within 10–15 minutes	1 hour	3–4 hours
Intermediate-acting (NPH, Lente)	Within 3 hours	4–14 hours (high peak)	14–24 hours
Long-acting (Ultralente)	Within 6–14 hours	14–24 hours	20–36 hours
Long-acting (Lantus)	½–1 hour	No peak	24 hours

as a healthy pancreas. The programmable device, about the size of a pager, can be slipped into a pocket. A thin catheter tube delivers the insulin into the tissue below the surface of the skin.

• **Drug therapy:** The current drug regimen for type 2 diabetes combines the *biguanide* agent metformin with a *sulfonylurea* (chloropropramide, glimepiride, glyburide, glypizide, tolbutamide, tolazamide). Biguanides prevent the liver from producing glucose, while sulfonylureas work by prevailing upon the pancreas to secrete more insulin. A third type, *glucosidase inhibitors* (acarbose), inhibits a key enzyme that reduces the intestines' absorption of carbohydrates. Side effects such as flatulence and bloating make this drug less than popular with the teen set.

• **Dietary measures:** Virtually all endocrinologists have a dietitian on staff to counsel teenage patients and their parents on making necessary changes in the diet. Current recommendations are for food intake to be at or under 30 percent as fat, 50 to 60 percent as carbohydrate and the rest protein. The teen should check with his physician and dietitian to work out a specific meal plan that is right for him.

• **Blood-glucose monitoring:** This simple blood test, performed several times daily, measures the concentration of sugar in the circulation. Based on the results, which are logged on a chart, the drug dosage and/or diet may be adjusted in order to help patients maintain control of their blood-glucose level. Most young people with diabetes are taught "carb counting" at mealtime and snack time, so that they can become adept at balancing the carbohydrate content of the food they eat and the amount of insulin they must take.

Controlling diabetes can be akin to piloting a ship between two icebergs. Veer off course in one direction, and your blood sugar rises alarmingly high. Stray too far the other way, and you're confronting an equally dangerous situation: blood-glucose deficiency, or *hypoglycemia,* the most common acute complication among young persons with diabetes. Even the most conscientious patients overshoot or undershoot their marks now and then, due to their own miscalculations of how much insulin to take or to complicating factors like physical illness, exercise or emotional stress.

Ironically enough, both insulin and oral diabetes medications can perform *too* well and bring about hypoglycemia, which is defined as a blood-sugar level below 40 to 50 mg/ml. These *insulin reactions* can be serious, so an endocri-

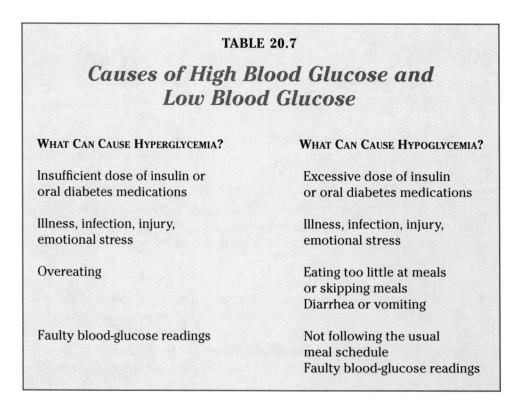

TABLE 20.7

Causes of High Blood Glucose and Low Blood Glucose

What Can Cause Hyperglycemia?	What Can Cause Hypoglycemia?
Insufficient dose of insulin or oral diabetes medications	Excessive dose of insulin or oral diabetes medications
Illness, infection, injury, emotional stress	Illness, infection, injury, emotional stress
Overeating	Eating too little at meals or skipping meals Diarrhea or vomiting
Faulty blood-glucose readings	Not following the usual meal schedule Faulty blood-glucose readings

nologist deciding on a target blood-sugar range for an adolescent usually builds in margins for error at both ends.

WHEN SYMPTOMS POINT TO HIGH BLOOD SUGAR
(IN A PERSON WITH DIABETES)

If the teen feels ill, contact your pediatrician or endocrinologist immediately for instructions. Otherwise, step one is to test the blood-glucose level.

If the concentration of sugar in the blood is higher than normal but under 240 mg/ml:

- Drink at least eight glasses of water a day.
- Eat according to the prescribed treatment program.
- Continue to check blood glucose four times a day until it returns to a safe level.
- Take extra short-acting insulin.

If blood sugar regularly exceeds 239 mg/ml, the teen is at risk for ketoacidosis and should:

- Test a urine sample for excess ketones (*ketonuria*). Testing strips are available over the counter in most pharmacies.
- If the urine tests negative for ketones or contains only a trace amount:

  Repeat blood and urine tests.
  Drink at least eight glasses of water a day until the urine is clear of ketones.

If the urine tests positive for ketones:

- Call your pediatrician or endocrinologist right away.
- Keep drinking plenty of water.
- Do not exercise. In this state, physical activity can nudge blood glucose higher still.

WHEN SYMPTOMS POINT TO LOW BLOOD SUGAR
(IN A PERSON WITH DIABETES)

Hypoglycemia, though usually mild, comes on suddenly. As with hyperglycemia, the blood should be tested at once, because the symptoms of low blood sugar mimic those of other medical conditions. Report repeated episodes to your doctor, who may need to adjust the dosage of insulin or oral diabetes medication.

If blood sugar is below 60 mg/ml, indicating hypoglycemia, and the teen is alert, *he should:*

- Eat or drink one of these rapidly digested starches, such as:

  glucose tablets
  orange juice
  non-diet soda
  grape jam, honey or sugar

- If the symptoms do not improve after fifteen minutes, call your pediatrician or endocrinologist for instructions. Continue feeding the teen sweets every fifteen minutes until the blood sugar climbs back up to at least 70 mg/ml.

- Once he is out of danger and feeling better, give him something more substantial to eat, such as bread or crackers with peanut butter or cheese, or a bowl of cereal with milk.

If the blood sugar is below 60 mg/ml and the teen is convulsing or too drowsy to swallow safely, or unconscious:

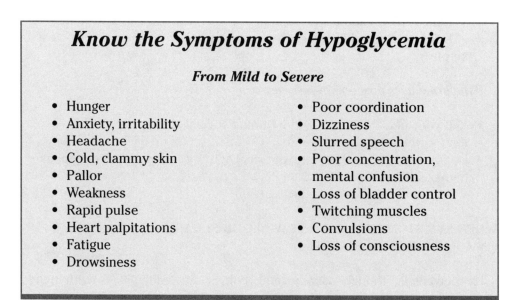

Know the Symptoms of Hypoglycemia

From Mild to Severe

- Hunger
- Anxiety, irritability
- Headache
- Cold, clammy skin
- Pallor
- Weakness
- Rapid pulse
- Heart palpitations
- Fatigue
- Drowsiness

- Poor coordination
- Dizziness
- Slurred speech
- Poor concentration, mental confusion
- Loss of bladder control
- Twitching muscles
- Convulsions
- Loss of consciousness

- A family member or friend should inject him with the hormone glucagon.
- Alert your pediatrician or endocrinologist immediately.

HELPING TEENAGERS HELP THEMSELVES

Youngsters with diabetes should be encouraged to observe the following recommendations:

- Know the warning signs of hyperglycemia, ketoacidosis and hypoglycemia (low blood sugar). Prompt treatment can spare patients from the dangerous symptoms of these acute complications.

- Wear a medical alert ID bracelet for diabetes, or keep one in their wallet.

- Always carry 15 grams of fast-acting carbohydrates to eat or drink in the event of a hypoglycemic episode.

- Get into the habit of reading labels on commercial food packages before eating. Sucrose, dextrose, high-fructose corn syrup, corn sweeteners, honey and molasses are all forms of sugar. If any of these are among the first ingredients listed, select something with less sugar. Other helpful information on today's labels: the total amount of carbohydrates.

Memo to Mom and Dad: Always make sure that you have glucagon and ketone test strips on hand, for emergencies. (See chapter 21, "When a Teenager Has a Chronic Illness or Disability.")

Thyroid Disorders (*Hypothyroidism/Hashimoto's Disease and Hyperthyroidism/Graves' Disease*)

In *hypothyroidism,* the most common thyroid illness, the butterfly-shaped thyroid gland produces too little thyroxine. *Hyperthyroidism* refers to an overactive thyroid that is making too much hormone. Both these autoimmune disorders are five to ten times more prevalent among women than among men.

Hashimoto's Thyroiditis (chronic lymphocytic thyroiditis), named for the physician who first described it, is the leading cause of hypothyroidism. *Graves' disease,* named for *its* discoverer, is a form of hyperthyroidism—and the type seen most frequently in adolescents and young adults. Some people afflicted with an autoimmune thyroid disease inherited the trait genetically, so there may be a family history.

SYMPTOMS THAT SUGGEST HYPOTHYROIDISM/ HASHIMOTO'S DISEASE MAY INCLUDE:

- Sluggishness, fatigue, drowsiness
- Depression
- Anxiety
- Constipation
- Dry, brittle hair
- Dry, itchy skin
- Muscle cramps
- Increased menstrual flow in young women
- A feeling of tightness or fullness in the neck
- Enlarged thyroid (goiter)
- Appetite loss
- Fluid retention, particularly around the eyes
- Anemia
- Numbness and tingling of the hands and feet
- Poor memory
- Deepened voice or hoarseness
- Impaired hearing
- Chest pain
- Irregular heartbeat
- Decreased sweating
- Frequent complaints of feeling cold
- Weight gain or weight loss

SYMPTOMS THAT SUGGEST HYPERTHYROIDISM/ GRAVES' DISEASE MAY INCLUDE:

- Hyperactivity, restlessness, anxiety, irritability
- Frequent complaints of feeling warm
- Flushed face
- Profuse perspiration
- Thinning, itchy skin
- Brittle hair
- Tremoring fingers
- Rapid, irregular heartbeat
- Insomnia
- Unexplained weight loss
- Fatigue
- Weakness, especially in the thighs and upper arms

- Insomnia
- Diarrhea
- Decreased menstrual flow and less frequent periods in young women

Additional symptoms associated with Graves' disease:

- Enlarged thyroid (goiter)
- Bulging eyes, sometimes accompanied by double vision

Youngsters with either an overactive or underactive thyroid may go for months without exhibiting symptoms. An enlarged thyroid, or *goiter,* may not develop until the disease is well advanced. Hashimoto's disease is the most common cause of thyroid enlargement in children.

HOW THYROID DISORDERS ARE DIAGNOSED

Physical examination and thorough medical history, plus one or more of the following procedures:

- Thyroid function blood tests to measure the circulating levels of thyroid hormone and thyroid-stimulating hormone (TSH)
- Nuclear scan of the thyroid, for which the patient first drinks a small amount of radioactive iodine

Thyroid disorders can often be diagnosed on the basis of laboratory tests alone, although a nuclear scan may be ordered. Thyroid hormone and thyroid-stimulating hormone act as "thermostats" for each other. Therefore, a youngster suffering from an overactive thyroid will have an overabundance of thyroxine and too little TSH, while in hypothyroidism the proportions will be reversed.

HOW THYROID DISORDERS ARE TREATED

HYPOTHYROIDISM

- **Hormone replacement therapy:** According to Dr. LaFranchi, a pediatric endocrinologist since the late 1970s, "The treatment for hypothyroidism is pretty straightforward. We compensate for the hormone deficiency by giving the teen a synthetic preparation called levothyroxine once a day. Sometimes it takes the physician a while to settle on the correct dose, but we use a formula based on body weight, so that gives us a good idea of where to start." As with insulin therapy in diabetes, *thyroid-hormone replacement* is for life. Fortunately, the majority of young people take the oral tablets without any problems. Once the TSH level is stabilized, thyroid function needs to be checked only once per year, barring any recurrences.

HYPERTHYROIDISM

• **Drug therapy:** "Hyperthyroidism is a little trickier to treat," says Dr. LaFranchi. "There are essentially three options. One is to give so-called *antithyroid* drugs [propylthiouracil, methimazole], which shut off production of excess thyroid hormone until the level is in a normal range." Twelve to eighteen months of therapy produce a prolonged remission in about one-fourth of all patients.

Another class of drugs, *beta-adrenergic blockers,* inhibits the action of thyroid hormone. While agents such as atenolol, metoprolol, nadolol and propranolol do not actually lower the excessive levels of circulating thyroid hormone, beta-blockers usually bring rapid relief from many of the disease's symptoms.

• **Radioiodine ablation:** Because drug therapy usually does not cure hyperthyroidism, it has been surpassed in recent years by *radioiodine ablation.* The thyroid appropriates iodine from the circulation in order to make thyroxine. In this ingenious therapy, the patient swallows a capsule or liquid containing radioactive iodine, known as I-131. The gland absorbs the *radionuclide,* which proceeds to destroy (*ablate*) the cells responsible for secreting thyroid hormone.

Perhaps the idea of ingesting a radioisotope sounds hazardous, but radioiodine ablation is an extremely safe procedure. Though the tasteless, odorless substance passes from the body in a matter of days, it generally takes three to six months for the thyroid to fully react by shrinking in size and allowing the concentration of thyroid hormone to return to normal. If necessary, a second dose can be given. Most patients treated this way develop *hypo*thyroidism anywhere from several months to many years later. At that point, they go on permanent thyroid-hormone replacement therapy.

• **Thyroid surgery:** The third option, rarely exercised, consists of an operation to remove part of the thyroid. *Thyroidectomy* is curative. However, patients who require extensive surgery may become hypothyroid some time in the future.

EYE CONDITIONS

Nearsightedness (Myopia)

Adolescence is the time of life when millions of boys and girls are found to be nearsighted. "*Myopia* is the most common eye problem of the teen years," says Dr. Harold P. Koller, a pediatric ophthalmologist from Meadowbrook, Pennsylvania, and clinical professor of ophthalmology at Thomas Jefferson University in Philadelphia, Pennsylvania.

"In kids who are genetically programmed to be nearsighted," he explains, "the eyeball grows too long from front to back, usually during the growth spurt." Consequently, the rays of light that make up optical images converge just short of the *retina,* the "movie screen" at the back of the eye. A *myopic* person can see clearly up close, but distant objects appear blurry.

Farsighted youngsters have the opposite problem: normal vision for things that are far away, difficulties seeing what may be right in front of them. That's because their eyeballs are abnormally short, causing the image to focus behind the retina. It is not unusual for children to develop *hyperopia* before age five or six. As they grow, the eyeball "catches up" with the rest of the body. If they'd required corrective lenses for farsightedness, they may be able to set them aside for several years—perhaps permanently. A small amount of farsightedness is considered normal in childhood. Myopia typically becomes more severe throughout adolescence, then starts to stabilize when a young person reaches her twenties.

SYMPTOMS THAT SUGGEST MYOPIA MAY INCLUDE:

- Recurrent headaches
- Incessant eye-rubbing
- Squinting in an attempt to help vision
- Unexplained drop in school performance

HOW MYOPIA IS DIAGNOSED

Myopia is diagnosed with an eye examination and vision screening conducted by an *ophthalmologist* or an *optometrist.* An ophthalmologist holds a degree in medicine (M.D. or D.O.)[1] and has received an additional three to five years train-

---

1 Doctor of Osteopathy

ing in the diagnosis and treatment of all eye disorders. That includes performing surgery. An *optometrist* has a degree in optometry (O.D.) and is qualified to prescribe and fit glasses and contacts, and to screen for, and treat, certain vision problems. An *optician* is trained to fit glasses and contacts, although the prescription must have been written by either an M.D., D.O. or O.D.

HOW MYOPIA IS TREATED

• **Corrective lenses:** Eyeglass frames, once merely functional, are now stylish enough to serve as fashion statements. Nevertheless, some teens are self-conscious about wearing glasses—and so they don't, ditching them at every opportunity. For them, contact lenses might be the preferable selection. But only on three conditions, advises Dr. Koller:

"Number one: The young person has no medical condition that would preclude him from wearing contacts, such as dry eye, severe allergies and frequent eye infections. Numbers two and three: The young person has to be sufficiently mature and motivated to handle and care for the lenses properly."

Soft contact lenses are relatively problem free, but they do need to be cleaned and disinfected each time they're taken out. Failure to practice adequate hygiene can lead to nasty eye infections. Here are some other precautions for teens to remember:

• Never put in contact lenses when the eyes are red and inflamed.
• After inserting the lenses in the eyes, rinse the plastic case with warm water and allow it to dry.
• Don't forget to take the lenses out at night.
• Keep a backup pair of contacts *and* a backup pair of eyeglasses, for emergencies.

Eye Trauma

"Trauma is the second most frequent eye problem that we see in the teenage years," says Dr. Koller, a pediatric ophthalmologist since 1971. Sports-related injuries are the leading cause, followed by bicycle spills and injuries involving BB guns and air rifles. Baseball is responsible for more eye injuries among children aged five to fourteen than any other sport—typically as a result of a batter being struck by the ball—while inadvertent elbow jabs and stabbing fingers account for the majority of eye injuries in basketball, which holds the same dubious distinction among fifteen-to-twenty-year-olds.

Treatment: Call your pediatrician or eye doctor at once. There are several different treatments for eye injuries ranging from mild to serious and your pediatrician or ophthalmologist can make the correct determination as to how to treat your teenager.

STEPS TO TAKE WHEN A TEENAGER SUFFERS AN EYE INJURY

Cuts and lacerations to the eye should be left untouched. Do not attempt to put medicine in the eye or flush it with water, and remind the young person not to rub his eyes. Gently place a bandage or gauze pad over the eye and head to the ophthalmologist right away.

Sports With the Highest Risk of Eye Injury

- Baseball
- Basketball
- Hockey
- Water polo
- Football
- Lacrosse
- Softball
- Racquet sports
- Soccer
- Fencing
- Paint ball
- Downhill skiing
- Boxing

Source: American Academy of Ophthalmology

HELPING TEENAGERS HELP THEMSELVES

Every year, some thirty-three thousand young athletes injure their eyes participating in sports. Nine in ten of those mishaps could have been avoided. Insist that your sports-minded youngster wear protective lenses made of *polycarbonate,* a rugged material that is twenty times stronger than conventional eyewear.

DISORDERS OF THE GENITOURINARY TRACT

Urinary-Tract Infections (*UTI*)

The urinary tract begins with the *kidneys,* two bean-shaped organs that skim waste products and excess water from the blood to create *urine.* A pair of narrow tubes called the *ureters* carries the urine to the baglike *bladder* for storage. From there it travels down another tube, the *urethra,* and leaves the body through the penis or the vulva.

In the process, the urine washes away germs from the opening of the urinary system. But sometimes microorganisms slip into the urethra and begin to multiply and inflame its inner lining. The culprit behind most urinary-tract infections (UTIs) is *Escherichia coli (E. coli)*, a bacteria that resides in the intestinal tract.

An infection confined to the urethra is called *urethritis.* However, many times the germs continue upward, landing in the bladder. *Cystitis,* the most common UTI, frequently occurs in tandem with urethritis. If not treated promptly, the infection can spread to the ureters and the kidneys. The medical term for this more serious condition is *pyelonephritis.*

Young women develop urinary-tract infections at more than three times the rate of young men. One probable reason why is that the female urethra, at just one and a half inches long, affords germs easy access to the bladder. The male urethra, in contrast, measures eight inches in length. A second factor is the close proximity of the urethral opening to the vagina and anus, both of which serve as fertile environments for bacteria. During intercourse, germs from the vagina may be pushed into the bladder. In fact, as Dr. Alain Joffe points out, a UTI may be a sign that a teenager is sexually active. "There is a significant overlap between the symptoms of urinary-tract infections and the symptoms of chlamydia, gonorrhea and other sexually transmitted diseases," says the director of adolescent medicine at Baltimore's Johns Hopkins School of Medicine.

SYMPTOMS THAT SUGGEST A URINARY-TRACT INFECTION MAY INCLUDE:

- Pain or burning sensation when urinating
- Frequent urge to urinate, though only a small amount is passed
- Fever and chills
- Pressure sensation
- Pain in the abdomen, pelvis or lower back
- Nausea and vomiting
- Blood or pus in the urine
- Urinary incontinence

HOW A URINARY-TRACT INFECTION IS DIAGNOSED

Physical examination and thorough medical history, plus one or more of the following procedures:

- Urinalysis, to detect the presence of bacteria and white blood cells (wbc's)
- Urine culture, to determine which antibiotic can be used to treat it

HOW A URINARY-TRACT INFECTION IS TREATED

• **Drug therapy:** Three days on an oral antibiotic usually clears up infections of the lower urinary tract. Once the kidneys are involved, however, treatment takes longer. Among the drugs most commonly ordered: trimethoprim, trimethoprim/sulfamethoxazole, amoxicillin, ampicillin, ofloxacin and nitrofurantoin. Additional medications may be prescribed to relieve pain and inflammation.

Approximately one in five female sufferers will experience at least one subsequent urinary-tract infection. The new illness usually stems from a different strain of *E. coli* or an entirely different bacteria.

HELPING TEENAGERS HELP THEMSELVES

The following measures may help prevent urinary-tract infections:

- Drink the equivalent of eight glasses of water a day.
- Don't resist the urge to urinate, void at frequent intervals (every 3 to 4 hours).
- Urinate after sexual intercourse.
- Change tampons and sanitary napkins frequently.
- Do not douche.
- Wipe front to back, or from urethra/vagina toward the anus.

Nighttime Incontinence (Nocturnal Enuresis)

By adolescence, only 4 percent of boys and 2 percent of girls wet the bed; the figures fall to 1.5 percent and 0.5 percent by age eighteen. So you can appreciate how distressing it is to be one of those teenagers who is still experiencing urinary incontinence at night. In most cases the lack of bladder control has been a problem since birth, as opposed to having resurfaced after six months or more of dryness. The former condition is called *primary nocturnal enuresis;* the latter, *secondary nocturnal enuresis.*

HOW NIGHTTIME INCONTINENCE IS EVALUATED

The cause for nocturnal enuresis is multifactoral. Contributing factors may include poor dietary control with excessive caffeine intake, a deep sleep pattern that can be part of normal adolescent development, inconsistent sleep schedule and limited hours sleeping. Other influencing factors include:

- Medications
- Caffeine
- Urinary-tract infections
- Diabetes and other chronic medical problems
- Family history

Primary nocturnal enuresis often follows a similar pattern. It is helpful to identify the age of nocturnal continence for both parents. If one parent was incontinent through a particular age, their children will have a similar problem approximately 40 percent of the time. If both parents have primary nocturnal enuresis through a particular age, their children have a 70 percent chance of following a similar pattern.

Secondary enuresis in older children or adolescence should prompt a review for urinary-tract infections, major medical illnesses, social stress factors and the potential for sexual abuse.

HOW NIGHTTIME INCONTINENCE IS TREATED

Treatment of nocturnal enuresis is based on differentiating primary from secondary nocturnal enuresis. Any factor that resulted in secondary nocturnal enuresis would need to be managed prior to concentrating on the enuretic event. A child who actively participates in their treatment has a better chance to improve their outcome.

PRACTICAL APPROACH

It is first important to educate the child and family on appropriate dietary intake. While totally restricting fluids is not practical, eliminating products with caffeine is essential and recommending moderate intake is appropriate. The child needs to routinely use the bathroom prior to going to bed and immediately upon waking in the morning. You can wake your teenager once during the night so he can urinate if necessary, but waking him more than once a night may disrupt his sleep pattern, which could lead to diminished school performance the following day.

BEHAVIOR MODIFICATION

Behavior modification through the use of an enuretic alarm is effective in approximately 70 percent of motivated children. The device contains moisture-sensitive sensors that result in buzzing or vibrating. Typically the expense for these alarms is sixty to a hundred dollars. This form of therapy requires active participation by an adult and long-term commitment. Strong office support should be provided in follow-up.

MEDICATIONS

There are only two medications that have been approved for nocturnal enuresis—imipramine and desmopressin. The exact action of imipramine is not completely understood, but it has been shown to be effective in approximately 50 percent of enuretic children. The dosing of imipramine is somewhat arbitrary and the family should be advised regarding the potential toxicity for overdose of the medication. A baseline EKG prior to initiating therapy is recommended although cardiac side effects have not been reported with doses used to treat bed-wetting. The family should also maintain strict control over dispensing the medication because of the potential for overdosing.

Desmopressin (DDAVP) is a synthetic antidiuretic hormone (ADH). Its mechanism of action is similar to ADH and is effective in improving nocturnal enuresis in approximately 40 to 60 percent of children. DDAVP is available in both nasal spray and pill forms. When continued long term, expense can become an issue with medication costing $80 to $120 for a month's supply.

Varicocele

As part of your periodic parent-son chats about sex and sexual development, stress that any sort of genital pain or swelling is cause for concern and should be brought to the immediate attention of Mom, Dad or the pediatrician.

One source of scrotal swelling is a *varicocele* within the *scrotum*. Like all veins, the veins in the spermatic cord have pairs of flipperlike valves interspersed along the inner walls. Their job: to keep blood moving in one direction, toward the heart. Any time the circulation starts to flow backward, the flaps of the valves swing shut.

Varicocele is set in motion when one or more valves fail to close properly. As a result, stagnant blood builds up in the vessel until the wall becomes swollen. The distended scrotal sac is said to resemble a "bag of worms": a reference to the bulging vessels inside.

A varicocele most often develops on the left side of the scrotum.

SYMPTOMS THAT SUGGEST VARICOCELE MAY INCLUDE:

Most varicoceles are painless and do not cause symptoms. Occasionally one may experience dull, persistent ache or sensation of heaviness in the scrotum—often most noticeable after physical exercise. There may be a reduction in testicular size (*atrophy*).

HOW VARICOCELE IS DIAGNOSED

The condition is diagnosed through physical examination and thorough medical history, including probing or palpating the area with the fingers. No radiographic studies are needed unless there is concern about obstruction as a cause. An ultrasound is done if the examiner feels the testicle on the affected side is too small. The varicocele may be apparent when standing.

HOW VARICOCELE IS MANAGED

Most pubertal or prepubertal varicoceles do not need to be treated. However, if the varicocele is associated with pain during physical exercise, repair may be needed. Even if there is no pain, the potential for problems of infertility, which has been noted in men with a varicocele, may cause some doctors to suggest surgical repair. There is no absolute test or study that will predetermine which child is at risk for infertility based on his varicocele. Some physicians would encourage repairing a varicocele if there is a noticeable size discrepancy between the two testicles. Therefore, it is important to closely monitor the growth and development of both testicles as a child progresses through puberty. When surgical correction has been recommended, the procedure can be performed in an outpatient setting. Recovery takes about one week; however, it will be another five weeks, on average, before full recovery can be expected.

Testicular Torsion

A sudden, excruciating pain on one side of the scrotum may indicate *testicular torsion,* in which the testicle twists one or more times on the spermatic cord attached to it. This diminishes or cuts off circulation to the testicle. If the injury isn't corrected surgically within six to twelve hours, the tissue will be irreversibly destroyed. Torsion can occur during exercise, but it is just as likely to come on while the young person is asleep; and although men of all ages are vulnerable, the highest incidence is among twelve-to-twenty-year-olds.

SYMPTOMS THAT SUGGEST TESTICULAR TORSION MAY INCLUDE:

- Pain in one testicle
- Swollen, red, tender scrotum

- Enlarged testicle
- Abdominal pain
- Nausea and vomiting

HOW TESTICULAR TORSION IS DIAGNOSED

- Physical examination by a urologist
- Urinalysis, to detect presence of white blood cells
- A radionuclide scan or scrotal doppler ultrasound, to assess blood flow to the testicles
- Some urologists will take a patient with typical symptoms of torsion directly to the operating room

HOW TESTICULAR TORSION IS TREATED

- **Surgery:** Immediate surgical intervention to untwist the testicle is required if there is any chance of salvaging the testicle. It is also necessary to secure the other testicle to prevent it from twisting.

HELPING TEENAGERS HELP THEMSELVES

As many as 50 percent of patients will have experienced previous episodes of acute testicular pain. Parents should report these occurrences to the youngsters' pediatrician.

A Medical Emergency

"I can't stress enough that testicular torsion is a surgical emergency and that time is of the utmost importance," says Dr. Joffe. "If a teenager starts to complain of testicular pain and it doesn't go away within an hour or so, get him to the emergency room to be checked out. Within six hours, we can usually salvage the entire testicle. If the surgery is performed within six to twelve hours, about 70 percent of patients have recovery of testicular function. After twelve hours, only 20 percent of patients have recovery."

GYNECOLOGIC CONDITIONS

Menstrual Disorders (*Dysmenorrhea and Dysfunctional Uterine Bleeding* [DUB])

> ### Words Worth Knowing
>
> **Endometrium:** the membranous inner lining of the uterus. Each month, the endometrium thickens in anticipation of a fertilized egg (*embryo*) entering the womb to begin its nine months of gestation. When conception fails to take place, the uterus sheds the unused extra tissue, which leaves the body through the vagina as part of menstrual fluid.

Within a year or two of their first period, 50 to 75 percent of young women begin to experience painful menstrual cramps, or *dysmenorrhea.*

Some cases of dysmenorrhea are eventually traced to the gynecologic disorder *endometriosis,* in which endometrial tissue is located in sites within the pelvic cavity other than the uterus. However, the majority of girls can be reassured that the cramping is related to the production of prostaglandins by the uterus, which is easily remedied, emphasizes Dr. Jennifer Johnson, a specialist in adolescent medicine at the University of California at Irvine.

"Some parents can be remarkably fatalistic about menstrual cramps, like it's something their daughters have to endure," she says. "I'll see girls who are missing a day of school every month because of dysmenorrhea, and when I ask if they're taking anything to relieve the symptoms, they'll shake their heads no. We have extremely effective, inexpensive medications for treating dysmenorrhea."

Heavy and irregular bleeding, referred to as *dysfunctional uterine bleeding* (DUB), can indicate serious underlying medical problems in teens. Dr. Johnson explains, "DUB is caused by a disturbance involving the hormones that regulate menstruation, but it is generally painless. But if it's not treated, patients can lose so much blood that they develop severe anemia."

SYMPTOMS THAT SUGGEST DYSMENORRHEA MAY INCLUDE:

- Severe cramping
- Occasional sharp pains in the lower abdomen, lower back and thighs
- Sweating
- Fatigue
- Headache
- Faintness

- Nausea and vomiting
- Diarrhea

SYMPTOMS THAT SUGGEST DYSFUNCTIONAL UTERINE BLEEDING MAY INCLUDE:

Bleeding more frequently than every twenty-one days (counting from the first day of one period to the first day of the next), less frequently than every thirty-five to forty-two days, or longer than seven days. Teens with these types of menstrual bleeding patterns should be medically evaluated.

HOW DYSMENORRHEA IS DIAGNOSED

Physical examination and thorough medical history (including menstrual history).

HOW DYSFUNCTIONAL UTERINE BLEEDING IS DIAGNOSED

Physical examination, including pelvic exam, and thorough medical history, plus one or more of the following procedures, to test for related complications or evidence of a mass or a sexually transmitted disease (STD).

- Complete blood count (CBC)
- Thyroid function tests
- STD laboratory tests
- Pregnancy test
- Measurement of gonadotropins, prolactin and androgens

HOW MENSTRUAL DISORDERS ARE TREATED

DRUG THERAPY

After exclusion of specific medical conditions, girls may be placed on medications. The cramping of dysmenorrhea is typically addressed with NSAID (nonsteroidal anti-inflammatory drug) *analgesics* such as ibuprofen, ketoprofen or naproxen. These medications block the uterus from releasing *prostaglandins,* naturally occurring chemicals that cause cramps. Oral contraceptives can also be used to relieve severe menstrual cramps. Hormone treatments, such as oral contraceptives, can also be used for dysfunctional uterine bleeding. NSAIDs may reduce bleeding to some extent, as well.

Vaginal Infections (*Vaginitis* [*Bacterial Vaginosis and Yeast Infections*])

Yeast infections are caused by the fungus *Candida albicans,* one of many fungi that reside harmlessly in the vagina, mouth, throat and skin. The slightly acidic chemical content of the vagina controls the balance between the bacteria and yeast that reside in the normal vagina. If the fragile balance between *acidity* and *alkalinity* is altered, the amount of yeast grows to the extent that a Candida infection (known as *candidiasis*) occurs.

A similarly uneasy truce exists between "friendly" bacteria (*lactobacilli*) and "unfriendly" bacteria (*anaerobes*). In bacterial vaginosis, the anaerobes multiply at a rapid pace until they've all but displaced many of the lactobacilli. As in candidiasis, the vaginal ecosystem changes from acidic to alkaline. "Nobody is absolutely sure what causes the bacterial overgrowth," says

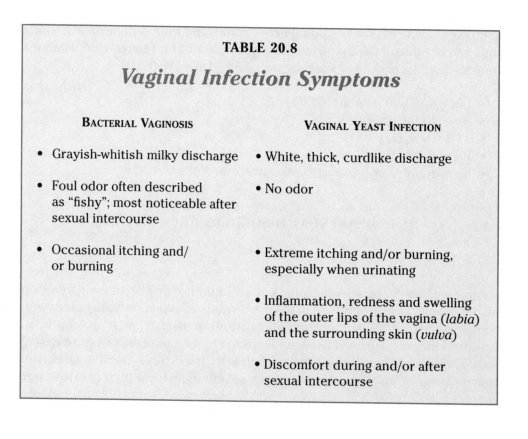

TABLE 20.8

Vaginal Infection Symptoms

BACTERIAL VAGINOSIS	VAGINAL YEAST INFECTION
• Grayish-whitish milky discharge	• White, thick, curdlike discharge
• Foul odor often described as "fishy"; most noticeable after sexual intercourse	• No odor
• Occasional itching and/or burning	• Extreme itching and/or burning, especially when urinating
	• Inflammation, redness and swelling of the outer lips of the vagina (*labia*) and the surrounding skin (*vulva*)
	• Discomfort during and/or after sexual intercourse

Dr. Meg Fisher, a pediatrician at St. Christopher's Hospital for Children, in Philadelphia. Interestingly, although bacterial vaginosis is not transmitted via intercourse, sexually active women have a higher rate of infection—and higher still if they've been intimate with multiple partners. (See chapter 12, "Sexuality.")

SYMPTOMS OF BACTERIAL VAGINOSIS AND VAGINAL YEAST INFECTIONS ARE LISTED IN TABLE 20.8

Physical examination, including pelvic exam, and thorough medical history, plus one or more of the following procedures: Microscopic laboratory analysis of vaginal fluid (your pediatrician may refer to these tests as *wet preparation* and *KOH preparation*) to rule out infection.

HOW VAGINAL INFECTIONS ARE TREATED

- **Drug therapy:** Yeast infections are managed with *antifungal* agents such as butoconazole, clotrimazole, miconazole and tioconazole, which come in the form of creams, ointments and suppositories. Fluconazole can be given orally. The shortest course consists of a single dose, which is 80 percent effective. For bacterial vaginosis, the *antibiotics* clindamycin and metronidazole are the mainstays of therapy.

INFECTIOUS DISEASES

Infectious Mononucleosis

The familiar nickname for mononucleosis (or mono), "the kissing disease," is somewhat misleading. While it is true that the *Epstein-Barr virus* (EBV) is responsible for 85 percent of mono diagnoses and can be contracted from another person's saliva, a teenager might acquire it through drinking out of the same glass or sharing a straw with a person who is infected. Because mono also travels via droplets of mucus, exposure can also come from sitting too close to an EBV carrier in the midst of a coughing spell or from sneezing.

An additional 10 percent of cases are caused by a second highly common virus from the *herpes* family: *cytomegalovirus* (CMV). Both CMV and EBV are *opportunistic infections*. They may stow away in a person's body for an entire lifetime without incident. It is only when the immune system isn't up to par that these viruses stir up trouble. "Once you've had mono, you usually don't get it again," explains Dr. Meg Fisher of St. Christopher's Hospital for Children, in Philadelphia. "However, you may never stop being contagious."

Mononucleosis can occur at almost any age, but the peak incidence is between ages fifteen and thirty. The rate of mono is high among college students, undoubtedly because they live in close quarters and tend to get run-down, particularly around finals time.

SIGNS AND SYMPTOMS THAT SUGGEST INFECTIOUS MONONUCLEOSIS MAY INCLUDE:

- Fever (101 to 104 degrees F) and chills
- Sore throat
- Fatigue
- Enlarged lymph glands in the groin and armpit, and particularly in back of the neck
- Achiness
- Appetite loss
- White patches at the back of the throat
- Headache
- Hypersensitivity to light
- Puffy eyelids
- Enlarged spleen and/or liver
- Anemia
- Rarely, yellow jaundice or a rash

The early symptoms of mononucleosis are often nondescript in teenagers and young adults. Many exhibit no symptoms at all. Adults and young children may develop atypical symptoms, which complicates the diagnostic process. Most adolescents, though, come down with the classic quartet of features: sore throat, fever, fatigue and swollen glands. The lymph nodes, tender yet firm to the touch, can grow to the size of small eggs.

HOW INFECTIOUS MONONUCLEOSIS IS DIAGNOSED

Physical examination and thorough medical history, plus one or more of the following procedures:

- Complete blood count (CBC), looking for increased numbers of white blood cells called *lymphocytes*

- Epstein-Barr virus antibody-titer blood test, to detect the presence of EBV antibodies
- Heterophile antibody-agglutination blood test, to screen for *heterophile antibodies,* a type of antibody common to EBV; also called the Monospot Test

HOW INFECTIOUS MONONUCLEOSIS IS TREATED

- **Bed rest, plenty of fluids, well-balanced diet:** There is no treatment for mono, per se. The therapies described in Table 20.9 are strictly for controlling the associated pain, fever and inflamed throat. The symptoms typically run their course within one to three weeks. Some youngsters, though, remain sick for months. "Mononucleosis is an incredibly variable disease," says Dr. Fisher, a member of the American Academy of Pediatrics's committee on infectious diseases. Even after the early effects disappear, fatigue and weakness may linger for several weeks or more.

Mono patients used to be confined to bed for four to six weeks, followed by another three months of limited activity. "Now," says Dr. Fisher, "some teen-

---

TABLE 20.9

Keeping Young Patients Comfortable: Treating the Common Symptoms of Mononucleosis

SYMPTOM(S)	TO MAKE YOUR YOUNGSTER FEEL BETTER, TRY THIS:
Pain/Fever	• Mild combination analgesics/fever reducers (aceta-minophen, ibuprofen) • *Children under 18 years of age should not be given aspirin, which heightens the risk of a life-threatening disease called* Reye's syndrome.
Sore Throat	• Warm-water-and-salt gargles • Cold drinks and frozen desserts • Throat lozenges and hard sucking candies
Strep Throat	• The antibiotic penicillin or erythromycin, prescribed by the pediatrician. (Remember that mono itself, being a virus, does not respond to antibiotics.)

agers feel better in a week and can go back to their full daily routines." Well, almost. Half of all patients develop an enlarged *spleen.* The glandlike organ, located in the upper-left portion of the abdomen, stores and filters the blood. If overexertion or traumatic impact to the body should cause the spleen to rupture, the internal hemorrhaging can be fatal. Fortunately, this complication is extremely rare. But as a precaution, adolescents recovering from mono must avoid heavy lifting, straining and competitive sports for approximately one month, or until their pediatrician gives them the go-ahead.

A sudden, violent pain in the upper-left abdomen that doesn't go away after five minutes warrants an immediate trip to the hospital emergency department or a phone call to the local emergency medical service.

Chronic Fatigue Syndrome (CFS)

Epstein-Barr, the virus responsible for mono, was once implicated in *chronic fatigue syndrome,* too. It has since been exonerated, leaving puzzled researchers without a definitive cause on which to pin CFS. Most likely, a combination of genetic, immunologic and psychological factors accounts for the debilitating illness, which may appear in the wake of an infection—among them, mono.

NEUROLOGICAL DISORDERS

Headaches

Mild to moderate pain from *tension headaches* is one of the most prevalent medical complaints of the teen years. A tension headache typically comes on over the course of the day, producing a viselike pressure on both sides of the scalp and down the neck. "What happens is that the scalp muscles tighten around the skull," explains Dr. John Kulig of Boston's New England Medical Center, "usually in response to stress."

Migraine headaches, seen in 10 percent of adolescents, particularly girls, are characterized as attacks—that's how severe they are. When the pounding pain on one side of the skull is preceded by a visual disturbance, a person is said to have a *migraine with aura.* "The person will see bright, flashing lights, pinwheels or zigzag patterns," says ophthalmologist Harold Koller, who adds that parents often mistakenly attribute the optical illusions and headaches to eye strain. An aura may subside within minutes or continue for hours, while the pain lasts for several hours, on average. A *migraine without aura* strikes suddenly and persists for anywhere from three hours to several days. Mi-

Causes of Headaches

Headaches often accompany illnesses such as viruses, strep throat, allergies, sinus infections and urinary-tract infections. Other common causes include:

- Extreme hunger or thirst
- Not getting enough sleep
- Specific foods and beverages, such as chocolate, hard and aged cheeses, pizza, yogurt, nuts, lima beans, processed meats, some fruits and fruit juices
- Food additives (monosodium glutamate, nitrates, nitrites)
- Certain nonprescription dietary supplements and medications, and prescription drugs (birth-control pills, tetracycline, excessive doses of vitamin A)
- Food products and beverages containing caffeine (sodas, coffee, chocolate)
- Alcohol, cocaine and other illicit substances
- Eye strain, including sun glare
- Fatigue
- Tooth infections or abscesses
- Hormonal changes during a girl's menstrual cycle
- Changes in the weather
- Emotional stress, depression, anxiety, intense anger, extreme excitement
- Noisy, hot, stuffy environments
- Flickering or glaring lights
- Strong aromas
- Clenching or grinding teeth
- Physical exertion
- Head injury

graines may occur frequently, as often as several times a week, or rarely, with years between episodes.

There are many possible causes or triggers of migraines, including stress, various foods and the constriction of blood vessels in the head and neck, which reduce circulation to the brain. In 2000, researchers at the National Institutes of Health discovered another cause: a malfunction in the back of the brain. Apparently, a trigger (see box on previous page) stirs abnormally excitable brain cells into firing off tiny impulses. The electrical charges ripple throughout the brain and brain stem, stimulating pain receptors along the way.

SYMPTOMS OF HEADACHES MAY INCLUDE:

TENSION HEADACHES

- Constant, dull ache on both sides of the forehead
- Sensation of tightness in the head, radiating down the neck

MIGRAINE HEADACHES

Migraine with aura:

- Visual disturbance called an aura
- Throbbing, incapacitating pain that starts on one side of the head and occasionally envelops the other side
- Drowsiness

Migraine without aura:

- Throbbing, incapacitating pain on one side of the head
- Mental dullness
- Moodiness
- Fatigue
- Fluid retention
- Sensitivity to light
- Diarrhea
- Nausea and vomiting
- Drowsiness

HOW HEADACHE CAUSES ARE DIAGNOSED

- Physical examination and thorough medical history
- More involved and/or invasive procedures such as CT scan, MRI scan, lumbar puncture, would be performed only if a serious condition was suspected

HOW HEADACHES ARE TREATED

Headaches respond best to treatment when they're still in their early stages. If your teen has a tension headache, encourage her to lie down and relax, with her head elevated slightly. A hot bath or shower can help to ease the pain, as can placing a warm or cold compress on the forehead and/or neck. For migraine sufferers, you want to minimize sensory stimulation: Turn off the lights in the room, close the curtains, ask family members to keep the noise level down and so on. A cold pack helps here too, but do not apply heat—that will only make the pain worse.

• **Drug therapy:** Tension headaches and migraines frequently respond well to a single dose of the over-the-counter analgesics acetaminophen or ibuprofen. According to the American Council on Headache Education, acetaminophen gets down to business more quickly, but ibuprofen appears to provide superior pain relief. If the symptoms recur, the next step might be a prescription for one of the "triptans": sumatriptan, zolmitriptan, naratriptan, rizatriptan. This family of drugs puts a halt to two in three migraines by blocking the action of the *neurotransmitter* serotonin. And because triptans are nonsedating, teens may be able to return to the classroom or to other activities more quickly, without having to sleep off the migraine.

We never want to *over*medicate, however, for fear of inducing *rebound headaches.* The phenomenon was discovered in the 1980s. Apparently, taking analgesics every day or every other day interferes with the brain's own ability to battle pain. The net effect is that over time the teenager begins to experience more headaches between doses. What's more, the medicines that once brought relief no longer seem as effective.

• **Put your finger on the trigger:** Your pediatrician may suggest keeping a "headache diary" to help pinpoint the cause of your teen's headaches. In it, she writes down the following information:

TEEN TIP:

Teenagers plagued by three or more migraines a month may be candidates for preventive (*prophylactic*) medicine, using antidepressants such as amitriptyline, as well as beta-blockers, calcium-channel blockers, or antiseizure medications.

- when the headache occurred
- how long it lasted
- what she was doing when the headache came on
- foods eaten that day
- amount of sleep the night before
- any observations on what seems to make the headaches better or worse

Identifying and eliminating the precipitating factor of migraines—be it a certain food, a medication, a situation—can significantly reduce their occurrence. Some triggers, though, can't be avoided, like the stress of school. When researchers at the Palm Beach Headache Center in Palm Beach, Florida, studied nineteen hundred migraine sufferers aged twelve to seventeen, they discovered a fascinating (though not entirely surprising) pattern: Of the seven days of the week, the rate of migraines was the lowest (9 percent) on Saturdays and peaked (20 percent) on Mondays.

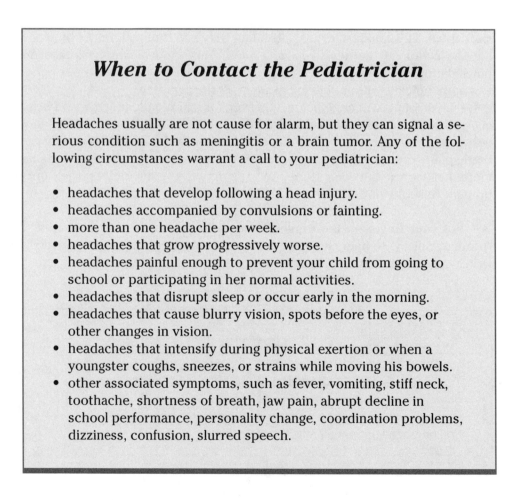

When to Contact the Pediatrician

Headaches usually are not cause for alarm, but they can signal a serious condition such as meningitis or a brain tumor. Any of the following circumstances warrant a call to your pediatrician:

- headaches that develop following a head injury.
- headaches accompanied by convulsions or fainting.
- more than one headache per week.
- headaches that grow progressively worse.
- headaches painful enough to prevent your child from going to school or participating in her normal activities.
- headaches that disrupt sleep or occur early in the morning.
- headaches that cause blurry vision, spots before the eyes, or other changes in vision.
- headaches that intensify during physical exertion or when a youngster coughs, sneezes, or strains while moving his bowels.
- other associated symptoms, such as fever, vomiting, stiff neck, toothache, shortness of breath, jaw pain, abrupt decline in school performance, personality change, coordination problems, dizziness, confusion, slurred speech.

Relaxation exercises, taught by your pediatrician or a mental health professional, can help kids to handle stress with greater resilience. Another mind-body technique, *biofeedback,* has proved useful in reducing both the frequency and the duration of migraine headaches. *Psychotherapy,* too, may play a part in treating migraines. (See "Anxiety Disorders" in chapter 15, "Emotional and Behavioral Problems.")

HELPING TEENAGERS HELP THEMSELVES

The tips below can help youngsters to avoid headaches:

- Get the proper amount of sleep.
- Eat regular meals, if possible. If not, snack frequently.
- Exercise regularly.
- Be aware of any pattern to your headaches that might help you to identify headache triggers.

Dizziness and Fainting Spells (*Syncope*)

A temporary decrease in blood flow to the brain results in unconsciousness, or *fainting.* Many disorders, some of them serious, can cause this. "In adolescents," says pediatric neurologist Dr. Patricia Crumrine of the University of Pittsburgh Medical Center, "fainting usually turns out to be due to *vasovagal syncope.*" Your pediatrician may also refer to it as *neurally mediated syncope.* The condition is not serious, although a child can incur head injuries and lacerations from collapsing.

Syncope can be set off by pain, fatigue, heat, exercise, stress—even intense emotions, like the shock of hearing some distressing news or watching a scary scene in a movie. In response, the heart contracts more forcefully than usual. The nervous system, sensing this, overreacts. It slows down the pumping action, inducing a sudden drop in blood pressure. At the same time, it

---

What to Do if a Youngster Faints

- If you can, try to catch him before he hits the floor.
- Gently lay him down on his back.
- If he has food in his mouth, lay him on his side with his face turned to the floor.
- Do not attempt to rouse the youngster with ammonia or ammonia capsules, or by dousing him with cold water or slapping his cheeks. He should come to on his own within several minutes.
- Inform your pediatrician.

narrows major blood vessels, including those that carry blood to the brain. Typically, young victims regain consciousness after a few minutes, with no lingering effects, and have full recall.

SYMPTOMS OF SYNCOPE

Sudden light-headedness, followed by loss of consciousness and collapse.

HOW SYNCOPE IS DIAGNOSED

- Physical examination and thorough medical history
- Tilt-table test

Vasovagal syncope runs through many family trees. "When we take the patient's family history," says Dr. Crumrine, "we often find that a close relative experienced similar symptoms at around the same age." A diagnosis can frequently be reached just on the basis of the history and possibly a *tilt-table test*. This simple, noninvasive procedure entails strapping a young patient to a mechanical table, then tilting it up to a near-standing position. She remains at this angle for ten to fifteen minutes. Fainting brought on by a rapid drop in blood pressure and heart rate is considered a positive result for vasovagal syncope. Rest assured that once the table is lowered, the patient's heartbeat and circulation return to normal, and she regains consciousness.

The physician may order a variety of additional tests to rule out other conditions, such as seizures (*epilepsy*) and cardiac disorders.

HOW SYNCOPE IS TREATED

- **Dietary measures:** Teenagers who are prone to fainting tend not to eat the recommended daily allowance of two thousand to three thousand milligrams of salt. While a diet high in sodium can eventually lead to hypertension, too little salt isn't healthy either, for two of the mineral's functions are to regulate blood pressure and retain fluid in the circulation.

Children often do not take in enough fluid. This, too, contributes to vasovagal syncope. Your youngster should be drinking the equivalent of at least eight cups of water and other fluids per day.

- **Drug therapy:** If medication is used, one of three drugs is typically called on to control the symptoms of vasovagal syncope. Fluorocortisone, a *mineralo-*

corticoid steroid, compels the kidneys to recirculate dietary salt instead of excrete it in the urine. Potassium is sacrificed instead; accordingly, a potassium supplement is often added when young patients begin the medication.

Atenolol works by way of an entirely different mechanism. The *beta-blocker* decelerates the heartbeat and prevents the powerful contractions that switch on the fainting reflex. Disopyramide, too, decreases the strength of the contraction, but it belongs to two different groups of agents: *antiarrhythmics* and *anticholinergics.*

Other Causes of Fainting in Teens

Two other common causes of dizziness and fainting in young people are *hyperventilation* (see "Respiratory Conditions," page 538) and *orthostatic hypotension.* "Orthostatic" means "caused by standing erect"; "hypotension," "low blood pressure." Adolescents with this condition may feel dizzy and weak if they stand up too quickly from a prone position. The drop in blood pressure is related to pubertal growth causing a rapidly rising center of gravity and expanding blood volume.

HELPING TEENAGERS HELP THEMSELVES

The measures below can help teens who are prone to fainting reduce the frequency of future episodes:

• Learn to recognize the early signs of a faint. A full swoon can be prevented by placing the head between the knees or by lying down.

• Minimize the amount of time spent in warm environments, such as showers and baths, and a hot midday sun. Saunas, hot tubs and Jacuzzis are to be avoided.

• When you are standing for long periods of time, shift your weight and flex your leg muscles, to keep the circulation moving. Even subtle movements, like bending forward from the waist, aid blood flow to the brain.

• When sitting for extended periods of time, sit in a low chair, lean forward with your hands on your knees or bring your knees up to your chest.

• Use pillows to elevate the head of the bed slightly.

• Avoid alcohol, which causes veins to widen, further reducing blood pressure.

Sleeping Problems

By the time most boys and girls enter adolescence, they've usually outgrown the common sleep problems of childhood. A young person who repeatedly tosses and turns at night should see her pediatrician. For occasional *insomnia,* help your teen sleep more soundly by encouraging her to improve her nighttime habits through the measures below.

• Eliminate long naps during the day, which can throw off the internal body clock that regulates the sleep cycle.

• Avoid caffeinated tea, soda, coffee and chocolate. Caffeine, a stimulant, can disrupt the normal sleep rhythm.

• Exercise during the day but not too close to bedtime. Physical activity energizes the body—hardly conducive to a good night's rest.

• An hour or two before bedtime, munch on a muffin, some crackers, a handful of cereal, fresh fruit or vegetables, popcorn, a small dish of sorbet or sherbet, or another food rich in carbohydrates. But don't eat heavy meals just prior to going to sleep.

• Take a warm, relaxing bath.

• Drink a glass of warm milk.

ORTHOPEDIC CONDITIONS

Repetitive Stress Injury

The National Academy of Sciences estimates that thirteen million to twenty million American adults are plagued by *repetitive stress injuries (RSIs),* the nation's number-one on-the-job hazard. Most RSIs involve the hands and wrists, and many cases are related to computer use. With more and more teenagers typing, clicking and dragging, it was inevitable that the epidemic would begin to make inroads in this age group.

All that time spent on-line has a cumulative effect on the soft tissues of the hands, wrists, elbows, shoulders, neck and back. (Another name for repetitive stress injury is *cumulative trauma disorder.*) Physicians are reporting growing numbers of pain complaints among cyberspace travelers in their twenties. The initial damage to nerves and tendons, however, was most likely sustained as many as five to ten years earlier, when they were teens.

SYMPTOMS THAT SUGGEST REPETITIVE STRESS INJURY MAY INCLUDE:

Minor aches and pain in the affected area; if left unchecked, may progress to:

- Sensations of tightness, soreness, numbness, tingling, burning, coldness in the hands, wrists, fingers, forearms and/or elbows
- Loss of hand strength and coordination
- Severe pain

Types of Repetitive Stress Injuries

- **Bursitis:** inflamed *bursa.* These tiny, fluid-filled sacs, located throughout the body, facilitate motion between soft tissues and bones. Bursitis occurs most often in the shoulder.
- **Carpal tunnel syndrome:** discomfort caused by compression of the major nerve that runs through the wrist and into the hand.
- **Tendinitis:** inflamed tendon.
- **Tenosynovitis:** inflamed tendon and the layer of tissue (*sheath*) around it.

HOW REPETITIVE STRESS INJURY IS DIAGNOSED

Physical examination and thorough medical history, plus one or more of the following procedures: (1) nerve conduction study and (2) X rays.

HOW REPETITIVE STRESS INJURY IS TREATED

- **Immobilization:** Mild cases of repetitive stress injury frequently heal just by resting the affected area. The young patient might have to be fitted with a lightweight *splint* or a more rigid *brace* temporarily. Be sure that he wears it as instructed; in a small study of people with carpal tunnel syndrome, researchers at the Medical College of Virginia in Richmond found that those who kept their splints on twenty-four hours a day improved more than the group that didn't wear the splint.

- **Drug therapy:** More severe cases of RSI may require over-the-counter or prescription oral *nonsteroidal anti-inflammatory drugs* (*NSAIDs*), to reduce swelling. Examples include naproxen and ibuprofen.

- **Surgery:** An operation is rarely necessary for treating bursitis, tendinitis and tenosynovitis. Carpal tunnel syndrome, though, does not always respond to nonsurgical interventions. If surgery is necessary, the surgeon performing the outpatient procedure cuts one of the ligaments in the wrist, to relieve the pressure on the *median* nerve.

HELPING TEENAGERS HELP THEMSELVES

Repetitive-stress injuries are infinitely easier to prevent than to treat. Mom and Dad, you can help. The next time your youngster's at the computer, check to see that she is observing the healthy habits below and write out a list of these habits, to be kept near the computer.

• Sit up straight in the chair (which should have a back support), shoulders relaxed.

• Keep both feet on the floor or on a small stool.

• Eye level should be even with the top of the monitor screen, so that your head is tilted slightly down, not with the chin jutting out.

• Keep your wrists straight and level with the keyboard. You shouldn't have to stretch your fingers to reach the keys.

• Don't contort your hands while typing; the fingers should form a straight line with your forearms.

• Wrist rests are for parking your hands only when taking a breather, not while typing.

• The keyboard should be tilted toward you, but slightly.

• Dance lightly over the keys, don't stomp on them. Similarly, refrain from gripping the mouse too hard. If possible, learn as many keyboard command codes as you can, so that you don't have to rely so heavily on the mouse.

• Use both hands to perform combination key strokes such as CTRL-K or ALT-F8.

• Both the monitor and the keyboard should be directly in front of you, not off to the side, forcing you to turn to see them.

- When using the mouse, try to move it with your hand and arm instead of with your hand and fingers.

- Don't let the room get too chilly; cold temperatures contribute to muscle stiffness.

- Don't talk on the phone while you're typing, with the receiver tucked between your shoulder and cheek. Invest in a headset or use the speakerphone function.

- Take a ten-minute break every hour that you're on the computer. Stand up and shake out your wrists. Step outside. If you get so immersed in your work or play that you tend to forget, set an alarm clock or watch.

- *If your teen complains of stiffness and other early signs of repetitive-stress injuries, consider purchasing a voice-recognition program, which allows the user to speak into a microphone and watch in amazement as his words appear on the screen.* (See "Overuse Syndromes" in chapter 19, "Physical Activity and Sports.")

Scoliosis

Our spine is naturally curved in order to distribute the weight of the body. A side-view X ray of a soldier standing rigidly at attention would show the *cervical* spine in his neck arched slightly forward. The twelve *thoracic vertebrae* curve gently to the rear. Then the *lumbar* spine, which bears most of our upper-body weight, arches forward as it nears the pelvis.

About one in twenty-five adolescent girls and one in two hundred teenage boys develop *scoliosis.* Captured on an X ray, their spines form, to varying degrees, a more pronounced *S* shape. When imaged from the back, a normal spine exhibits no curvature. A youngster is said to have scoliosis if her curvature is greater than ten degrees.

The condition can occur as a complication of polio, muscular dystrophy and other central nervous system disorders, but four in five cases among teenage girls are *idiopathic*—that is, of unknown cause. Very often, though, a family member will also have had scoliosis.

SYMPTOMS SUGGESTIVE OF SCOLIOSIS MAY INCLUDE:

- Conspicuous curving of the upper body
- Uneven, rounded shoulders
- Sunken chest

- Leaning to one side
- Back pain (rare)

Scoliosis can develop quietly for months to years so it may only be picked up by the pediatrician during an examination of the teen's back. Progression may occur quickly during the teen's growth spurt. One in seven young people with scoliosis have such severe curvature that they require treatment.

Backpack Flak

Back pain is becoming an increasingly common diagnosis among young people. By age twelve, about one in eight kids complain of back pain; by age eighteen, more than half have the problem. Overstuffed backpacks are partly to blame. Teenagers now tramp off to school looking like piano movers. They're loaded down with so much paraphernalia, you'd think they were heading off for a month in the Alaskan wilderness. It's not unusual for youngsters to cram twenty or more pounds of books, food items, sports gear and so on into their backpacks. This exerts pressure on the *vertebral* discs in the spine along with the vertebrae and muscles of the back.

The American Academy of Orthopedic Surgeons recommends the following guidelines for avoiding injury:

- A backpack should weigh no more than 10 to 15 percent of the carrier's weight.
- Choose a model that boasts features such as wide, padded shoulder straps and a padded back. How about a backpack with wheels?
- When packing the bag, place the heaviest items in back, so that they rest against your back. Try to pack them tightly, too; we don't want items shifting while you're walking.
- Slip on both straps, not just one. The pack should hang two inches above the waist.
- Make frequent trips to your locker every day, so that you're not always lugging a full bag around the halls.

If pain persists, interferes with or limits activities or is associated with other problems, the adolescent should be examined by her pediatrician.

HOW SCOLIOSIS IS DIAGNOSED

- Physical examination and thorough medical history
- X rays

HOW SCOLIOSIS IS TREATED

• **Bracing:** Many such cases never progress to the point that treatment is necessary. Follow-up visits are scheduled approximately every six months for those diagnosed with curves between fifteen and twenty degrees.

Curvature above twenty-five degrees may call for *bracing*. There are two main types of orthopedic back braces. The *Milwaukee brace* has a neck ring and can correct curves anywhere in the spine; the *thoracolumbosacral orthosis* (TLSO for short, thankfully) is for deformities involving the vertebrae of the thoracic spine and below. The device fits under the arm and wraps around the ribs, hips and lower back.

Scoliosis patients can expect to wear the brace all but a few hours a day until their spinal bone growth is complete; usually that's about ages seventeen to eighteen for girls, and eighteen to nineteen for boys. The braces are more cosmetically appealing than they used to be and can be hidden easily under clothing. Having to wear an orthopedic brace interferes only minimally with physical activity. Only contact sports and trampolining are off-limits for the time being.

• **Surgery:** *Posterior spinal fusion and instrumentation,* the operation to surgically correct scoliosis, is typically recommended when the spine's curvature is fifty degrees or more. The surgical procedure fuses the affected vertebrae using metal rods and screws to stabilize that part of the spine until it has fused together completely. On average, this takes about twelve months. Although teenagers who have the surgery still face some restrictions on physical activity, they can say good-bye to the brace.

TEEN TIP:

Don't worry [*crack!*] if your teenager has a habit of cracking his knuckles. The sound may drive you to distraction [*crack!*], but it does not cause any permanent harm [*crack!*] to joints.

HELPING TEENS HELP THEMSELVES

Only about 50 percent of young scoliosis patients wear their braces. Parents need to convey the importance of complying with the doctor's instructions. At the same time, they should be sensitive to the tremendous impact the condition can inflict on a teenager's body image, which at this age is inextricably entwined with self-identity and self-confidence. You might want to consider asking your pediatrician or orthopedist for a referral to a mental-health professional experienced in counseling children with chronic medical problems. A patient support group, like those run by the Scoliosis Association may also be helpful.

RESPIRATORY CONDITIONS

Asthma

One in ten adolescents and young adults in the United States suffer from *asthma,* a breathing disorder that typically strikes during childhood. Asthma can be described as hypersensitivity of the *bronchial tubes* that carry air throughout the lungs. Either a respiratory infection or irritants in the environment cause these passageways to spasm. At the same time, their inner linings become inflamed and swollen. Mucus from the lungs clogs the ever-narrowing openings. The net effect is that fresh air bearing oxygen can't get in, and stale carbon-dioxide–laden air can't escape. An *asthma attack* can be frightening, for both youngsters and parents. In severe episodes, wheezing and coughing give way to desperate gasps for air. Although asthma rarely proves fatal, it should be regarded as a potential medical emergency.

Recent findings have refuted many long-held views of asthma. For instance, it was once thought that about half of all young sufferers outgrew the disease by their midteens. We now know that although asthma may go into hiding—leaving patients symptom-free for years at a time, it never completely goes away.

> ### *Words Worth Knowing*
>
> **Pulmonology:** the study of the lungs and lung-related medical conditions.

SYMPTOMS SUGGESTIVE OF AN ASTHMA ATTACK MAY INCLUDE:

MILD ATTACK

- Mild difficulty breathing
- Slightly increased respiration

- Mild wheezing upon exhaling only, coughing, shortness of breath, tightness in chest
- Mild retraction of the *intercostal* muscles between the ribs, to facilitate breathing
- Peak air flow rate (see "Self-monitoring" on page 541) is 80 percent or more of teen's highest reading

MODERATE ATTACK

- Moderate difficulty breathing
- Increased respiration
- Moderate wheezing upon inhaling and exhaling, cough, shortness of breath and tightness in chest
- Peak air flow rate is 50 to 80 percent of teen's highest reading
- Moderate retraction of the intercostal muscles, to facilitate breathing
- Shortness of breath making it hard to speak in anything more than single words or brief phrases
- Pale skin color

SEVERE ATTACK

- Extreme difficulty breathing
- Labored and rapid respiration
- Coughing, shortness of breath, tightness in chest
- Peak air flow rate is less than 50 percent of teen's highest reading
- Shortness of breath making it hard to speak in anything more than single words or partial sentences
- Moderate retractions of the intercostal muscles and other muscles in the neck, abdomen and chest, to facilitate breathing
- Skin may take on a bluish tinge (*cyanosis*)
- Inaudible breath sounds

HOW ASTHMA IS DIAGNOSED

- Blood gas analysis, to measure levels of oxygen and carbon dioxide in the blood
- Pulmonary function tests
- Bronchial provocation test
- Chest X ray

HOW ASTHMA IS TREATED

• **Drug therapy:** Pediatricians adopt a double-barreled approach to controlling asthma. "For prevention and long-term management," says Dr. Howenstine of Riley Children's Hospital in Indianapolis, "we have the anti-inflammatory medications, which are taken daily." There are three types: *inhaled corticosteroids* such as beclomethasone, budesonide, fluticasone, flunisolide and triamcinolone; the *nonsteroidal* agent cromolyn; and a novel group of oral drugs called *leukotriene modifiers.* Upon their introduction in the late 1990s, montelukast, zafirlukast and zileuton became the first new therapies for chronic asthma in twenty years.

The antileukotrienes reduce both airway inflammation *and* constriction. In clinical studies testing the effectiveness of leukotriene modifiers and inhaled corticosteroids, patients who took the corticosteroids fared slightly better. However, the newer agents hold one major advantage in that they come in tablet and chewable-tablet forms; with steroids, the young person breathes in the medicine through a handheld device or nebulizer (see box below). Not all kids adjust to using the inhaler, however, and so for them these oral medications might be preferable.

What's more, moderate to high doses of inhaled steroids are believed to stunt the growth of some teenagers. Adding a leukotriene modifier to a corticosteroid allows for the steroid medication's dosage to be lowered by as much as half. A leukotriene modifier may be used in place of a corticosteroid if a boy or girl with asthma has not responded to the previous medication.

Metered-dose inhaler: an aerosol device that is placed in the mouth. With the press of a button, a precise dose of medication is delivered down the throat and into the airways.

When an asthma attack occurs, the patient reaches for a *bronchodilator,* which relieves the spasming and reopens the narrowed passageways. These medications include albuterol, metaproterenol, pirbuterol and terbulaline. They, too, are administered through an inhaler. Using asthma medications

TEEN TIP:

Administering cromolyn and/or albuterol about twenty minutes before physical activity helps to prevent exercise-induced asthma.

carefully enables the majority of young people with this respiratory condition to lead full, active lives.

• **Self-monitoring:** *Peak-flow measurement,* a simple home test for assessing lung function, enables asthmatics to control their disease more effectively. It warns of impending attacks and also helps patients to identify which precipitants in the environment cause their airways to constrict and therefore are to be avoided.

Your pediatrician will show your teen (and you) how to use the *peak-flow meter.* It is a cylindrical handheld device that resembles an oversized kazoo. The patient inhales deeply, then blows as hard as he can into the mouthpiece. A scale on the meter registers how many liters of air were expelled per minute, from 0 L/min (liters per minute) to 600 L/min. This is the *peak expiratory flow rate,* or PEFR.

The first time your youngster performs the procedure, she takes three separate readings. The highest PEFR becomes her *baseline* flow rate: the standard against which future tests are compared. Naturally the baseline must be readjusted periodically to reflect physical growth and as asthma control improves.

An adolescent's peak flow rate is expressed as a percentage of the baseline value. Most doctors additionally use a zone system to help them interpret the results for patients and parents. To give you an example, let's say that a fifteen-year-old's normal peak-flow rate is four hundred liters of air expelled per minute:

TABLE 20.10

Peak-Flow Measurement Meanings

ZONE	PEAK EXPIRATORY FLOW RATE	WHAT THIS MEANS/ WHAT YOU SHOULD DO
Green Zone	80 to 100% of the peak flow (*320 L/min to 400 L/min*)	Asthma is reasonably well controlled, producing symptoms only occasionally.
Yellow Zone	50 to 80% of the peak flow (*200 L/min to 320 L/min*)	Caution: Air passages are narrowing and may require additional therapy.
Red Zone	Less than 50% of the peak flow (*Less than 200 L/min*)	Call your pediatrician, who can counsel you on what to do.

Your pediatrician will advise your teen on how often to perform peak-flow measurement. Typically, the schedule is once in the morning and once in the evening, as well as anytime symptoms arise. Readings taken before and after administering asthma medications can yield valuable information for the doctor about how well the treatment is working.

MEASURING PEAK-FLOW RATE, STEP BY STEP

1. Stand up straight.
2. Take a deep breath.
3. Place your lips tightly around the mouthpiece and blow as fast and as hard as you can for one to two seconds.
4. Read the number on the meter scale and write it down on the preprinted graph that came with the device.
5. To ensure the meter's accuracy, follow all care and cleaning instructions.

• **Avoiding asthma triggers:** Another tactic for people with asthma is to identify which environmental offenders, foods and activities provoke attacks. Here are suggested strategies for eliminating or avoiding the most common asthma agitators in and around the home:

GENERAL PREVENTIVE MEASURES

• Use a powerful vacuum cleaner fitted with a HEPA (high-efficiency particulate air) filter; don't use brooms and dusters, which raise dust.

• Rid the home of any pillows, bedding and furniture stuffed with *kapok,* the silky down from the seeds of silk-cotton trees.

• Encourage your teen to stay indoors on days when the air-pollution count or the pollen count is high.

• Regularly replace filters on air conditioners, furnaces and air filters, so that mold and dust don't build up and get blown into the air. Consider using HEPA filters for the furnace and the AC too.

• Air-conditioning does more for asthmatic children than merely keep them cool. One, it allows you to shut the windows and doors, keeping out pollen from flowers, trees, grasses, hay and ragweed, and mold spores. And, two, it lowers the humidity, which helps to control dust mites and household mold.

But don't set the temperature *too* low: Some kids with asthma cannot tolerate cold air, especially when they come in from outside on warm days.

• Cover bedroom air vents with several layers of cheesecloth to reduce the the number of large allergen particles invading the room.

• Try to limit the number of flat surfaces in your child's room (horizontal blinds, bookcases and so on), which collect dust.

• Make schoolteachers aware of your teen's asthma triggers and ask them to help him avoid them. According to a 2000 survey by the American Academy of Allergy, Asthma and Immunology, two in five pediatric asthma patients had as many as three attacks a month. Common classroom allergens include chalk dust, pollen, dust, mold spores and animal dander.

INDOOR TRIGGERS

Animal Dander

Dander is the loose scales shed from the coat or feathers of warm-blooded pets such as dogs, cats, birds and rodents.

• The least-popular solution as far as your family is concerned is to give away the pet.
• The least-popular solution as far as your pet is concerned is to bathe the animal once a week.
• Keep pets out of the youngster's bedroom at all times; if your home has forced-air heating, close the bedroom's air vents.
• Make sure that your teen takes his asthma medication before visiting friends and relatives who have pets.
• Choose pets without fur or feathers, like fish or snakes.
• Don't buy pillows, comforters, or other products made with feathers or down.

Cockroaches

Dead roaches and roach droppings collect in household dust and can induce asthma attacks. The insects typically congregate in dark, moist areas, such as basements, attics, crawl spaces, floor drains, in and around bathtubs, hampers and sewers. It is highly recommended that you exterminate roaches with insecticide sprays, baits or dusts, or hire a pest-control professional to do the job. Children with asthma should not be present when the home is being treated.

Dust Mites

These microscopic creatures, one of the chief nuisances for asthmatics, make their homes in household dust. Thousands of them can crowd onto a single speck. Ask your pediatrician or pharmacist to recommend a cleaning solution specially formulated to kill the mite.

- Wash your teen's pillows and bedcovers in hot water once a week.

- Encase his mattress and box spring in airtight plastic covers; then place duct tape or clear plastic tape over the lengths of the zippers. You can buy similar covers for pillows, too.

- Take up carpets in the youngster's bedroom.

- A child with asthma should not be in the same room when you're vacuuming (or cleaning). Nor should he run the vacuum himself. If necessary, though, make sure he wears a dust mask.

- Wipe up surface dust as frequently as possible, using a damp mop or cloth, but no spray or aerosol cleaners.

- Window curtains and shades made from washable materials like plastic attract less dust and are easier to clean than other types of window coverings.

- Remove cloth-upholstered furniture from the home if it appears to be a trigger.

Household Odors and Products

- When painting the interior of your home, arrange for your teenager with asthma to be elsewhere until the paint is sufficiently dry. Open windows and turn on fans to disperse the fumes. Other common household products that may need to be avoided include paint thinner, cleaning solvents and furniture polish.

- Hair sprays, perfumes, talcum powder and scented cosmetics can set off asthma attacks and therefore should be used in small amounts or not at all.

- Do not use room deodorizers.

- Purchase unscented detergents, bleaches, starches and other laundry products whenever possible.

- Even strong cooking odors can instigate an attack, so open the kitchen windows and turn on a fan when cooking.

Molds

- Bathrooms, kitchens and basements should be well ventilated and cleaned regularly.
- Molds thrive under damp, moist conditions, so if you have a humidifier, turn it off.
- Dehumidifiers, on the other hand, are ideal for damp basement areas. Be sure to empty and clean the unit regularly, to prevent mildew from forming.
- Molds also occupy houseplants, so inspect them frequently. You may have to move all plants outdoors.

Tobacco Smoke

It goes without saying that no teen should smoke, much less those suffering from asthma. Tobacco smoke is a major irritant to the bronchial tubes.

Don't allow smoking in your home *at all.* If anyone needs to have a cigarette, ask him politely to please light up outside. That includes moms and dads. According to a study conducted at Tulane University in New Orleans, reducing an asthmatic child's exposure to cigarette smoke at home may improve lung function and reduce asthma symptoms. The study, the first of its kind, continuously monitored sixteen households. In all, there were twenty-one adult smokers and eighteen kids with asthma.

During the first three months, the adults smoked as they normally would. For the second three-month phase, the smokers were asked to abstain from using tobacco in the home. Not all were able to comply, but the average number of cigarettes smoked fell from nineteen per day to fewer than one a day. The impact on the youngsters' health was dramatic. They enjoyed more days of normal activity and sleep and less coughing and wheezing. Their need for medication dropped by 40 percent. Finally, in the peak-flow monitoring test, nearly nine in ten of the children improved their peak expiratory flow rate by 11 percent.

What more do you need to know?

OUTDOOR TRIGGERS

Cold Weather

On cold, windy days, asthmatic teenagers should keep their mouths and noses covered. Scarves work well, as does deploying that turtleneck sweater in its upright position.

Pollen and Molds

- When the pollen count is high, your youngster should consider staying inside from midday through the afternoon.
- During pollen season, keep windows closed and turn on the air conditioner.
- Wet leaves and garden debris often harbor molds and should be avoided.

OTHER ASTHMA TRIGGERS

Colds and Infections

Young people with asthma will want to take these precautions to ward off germs:

- Stay away from people with colds or the flu.

- Eat a balanced, nutritious diet, exercise regularly and get the proper amount of rest, all of which enhance immunity against infection.

- In the fall, ask your pediatrician whether or not your teen would benefit from receiving the flu shot.

- Also be sure to check with the pediatrician before giving your teenager over-the-counter cold remedies, such as antihistamines and cough syrup. Allergies and interactions with other medications can contribute to asthma attacks.

Exercise

- Asthmatic youngsters sometimes develop *exercise-induced asthma,* in which exertion causes them to start wheezing, particularly in cold weather. Your pediatrician can prescribe medication, to be taken daily or prior to exercise, that will allow your child to remain physically active.

- Teens should always warm up and cool down before and after exercising.

Emotions

Powerful emotions such as anger, fear, frustration, crying—even hearty laughter—can trigger an asthma attack. A counselor knowledgeable in teaching youngsters self-calming techniques and relaxation exercises could prove valuable. Ask your pediatrician for a referral.

HELPING TEENAGERS HELP THEMSELVES

Youngsters stricken with asthma should know the following about living with their disease:

• Learn to recognize the warning signs of an asthma attack (see box), so that they can act promptly. Waiting too long before initiating treatment can land kids in the hospital. They should stick exactly to the prescribed dose and neither undermedicate nor overmedicate themselves.

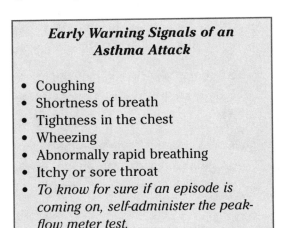

Early Warning Signals of an Asthma Attack

- Coughing
- Shortness of breath
- Tightness in the chest
- Wheezing
- Abnormally rapid breathing
- Itchy or sore throat
- *To know for sure if an episode is coming on, self-administer the peak-flow meter test.*

• They need to know what to do next. First, take the preventive medication ordered by their pediatrician. Then sit down in a chair, close their eyes and practice breathing slowly. It's normal to be anxious, says Dr. Howenstine, "but this makes it even harder to breathe. From there it can become a self-perpetuating cycle, because if you can't breathe, you get *more* nervous and have still more trouble breathing." While teens wait for the medication to take effect, they should drink plenty of fluids. This thins out the secretions from the lungs.

• Ask your pediatrician to show your teen *pursed-lip breathing,* a technique for emptying the lungs of trapped "used" air; as well as tricks for effective coughing—by that we mean a cough that brings up airway-plugging mucus.

• Remind your teen to have his bronchodilator on hand at all times. The medicine won't do an asthma sufferer much good if he feels an attack coming on while at school, and the inhaler is sitting at home on his desk.

• *If the doctor-prescribed medications don't relieve the spasming and open the airways, call your pediatrician or one of her associates. You can also contact the emergency department at a local hospital and ask to speak to the pediatrician on call.*

Hyperventilation

Hyperventilation—deep, heavy breathing triggered by anxiety—is common in adolescents. It is often accompanied by many of the same symptoms as an asthma attack (weakness, tightness in the chest, air hunger). Unlike an asthmatic episode, however, a youngster who is hyperventilating does not wheeze.

To stop the hyperventilation, have the teenager breathe into a paper bag. This seems to work for two reasons, says Dr. Howenstine. "Physiologically, because you're rebreathing your own air, your carbon dioxide can't be blown off so easily. But, also, it usually distracts the teenager from whatever stress brought this on in the first place."

If a child starts to hyperventilate before going on stage—a classic scenario—but quickly recovers, there is probably no need for a pediatric evaluation, according to Dr. Howenstine. "However," she adds, "it's important to sit down with the youngster and explain what happened to her body and why." But recurrent episodes may indicate a physical problem or panic disorder and should be brought to a doctor's attention. (See "Dizziness and Fainting Spells (Syncope)" on page 529.)

SEXUALLY TRANSMITTED DISEASES

Since 1981, when a mysterious sexually transmitted virus originally known as the "gay men's cancer" first came to light, AIDS (acquired immune deficiency syndrome) has cast an ominous shadow over the lives of teenagers—and their worried parents, too.

And yet, interestingly, adolescents make up just 0.5 percent of the total number of men and women to have been diagnosed with AIDS. As of 1999, nearly twenty years into the epidemic, only 3,423 youngsters between the ages of thirteen and nineteen had contracted the virus. (The figures ascend quickly, however, with 24,437 infections among the twenty-to-twenty-four age bracket.)

Still, since it remains incurable, despite significant advances in treatment, it's understandable that AIDS should command so much attention and dollars for research. Unfortunately, the specter of AIDS has tended to obscure the reality that a teenager is far more likely to contract several other sexually transmitted

---

TABLE 20.11

Sexually Transmitted Diseases:

Number of Cases Diagnosed Annually in the United States

- *At least 1 in 4 STDs diagnosed each year occurs in teenagers. That's a minimum of 4 million teens annually.*
- *Approximately 2 of the 3 STDs diagnosed each year infect young people under age twenty-five.*

STD	No. of Cases
1. Genital warts due to *Human Papillomavirus* (HPV)	5.5 million
2. Trichomonias due to *Trichomonas vaginalis*	5 million
3. Chlamydia infection due to *Chlamydia trachomatis*	3 million
4. Pelvic inflammatory disease (PID) due to various agents, including those causing *chlamydia* and *gonorrhea*	1 million
5. Genital herpes due to the *Herpes Simplex virus*	1 million
6. Gonorrhea due to *Neisseria gonorrhoeae*	650,000
7. Acquired immune deficiency syndrome (AIDS) due to *Human Immunodeficiency Virus* (HIV)	40,000
8. Syphilis due to *Treponema pallidum*	11,300
Approximate total:	15.3 million to 16.5 million

Source: National Institute of Allergy and Infectious Diseases

---

diseases (STDs). Though fatalities are rare among these other STDs, they can lead to infertility and ectopic pregnancies—the latter of which *is* potentially life threatening.

In addition, several of these lesser known STDs—including chlamydia, gonorrhea, herpes and syphilis—also make those who are infected with them more vulnerable to HIV infection.

Human Immunodeficiency Virus (HIV)
and Acquired Immune Deficiency Syndrome (AIDS)

AIDS is caused by the human immunodeficiency virus (HIV), which is spread through unprotected sexual intercourse with an infected person or through using a contaminated needle to inject drugs. A third potential route of transmission, tainted blood received via transfusion, is extraordinarily rare; the odds of incurring HIV this way are one in one million.

Upon entering the circulation, the HIV microorganisms abduct a type of white blood cell known as *T-lymphocyte helpers*. They go by other names, including *T-cells, CD4 cells* and *helper-Ts*. In a person with a healthy immune system, T-cells band together to help defend the body against foreign invaders, or *antigens*. But the hijacked T-cells are forced to mass-produce copies of HIV. This eventually depletes the ranks of normal helper-Ts.

Ordinarily, each cubic milliliter of blood contains around one thousand T-cells. A person who's tested positive for HIV is declared to have full-fledged AIDS when his T-cell count falls below two hundred, *or* if he develops any of twenty-five *opportunistic* infections and cancers. The five most common of these are *Pneumocystis carinii pneumonia, HIV wasting syndrome, candidiasis of the esophagus, tuberculosis* and *Kaposi's sarcoma*. Opportunistic illnesses pose minimal threat when the immune system is functioning properly. But when the body's defenses are down, as in AIDS, they seize the opportunity to create havoc.

For the first ten years of the AIDS crisis, the disease was a virtual death sentence for most of its victims. Few survived more than two years, on average. However, the 1990s brought several major breakthroughs: two new classes of antiviral drugs to act directly on the virus, and improved therapies for managing the associated illnesses.

According to the Centers for Disease Control and Prevention, from 1995 through 1998 the death rate from AIDS dropped 70 percent. The number of new infections per year has plummeted too, from about 140,000 annually in the mid- to late 1980s to 40,000. However, about one in three HIV-positive patients will not respond to current treatments. It is also unclear how long the new treatments will keep people alive. AIDS remains a serious public health threat, managed—when it can be—by a lifelong course of extremely expensive medications. It is a danger not only to partners of the infected person, but to the fetus in the womb of any pregnant woman who is infected, because the infection can be passed from mother to baby during childbirth.

Chlamydia

Chlamydia, the most prevalent bacterial STD in the United States, is the result of the *Chlamydia trachomatis* bacterium, which can infect the urethra (bladder opening) and cervix (uterus opening). It is common in youngsters aged fifteen to nineteen. The disease is easily treated, but like other sexually transmitted infections, chlamydia tends to be silent and therefore go undiagnosed until it becomes more serious than in its early stages. Three in four women and one in two men have no symptoms. In 40 percent of cases, by the time a girl seeks medical attention, the disease has progressed to *pelvic inflammatory disease* (PID, described below), a major cause of female infertility and pelvic pain.

Gonorrhea

Chlamydia infection is sometimes confused with gonorrhea, another bacterial infection transmitted through vaginal and anal intercourse, and oral sex. Not only do they share many of the same symptoms, the two diseases can occur together.

Gonorrhea usually begins in the urethra (bladder opening) or the cervix. However, the rapidly proliferating *Neisseria gonorrhoea* bacterium can migrate to the uterus and the fallopian tubes, giving rise to pelvic inflammatory disease (PID). The infection, like chlamydia, may also involve the rectum.

Pelvic Inflammatory Disease (PID)

A number of different microorganisms can cause pelvic inflammatory disease of the upper female reproductive tract. The two most common culprits are *Chlamydia trachomatis* and *Neisseria gonorrhoea,* which account for four in five cases.

Sexually active girls aged fifteen to nineteen are the most vulnerable population, partly because they are more likely than other age groups to have multiple sex partners.

PID from chlamydia infection typically produces mild symptoms or none at all, but should be treated promptly. Otherwise, like other forms of PID, it can inflame and scar the ovaries and the fallopian tubes. PID from gonorrhea, on the other hand, can produce what Dr. Meg Fisher of Philadelphia's St. Christopher's Hospital for Children characterizes as "the worst lower-abdominal pain a girl has ever had. That's what brings most of them in to the doctor."

Because PID affects the fallopian tubes, where conception takes place, if the scarring is severe enough, the male sperm may be prevented from reaching the female egg. In other words, sterility can be the final outcome of PID.

Genital Warts and Human Papillomavirus (HPV)

Scientists have identified more than one hundred types of this virus. A number of them are passed from one person to another during unprotected sex and cause benign genital warts (*condylomata acuminata*). Other human papillomaviruses are responsible for four in five cases of cervical cancer, in addition to several other genital malignancies.

HPV is another, often silent, STD. According to the National Institute of AIDS and Infectious Diseases, almost half the women harboring the virus exhibit no symptoms at all. Genital warts typically appear in clusters inside and outside the vagina, the cervix and/or the anus. Male venereal warts, which are far less common, form on the penis, the scrotum and/or around the anus. The pinkish or flesh-colored growths often vanish on their own.

The interventions for genital warts differ from those for other STDs. Most cases can be managed with topical treatment of the warts, though the lesions tend to return. Large warts may have to be removed using one of several surgical procedures: *cryosurgery* (freezing), *electrocautery* (burning) or *laser surgery.*

Genital Herpes (HSV-1, HSV-2)

There are two types of herpes simplex viruses, the highly contagious virus that causes genital herpes. "Herpes simplex 2 usually occurs on or around the vagina, the penis, the anus or on the buttocks and thighs," says Dr. Fisher, "whereas herpes simplex type 1 generally causes cold sores around the outside of the mouth, or blisters on the gums or in the throat." However, HSV-1 sometimes infects the genital-anal area, while both types can be transmitted to the mouth via oral sex.

Because the virus permanently inhabits sensory nerves at the base of the *spinal cord,* genital herpes is a chronic, lifelong condition. Most of the time, HSV lies dormant. But it is reactivated periodically and produces sores or vessicles—most notably, clusters of tiny ulcers that resemble cold sores. These outbreaks, which typically last about one week, should be taken as a warning that the disease is contagious. The virus travels up the nerves that lead to the surface of the skin, where it proliferates, giving rise to new sores. (Initial symptoms of genital herpes tend to be more severe and longer-lasting than subsequent episodes.) The disease can be infectious even if no sores or lesions are present.

Teenagers need to know that "at least half the time, active herpes produces no symptoms at all," Dr. Fisher emphasizes. "So the virus can easily be transmitted sexually without either partner being aware that the carrier has active disease." Recurrences flare up regularly in some people but can be unpredictable in others. Why they occur remains a mystery, although stress, menstruation, illness and sunlight exposure appear to be possible triggers.

Syphilis

Until the early 1940s, when the *antibiotic* penicillin entered into widespread commercial use, epidemics of syphilis had been reported for centuries. Even today the onetime scourge can be fatal if left untreated. The bacterium *Treponema pallidum* eventually slips into the bloodstream, which sends it to organs outside the reproductive tract.

Physicians divide the course of the disease into three stages: *primary* (stage 1), *secondary* (stage 2) and *tertiary* (stage 3). The first evidence of syphilis is a hard, round open sore known as a *chancre* (pronounced "*shan*-ker") in the genital area. Young women often don't realize that they are infected, says Dr. Fisher, "because the initial chancre typically may develop inside the vagina; whereas with boys, it forms on the outside of the penis and is noticed immediately."

Since syphilis chancres aren't painful and typically heal within four to six weeks, most boys don't see a doctor. They assume the mysterious sore is gone for good, but one-third of men and women exposed to primary syphilis progress to a secondary infection. A few weeks after the chancre heals, they come down with a rash on the palms of their hands and the soles of their feet. The reddish-brown spots, about the size of a penny, can spread anywhere on the body. Other unwanted symptoms soon follow. Syphilis is still highly treatable at this point. However, a pregnant woman with primary or secondary syphilis will almost certainly transmit the bacterium to her fetus. Infection early in fetal life leads to death and abortion; infection later in pregnancy leads to a variety of problems including anemia, bleeding, swollen glands and infection of the various organs, such as the lungs, spleen and brain.

SYMPTOMS THAT SUGGEST SEXUALLY TRANSMITTED DISEASES MAY INCLUDE:

HIV/AIDS

- Headaches
- Difficulty swallowing
- Fever
- Night sweats
- Fatigue/weakness
- Appetite loss
- Weight loss
- Chronic diarrhea
- Nausea/vomiting
- Itchy, rashy skin/skin lesions
- Chronic coughing
- Confusion/delirium
- Difficulty breathing

CHLAMYDIAL INFECTION

Symptoms typically occur one to three weeks after exposure.

Women:

- Abnormal vaginal discharge
- Mild pain when urinating
- Progression to pelvic inflammatory disease

Men:

- Penile discharge
- Mild pain when urinating
- Progression to *epididymitis,* an inflammation of the tubelike structure that stores and transports sperm

GONORRHEA

Symptoms typically occur two to ten days after exposure.

Men:

- Penile discharge
- Mild to severe burning sensation when urinating
- Can progress to epididymitis

Women:

- Painful or burning sensation when urinating and/or yellow or bloody vaginal discharge
- Abdominal pain
- Bleeding between menstrual periods
- Vomiting
- Fever
- Progression to pelvic inflammatory disease

Rectal Infection:

- Anal discharge
- Anal itching
- Painful bowel movements

PELVIC INFLAMMATORY DISEASE (PID)

- Lower abdominal pain
- Abnormal vaginal discharge
- Fever
- Painful intercourse
- Irregular menstrual bleeding

GENITAL WARTS/HUMAN PAPILLOMAVIRUS (HPV)

Symptoms typically occur three months after exposure.
    Women: Clusters of tiny warts outside and inside of the vagina, on the cervix or around the anus
    Men: Clusters of tiny warts on the penis, scrotum or anus

GENITAL HERPES

Symptoms typically occur two to ten days after exposure.
    Initial episode, typically lasting two to three weeks:

- Itching or burning sensation in the genitals or anus
- Pain in the genitals, buttocks, legs
- Vaginal discharge
- Feeling of pressure in the abdomen
- Tiny red bumps involving the vagina, cervix, penis and/or anal area; these turn into blisters and then become painful open sores
- Fever
- Headache
- Muscle aches
- Painful or difficult urination
- Swollen glands in the groin

Recurrences, typically lasting about one week:

- Itching or tingling sensation in the genitals, buttocks or legs
- Small blisters or open sores at the site of infection

SYPHILIS

Stage 1: Primary Syphilis

Initial symptoms typically occur two to six weeks after exposure and last four to six weeks.

Teenagers and the Law

Testing and Treatment for STDs: Their Rights, Your Rights

One reason that so many young people refuse to seek STD testing is their fear that Mom and Dad will find out. But they won't; not unless the teen decides to tell them herself.

"Federal law allows minors to receive treatment for STDs without their parents' consent," explains Dr. Robert Brown of Children's Hospital in Columbus, Ohio. "All information is kept confidential."

Naturally, we would hope that a child diagnosed with a sexually transmitted disease would inform his mother and father. For one thing, he will need his parents' advice and support. But because the consequences of these infections can be so devastating, eliminating obstacles to testing—even psychological ones—has to take precedence over a parent's right to know.

- Painless chancre on the penis, vulva, vagina, cervix or around the mouth
- Inflamed lymph nodes

Stage 2: Secondary Syphilis

Symptoms typically occur one to six weeks after the chancre heals and last three to six months.

- Light rash with brown sores roughly the size of a penny, typically on the palms of the hands and soles of the feet; may also cover the rest of the body
- Sores in or around the genitals or anus
- Mild fever
- Fatigue
- Headaches
- Sore throat
- Patchy hair loss
- Appetite loss
- Weight loss

Stage 3: Tertiary Stage

Symptoms typically occur anywhere from two years to more than forty years after the onset of infection.

Syphilis in multiple systems, including the heart and blood vessels, skin, bones and brain.

HOW SEXUALLY TRANSMITTED DISEASES ARE DIAGNOSED

STDs are usually detected on the basis of laboratory tests and a physician's clinical examination. Sexually active young people are notoriously lax about getting themselves tested, undoubtedly due to fear of learning that they've been infected. For instance, young people under twenty-five account for fully half the new cases of HIV infections in the United States, according to the Centers of Disease Control and Prevention. Yet only one in four sexually active boys and girls have been screened for the HIV antibodies produced in response to the virus's presence.[1]

Teens need to hear from parents and pediatricians that it is always better to know your disease status than to bury your head in the sand, *especially* in the event that the test comes back positive. Early detection and prompt treatment can significantly improve a young person's prospects for a cure (or, in the case of AIDS, for reducing the odds of suffering a potentially deadly complication). To give you an example, a health-maintenance organization studied the benefits of screening for chlamydia. One group of patients underwent testing, the other group did not. Over the next year, the incidence of pelvic inflammatory disease among the screened volunteers was approximately half that of the unscreened participants.

A teen who tests positive for any sexually transmitted disease should inform sex partners of his or her status. They, too, should be screened—even if they do not have symptoms—so that no more links are added to the chain of infections.

HOW SEXUALLY TRANSMITTED DISEASES ARE TREATED

• **Drug therapy:** With the exception of HIV/AIDS, treatment for the sexually transmitted diseases discussed here consists of antibiotic, antiviral or antiparasitic medications, depending on the nature of the infectious microorganism.

---

1 The blood test for HIV does not actually detect the virus itself but rather the level of HIV antibodies manufactured by the body's immune system.

TABLE 20.12

Diagnostic Testing for Sexually Transmitted Diseases

STD	TYPE OF DIAGNOSTIC PROCEDURES THAT MAY BE ORDERED
HIV/AIDS	Physical examination, including pelvic exam in young women, and thorough medical history, plus one or more of the following blood tests: *ELISA (Enzyme-Linked Immunosorbent Assay)* antibody blood test. If the sample tests positive for HIV, the more-accurate *Western blot* antibody blood test is performed to confirm a diagnosis.
Chlamydia	Physical examination, including pelvic exam in young women, and thorough medical history, plus laboratory analysis of cervical secretions or urine, to detect presence of *C. trachomatis.*
Gonorrhea	Physical examination, including pelvic exam in young women, and thorough medical history, plus laboratory testing of cervical, vaginal or penile secretions.
Pelvic Inflammatory Disease (PID)	Physical examination, including pelvic exam in young women, and thorough medical history, plus one or more laboratory tests of cervical or vaginal secretions, ultrasound imaging exam. *Severely ill patients may be hospitalized and given antibiotics intravenously.*
Genital Warts/Human Papillomavirus (HPV)	Physical examination, including pelvic exam in young women, and thorough medical history, plus a Pap smear. If the Pap smear is abnormal, colposcopy and cervical biopsy may be done.
Genital Herpes	Physical examination, including pelvic exam in young women, and thorough medical history, herpes virus blood test and culture.
Syphilis	Physical examination, including pelvic exam, and thorough medical history, plus one or more of the following blood tests: VDRL (Venereal Disease Research Laboratory) blood test or RPR (Rapid Plasma Reagin) blood test, (FTA-ABS) Fluorescent Treponemal Antibody-Absorption antibody blood test or (TPHA) *T. pallidum* hemagglutination assay, to confirm a positive finding on the VDRL or RPR test.

Early on in the AIDS crisis, doctors had little to offer their patients. The first drug designed to suppress the human immunodeficiency virus, the *nucleoside reverse transcriptase inhibitor* AZT (now called zidovudine, or ZDV), wasn't approved until 1986. Ten years later, a second family of medications, *protease inhibitors,* emerged, soon to be joined by a third class, the *nonnucleoside reverse transcriptase inhibitors.* Each of these antivirals interrupts HIV's ability to multiply, but at a different stage of its life cycle.

The current standard treatment, "Highly Active Anti-Retroviral Therapy" (HAART), incorporates medications from all three categories. Based on a study made public in 2000, giving youngsters four drugs several times a day seems to be superior to a three-drug regimen. In the trial, conducted at Jacobi Medical Center in the Bronx, New York, 181 HIV-positive children were assigned to one of four groups. After twenty-four weeks, more boys and girls in the group that received the most aggressive treatment had undetectable levels of HIV in their bloodstream; the four-drug arm also exhibited the greatest increase in T-cells.

The use of these so-called "AIDS cocktails" is not without problems. For one thing, the drugs are extremely expensive—prohibitively so for some families. "The medicines can also be very hard for teenagers to take," observes Dr. Donna Futterman. "That is why it is so important to get kids into care sufficiently early so that we can work with them to be able to juggle the medicines and help them learn to cope with the disease."

AIDS therapy is also waged on a second front. While antivirals act against the virus itself, physicians can draw upon an ever-expanding arsenal of agents to treat or prevent life-threatening complications. For example, *pneumocystis carinii* pneumonia (PCP), once a lethal opportunistic infection, is now readily treatable through medication and mechanical ventilation. A multicenter study involving seventy hospitals evaluated the outcomes of roughly sixteen hundred people treated for PCP over a three-year period, beginning in 1995. The prospects for surviving respiratory failure were about twice as high as they had been just five years earlier, said the researchers.

HELPING TEENAGERS HELP THEMSELVES

Although AIDS may be more treatable than at any time since it entered the national consciousness like a bad dream, a cure may still be years or decades away. Experts worry that boys and girls who are coming of age during this era of improved medical care for HIV may begin to let down their guard, leading to a second wave of infections among young people. It is critical for parents to spend time talking to their child about how to prevent sexually transmitted diseases, a topic discussed in depth in chapter 12, "Sexuality."

TABLE 20.13

Medications Typically Prescribed for Treating Sexually Transmitted Diseases

STD	TYPE OF MEDICATION(S) THAT MAY BE PRESCRIBED
HIV/AIDS	*Nucleoside Reverse Transcriptase Inhibitors* abacavir • didanosine (ddl) • lamivudine (3TC) • stavudine (d4T) • zalcitabine (ddC) • zidovudine (ZDV) *Protease Inhibitors* indinavir • nelfinavir • ritonavir • saquinavir • lopinavir *plus* ritonavir *Nonnucleoside Reverse Transcriptase Inhibitors* delavirdine • efavirenz • nevirapine
Chlamydia	*Antibiotics* azithromycin • erythromycin • doxycycline
Gonorrhea	*Antibiotics* ceftriaxone • cefixime • ciprofloxacin • ofloxacin[2] *Gonorrhea and chlamydia can occur in tandem, in which event the doctor might prescribe a regimen of ceftriaxone plus doxycycline or azithromycin.*
Pelvic Inflammatory Disease (PID)	*Antibiotics* cefotetan *or* cefoxitin *plus* doxycycline • clindamycin *plus* gentamicin • ofloxacin *plus* metronidazole • others *Typically, two antibiotics are prescribed.*
Human Papillomavirus (HPV)	*Topical Preparations* (creams and solutions that the patient applies directly to the affected area) imiquimod • podophyllin • podofilox • fluorouracil (5-FU)[3] • trichloroacetic acid (TCA) • interferon
Genital Herpes	*Antivirals* acyclovir • famciclovir • valacyclovir
Syphilis	*Antibiotics* penicillin—doxycycline or tetracycline only if allergic to penicillin

---

2 Girls aged 17 and younger should not take ofloxacin or ciprofloxacin; nor should pregnant women of any age.
3 Pregnant women should not use 5-FU, podofilox or podophyllin.

SKIN CONDITIONS

Acne Vulgaris

From a teenager's point of view, medicine's greatest achievement of the past one hundred years isn't the discovery of penicillin or Dr. Jonas Salk's polio vaccine, it's the strides made in treating that adolescent rite of passage: acne.

The National Institute of Arthritis and Musculoskeletal and Skin Diseases (NIAMS) estimates that the chronic skin condition afflicts 85 percent of young people between the ages of twelve and twenty-four. Most cases are mild, but that is small consolation to a teenager who's awakened to find what he perceives to be a huge, grotesque pimple in the middle of his forehead (when actually, it's a small blemish, barely noticeable). Inevitably, this happens to be the day of the senior class picture, a first date or another much-anticipated occasion.

Let's never underestimate the impact a poor complexion can have on a teenager's self-image, confidence level and social interactions. "It has a *tremendous* impact," says Dr. Lawrence F. Eichenfield, chief of the division of pediatric dermatology at San Diego's Children's Hospital. "Adolescence is a time of great concern about physical appearance. We constantly see children with severe acne who are clinically depressed or withdrawing socially at school. In talking to them, you hear how distressed they are over their acne."

"But with proper treatment, they often bloom," he adds. "It can literally change their lives."

WHAT CAUSES ACNE?

Although a number of factors contribute to acne, the initiating event is hormonal stimulation of the *sebaceous glands* beneath the skin. "The sebaceous glands produce *sebum,* the oily substance that gets transmitted onto the skin's surface," explains Dr. Eichenfield. Each bulb-shaped gland leads to a narrow duct called a *follicle;* each follicle contains a strand of hair.

"Once kids reach puberty," he continues, "not only do the glands become more active, but the chemical composition of the sebum changes." Ordinarily, a follicle's inner lining sheds dead cells into the sebum, which gets deposited onto the skin, waiting to be scrubbed away.

For reasons that aren't clear, in acne the cells clump together and plug the opening, or *pore.* This prevents the oil from escaping. It also forces bacteria that normally reside in the skin (called *Propionibacterium acnes,* or *P. acnes*), to proliferate inside the narrow follicle. Eventually the sebum seeps out of the opening. If chemicals produced by P. acnes inflame the skin, a reddish pus-filled *pimple* begins to grow there.

Acne, whiteheads and blackheads are all by-products of the same process. *Acne* refers to an enlarged follicle that protrudes from the surface of the skin; *whitehead* describes a plugged follicle that remains just beneath the surface. When the follicle opens partially to reveal a black speck the size of a pinhead, it is called a *blackhead.* Contrary to popular myth, "the discoloration is pigment, *not* accumulated dirt," stresses Dr. Eichenfield. "Blackheads are just another type of acne." Still other acne lesions include:

- **Paranasal erythema:** an early form of acne commonly seen in kids on the cusp of puberty.
- **Papule:** an inflamed, small, pink bump that is tender to the touch.
- **Nodule:** a large, solid lesion lodged far below the skin's surface; is frequently painful.
- **Cyst:** another painful deep-seated lesion. Cysts, however, are inflamed and contain pus. They can also leave scars. Only one in twenty cases of acne are this severe.

POPPING THE MYTHS SURROUNDING PIMPLES AND ACNE

Before we examine the causes of acne, let's dismiss the long-standing charges against the following:

- Greasy foods like pizza and french fries, chocolate, soft drinks
- Poor personal hygiene. In fact, harsh scrubbing can irritate the skin, aggravating the condition
- Masturbation or the harboring of sexual thoughts

Surprised? Many parents probably wouldn't be, since these superstitions have been in circulation for decades. Heredity and hormonal changes are at the root of acne, although other catalysts may enter the picture, such as emotional stress or the use of pore-clogging makeup, face creams or oily hair products. The helmet chin-straps worn by young football players often invite pimples, as can headbands, hair swept across the forehead—anything that rubs against the skin.

Timing Is Everything

A child's age at the onset of acne is a partial predictor of how mild or severe it will be. Youngsters whose first blemishes predate puberty face a greater likelihood of developing serious skin problems than those who don't get pimples until their midteens.

HOW ACNE IS TREATED

DRUG THERAPY

The skin-care products available today "are vastly superior to what they used to be," says Dr. Eichenfield. Over-the-counter medications (see box on p. 564) may be more than adequate for managing mild to moderate acne. "Topical benzoyl peroxide is usually recommended as a first-line treatment," he says. "It works mainly by reducing the bacteria in the skin." As a *keratolytic* agent, benzoyl peroxide also slows down the sloughing off of follicle cells. You can find many brands of this preparation, which comes in various forms (creams, gels, lotions, pads, washes) as well as in 2.5 percent, 5 percent and 10 percent strengths.

"Often," says Dr. Eichenfield, "the lower-strength benzoyl peroxide is just as effective, and with fewer side effects." When using a topical medication, your teen should apply a thin film to the entire area where pimples might sprout, not just dab it on current blemishes. Acne products tend to dry out the skin, so it's best to avoid the delicate areas around the eyes, mouth and nostrils. After four to six weeks without satisfactory results, a youngster can try one of the higher-strength products.

More severe acne may call for a prescription medication. "The classes that are most effective are the *retinoids* [tretinoin, isotretinoin] and the retinoid-like agents [adapalene, tazarotene]," says Dr. Eichenfield. These derivatives of vitamin A (all topical except for isotretinoin, which is a systemic tablet) "stop the blockage in the skin," he explains. "They also bring whiteheads to the surface and prevent new whiteheads from forming."

Isotretinoin is usually reserved for extremely severe acne that has not responded to therapy with topical or systemic antibiotics, and/or has caused scarring. Dr. Eichenfield calls it "absolutely the most potent medicine that we have." The drawback to isotretinoin, however, is its side effects, which include birth defects and possibly depression. Isotretinoin should be used under the supervision of a clinician well versed in prescribing the drug. It is *never* to be taken during pregnancy. Female patients are typically placed on birth control pills (which themselves may improve acne) before and during isotretinoin use.

For any acne product to work, teenagers must follow the manufacturer's instructions to the letter. That includes resisting the temptation to slather on the medication, on the mistaken assumption that using more than the recommended amount will bring better/quicker results. Applying too much can damage skin to the extent that the doctor has to discontinue the drug temporarily. Let's also remind kids to be patient: It typically takes six to eight weeks before they can expect to see any improvement.

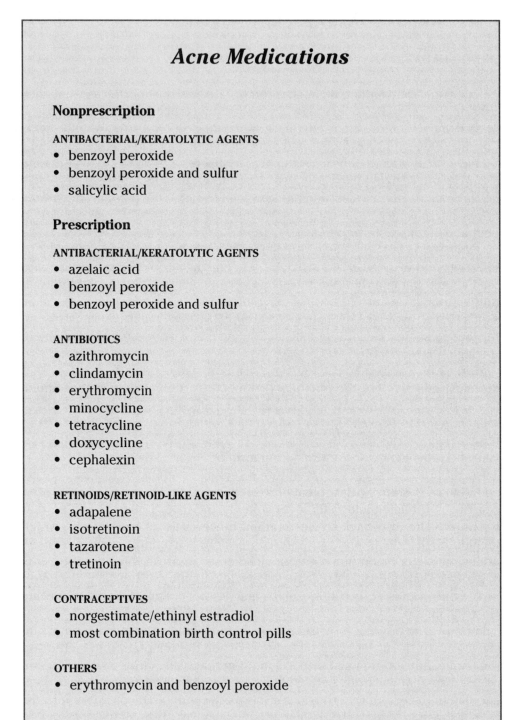

Acne Medications

Nonprescription

ANTIBACTERIAL/KERATOLYTIC AGENTS
- benzoyl peroxide
- benzoyl peroxide and sulfur
- salicylic acid

Prescription

ANTIBACTERIAL/KERATOLYTIC AGENTS
- azelaic acid
- benzoyl peroxide
- benzoyl peroxide and sulfur

ANTIBIOTICS
- azithromycin
- clindamycin
- erythromycin
- minocycline
- tetracycline
- doxycycline
- cephalexin

RETINOIDS/RETINOID-LIKE AGENTS
- adapalene
- isotretinoin
- tazarotene
- tretinoin

CONTRACEPTIVES
- norgestimate/ethinyl estradiol
- most combination birth control pills

OTHERS
- erythromycin and benzoyl peroxide

SURGERY

Because the medications described above eradicate acne so effectively, says Dr. Eichenfield, "surgical procedures are far less common than they used to be." A *dermatologist* might occasionally use a small needle and an instrument called an extractor to pierce (*lance*) whiteheads and blackheads, but surgery's current role in acne treatment is mainly to minimize residual scars. Techniques include *dermabrasion* and *laser resurfacing.*

In dermabrasion, the physician uses a high-speed rotary instrument with a sandpaper-like wheel or brush to smooth rough, pitted skin. A new layer of skin replaces the *abraded* layer. Laser resurfacing, too, removes old skin cells so that fresh cells grow there. The intense beam of laser light literally vaporizes unwanted scar tissue. Both procedures are performed on an outpatient basis.

HELPING TEENAGERS HELP THEMSELVES

Youngsters who have acne should be encouraged to practice the following steps for scrupulous skin care:

- Avoid manipulating, or squeezing, pimples.

- Squeezing a zit only inflames surrounding healthy skin. Practitioners of this adolescent ritual also run the risk of developing scars.

- Wash skin gently with a mild soap. The doctor can recommend which brands to buy. Avoid hard scrubbing, which can aggravate the condition.

- Wash hair regularly. Youngsters with oily hair would benefit from shampooing every day.

- Take appropriate precautions against excessive sun exposure. A national online survey of 1,186 teenagers revealed that many young people believe that the sun helps to clear up acne. According to the American Academy of Dermatology, the sun's ultraviolet rays may in fact kill the *P. acnes* bacterium. Nevertheless, this possible benefit is more than offset by the sun's damaging effects, which include premature aging of skin tissue and a heightened risk of skin cancer.

- Use only cosmetics labeled as nonacnegenic or noncomedogenic, as they are less likely to block pores and thus fuel acne.

Pityriasis Rosea

The inflammatory skin disorder *pityriasis rosea* peaks in incidence during adolescence and young adulthood. It typically begins as a large (three-quarters of an inch to two inches in diameter) pink rash on the chest or back. This is called a "herald patch," because it is indeed a harbinger of what is to follow.

Within one to two weeks, the youngster breaks out in dozens, if not hundreds, of smaller faint-pink rashes. The trunk, arms, legs and neck may be affected, but rarely the face. Parents often confuse pityriasis rosea with ringworm, a fungal infection. Pityriasis rosea's cause isn't known, but it is *not* a fungal infection and therefore isn't helped by antifungal medications. One way to recognize the disorder is to examine the chest or back for the distinctive Christmas-tree-shaped pattern of its flat, oval-shaped lesions.

Pityriasis rosea presents differently in African Americans, who tend to develop raised patches on their face and extremities more so than on their torsos. The color usually differs, too: light-brown instead of pink, and with a coarse, granular center.

SYMPTOMS THAT SUGGEST PITYRIASIS ROSEA MAY INCLUDE:

Large pink patch, typically on the torso, followed by:

- Multiple smaller rashes
- Mild fatigue
- Mild itching

HOW PITYRIASIS ROSEA IS DIAGNOSED

Physical examination and thorough medical history, plus KOH prep, in which a tiny sample of tissue from one of the spots is scraped off and examined under a microscope to rule out fungal infection.

HOW PITYRIASIS ROSEA IS TREATED

Pityriasis rosea is not contagious and does not pose any danger, usually running its course within three to nine weeks. Expect new spots to erupt during that time. Until the rashes fade and disappear—leaving no scars, happily—your pediatrician will focus on controlling symptoms. For example, lotions or antihistamines may be prescribed to relieve the itching. Exposure to sunlight or ultraviolet light treatments are sometimes recommended to hasten resolution of the rashes.

HELPING TEENAGERS HELP THEMSELVES

Youngsters with symptomatic pityriasis rosea may wish to avoid strenuous physical activity, which can exacerbate existing rashes. Bathing in lukewarm water, not hot water, is also recommended.

Warts

Warts, often known as verrucae, are benign (noncancerous) tumors of the outer skin layer, and can occur at any time in life. They are most prevalent, however, during early to middle adolescence, infecting approximately one in twenty teens. A break in the skin allows one of several *human papillomaviruses* (HPV) to invade the body. Months later, several tiny, firm bumps with well-defined borders start to grow nearby. The most common sites include the fingers, hands, forearms and feet. Warts often emerge in clusters, with several small verrucae encircling a larger growth. Other members of the HPV family cause *genital warts,* a sexually transmitted disease. Although common warts also can be spread via sexual contact, they are usually passed from one person to another through casual contact, like shaking hands or using towels or other items that were touched by someone who has warts.

Warts generally do not cause itching, nor are they painful, except when they grow on the soles of the feet. These are called *plantar warts*—"plantar" being the medical term for this part of the foot.

SYMPTOMS THAT SUGGEST WARTS MAY INCLUDE:

Clusters of tiny raised growths the same color as the skin or darker.

HOW WARTS ARE DIAGNOSED

Physical examination and thorough medical history.

HOW WARTS ARE TREATED

Two-thirds of all cases resolve on their own within two years, while approximately one in four youngsters see their warts disappear spontaneously within just six months. Rarely do the growths remain more than five years. One benefit of treatment, however, is that you eliminate the risk of the warts spreading to other areas of the body, as well as the risk of transmitting the virus to someone else. As with acne therapy, teenagers may need occasional reminding that the techniques for wart removal are carried out over a period of weeks or months.

• **Drug therapy:** Common warts and *flat warts* (usually tan to yellow-pink in color) respond well to some of the same topical medications used to heal acne: salicylic acid, tretinoin and benzoyl peroxide. Other candidates include trichloroacetic acid, a keratolytic, and cantharidin. The latter is a *vesicant:* When brushed on warts and left there for several hours or more, the chemical causes the tiny tumors to blister. Then the physician removes the dead tissue at the next office visit. This may be repeated for several weeks.

• **Surgery:** Of all the office procedures for removing warts, only *curettage* actually involves the use of a scalpel. In *cryosurgery,* the warts are swabbed with liquid nitrogen or another freezing agent, which destroys the tissue little by little. Or the doctor freezes the warts using a handheld *cryogenic* probe. After two to four appointments, the growths are often completely gone.

Warts can also be burned away with an electrical instrument (*electrofulguration*) or an electrically heated device (*electrocautery*), or eradicated with a laser wand. Because these techniques can leave scars, you and your child will want to discuss with the doctor—and with one another—the pros and cons of each approach before making your decision.

Plantar warts are among the most stubborn skin conditions to treat. In general, the smaller the lesion, the greater the chances for success. Often a physician will take a surgical knife and pare down the tissue, then apply salicylic acid, or other agents (such as liquid nitrogen) over the course of several weeks.

HELPING TEENAGERS HELP THEMSELVES

The following tips can help prevent warts from cropping up elsewhere:

- Don't scratch or pick at a wart. Doing so can spread the infection to small cuts and other breaks in the skin.
- Wash hands frequently and moisturize the skin liberally; dry skin cracks more easily, opening the door to infection.
- Don't walk a mile—or even one foot—in someone else's shoes.
- Always wear footwear in gym locker rooms and showers.

Practicing Sun Safety

Adults and teenagers alike frequently underestimate the potential hazards of the sun. To assess parents' attitudes toward sun safety, researchers at Chicago's Loyola University Medical Center, New York University and the University of Tennessee randomly surveyed approximately five hundred households. One in eight children reported having been sunburned during the previous weekend, as did one in eleven adults. What's more, nearly half the mothers and fathers who participated in the poll said that their children appeared healthier with a tan. Pediatricians know otherwise.

Tan skin is actually the skin's response to irreversible damage from the sun's harmful *ultraviolet* rays; to safeguard against further injury, cells called *melanocytes* donate *melanin* to cells that don't produce the protective pigment. (Melanin also lends skin its color.)

Excessive sun exposure is far and away the leading cause of the major skin cancers *basal-cell carcinoma, squamous-cell carcinoma* and *malignant melanoma* (see box), which together afflict more than one million Americans each year. The vast majority are adults. But 80 percent of a person's lifetime sun injury occurs by the time he or she is eighteen. Fifty percent of men and women who

---

The Major Types of Skin Cancers

Basal-Cell Carcinoma: The most common of all cancers, BCC arises in the tiny, round *basal cells* of the upper layer of the skin, or *epidermis.* Usually discovered on the face, ears, lips and around the mouth, basal-cell cancer rarely spreads and is nearly 100 percent curable when treated early. If missed, however, it can cause disfigurement. Affects approximately 800,000 Americans annually.

Squamous-Cell Carcinoma: forms in the flat scalelike *squamous cells* of the epidermis. Typically found on the face, ears, lips, mouth, neck, hands, arms and back. Unlike basal-cell carcinoma, SCC can spread to other parts of the body. With early treatment, is 95 percent curable. Affects approximately 225,000 Americans annually, claiming 2,000 lives.

Malignant Melanoma: the most rapidly increasing malignant tumor in the United States. Melanoma is a cancer of the melanocytes. The disease may develop as a new mole (a mole is merely a cluster of melanocytes) or as part of a preexisting mole. Highly curable if diagnosed and treated early. When it spreads (metastasizes), typically to the lungs or liver, can be extremely difficult to cure. Affects approximately 48,000 Americans annually, claiming 9,600 lives.

reach age sixty-five will incur skin cancer. Therefore, to allow kids to frolic in the sun without taking precautions is to increase their future risk of becoming a victim. Possibly their present risk, too: One worrisome trend has been the slow but steady rise in childhood skin malignancies.

Fortunately, teenagers are young enough that the window of opportunity for reducing their odds of developing skin cancer is still wide open. Although anyone can get skin cancer, people with certain characteristics are more sensitive to the negative effects of UV rays. The American Academy of Dermatology identifies six skin types, based on the tendency to burn:

HIGH RISK

- **Type I (extremely sun-sensitive skin)**—a youngster who burns frequently but never seems to tan. Typically fair-skinned and freckled, with red or blond hair.
- **Type II (very sun-sensitive skin)**—burns readily, tans minimally. Typically fair-skinned and fair-haired, with blue, green or gray eyes.

AVERAGE RISK

- **Type III (sun-sensitive skin)**—sometimes burns, and tans gradually to a light brown.
- **Type IV (minimally sun-sensitive skin)**—burns minimally, and always tans to a moderate brown.

LITTLE RISK

- **Type V (sun-insensitive skin)**—rarely burns, and tans well. This describes many people from the Middle East and some Hispanics and African Americans.
- **Type VI (deeply pigmented sun-insensitive skin)**—never burns but tans darkly. Most African Americans belong to this category.

Additional factors predispose an adolescent to skin cancer. Checking just *one* of the following boxes places your son or daughter at elevated risk:

☐   A greater-than-average number of moles.

☐   Unusual-looking moles (*atypical nevi*).

☐ An unusually large *congenital* mole (one that is present at birth).

☐ Family history of any of the following skin diseases: melanoma, xeroderma pigmentosum, dysplastic nevus syndrome, familial atypical multiple mole melanoma (FAMMM).

☐ Personal history of skin cancer or impaired immunity as a result of disease or medical treatment that compromises the immune system.

☐ One or more blistering sunburns during childhood or adolescence.

☐ Living in a sun-drenched climate close to the equator. For instance, Floridians receive 150 percent more ultraviolet rays than citizens of Maine.

PROTECTING TEENS FROM THE HARMFUL EFFECTS OF THE SUN (WITHOUT BEING ACCUSED OF RUINING ALL THEIR FUN)

Encourage your teen to avoid solar radiation between 10 A.M. and 4 P.M., when the ultraviolet rays are the harshest. The safest measure—stay indoors or seek shade—isn't always practical. Next best? Protect that skin by wearing the proper clothing and sunscreen.

Light-colored, tightly woven clothing reflects sunlight rather than absorbs it. A hat with a brim at least three inches wide also affords protection.

Get your teen into the habit of applying sunscreen. And not just when she goes to the beach and not just on bright, sunny days. Even when clouds obscure the sun, 80 percent of its UV light reaches the earth. You can singe your skin during the winter, too, since snow reflects 80 percent of the sun's rays.

Sunscreens used to be classified according to their sun protection strength, which was expressed as a Sun Protection Factor (SPF) ranging from 2 to 50. The higher the number, the longer the user can stay in the sun without burning. So let's say that your youngster typically burns in about fifteen minutes. A sunblock with an SPF of 15 would afford him 225 minutes (just under four hours) of safe exposure. If he is dark-complexioned and generally doesn't burn for, say, forty minutes, the same product would enable him to spend six hundred worry-free minutes outdoors. Having said that, *no one* should bake in the sun for that long, regardless of how much sunscreen he slathers on his skin.

The U.S. Food and Drug Administration has since pared down the categories to just three strengths: minimum (which corresponds to 2 SPF to 12

What About Tanning Salons?

Every day one million Americans, mostly young people, pay for the opportunity to be encased in a coffin-shaped tanning bed and bombarded with ultraviolet rays.

They are by no means safe. Most sunlamps emit rays that are 95 percent UVA and 5 percent UVB. As noted elsewhere on this page, UVA radiation is responsible for the leathery, sagging skin you see on many confirmed denizens of the beach. And just 1 percent of UVB rays is sufficient to increase a person's skin-cancer risk.

SPF), moderate (12 SPF to 30 SPF) and high (30 SPF or greater). Moderate strength is the sensible choice for most people.

Memo to Mom and Dad: Before purchasing sunscreen, look for the words "broad-spectrum" on the label; this assures you that the product screens out both types of ultraviolet light: *UVA* and *UVB*. UVA radiation doesn't burn skin as readily as UVB—and the jury is still out on whether or not it contributes to skin cancer—but we do know that UVA rays penetrate tissue more deeply and age the skin.

Buying sunscreen is the first step; using it correctly is the second. Studies show than most sun worshipers use only about one-fifth to one-half as much sunscreen as they should. To thoroughly cover the entire body—including the ears and hands, which most people neglect—the general rule of thumb is to apply about one ounce of water-resistant lotion or cream fifteen to thirty minutes before going outdoors. Then generously reapply every two hours and immediately after swimming or strenuous activities.

Protect the eyes too. According to the American Optometric Association, sunglasses should block out 99 to 100 percent of both UVA and UVB radiation and screen out 75 to 90 percent of visible light. Gray, green or brown lenses work best.

The American Academy of Dermatology recommends that teens periodically inspect their bodies for suspicious-looking moles. To do this, they'll need a full-length mirror, a hand mirror, and a well-lit room.

TABLE 20.14

The Signs of Skin Cancer

BASAL-CELL CARCINOMA	SQUAMOUS-CELL CARCINOMA/ ACTINIC KERATOSIS	MALIGNANT MELANOMA
Look for a reddish patch or a shiny pink, red, or pearly white bump. May have an open sore that refuses to heal. Bleeding, oozing and crusting are common.	Look for a raised red or pink scaly patch or a wartlike bump with an open sore in the middle. *Actinic keratosis,* a premalignant lesion, appears as a slightly raised, hardened patch—tan, red, brownish or grayish in color. If not treated, about 1 in 20 actinic keratoses progress to squamous-cell carcinoma.	Look for a mole with any of the following characteristics: (1) asymmetrical shape, (2) larger than ¼", (3) poorly defined border, (4) uneven color. Melanomas typically begin as mottled brown or black but may eventually turn blue, red or white.

1. Standing in front of the full-length mirror, examine the front and back of the body. Then, with arms raised, do the same for the left side and the right side.
2. Bend both elbows and carefully inspect the forearms, the back of the upper arms, and the palms of the hands.
3. Next, look at the backs of the legs and the feet, the spaces between toes, and the soles of the feet.
4. Hold up the hand mirror and examine the back of the neck and the scalp. Part hair to lift.
5. Finally, check the back and the buttocks with the hand mirror.
6. If you spot any unusual-looking moles, immediately make an appointment with your pediatrician. Skin cancers are eminently treatable when caught early.

21

WHEN A TEENAGER HAS A CHRONIC ILLNESS OR DISABILITY

Ten to twenty million children and adolescents in the United States have some form of chronic illness or disability. *Chronic* refers to a health condition that lasts anywhere from three months to a lifetime. For one in sixteen teens, the ailment is severe enough to affect their day-to-day lives. This chapter is about them.

As much as possible, a teenager who is chronically ill or disabled needs to be treated as a *teenager* first and *chronically ill* or *disabled* second. Whatever his health problem, he must still master the tasks that will transform him from an adolescent to an adult, such as learning to feel comfortable with his changing body, separating emotionally from Mom and Dad, forming friendships and possibly romantic relationships, and striving toward economic self-sufficiency.

The teen years can be challenging enough without the considerable stresses and strains imposed by illness or disability. Parents would be unrealistic not to anticipate some rocky times ahead. Kids diagnosed with a chronic medical condition frequently leapfrog from shock to denial to anger to depression to regression—not necessarily in that order. Sometimes *all* of those emotions may well up in the course of a single day.

Fortunately, adolescents tend to be remarkably resilient. With Mom and Dad's guidance and support, most come to accept their condition. But if your son or daughter seems unusually withdrawn or exhibits other signs of emotional distress, consult your pediatrician to determine whether help from a mental-health professional is warranted.

How well youngsters adapt depends partly on their personality, temperament, and previous responses to crises in general. Other determining factors include:

The age at which they were diagnosed. Studies have found that teenagers seem to adjust better to a chronic health problem that emerged prior to adolescence or that occurs during the late teens. Being diagnosed early in life gives a child ample practice at overcoming the hurdles presented by disease or disability, while an older adolescent generally possesses greater coping skills—as well as a more fully formed self-identity—than your average twelve- or thirteen-year-old.

The disorder's stability or unpredictability. A condition that isn't expected to change, like an amputated limb, is often easier for a young person to handle emotionally than an illness that can get out of control (an episode of high blood sugar in a diabetic, for instance) or one that progresses, triggering new, unfamiliar symptoms.

The extent to which the condition interferes with the teen's daily life. A youngster who is paralyzed from the waist down, for example, may not be able to participate in certain activities with his friends because the venues aren't accessible to wheelchairs. Other disabilities may require such significant commitments of time and energy to manage that they make it difficult for the teenager to remain in the social loop.

Whether the health problem is evident to others. Visible signs of their illness or disability may upset adolescents more so than preteens, because of the importance teens place on appearance. On the other hand, when a condition can't readily be seen (asthma, anemia, diabetes, among others), young patients may slip into denying its severity and neglect to take medicine as directed.

Often these determinants can be addressed successfully if the team caring for your child includes someone knowledgeable about adolescent development.

THE STRESSES FACED BY TEENAGERS WHO ARE CHRONICALLY ILL OR DISABLED

In the immediate aftermath of a diagnosis, expect your teen to ask countless questions:

> *"Is this going to affect the way I look?"*
> *"Am I going to have to miss a lot of school?"*
> *"Don't tell me I won't be able to go out for the lacrosse team this year!"*
> *"What if the other kids laugh at me because the chemotherapy makes my hair fall out?"*

These questions may demand thoughtful, well-informed answers. Bear in mind that young people's fears about medical matters may be based on misinformation. For instance, a patient recently diagnosed with Hodgkin's disease might sadly conclude that he doesn't have long to live. After all, everyone knows that cancer is deadly; only the year before, his favorite aunt died of ovarian cancer.

What he needs to hear from both his doctor and his parents is that there are more than one hundred forms of cancer—many of them highly treatable. In addition, the outlook for children's malignancies tends to be more favorable than for adult tumors. Hodgkin's disease happens to be the most curable pediatric cancer; nine in ten kids live five years from the time of diagnosis, at which point they can essentially be declared cured.

Another frequent source of anxiety is upcoming medical tests and procedures. A fourteen-year-old boy slated to undergo magnetic resonance imaging (MRI) is utterly convinced that the scan is going to hurt. It's *got* to: Did you see the *size* of that machine? *Or what if it zaps me and I become radioactive?!*

The scanner *is* an imposing piece of equipment, to be sure. But he'll be relieved to hear that an MRI uses electromagnetic energy, not radiation, to visualize the body. He won't feel any pain, and he most certainly won't glow in the dark. A kid who is prone to claustrophobia, though, may turn panicky when the portable examining table draws her into the narrow tunnel. Mom and Dad, as her *advocates* within the medical system, should alert the doctor ahead of time about her aversion to confined spaces. He might prescribe a mild short-acting sedative to be taken prior to the test or arrange for an "open" MRI scanner to be used.

To find out what your child can expect, ask the physician or one of the nurses to describe the procedure step by step. Many medical practices routinely provide informative, illustrated pamphlets beforehand.

An adolescent should feel that he can always share what is worrying him. But as explored elsewhere in *Caring for Your Teenager,* kids don't always say what's on their minds. In addition to being active, empathetic listeners, we need to anticipate what they may be feeling.

"Honey, you seem a bit down today. I know that having diabetes is hard for you sometimes . . ."

"Yeah, a little down. . . . *A lot,* really."

"What is it exactly that's bothering you? Maybe I can help."

"I'm just scared, that's all."

"Scared about the future?"

"Yeah, that. What if one of those terrible things that happens to people with diabetes happens to me, like losing my sight? Or what if the diabetes messes up my kidneys? I don't want to have to go on one of those artificial kidney machines. I can't believe I'm seventeen and have to worry about this stuff. It's not fair!"

Tips for Reducing Anxieties

Techniques such as *deep breathing, progressive muscle relaxation* and *visualization* can help to soothe jangled nerves before and during medical procedures.

Tell your teenager about *thought stopping,* which will allow him to control the mind instead of the other way around. Each time a negative thought comes a-knocking—about an impending needle stick, for example—the teenager literally orders his brain to switch channels.

"Okay, stop it! Turn off that thought right now! Think about something else." It may sound overly simplistic, but with practice, this method can be extremely effective.

Perhaps nothing we say will dispel our child's sadness or resentment or rage at being saddled with a health problem. However, listening nonjudgmentally and letting our children know they can talk to us any time is beneficial. For a young person, the realization that he can express his feelings freely, without being told, "You shouldn't be _____ (angry, depressed, etc.)," is psychologically therapeutic in itself.

Honesty *Is* the Best Policy

Some mothers and fathers deliberately conceal all details of the illness from the young patient, operating under the misconception that they are safeguarding their child from potentially devastating news. Seriously ill teenagers instinctively know about their condition. Ironically, they frequently refrain from discussing this with Mom and Dad for much the same reason: to protect their grief-stricken parents.

How do they know? Their bodies tell them. In addition, no matter how careful the adults around them are, kids glean fragments of conversations and take notice of grim expressions. Ultimately, to deny a sick person the truth about his condition is an unintentionally selfish act; all the more so in the setting of a terminal disease. Children need to talk about what they're feeling—including their fears, their conceptions of death and dying; whatever is on their minds. No one should take away their right to talk about these issues.

On the other hand, while it's important to answer questions honestly, try to emphasize the positive whenever possible. Let's return to the earlier example of the adolescent diabetic who is concerned that he might develop a serious long-term complication. His mother and father might say something like this:

"The doctor doesn't know for sure what's going to happen years from now. But most kids with diabetes go on to live normal life spans. We're confident that you will, too. The best thing we can do is to make sure that you stay healthy by keeping your blood sugars within a normal range. Never think that you're all alone in this; we're here to help you, and so are your brothers and sister."

Ensuring Adequate Pain Control

"Mom, is it going to hurt?"

Pain is not an inevitable consequence of illness or disability. But in cases where a young patient does experience chronic discomfort, parents should never accept a health-care practitioner's opinion that "nothing can be done" and that he or she will have to learn to "live with it."

In the first place, that is no way for anyone to live, much less an adolescent. Second, advances in pain control have made it possible to relieve most people's discomfort and make it manageable. If a teenager is in pain, chances are it isn't being managed aggressively enough. Parents have every right to insist that the primary physician either explore other options or else refer them to a pain specialist.

In the event that relief still proves elusive, request a consultation with a *multidisciplinary* pain-care team. The multidisciplinary approach incorporates the perspectives of several professionals; typically, a pediatrician, an anesthesiologist, a neurologist and perhaps a psychiatrist and/or a social worker. The premise of multidisciplinary care is that two, three or four heads are better than one.

Few medical centers offer this feature, however. You may have to search out individual pain specialists or pain clinics in your area.

CHRONIC ILLNESS OR DISABILITY AND YOUR TEENAGER'S EMOTIONAL, SOCIAL AND SEXUAL DEVELOPMENT

A Bump in the Road to Independence: Respecting the Need for Autonomy While Maintaining Discipline

A chronic disorder or disability can thwart the natural process of achieving autonomy. While most kids are beginning to savor the sweet taste of freedom from Mom and Dad, illness may force an adolescent to rely on his parents nearly as much as when he was a younger child. This can set the stage for parent-teen conflict.

One way that some adolescents sometimes attempt to assert their independence is to balk at taking proper care of themselves. No doubt an element of adolescent risk-taking behavior also plays a part in decisions to disregard medication schedules or restrictive diets. Unfortunately, the consequences of such actions can be deadly.

The helpless feeling that accompanies a prolonged or serious illness is difficult to handle for patients of all ages. A parent's top priority is to restore a youngster's feeling of control over her life—within the boundaries dictated by the health problem, of course. The first step is to include your son or daughter in medical decision making.

For instance, maybe you always tend to supervise him when he takes his medications. "It's eight o'clock! Did you remember to take your insulin?" Why not offer him the flexibility of injecting himself anytime between, say, seven o'clock and eight-thirty? It may seem like a trivial matter, but it's not. Handing a teenager increasing responsibility for his own health care allows him to feel grown-up and not quite so powerless.

It's easy to understand why parents of an ailing child might waver in enforcing discipline at times. *The poor kid is going through so much,* they reason, *let's cut him some slack.* There's nothing wrong with making allowances now and then. But as a general rule, mothers and fathers should employ the same style of discipline they've always used. Parents who cater to every whim or fail to correct misbehavior are ultimately doing their son or daughter a disservice. Children appreciate being treated like their peers.

Square Pegs, Round Holes: The Effects of Chronic Illness and Disability on Socialization, Sexual Identity and Intimacy

Adolescents want nothing more than to feel accepted by their peers and to not be perceived as "different" or "weird." But blending in with the crowd can be an improbable feat for the paraplegic teenager who must maneuver her wheelchair through hallway traffic between classes; or the youngster whose severe asthma forces him to watch enviously from the sidelines while his buddies play touch football on a crisp fall afternoon; or the baby-faced boy who looks several years younger than his classmates on account of sickle-cell anemia, which has delayed his sexual maturity.

Teens who are chronically ill or disabled tend to pal around less with other kids outside of school. As noted earlier in this chapter, the logistics of getting around and the time demands of managing an illness can pose a problem. But most of these teens are desperate for contact with their peers—and, as they grow older, romantic intimacy. They have the same curiosity (and anxiety) about dating, sex, their bodies, as other adolescents, a fact that parents and pediatricians don't always appreciate.

Chapter 12's guidelines for discussing sex and sexuality with teenagers pertains to all adolescents. Kids with long-term health problems may have more than the usual worries, though, about their attractiveness to potential romantic partners. "This boy at school asked me out to a movie. I really like him, and I want to go. But what if I have an epileptic seizure while we're out? I'm afraid he might panic and never call me again." If you aren't comfortable answering these types of painfully blunt questions, ask your pediatrician to initiate the discussion during your teen's next office visit.

School Disruptions: Easing the Transition Back

Lengthy hospitalizations or periods spent convalescing at home can lead to significant problems at school, not only academically but socially. Following a prolonged absence, even teenagers who normally aren't all that fond of school may be moved to kneel and kiss the scuff-marked linoleum inside the front entrance, if for no other reason than to be among their peers again. The reverse situation is also seen, where perennially conscientious students become almost phobic about returning to school.

Parents can help to ease their youngster's transition from patient to pupil well in advance of the first day back. Ideally, you don't allow your child to fall too far behind in her classes, provided, of course, that she is well enough to tackle the work. Here's what else you can do:

• When a youngster has a serious condition that changes his appearance or can be expected to impair his academic performance, consider asking the clinic nurse to update the school nurse, counselors and teachers about the nature of his illness and what he's gone through during the past weeks or months, and suggest ways that they can assist the returning pupil. Parents also can assume this role. Or perhaps the young patient would like to address his peers personally. Before proceeding with this plan, however, be sure to clear it with your teenager first.

- If your child must take medication while at school, contact the nurse's office and ask for the parental-permission forms to be sent or mailed home well before the return date. Teachers should be made aware of disease symptoms and/or treatment side effects that may leave the student fatigued or unable to pay attention in class.

- Prepare your youngster for the return to school by role-playing possible situations: "Okay: If a friend asks why you were in the hospital, how much do you feel comfortable telling her?" "What if some kid starts teasing you because your face is a little pudgy from the medication you're taking? What would you say to him?"

- Request that teachers send the teen weekly notes updating him about what went on in class, in addition to all of his homework assignments. Other creative alternatives are to have lessons tape-recorded or video-recorded; have video cameras set up in class and at home so that the patient can interact with his teachers and classmates.

- Discuss with your school district the possibility of its hiring an in-home tutor for your child. In some school districts this is required. The use of computers with e-mail can be very helpful in this regard.

COMMON COPING STYLES OF TEENS WHO ARE CHRONICALLY ILL OR DISABLED

Denial

An example of denial in action is the teen with diabetes who wolfs down two pieces of birthday cake at a party, knowing full well that she's going to regret it later; or the young person with hemophilia who insists on performing daredevil stunts on his dirt bike. But suppressing the reality of a health condition is also an effective coping strategy that allows people to go on living productively. Denial becomes a problem only when it leads to dangerous outcomes.

Intellectualization

This defense mechanism, seen mainly with younger adolescents, consists of *partial* denial. The teenager accepts her condition and often exhibits a first-year medical student's knowledge about it, but chooses to block out how she *feels* about it. Intellectualization can be useful when employed as a delay tactic; it gives the young patient time to sort out and deal with her emotions. But if it persists, the adolescent never truly comes to grips with her situation. She may also fall into a pattern of shutting out all uncomfortable feelings, at which point intervention from a health-care professional is certainly warranted.

Regression

When the going gets tough, even the most outwardly stoic youth may revert to childish behavior. Regression provides temporary escape from stressful situations. The proper parental response? Be firm about what you will and will not tolerate, but show plenty of caring and patience. In time, the young person will learn to cope with his circumstances in a more mature fashion.

Acting-Out Behavior

This is another short-term survival tool, frequently wielded like a battering ram. Defiance, combativeness and testing limits at home and at school are all expressions of a teenager's anger and depression over his predicament: *I'm furious that I have this stupid disease! And even though I know it's irrational, Mom and Dad, sometimes I can't help venting my rage in your direction.* Acting-out behavior can be hurtful to anyone who stumbles into its path. It may also manifest in self-destructive ways, such as poor performance in school, experimenting with substances and/or sex and run-ins with the law. Involving a mental-health expert from the beginning can help to prevent things from spinning out of control.

KNOW YOUR RIGHTS: TEENS AT WORK AND SCHOOL

The Americans with Disabilities Act (ADA) of 1990 is one of several federal laws that were enacted to secure the rights of people with physical or mental impairments. ADA alone prohibits discrimination on a number of fronts: recruitment, hiring, promotions, training, pay, social activities and other privileges of employment; state and local government; public accommodations; commercial facilities; transportation; and telecommunications.

Here's an example: Under the Americans with Disabilities Act, employers with fifteen or more workers are required to make what is termed *reasonable accommodation:* that is, to modify the work environment or revise the job description to accommodate qualified applicants or employees with a disability. The safeguards even extend to the job interview, with prospective employers restricted in the questions they can ask about an applicant's disability before a job offer is made.

Violations of this or other protections must be filed with the U.S. Equal Employment Opportunity Commission (EEOC), which investigates the complaint and, if it is found to be valid, takes action against the employer. As with many government agencies, however, the number of cases far exceeds the EEOC's staffing, resulting in an often frustratingly slow process.

A teen who is disabled must also be provided reasonable accommodation in public schools. The Individuals with Disabilities Education Act (IDEA), formerly known as PL 94-142, requires public schools to make available to all eligible children with disabilities a free, appropriate public education in the least restrictive environment appropriate to their individual needs. For more on the IDEA, see chapter 10, "Learning Problems."

CHRONIC ILLNESS OR DISABILITY: A FAMILY AFFAIR

A teenager's chronic illness or disability can't help but disrupt the lives of everyone in the household. The question is, to what extent will you let it intrude?

Try not to let your child's health problem color every aspect of family life, particularly your marriage. Allow yourselves time away from your caretaker roles. Go out to dinner or to a movie—and turn the conversation to topics other than your teenager's problems. Take a vacation now and then—and don't feel guilty about it. Arrange for a caretaker or a family member knowledgeable about your child's condition to be available while you are away. Being good to yourselves will provide the needed emotional and physical energy necessary to give your ailing youngster the love and support that *she* needs.

All caregivers, though, feel overwhelmed at times by the immense responsibility of overseeing a child's medical care. When we feel ourselves being swallowed up by stress and physical fatigue, our minds often fill with worry, anger, sadness—even guilt—that we somehow are responsible for what's happened.

If you feel on the brink of burnout (and it happens to the best of parents), don't hesitate to get some help. In addition to accessing the mental-health-care system, consider joining a support group for parents of children with a chronic illness or disability. These groups can provide a safe haven in which to voice frustrations, draw encouragement and share practical information about how to ease the burdens of caring for a sick teenager. Nowadays, you don't even need to leave your home to find a support group; many if not most of these organizations have established on-line support communities for the many parents who otherwise would not have the time to attend in person.

One piece of advice you'll almost certainly take away from a support group is the importance of not neglecting your other children. So much energy gets channeled into caring for the youngster who is chronically ill that it's easy to overlook their needs. Above all else, "Just appreciate that this isn't how everybody else is growing up," advises Dr. John Rowlett, an adolescent medicine physician living in Savannah, Georgia. "The other kids at school don't have a brother or sister who's dying from cardiomyopathy and can't get a heart transplant, or has cancer, or another chronic illness. They get to go on family vacations, and both their moms and dads can show up at school functions, while these kids don't."

Younger siblings in particular sometimes conclude that they're somehow to blame for their brother's or sister's misfortune. *That* must be why Mom and Dad are ignoring me. Another common pattern is for older siblings to act out, out of resentment for the attention being showered on the patient. This problem is compounded when healthy siblings are overburdened with new responsibilities. It is reasonable for parents to expect everyone to pitch in around the household and take on additional chores, but kids should never be thrust into a parenting role.

The American Academy of Pediatrics is an organization of 57,000 primary care pediatricians, pediatric medical subspecialists and pediatric specialists dedicated to the health, safety and well-being of infants, children, adolescents and young adults. AAP books with Bantam include *Caring for Your Baby and Young Child Birth to Five, Caring for Your School-Age Child Ages 5 to 12, Your Baby's First Year, Guide to Toilet Training,* and *New Mother's Guide to Breastfeeding.*

Donald E. Greydanus M.D., F.A.A.P., F.S.A.M., is Director of the Pediatrics Residency Program at Michigan State University/Kalamazoo Center for Medical Studies, and Professor of Pediatrics and Human Development at Michigan State University College of Human Medicine. Dr. Greydanus has edited or written eight books and published over 200 articles on adolescent health. He lectures on caring for adolescents internationally, and has received a number of awards for his work in adolescent medicine from such organizations as the American Academy of Pediatrics and the Mayo Graduate School of Medicine. He and his wife Katherine have raised four daughters who are now remarkable young adults, having survived their own adolescent years.

Philip Bashe is the author or coauthor of seventeen books, including *The Complete Cancer Survival Guide, Dog Days: The New York Yankees' Fall From Grace and Return to Glory, 1964–1976, When Saying No Isn't Enough: How to Keep the Children You Love Off Drugs,* and *The Complete Bedside Companion: No-Nonsense Advice on Caring for the Seriously Ill.*

Index